W9-CGN-282

LET'S GO

■ THE RESOURCE FOR THE INDEPENDENT TRAVELER

"The guides are aimed not only at young budget travelers but at the independent traveler; a sort of streetwise cookbook for traveling alone."
—*The New York Times*

"Unbeatable; good sight-seeing advice; up-to-date info on restaurants, hotels, and inns; a commitment to money-saving travel; and a wry style that brightens nearly every page."
—*The Washington Post*

"Lighthearted and sophisticated, informative and fun to read. [Let's Go] helps the novice traveler navigate like a knowledgeable old hand."
—*Atlanta Journal-Constitution*

"A world-wise traveling companion—always ready with friendly advice and helpful hints, all sprinkled with a bit of wit."
—*The Philadelphia Inquirer*

■ THE BEST TRAVEL BARGAINS IN YOUR PRICE RANGE

"All the dirt, dirt cheap."
—*People*

"Anything you need to know about budget traveling is detailed in this book."
—*The Chicago Sun-Times*

"Let's Go follows the creed that you don't have to toss your life's savings to the wind to travel—unless you want to."
—*The Salt Lake Tribune*

■ REAL ADVICE FOR REAL EXPERIENCES

"The writers seem to have experienced every rooster-packed bus and lunar-surfaced mattress about which they write."
—*The New York Times*

"A guide should tell you what to expect from a destination. Here Let's Go shines."
—*The Chicago Tribune*

"[Let's Go's] devoted updaters really walk the walk (and thumb the ride, and trek the trail). Learn how to fish, haggle, find work—anywhere."
—*Food & Wine*

LET'S GO PUBLICATIONS

TRAVEL GUIDES
Alaska 1st edition **NEW TITLE**
Australia 2004
Austria & Switzerland 2004
Brazil 1st edition **NEW TITLE**
Britain & Ireland 2004
California 2004
Central America 8th edition
Chile 1st edition
China 4th edition
Costa Rica 1st edition
Eastern Europe 2004
Egypt 2nd edition
Europe 2004
France 2004
Germany 2004
Greece 2004
Hawaii 2004
India & Nepal 8th edition
Ireland 2004
Israel 4th edition
Italy 2004
Japan 1st edition **NEW TITLE**
Mexico 20th edition
Middle East 4th edition
New Zealand 6th edition
Pacific Northwest 1st edition **NEW TITLE**
Peru, Ecuador & Bolivia 3rd edition
Puerto Rico 1st edition **NEW TITLE**
South Africa 5th edition
Southeast Asia 8th edition
Southwest USA 3rd edition
Spain & Portugal 2004
Thailand 1st edition
Turkey 5th edition
USA 2004
Western Europe 2004

CITY GUIDES
Amsterdam 3rd edition
Barcelona 3rd edition
Boston 4th edition
London 2004
New York City 2004
Paris 2004
Rome 12th edition
San Francisco 4th edition
Washington, D.C. 13th edition

MAP GUIDES
Amsterdam
Berlin
Boston
Chicago
Dublin
Florence
Hong Kong
London
Los Angeles
Madrid
New Orleans
New York City
Paris
Prague
Rome
San Francisco
Seattle
Sydney
Venice
Washington, D.C.

COMING SOON:
Road Trip USA

SAN FRANCISCO

MICHAEL B. MURPHY EDITOR
MIRANDA I. LASH ASSOCIATE EDITOR

RESEARCHER-WRITERS
CAITLIN CASEY
HEATHER JACKIE THOMASON
JORDAN BLAIR WOODS

TZU-HUAN LO MAP EDITOR
MEGAN BRUMAGIM MANAGING EDITOR

ST. MARTIN'S PRESS ✄ NEW YORK

Maps by David Lindroth copyright © 2004 by St. Martin's Press.

Distributed outside the USA and Canada by Macmillan.

ISBN: 0-312-31997-5

First edition
10 9 8 7 6 5 4 3 2 1

Let's Go: San Francisco is written by Let's Go Publications, 67 Mount Auburn Street, Cambridge, MA 02138, USA.

Contents

Bold denotes a map.

v

▐ accommodations 191

▶ daytripping 207

✈ planning your trip 277

▐᠁ alternatives to tourism 297

▞ service directory 311

▐ index 319

▞ map appendix

1 2 3 4 5
PRICE RANGES >> San Francisco

Our researchers list establishments in order of value, beginning with the best; our favorites are denoted by the Let's Go thumbs-up (🔖). Since the best value is not always the cheapest price, we have incorporated a system of price ranges for quick reference. Our price ranges are based on a rough expectation of what you will spend. For **accommodations,** we base our price range on the cheapest price for which a single traveler can stay for one night. For **restaurants** and other dining establishments, we estimate the average amount that you will spend in that restaurant. The table below tells you what you will *typically* find in San Francisco at the corresponding price range; keep in mind that a particularly expensive ice cream stand may only be marked a ❷, depending on what you will spend.

ACCOMMODATIONS	RANGE	WHAT YOU'RE *LIKELY* TO FIND
❶	under $40	Camping; most dorm rooms, such as HI or other hostels or university dorm rooms. Expect bunk beds and a communal bath; you may have to provide or rent towels and sheets.
❷	$41-60	Upper-end hostels or small hotels. You may have a private bathroom, or there may be a sink in your room and communal shower in the hall.
❸	$61-80	A small room with a private bath. Should have decent amenities, such as phone and TV. Breakfast may be included in the price of the room.
❹	$81-120	Similar to 3, but may have more amenities or be in a more touristed area.
❺	$121+	Large hotels or upscale chains. If it's a 5 and it doesn't have the perks you want, you've paid too much.

FOOD	RANGE	WHAT YOU'RE *LIKELY* TO FIND
❶	under $7	Mostly street-corner stands, pizza places, or fast-food joints. Rarely ever a sit-down meal.
❷	$8-12	Sandwiches, appetizers at a bar, or low-priced entrees. You may have the option of sitting down or getting takeout.
❸	$13-16	Mid-priced entrees, possibly coming with a soup or salad. Tip will bump you up a couple dollars, since you'll probably have a server.
❹	$17-22	A somewhat fancy restaurant or a steakhouse. Either way, you'll have a special knife. Few restaurants in this range have a dress code, but some may look down on t-shirt and jeans.
❺	$23+	Food with foreign names and a decent wine list. Slacks and dress shirts may be expected. Don't order PB&J.

RESEARCHER-WRITERS

Caitlin Casey
Union Sq., Presidio, Chinatown, Sausalito
Tenderloin, Potrero Hill, SoMa, Haight, Noe Valley

A history & literature concentrator specializing in the writing of activists, this D.C. area native made a seamless transition into San Francisco life. She traipsed through art galleries with the ease of a connoisseur and hopped clubs with the sass of a local. Caitlin left hoping to discover the ghosts of the Summer of Love and returned having tapped into the pulse of the city's current incarnation.

Heather Jackie Thomason
Berkeley, Half Moon Bay, Mission,
Oakland, Lake Tahoe, Marin Coast & Headlands

After a summer stint as a Berkeley resident, Heather couldn't help but return (and revamp its coverage). This senior women's studies concentrator mined the Bay Area's best bookstores for the cheap, the rare, and the downright strange. From the Mission to Lake Tahoe, Heather brought a hip sensibility and sharp, descriptive prose to the sights and scenes of San Francisco.

Jordan Blair Woods
Pac. Heights, Fish. Wharf, Fin. Dist., GG Park,
Castro, Palo Alto, Mill Valley, North Beach

Wide-eyed and armed with an almost frightening knack for detail, this sophomore sociology concentrator and Catskills native headed cross-country to discover what that west coast vibe is all about. Jordan cruised the Castro, trailed Angel Island, and conquered a few pulled muscles, all the while infusing the write-ups of even the most patently touristed locales with his signature humor.

CONTRIBUTING WRITERS

Kristin McCloskey, Researcher-Writer, Let's Go: California 2004   *Wine Country*

Bryden Sweeney-Taylor, Researcher-Writer, Let's Go: Southwest USA 2004   *Lake Tahoe*

Susan Gray   *Scholarly Article: "Gay San Francisco: A Quick History"*
Susan Gray was a Researcher-Writer for *Let's Go: Greece 1994* and *Let's Go: Turkey 1995*. She is now a law student living in San Francisco.

Matt Heid   *Scholarly Article: "Going Hiking? Quick Equipment Tips"*
Matt Heid was a Researcher-Writer for *Let's Go: Alaska and Western Canada 1993*, *Europe 1995*, and *New Zealand 1998*. He is the author of *101 Hikes in Northern California* and *Camping and Backpacking the San Francisco Bay Area* (Wilderness Press).

Peggy Phelan   *Scholarly Article: "Walking Performances"*
Peggy Phelan is the Ann O'Day Maples Chair in the Arts at Stanford University. She is the author of *Unmarked: The Politics of Performance* (1993) and *Mourning Sex: Performing Public Memories* (1997) and the co-editor of *Art and Feminism* (2001).

Erica Silverstein   *Sidebar Feature: "Summer in the City: A Guide to SF Street Fairs"*

Stephanie Smith   *Sidebar Feature: "Beyond City Lights: A Guide to SF's Beat Culture"*

HOW TO USE THIS BOOK

PRICE DIVERSITY AND RANKINGS. We list establishments in order of value from best to worst. Our absolute favorites are denoted by the Let's Go thumbs-up (🖐). Since the best value does not always mean the cheapest, we have incorporated a system of price ranges in the guide. Each listing is followed by a price icon, from ❶ to ❺. You can find an explanation of these ranges on page xi.

ORGANIZATION. The coverage in this book is divided into 26 neighborhoods. All neighborhood-based listings in this book move roughly from the tourist-laden western section of downtown, through the neighborhoods in the south, and then over to the residential sections in the east. Read the neighborhood section of **Discover** to get acquainted with the neighborhoods.

FEATURES AND ARTICLES. Throughout this book, you'll find sidebars in black boxes and longer articles—built-in reading material for the airplane, long lines, or afternoons at a café. You can read researchers' tales **From the Road**, get **The Local Story** from San Franciscans themselves, learn what's been going on **In Recent News**, hear about some of the city's **Local Legends**, find explanations of items that you'll see **On the Menu**, discover the best ways to blow your budget on **Big Splurges**, and indulge in **All Play No Work** with SF's coolest festivals. Don't miss the book's extended **Articles:** a history of gay culture in SF dating back to the Gold Rush (p. 63), a comparison of performance art to walking in the city (p. 84), and a discussion of tips for hiking in the Bay Area (p. 233).

WHEN TO USE IT

ONE-TWO MONTHS BEFORE YOU GO. Planning Your Trip (p. 277) has advice about passports, plane tickets, insurance, and more. **Accommodations** (p. 191) can help you with booking a room from home.

2 WEEKS BEFORE YOU GO. Start thinking about your ideal trip. **Discover San Francisco** (p. 1) lists the city's top 25 sights, along with suggested itineraries, walking tours, Let's Go Picks (the best and quirkiest that SF has to offer), and the scoop on each of the city's neighborhoods. Read up on San Francisco history and culture in the **Life & Times** chapter (p. 51).

ON THE ROAD. Once in San Francisco (p. 33) will be your best friend once you've arrived, with all the practical information you'll need. When you feel like striking out of the city, the **Daytripping** chapter will help; it provides options for daytrips, weekend trips, and roadtrips in the Bay Area and beyond. The **Service Directory** contains a list of local services. Should you decide that you want to do something more than see the sights, turn to **Alternatives to Tourism** for information on volunteering, studying, and working in San Francisco. Finally, just remember to put down this guide once in a while and explore on your own; you'll be glad you did.

ABOUT LET'S GO

GUIDES FOR THE INDEPENDENT TRAVELER

Budget travel is more than a vacation. At *Let's Go*, we see every trip as the chance of a lifetime. If your dream is to grab a knapsack and a machete and forge through the jungles of Brazil, we can take you there. Or, if you'd rather enjoy the Riviera sun at a beachside cafe, we'll set you a table. If you know what you're doing, you can have any experience you want—whether it's camping among lions or sampling Tuscan desserts—without maxing out your credit card. We'll show you just how far your coins can go, and prove that the greatest limitation on your adventure is not your wallet, but your imagination. That said, we understand that you may want the occasional indulgence after a week of hostels and kebab stands, so we've added "Big Splurges" to let you know which establishments are worth those extra euros, as well as price ranges to help you quickly determine whether an accommodation or restaurant will break the bank. While we may have diversified, our emphasis will always be on finding the best values for your budget, giving you all the info you need to spend six days in London or six months in Tasmania.

BEYOND THE TOURIST EXPERIENCE

We write for travelers who know there's more to a vacation than riding double-deckers with tourists. Our researchers give you the heads-up on both world-renowned and lesser-known attractions, on the best local eats and the hottest nightclub beats. In our travels, we talk to everybody; we provide a snapshot of real life in the places you visit with our sidebars on topics like regional cuisine, local festivals, and hot political issues. We've opened our pages to respected writers and scholars to show you their take on a given destination, and turned to lifelong residents to learn the little things that make their city worth calling home. And we've even given you Alternatives to Tourism—ideas for how to give back to local communities through responsible travel and volunteering.

OVER FORTY YEARS OF WISDOM

When we started, way back in 1960, Let's Go consisted of a small group of well-traveled friends who compiled their budget travel tips into a 20-page packet for students on charter flights to Europe. Since then, we've expanded to suit all kinds of travelers, now publishing guides to six continents, including our newest guides: *Let's Go: Japan* and *Let's Go: Brazil*. Our guides are still annually researched and written entirely by students on shoe-string budgets, adventurous travelers who know that train strikes, stolen luggage, food poisoning, and marriage proposals are all part of a day's work. Even as you read this, work on next year's editions is well underway. Whether you're reading one of our new titles, like *Let's Go: Puerto Rico* or *Let's Go Adventure Guide: Alaska*, or our original best-seller, *Let's Go: Europe*, you'll find the same spirit of adventure that has made *Let's Go* the guide of choice for travelers the world over since 1960.

GETTING IN TOUCH

The best discoveries are often those you make yourself; on the road, when you find something worth sharing, please drop us a line. We're Let's Go Publications, 67 Mt. Auburn St., Cambridge, MA 02138, USA (feedback@letsgo.com).

For more info, visit our website: www.letsgo.com.

ACKNOWLEDGMENTS

Michael thanks: Caitlin, Heather, and Jordan for amazing research, allowing me to sleep on their floor, entertaining my talk of ephemera and authenticity, and allowing the book to happen. Megan and Scrobins for being the most incredible (and patient) bosses one could expect; I could never thank you enough. TLo for his sharp eye and excellent mapping. Miranda for all her work and for conveying some alternatives to tourism to the world. Peggy Phelan for her wonderful and much-appreciated contribution. All of my fellow city guide editors for the shared nights and the sublimely manic office environment. To the rest of the Dane St. Gang (Abigail, Dan, Oussama, Tim) for providing some outstanding dinners and long walks to work. Ralph for keeping it real. Meghana and Eric for early advice. Abigail, Allie, and Kara for beautiful friendships (now that's an interesting relational mode), talk of torment, and future domiciles. Kevin Williamson for syndicated episodes. My family and Max. And, of course, performative quotation marks and shame.

Miranda thanks: Mike, Tzu-Huan, Sarah, and our RWs for their hard work. Love to the City Guide buds. Big hug to Cristina, who brightened my summer. To Becky for making life fun. To my parents for their love and support. To Danny for friendship and affection. You gave me an extra boost when I need it most.

Tzu-Huan thanks: Mike, Miranda, Caitlin, Heather & Jordan for making this book happen, and family & friends, especially MK and JPJ for making summer doldrums bearable. Special thanks to my predecessor, Mr. Hartzell, for making the book a joy to edit. AMDG

Editor
Michael B. Murphy
Associate Editors
Miranda I. Lash
Managing Editor
Megan Brumagim
Map Editor
Tzu-Huan Lo
Typesetter
Jeffrey Hoffman Yip

Discover San Francisco

If California is a state of mind, San Francisco is chaotic euphoria. Welcome to the city that will take you to new highs, leaving your mind spinning, your tastebuds tingling, and your calves aching. Though it's smaller than most "big" cities, the City by the Bay more than compensates for its size with personality that simply won't quit. The dazzling views, daunting hills, one-of-a-kind neighborhoods, and laid-back, friendly people create a kind of charisma that continues to fascinate visitors and residents. The city manages to pack an incredible amount of vitality into its 47 square miles, running from its thriving art communities and bustling shops, to the pulsing beats in some of the country's hippest nightclubs and bars. Everyone finds something to love here and a reason to return.

By California standards, San Francisco is steeped in history—but it's a history of oddballs and eccentrics that resonates more strongly today in street culture than in museums and galleries. The lineage of free spirits and troublemakers dates back to the 19th century, with the smugglers and pirates of the Barbary Coast and the 49ers who flocked here during the mad boom of the California Gold Rush. As the last stop in America's voracious westward expansion, San Francisco has always attracted artists, dreamers, and outsiders. In the 1950s came the Beats—brilliant, angry young writers who captured the rhythms of be-bop jazz in their poetry and discontent. The late 60s ushered in the most famous of SF rabble rousers—hippies and flower children, who turned on one generation and freaked out another by making love, not war.

The tradition of free spirit and subversion persists in the city's memory. Anti-establishment politics have almost become establishment here, as rallies and movements continue to fill the streets and newspapers. The queer community became undeniably visible in the

1

California

70s as one of the city's most visible and powerful groups. In addition, Mexican, Central American, and Asian immigrants have made San Francisco one of the most racially diverse cities in the United States. And then in a wave of mid-90s, computer-crazed prosperity, young computer workers ditched the bland suburbs of Silicon Valley for the cooler breezes of San Francisco, with upstart Internet companies infiltrating the forgotten spaces of lower-rent neighborhoods. For a while, the Frisco fight was old-timers and hippies vs. dot-commers, but when the Clinton-era and the national surplus went the way of the dodo, high-end yuppification collapsed, leaving neighborhoods to reassess their futures. Like so many chameleons, San Francisco is changing with the times, but fortunately, some things stay the same: the Bay is foggy, the hills are steep, and tourists are the only ones wearing shorts.

TOP 25 REASONS TO VISIT SF

25. THE SEA LIONS AT PIER 39. They bark, roll over, nap in the sun, and dive into the deep less than five feet from the pier (p. 65).

24. FORT POINT. The Spaniards chose this as a military outpost because it's the best spot to survey the entrance to the Bay. It still has one of the best views of the Bridge and the water (p. 77).

23. VAILLANCOURT FOUNTAIN AND JUSTIN HERMAN PLAZA. On those rare roasting hot days, cool off in the mists of a 1970s architectural oddity. On weekends, take in a lunchtime protest (p. 89).

22. AQUARIUM OF THE BAY. Gaze above at marine species in amazing tunnels below the Bay (p. 66).

21. STERN GROVE AMPHITHEATER. Bathe your ears in the amazing acoustics of a eucalyptus soundboard. Check out free Sunday concerts in summer (p. 109).

20. THE HAIGHT. Though most of the flower children have packed up their guitars and moved on, you can still see the places where cultural history (and love) was made, including the homes of Janis Joplin and the Grateful Dead (p. 97).

19. PALACE OF FINE ARTS. Built for the 1915 Panama-Pacific Exposition (and often serving as the backdrop for weddings), this beautiful domed rotunda makes for a beautiful picnic spot (p. 68).

18. COIT TOWER. Commissioned by firefighter fan Lillie Hitchcock Coit and designed to look like a fireman's um, nozzle, 180 ft. Coit Tower commands spectacular views of the city and the Bay. Vibrant WPA-sponsored murals adorn the interior (p. 103).

Top Ten Ways to Turn Heads in SF

After a long day of touring and gazing, why not create a spectacle and attract some attention yourself?

10. Show off your moves during free tango lessons at **Tango Gelato** (p. 129) in Pacific Heights.

9. Opt to keep your shirt *on* at an unforgettable (and unforgettably late) Friday at **The EndUp** (p. 152) in SoMa.

8. Connect with history and lead your own protest (or revolution) in **Sproul Plaza** (p. 215) in Berkeley.

7. Keep your swimsuit *on*, or let your eyes linger too long at **Baker Beach** (p. 77).

6. Be a little "too old" to play in the Tactile Dome at the **Exploratorium** (p. 68).

5. Show off your knowledge of Beatnik literary culture at **City Lights Bookstore** (p. 177) in North Beach.

4. Join a waitress for a runway show during dinner at **Asia SF** (p. 153) in SoMa.

3. Escape the crowds with your drink and climb the ladder to "jail" at **Odeon Bar** (p. 159) in the Mission.

2. Sport your best Frankenfurter get-up on Th night—even though *The Rocky Horror Picture Show* (p. 228) plays on F in Oakland.

1. Look fabulous and strut your stuff down **Castro Street** (p. 155) on a weekend evening.

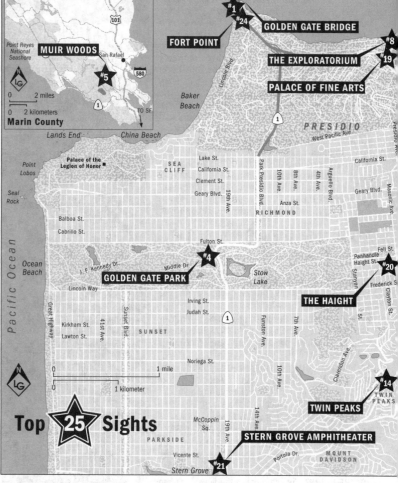

17. CITY GUIDES WALKING TOURS. Volunteer tour guides do it for love of SF! See the neighborhoods and sights through the eyes of residents (p. 103).

16. BURRITOS IN THE MISSION. So delicious! And so cheap! Without a doubt, the best bite for your buck, and maybe just the best bite, period (p. 135).

15. CITY LIGHTS BOOKSTORE. (cue bongos) City Lights (ba-bum). Nifty books (ba-bum). Winding staircase (ba-bum). Cozy nooks (ba-bum). Beat culture (ba-bum). The beat goes on (p. 70).

14. TWIN PEAKS. Perfect 360° views. At night, glittering lights below meet glimmering stars above, yielding the most romantic spot around (p. 101).

13. CABLE CARS. Get in line early and hang on! Not only are the cars themselves classic SF icons, but they'll also take you up to some of the city's best views (p. 37).

12. POTRERO HILL. Tucked between freeways and seemingly far from downtown's bustle, this middle-class neighborhood gives off the artsy yet unpretentious vibe of a communal Main St., USA. It's also a sunny fog-free spot to snap your own picture of the city skyline (p. 19).

SEA LIONS AT PIER 39 #25

AQUARIUM OF THE BAY #22

COIT TOWER #7

THE SF ART INSTITUTE ALCATRAZ

San Francisco Bay

Marina Blvd.

Beach St.

MARINA

Chestnut St.

Lombard St.

Franklin St.

Van Ness Ave.

#11 #6

#18

NORTH BEACH

DIM SUM IN CHINATOWN

RUSSIAN HILL

#15

CHINA-TOWN

LOMBARD STREET

Taylor St.

#9

Broadway

Pacific Ave.

CITY LIGHTS BOOKSTORE

#23

Bay Bridge

TO OAKLAND

80

PACIFIC HEIGHTS

Alta Park

Lafayette Park

101

California St.

NOB HILL

CABLE CARS

Main St.

VAILLANCOURT FOUNTAIN & JUSTIN HERMAN PLAZA

China Basin

Pine St.

Bush St.

JAPAN-TOWN

Gough St.

Geary Expressway

Post St.

Divisadero St.

Fillmore St.

Steiner St.

Laguna St.

Hyde St.

Larkin St.

Geary St.

#13

2nd St.

3rd St.

Turk St.

Golden Gate Ave.

TENDER LOIN

Turk St.

Market St.

Mission St.

Howard St.

4th St.

5th St.

6th St.

WESTERN ADDITION

#17

CIVIC CENTER

8th St.

9th St.

SOMA

Folsom St.

80

Brannan St.

Townsend

Berry St.

#2

China Basin

CITY GUIDES WALKING TOURS

10th St.

PACIFIC BELL PARK

7th St.

CHINA BASIN

Central Basin

Buena Vista Park

Duboce Ave.

Castro St.

Market St.

101

BURRITOS IN THE MISSION

Potrero St.

Mariposa St.

280

Indiana St.

16th St.

Mission Dolores

#10

#16

S. Van Ness Ave.

20th St.

#12

CASTRO

Noe St.

Diamond St.

CASTRO STREET

Dolores St.

Guerrero St.

Harrison St.

Treat Ave.

SF General Hospital

POTRERO HILL

POTRERO

Market St.

Clipper St.

#3

Valencia St.

MISSION

25th St.

MISSION MURALS

Cesar Chavez St.

Cesar Chavez St.

NOE VALLEY

Mission St.

San Jose Ave.

Bernal Heights Park

BAY VIEW

Quint St.

3rd St.

30th St.

Jerrold Ave.

Oakdale Ave.

280

Cortland Ave.

11. THE CROOKEDEST STREET IN THE WORLD (LOMBARD STREET). The famous curves of Lombard St. were installed in the 1920s so that horse-drawn carriages could negotiate the extremely steep hill. Bright, beautiful flowers adorn each level, and crazy in-line skaters sometimes whiz past (p. 73).

10. CASTRO STREET ON FRIDAY AND SATURDAY NIGHTS. Before they duck into bars or head to SoMa for the clubs, San Francisco's beautiful gay boys and girls stroll Castro St. Don't come expecting a freakish spectacle—this is high-class and happy (p. 155).

9. DIM SUM IN CHINATOWN. Sample delectable Chinese brunch delights. Be brave and try chicken feet, or stick to savory shrimp dumplings. Just about any restaurant in Chinatown will suffice (p. 120).

8. THE EXPLORATORIUM. Hands-on science at this museum will captivate kids as well as kids-at-heart. The huge space is crammed with cool contraptions to climb through and play with (p. 68).

✍ LET'S GO PICKS

Forget the Golden Gate Bridge for a moment—the following unsung heroes of San Francisco deserve a mention, and a visit.

Best desserts: Stella Pasticceria e Caffé in North Beach (p. 119).

Best gay club: SF Badlands in the Castro (p. 157).

Best places to collapse for a nap: Alta Plaza in Pacific Heights (p. 96) and Limantour Beach.

Best place to be meditatively intellectual (or at least pretend): Shakespeare Garden in Golden Gate Park (p. 87).

Best place to wait for the Night Owl: The Mission.

Best street for toning your calves (or ass): Gough St., between Union and Sacramento.

Best meal for under $7: Kate's Kitchen in the Haight (p. 131).

Best place to mourn your poverty: Top of the Mark in Nob Hill (p. 75).

Best place to amuse yourself: Good Vibrations in the Mission (p. 188).

Best place to buy a pipe: Pipe Dreams in the Haight (p. 186).

Best way to spend a rainy afternoon: Picnic in the Public Art Space in SoMa (p. 95).

(cont'd on next pg.)

7. ALCATRAZ. Cheesy Bruckheimer flicks aside, "The Rock" is the coolest attraction in the Bay. First a military detention hall and then the original high security civilian prison, this sight has enough ghost stories to keep you up for days. Squeeze into a cell...if you're into that kind of thing (p. 109).

6. THE SAN FRANCISCO ART INSTITUTE. Among the many artist hot shots to have studied and taught at this gorgeous hilltop hideaway, Diego Rivera left his mark in 1931 with a fresco depicting the city (p. 73).

5. MUIR WOODS. Experience the mysterious, magical stillness of these centuries-old redwoods that loom above you in silence. George Lucas was so impressed that he filmed *Return of the Jedi* here (p. 238).

4. GOLDEN GATE PARK. GG Park is the largest urban park in the United States. Central what? Spend an entire day (or five) seeing the sights and the bison in this lush paradise (p. 83).

3. MISSION MURALS. This urban street art brilliantly combines artistic excellence, technical perfection, and community politics. Standouts include Balmy Alley and a three-building tribute to guitar god Carlos Santana (p. 102).

2. A GIANTS GAME AT PACIFIC BELL PARK. Not only do you get to cheer on the Giants (and maybe see a right-field homer make a splash), but the bleacher seats come with fabulous views of the game, the city, and the Bay (p. 172).

1. GOLDEN GATE BRIDGE. You're kidding?!? The Golden Gate Bridge is in San Francisco? I had no idea! I'll have to go check that out! You can see the bridge from around the city (and on two out of every three postcards), but to truly know its immense beauty, you have to be there. Don't forget your windbreaker (p. 77).

NEIGHBORHOODS

Like all of the neighborhood-based listings in this book, the following descriptions will move roughly from the tourist-laden western section of downtown San Francisco, to the neighborhoods in the south, and then over to the residential sections in the east. If you find that neighborhood boundaries are getting a bit confusing, don't stress—San Francisco, like any living, breathing city, doesn't follow the imaginary boundaries that books like this one need to rely on. Still, the neighborhoods of San Francisco exhibit a fascinating sense of place and locality to be explored. A good map is a must.

FISHERMAN'S WHARF & THE PIERS

🔍 *NEIGHBORHOOD QUICKFIND:*
Sights, p. 65; **Food & Drink,** p. 116.

🔲 **Orientation:** *Fisherman's Wharf is anchored by the shopping complexes of Pier 39 to the east and Ghirardelli Sq. to the west, and extends down to Bay* see map p. 338 *St. to the south.* **Public Transportation:** *MUNI buses # 10, 15, 30, 39, 47, and F and the Powell-Mason and Powell-Hyde cable cars run to the Wharf; buses #19, 47, and 49 run across town to Ghirardelli Sq.* **Driving:** *Driving in this area is not recommended. If you must, use The Embarcadero and a parking garage (****Service Directory*** *p. 316).* **Contact:** *www.fishermanswharf.org.*

The eastern portion of San Francisco's waterfront is one of its most visited—and most reviled—tourist destinations. Fisherman's Wharf remained obscure until the 1930s, when a fisherman from the area ditched his bait and tackle and decided that he could catch other things— namely baseballs and shapely Hollywood starlets. Fisherman's Wharf is home to eight blocks of touristy carnival-esque aquatic splendor. Cheesy t-shirt shops and garish storefronts share the area with rich maritime tradition and several surprisingly fun museums. Aside from the while-you-wait caricature artists, "olde-fashioned fudge shoppes," and penny-flattening machines, the only natives you're likely to find here are the sea lions. **Piers 39** through **45** house some of San Francisco's most iconic attractions. **Alcatraz** and the **Hyde St. Pier** harbor some of the Bay's fascinating history. **Ghirardelli Square,** the **Cannery,** and the western edge of the wharf are generally calmer than Pier 39, offering stunning Bay views, sultry courtyard jazz, and some tasty eateries.

MARINA, FORT MASON & COW HOLLOW

MARINA

🔍 *NEIGHBORHOOD QUICKFIND:*
Sights, p. 68; **Food & Drink,** p. 117; **Nightlife,** p. 144; **Accommodations,** p. 191.

🔲 **Orientation:** *From the busy shopping area along Chestnut St., the Marina reaches north to the* see map p. 338 *waterfront, bordered to the east by Van Ness Ave. and to the west by the Presidio.* **Public Transportation:** *MUNI bus #30 runs all the way along Chestnut*

(cont'd from previous pg.)

Best places to see a drag show: Marlena's in Hayes Valley (p. 150) and Asia SF in SoMA (p. 153). Or your local laundromat, of course.

Best bar in which to pass out: The Royal Oak (p. 147) in Russian Hill.

Best place to get hot and sweaty: Funky Door Yoga (p. 175).

Best places to relive your childhood: Zeum in SoMA (p. 95) and the Exploratorium in the Marina (p. 68).

Best place to feel like a prude: Folsom Street Fair (p. 10).

Best places to remember your sunscreen: The Presidio and the Amphitheater in Stern Grove (p. 109).

Best place to haggle: Stockton Street in Chinatown (p. 72).

Best place to nurse a hangover: Lori's Diner in Union Square (p. 123).

Best place to meet smokers: any bar with an outdoor patio or out on the street after dark.

Best place to love meat: Tommy's Joynt in the Tenderloin.

Best place to feel nostalgic: Pet Cemetery in the Presidio (p. 76).

Best place to get stuck in rush hour traffic: Golden Gate Bridge (p. 77).

Best places to cruise: SF Badlands in the Castro (p. 157) and Bambuddha Lounge in the Tenderloin (p. 150).

*St. to Divisadero St., where it turns north and runs to Jefferson St., 1 block from the waterfront. MUNI bus #45 runs down Union St. **Driving:** Avoid staying on congested Chestnut St. and head a block or 2 toward the water for street parking.*

The residential Marina, between Fort Mason to the east and the expansive Presidio to the west, is home to more young, wealthy professionals (and failed dot-commers) than any other part of San Francisco. Pastel stucco houses with lavish gardens, **stunning views** of Marin, and a high quotient of young, beautiful socialites characterize these residential neighborhoods. You would never know that the area was one of those hit hardest by the 1989 earthquake.

FORT MASON

◻ *NEIGHBORHOOD QUICKFIND: **Sights**, p. 68; **Food & Drink**, p. 117; **Nightlife**, p. 144; **Accommodations**, p. 191.*

◻ ***Orientation:** Fort Mason hangs out over the water in the northeast corner of the Marina, at Laguna and Marina St., east of Marina Green, and west of Fisherman's Wharf's Municipal Pier. There are entrances at Bay and Franklin St., 1 block west of Van Ness Ave., and on McDowell St. on the water side. **Public Transportation:** MUNI bus #28 has its terminal just inside Fort Mason; #30 and 42 stop on North Point St. and Van Ness Ave. at the southeast corner. **Driving:** Take Van Ness Ave. to Bay St. Parking is available at 2 lots in Fort Mason.*

Fort Mason, with an abundance of theaters and museums, provides a culturally rich counterbalance to the wealth of the Marina. Directly across the lengthy Marina Green near the Presidio stands the breathtaking **Palace of Fine Arts** and the **Exploratorium** (fun-for-kids-of-all-ages). On the southern border of the Marina, Chestnut St. bustles with shops and eateries, while Lombard St. is a restful destination for motel-seekers.

COW HOLLOW

◻ *NEIGHBORHOOD QUICKFIND: **Food & Drink**, p. 117; **Nightlife**, p. 144; **Accommodations**, p. 191.*

◻ ***Orientation:** Cow Hollow is south of the Marina. **Public Transportation:** Bus #22 runs straight up Fillmore through Pacific Heights and Cow Hollow to the Marina Green.*

A few blocks farther south, Cow Hollow primarily caters to crowds of San Francisco's elites. Some medium-priced stores speckle the landscape, but the pricey boutiques, hair and nail salons, and furniture galleries make this section of the city less budget-friendly than the Marina. There are a few cheap eats that make the trip worthwhile, however, and window shopping is always a no-commitment option. By dinner time and into the night, the **swinging singles scene** picks up, and the area's trendy bars serve as leveling ground for illustrious people of all kinds.

NORTH BEACH

◻ *NEIGHBORHOOD QUICKFIND: **Sights**, p. 70; **Food & Drink**, p. 118; **Nightlife**, p. 144; **Accommodations**, p. 193.*

◻ ***Orientation:** North Beach is centered along Columbus Ave., extending east to Telegraph Hill. It is bounded to the south by Chinatown and to the west by Russian Hill. To the north it eventually dissipates into the Wharf area. **Public Transportation:** MUNI buses #15, 30, 39, 41, 42, 45,*

see map p. 339 *and 83 and the Bay and Taylor cable car line serve North Beach. **Driving:** Parking is nearly impossible, but you can try for metered parking or* look into one of the several packed and pricey parking lots (**Service Directory**, p. 316).

When Water St. marked the end of San Francisco and the beginning of the Bay, sunny North Beach served as a first stop for waves of immigrants in the 19th and early 20th centuries. The Italian community stuck around, and the neighborhood teems with home-style Italian restaurants. The numerous Old World cafes, many of which have been around for generations, sustained the drinking habits of the Beats. In the early 1950s, poets and writers (including Jack Kerouac, Allen Ginsberg, Maynard Krebs, and Lawrence Ferlinghetti) came here to write, drink, and raise hell.

They lashed out at the conformity of postwar America, embraced Eastern religions and bebop jazz, and lit a fuse that set off the counterculture explosion of the late 1960s. Since then, North Beach has experienced a major nightlife surge. Finely clad peninsula- and city-dwellers flock to the zillions of Italian restaurants around Columbus Ave. and stay for the cozy bars and hot live acts around Broadway and Kearny St. Meanwhile, the internationals who staff the area head to tiny, laid-back bars on Grant St., while herds of wandering trans folk duck into the Broadway strip clubs.

CHINATOWN

⚑ *NEIGHBORHOOD QUICKFIND:* **Sights,** p. 71; **Food & Drink,** p. 120; **Nightlife,** p. 146; **Accommodations,** p. 193.

⬛ Orientation: *Chinatown activity centers around Grant Ave. It is bounded roughly by Columbus Ave. and North Beach to the north, Kearny St. to the east, Mason St. to the west, and the Financial District to the south.* **Public Transportation:** *MUNI buses #30 and 45 run along Stockton St. 1 block west of Grant Ave.; #15 goes along Kearny St.* **Driving:** *Don't. The area is congested and the only parking to be found is in garages (Service Directory: p. 316).*

see map p. 339

The largest Chinese community outside of Asia (over 100,000 people), Chinatown is also the most densely populated of San Francisco's neighborhoods. Chinese laborers began coming to San Francisco in the mid-19th century as refugees from the Opium Wars between Britain and China, and were put to work constructing the railroads of the West. Racism swelled after the tracks had been laid and Gold Rush prosperity dissipated. In the 1880s, white Californians secured laws against further Chinese immigration to prevent the so-called "Yellow Peril." Stranded in San Francisco, Chinese-Americans banded together to protect themselves in this small section of the city. As the city grew, speculators tried to take over the increasingly valuable land, but the residents refused to leave. To this day Chinatown's residents remain mostly Chinese or of Chinese descent, although it has attracted visitors since the 1850s. Today tourists are drawn to its alleyways and markets, which pulse with the sights and smells of Chinese-American culture.

Locals of all backgrounds bargain in Chinatown's markets and feast in its abundance of **affordable eateries.** Note, however, that today's Chinatown is one that celebrates Chinese-American culture. Chinatown residents caution against mistaking Chinatown for a re-creation of China (if anything, Chinatown is more of a snapshot of Chinese life forty years ago, preserved by immigrants who remember that China). Navigating the markets and alleyways of the neighborhood brings you up close and personal with San Francisco's infamous hills. No matter which temple or park you are looking for, always remember to look around—some of the best sights in Chinatown are the Chinese-influenced building facades, which you might otherwise miss as you maneuver through the crowded streets.

NOB HILL & RUSSIAN HILL

⚑ *NEIGHBORHOOD QUICKFIND:* **Sights,** p. 73; **Food & Drink,** p. 121; **Nightlife,** p. 147; **Accommodations,** p. 194.

⬛ Orientation: *Nob Hill rises above Union Sq. and the Tenderloin to the south and Chinatown to the east. Russian Hill stands north of Nob Hill, toward Fisherman's Wharf and just west of North Beach.* **Public Transportation:** *MUNI bus #45 follows Union St. between the 2 hills. The Powell-Hyde and Powell-Mason cable cars run up Powell St. just east of Nob Hill. They continue along Hyde and Mason St., respectively, on either side of Russian Hill.* **Driving:** *Polk, Larkin, Hyde, Leavenworth, Jones, Taylor, and Mason St. all run north-south through the area. East-west streets often have one-way blocks. Street parking can be found.*

see map p. 342

In the late 19th-century, Nob Hill attracted the West's great railroad magnates and robber barons. Today, their **ostentatious mansions** continue to make it one of the nation's most prestigious addresses. Fancy hotels, a lovely little park, and an impres-

Summer in the City

One of the best ways to explore the unique culture and neighborhoods of this community-oriented city is to hit one of the many **street festivals** from June through September.

Street fairs feature arts and crafts, ethnic food vendors, and music. Original art and jewelry may be too expensive for the budget traveler, but the browsing is top-notch, and the people-watching couldn't be better. Many of the same vendors appear at every street fair, so you won't miss out if you need to skip a festival or three.

Summer festival highlights:

Union Street Art Fair: Ditch comfort for fashion (if only for a day!) and join the Marina throngs in trendy tops and high-heeled strappy sandals for this art festival. The young, the rich, and the preppy come out in full force (over 100,000 attendees) to "ooh" and "ah" over handmade jewelry and professional photography. Gourmet food. Parking at Bay St. and Webster St. *(Union between Steiner and Gough. www.unionstreetfestival.com. 1st weekend in June.)*

Haight Street Fair: The Summer of Love may have ended, but Haight Street still sports colorful characters and lots of tie-dye. Two stages boast musical acts from rock to reggae to blues. Once you've had your fill of crowded beer gardens, pop into one of the many vintage clothing stores and search for next year's

(cont'd next pg.)

sive cathedral grace the peak at California and Taylor St. Russian Hill, to the north, is named after Russian sailors who died during an expedition in the early 1800s and were buried on the southeast crest. Largely residential, Nob and Russian Hills themselves are great places to catch the views and grab a bite to eat, but there are more interesting happenings to be found on the streets running to and beyond them.

UNION SQUARE

🔎 *NEIGHBORHOOD QUICKFIND:* **Sights,** *p. 80;* **Food & Drink,** *p. 122;* **Nightlife,** *p. 148;* **Accommodations,** *p. 194.*

📍 *Orientation: Bordered clearly to the north by Bush St. and the gates to Chinatown, and to the south by Market St., Union Sq.*

see map p. 343

sprawls considerably to the east and west. The world-class theaters and strip clubs mark the border of the seedy Tenderloin around Taylor St. to the east, while towering banks mark the start of the Financial District around Grant St. to the west. **Public Transportation:** *Take BART or any MUNI to the Powell St. Station at Hallidie Plaza.* **Driving:** *Market or Powell St. will get you there from anywhere, but there's almost no street parking. Garage parking is plentiful, but expensive.*

Union Square itself is a square block of manicured park presided over by a bronze statue of the Goddess of Victory, erected in 1903. However, when people refer to Union Square they are usually talking about the plethora of **chic shops,** ritzy hotels, and prestigious **art galleries** housed in the three-block radius around the park. The area is also home to Geary St. and Mason St., the heart of San Francisco's **theater district.** Enticements for the budget traveler also abound: affordable accommodations, nighttime fun, and—of course—window shopping.

GOLDEN GATE BRIDGE & THE PRESIDIO

🔎 *NEIGHBORHOOD QUICKFIND:* **Sights,** *p. 77.*

📍 *Orientation: At the northwest tip of San Francisco, the Presidio leads to the Golden Gate Bridge, which connects San Francisco to its northern neighbor, Marin County. The Presidio is bounded*

see map p. 78

to the east by the Marina and to the south by the Richmond. Lincoln Blvd. runs through the western side of the Presidio, Park Presidio (Rte. 1) crosses it in the middle, and Doyle Dr. (US 101) runs along its northern edge.

Public Transportation: MUNI bus #29 runs along Park Presidio and Lincoln Blvd., but can be unreliable due to traffic; #28 follows Doyle Dr.; #43 enters the eastern tip of the park on Lombard St. Golden Gate Transit buses cross the bridge. The newly expanded free PresidiGo shuttle service is reliable and stops at all major destinations in the park every 30min. (Schedules available: ☎561-5300; www.presidiotrust.gov/shuttle.) *Driving:* Numerous small roads loop off the major arteries and are confusing to navigate, but traffic is light and the views are always pretty. Parking available.

The great span of the Golden Gate Bridge reaches across the San Francisco Bay from Marin County to the Presidio. Originally the northernmost Spanish military garrison in California, the Presidio served first the Mexican and then the American army until the 1990s. Most of the former military buildings have been converted for civilian use, but the Presidio can still feel rather deserted. Its miles of **paths** and **hills,** however, are wide open to the public and worth a visit. At 76,000 acres, it is the largest urban park in the US and is recognized by the United Nations as the Golden Gate Biosphere Reserve. **Crissy Field,** in particular, is a newly restored and beautiful shoreline park that serves sunbathers, ballplayers, and nature lovers.

LINCOLN PARK

🔳 *NEIGHBORHOOD QUICKFIND:* **Sights,** p. 80.

🔳 *Orientation:* Lincoln Park covers the northwest point of the city, just south of the Presidio and the Golden Gate Bridge. *Public Transportation:* MUNI bus #2 offers access to the eastern part of the park; #18 will take you to the Palace of the Legion of Honor; #38 lets you off near the Cliff House. *Driving:* The best points of entry are at Point Lobos and 48th Ave. (there are parking lots at Merrie Way and Fort Miley), or at Clement St. and 34th Ave., through the Lincoln Park Golf course (there is a parking lot at the California Palace of the Legion of Honor). All parking lots are free.

see map p. 341

Lincoln Park's great chunk of green is perfectly positioned for snapping a shot of the Golden Gate Bridge and the Bay. The collection of meandering paths and historical sights make it a fabulous place for an afternoon hike or summertime picnic. Here you can catch a glimpse of the closest thing California has to offer in the way of "ancient ruins" at the **Sutro Baths.** The **California Palace of the Legion of Honor** is an oasis of high culture and stunning architecture in the midst of rugged trails and manicured golf greens. Hikers can follow the **Coastal Trail** to **Land's End,** which

(cont'd from previous pg.)

Halloween costume. (Haight St. between Masonic and Stanyan. www.haightstreetfair.org. 2nd weekend in June.)

North Beach Festival: Come to San Francisco's Little Italy for the oldest urban street fair in the country, where Italian scents meet the birthplace of beat poetry. Enjoy swing dancing in the park, spoken word performances in the street, or cappuccino outside one of the many fabulous Italian restaurants. (North Beach. www.sfnorthbeach.org/festival. 3rd weekend in June.)

Ghirardelli Sq. Chocolate Festival: A must-see for every sweet-toothed visitor in SF. Overload your senses with chocolate candy, ice cream, baked goods, and even chocolate-covered fruit from prominent hotels, restaurants, chocolate manufacturers, and of course, the Ghirardelli Chocolate Store. Enter the "Earthquake" ice-cream eating contest; winner wins her weight in Ghirardelli chocolate. (Ghirardelli Sq. www.ghirardellisq.com. 1st weekend in Sept.)

Folsom Street Fair: Leave shyness behind as you join San Francisco's more sexually liberated folk as they show off their leather, bondage gear, whips, and chains. The more skin, the better! So polish your piercings, put a leash on your travel buddy, and ogle the kinkiest crowd you'll ever see parading in public. (Folsom St. between 7th and 12th Streets. 4th weekend in Sept.)

— Erica Silverstein

Botanical Gardens

Fisherman's Wharf

offers unparalleled views of the bridge and the Bay area's best nude beach according to the 2003 *Guardian* poll.

GOLDEN GATE PARK

⁊ *NEIGHBORHOOD QUICK-FIND:* **Sights,** *p. 83;* **Entertainment,** *p. 172.*

⊞ Orientation: *Bordered to the north and south by the residential Richmond and Sunset districts, the park reaches from Ocean Beach to the Haight.*

see map p. 82-83

Public Transportation: *Take MUNI bus #5, 16, 21, or 71 from downtown. MUNI buses #18, 28, 29, and 44 pass through the park north and south and intersect the surface Metro south of the park. MUNI N (Judah St.) runs from Market St. down to Arguello Blvd. near the southeast corner of the park.* **Driving:** *Park Presidio Blvd. runs straight through the park. Parking is readily available alongside the park, if not on Fulton or Lincoln St., then on any one of the cross-streets.* **Contact:** *Friends of Recreation and Parks,* ☎ *263-0991; www.frp.org.* **Park headquarters:** ☎ *831-2700; www.ci.sf.ca.us/recpark. Open daily 8am-5pm.* **Visitors Center:** ☎ *751-2766. Open daily 9am-6pm.*

Golden Gate Park originated in the 1870s when city leaders, ignoring the Spanish land-claim, convinced the courts that this area of sand and dunes belonged to San Francisco. In the following decades, the desert-like region was transformed into a vibrant, green patch of loveliness. Today gardens, groves, and lush greenery beckon San Fran natives and visitors alike to the 5 square miles perfect for bike rides, in-line skating, archery, or lawn bowling. The park is bounded by Fulton St. to the north, Stanyan St. to the east, Lincoln Way to the south, and Ocean Beach to the west, except for a strip called the Panhandle, which juts east between Fell and Oak St. into the Haight. Originally the "carriage entrance," the Panhandle contains the oldest trees in the park. The heavily trafficked section of Rte. 1 running through the park is called Park Presidio By-Pass Dr. heading north and Cross-Over Dr. heading south. On Sundays, traffic is banned from 10am-5pm on park roads, and bicycles and in-line skates come out in full force. The **Academy of Sciences** (p. 83) offers an aquarium, natural history museum, and planetarium under one roof.

Chinatown

FINANCIAL DISTRICT & THE EMBARCADERO

⚑ NEIGHBORHOOD QUICKFIND:
Food & Drink, p. 124; **Nightlife,** p. 149; **Accommodations,** p. 195.

▪ Orientation: *The Financial District is bordered by Market St. to the south, Washington St. to the north, Grant St. to the west,*

see map p. 344

and the Embarcadero and Ferry Building to the east. **Public Transportation:** *Take MUNI J, K, L, M, or N or BART to the Montgomery St. or Embarcadero Station. A slower route to the district is the California St. cable car.* **Driving:** *Parking is very difficult during business hours. If you must drive, park in SoMa and walk or ride the MUNI to Montgomery St.*

Although much of modern-day Bay Area business may be conducted online, the city still has its share of pressed suits and corner offices. The Financial District is a chilly concrete world where towering banks blot out the sun and corporate workers rush between meetings, giving the area an impersonal atmosphere. When the workday finishes at 7:30pm, the district becomes a ghost-town with empty streets. The walk up Columbus St. toward Broadway at dusk offers a spectacular view of the **Transamerica Pyramid,** provided it isn't too foggy. To seek solace from the sunless streets, wander through one of the verdant parks, nurse a beer in a backstreet bar, or feast in one of many fancy restaurants.

Presidio Waters

Palace of Fine Arts

CIVIC CENTER

⚑ NEIGHBORHOOD QUICKFIND:
Sights, p. 90; **Food & Drink,** p. 124; **Accommodations,** p. 196.

▪ Orientation: *The Civic Center lies at Market St. and Van Ness Ave.* **Public Transportation:** *Take MUNI J, K, L, M, or N to the Civic Center stop or Van Ness Station.*

see map p. 345

Most MUNI buses and Golden Gate Transit buses (#10, 20, 50, and 70) also stop at the Civic Center. **Driving:** *Take either Market or Van Ness. Parking meters and lots around the Civic Center are plentiful but pricey.*

There's no mistaking the colossal Civic Center, with its mammoth classical buildings arranged around two vast plazas. Home to the opera, symphony, and most of San Francisco's major theater, the district is grandest at night, when beautifully lit flags and fountains flank bumper-to-bumper limousine traffic.

Embarcadero Plaza

from the road

Gentle People Here

I stepped out of the cab, ready to engage with a new coast and culture. Inevitably, my grand entrance was spoiled as my luggage broke, spilling my clothing for the next two months in front of a parking garage entrance on one of the many SF hills. Rushing to gather my things, I was startled by the lights of a red truck coming to a quick stop in my path. As I caught my breath, I prepared myself for some verbal abuse. But, the driver looked at me with a bright smile on his face, and yelled, "Get out of the way sunshine!"

I decided not to let a rough start get in the way of a first day of street exploration. Walking down Fillmore St., I was struck by the way people seemed to carry themselves. People walked with purpose, but without the sense of frenetic chaos I was used to in New York.

I ended my first day in SF in the Castro. Rainbow flags lined the streets as emblems of the city's diversity and history. I chatted with a few residents in a cafe about my initial impressions and expectations of the city, noting that I expected to miss the tenseness and energy of NY. They merely laughed and sent me back to my apartment, reminding me that many San Franciscans were still "gentle people," whether or not they had "flowers in their hair."

—Jordan Woods

14

HAYES VALLEY

🔎 NEIGHBORHOOD QUICKFIND: **Sights,** p. 92; **Food & Drink,** p. 126; **Nightlife,** p. 149; **Accommodations,** p. 196.

see map p. 345

📍 **Orientation:** Hayes Valley lies just west of the Civic Center, between Franklin and Laguna St., bordered to the north and south by Grove and Fell St., respectively. **Public Transportation:** Take MUNI bus #21, which runs down Hayes St. Bus #22 runs on Fillmore St. and also stops at Hayes St.; walk east on Hayes St. to get to Hayes Valley. You can also take BART to the Civic Center Station or MUNI J, K, L, M, or N to the Van Ness Station. From there, walk down Market St., take a right onto Franklin St., and turn left onto Hayes St. where a huge sign for the neighborhood greets you. **Driving:** Streets are easy to navigate, but parking will only be found on the outskirts.

The hipster is king to the west of the Civic Center. Recently gentrified **Hayes Valley** is small, glitzy, and increasingly upscale. Formerly two distinct areas divided by a looming freeway, Hayes Valley's east side harbored trendy stores and eateries, while the west side functioned as the business grounds for prostitutes and drug dealers. The 1989 earthquake brought the freeway down, and the rebuilding process brought artists in. Because the architects, interior designers, and fashionistas who call Hayes home needed studios to work in, cafes to chat in, and pads to sleep in, the area got a bit more pricey and the seedier elements moved to tiny Tenderloin. Success has brought higher prices, but the coffee's still cheap, and gallery-hopping and window-shopping remain delightfully free of charge, so the increasingly high-end Hayes St. still allows for bouts of bohemia.

TENDERLOIN

🔎 NEIGHBORHOOD QUICKFIND: **Sights,** p. 93; **Food & Drink,** p. 127; **Nightlife,** p. 150; **Accommodations,** p. 197.

see map p. 345

📍 **Orientation:** The area begins north of Market St. and stretches roughly from Van Ness Ave. north of Golden Gate Ave. to Taylor St., and north toward Post St. **Public Transportation:** Take BART or MUNI J, K, L, M, or N to the Powell St. Station. **Driving:** Public transportation is better. If you drive, park in SoMa and walk to the Tenderloin.

The amorphous region known as the Tenderloin is economic light-years away from its neighbors, upscale Union Sq. and cultural heavyweight Civic Center. Though many of the posh hotels in Union Sq. actually fall within the Tenderloin for administrative purposes, for all practical purposes, the area is defined socially—as one native put it, "if something good happens, then we're Nob Hill, but if it's mildly negative, then we're Tenderloin." As low-income neighborhoods go, this one is smaller than its counterparts in Oakland or Los Angeles, and sporadic attempts at **urban renewal** have done a bit to improve the poverty of the quarter and its residents. Also, because Geary, Polk, and Van Ness serve as major thoroughfares in the city, the Tenderloin's streets are rarely completely deserted. Nevertheless, **avoid walking here alone, especially in the rectangle formed by Ellis St., Van Ness Ave., Taylor St., and Golden Gate Ave. and the stripclub-lined stretch of Market St. from 5th to 8th St.** If you find yourself in this area at night (for example, if you're heading home from one of the hot nightspots), don't linger, and walk briskly (preferably with a companion).

SOUTH OF MARKET AREA (SOMA)

🔢 NEIGHBORHOOD QUICKFIND: **Sights,** p. 94; **Food & Drink,** p. 127; **Nightlife,** p. 151; **Accommodations,** p. 198.

⬛ Orientation: South of Market Area extends west to South Van Ness Ave. and south and east to the ocean. **Public Transportation:** Take BART or MUNI to the Civic Center and walk down 7th or 8th St.; alternatively, from the Powell St. Station, walk down 4th St. **Driving:** Howard, Folsom, Harrison, and Bryant St. all run one-way in alternating directions. Parking is relatively plentiful by day on the long, deserted streets. Watch for street-cleaning prohibitions beginning around midnight. **Garages: Service Directory,** p. 316.

see map p. 347

Although the South of Market Area (usually abbreviated **SoMa**) may seem like a bleak expanse of industrial warehouses and intermittent homelessness, it has served as landscape for three rich spheres of life and culture. This is where the **Leather and Levi's** community congregated in the 1940s and 50s, from which a wild and wonderful nightlife scene burgeoned (p. 184). The leather and whips still pulse in some bars like **Hole in the Wall** (p. 152) and **The Stud** (p. 153) and come out full force at the annual Folsom St. Fair (p. 30). The area is now also home to a wide variety of hip **nightlife** for all types and vibrant daytime **art venues.** A well-visited cultural area lies north of Folsom St., between 2nd and 4th St. These blocks are filled with the concrete and glass expanses of **Yerba Buena Gardens,** Metreon, and the Moscone Convention Center. The **San Francisco Museum of Modern Art** (SFMOMA) presides over the cultural milieu. Several blocks south, between **Pacific Bell Park** (home of the San Francisco Giants, p. 172) and the freeway, the tiny but vibrant South Park is surrounded by old and new eateries as well as the "cyberspace gulch" of upstart Internet and design companies. Finally, the stretch from 6th to 12th St. along Folsom St., toward the Mission, is known for being hip and clubby. Its trendy cafes, inexpensive restaurants, myriad clubs, and establishments dedicated to the wearing and selling of leather are unfortunately threatened by rising rents. Many small businesses have shut down, and battles still rage in the newspapers over who should have priority—late night clubbers or ear-plugged tenants.

PACIFIC HEIGHTS & JAPANTOWN

PACIFIC HEIGHTS

🔢 NEIGHBORHOOD QUICKFIND: **Sights,** p. 95; **Food & Drink,** p. 129; **Accommodations,** p. 198.

⬛ Orientation: Pacific Heights is bordered by Bush St. to the south, Lyon St. to the west, Van Ness Ave. to the east, and Union St. to the north. **Public Transportation:** Take MUNI bus #1, 3, 12, or 45 to Fillmore St., or the #22 up Fillmore St. From downtown, take MUNI bus #27 from Cyril Magnin St. going away from Market St. and get off at Jackson and Van Ness. **Driving:** Divisadero St. runs both ways from the Marina through Pacific Heights and down to the Haight, where it turns into Castro St. and continues down to Noe Valley. Street parking is plentiful in Pacific Heights.

see map p. 348

Stunning views of both the city and the Bay, the legendary **Fillmore St. jazz scene,** and elegantly restored **Victorian homes** all put Pacific Heights on the map. Because this region of the city escaped serious damage in the 1906 earthquake and benefited from modern restoration technology by the time the 1989 rumbler hit, Pacific Heights boasts one of the city's largest sections of turn-of-the-century architecture. Mansions used as foreign consulates, as well as an abundance of other grand homes, can be found around Pierce and Clay St. The **Public Library** offers free tours of Pacific Heights mansions during the summer. Hip clothing vendors and tasty restaurants line Fillmore St. and spill over onto Union St. in northern Pacific Heights. South toward Geary Expwy., sounds of the 1950s Fillmore live on in top jazz and blues bars.

JAPANTOWN (NIHONMACHI)

⬛ NEIGHBORHOOD QUICKFIND: Sights, p. 15; **Food & Drink,** p. 129.

⬛ Orientation: One mile west of downtown, Japantown is bordered to the north by Bush St., to the west by Fillmore St., to the east by Laguna St., and to the south by Geary Expwy. **Public Transportation:** Take MUNI bus #2, 3, or 4 to Sutter St., #38 to Geary Blvd., or #22 down Fillmore St. **Driving:** Sutter and Post St. run one-way in opposite directions. Fillmore, Webster, and Laguna St. connect them. Street parking available.

After the area was destroyed by the 1906 earthquake, Japanese immigrants started to reside in the area known as Japantown, just south of Pacific Heights. For a time, its closely packed homes and shops comprised one of the largest Japanese enclaves outside of Japan. Few returned after the community was broken apart by internment during WWII, but the name remained. Even though less than 4% of San Francisco's Japanese population currently resides in Japantown, the shopping malls and traditional shops convey interesting aspects of Japanese-American culture. Seeing Japantown by foot takes just minutes. Stores hawk the latest Asian popstar and animé paraphernalia, and patrons warble J-pop in karaoke bars along Post St. near the **Japan Center.**

HAIGHT-ASHBURY

see map p. 349

⬛ NEIGHBORHOOD QUICKFIND: Sights, p. 97; **Food & Drink,** p. 130; **Nightlife,** p. 154; **Accommodations,** p. 198.

⬛ Orientation: Centered around the intersection of Haight and Ashbury St., the area is divided into the **Upper Haight,** between Golden Gate Park and Divisadero St., and the **Lower Haight,** east of Divisadero St. to about Fillmore St. **Public transportation:** MUNI buses #6, 7, 16, 22, 24, 33, 43, 66, and 71 all serve the Haight, while Metro line N runs along Carl St., 4 blocks to the south. **Driving:** Page and Haight St. run both ways the length of the Haight. Parking is available on cross-streets, at least a few blocks from Haight St.

East of Golden Gate Park, smack dab in the center of the city, the Haight has aged with uneven grace since its **hippie** heyday. The neighborhood's large Victorian houses began to attract post-Beat **Bohemians** in the early 1960s for communal living (**Life & Times,** p. 56). At one time a haven for conscientious objectors, "Hashbury" subsequently embraced drug-use and Eastern philosophies as well as anti-war protests and marches. The hippie voyage reached its apogee in 1967's **"Summer of Love,"** when Janis Joplin, the Grateful Dead, and Jefferson Airplane all made music and love here within a few blocks of each other. Flamboyant dress scared off the traditionalists, LSD permeated local consciousness, and young people from across the country converged on the grassy panhandle for the celebrated **Be-Ins.** To some, the Haight seemed the very confluence of spiritual power; to others, it was just one hell of a party.

Today the counterculture hangs out side-by-side with the tourist culture, especially in the Upper Haight, where the 60s, its ideals firmly emblazoned on consumer products, live on in the forms of tie-dyed t-shirts, hemp jewelry, cuddly Grateful Dead bears, and water pipes. The Lower Haight, on the other hand, still clings to the good ol' days despite the latest additions of Internet cafes and smoothie joints. Fewer tourists venture below Divisadero St., leaving the area with a much more mellow atmosphere, preferred by those seeking a less commodified glimpse of the past.

CASTRO

⚑ NEIGHBORHOOD QUICKFIND:
Sights, p. 99; *Food & Drink,* p. 132; *Nightlife,* p. 155; *Accommodations,* p. 199.

see map p. 350

▣ Orientation: *Most people here seem sure of their orientation (or lack thereof), but in case you need a little help, the center of the Castro, also called Castro Village, runs along Castro St. from Harvey Milk Plaza at Market St. down to 19th St. The other major shopping, munching, and cruising area stretches up Market St. from Milk Plaza to the intersection of Church and 14th St.* **Public Transportation:** *Take MUNI F, K, L, or M or MUNI bus #37 down Market St. to the Castro St. station. Bus #24 runs along Castro St. between 14th and 26th St.* **Driving:** *Go southwest from downtown on Market St. 1hr. meters and 2hr. street parking can sometimes be found on the blocks surrounding Castro St. Spots are more available further from the main drag.*

Scout's honor, *this* is where the boys are. Much of San Francisco's **queer community** (mostly male as well as a smaller number of hip young lesbians) make the Castro home. The wild days of the 1970s, when discos throbbed all night and day, have come and gone, but **Harvey Milk Plaza,** at Castro and Market St., remains the pulsing heart of gay San Francisco. Cruisey bars and cafes are everywhere, same-sex public displays of affection raise nary an eyebrow, and tank tops and chiseled abs are a must. Besides the sights of the gorgeous and the good-looking, the Castro also boasts rhetoric of community and great views of the city. Halfway down the hill from the Castro MUNI stop at the intersection of Market and 17th St. are views across the Noe and Eureka Valleys to the south, and the hills around Buena Vista Park and Twin Peaks to the northwest. Away from the hubbub of Castro St., affluent guppies (yes, gay yuppies) live on quiet streets lined with trees and rainbow flags south from Market St. to Noe Valley and west from Mission St. to Portola Dr. and Twin Peaks.

GIVING BACK

Kay Rodriguez, a youth program director, talks about the role she plays in the lives of inner-city kids.

I've been working here for seven years. They used to say that this area had the highest concentration of children in the city, and it makes a difference when kids have a place to run free. [Here] kids feel support, they get a chance to act, a little more positive feedback, and a sense of right and wrong. As a rec director, you get really close to the kids. You can't really avoid it...why would you be in this business if you wanted to avoid it? I got to the point in my life where I needed more security and working with kids interested me the most. When you make a kid smile, you feel good.

Sometimes you think: "Look at all these poor children, these prostitutes and drug dealers." But when you see what is happening with one child...his mother who's the prostitute on the corner [but] doing a really good job raising him. When she comes here she is just a mother. When [she] crosses our threshold, she's not what the community perceives her to be. She's a parent in our community, doing what she can to raise her kid the best she can.

(Tenderloin Park & Recreation Center, 570 Ellis St. ☎ 292-2162 for volunteer info.)

Alamo Square

Washington Square

NOE VALLEY

see map p. 350

🚩 NEIGHBORHOOD QUICKFIND: **Sights,** p. 100; **Food & Drink,** p. 133; **Nightlife,** p. 158; **Accommodations,** p. 201.

🚩 **Orientation:** Noe Valley's main drag is 24th St. between Guerrero and Diamond St. **Public Transportation:** Take MUNI J or bus #24 to 24th St. **Driving:** Getting to Noe Valley is easy: the streets from Church to Guerrero run both ways to Market St. Once you get there, though, parking is a pain. Search for meters on 24th St. or in the metered lot between Noe and Castro St.

Named after a local Mexican rancher, Don Jose de Jesus Noe, Noe Valley (pronounced NO-ee) has seen many incarnations. Its early days were spent as dairy land. Isolated due to the lack of public transportation, the area developed a strong sense of community, driven by the Irish working class as well as German, Italian, and Hispanic immigrants. The place started hopping when hippies and fresh folk discovered the allure of the scenic architecture and fabulous weather. The trend continued into the 1980s, when young couples made it their home-of-choice. Noe Valley now overflows with rosy-cheeked, upwardly mobile people (and their babies) and the charming bakeries, salons, and restaurants that often follow in their wake.

MISSION

see map p. 352

🚩 NEIGHBORHOOD QUICKFIND: **Sights,** p. 102; **Food & Drink,** p. 135; **Nightlife,** p. 158; **Accommodations,** p. 202.

🚩 **Orientation:** The Mission lies south of Market St. and is roughly bordered by 16th St. to the north, US 101 to the east, César Chavez (formerly Army) St. to the south, and the Castro to the west. Activity centered on Mission and Valencia St. extends toward the Castro on 16th and 20th St. **Public Transportation:** BART has stops at 16th and 24th St. ($1.10 from downtown). MUNI buses #9, 12, 14, 22, 26, 27, 33, 53, and 67 trace the area. MUNI J runs down Church St. to the west. SamTrans runs throughout the district. **Driving:** Mission and Valencia St. are both easy to navigate. Parking is plentiful on cross-streets, except on 16th and 20th St.

Founded by Spanish settlers in 1776, the Mission district is home to some of the city's **oldest structures,** as well as some of the hottest young people and places around. Colorful **murals** celebrate the prominent Latino presence that has long defined the Mission. The area grows increasingly diverse and gentrified along **Valencia St.** Politically, the Mission is the city's most radical pocket, marked by left-wing bookstores, active labor associations, and bohemian bars and cafes filled with hipsters and hippies. The area is also home to a cohesive lesbian community and gay male presence. Outgrowing its reputation as one of the most under-appreciated neighborhoods in the city, the Mission prides itself on a virtual micro-climate that stays sunny and smiling while the rest of Frisco sulks in a fog. Beyond the fabulous food and kickin' nightlife, the Mission is home to a vibrant community of painters and writers struggling to keep their messages heard.

BERNAL HEIGHTS

⊠ *NEIGHBORHOOD QUICKFIND:* ***Sights,*** *p. 104;* ***Food & Drink,*** *p. 136;* ***Nightlife,*** *p. 160.*

⊠ Orientation: *Bernal Heights is roughly bounded by César Chavez St. to the north, San Jose Ave. to the west, Alemany Blvd. to the south, and Bayshore Blvd. to the east.* ***Public Transportation:*** *Take BART to 24th St. Mission, then take the #14 bus to the bottom of Cortland Ave. MUNI bus #24 runs crosstown along Cortland; #23 traverses the southern part of Bernal Heights; #67 runs down Market St. to 24th St.*

see map p. 352

where it continues down Folsom St. through Cortland Ave. ***Driving:*** *Turn left off Mission St. onto César Chavez St., and then right up Folsom or Alabama St. Parking is plentiful.*

A product of rapid gentrification, Bernal Heights has changed so much over the past few years that many long-time residents still don't know what hit them. Formerly ranking with the Tenderloin as one of the more undesirable neighborhoods in town, Bernal Heights is now overflowing with young families and professionals who savor the convenience of the nearby Mission's activities from the quiet of the hills. You should still exercise caution at night around Bernal Heights Park—roads are curvy and deserted and may be dangerous.

POTRERO HILL

⊠ *NEIGHBORHOOD QUICKFIND:* ***Sights,*** *p. 104;* ***Food & Drink,*** *p. 137;* ***Nightlife,*** *p. 160.*

⊠ Orientation: *Flanked by freeways (US 101 and I-280), Potrero Hill stretches north from 16th St. and rises to 22nd St. before sloping south down to César Chavez St.* ***Public Transportation:*** *MUNI bus #19 follows Rhode Island St. south from SoMa (and goes back downtown via De Haro St.), crossing line #22 at 17th St. and continuing south.*

see map p. 353

MUNI bus #22's lengthy but convenient route traces a crooked east-west path ending at 3rd St. near the waterfront. ***Driving:*** *State-named streets run one-way north-south from the bottom of the hill to the top. East-west streets are numbered and run both ways. Street parking is ample.*

Residential and quaint Potrero Hill hides its communal **small-town warmth** between two freeways that (in)conveniently bypass this treasure for a more bustling downtown. Victorian homes have survived earthquakes in this stable location, where the visibly buxom Twin Peaks to the west divert fog north toward the city skyline. Today, the neighborhood where O.J. Simpson grew up has retained the best pieces of its upbringing and projects an unassuming, diversely artsy, middle-class demeanor. The placid bustle of 18th St. could double as the Main St. of some small town, but with one delightfully insistent bonus—Potrero's distant elevation south of downtown affords the best postcard **panoramic view** of the San Francisco skyline. Walk up DeHaro or Carolina St. toward 22nd St. for even more sweeping views of Twin Peaks and the East Bay.

RICHMOND

⚑ *NEIGHBORHOOD QUICKFIND:* **Food & Drink,** *p. 139;* **Nightlife,** *p. 160;* **Accommodations,** *p. 202.*

⬧ Orientation: *The Richmond extends east from Point Lobos to Arguello Blvd. The* **Inner Richmond** *lies between Arguello Blvd. and Park Presidio Blvd. Between Park Presidio Blvd. and the beach is the* **Outer Richmond,** *which extends east from Pt. Lobos to Arguello Blvd.*

see map p. 341   *Geary Blvd. is the Richmond's main thoroughfare. Clement St. is the principal shopping and dining strip.* **Public Transportation:** *MUNI bus #2 runs along Clement St. from Lincoln Park to Sutter St. and eventually Union Sq. Bus #38 transverses the entire city via Geary Blvd. from the Transbay Terminal in the east to Pt. Lobos in the west.* **Driving:** *Parking is plentiful.*

Beneath its fog and blank facade of stuccoed buildings, the Richmond is a riot of immigrant history and student life. This mainly residential area is home to Irish-, Russian-, and Chinese-Americans. East of Park Presidio Blvd., the **Inner Richmond**, festooned with cut-price grocery stores and excellent ethnic cuisine, is known as **"New Chinatown."** The **Outer Richmond** holds a handful of Russian delis, an abundance of Irish pubs, and an imposing orthodox church.

SUNSET

⚑ *NEIGHBORHOOD QUICKFIND:* **Sights,** *p. 105;* **Food & Drink,** *p. 140;* **Nightlife,** *p. 161.*

⬧ Orientation: *Stretching from Golden Gate Park to Stern Grove, the* **Inner Sunset** *lies east of Sunset Blvd., while the* **Outer Sunset** *reaches to the ocean.* **Public Transportation:** *The fastest way to get into the Sunset is to take the MUNI N (Judah St.), which runs from Market St.*

see map p. 341   *down to Arguello Blvd. near the southeast corner of the park, then through the northern Sunset. MUNI buses #1, 2, 31, and 71 run east-west toward MUNI bus #28. #28 runs south on Park Presidio Blvd., through Golden Gate Park, down to the heart of Sunset at Irving St.* **Driving:** *Driving and parking are very easy here. Numbered avenues run north-south, and cross streets are named alphabetically from Irving St. near Golden Gate Park to Wawona St., by Stern Grove.*

It may look like a flat, suburban sprawl on the map, but the Sunset has a lot to offer. Unspoiled by tourists and real estate madness, this middle-class and student-heavy district is an untarnished slice of "real life." Golden Gate Park, with its recreational facilities, museums, and gardens of greenery, lies one block north of Irving St. For the visitor, fantastic cheap food, used bookstores, lively cafes, and laid-back bars are worth the 15min. MUNI ride from Haight-Ashbury.

OCEAN BEACH

⚑ *NEIGHBORHOOD QUICKFIND:* **Sights,** *p. 106.*

⬧ Orientation: *Ocean Beach begins south of Pt. Lobos and Lincoln Park's Cliff House and extends down the northwestern edge of the city's coast for 4 mi. to Fort Funston.* **Public Transportation:** *MUNI bus #18 runs the length of Ocean Beach within 3 blocks of the water. #48 and 71 routes terminate right at Ocean Beach.* **Driving:** *The Great Hwy. runs north-south*

see map p. 341   *alongside Ocean Beach. Street parking is plentiful.*

On the extreme western edge of the city, running parallel to the Great Highway (and, of course, the Pacific), Ocean Beach attracts crowds despite its frigid waters and dangerous riptides. The largest and most popular of San Francisco's beaches, Ocean Beach's golden sand can stretch 100 yards to the ocean's edge during low tide. The lighting here is frequently diffuse and hazy—a combination of city smog and ocean fog—making the beach seem like an ethereal movie set.

enough already...
Get a room.

Book your next hotel with the people who know what you want.

ZOO, LAKE MERCED, FORT FUNSTON & STERN GROVE

🔎 *NEIGHBORHOOD QUICKFIND:* **Sights,** *p. 106;* **Food & Drink,** *p. 141.*

📍 *Orientation: In the southwest corner of the city, the Zoo, Lake Merced, Fort Funston, and Stern Grove lie just south of Sunset and extend to Daly City. Skyline Blvd. and Lake Merced Blvd. run around Lake Merced. Sloat Blvd. runs along the Zoo at the northern tip of the area, and then along the southern edge of Stern Grove.* **Public Transportation:** *MUNI L follows Taraval St. and ends at 46th Ave. and Wawona St., 1 block north of Sloat Blvd. MUNI K and M have stops*

see map p. 353

passing through West Portal and at St. Francis Circle, 4 blocks east of Stern Grove entrance. MUNI bus #23 follows Sloat Blvd.; #18 circles Lake Merced on Lake Merced Blvd. and Skyline Blvd. **Driving:** *Sloat, Skyline, and Lake Merced Blvd. are easy to reach from the Great Hwy., 46th Ave., Sunset Blvd., and 19th Ave. Parking in the area is plentiful.*

The southern end of Ocean Beach opens up into the wild and windswept sand-dunes of **Fort Funston,** yet another abandoned military garrison. Just to the north, you can gawk at non-native species in the **San Francisco Zoo.** For a few hours away from the screeching of monkeys, parrots, and kids, **Lake Merced** is a peaceful place to walk, fish, or row. Just north of the lake, **Stern Grove** draws crowds to the fantastic summer music festival from June-August in its foresty outdoor **amphitheater.**

IN THE BAY

ALCATRAZ

🔎 *ISLAND QUICKFIND:* **Sights,** *p. 109.*

📍 *Orientation: Alcatraz lies just north of Fisherman's Wharf. Assistance is available for those with disabilities.* **Transportation:** *To get to Alcatraz or Angel Island, take the Blue and Gold Fleet (☎ 773-1188, tickets ☎ 705-5555; www.blueandgoldfleet.com), from Pier 41 (p. 65). Ticket lines can be painfully long. Reserve tickets at least a day (and preferably a week) in advance, especially in summer. If all else fails, the Blue and*

see map p. 336

Gold ticket counter in the basement of the DFS Galleria in Union Square on Geary St. and Stockton St. offers a number of "extra" tickets on sold out days for a $2.25 mark-up. First boat departs pier 41 at 9:30, then 10:15am and every 30 min. until 4:15pm. Arrive 20min. before departure. Adults $9.25, seniors $7.50, ages 5-11 $6. **Contact:** *www.nps.gov/alcatraz.* **Audio tours:** *Adults $4, ages 5-11 $2.* **Alcatraz after dark:** *call for times and availability. Adults $20.75, seniors and ages 12-17 $18, ages 5-11 $11.50 (includes audio tour).* **Park Ranger guided tours:** *Free. Offered daily. See Alcatraz dock for daily schedule. Other boating companies run shorter tours up to and around—but not onto—the island for about $10 per person.* **Ferries:** *p. 109.*

This former military outpost and federal prison—named by Spanish explorers after the small cormorant *alcatraceo* (and not for flocks of *alcatraces*, or pelicans, as is widely believed), Alcatraz Island looms over the San Francisco Bay, 1½ mi. from Fisherman's Wharf. In its 29 years as a maximum security federal penitentiary, 36 criminals tried to escape; only one was known to survive the swim while five were never heard of again. From 1969-1971, Native American political activists occupied Alcatraz to raise awareness of issues surrounding Native American civil rights. Alcatraz is now a **National Park area** and a great place to appreciate its present reincarnation as a haven for wildlife.

ANGEL ISLAND

🔎 *ISLAND QUICKFIND:* **Sights,** *p. 109.*

📍 *Orientation: Angel Island, a few miles north of Alcatraz, is the largest of the 14 islands in the Bay. Assistance available for those with disabilities.* **Transportation:** *see above.* **State Park:** *☎ 435-1915.* **Contact:** *historical info: www.angelisland.org; commercial info: www.angelis-land.com.* **Tours:** *☎ 897-0715. 1hr. historic TramTours depart from Ayala Cove Apr.-Nov. M-F*

Protests at Pride

Outdoor Garden

St. Patrick's Church

10:30am, 12:15, 1:30pm; Sa-Su and holidays 10:30am, 12:15, 1:30, and 3:15. Adults $11.50, seniors $10.50, ages 6-12 $7.50, under 5 free. Self-guided audio tours ($5.75) also available. State park, docent-led tours of historic sites available May-Oct. Sa-Su. (☎ 435-3522). **Kayak tours:** *☎ 448-1000; www.seatrekkayak.com. Led by Sausalito-based SeaTrek Kayak; May-Oct. 10:30am-1pm and 1:30-4pm every Su. Includes instruction, tour, and equipment ($75).*

Much larger and less-visited, Angel Island offers a **serene getaway** with miles of hiking and biking trails and spectacular views. During the early 1900s, the island was labeled the "Ellis Island of the West" but actually served as a detention center after the Chinese Exclusion Act of 1882 was passed to prevent Chinese immigrants from entering the US. During WWII, the grounds primarily served as a prisoner-of-war camp for German and Japanese prisoners.

SUGGESTED ITINERARIES

San Francisco is a complex, multi-flavored city bursting at the seams with things to see and do. Try these 3-, 5-, and 7-day tours if you're here for a week or less and are too overwhelmed by the city's offerings to prioritize.

THREE DAYS

DAY ONE: DIVE RIGHT IN. Kick off your whirlwind tour by plunging headfirst into the heart of the city. Start your day with breakfast at **Squat and Gobble** or another **Haight-Ashbury** joint (p. 131). Get a taste of Haight's history with one of the area's walking tours (p. 27) or check out the houses of the weird and famous on your own (p. 83). Just west of the Haight lies the largest urban park in the United States. Get up close and personal with **Golden Gate Park's** bison or explore all of the museums and gardens along the way (p. 83). Break out the munchies on **Strawberry Hill** in the middle of the park. When you reach the beach, hang a right and finish off the afternoon with the museums and sights in the **Cliff House** (p. 137). For a little nighttime fun, take MUNI bus #30 to **SoMa's** hopping clubs and bars (p. 151).

DAY TWO: ANCHORS AWAY. Eat an excellent breakfast in the **Marina** at **Home Plate** (p. 117). Wander around the **Marina** gawking at the fancy homes and poking your head into the cool shops

(p. 185). While you're there, make a stop at **Marina Safeway** (p. 117) and get provisions for a picnic lunch as you follow the **On the Waterfront Walking Tour** (p. 29). When you finish, take MUNI bus #28 to the Marina and change to #30 to Market St. From Market St., you can take BART into the **Mission** to **burrito heaven** (p. 135). After your meal, hit one of the Mission's many **nightlife hotspots** (p. 158).

DAY THREE: BE A TOURIST, BE (AND SEE) A STAR. Catch a quick breakfast bite at **Pat's Café** (p. 116). While following the **Tourist Trap Walking Tour** for the first half of your day (p. 27), pick up ferry tickets for Alcatraz, where you can spend the afternoon (p. 109). When you escape in the evening, take MUNI bus #32 to the Embarcadero station, where you'll change for MUNI J. Take it to the end of the line in **Noe Valley** (p. 100) and dine in style (p. 133). When the stars come out, put away your dancing shoes and take out your boots to hike up to the top of **Twin Peaks** for views and romance (p. 101).

FIVE DAYS

If the first three days were just enough to whet your appetite, try these additional two as a generous course.

DAY FOUR: MAKE LIKE YOGURT (CULTURE YOURSELF). Grab a bite to eat at **Dottie's True Blue Cafe** (p. 122) in **Union Sq.** and then head over to **Post** or **Sutter St.** where small **galleries** line the streets (p. 76). Grab dinner at the **Sotano Grill** (p. 123) or another veggie-friendly restaurant and then a taste of live blues at one of Union Square's hip clubs like **Blue Lamp** (p. 166). After dinner, hop on MUNI bus #2 to Market St. and the **Civic Center.** See what's happening at **Justice League** (p. 167), or sit back and relax at a **symphony** or **ballet** (p. 166).

DAY FIVE: MORNIN', SUNSHINE. HOW 'BOUT A DRIVE?
Whether you've got a car or are relying on public transportation, a daytrip to **Berkeley** is definitely in order (p. 209). Start with a sumptuous meal in the **Gourmet Ghetto** or at another posh restaurant (p. 212) and then head over to the university and check out all Cal has to offer (p. 215). With its funky shops and counterculture bent, Berkeley is a great place to flex the credit card power; shopping is best on **Telegraph Ave.** (p. 220). Finish off the evening with dinner at **The Blue Nile** (p. 213) or another fine ethnic restaurant and catch a show at one of the area's theaters (p. 227).

SEVEN DAYS

Finishing up the suggested itineraries with days six and seven will practically ensure that you'll leave a San Francisco "native."

DAY SIX: HERE, THERE, AND EVERYWHERE. Have breakfast with a view on **Nob** or **Russian Hill** (p. 121). Meander down Jones or Leavenworth St. to peep into the **Tenderloin**—you might not catch all of the wild nighttime sights, but you'll benefit from the safety of daylight (p. 93). Spend a few hours enjoying the architecture, museums, and galleries of the **Civic Center** and Hayes Valley (p. 80). Move on down Mission St. to 16th or 20th St. for an excellent lunch selection (p. 135). Follow 16th St. to Dolores and duck into the **Mission Dolores** (p. 102). Then go up to 18th St. and continue on past **Mission Dolores Park** (p. 103) into the **Castro** (p. 99). Cruise the scene and novelty shops of one of the world's most famous queer neighborhoods, then break for dinner (p. 132). In the evening, either toss back a few drinks at a local bar (p. 155) or catch an organ show and a flick at the **Castro Theatre** (p. 170).

DAY SEVEN: CLIMB EVERY MOUNTAIN (WELL, JUST ONE). Pack a picnic, and then rent a car or hop a bus to **Mount Tamalpais State Park** (p. 238). If it's lunchtime and you're hungry, break out the basket in the **Bootjack Picnic Area** (p. 238). Swing by the **Pan Toll Rangers Station** to pick up some trail maps and start a-hikin' (p. 238). On clear days, look for fabulous views of the entire San Francisco coastline, the East Bay, the Golden Gate Bridge, and the sparkling blue waters below. Hike on into the center of the park to **Muir Woods** and stand in a hush under the giant, regal redwoods (p. 239). When you've taken in all the natural beauty you can in a day, head back to the city, take a good shower, put up your feet, and relax.

SEASONAL EVENTS

No matter the time of year, San Francisco hosts an astounding array of seasonal events, though the summer is an especially busy time. Events like Pride (can draw as many as 700,000 people, nearly doubling the city's population and making little things like a hotel reservation or a parking space worth their weights in gold. Plan early, keep an open mind, and enjoy. Events below are listed chronologically; in addition, the Visitors Center has a recording of current events (☎391-2001).

SPRING

Examiner Bay to Breakers (☎359-2800; www.baytobreakers.com), on the 3rd Su in May starting at the Embarcadero at 8am. The largest foot race in the US, with up to 100,000 participants, covers 7½ mi. in inimitable San Francisco style. Runners win not only on their times but on their costumes as well. Special centipede category.

Tulipmania (☎705-5500), Pier 39. Tiptoe through 39,000 tulips from around the world. Free.

International Asian American Film Festival (☎255-4299; www.naatanet.org), in mid-Mar., AMC Kabuki 8 Theater, Japantown. Plays over 50 Asian and Asian-American feature and short films, most $8-15.

St. Patrick's Day Parade (☎675-9885). One of SF's biggest annual parades and one of the longest-running in the US. Starts at noon at 2nd and Market St. and ends at City Hall.

Cherry Blossom Festival (☎563-2313), Japantown. A Japanese cultural festival on 2 consecutive weekends in April featuring hundreds of performers.

Spike and Mike's Festival of Animation (☎621-6120; www.spikeandmike.com), Apr.-May, Palace of Fine Arts and the Castro Theatre. Shows animated films from *Wallace and Grommit* to *Lupo the Butcher.* Check website for schedule.

San Francisco International Film Festival (☎561-5000; www.sffs.org), Apr.-May, Kabuki and Castro Theaters. The oldest film festival in North America, showing more than 100 international films of all genres over 2 weeks, most $9.

A Fair to Remember (☎750-8340), early May, in Golden Gate Park. Features crafts, food, entertainment, and an auction held to raise funds for the AIDS National Grove endowment.

Cinco de Mayo (☎256-3005), during the weekend nearest May 5. The Mission explodes with colorful costumes and mariachi bands to celebrate Mexican Independence.

Carnaval (☎920-0125; www.carnavalSF.com), Memorial Day weekend. San Francisco's take on Mardi Gras, featuring Latino, jazz, and samba Caribbean music and more.

SUMMER

San Francisco International Gay and Lesbian Film Festival (☎703-8650; www.frameline.org), during the 11 days leading up to Pride Day (June 26-27 in 2004), at the Roxie (at 16th and Valencia St.) and Castro Theatre (at Castro and Market St.). California's 2nd-largest film festival and the world's largest lesbian and gay media event. Tickets go fast. $6-15.

Stern Grove San Francisco Midsummer Music Festival (☎252-6252; www.sterngrove.org), for 10 weeks from June-Aug., in Stern Grove, south of Golden Gate Park. Free opera, ballet, jazz, world music, and *a capella* on Sundays. Arrive early for best seating. Performances 2pm; pre-performance talks 11am.

San Francisco Black Film Festival (☎346-0199; www.juneteenthfilmfestival.org), the weekend closest to June 14 (June 11-13 in 2004), location TBA. Celebrates black indie film.

Pride Day (☎864-3733; www.sfpride.org), on the last Su in June (June 27 in 2004). The High Holy Day of the queer calendar. Officially it's called Lesbian, Gay, Bisexual, Transgender Pride Day, with a **parade** and events downtown starting at 10:30am. Pink Saturday, the night before, brings a sea of bodies to the Castro, where the party actually lasts 12 months.

Fourth of July Waterfront Festival (☎705-5500; www.pier39.com), fireworks on the waterfront starting around 9pm. About as American as you can get.

San Francisco Jewish Film Festival (☎621-0556; www.sfjff.org), from mid-July to early Aug. An area-wide festival, the oldest in the world.

Cable Car Bell-Ringing Championship (☎923-6217; www.sfmuni.com), on the 3rd Th in July (July 15 in 2004), Fisherman's Wharf or Union Sq. Where people who have spent years perfecting their clang go to get recognition.

North Beach Jazz Festival (☎771-2061; www.nbjazzfest.org), the last week of July or beginning of August at venues from Washington Sq. Park to Telegraph Hill. Assortment of musicians. Every Sa afternoon June-Sept. at the Cannery free jazz performances. Free-$15.

Nihonmachi Street Fair (☎771-9861), in early Aug. in Japantown. Lion dancers, *taiko* drummers, and karaoke wars.

FALL

San Francisco Shakespeare Festival (☎865-4434), every Sa and Su in September, in Golden Gate Park. Shows begin at 1:30pm, but get there at noon for a seat. Free.

▧ **San Francisco Fringe Festival** (☎931-1094; www.sffringe.org), starting the 1st Th after Labor Day (Sept. 9 in 2004), at several theaters downtown, all within walking distance of each other. Experimental

NO **WORK** ALL **PLAY**

A Matter of Pride

Each summer SF celebrates Pride, drawing enough queer pilgrims to nearly double the city's population (www.sfpride.com; June 27 in 2004). Rainbow flags are hoisted above the streets; stores highlight gay literature and history; and the streets, clubs, bars, and hotels burst at the seems to accommodate gay revelers. In 2003, "Let the Queer Revolution Begin" signs were brandished as the Supreme Court overturned a Texas anti-sodomy law.

Expressing "pride," though, is not such a simple matter for all queers. As Pride celebrations have increased in size and lavishness, queer folk have begun to resist the commodified, consumerist ideals they seem to elevate. Pride, they argue, should not be a matter of your ability to pay entrance at the hottest club or obtain corporate sponsorship, but should celebrate diversity and justice within and outside the queer community.

Enter the **Gay Shame Awards.** Shame events around the country offer alternative spaces to consider and celebrate the queer experience. Past SF winners include a gay-owned real estate company who evicted tenants with AIDS, Mary Cheney, and the entire Castro neighborhood for resisting a queer youth shelter. The Awards are often followed by free, impromptu street parties.

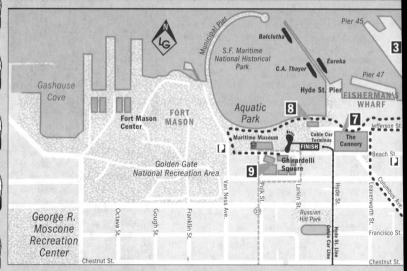

Even the most hardened budget travelers must be wondering why so many tourists flock to Fisherman's Wharf. Why not leave your boots and backpack behind for the day, slip on some flip-flops and shades, and take it like a tourist?

1 PAT'S CAFÉ. Fuel up for the Fisherman's Wharf trail with breakfast or lunch in the bright yellow building (p. 116). Home-cooked eats and huge portions will keep you going for a day in the trap.

2 LEAVENWORTH AND JONES ST. With a belly-full of goodness, wander down Leavenworth St. toward the docks. Turn right on Jefferson where you can pick up some postcards, an "Alcatraz Reject: Too Cute" t-shirt, or flatten your very own souvenir penny. Pause at Jones St. for some voyeuristic fun; a local panhandler known as the Bushman often sets up camp on the wharf side of the street, leaping out from behind two leafy twigs, and scaring unsuspecting passers-by.

TIME: Approximately 4hr.

DISTANCE: Approximately 25 blocks, from 2330 Taylor St. to Ghirardelli Sq.

WHEN TO GO: For the sake of your sanity, M-F 10:30am-2:30pm. Or, for a true tourist trap feel, try a weekend afternoon.

PUBLIC TRANSPORTATION from start: F St. car along Embarcadero.

PUBLIC TRANSPORTATION from finish: MUNI bus #19 or the Powell-Hyde cable car.

PARKING: Street parking near beginning and end of tour is ridiculously difficult to find and garage parking is expensive.

NEIGHBORHOOD QUICKFIND: Sights, p. 65; Food & Drink, p. 116.

3 USS PAMPANITO. Continue along Pier 41 and anchor your sea-legs aboard the USS *Pampanito*. Armed with an audio-tour, you can crawl around the 312 ft. navy submarine that sank six enemy ships on its World War II Pacific patrols. Resurface at the base of Pier 41 if you're planning a trip to Alcatraz or a ferry ride across the bay. The **Blue and Gold Fleet** ticket booth (p. 42) can assist with schedules or reservations.

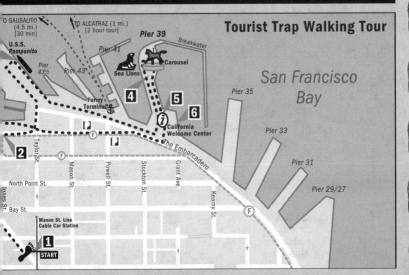

Tourist Trap Walking Tour

TO SAUSALITO (4.5 mi.) [30 min]

TO ALCATRAZ (1 mi.) [2 hour tour]

U.S.S. *Pampanito*

Pier 43½

Pier 43

Pier 41

Pier 39

Breakwater

Carousel

Sea Lions

San Francisco Bay

Pier 35

Pier 33

Pier 31

Pier 29/27

Ferry Terminal

California Welcome Center

The Embarcadero

Taylor St.

Mason St.

Powell St.

Stockton St.

Grant Ave.

Kearny St.

Innes St.

North Point St.

Bay St.

Mason St. Line Cable Car Station

START

4 PIER 39. If you've decided to save the jaunt across the bay for another day, the people-packed pier should be in sight after you leave the USS *Pampanito*. Stroll along the eastern walkway for a photo-opportunity of the world-famous **sea lions**—they'll entertain you for awhile with their splashing, squabbling, and snorting. Heading into the pier's center stage, take a ride on the **Venetian Carousel** (p. 65), watch some juggling and magic shows, or visit the **Peter Lik Gallery** (p. 68) to see some dazzling photos of San Francisco.

5 CALIFORNIA WELCOME CENTER AND INTERNET CAFE. Swing by the Welcome Center (p. 65) for a quick mid-tour stop. This is a great place to make evening reservations, pick up a brochure, check email, and get a quick bite or something to drink.

6 CINEMAX THEATER. Elbowing your way to the base of the Pier, make a stop at the Cinemax Theater's Great San Francisco Adventure (p. 65). In 30 minutes, you'll be taken on a surround-screen whistle-stop tour of the city. If you've never seen Cinemax it's worth the splurge. Adults $7.50, children $4.50.

7 THE CANNERY. Leave the Pier behind and walk westward toward the more serene side of the wharf. The Cannery (p. 67), on the corner of Jefferson and Leavenworth, houses a European-market-style mall in the walls of the original Del Monte canning factory. Garden courtyard seating and rooftop bars with views will tempt you to take some weight off your feet.

8 AQUATIC PARK. Step out into the Victorian gardens adjoining Aquatic Park. On a hot day, cool off with a dip in the chilly bay water, then thaw out in the sauna of the Dolphin Swimming and Boating Club (p. 67). If you start shivering at the sight of the sea-bathers, continue along Beach St. to Ghirardelli Sq.

9 GHIRARDELLI SQUARE. The Ghirardelli soda fountain (p. 67) sells huge sundaes, piled with homemade fudge sauce. But if you're looking for something a little smaller, file through either the chocolate factory or the chocolate shop and caffe for a ◧ **free sample.** What a sweet ending to an action-filled day in one of San Francisco's biggest tourist traps!

WALKING TOUR

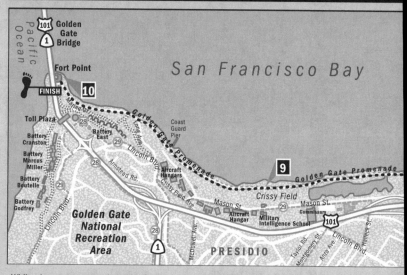

While almost everyone who visits San Francisco makes a stop at the Golden Gate Bridge and many venture part-way across, few make a longer walk of it. Those who do are rewarded with fantastic views, excellent museums, and a refreshing lack of overly earnest tourists. The gorgeous three-mile walk from Fort Mason to the Bridge should take about two hours. Add in stops at museums and a well-deserved rest and picnic in the Presidio and you have an invigorating day of sightseeing off the beaten path.

1. FORT MASON. Wander around the Fort and contemplate the 1906 earthquake, whose effects left the city in shambles but also gave rise to the culturally packed grounds of the fort (p. 69).

2. MUSEO ITALO AMERICANO. Take the time to visit the Fort's collection of tiny but densely-packed and amazing museums. Each museum can be visited in about half an hour.

TIME: Approximately 5hr., including all museums.

DISTANCE: Approximately 3 mi. from the Fort Mason Center to the Golden Gate Bridge.

WHEN TO GO: W-Su 11:30am-7:30pm.

PUBLIC TRANSPORTATION to start: MUNI bus #28, 30, 37, or 49 to the corner of North Point St. and Van Ness Ave.

PUBLIC TRANSPORTATION from finish: MUNI bus #28 or 29.

PARKING: Street parking near the beginning of the tour by the Marina Green is abundant.

NEIGHBORHOOD QUICKFIND: Sights, p. 68; Food & Drink, p. 117.

Learn the difference between *farfalle* and *fusili,* and glimpse the vibrancy of the Italian-American artistic community at the Museo Italo Americano, the world's only museum dedicated solely to Italian and Italian-American art (p. 70).

3. AFRICAN-AMERICAN HISTORICAL AND CULTURAL SOCIETY MUSEUM. Enjoy the Museum's collection, which ranges from ancient artifacts to new work by local and African artists (p. 70).

4. MUSEUM OF CRAFT AND FOLK ART. Spanning both distance and time, the Museum of Craft and Folk Art brings together a fascinating collection of past and contemporary creations from around the world (p. 69).

WALKING TOUR

On the Waterfront Walking Tour

0   1/2 mi

0   1/2 km

5. GREENS-TO-GO. When you're ready to head back outside, swing back by Greens Restaurant in building A and pick up some light picnicking supplies. (p. 117)

6. MARINA GREEN. Goodies in hand, follow the San Francisco Bay Trail through the Marina Green where on a breezy day you can watch expert kite-fliers guide their colorful creations through the air. Drop anchor and enjoy your lunch here (p. 68).

7. PALACE OF FINE ARTS AND EXPLORATORIUM. Continue past the Marina Small Craft harbor at Lyon St. and cross Marina Blvd. to reach one of the best picnic spots in the city: the grounds of the Palace of Fine Arts (p. 68). A remnant of the 1915 Panama-Pacific International Exposition, the Palace was designed to resemble classic ruins. After lunch go from faux-ancient to groundbreakingly modern when you visit the Exploratorium (p. 68), a hands-on science museum that will delight children and parents alike (as well as childless 20-somethings who think rearing another human being is both frightening and overly time-consuming).

8. WAVE ORGAN. When you've had your fill of cow eyes and computers, meander back to the trail and out along the jetty, past the Golden Gate Yacht Club to the Wave Organ (p. 69), a huge pipe sculpture that makes music when waves crash upon it. Let the music of the bay inspire you to walk along the water's edge.

9. GOLDEN GATE PROMENADE. As you look out to sea from the Golden Gate Promenade, scan for sailboats and windsurfers navigating the choppy waters. Pass San Francisco's first military airstrip, **Crissy Field.** On a chilly day, stop by the Warming Hut—a bookstore and cafe offering snacks and hot drinks—to thaw out before the final push. Continue on to Fort Point (p. 77).

10. FORT POINT. After an incarnation as a Spanish Fort from 1776 to 1848, this site served as a US military garrison from 1848 to 1887, and again during the two World Wars. From the Fort, look for spectacular photo opportunities of the Golden Gate Bridge and the city (p. 77).

WALKING TOUR

theater at its finest, with 62 international companies presenting shows under an hour, all less than $8.

Ghirardelli Square Chocolate Festival (☎ 775-5500; www.ghirardellisq.com), in early Sept., in Ghirardelli Sq. Welcome to chocolate heaven. All kinds of chocolate goodies to be sampled, with proceeds going to Project Open Hand.

Vivas Las Americas! (☎ 705-5500; www.pier39.com), in mid-Sept. at Pier 39. Music and dance performances celebrating Hispanic heritage.

San Francisco Blues Festival (979-5588; www.sfblues.com), during the 3rd weekend in Sept., Fort Mason. The oldest blues festival in America attracts some of the biggest names in the business.

Chinatown Autumn Moon Festival (☎ 982-6306; www.moonfestival.org), late Sept., on Grant Ave. Martial arts, lion dancing, and tons of bean-cake-happy spectators.

Folsom Street Fair (☎ 861-3247; www.folsomstreetfair.com), on the last Su in Sept. (Sept. 26 in 2004), on Folsom St. between 7th and 11th St. Pride Day's ruder, raunchier, rowdier brother. The Hole in the Wall gang lets it all hang out in leather and chains (p. 10).

Great Pumpkin Weigh-Off (☎ 650-726-9652), in late Oct., location TBA, followed by **Halloween San Francisco** (☎ 826-1401) on Halloween Day, at Civic Center, with a laser show, music, dancing, and food. For a crazier party, check out the Castro.

Castro Street Fair (☎ 841-1824; www.castrostreetfair.org), on the 1st Su in Oct., in the Castro. Food, live music, and art.

Día de los Muertos (Day of the Dead; ☎ 821-1155), Mission. Follow the drummers and dancing skeletons to the festive Mexican celebration of the dead (Nov. 2). The party starts in the evening at the Mission Cultural Center, on Mission at 25th St.

Italian Heritage Parade and Festival (☎ 434-1492), on Columbus Day in North Beach.

San Francisco Jazz Festival, See p. 165.

WINTER

Fantasy of Lights (☎ 885-1335), a month long festival starting on the Sa after Thanksgiving at sunset. Light parade complements illuminated buildings in Union Sq.

Festival of Lights (☎ 346-8959), in Dec., at Union Sq. Festivities lead up to the lighting of a huge menorah.

Messiah (☎ 864-4000), in Dec., Symphony Hall. Also at the Symphony: some say San Franciscans can't keep their mouths shut. At the **Sing-It-Yourself-Messiah** (☎ 564-8086) they don't have to. $30-70.

San Francisco Independent Film Festival (☎ 820-3907) in Jan. or Feb. The best of Bay Area indie films at various locations.

Dr. Martin Luther King Jr.'s Birthday Celebration (☎ 510-268-3777; contact Jackie Keys-Guidry), Jan. 19-21, in Yerba Buena Gardens. Includes a candlelight vigil and "Making the Dream Real" march and rally on Jan. 21 to honor the great civil rights leader.

Pacific Orchid Exposition, (665-2468), during Feb., in the Festival Pavilion at Fort Mason Center. The San Francisco Orchid Society displays breathtaking floral collections. Free.

Chinese New Year Celebration (☎ 982-3000) and **Parade** (☎ 391-9680; www.chineseparade.com), during the month of Feb., in Chinatown. North America's largest Chinese community celebrates the Year of the Sheep in San Francisco's largest festival. Flower Fair, Miss Chinatown USA Pageant, a Coronation Ball, and a Community Street Fair are among the festivities. Watch the **Parade** (starting around 5:30pm) from Market and 2nd St. to Columbus Ave. Don't miss the Chinese New Year Treasure Hunt (www.sftreasurehunt.com). Free.

🔲 **Sex Tour 2004** (☎ 753-7165; www.sfzoo.org), weekends during mid.-Feb. at the San Francisco Zoo. Birds, bees, giraffes, and monkeys show you how the *rest* of the animal kingdom gets it on. Reservations required. $55.

NATIONAL HOLIDAYS

HOLIDAY	DATE OBSERVED
New Year's Day	Jan. 1
Martin Luther King, Jr. Day	3rd M in Jan.
President's Day & Washington's Birthday	3rd M in Feb.
Patriot's Day	3rd M in Apr.
Memorial Day	Last M in May
Independence Day	July 4
Labor Day	1st M in Sept.
Columbus Day	2nd M in Oct.
Veterans' Day	Nov. 11
Thanksgiving Day	4th Th in Nov.
Christmas Day	Dec. 25

Once in SF

GETTING INTO SF

SAN FRANCISCO INT'L AIRPORT (SFO)

The main port of entry into SF is **San Francisco International Airport** (SFO; ☎650-821-8211), which is 15 mi. south of downtown by US 101. Plan your transportation from the airport by calling SFO Travelers Aid (☎650-821-2735; open daily 9am-9pm) or TravInfo (☎817-1717), or by accessing the ground transport section of www.flysfo.com, which includes links to the websites of all public transportation services as well as a driving route planner. Information booths, located on the arrivals levels of all terminals (10am-9pm) and in the international departures terminal (10am-9pm), offer detailed fare and schedule info. Travelers Aid Society booths are on the departures levels of all terminals (9am-9pm).

GETTING FROM SFO TO DOWNTOWN

BY PUBLIC TRANSPORTATION
San Mateo County Transit (SamTrans; from the Bay Area ☎800-660-4287, from outside the Bay Area 650-817-1717; www.samtrans.com) runs two buses between SFO (from the lower level, in front of Swissair) and downtown San Francisco. Express bus KX reaches the Transbay Terminal with a few stops along Mission St. and allows

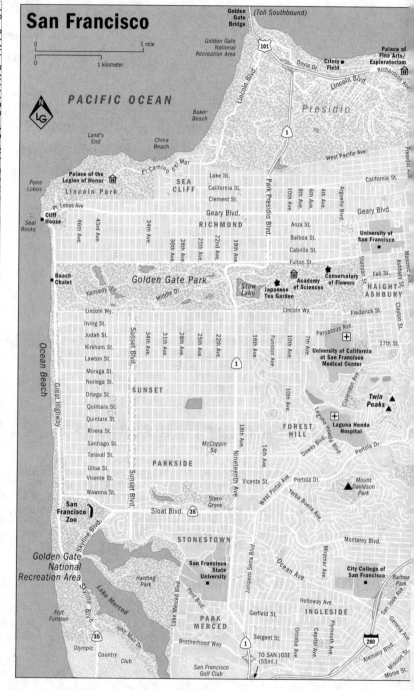

San Francisco

Golden Gate Bridge (Toll Southbound)

0 — 1 mile
0 — 1 kilometer

PACIFIC OCEAN

Golden Gate National Recreation Area

Crissy Field

Palace of Fine Arts/ Exploratorium

Richardson Ave.

Presidio

Baker Beach

Land's End

China Beach

El Camino del Mar

West Pacific Ave.

Point Lobos

Palace of the Legion of Honor

Lincoln Park

SEA CLIFF

Lake St.
California St.
Clement St.
Geary Blvd.

California St.

Cliff House

Seal Rocks

Pt. Lobos Ave.

46th Ave. 43rd Ave. 34th Ave. 30th Ave. 28th Ave. 25th Ave. 22nd Ave. 19th Ave.

RICHMOND

Anza St.
Balboa St.
Cabrillo St.
Fulton St.

10th Ave. 8th Ave. 6th Ave. 4th Ave.

Arguello Blvd.

Geary Blvd.

University of San Francisco

Masonic Ave. Ashbury St.

Beach Chalet

Golden Gate Park

Kennedy Dr.
Middle Dr.

Stow Lake

Japanese Tea Garden

Academy of Sciences

Conservatory of Flowers

Fell St.

HAIGHT ASHBURY

Clayton St.

Ocean Beach

Lincoln Wy.
Irving St.
Judah St.
Kirkham St.
Lawton St.
Moraga St.
Noriega St.
Ortega St.
Quintara St.
Quintara St.
Rivera St.
Santiago St.
Taraval St.
Ulloa St.
Vicente St.
Wawona St.

Lincoln Wy.

Frederick St.

Parnassus Ave.

17th St.

Sunset Blvd. 34th Ave. 31th Ave. 28th Ave. 25th Ave. 22nd Ave.

16th Ave.

Funston Ave. 10th Ave. 7th Ave.

University of California at San Francisco Medical Center

SUNSET

McCoppin Sq.

18th Ave.

14th Ave.

10th Ave.

Claremont Ave.

Twin Peaks

FOREST HILL

Laguna Honda Hospital

Laguna Honda Blvd.

Dewey Blvd.

Portola Dr.

Great Highway

PARKSIDE

Nineteenth Ave.

Vicente St.

West Portal Ave.

Portola Dr.

Yerba Buena Ave.

Mount Davidson Park

Sunset Blvd.

Stern Grove

Sloat Blvd. 35

San Francisco Zoo

Skyline Blvd.

STONESTOWN

San Francisco State University

Juniper Serra Blvd.

Ocean Ave.

Monterey Blvd.

City College of San Francisco

Balboa Park

Golden Gate National Recreation Area

Harding Park

Lake Merced

Lake Merced Blvd.

Font Blvd.

Holloway Ave.

INGLESIDE

Miramar Ave.

Plymouth Ave. Capitol Ave.

San Jose Ave.

Geneva Ave.

Fort Funston

Skyline Blvd.

35

John Muir Dr.

PARK MERCED

Garfield St.

Sargent St.

Brotherhood Way

Orizaba Ave.

280

Alemany Blvd.

Mission St.

Morse St.

Olympic Country Club

San Francisco Golf Club

San Francisco Golf Club

TO SAN JOSE (55mi.)

TO ALCATRAZ
TO SAUSALITO
TO LARKSPUR

Pier 39

Marina Park

Aquatic
Park

**San
Francisco
Bay**

Marina Blvd.

Fort
Mason

Beach St.

**FISHERMAN'S
WHARF**

MARINA

Chestnut St.

Lombard St.

101

Bay St.

Leavenworth St.

Columbus Ave.

Powell St.

Stockton St.

**TELEGRAPH
HILL**

**Colt
Tower**

The Embarcadero

TO
OAKLAND
& THE
EAST BAY

Van Ness Ave.

Larkin St.

Polk St.

Taylor St.

Jones St.

**NORTH
BEACH**

Kearny St.

Sansome St.

Battery St.

Drumm St.

Davis St.

Front St.

**Ferry
Building**

Bay Bridge
(toll westbound)

80

enwich St.

Filbert St.

on St.

Green St.

Franklin St.

**RUSSIAN
HILL**

Vallejo St.

Broadway

**CHINA-
TOWN**

Montgomery St.

Grant Ave.

Steuart St.

Main St.

ilejo St.

Broadway

ific St.

**PACIFIC
HEIGHTS**

Pacific Ave.

Washington St.

Jackson St.

Clay St.

Alta Plaza
Park

Lafayette
Park

Sacramento St.

California St.

**Transbay
Terminal**

2nd St.

e St.

n St.

Divisadero St.

t St.

Gough St.

NOB HILL

**UNION
SQUARE**

Market St.

**JAPAN-
TOWN**

101

Hyde St.

Larkin St.

Geary St.

Turk St.

Mission St.

Howard St.

SFMoMA

3rd St.

Geary Expressway

Laguna St.

Buchanan St.

Webster St.

Fillmore St.

Steiner St.

**TENDER-
LOIN**

4th St.

5th St.

rk St.

olden Gate Ave.

**CIVIC
CENTER**

SOMA

Bryant St.

**China
Basin**

**WESTERN
ADDITION**

Alamo
Square

Hayes St.

HAYES VALLEY

8th St.

9th St.

6th St.

Folsom St.

Harrison St.

Branman St.

Townsend St.

King St.

Pacific Bell Park

ak St.

Page St.

10th St.

7th St.

Caltrain

aight St.

Divisadero St.

Duboce Ave.

101

**CHINA
BASIN**

China Basin

uena
Vista
Park

Market St.

16th St.

Potrero St.

280

16th St.

De Mariposa St.

China Basin St.

Central Basin

Castro St.

**Mission
Dolores**

Treat Ave.

Connecticut St.

Indiana St.

3rd St.

18th St.

19th St.

Mission
Dolores
Park

MISSION

20th St.

S Van Ness Ave.

Harrison St.

20th St.

Caltrain

CASTRO

Noe St.

Sanchez St.

Church St.

Dolores St.

Guerrero St.

Valencia St.

Mission St.

**SF
General
Hospital**

**POTRERO
HILL**

Diamond St.

Castro St.

24th St.

25th St.

101

Douglass St.

**NOE
VALLEY**

Clipper St.

César Chavez St. (Army St.)

César Chavez St.

(Army St.)

**Port of San Francisco
North Container Terminal**

30th St.

Mission St.

Bernal Heights
Park

**BERNAL
HEIGHTS**

Cortland Ave.

Jerrold Ave.

Toland St.

**BAY
VIEW**

**Port of San Francisco
Intermodal Container
Transfer Facility**

len
nyon
ark

**GLEN
PARK**

San Jose Ave.

Park
St.

Industrial St.

Oakdale Ave.

3rd St.

Mendell St.

Evans Ave.

**Port of San Francisco
South Container Terminal**

**Heron's Head
Park**

**India
Basin**

osworth St.

Alemany Blvd.

Silver Ave.

Silver Ave.

Thornton Ave.

Revere Ave.

**HUNTERS
POINT**

Innes Ave.

Alemany Blvd.

Mission St.

Brazil Ave.

Felton Ave.

San Bruno Ave.

BAYVIEW

Jennings St.

Ingalls St.

Crisp Ave.

ean Ave.

EXCELSIOR

Persia Ave.

Russia Ave.

France Ave.

Prague Ave.

Cambridge St.

Yale St.

University St.

Holyoke St.

Bayshore Blvd.

Carroll Ave.

Gilman Ave.

Spear Ave.

**McLaren
Park**

Dwight St.

Caltrain

Jamestown Ave.

**South
Basin**

taly Ave.

Golf
Course

Mansell St.

**VISITACION
VALLEY**

Sunnydale Ave.

Visitacion
Ave.

TO SFO
(6mi.)

Bay View
Park

Bay View Ave.

**3Com
(Candlestick)
Park**

**Candlestick Point
Recreation Area**

ordova
St.

Haight-Ashbury Intersection

Pier 39

one small carry-on bag per passenger (35min.; 5:30am-12:50am; adults $3, seniors at off-peak times $1.25, under 17 $1.25). Bus #292 makes frequent stops on Mission St. and allows all luggage (1hr.; 4:30am-12:45am; adults $2.20, seniors at off-peak times 50¢, under 17 $1.50). Another option is a SamTrans bus to the Bay Area Rapid Transit (BART) system (**Getting Around,** p. 37), which runs through the city and to other Bay Area destinations. Three BART stops in San Francisco connect to the San Francisco Municipal Railway (MUNI), the city's public transportation system (p. 37). SamTrans bus BX runs from the airport to the Colma BART station just south of the city (20min.; every 20-30min. M-F 5:45am-11:30pm, Sa-Su 6:30am-11:30pm; adults $1.10, under 17 75¢, seniors 50¢).

BY SHUTTLE

The most convenient way of getting downtown are van services, which take you from the airport to your hotel or hostel (around $10-15). Most shuttles circulate regularly at the airport around the lower level central island—outside the baggage claim—and do not require reservations. For a more complete list of shuttles, see the **Service Directory** (p. 311) or ask at the SFO Info Booth.

BY TAXI

Taxis to downtown (about $30) from SFO depart from the center island in all terminals—outside the baggage claim area. Check free area guides for coupons (**Publications,** p. 49). Any San Francisco taxi will take you to the airport, but it is better to call to arrange a pickup. See the **Service Directory** (p. 317) for companies and numbers.

BY CAR

To drive from SFO to downtown San Francisco, take the **US 101 North/I-380 West** ramp toward San Francisco (I-280/San Bruno); bear left at the fork in the ramp and merge onto US 101 North. To reach SFO from the city, take **US 101 South** toward San Jose and take the **North Access Road/ San Bruno/SF Int'l Airport** exit.

OAKLAND INT'L AIRPORT

Oakland International Airport (OAK) is located across the Bay from San Francisco, about 19 mi. driving distance east of the city. The Oakland airport's website (www.flyoakland.com)has a ground transportation section that describes and links to **public transportation, shuttle,** and **taxi** services, and **driving directions.**

GETTING AROUND SF
BY PUBLIC TRANSPORTATION

San Francisco's main public transportation systems are the **MUNI Metro subway and bus system** and **BART**, which provides wider coverage of the Bay Area and speedy but limited service in San Francisco. Each system is described below; all overseen by the **Metropolitan Transportation Commission** (☎510-464-7700; www.transitinfo.org), which provides transit information for the nine-county San Francisco Bay Area.

BAY AREA RAPID TRANSIT (BART)

BART (☎415-989-2278; www.bart.org) runs five main lines throughout the Bay Area, four of which stop at the six main San Francisco stations (from southwest to northeast: **24th St. Mission, 16th St. Mission, Civic Center, Powell St., Montgomery St.,** and **Embarcadero**). **Maps** and **schedules** are available online and at all stations.

BART **tickets** are like debit cards; when you take a trip, your fare is automatically deducted until the stored value is depleted. All BART stations sell tickets through automatic ticket machines that accept coins as well as bills up to $20. Credit cards can also be used at Charge-A-Ticket (CAT) machines in selected stations. You can also buy tickets online (www.cdsnet-inc.net/tickets2go/bart.htm), by mail, and at many banks and stores throughout the city. BART's fare structure is built on a mileage-based formula (from $1.15-4.90), so weekly or monthly passes for BART fare are not available. Service runs weekdays 4am to midnight, Saturdays 6am to midnight, and Sundays 8am to midnight, although times at individual stops may vary.

MUNI, BUS, AND CABLE CARS

San Francisco's public transit systems may be slower and less developed than their counterparts on the East Coast and in Europe, but the city is so walkable that most find a mix of foot and public transport perfect for getting around the city.

Most transportation within the city falls under the authority of the **San Francisco Municipal Railway** (MUNI; pronounced MEW-nee; ☎673-6864; www.sfmuni.com)—something of a misnomer since the system includes **buses** (electric trolley and diesel), **cable cars** (the only ones in the world still operating), a **subway**, and **streetcars**. In operation since 1912, MUNI was the first publicly owned streetcar system in a major city in the US and remains the seventh-largest today. Though a majority of riders (58%) expressed satisfaction with MUNI in a 2001 survey, numerous advocacy groups are fighting to make MUNI more efficient, safe, and responsive to customers.

The official, super-handy **MUNI maps** cover all regional bus and subway services and double as excellent street maps. You can pick one up at a ticket booth at Powell and Market St. in Union Sq., in Victoria Park at Beach and Hyde St. in Fisherman's Wharf, at 949 Presidio at Geary Ave. and Presidio St., or in City Hall (Rm. 140) in the Civic Center. They are also available at many bookstores ($2) and online (free). Many lines run less frequently after 7pm. The **Owl Service** provides a core series of routes from 1am to 5am. **Wheelchair accessibility** varies among bus routes. All below-ground subway stations are accessible; new trolleys will arrive over the next two years to complete MUNI's wheelchair accessibility.

FARES

Single-ride fares on MUNI buses, streetcars, and the subway cost $1.25 (seniors and ages 5-17 35¢, under 4 free); if you need one, ask for a **free transfer** (valid for 2 additional rides, including BART, within a 90min. period). Single-ride fares on the cable cars are pricier (adults $3, seniors and disabled $2, children under 6 free; before 7am and after 9pm $1), with no transfers. **MUNI passports**, sold at the Powell St. Visitors Center and at

San Francisco Public Transportation

- —— MUNI Bus Service
- ‑‑‑ MUNI Metro Service
- +‑+‑+ Cable Car Route
- +■+■+ Waterfront Streetcar Service
- +—+—+ CalTrain
- ▭▭▭ BART
- ■ End of Line
- ○ Route Number

0 _____ 1 mile
0 _____ 1 kilometer

San Francisco Bay

Marina Park
Pier 39
F
To OAKLAND
80

Fort Mason
49 19
15

MARINA
30
22
28
Marina Blvd
Lombard St
30
Union St

TELEGRAPH HILL
Coit Tower
15
NORTH BEACH
15

POWELL-HYDE CABLE CAR LINE
POWELL-MASON CABLE CAR LINE
RUSSIAN HILL

Jackson Square

Ferry Building
F

22
49 28
30
22
Broadway
CHINA TOWN
30
15

PACIFIC HEIGHTS
24
24
Washington St
California St
JAPAN TOWN
NOB HILL
CALIFORNIA ST CABLE CAR LINE

71
b
7 14 71
7
J K L M
N

38
Embarcadero Station
Transbay Terminal
38
b

22
38
22
24
5
49
Information
Turk St
38
30
30
15

N

WESTERN ADDITION
5
22
Alamo Square
19
19

7 71 7 71
7 71
37
N

CalTrain Station (4th & King)
N
30
30
15

16th St
b
Mission Dolores
22
22 33
22

MISSION
33
33
Mission Dolores
33
20th St
19
22
15

CHINA BASIN
Central Basin
15
22
22

CASTRO
24
24
Noe St
Castro St
24th St.
b
25th St
SF General Hospital
33
C. Chavez St (Army St.)
POTRERO
CalTrain Station (22nd St.)
15

NOE VALLEY
J
Bernal Heights Park
19
BAY VIEW
15

Glen Park
b J
24
24
Cortland Ave
24

GLEN PARK
49 14
Silver Ave
280
24
24
19
HUNTERS POINT

19 at Hunter's Point Naval Reserve (1.3mi.)

India Basin

John McLaren Park
49
14

VISITACION VALLEY
CalTrain Station (Paul Ave.)
101
15
15
15

TO SAN FRANCISCO INT'L AIRPORT & SAN JOSE
3Com (Candlestick) Park
Candlestick Point Recreation Area
South Basin

39

Night Owl Bus Service
■ End of Line
☆ Timed Transfer
○ Route Number
All routes operate half-hourly
from 1:00 a.m. to 5:00 a.m.

Night Owl Service

some accommodations, are valid on all MUNI vehicles, including cable cars (1-day $9, 3-day $15, 7-day $20). The **Weekly Pass** is cheaper ($12), but must be purchased for a single work week and requires an additional $1 to ride the cable cars. The **Monthly FastPass** (adults $45; seniors, disabled, and ages 5-17 $10) includes in-town BART trips (from Embarcadero to Balboa Park) and cable cars.

MUNI METRO LINES

The MUNI Metro system, whose cars alternate between subway (below ground) and surface-rail (above ground) transportation, offers more limited but speedier service than the MUNI bus system. Downtown, all six Metro lines (F, J, N, L, M, and K) travel underground along a central artery: **Market St.** With the exception of the F line, they all travel underground from the **Embarcadero Station** to at least the **Church St. Station.** (The **F** line runs antique streetcars above ground along Market St., from the **Embarcadero** to the **Castro St. Station** and also connects to Fisherman's Wharf via the Northern Waterfront/ Embarcadero.) As they travel "outbound" (i.e., away from the Ferry Terminal and the Embarcadero), they all stop at the **Embarcadero, Powell, Civic Center, Van Ness,** and **Church St. Stations,** so any line is sufficient. If you're heading any farther, however, you should take care to snag the appropriate car before the lines split off from one another. The **J** and **N** emerge from the tunnel at **Church St.,** while the **K, L,** and **M** routes continue underground past **Castro St.** and emerge above ground at the **West Portal Station.** See the chart below for more detailed information.

MUNI METRO LINES

F—MARKET: Outbound cars travel from Jones and Beach St. near the Embarcadero down **Market St.** via Steuart St., Noe St., 17th St., Church St., and 17th St. to the **Castro St. Station** (at 17th St. and Castro). Inbound cars return via Market and 1st St. to **the Embarcadero.** The recent extension of this line travels from **Downtown** along the Northern Waterfront all the way to **Fisherman's Wharf** at Jones and Beach St.

J—CHURCH: Outbound cars travel from the CalTrain Depot at **King and 4th St.** in SoMa up to the **Embarcadero Station** and then southwest down **Market St.** to Duboce Ave. and Church St., then travel south down Church St. (through the Castro and Noe Valley) to **30th St.** before finally terminating at the **Balboa Park BART station,** at Geneva and San Jose Ave.

N—JUDAH: Outbound cars run from the CalTrain Depot (see above) up to the **Embarcadero Station** before heading southwest down **Market St.** to Duboce ave. and Church St. From there, N cars bust west through **Haight-Ashbury,** continuing past the UCSF Medical Center at 2nd and Irving St., all the way down **Judah St.** through the Sunset (parallel to the south side of Golden Gate Park) to **Ocean Beach.** Offers **Owl** service.

L—TARAVAL: Outbound cars from the Embarcadero Station run all the way down **Market St.** and continue southwest beneath Twin Peaks to **West Portal Station,** where they split off from K and M cars and head west almost all the way down **Taraval Ave.** through the southern Sunset before terminating at Wawona St. and 46th Ave. near the **Zoo.** Offers **Owl** service.

K—INGLESIDE AND M—OCEAN VIEW: Outbound K and M cars split from L cars at **West Portal** (see above), continuing down West Portal Ave. to **St. Francis Circle.** At that point, the two lines split—the M makes a bee-line for **19th Ave.** (passing Stonestown and SFSU), while the K wanders up **Ocean Ave.** through **Ingleside**—before being reunited at the **Balboa Park** BART Station at Geneva Ave. Offers **Owl** service.

MAJOR MUNI BUS LINES

MUNI buses fill in the gaps in San Francisco's Metro system. The most important bus lines for visitors are outlined in the following chart.

MAJOR MUNI BUS LINES

#14. MISSION. Follows **Mission St.** all the way from near the Embarcadero through **SoMa** and the **Mission,** skirting **Noe Valley** and **Bernal Heights** on its way to Crocker Ave. on the southern fringes of the city. Offers **Owl** service.

#15: 3RD ST. The most relevant portion runs from 3rd St. in **SoMa** through the **Financial District** via Kearny St. and **North Beach** via Columbus Ave., then along Powell St. toward **Fisherman's Wharf.** Heading outbound instead of inbound from 3rd St. will bring you in a loop around the southeast part of the city and finally drop you at Ocean Ave. For express service, catch line 9X, 9AX, or 9BX. Line 9X offers **Owl** service.

#18: 46TH AVE. Travels from the **Palace of the Legion of Honor** past Sutro Baths down the west coast of SF along the **Great Highway,** past the **San Francisco Zoo** and around **Lake Merced.**

#19: POLK. Runs from **Ghirardelli Sq.** south along Polk St., passes by the **Civic Center Station,** and ends up at **César Chavez (Army) St.**

#22: FILLMORE. Travels from **Potrero Hill** west down 16th St. through the **Mission,** then heads north up **Church** and **Fillmore St.** past Japantown to the **Marina.** Offers **Owl** Service.

#24: DIVISADERO. Travels from Noe St. in **Noe Valley** north along **Castro St.,** then follows Divisadero and then Jackson St. to **Pacific Heights.** Offers **Owl** Service.

#28: 19TH AVE. Travels from **Fort Mason** west into the **Presidio,** then south on Park Presidio Blvd. through the **Richmond District** and **Golden Gate Park.** Continues south on **19th Ave.** through the **Sunset District** all the way to the **Daly City** BART station.

#30: STOCKTON. Runs from the CalTrain Depot in **SoMa** along 3rd and Market St., then proceeds up Stockton St. through **Chinatown** and Columbus Ave. through **North Beach,** passing **Fisherman's Wharf** and Fort Mason en route to the **Palace of Fine Arts.** Offers **Owl** service.

#33: STANYAN. Runs from **Potrero Hill** through the **Mission** on 16th and then 18th St., through the **Castro** up to Market St., up Clayton St. into the **Haight-Ashbury,** then up Stanyan St. along the eastern edge of **Golden Gate Park** and finally up Arguello Blvd. in the **Richmond District.**

#37: CORBETT. Winds from **Masonic** and **Haight St.** to **Twin Peaks** via Buena Vista Park. From there it goes on to 14th St., Market St., and ends at Burnett St.

#38: GEARY. Starts at the Transbay Terminal in **SoMa,** then follows **Geary Blvd.** all the way from **Market St.** to the **Cliff House** and **Pt. Lobos.** Returns part of the way along Balboa St.

#71: HAIGHT-NORIEGA. Travels from the Ferry Building down **Market St.,** then heads west through the **Haight-Ashbury** on Haight St. before hugging the south side of **Golden Gate Park** (along Lincoln Way), heading south on 23rd St., and following **Noriega St.** west to the ocean.

CABLE CAR ROUTES

MUNI's cable cars are an emblem of San Francisco. Declared a national historic landmark in 1964, the colorful cable cars are about image, not practicality. They are noisy, slow (9½ mph), expensive (**Fares,** above), and usually crammed, making them an unreliable method of getting around. You won't be the first person to think of taking one to Fisherman's Wharf. Still, there is something charming about these relics, and you'll probably want to try them, especially if you have a MUNI passport. To avoid the mobs, get up early and climb the hills with the sunrise. All lines run daily from 6am to 1:30am. Choose one of the three lines detailed below.

CABLE CAR ROUTES
POWELL-MASON (PM): Climbs from the **Hallidie Plaza** turnaround (at the intersection of Market and Powell St.) up **Powell St.** past **Union Sq.** before heading one block west along **Jackson St.** and then descending north down Mason, Columbus, and Taylor St. toward **Fisherman's Wharf.** Always the most popular route.
CALIFORNIA STREET (C): Runs from the **Embarcadero** turnaround at Market and Davis St. straight west up **California St.** (though the Financial District, Chinatown, and Nob Hill) to **Van Ness Ave.** Usually the least crowded route.
POWELL-HYDE (PH): Starts out following the PM line, but heads west down Jackson St. for four additional blocks before turning north down **Hyde St.** and terminating on **Beach St.** between Ghirardelli Sq. and the Cannery. With the steepest hills and the sharpest turns, this line may be the most fun.

BY FERRY

Golden Gate Ferry (☎ 923-2000; www.goldengateferry.org) sails across the Bay to Marin County from the **Ferry Building** at the foot of Market St., east of Pier 1. Ferries serve **Larkspur** (M-F 20 trips per day, first ferry leaves SF 6:35am, last ferry leaves Larkspur 8:15pm; adults $3.25, seniors $1.60, ages 6-12 $2.45; Sa-Su and holidays 5 trips per day, first ferry leaves SF 10:40am, last ferry leaves Larkspur 5:40pm; $5.30) and **Sausalito** (M-F 9 trips per day, first ferry leaves SF 7:40am, last ferry leaves Sausalito 7:20pm; adults $5.60, seniors $2.80, ages 6-12 $4.20, under 5 free; Sa-Su 6 trips per day, first ferry leaves SF 11:30am, last ferry leaves Sausalito 6:10pm; $5.30; increased service May-Sept.). Both lines are wheelchair accessible. Transfers are free between bus routes and ferries.

The **Blue and Gold Fleet** (☎ 705-8200, tickets ☎ 705-5555; www.blueandgold-fleet.com) runs to Alcatraz (14 trips per day; $9.25 round-trip, seniors $7.50, ages 5-11 $6; audio tour $4, for children $2; AmEx/D/MC/V) and Angel Island (M-F 4 per day, Sa-Su 3 per day; $12 round-trip, ages 6-12 $6.50, under 6 free) and between SF and Tiburon, Vallejo, Alameda, and Oakland. The Blue and Gold Fleet also offers an Island Hop to Alcatraz and Angel Island. (Sept.-June daily, May-June M and Th-Su; adults $36.75, seniors $34, ages 5-11 $22, under 5 free; includes audio tour on Alcatraz and TramTour on Angel Island). The **Harbor Bay Ferry** (☎ 510-769-5500; www.harborbayferry.com) goes between SF and Alameda. The **Red and White Ferry** (☎ 673-2900; www.redandwhite.com) runs between SF and Point Richmond; the **Baylink Ferry** (☎ 877-643-3779; www.baylinkferry.com) services SF to Vallejo with connecting bus to Sacramento. All ferries leave the **Ferry Building** near the Embarcadero.

BY BIKE

Despite the predictably punishing hills, San Francisco is a great city to traverse by bike or in-line skate. Even the hardiest bike couriers have been spotted walking their bikes up the especially steep grades. Check out our topographical map of downtown (in the color insert in the middle of the book) to plan a flatter route. Most modes of public transportation in the Bay Area accommodate bicycles. Beware, when riding on roads also used by cable cars and trains, of getting your tires stuck in their grooves. Check (**Service Directory,** p. 312) for the bike or skate rental nearest you.

The Department of Parking and Traffic runs the **SF Bicycle Program** (☎ 585-2453; www.bicycle.sfgov.org), which organizes numbered **bike routes** around the city. Rectangular signs with a silhouette bike and the Golden Gate Bridge mark the routes. Even numbers refer to north/south routes, with the numbers increasing from east to west; odd numbers refer to east/west routes, with the numbers increasing from north to south; three-digit numbers indicate connector routes; and green signs are for local routes, while signs with a red Golden Gate Bridge icon indicate crosstown routes. Bike paths may run separate from motor vehicle traffic, alongside traffic in the street in a marked bike lane, or with traffic on a street with a wide-curb lane. The SFBP hotline has info on bike lockers, MUNI racks, and safety resources.

The non-profit **SF Bicycle Coalition** (☎431-2453; www.sfbike.org) promotes bike use, advocates for transit improvement, and gets members bike shop discounts. Safe and secure cycling requires a quality **helmet** (required by state law) and **lock**. A good helmet costs about $40—much cheaper than critical head surgery—and is also usually available for rental. U-shaped **Kryptonite** or **Citadel** locks ($30-60) carry **insurance** against theft for one or two years if your bike is registered with the police.

BY TAXI

Taxis are not as easy to hail on the street in San Francisco as they are in many American cities, so it might be helpful to carry the phone numbers for taxi agencies (**Service Directory**, p. 317).

BY CAR

A car is not necessary for getting around the area and may be more trouble than it's worth, unless you would like the convenience of your own wheels on a daytrip. See **Planning Your Trip** (p. 291) for information on obtaining an international driving permit. **Seat belts** in cars and **helmets** on motorcycles and mopeds are required by law. Children under 40 lbs. must ride in a specially designed **car seat,** available for a small fee at most car rental agencies. Study routes before you hit the road.

Parking in San Francisco is rare and expensive even where legal, and a network of zealous traffic cops doles out copious tickets, despite local protests against the city's rigorous regulations. The many broken parking meters indicate an irate citizenry, but the time limit still applies to such spaces, and you may be ticketed up to three times for a single offense. Whatever you do, don't block a sidewalk disabled-access ramp—the ticket is a whopping $250. You can stow your car all day in the residential Richmond or Sunset districts—just make certain you heed signs indicating weekly street-cleaning times. To park near a popular area, your best bet may be a **parking garage** (**Service Directory**, p. 316).

As evidenced by the terrain, driving in San Francisco demands a certain conscientiousness. Contending with the treacherous **hills** is the first task; if you've arrived in a standard (manual) transmission vehicle, you'll need to develop a fast clutch foot, since all hills have stop signs at the crests. If you're renting, get an automatic transmission. Make sure to stop for cable cars, because they won't stop for you.

Trolley

Fisherman's Wharf

Castro District

RENTING

Most major **car rental** companies have offices at airports and throughout the city. Smaller companies often offer better deals, but may not always have availability. **You must be 21 years of age to rent a car.** If you are **under 25,** beware that most companies add hefty daily surcharges, while some still flat-out refuse to rent to you.

RENTAL AGENCIES. Car rental agencies fall into two categories: national companies and local agencies that serve only one city or region. National chains usually allow you to pick up a car in one city and drop it off in another (for a hefty charge, sometimes over $1000). By calling ahead, you can reserve a car anywhere in the country. Rental fees change constantly and often require scouting around for the best rate. Generally, airport branches have more expensive rates. A compact car generally rents for $35-45 per day. See the **Service Directory,** p. 312 for agencies.

INSURANCE AND ASSISTANCE. Drivers are required to carry **insurance** in the state of California. If you already have insurance on your car, it will apply to your rental as well. Otherwise, you can purchase insurance from the rental agency. There may be an additional charge for a collision and damage waiver (CDW), usually $12-15 per day. Major credit cards (including MC and AmEx) will sometimes cover the CDW if you use their card to rent a car; call your credit card company for specifics.

The **American Automobile Association (AAA)** provides free trip-planning services, maps, guidebooks, commission-free American Express Traveler's Cheques, free towing, and 24hr. emergency road service. (☎800-AAA-HELP/222-4357.) Cardholders get discounts on Hertz car rental (5-20%) and various motels and theme parks. AAA has agreements with the auto associations of other countries, which often provide full benefits while in the US. Check with your auto association for details. Membership for the California branch costs $49 to join and $17 yearly. To sign up, call ☎800-922-8228 or visit www.aaa.com.

BY REGIONAL PUBLIC TRANSPORTATION

BY BUS

All regional buses operate from the **Transbay Terminal,** 425 Mission St., at 1st St. An information center on the second floor has maps and free phone lines for bus information. (☎495-1569. Open daily 4:30am-12:30am.) **Golden Gate Transit** provides regional fixed-route bus service in San Francisco, Marin, and Sonoma Counties. Limited service is also available between Central Marin and Western Contra Costa Counties. (☎923-2000; www.goldengatetransit.org. M-F 6am-10pm, Sa-Su reduced service; $1.50-6.30 depending on distance; discounts for seniors, disabled, and youth.) **Alameda County (AC) Transit** operates bus service to and in Oakland and Berkeley. (☎800-448-9790; www.actransit.org; $1.35-2.75 (transbay fares); discounts for seniors, disabled, and youth.) **San Mateo Transit (SamTrans)** serves the peninsula with hundreds of trips along the Bayshore corridor between Palo Alto and downtown San Francisco. Additional frequent SF service is provided along El Camino Real and Mission St. Hundreds of other daily trips serve SFO, Daly City, Hayward, and 20 other cities in the county. (☎800-660-4287 or ☎650-817-1717; www.samtrans.com. Most routes daily 6am-6pm; $1-3, discounts for seniors and youth.)

BY TRAIN

Caltrain (in Bay Area ☎800-660-4287, from elsewhere ☎510-817-1717; www.caltrain.com leaves SF from the **Caltrain Depot** at 4th & King St. in SoMa (M-F 5am-midnight, Sa 7am-midnight, Su 8am-10pm), and runs south to Palo Alto ($4.50, seniors and under 12 $2.25) and San Jose ($6, seniors and under 12 $3), making many stops along the way. Fares are calculated on the basis of zones and monthly passes are available. Be sure to check ahead as service is somewhat unreliable due to construction.

ℹ ESSENTIAL
INFORMATION

CALLING WITHIN THE 415 AREA CODE

To place a call within the 415 area code, just dial the 7-digit number.

CALLING OUTSIDE THE 415 AREA CODE

To place a call within the US but outside the 415 area code, dial:

a. 1

b. 3-digit area code

c. 7-digit number

CALLING OUTSIDE THE US

To place an international call, dial:

a. 011

b. The country code. Australia (61); the Republic of Ireland (353); New Zealand (64); South Africa (27); the UK (44).

c. The city code. If the first digit is a zero, omit it.

d. the local number.

e.g., calling London from San Fran dial: 011-4420–7499-8967

CONSULAR SERVICES IN SF

See the **Service Directory,** p. 312 for listings of foreign consulates in San Francisco.

KEEPING IN TOUCH

BY MAIL

SENDING MAIL HOME FROM SAN FRANCISCO

First-class letters sent and received within the US take 1-3 days and cost 37¢; **Priority Mail** packages up to 1 lb. generally take 2 days and cost $3.85, up to 5 lb. $7.70. **All days specified denote business days.** For details, see www.usps.com. **Airmail** is the best way to send mail home from the US. **Aerogrammes** are printed sheets that fold into envelopes and are available at post offices. Write "*par avion*" or "air mail" on the front. Most post offices will charge exorbitant fees or simply refuse to send aerogrammes with enclosures. **Surface mail** is by far the cheapest and slowest way to send mail. It takes one to three months to cross the Atlantic and two to four to

Victorians

Shopping

Yerba Buena

cross the Pacific—good for items you won't need to see for a while, such as souvenirs These are standard rates for mail from the US to:

Australia: Allow 4-7 days for regular airmail home. Postcards/aerogrammes 70¢. Letters up to 1 oz. 80¢; packages up to 1 lb. $14.50, up to 5 lb. $32.75.

Canada: Allow 4-7 days for regular airmail home. Postcards/aerogrammes 50¢. Letters up to 1 oz. 60¢; packages up to 1 lb. $13.25, up to 5 lb. $16.75.

Ireland: Allow 4-7 days for regular airmail home. Postcards/aerogrammes 70¢. Letters up to 1 oz. 80¢; packages up to 1 lb. $14, up to 5 lb. $22.75.

New Zealand: Allow 4-7 days for regular airmail home. Postcards/aerogrammes 70¢. Letters up to 1 oz. 80¢; packages up to 1 lb. $12.50, up to 5 lb. $28.75.

The UK: Allow 4-7 days for regular airmail home. Postcards/aerogrammes 70¢. Letters up to 1 oz. 80¢; packages up to 1 lb. $16, up to 5 lb. $32.

RECEIVING MAIL IN SF

Mail can be sent via **General Delivery** to almost any city or town with a post office. Address letters to:

Victor VICTORIA
c/o General Delivery
123 Any St.
San Francisco, CA 94130

The mail will go to a special desk in the central post office, unless you specify a post office by street address or postal code. It's best to use the largest post office, since mail may be sent there regardless of what is written on the envelope. It is usually safer and quicker to send mail express or registered. When picking up your mail, bring a form of photo ID, preferably a passport.

BY TELEPHONE

Phone rates tend to be highest from 8am to 7pm, lower from 7 to 11pm, and lowest after 11pm and on Sundays and holidays.

CALLING HOME FROM SAN FRANCISCO

A **calling card** is probably your cheapest bet. Calls are billed collect or to your account. You can often also make direct international calls from pay phones, but if you aren't using a calling card, you may need to drop coins as quickly as your words. Where available, prepaid phone cards and occasionally major credit cards can be used for direct international calls, but they are less cost-effective.

CALLING WITHIN SAN FRANCISCO

The simplest way to call within the city is to drop change into a coin-operated public pay phone. Most charge 35¢ for three minutes. As time runs out, a voice will inform you of how much money to insert in order to remain on the line.

Let's Go has recently partnered with ekit.com to provide a calling card that offers a number of services, including email and voice messaging. Before purchasing any calling card, always be sure to compare rates with other cards, and to make sure it serves your needs (a local phonecard is generally better for local calls, for instance). For more information, visit www.letsgo.ekit.com.

Directory Assistance: ☎411.

Operator: ☎0.

BY EMAIL AND THE WEB

San Franciscans are certainly hip to the cyberage. In fact, so many are wired at home, at work, in the car, and on their PDAs that the number of **cybercafes** in San Francisco is actually diminishing. Still, places like **Cafe.com** (sanfranciscocafe.com), **Chat Cafe** (www.sfchatcafe.com), and **Global Bazaar Internet Cafe** provide Internet connections and terminals for those who have a jonesin' for the web. For additional cybercafes in SF, see the **Service Directory** (p. 314). **Cybercafe Guide** locates cybercafes throughout the Golden State (www.cyberiacafe.net/cyberia/guide/ccafe.htm). Most public libraries and some universities also offer free, although sometimes slower and more limited, Internet terminals.

GETTING MONEY FROM HOME

If you run out of money, the easiest and cheapest solution is to have someone make a deposit to your credit card or cash (ATM) card. Failing that, consider:

WIRING MONEY. It is possible to arrange a **bank money transfer** in which a bank back home wires money to one in SF. This is the cheapest way to transfer cash, but also the slowest, taking several days or more. Note that some banks may only release your funds in local currency, potentially sticking you with a poor exchange rate; inquire in advance. Services like **Western Union** are faster and more convenient than bank transfers—but also much pricier. To find a Western Union location, visit www.westernunion.com, or call in the US ☎800-325-6000, in Canada ☎800-235-0000, in the UK ☎0800 83 38 33, in Australia ☎800 501 500, in New Zealand ☎800 27 0000, in South Africa ☎0860 100031. Money transfer services are also available at **American Express** and **Thomas Cook** offices.

Sky's Up

Maiden Lane

Lombard Street

ETIQUETTE

TIPPING AND BARGAINING. In the US, it is customary to **tip** waitstaff and cab drivers **15-20%**, at your discretion. Tips are usually not included in restaurant bills, unless you are in a party of six or more—check the menu or ask the maitre d' about tipping if you are in a large party. At the airport and in hotels, porters expect a tip of at least $1 per bag to carry your baggage. **Bargaining** is generally frowned upon and fruitless, unless you are at a flea market or a street vendor in Chinatown.

SMOKING. The state of California banned smoking in restaurants in 1995—many American cities have since followed suit—and the domain of the smoker has grown smaller and smaller. Today, smoking is prohibited in virtually all enclosed public places, including bars. So, grab a coat and enjoy that cigarette outdoors, though some bars and restaurants have smoker-friendly patios.

TAXES. Sales tax in San Francisco, the equivalent of the European Value-Added Tax, is **8.5%** on normal consumer items. There are additional federal taxes on tobacco products and alcoholic beverages. Most grocery items in California are not taxed; clothing items are taxed. *Let's Go* does not usually include taxes (e.g.,. on accommodations) in listed prices.

LOCAL MEDIA

RADIO

Talk Radio, KQED 88.5FM National Public Radio, KAWL 91.7FM National Public Radio/BBC/CBC, KCBS 740AM all news.

Classical, KDFC 102.1FM.

Jazz, KCSM 91.1FM

College/Indie/Alternative/Popular, KUSF 90.3FM, KLLC "Alice" 97.3FM, KFOG 104.5FM.

Classic Rock, KSAN 107.7FM.

Top 40, KZQZ 95.7FM.

Hip-Hop/R&B/Soul, KMEL 106.1FM, KYLD 94.9FM.

Oldies, KFRC 99.7FM.

Latino/Spanish Language, KIQI 1010AM talk radio, KSOL 98.9FM, KBRG 104.9FM.

PUBLICATIONS

Free publications flood San Francisco cafes, visitors centers, and sidewalk boxes, and offer a local spin on upcoming events and activities. The progressive **San Francisco Bay Guardian** (www.sfbg.com) comes out on Wednesdays, as does **S.F. Weekly** (www.sfweekly.com), its major competitor, which has similar politics but a more skeptical tone and proudly limits itself to the city proper for its listings and distribution. Both have comprehensive nightlife listings. Harder to find, but worth the effort, are two special-interest rags: **Poetry Flash**, available at discerning bookstores, has the skinny on literary happenings in the Bay Area and beyond, while the **Bay Area Music (BAM)** magazine is available at livelier cafes and restaurants in town.

Various tourist-targeting, **coupon-filled free glossies** are available in sidewalk boxes in the busy Fisherman's Wharf and Union Sq. areas, as well as at visitors centers. Among them are the **Bay City Guide**, the **San Francisco Guide**, and the **San Francisco Quick Guide.** The annual **Chaperon** introduces San Francisco in German, French, Spanish, and Italian. The city administrators print a **Lodging Guide** and **The San Francisco Book**, excellent compilations of tourist info.

The largest Bay Area **daily** is the **San Francisco Chronicle** (www.sfchron.com; 50¢). The **San Francisco Examiner** (www.examiner.com), started by yellow journalist William Randolph Hearst and currently run by Phil Bronstein, best known for once being married to Sharon Stone, has lunchtime and evening editions. The two papers share a Sunday edition ($1.50). The **Datebook** in the Sunday edition is also a worthwhile entertainment resource.

Lastly, San Francisco has several free gay and lesbian publications. The **Bay Times** appears monthly with a thorough entertainment section and the work of talented cartoonists. The **Bay Area Reporter** appears every Thursday and contains articles on gay pride as well as a highly varied "Arts & Entertainment" section. **Odyssey** appears every other Friday and is an excellent guide for gay bars, clubs, and stores. Every other Thursday **SF Frontiers Magazine** is published—a glossy with interest articles and nightlife listings. For $10.95, **Betty and Pansy's Queer Review of San Francisco,** a kind of travel guide to gay San Francisco, is both hysterically funny and brutally frank. These publications can be found in cafes and bars around the Castro and Polk St. and at A Different Light Bookstore (p. 177).

Life & Times

THE SAN FRANCISCO STORY

THE EARLY YEARS AND EXPLORATION

NATIVE CALIFORNIANS

The Coast Miwoks, Ohlones, and Wintuns were the first people to colonize the Bay Area, establishing small tribal societies nearly 60,000 years ago. The land we currently know and love as California was originally home to more than 100 Native American tribes who were descendants of the original Paleo-Siberian immigrants and who made up the densest population north of Mesoamerica. Despite a lack of written records, anthropological evidence suggests that their social order was stable and successful enough to remain virtually unchanged for thousands of years. Their spiritual beliefs revolved around animal gods and the natural world. Coyote, his grandson Falcon, and his wife Frog-Woman were the principle deities of the Miwoks.

BURGLARY OF THE BAY

The Portuguese conquistador Estevan Juan Rodriguez Cabrillo was the first European to sail the west coast of North America and make contact with California tribes in 1542. Cabrillo's mission— to find the mythical Strait of Anian—was considered a failure even though the exploration party reached as far as the Oregon coast, bringing the unwitting team past San Francisco Bay.

1587
Sir Francis Drake claims the land in the SF Bay Area for Queen Elizabeth I of England.

Queen Elizabeth I of England soon sent seadog **Sir Francis Drake** to raid Spanish galleons on the Pacific Coast. He encountered the Miwoks in 1587 during an emergency landing near present-day San Francisco. Drake was impressed with the skilled hunters, but not enough so to recognize their right to the land. Always thinking of his queen, Drake claimed the land—which he called "Nova Albion." As is usually the case, European diseases, more so than colonial aggression, turned out to be the California natives' biggest problem. Between 25 and 50% of California's native population died from smallpox, tuberculosis, and measles.

MEN ON A MISSION

1769
King Charles III orders colonization of the Bay Area for Spain.

1776
Mission San Francisco de Asis established by Father Junipero Serra.

Europeans began settling the Bay Area en masse when Spain's King Charles III ordered colonization in 1769. Coastal cities cropped up alongside Catholic missions which were started by **Father Junipero Serra.** In order to fortify these outposts, a Spanish military garrison built near **Fort Point** went into operation on September 17, 1776. Less than one month later, Father Junipero Serra established **La Misión de San Francisco de Asis,** named after the holy order that controlled northern California. The mission's purpose was to assist in the crusade to "civilize" and Christianize the indigenous peoples. Over time, the mission became known as **Misión Dolores** (p. 102) and subjected the tribes to harsh treatment (the Spanish referred to the Native peoples as *bestias* or beasts), forced labor, and illness. In a few short years an estimated 75% of cultures that had survived for millennia were decimated.

THE NINETEENTH CENTURY: BUILDING A CITY

AMERICAN MANIFEST DESTINY

1812
Earthquake.

Like something out of a Doomsday prophecy, the 1812 earthquake destroyed many of California's missions. What's more, the Spanish met with competition from Russian fur traders who had established themselves as a presence at Fort Ross (1812-41), just north of San Francisco. Once the Independent Republic of Mexico was declared and the Mexicans no longer feared aggression from the short-lived Russian occupation, the up-and-coming United States decided to get a bit testy and take action.

1845
Texas declared independence from Mexico and was then annexed by the United States.

In 1835, the United States attempted to buy the whole Bay Area from the Mexicans—an offer promptly refused by Mexico. Not long after Mexico won it's independence, though, the United States annexed the land in 1845 in the name of Manifest Destiny. The Mexicans were less than pleased, and soon after the Mexican-American War began. In other news, idealist **Captain John Fremont** convinced a small band of hoodlums to take over San Francisco's abandoned **Presidio** (p. 77) in the name of the Bear Flag Republic and declare independence. Fremont coined the term **"Golden Gate"** for the mouth of the San Francisco Bay, after Istanbul's Golden Horn. Although Fremont's rule was extremely short-lived, the nickname managed to stick—not because of the Bay's resemblance to any Turkish harbors, but thanks rather to the discovery of gold only three years later.

Manifest Destiny—the idea that it was necessary and right to expand the US to the continent's western edge—was all the rage. The acquisition of California was supported by public figures ranging from President Polk to poet Walt Whitman. Published in the *Brooklyn Eagle*, Whitman wrote "Mexico must be thoroughly chastised!...Let our arms now be carried with a spirit which shall teach the world that...America knows how to crush, as well as how to expand!" Under such severe pressure, Mexico eventually surrendered. In the **Treaty of Guadalupe Hidalgo** of 1848, Mexico ceded half of its territory, including California and parts of New Mexico and Texas, to the US. The timing—it turned out—was golden.

ALL THAT GLITTERS

While the treaty was being negotiated, the seeds of **gold rush** were beginning to sprout nearby. When gold was discovered in January 1848 at General John **Sutter's Mill** near Coloma by Sutter's carpenter, James Marshall, the rush was on. The number of fortune-seekers reached a feverish pitch as bands of men—known collectively as the **Forty-Niners**—flooded the region. The massive influx of prospectors caused the non-native population to multiply six-fold within four years. The miners' demands for food and supplies created an economic boom, and turned San Francisco into an international port. Within a decade, over 28 million ounces of gold (worth about $10 billion today!) had been mined. The journey westward is not to be underestimated, however. Like thousands of would-be settlers looking to the coast, the **Donner Party** faced hardship because of fierce winter conditions and diminished supplies. During the winter of 1846-47, they were forced to madness and cannibalism at a snowbound outpost near what is now called Donner Lake in Sierra Nevada.

The Forty-Niners quickly discovered that their thirst for wealth was met not with mountains of gold, but with hardship and skyrocketing prices. Everyone except miners seemed to be getting rich, especially the merchants who could charge essentially whatever they wanted for goods.

Meanwhile, with only the slightest semblance of governmental order, **vigilante justice** became the name of the game. In 1856, the *Sacramento Union* noted that there had been "some fourteen hundred murders in San Francisco in six years, and only three of the murderers hung, and one of these was a friendless Mexican." San Francisco mayor **John White Geary** tried to crack down on the lawlessness, guns, violence, prostitution, and gambling that had become commonplace, but his crude, extralegal policies were hardly better than the vigilante rule he was combating.

"PERFECTLY INSANE PEOPLE"

In 1859, the silver **Comstock Lode** was discovered in Nevada and helped abate the financial hardships of the late 1850s. The millions of dollars worth of silver mined from the hills

1848
Treaty of Guadalupe Hidalgo is signed; Mexico cedes California to the US.

1848
Gold discovered at Sutter's Mill.

1859
Silver Comstock Lode
discovered in Nevada.

changed the face of the San Francisco citizenry. Instead of miners, fleecing merchants, and dilapidated shacks, the population was soon typified by bankers, lawyers, and rich speculators who were prepared to transform the town into a thriving metropolis with beautiful hotels, luxurious restaurants, and mansions high atop the city's hills.

When former **outlaws** and **vagrants** got rich, they were not concerned with recreating the east-coast Puritanical, Boston Brahmin mentality. They were hell-bent on glitzy glamor and a good time; opium, loose women, and booze were their self-destructive weapons of choice. The intoxicating nature of San Francisco led historian-moralist B.E. Lloyd to warn parents in 1876 to "look closer to their daughters, for they know not the many dangers to which they are exposed...and to mildly counsel their sons, for when upon the streets of this gay city they are wandering among many temptations." Twenty years later, **Rudyard Kipling** observed an even wilder metropolis: "San Francisco is a **mad city,** inhabited for the most part by perfectly insane people..."

JOINING THE COASTS

Beginning in 1860-61, the riders of the **Pony Express** carried mail between Missouri and San Francisco in 10-day trips. By 1861, however, the completion of a transcontinental **telegraph system** linked California electrically with the East and sent the ponies out to pasture.

1869
Transcontinental Railroad
completed.

Emerging industrialists twisted their greasy black handlebar moustaches and formed the **Central Pacific Railroad**—importing and abusing cheap Chinese labor to lay tracks eastward. The meeting of the Central Pacific and Union Pacific Railroads in 1869 formed the **Transcontinental Railroad,** which transformed traveling cross-country to California from a month-long venture by stagecoach to a quick five-day trip—a viable option for fortune-seekers everywhere. After its completion, 15,000 luckless Chinese railroad workers found themselves unemployed and were subsequently blamed in the mid-1870s for causing a **nationwide depression.**

THE 20TH CENTURY: BRIDGES TO THE FUTURE

SOMEONE ELSE'S FAULT

1906
Great Earthquake.

On the morning of April 18, 1906, the **Great Earthquake** struck with a vengeance. The **San Andreas Fault** (p. 95) ripped open the Californian coastline as the quake caused 74hr. fires that only subsided when a change in wind direction brought a desperately needed rainstorm. Three days of catastrophe took a high toll on the city: several thousand dead, 750,000 homeless, and 3,500 developed acres reduced to ashes. At the same time, the largest extortion scandal in the country's history was exposed and rebuilding was entrusted to reformers. The press surrounding the investigation sparked a state-wide movement for governmental reform.

DEPRESSION, IMPRESSION, AND OPPRESSION

San Francisco doesn't corner the market on suffering here—the **Great Depression** (following the 1929 stock market crash) hit everyone hard, although the Bay area experienced particularly difficult times. The city's weak spot was its reliance on port business; trade plummeted and 70% of the workforce was laid off. On May 9, 1934, in response to financial hardship and with the support of other sympathetic unions, the International Longshoremen's Association went on strike all along the West Coast. The industrialists attempted to break the picket lines with scab crews, but the results were disastrous. On July 5th—**Bloody Thursday**—the docks erupted in violence and the police responded by opening fire on the strikers, killing two and wounding over 25. As a result, the entire labor force went on strike for three days, shutting the city down completely.

The 1930s saw the construction of two enormous bridges in the Bay Area: the **San Francisco-Oakland Bay Bridge** and the **Golden Gate Bridge** (p. 77). Completed in 1936, the Bay Bridge tunnelled through Yerba Buena Island to connect two enormous suspension bridges. Less than a year later, the gorgeous, deep-orange-colored Golden Gate Bridge stretched out across the Bay. Other construction accomplishments of the period included the **San Francisco War Memorial Opera House** (p. 91)—completed in 1932—which would house the drafting committee for the United Nations Charter thirteen years later. In addition, a maximum security prison opened on **Alcatraz Island** in 1933. By the time the Rock shut down in 1963, 36 men had tried to escape from its cells on 14 separate occasions. Of those 36, only five remain unaccounted for. The bay's frigid water and notoriously strong currents have led to the official presumption that these men drowned, though one escapee did survive the swim before his recapture.

World War II helped San Francisco prosper, as huge shipyards were built around the bay and war-related industries took off. Hundreds of thousands of people flocked to the job opportunities in the Bay Area, and many of them stayed on permanently. San Francisco was also the **birthplace of the United Nations,** which signed its charter in 1945.

There was, tragically, a much darker side to the influence of the war in San Francisco. Anti-Japanese sentiment began to build when Pearl Harbor was bombed in 1941. That fear-driven sentiment reached its zenith when President Roosevelt issued **Executive Order 9066** in 1947, which sent all people with Japanese ancestry into **internment camps,** or "relocation centers," in the interior of the state. After the US gained command of the Pacific waters and danger of a Japanese invasion had passed, the relocated Japanese were allowed back into society, at which point tightly knit communities that centered in **Japantown** (p. 15) were established. Thousands of **Nisei** (second-generation Japanese) were accepted into the US armed forces, and many of their units were later honored for bravery. In 1988,

1934
Depression and labor unrest.

1936-37
Golden Gate and Bay Bridges completed.

1945
United Nations founded.

1947
Executive Order 9066 forces Japanese Americans into relocation centers.

the government apologized for the internments and offered some monetary reparations to the 60,000 surviving Japanese-Americans who had been relocated.

RESTLESSNESS BY THE BAY

In the 1950s, while June Cleaver vacuumed in pearls and the government heralded the reign of nuclear supremacy, San Francisco's **North Beach** became home to a group of bearded, beret-wearing iconoclasts. Lawrence Ferlinghetti and Peter Martin opened the **City Lights Book Store** (p. 70) in 1953, a cultural center for the **Beat Generation.** Proclaiming themselves "angelheaded hipsters," Beatniks packed City Lights to hear **Jack Kerouac, Allen Ginsberg,** and others read the poems and prose that had the Ward and June Cleavers so nervous. They were both world-weary and awe-inspiring, awestruck and jaded, and seemed to threaten everything deemed decent by the norms of 1950s American civilization.

1953

Lawrence Ferlinghetti and Peter Martin open the City Lights Book Store, cultural center of the Beat Generation.

Across the bay, after returning to college from a summer of civil rights protesting in the South, student activists clashed with the **University of California, Berkeley** (p. 215) administration officials over their right to use facilities for their campaigns. The unrest became known as the **Free Speech Movement**—only the beginning of activism at a university dubbed the "People's Republic of Berkeley" by Pat Buchanan. The resulting confrontation marked the beginning of a new wave of student protests as civil rights took a back seat to the antiwar movement. The drama erupted in December 1964 when over 800 students were arrested for occupying the UC Administration Building, at that time the largest mass arrest of students in US history.

1967

Summer of Love marks the hippie heyday.

The hippies of San Francisco's Haight-Ashbury neighborhood (p. 16) declared a **"Summer of Love"** during which young people voiced their disgust with the Establishment by (in Timothy Leary's words) "turning on, tuning in, and dropping out." **Jerry Garcia** and the **Grateful Dead, Janis Joplin,** and **Jefferson Airplane** (among others) experimented with their guitars and their LSD in an open environment in which sex, drugs, and rock 'n' roll blended into blissful psychedelic euphoria. In the midst of mounting antiwar protests, the black empowerment coalition known as the **Black Panthers,** based in Oakland (p. 221), terrorized white residents in the Bay Area. In 1974, the **Symbionese Liberation Army,** the most prominent of the new revolutionary groups, kidnapped newspaper heiress Patty Hearst and converted her to their cause. In the late 70s, the **People's Temple of San Francisco** gained international focus when its leader, Jim Jones, poisoned and killed some 900 members in a mass-suicide service at his religious retreat in Guyana.

1974

Symbionese Liberation Army kidnaps Patty Hearst.

The 1970s also witnessed the emergence of the modern **Gay Liberation Movement,** which put San Francisco at the forefront of yet another cutting-edge social movement. The country's first openly gay elected official, San Francisco supervisor **Harvey Milk,** was elected on his third bid for the position in 1977. A year later, he and mayor **George Moscone** were assassinated by former police officer Dan

White, who pled temporary insanity caused by eating too much junk food along with some "moral outrage"—a plea that became known as the infamous **Twinkie Defense**. White was punished with a very light prison sentence for voluntary manslaughter (see p. 63), prompting the **"White Night Riot."** Despite his brief time in office, Milk changed the face of the nation's politics, and left a lasting mark for tolerance on San Francisco with his **Human Rights Ordinance** which prohibited anti-gay discrimination by companies doing business with the city. In 1990, the City of San Francisco passed a **domestic partnership** bill, and in 1996 it passed a regulation requiring all companies and businesses doing business in the city to provide domestic partner benefits. The SF queer community has also had to rally around more tragic happenings. To date, almost 20,000 residents (both straight and gay) have died from the **AIDS epidemic,** with tens of thousands more HIV positive. But the city and community have come together in response to the crisis by providing extensive hospice and support services when necessary, and by spearheading national awareness campaigns such as the **AIDS Quilt** and the **Stop AIDS Project.**

With so many social movements dominating the attention of liberal San Franciscans, it is easy to forget that natural catastrophes can be just as damaging as any conservative legislation. The **Loma Prieta earthquake** in 1989 hit 7.1 on the Richter scale, leveling much of the Bay Area and disrupting **World Series** baseball action between local rivals the Oakland Athletics and the San Francisco Giants (see p. 172). Only two years later, a massive fire in Oakland burned over 2000 homes.

In 2001, California was struck by an **energy crisis,** caused by the government's failed attempt to deregulate the electricity market. As caps on prices were lifted, consumers saw their bills as much as double and triple. The state's electricity did not meet consumer demand, and energy reserves dipped to extremely low levels; rolling blackouts were implemented to keep energy from running out completely. In January, the state began purchasing electricity on behalf of financially depleted utilities, and governor **Gray Davis** (now infamously recalled) suggested to President George W. Bush that the whole nation may experience the same crisis that California did if price caps continue to be lifted. In a salute to the conservation cause, NBC and Jay Leno decided to tape the June 12th episode of *The Tonight Show* virtually in the dark, without studio lights, amplifiers, or other power-eaters. NBC stated that the power used to tape one episode of *The Tonight Show* is equal to the amount of power the average family home uses in a month. Lighted or not, the party continues in the City by the Bay.

Recent events in San Francisco have continued to test the political arena, both locally and nationally. During the political reshuffling after the 2002 election, **Nancy Pelosi**—congressional representative for most of San Francisco—was overwhelmingly elected as Democratic Leader of the US House of Representatives, making her the highest ranking

1977

San Francisco supervisor Harvey Milk becomes the nation's first openly gay elected official.

1989

Earthquake.

1990

Domestic Partnership Bill passed.

woman in the Congress's history and the first woman to lead a major national political party. In 2003, many San Franciscans once again took to the streets to have their voices heard–this time to protest the United States **war on Iraq.** San Francisco was perhaps the most vocal and active enclave of anti-war sentiment in the country. Thousands of protestors flocked to Downtown San Francisco and the Civic Center during the week that war broke out. While essentially peaceful, tension in the city heightened as police arrested 2,300 protestors over the course of the demonstrations. The city estimates that $3.5 million were lost in expenses and revenue due to the protests.

2003

Anti-war protests shake San Francisco.

WHO'S WHO, SAN FRANCISCO STYLE

LITERARY GIANTS

Mark Twain: The southern author made his literary debut writing for San Francisco papers. Twain even wrote travel advice in the *San Francisco Daily Morning Call,* recommending, "If one tires of the drudgeries and scenes of the city, and would breathe the fresh air of the sea, let him take the cars and omnibuses, or, better still, a buggy and pleasant steed, and, ere the sea breeze sets in, glide out to the Cliff House" (p. 137).

Jack London: Oakland's literary native son spent some time panning for gold and writing pastoral short stories on the side. "The Valley of the Moon" provides an evocative portrait of the Sonoma and San Joaquin Valleys before they were consumed by wineries and agribusiness. Oakland still honors him with a square and a museum (p. 226).

William Randolph Hearst: Toward the end of the Gold Rush, Hearst–of **Citizen Kane** fame–took over his father's *San Francisco Examiner,* which soon became one of the nation's leading papers.

John Dos Pasos: Pasos wrote the massive trilogy *U.S.A.,* setting much of the first volume in San Francisco's **Sutro Heights** (p. 81) as the "lost generation" of post-WWI writers tried to define what it meant to be American.

Gertrude Stein: This Oakland-raised author and art critic (along with her life-long companion, author **Alice B. Toklas**) left the Bay Area for Europe, but continued to write about it as a progenitor of modernism.

Dashiel Hammett: As the 20th century brought crime to the literary forefront, Hammett found his inspiration for works such as *The Maltese Falcon* working in a San Francisco detective agency.

Jack Kerouac: During the 1950s, Kerouac penned a candid autobiography, *Dharma Bums,* and hipster classic, *On the Road,* that chronicle his free-spirited life on the road and help usher in the Beat Generation.

Allen Ginsberg: The poetic voice of the Beat Generation, Ginsberg howled his way into a 50s courtroom drama and the hearts and minds of Beatniks (and later academics) everywhere.

Bob Kaufman: Inspired by bebop and readings in **Lawrence Ferlinghetti's** City Lights Bookstore (p. 177), Kaufman's poetry often featured jazz accompaniments.

Hunter S. Thompson: In the 1970s, Thompson moved to San Francisco to live and research the city's Hell's Angels motorcycle gangs. Provoking fights with both Beatniks and police, he took the roadtrip motif in a new direction with his narcotic-laden tour through southern California's barren Mojave Desert.

Herb Caen: Continuing the city's tradition of literary journalism, Caen's 58-year column in the *San Francisco Chronicle* delighted readers and won a Pulitzer Prize with such astute observations as, "We are all in awe of the bitch-goddess San Francisco: so cool, so grand and elegant, so careless of its many treasures."

Alice Walker: Although famous for writing about the South, Walker resides in San Fran and wrote *The Color Purple* in her Alamo Sq. (p. 97) Victorian.

Dorothy Allison: Most famous for her painfully true-to-life novel, *Bastard Out of Carolina*, Allison, formerly a poverty-stricken South Carolina youth, now calls San Francisco her home.

Isabel Allende: Renowned for her magical Chilean family sagas, Allende describes her move to the Bay Area in *Paula*.

Amy Tan: As a native, Tan writes about San Francisco's Chinese-American community in *The Joy Luck Club,* as do **Maxine Hong Kingston** in *The Woman Warrior* and **Fae Myenne Ng** in *Bone*.

Carol Queen: Co-editor of *PoMosexuals* and *Switch Hitter*s, and producer of ground breaking instructional videos *Bend Over Boyfriend (1 and 2)* and the newly-released *Beyond Vanilla,* Queen is one of the most prominent members of San Francisco's current "sex-positive" activist community interested in destabilizing notions of gender and sexuality. She is also a worker/owner at Bay area sex store, Good Vibrations (p. 188)

MUSICAL GIANTS

Tony Bennett: When Bennett put his crooning to George Cory and Douglas Cross's "I Left My Heart in San Francisco," his signature song was born. Bennett used to show up in **Union Sq.** (p. 80) with a mic to pay tribute to the city.

Otis Redding: The singer-songwriter found inspiration in San Fran and wrote his mellow hit "Sittin' on the Dock of the Bay."

Janis Joplin: The doomed rocker and hippie helped establish a nationally recognized San Francisco sound with her early blues band, Big Brother and the Holding Company. Other big names in the 60s San Francisco scene were Latin rocker **Carlos Santana,** and the folksy **Grateful Dead.**

Jefferson Starship: In 1965, the Starship, then Jefferson Airplane, made their debut at their very own Matrix club on Fillmore St.

The Beatles: Right, the Beatles are Brits, but they did choose San Francisco's Candlestick Park (p. 172) to end their touring career.

Joan Baez: The sultry folk singer helped traditional folk flourish in the City by the Bay, as did others like **Kate Wolf.**

Creedence Clearwater Revival: Though they were El Cerrito boys, CCR credibly impersonated bayou swamp rats and gave a voice to antiwar angst.

Tower of Power: The Tower invented the Oakland Soul Sound in the 60s, making way for the city's rappers **(Digital Underground, Too $hort, 2Pac)** to build the loping Oaktown sound on Larry Graham's hefty bass foundation.

Counting Crows: Front man Adam Duritz cashed in on his mellow Berkeley vibe with hits like "Hanging Around," and "Mr. Jones."

Windsurfing

Buena Vista Park

Alcatraz

ARTISTIC GIANTS

Diego Rivera: Lured to the City by the Bay because of its breathtaking coastline, its valleys and its vistas, Rivera (along with his lover, painter **Frida Kahlo**) would visit often, fascinating American society and adorning the city with Mexican-influenced murals.

Robert Crumb: Crumb's demently insightful comics about the sex, drugs, and rock 'n' roll scene in San Francisco helped fuel the euphoric introspection of late-60s counterculture; his cartoon histories of the blues redefined the comic genre.

Ansel Adams: Born in SF, Adams won three Guggenheim grants to photograph the national parks from 1944-58. His pictures of Yosemite National Park and the Sierras have graced calendar pages everywhere and become among the most recognized photos in the United States.

Julia Morgan: A San Francisco native and one of the most prolific and important woman architects to ever work in the United States designed over 600 homes, among them the famous Hearst castle in the 1930s.

Frank Lloyd Wright: One of the 20th century's most experimental architects, Wright designed the huge complex constituting the Marin Civic Center and used his Maiden Lane building (p. 75) as practice for building the Guggenheim Museum in New York.

SPORTS GIANTS...HEY, WAIT A MINUTE

BASEBALL

San Francisco Giants: Once stationed in NY and once the team of **Willie Mays,** arguably the best all-around player in the history of the game. Today, the Giants have another one of the game's greatest athletes, outfielder (and Willie's godson) **Barry Bonds,** all-time record holder for home runs in a single season. Today the Giants play in one of baseball's best stadiums, the newly opened **Pacific Bell Park** in SoMa, (p. 172) near the water off King St. Tickets $10-42. Tours $10, $8 online (www.sfgiants.com). You can also get a free bird's-eye view of the game from The Portwalk, located beyond the outfield wall along the water.

The Oakland A's: The A's (athletics.mlb.com) dominated baseball in the early 1970s, winning five division titles, three consecutive pennants, and the World Series. They gave **Mark McGwire** his start, and have been home to such baseball greats as Jose Canseco, Dennis Eckersly, and Dave Stewart. The A's went to the World Series in 1988 and won it in 1989 (the "Earthquake Series"), beating their Bay Area rivals, the Giants. Today, the A's have returned to the Bash Brother days of the early 90s with a team of young, portly sluggers. The A's play at the **Coliseum,** accessible by BART and by taking I-880 to the 66th Ave. east to the main entrance (p. 228).

BASKETBALL

Golden State Warriors: Oakland also reaches for basketball fame with its Warriors (originally the San Francisco Warriors), who finished the 2001 season last in the Pacific Division. Led by coach and former Celtic Dave Cowens, the consistently injury-plagued Warriors will probably finish at the bottom of the standings for many years to come. The Warriors battle (unsuccessfully generally) in the **Oakland Coliseum Arena,** located just off I-880 at the Hegenberger Rd. exit in southern Oakland (p. 228).

FOOTBALL

San Francisco 49ers: When **Joe Montana** was quarterback, the 49ers dominated the NFL, winning Super Bowls XVI, XIX, XXIII, XXIV. Montana thought four rings were enough and handed the old pigskin to the Salt-Lake-City-raised Mormon **Steve Young.** Under his concussion-laden leadership, the Niners won Super Bowl XXIX. **Jerry Rice,** considered by many the best wide-receiver in NFL history, was released from the 49ers in June 2001 after 16 years of stellar playing. Following the big money across the bay, Rice moved to the...

Oakland Raiders: Based out of Los Angeles from 1982-1995, the Raiders, despite the death of defensive back Eric Turner, have continued to play great seasons. Now, the consistently .500 team features a record five Heisman Trophy Award winners, including Pro Bowlers **Charles Woodson** and **Tim Brown.**

SF ON THE SILVER SCREEN

ACTION/THRILLER

THE MALTESE FALCON (1941). Humphrey Bogart plays Sam Spade, San Fran detective of Dashiel Hammet's creation.

THE BIG SLEEP (1946). A classic detective story, starring Lauren Bacall and Humphrey Bogart, who plays Raymond Chandler's hard-boiled Philip Marlowe. Mucho chiaroscuro lighting and an incomprehensible script co-written by William Faulkner.

VERTIGO (1958). Alfred Hitchcock's complex story about a San Francisco detective and his psychological troubles with acrophobia and a woman.

THE BIRDS (1963). A troubling Hitchcock story: a young woman follows a man out of a San Francisco pet shop to his Bodega Bay home where she and soon the entire town are attacked by sea gulls.

Oh Willie!

Popularly known as "Da Mayor," Willie L. Brown, Jr. is currently serving his second term in office as executive of San Francisco.

How did he make it through the debates of two campaigns? In September 1999, he explained, "I just keep making shit up...I use a little bit of ebonics...and then come to the punch line."

Brown continues the tradition of liberal politics established by his predecessors George Moscone and Dianne Feinstein. While issues such as the MUNI public transportation system (p. 37), homelessness, and a number of alleged scandals have continued to plague Brown's leadership, he has successfully delivered on his commitments to civil rights, the environment, and community safety.

He also keeps the press and gossip-mongers happy with a sharp wit, a flare for showmanship, and a quick temper that has led him to such gaffes as calling 49ers quarterback Elvis Grbac an "embarrassment to humankind" (a comment for which he later apologized).

Positively Haight Street

Gay Pride Parade

United Nations Plaza

DIRTY HARRY (1971). In a film based on the escapades of the real-life Zodiac Killer, Clint Eastwood played San Francisco's Dirty Harry.

BASIC INSTINCT (1992). Sharon Stone does girls and boys and (maybe) kills them all. A SF cop played by Michael Douglas tries to figure it out and get some at the same time. The movie was boycotted by lesbian and gay activists at its release for the lesbian-psycho-killer pathology depicted.

THE ROCK (1996). "Gentleman, welcome to the Rock." The plot is secondary to the explosions, Connery one-liners, and panoramic shots of the bay. And yes, Bruckheimer directed the Lamborghini chase scene in the city.

DRAMA

BIRD MAN OF ALCATRAZ (1962). John Frankenheimer's film was based on the true story of convicted killer Robert Stroud, played by Burt Lancaster. Stroud, who was sentenced to death for killing a prison guard, wrote two books on bird diseases after his sentence was commuted to life in prison by President Wilson.

THE GRADUATE (1967). Dustin Hoffman is a recent college grad in a meaningless, topsy-turvy, psychoerotic void, set to the tune of Simon and Garfunkel's acoustic caterwauling. Watch for the shot of the Bay Bridge, and notice our hero driving the wrong way.

HAROLD AND MAUDE (1971). A classic love story between a bored rich teenager and a vivacious old lady who meet on a SF hilltop at the funeral of someone neither knows. The film is considered one of the most touching romances of the century.

THE JOY LUCK CLUB (1993). Based on author Amy Tan's novel of the same name, this drama captures the disparate experiences of four Chinese-American girls and their mothers.

MUSICAL & COMEDY

SAN FRANCISCO (1936). Clark Gable and Mary Blake star in this MGM disaster musical whose earthquake scene is so realistic that at the premiere several 1906 survivors got sick and had to leave the theater. See what it does to you on April 18—it's shown at the **Castro Theatre** (p. 170) every year to commemorate the Great Earthquake and fire.

WHAT'S UP, DOC? (1972). This hilarious slapstick comedy set in San Francisco (hills are funny) stars Madeline Kahn and Barbara Streisand.

MRS. DOUBTFIRE (1993). Robin Williams pays a displaced dad who cross-dresses as an old British nanny to spend time with his kids. Could this be based on a true story? It *is* set in San Francisco, after all.

A Quick History

When confronted with the exuberant face of San Francisco's gay population, one might easily imagine an early prospector triumphantly striking gold…gold lamé, that is. Although it would have been difficult to pan for gold platform go-go boots, the Gold Rush of 1849 indeed helped lay the foundation for SF's image as a beacon of tolerance.

By late 1849, "Gold Fever" had attracted upwards of 40,000 fortune-seekers. Due to this steady influx of miners, the population of San Francisco was roughly 90 percent male throughout the 1850s and remained disproportionately high for years. Mine work meant laboring in a remote location with long absences from women; such conditions helped foster a homosexual subculture. Tales of all-male barn dances, where the partner dancing the woman's steps wore a red bandana on his arm, circulate in gay folklore as a possible source of the contemporary "hanky code." San Francisco's new arrivals mingled with sailors, transients, and travelers. They patronized the saloons and brothels of the infamous Barbary Coast, a subversive action for the time, earning the city one of its earliest nicknames, "Sodom By The Sea." By the late 19th century, some establishments catered exclusively to a gay clientele; the city's earliest gay bar, The Dash, was located at 574 Pacific Street. The saloon, with a dance hall that featured female impersonators, was shut down by city officials in 1908.

The onset of World War II contributed to the city's reputation as a haven for "outlaws" of traditional society. The Bay was a point of departure and reentry for over 1.5 million servicemen in the war, thousands of whom were discharged by the military for homosexuality; rather than return home, many opted to remain in San Francisco. The number of gay bars and restaurants in the city flourished during the war years. Military personnel seeking out such establishments got inadvertent assistance from the armed services themselves—lists of off-limits bars were routinely posted on military bases.

In the 1950s, right-wing politicians like Joseph McCarthy and Californian Richard Nixon promoted a discourse in which homosexuality was on par with communism as an "anti-American" threat. At the same time, the Beat movement gained momentum, which influenced and was influenced by the attitudes and social scene of the emerging gay culture. Jack Kerouac immortalized one of SF's best-known gay bars, the Black Cat Café, as the bohemian bar in *On The Road*. Establishments which catered to a gay and lesbian clientele in the 40s and featured drag shows throughout the 50s bore the brunt of officially sanctioned anti-gay activity. Because homosexuality was illegal, the state Alcoholic Beverage Commission would police gay bars and close them for serving drinks to self-identified homosexuals. In response to such harassment, owners of primarily gay establishments formed the Tavern Guild in 1962. The Guild became the first overtly gay business association in the country and offered a backbone for the gay community.

San Francisco's gay population found further political empowerment during the mayoral election of 1960. Incumbent conservative George Christopher was accused by his opponent of allowing the city to become a safe harbor for homosexuals. The smear tactic failed and Christopher was reelected, but in the course of the debate both candidates' homophobia alienated voters. In 1964, Life Magazine ran a full-photo feature naming San Francisco the country's "Gay Capital." During the 60s, gays found the counterculture and anti-war movements sympathetic to their own struggle. New York's watershed Stonewall Riot in 1969 led to explosive progress in gay consciousness and activism. The growing identity of the gay community manifested itself publicly in 1970 with the first annual Gay Pride Parade. In 1978, local artist Gilbert Baker designed a visual symbol for the community by creating the Rainbow Flag. The flag is now recognized by the International Congress of Flag Makers.

The best-known figure of SF's gay social and political scene was Harvey Milk, who in 1977 became the first openly gay member of the city's Board of Supervisors. Milk, along with Mayor George Moscone, worked to successfully defeat the Briggs Initiative (a proposal barring the employment of gay people as teachers). But on November 27, 1978, Milk and Moscone were murdered by ex-Supervisor and anti-gay spokesperson Dan White. White escaped first-degree murder charges and received a lighter manslaughter sentence after his attorney presented a "Twinkie Defense," arguing that his client could not be held accountable for his actions due to a sugar high from eating cupcakes and drinking Coke. When the sentence was announced, enraged citizens staged one of the biggest riots in San Francisco history, known as White Night.

For further reading try *Gay by the Bay: A History of Queer Culture in the San Francisco Bay Area* (1996) by Susan Stryker, et al.

Susan Gray was a Researcher-Writer for Let's Go: Greece 1994 *and* Let's Go: Turkey 1995. *She is now a law student living in San Francisco.*

Sights

FISHERMAN'S WHARF & THE PIERS

◪ *NEIGHBORHOOD QUICKFIND:* **Discover,** *p. 7;* **Walking Tour,** *p. 27;* **Food & Drink,** *p. 116.*

see map p. 338

PIER 39

◪ ☎ *981-7437. Shops, attractions, and fast food open Su-Th 10am-9pm, F-Sa 10am-10pm; restaurants open Su-Th 11:30am-10pm, F-Sa 11:30am-11pm.* **Cinemax:** ☎ *956-3456. Shows every 45min. First show 10am. Adults $7.50, seniors $6, children $4.50.* **California Welcome Center and Internet Cafe:** ☎ *956-3493. Open Su-Th 9am-9pm, F-Sa 9am-10pm.*

Self-titled "San Francisco's Number One Attraction," Pier 39 is a shamelessly commercial collection of 110 speciality shops, restaurants, fast-food vendors, and entertainment. Even the world-famous sea lions—found by the eastern tip of the pier—seem to put on a spectacle of splashing and snorting for the benefit of tourists. The **California Welcome Center,** located at the top of the Marina Plaza stairs, features an Internet cafe, snacks, info, and occasional discounts for attractions in the city and beyond. For a whirlwind city-tour, experience **The Great San Francisco Adventure** at **Pier 39 Cinemax.** In huge-screen format, you can fly over the Golden Gate Bridge, feel a 3.0 scale earthquake, race down Lombard St., watch a 49ers game, and dive to the ocean depths—in only 30 minutes! If that leaves

The Local LEGEND

Domingo and the Chocolate Factory

The world-famous **Ghirardelli Chocolate Company,** the oldest chocolate manufacturer in America, has called San Francisco home since 1852. Its founder, Domingo Ghirardelli (GEAR-a-dell-ee), discovered his love of chocolate at a young age when he apprenticed with his father, a celebrated Italian chocolatier.

In 1849, Ghirardelli was lured to California by tales of the Gold Rush. Discouraged with prospecting for gold, he relocated to Sacramento to supply chocolate and provisions to the miners and vagrants. In 1852, Domingo Ghirardelli moved to San Francisco and opened the Ghirardelli Chocolate Company. His chocolate, like liquid gold, quickly became renowned in San Francisco and beyond—Let's Go recommends the lush creamy chocolate chunks.

The Ghirardelli Chocolate Company is found today in **Ghirardelli Square,** now a San Francisco landmark and the site of the **Ghirardelli Manufactory & Soda Fountain**. You can still see original equipment from the manufacturer and taste free samples (p. 67).

you feeling giddy, head to the end of the pier to unwind with live street performances at **Center Stage** or a jaunt on the **Venetian Carousel.**

AQUARIUM OF THE BAY

🔎 *Pier 39:* ☎ 888-732-3483 or 623-5300; www.aquariumofthebay.com. Open June-Aug. daily 9am-8pm; Sept.-May M-Th 10am-6pm, F-Su 10am-7pm. Adult $12.95, seniors and children $6.50, family $29.95 (2 adults and 2 children), behind-the-scenes tour $25.

Find out what lurks beneath the Bay at this eco-friendly facility. Gaze at silvery shoals and circling sharks along 300 ft. of tunnels, complete with moving walkway. A series of touching pools allows you to caress a sea-cucumber or tickle a shark. The aquarium is a perfect way to spend time with the family, or unwind after visiting one of the wharf's restaurants at **Pier 39**.

PIER 45

🔎 *Pampanito:* ☎ 775-1943. Open June-Sept. M-Th 9am-6pm, F-Su 9am-8pm; Oct.-May M-Tu and Th-Su 9am-8pm, W 9am-6pm. Adults $7, seniors $5, ages 6-12 $4, under 6 free.

Still used by fishermen in the early morning hours, Pier 45 is also home to the **USS Pampanito** (SS-383). In retirement after sinking six enemy ships during its Pacific patrols, this World War II *Balao*-class fleet submarine now serves as a National Historic Park museum.

FERRIES AND CRUISES

🔎 *Blue and Gold Fleet:* Piers 39 and 41. Info ☎ 773-1188, tickets 705-5555; www.blueandgoldfleet.com. Ticket office open in summer daily 9am-4:30pm. Admission included in San Francisco CityPass (p. 92). *Red and White Ferry:* Pier 43.5. Info ☎ 673-2900, tickets 800-229-2784; www.redandwhite.com. Ticket office open daily 9am-6:15pm (summer). AmEx/D/MC/V.

The **Blue and Gold Fleet** and the **Red and White Fleet,** named after the Bay Area rival universities Berkeley and Stanford, offer sea-faring and landscape-scoping opportunities. The Red and White departs Pier 43.5 for a 1hr. cruise skirting Alcatraz, Angel Island, and the Golden Gate Bridge. The tour (adult $19, seniors and ages 12-18 $15, ages 5-11 $11) is fully narrated with headsets. The Blue and Gold offers a similar 1hr. cruise, with narrated highlights (adults $18, seniors and ages 12-18 $14, ages 5-11 $10). Both run daily with frequent departures (call for times). The Blue and Gold also runs coach trips and ferries to Sausalito, Tiburon, Angel Island, and Alcatraz.

GHIRARDELLI SQUARE

🏢 *Mall:* 900 North Point St. ☎ 775-5500. Stores open M-Sa 10am-9pm, Su 10am-6pm. *Ghirardelli Chocolate Manufactory:* ☎ 771-4903. Open Su-Th 10am-11pm, F-Sa 10am-midnight. *Soda fountain:* Open Su-Th 10am-11pm, F-Sa 10am-midnight. *Chocolate Shop and Caffe:* ☎ 474-1414. Open M-Th 8:30am-9pm, F 8:30am-10pm, Sa 9pm-10pm, Su 9am-9pm. AmEx/MC/V.

Chocolate-lovers' heaven, Ghirardelli Square, houses a mall in what used to be a chocolate factory. Don't worry, you don't need a Willy Wonka golden ticket to sample the savory sweets; visit the **Ghirardelli Chocolate Manufactory,** with its vast selection of chocolatey goodies, or the **Ghirardelli Chocolate Shop and Caffe,** with drinks, frozen yogurt, and a smaller selection of chocolates. Both hand out **free samples** of chocolate at the door, but on tourist-heavy days, the Caffe is often less crowded. The **soda fountain,** an old-fashioned ice-cream parlor, serves huge sundaes ($6.25) smothered with its world-famous hot fudge sauce. For the metabolically blessed, try the Earthquake Sundae: eight scoops (all different flavors!) of ice cream, eight toppings, bananas, whipped cream, nuts, and cherries ($20).

RIPLEY'S BELIEVE IT OR NOT MUSEUM

🏢 175 Jefferson St. ☎ 771-6188; www.ripleysf.com. Open summer Su-Th 9am-11pm, F-Sa 9am-midnight; Labor Day to mid-June Su-Th 10am-10pm, F-Sa 10am-midnight. Adults $10.95, seniors $8.50, students $8.95, ages 5-12 $7.95, under 5 free. AmEx/MC/V.

Named after eccentric man-of-all-trades Robert Ripley, the museum contains bizarrely fascinating documents, artifacts, and folklore from his 19 trips around the world. Not for the overly skeptical or weak of constitution. Exhibits include a kaleidoscope tunnel, shrunken torsos, a portrait of Van Gogh made entirely of toast, and a video portraying the trials and tribulations of being an 8'11" man.

WAX MUSEUM

🏢 145 Jefferson St. ☎ 800-439-4305; www.waxmuseum.com. Open M-F 10am-10pm, Sa-Su 9am-midnight (last tickets sold 1hr. before closing). Adults $10.95, seniors $10.55, ages 4-11 $6.95.

If you only have time to visit one of the two "eccentric" museums, Ripley's is the way to go. But if you haven't had your fill of sculpted bees' wax, human hair, and medical-quality glass eyes, this collection of over 250 life-size figures should be creepily satisfying. Stroll by the famous and infamous from history—world leaders, dictators, film stars, royals, scientists, and athletes. New additions include Princess Diana, Ricky Martin, and Britney Spears. Selective narrations provide biographic details. The Chamber of Horrors features sadistic scenes of torture and iconic figures of evil.

HYDE STREET PIER & NATIONAL HISTORIC PARK

🏢 On Hyde St. ☎ 561-7100. Open 9:30am-5:30pm. Adults $5, under 16 free. Guided Pier Walks offered 4 times daily; call for times. *Dolphin Club:* 502 Jefferson St. ☎ 441-9329. Open in summer W 11am-6pm; in winter 10am-5pm. *South End Rowing Club:* 500 Jefferson St. ☎ 929-9656. Open in summer Tu, Th, and Sa 11am-6pm; in winter 10am-5pm. *Boating Class:* ☎ 929-0202.

Along with the curving Municipal Pier, Hyde Street Pier encloses an area of the Bay known as the Aquatic Park. Sittin' on the dock of the Bay, you can watch the daring locals swim laps in frigid 50°F water. If you feel like joining, the South End Rowing Club and the Dolphin Club are open to the public on alternate days for $6.50 where you can thaw out in their saunas. Rich with maritime tradition, Hyde Street Pier is also part of the National Historic Park, offering guided tours of the vessels, schooners, and ferryboats as well as a boat-building class to satisfy your nautical needs.

THE CANNERY

🏢 2801 Leavenworth St. www.thecannery.com.

Built in 1907 as the del Monte canning factory, once the largest peach cannery in the world, **The Cannery** has been converted into a marketplace-style plaza. Its maze of shady terraces and European-inspired garden courtyards offers respite from wharfside hubbub and ballyhoo. Three levels of balconies, bridges, and walkways house some charming restaurants, shops, and entertainment.

PETER LIK GALLERY

🚩 *Pier 39, shop K105. ☎ 765-7515; www.peterlik.com. Open Su-Th 9am-9pm, F-Sa 9am-10pm. Free admission. AmEx/D/MC/V.*

Take a break from touristy trinkets in this stylish gallery of spectacular photography, which displays and sells work by Peter Lik, one of the world's most famous landscape photographers. See the much-photographed images of San Francisco from a new, more nuanced perspective, or dream of distant sun-drenched shores in the shots of Australia.

MARINA & FORT MASON

MARINA

see map p. 338

🚩 NEIGHBORHOOD QUICKFIND: **Discover,** *p. 7;* **Food & Drink,** *p. 117;* **Nightlife,** *p. 144;* **Accommodations,** *p. 191.*

🔲 EXPLORATORIUM

🚩 *3601 Lyon St. ☎ 563-7337 or 561-0360; www.exploratorium.edu. Open Tu-Su 10am-5pm. Adults $12; students, seniors, disabled, and youth 9-17 $9.50; children 4-8 $8.00, under 3 free. Free 1st W of each month. Admission included in San Francisco CityPass (p. 92).* **Tactile Dome:** *reservations ☎ 561-0362; reservations@exploratorium.edu. $15 (includes general admission). Open during museum hours. Credit card required for reservation; book at least one day in advance.*

The Exploratorium can hold over 4,000 people, and on the first Wednesday of every month when admission is free, it usually does. Over 650 interactive displays—including miniature tornadoes, computer-simulated planet-managing, and giant bubble-makers—explain the wonders of the world, from the five senses to the mysteries of the cosmos. The cow's eye dissection is not to be missed, though the faint of stomach should hold off if it's almost lunchtime. On-site classrooms with windows allow museum-goers to watch scientists while they innovate. Ever-changing special exhibits with accompanying theme-related programs are a real treat. New features include the self-guided "Arts Tour" and the "Traits of Life" laboratory with over 30 living organisms. If you ever find yourself near the Exploratorium during a solar eclipse, consider watching a live, color broadcast of the celestial event. On the second Wednesday of each month from November to March, the Exploratorium hosts avant-garde **art-themed cocktail nights** (regular admission price, check website for more details) that feature Bay area artists, a DJ and bar, and attract a 20s-30s crowd. Inside the Exploratorium, the **Tactile Dome**—a dark maze of tunnels, slides, nooks, and crannies—helps refine your sense of touch. Claustrophobes beware.

🔲 PALACE OF FINE ARTS

🚩 *On Baker St., between Jefferson and Bay St. next to the Exploratorium. Open daily 6am-9pm. Free.* **Theater:** *☎ 569-6504; www.palaceoffinearts.com. Call for shows, times, and ticket prices.*

With its open-air domed structure and curving colonnades, The Palace of Fine Arts is one of the best picnic spots in the city. It was reconstructed from remnants of the 1915 Panama-Pacific Exposition, which had been built to commemorate the opening of the Panama Canal and exemplify San Francisco's recovery from the 1906 earthquake. Shakespearean plays are often performed here during the summer, and the nighttime illumination is glorious. Additionally, the **Palace of Fine Arts Theater,** located directly behind the rotunda, hosts various dance and theater performances and film festivals.

MARINA GREEN

Along the water, joggers and walkers crowd the windy Marina Green, which on a clear day offers unrivaled views of nearby Golden Gate Bridge and Marin, not to mention the expensive yachts lining the harbor. Though cleats aren't allowed on the main stretch, kite-flying (some of San Francisco's best) and picnicking are. On Saturdays, volleyball nets fill the small patch of the green near Baker St. at Marina Blvd. A small concession stand (drinks, snacks, sandwiches under $5) keeps athletes and onlookers refreshed.

FORT MASON

NEIGHBORHOOD QUICKFIND: ***Discover,*** *p. 7;* ***Food & Drink,*** *p. 117;* ***Accommodations,*** *p. 191.*

FORT MASON CENTER

The eastern portion of Fort Mason, near Gashouse Cove. ☎ 441-3400, ext. 3; www.fortmason.org.

Fort Mason Center is home to the original headquarters of the 1906 earthquake relief site. Its initial purpose, quite singular in scope, contrasts now with the diverse cultural museums and resources that inhabit the Fort. From theatre and craft, to Italian and African-American art, the innovative and impressive array of outstanding attractions in Fort Mason remains relatively unknown to travelers and locals alike. Fort Mason Center is a quiet waterfront counterpart to the tourist blitz of nearby Fisherman's Wharf. On the **first Wednesday of every month all museums are free** and open until 7pm. The grounds are also home to a popular hostel and the headquarters of the **Golden Gate National Recreation Area (GGNRA).** While not nearly as spectacular as some other lands under the GGNRA's aegis, these manicured greens make a swell spot for strolling and picnicking.

MUSEUM OF CRAFT AND FOLK ART

Bldg. A., 1st fl. ☎ 775-0991; www.mocfa.org. Open Tu-F and Su 11am-5pm, Sa 10am-5pm. Adults $4, students and seniors $3, under 18 free. Free Sa 10am-noon and 1st W of each month 11am-7pm.

The tiny but culturally rich MOCFA houses a fascinating collection of crafts and functional art (vessels, clothing, furniture, and jewelry) from past and present, near and far. The museum showcases everything from 19th century Chinese children's hats to war-time commentary made through lightbulbs. Second floor is not wheelchair-accessible.

SF MUSEUM OF MODERN ART ARTISTS GALLERY

Bldg. A, 1st fl. ☎ 441-4777; www.sfmoma.org. Open Tu-Sa 11:30am-5:30pm. Free.

Over 1,200 Bay Area artists show, rent, and sell their work in this rental space. Monthly curated exhibits are on display downstairs, while most other pieces are sold upstairs, with proceeds split between the artist and the Museum. Every May the gallery hosts a **benefit sale** in which all works are sold for half-off.

Ultimate Surround Sound

On any given day, a trip to the waterfront will provide a view of the crashing waves and a few solitary joggers. But just past the Marina Green, near the Golden Gate Yacht club, stands one of San Francisco's strangest and most natural musical instruments.

What most people don't realize is that one of San Francisco's best hidden treasures, the **Wave Organ,** rests among the rocks. A magnificent interplay between art and nature, the wave organ is an acoustic environmental sculpture consisting of 25 pipes jutting out of the ocean. Each pipe creates a different musical sound as waves crash against it.

Conceived by Peter Richards, the project was completed in 1986. George Gonzalez, a sculptor and stone mason, designed the seating area around the pipes using granite and marble pieces from an old decimated cemetery. Far from morbid though, the effect is rather meditatively intriguing. A series of carvings can be discerned if you look closely enough at the structure.

The music itself is quite subtle, like listening to a sea shell, and is best heard at high tide. If you take the time to sit for a while, tones from the organ will begin to harmonize with the clinking boat masts, fog horns, and sea gulls, synthesizing into a sublime oceanic symphony.

THE COFFEE GALLERY

⚐ *Bldg. B, 1st fl. ☎ 561-1840; www.ccsf.org. Open M-Th 8am-11pm, F-Su 8am-midnight. Free.*

The halls and seating areas on the first floor of Building B display artwork produced by students and instructors of the City College of San Francisco Fort Mason Art Campus. Bring your chess board and enjoy an extended coffee stop without abandoning your pursuit of art and culture.

AFRICAN-AMERICAN HISTORICAL AND CULTURAL SOCIETY MUSEUM

⚐ *Bldg. C, #165. ☎ 441-0640. Open W-Su noon-5pm. Adults $3, seniors and children over 12 $1, under 12 free. 1st W of each month free.*

The African-American Historical and Cultural Society Museum displays historic artifacts and artwork as well as modern works by African and African-American artists. The museum also has a permanent collection by local artists.

MUSEO ITALO AMERICANO

⚐ *Bldg. C, #100. ☎ 673-2200; www.museoitaloamericano.org. Open W-Su noon-5pm. Adults $3, students and seniors $2, under 12 free.*

The only museum in the country dedicated solely to Italian and Italian-American art, Museo Italo Americano is home to a small collection by artists from several centuries and offers a selection of cultural programs, such as language classes and lectures.

NORTH BEACH

see map p. 339

⚐ *NEIGHBORHOOD QUICKFIND:* **Discover,** *p. 8;* **Food & Drink,** *p. 118;* **Accommodations,** *p. 144;* **Nightlife,** *p. 144.*

WASHINGTON SQUARE

⚐ *Church: 666 Filbert St., to the north of the square. ☎ 421-0809. Mass M-Sa 7:30, 9am, and 12:15pm. Su 7:30, 8:45, 10:15am (Cantonese), 11:45am (Italian), 1, and 5pm. Open daily 7am-4pm.*

Washington Sq., bordered by Union, Filbert, Stockton, and Powell St., is North Beach's *piazza*, a pretty, not-quite-square, tree-lined lawn. The statue in Washington Sq. is of Benjamin Franklin. The wedding site of Marilyn Monroe and Joe DiMaggio, the park fills every morning with men and women from Chinatown practicing *tai chi.* By noon, sunbathers, picnickers, and bocce-ball players take over. At 666 Filbert St., the **St. Peter and St. Paul Catholic Church** beckons tired sightseers to take refuge in its dark, wooden nave. Turn-of-the-century San Francisco philanthropist and party-girl Lillie Hitchcock Coit donated the **Volunteer Firemen Memorial** in the middle of the square after being rescued from a fire as a young girl.

CITY LIGHTS BOOKSTORE

⚐ *261 Columbus Ave. ☎ 362-8193. Open daily 10am-midnight.*

Drawn by low rents and cheap bars, the Beat writers came to national attention when Lawrence Ferlinghetti's City Lights Bookstore, opened in 1953, published Allen Ginsberg's *Howl.* Banned in 1956, and then subjected to an extended trial at the end of which a judge found the poem "not obscene," the book and its publisher vaulted the Beats into literary infamy. City Lights has expanded since its Beat days and widely now stocks fiction and poetry, but it remains committed to publishing young poets and writers under its own imprint. Black and white signs beckon visitors to sit down, turn off their "sell-phones," and flip through the books. Index card boxes in the back stairwell hold postings for jobs, housing, and rides, and writers without permanent addresses can have their mail held in the store (**Shopping,** p. 177).

NORTH BEACH MUSEUM

⚐ *1435 Stockton St., at Columbus Ave. inside Bay View Bank. ☎626-7070. Open M-Th 9am-5pm, F 9am-6pm, Sa 9am-1pm. Free.*

The tiny North Beach Museum depicts the neighborhood of yesteryear in photographs, including some impressive shots of the 1906 earthquake and fire. Most of the pictures long predate the Beats, but a handwritten manuscript of Ferlinghetti's *The Old Italians Dying* is on display. Photos of some of North Beach's most famous citizens, such as NY Yankee teammates Joe DiMaggio, Frankie Crosetti, and Tony Lazzori, hang alongside lesser-known local boxers and opera stars.

LYLE TUTTLE'S TATTOO ART STUDIO

⚐ *841 Columbus Ave. (☎775-4991). Open in summer M-Th noon-9pm, F-Su noon-10pm; off-season F-Su noon-9pm.*

Lyle Tuttle opened his modern, clean tattoo studio in the 1960s, permanently decorating the skins of Janis Joplin, Joan Baez, and Cher. While the eminently professional Tuttle, age 72, himself covered in tattoos from head to foot, no longer tattoos behind the bar, his proteges continue the tradition, amidst a small, but impressive collection of tattoo memorabilia—consider it an added bonus if you drop by when someone's under the needle behind the bar. Tattoos start at $60. Open daily noon-9pm No credit cards.

CHINATOWN

⚐ *NEIGHBORHOOD QUICKFIND:*
Discover, *p. 9;* ***Food & Drink,*** *p. 120;* ***Nightlife,*** *p. 146;* ***Accommodations,*** *p. 193.*

see map p. 339

🏛 WAVERLY PLACE

⚐ *Between Sacramento and Washington St., and between Stockton St. and Grant Ave.* ***Tien Hou Temple:*** *125 Waverly Pl. Open Su-W and F-Sa 9:30am-3:30pm.*

This alley is well worth a visit for its multitude of shops and restaurants and the traditional Chinese architectural details on the facades of the buildings. The fire escapes are painted in bright pinks and greens and connected by railings cast in intricate patterns. You won't find any souvenir shops on Waverly, but you can visit the demure **Tien Hou Temple**—the oldest Taoist place of worship in San Francisco. Walk up three flights of stairs to the sacred wood carvings, fragrant incense, and serene atmosphere.

the local story

An Age of Change

Vivian Chang, a Chinatown resident, reflects on its recent changes.

Chinatown's residents have a reputation for being reserved and old-fashioned. Their initial mistrust of outsiders does not come by nature, but through fear and the insecurity of their position [in the city]. When I moved here from China in the 70s, I had to overcome the language barrier [because] I spoke Mandarin and in Chinatown people spoke Cantonese. No one understood me. It wasn't until I learned Chinatown's Chinese that [the community] finally accepted me.

Women [in Chinatown] are more aggressive now. They put profession first and then family. The younger generation is also more open. They still respect Chinese filial duty, but they leave home early. They go to public school...college...or move to the suburbs as soon as financially possible because they know there's more to life than this.

Chinatown has maintained its exterior, but it's a business. It has become an elderly community. Fifty years ago, [young people] were willing to carry on for the family. Now they want a contemporary life; they come to Chinatown to eat.

GRANT AVENUE

⁊ *At Bush St. and Grant Ave.*

The oldest street in San Francisco is a sea of Chinese banners, signs, and architecture. During the day, Grant Ave. and nearby streets are brimming with tourists, who stop at every block to buy health balls and chirping boxes and pretend not to notice the Chinese porn mags lining some shop windows. At Bush St. and Grant Ave. stands the ornate, dragon-crested **Gateway to Chinatown,** a gift from Taiwan in 1970. "Everything in the world is in just proportion," say the Chinese characters above the gate. Most of the picturesque pagodas punctuating the blocks were designed around or after 1900, not as authentic replicas of Chinese architecture, but as temptations for Western tourists. While Grant Ave. is the center of many Chinatown activities, to get a true taste of the neighborhood you must venture off into the alleys and side-streets.

ROSS ALLEY

⁊ *From Jackson to Washington St. between Grant and Stockton St.* **Golden Gate Cookie Co.:** *56 Ross Alley.* ☎ *781-3956. Bag of cookies $3, with "funny," "sexy," or "lucky" fortunes $5. Open daily 10am-8pm.*

Ross Alley was once lined with brothels and gambling houses; today, it has the cramped look of old Chinatown. The narrow street has stood in for the Orient in such films as *Big Trouble in Little China, Karate Kid II,* and *Indiana Jones and the Temple of Doom.* Squeeze into a tiny doorway to watch fortune cookies being shaped by hand at the **Golden Gate Cookie Company,** which has practiced its craft since opening in 1962. All cookies that don't come out according to the baker's high standards are put in big tins for free taste-testing by the hungry crowds that gather around the doorway.

CHINESE HISTORICAL SOCIETY OF AMERICA

⁊ *965 Clay St., between Powell and Stockton St.* ☎ *391-1188; www.chsa.org. Open Tu-F 11am-4pm, Sa-Su noon-4pm. Adults $3, seniors and students with ID $2, ages 6-17 $1, under 5 free. Free first Th of every month.*

Founded in 1963 to educate and foster an understanding of the Chinese experience in America, this combined museum and learning center houses books, artifacts, and impressive displays. Exhibits deal with Chinese-American fashion, food, and labor issues from the railroad boom to the dot-com bust. The society, actually a former YWCA residence, also hosts rotating exhibits of Chinese-American artists and a free monthly lecture series.

CHINESE CULTURAL CENTER

⁊ *750 Kearny St., on the 3rd fl. of the Holiday Inn; also accessible directly from Portsmouth Sq. by pedestrian overpass.* ☎ *986-1822; www.c-c-c.org. Open Tu-Sa 10am-4pm.* **Heritage Walk:** *Sa-Su 2pm. Adults $15, under 18 $8. Groups (4+) of adults can call ahead for* **private Heritage Walk** *and Culinary Walk tours.* **Culinary walk:** *Adults $30, under 18 $15. Includes dim sum luncheon. Reserve at least 24hr. in advance.*

A stone bridge leads from the park at Portsmouth Sq. to the other side of Kearny St., where the Chinese Cultural Center hosts two small galleries of Chinese-American art and offers classes in music, painting, Mandarin, and kung fu. The center also sponsors two **walking tours** of Chinatown: the **Heritage Walk** surveys the history and culture of Chinatown, while the **Culinary Walk** explores different styles of Chinese cooking, food, shopping, and eating (at a specially prepared dim sum luncheon).

OTHER SIGHTS

Old Saint Mary's, 660 California St., at Grant Ave., was built from Chinese granite and New England brick in 1854. The first church in the world dedicated to St. Mary, it served as California's only cathedral until 1891. Now, this historic site is in the process of raising $8 million to pay for seismic retrofit renovations or risk being torn down by the city. (Open M-F 7am-4:30pm, Sa 7:30am-6pm, Su 8am-3:30pm). **Buddha's Universal Church** at 720 Washington St., at Kearny St; (☎982-6116) is a five-story, hand-built temple with tiled mosaics and murals. For a truly intense taste of neighborhood culture, bustling upper **Stockton St.**, between Jackson St. and Broadway, packs its sidewalks with outdoor grocery stalls and crowds of haggling local residents doing their daily shopping, all in an invigorating urban jumble. Reasonably priced papaya, bok choy, and pig's foot all come fresh daily, but English and credit cards are not commonly understood. (Most markets open around 7am and close by 6pm).

NOB HILL & RUSSIAN HILL

🚩 *NEIGHBORHOOD QUICKFIND:* **Discover,** *p. 9;* **Food & Drink,** *p. 121;* **Nightlife,** *p. 147;* **Accommodations,** *p. 194.*

THE CROOKEDEST STREET IN THE WORLD

see map p. 342

🚩 *Between Hyde and Leavenworth St., running down Russian Hill.*

The famous curves of **Lombard St.** seem to grace nearly half of San Francisco's postcards, and rightfully so. The flowerbeds along the curves are beautifully manicured, and the eight curves themselves—installed in the 1920s so that horse-drawn carriages could negotiate the extremely steep hill—are uniquely San Francisco. From the top of Lombard St., pedestrians and passengers alike enjoy a fantastic view of the city and harbor. The view north along Hyde St.—a steep drop to Fisherman's Wharf and lonely Alcatraz floating in the bay—isn't too shabby either.

SAN FRANCISCO ART INSTITUTE

🚩 *800 Chestnut St., between Leavenworth and Jones St.* ☎ *771-7020 or 800-345-7324; www.sfai.edu.* **Diego Rivera Gallery:** *Open daily June-Aug. 9am-8pm; Sept.-May 9am-9pm.* **Walter and McBean Galleries:** *Open Tu-Sa 11am-6pm but call ahead because not always in use.* **Pete's Cafe:** *Open June-Aug. M-F 10am-2pm; Sept.-May M-Th 8am-4pm, F 8am-2pm.*

The oldest art school west of the Mississippi, the San Francisco Art Institute is lodged in a converted mission and has produced a number of American greats including Mark Rothko, Ansel

SF on TV

San Francisco's beautiful and distinctive landscape has played backdrop to many memorable stories and scenes of writers and filmmakers. The images of three television shows in particular continue to permeate the hills and streets of SF, despite their cancellation.

For years **Full House** served as centerpiece to ABC's wildly popular TGIF. The Tanners' non-traditional household offered images of the Golden Gate Bridge and delight to Americans from fictional 1882 Gerard St. (filming actually took place in LA). Although a new episode hasn't aired since 1995, it lives on in syndication and through the careers of Bob Saget, Candace Cameron, Jodie Sweetin, and of course the Olson twins.

The third season of MTV's **Real World,** set in San Francisco, boosted the reality series into the limelight and readied the nation for the art of voyeuristic television. Pedro, Pam, Puck, Judd, Rachel, Mohammed, and Cory exposed viewers to the "realities" of racism, HIV, and living with someone who farts in the living room. *Real World* zealots can view the exterior of the group's Russian Hill apartment at 949 Lombard St., between Leavenworth and Jones St.

The Salingers redefined the family drama genre in Fox's **Party of Five.** Charlie, Bailey, Julia, Claudia, and Owen hold together despite the tragic death of their parents and struggles with alcoholism, cancer, depression, and infertility...all from their Pacific Heights apartment at 2311 Broadway, between Fillmore and Steiner St. Visit www.po5.co.uk/sf.htm for a PO5 guide to SF.

GET sm**art**

Adams, Imogen Cunningham, Dorothea Lange, and James Weeks, to name a few. Student projects hang throughout the school, and given the place's history, you never know whom you might discover. As you enter, to the left is the **Diego Rivera Gallery,** one wall of which is covered by a huge 1931 Rivera mural. The gallery hosts weekly student exhibits with receptions every other Tuesday night from 5-7pm. Farther down the lefthand hallway are the **Walter and McBean Galleries,** which show professional exhibits. Outside these galleries and across the airy modern "quadrangle," **Pete's Cafe** serves up cheap burgers and sandwiches ($4.50), making for a nice picnic spot with fantastic views of the bay.

GRACE CATHEDRAL AND HUNTINGTON PARK

🛈 *Cathedral: 1100 California St., between Jones and Taylor St. ☎749-6300; www.gracecathedral.org. Open Su-F 7am-6pm, Sa 8am-6pm. **Services:** Su 7:30, 8:15, 11am, 3, and 6pm; M-F 7:30, 9am, 12:10, and 5:15pm; Sa 9, 11am, and 3pm. Tour guides available M-F 1-3pm, Sa 11:30am-1:30pm, Su 1:30-2pm. Suggested donation $3.*

The largest Gothic edifice west of the Mississippi, **Grace Cathedral** is Nob Hill's stained glass-studded crown. A labyrinthine entryway helps clear the minds of entering devotees. The main doors that beckon visitors in are replicas cast from Lorenzo Ghiberti's Doors on Paradise in Florence's famed Duomo Cathedral. Inside, modern murals mix San Franciscan and national historical events with saintly scenes. The altar of the AIDS Interfaith Memorial Chapel celebrates the church's "inclusive community of love" with a lustrously intricate Keith Haring triptych. Outside, this all-accepting behemoth of Christian modernity looks onto the neatly manicured turf and trees of **Huntington Park,** equipped with a park and playground.

CABLE CAR POWERHOUSE AND MUSEUM

🛈 *1201 Mason St., at Washington St. ☎474-1887. Open Apr.-Oct. daily 10am-6pm; Nov.-Mar. 10am-5pm. Free.*

After the journey up Nob Hill, you'll understand what inspired the development of the vehicles celebrated at this museum. More an educational breather than a destination in its own right, the modest building is the working center of San Francisco's cable car system. Look down on 57,300 ft. of cable whizzing by, or view displays to learn more about the cars, some of which date back to 1873.

BARS WITH A VIEW

⚑ Top of the Mark: *999 California St., at Mason St. in the Mark Hopkins Hotel.* ☎ *616-6916; www.topofthemark.com. Cocktails Su-Th 5pm-midnight, F-Sa 4pm-1am. Live piano music Su-W 6-10pm, live swing bands Th 9pm, jazz F-Sa. Cover after 8:30pm Su-Th $5, F-Sa $10.* **Tonga Room:** *In the Fairmont Hotel.* (**Nightlife,** *p. 148*).

Once the site of the enormous mansions of the four mining and railroad magnates who "settled" Nob Hill (Charles Crocker, Mark Hopkins, Leland Stanford, and Collis Huntington), the hilltop is now home to opulent hotels and their tourist- (but not wallet-) friendly bars. Perched at the literal tip-top of the food and drink chain is **Top of the Mark.** The view from the dance floor is awesome, but the prices are nearly as steep as the hill ($10 cover F-Sa, $6.50 beer, $10 martinis). Kitsch connoisseurs must not descend the hill without checking out the **Tonga Room.** In a city blessed with several faux-Polynesian tiki bars, King Tonga's lagoon has to be seen to be believed.

UNION SQUARE

⚑ *NEIGHBORHOOD QUICKFIND:* **Discover,** *p. 10;* **Food & Drink,** *p. 122;* **Nightlife,** *p. 148;* **Accommodations,** *p. 194.*

MAIDEN LANE

When the Barbary Coast (now the Financial District) was down and dirty, Union Square's **Morton Alley** was dirtier. Around 1900, murders on the Alley averaged one per week and prostitutes waved to their favorite customers from 2nd-see map p. 343
story windows. After the 1906 earthquake and fires destroyed most of the brothels and tenements, merchants moved in and renamed the area Maiden Lane in hopes of transforming the street's image. It worked. Today, the pedestrian street that extends two blocks from Stockton St. to Kearny St. on Union Square's eastern side is as virtuous as they come and makes for a pleasant place to stroll or sip espresso with your newly purchased Gucci shades.

FRANK LLOYD WRIGHT BUILDING

⚑ *140 Maiden Ln.* **Xanadu Gallery:** ☎ *392-9999; fax 984-5856. Open M-Sa 10am-6pm.*

Maiden Ln.'s main architectural attraction is the Frank Lloyd Wright Building, the city's only Wright-designed structure and one of 17 buildings that the American Institute of Architects recognizes as representative of his contribution to American design culture. It was built as the V.C. Shop in 1948 out of unreinforced masonry, complete with original wood cabinetry, gravity defying pneumatic tubes, and a cubbyhole for the Morris family cat. Wright left the square facade windowless and unobtrusive so that his building would sit comfortably alongside the other warehouses on the street. Inside, a graceful, spiraling ramp, similar to the one Wright designed for New York's Guggenheim Museum in 1943, connects the two floors. The space now houses the **Xanadu Gallery,** which displays an eclectic collection of African tribal art, Han Dynasty vases, Pacific Rim sculptures, and Pre-Columbian pottery. Sign the guest book and get a free invite to wine-and-cheese openings.

VIEWS

⚑ *Grandviews: 345 Stockton St., near Sutter St. 36th floor of the Hyatt.* ☎ *403-4847. Open daily 11am-2am. AmEx/D/MC/V.*

The swift ascent of the glass elevators at the **Westin St. Francis Hotel,** 335 Powell St., at Geary St., where Squeaky Fromme tried to assassinate President Gerald Ford, brings the entire East Bay into view. *Let's Go* recommends ▨ **a free twilight elevator trip,** where cosmopolitan San Francisco lights up in stellar panorama. If you happen to be decked out in appropriately chic attire, the **Grandviews Lounge** in the nearby Hyatt offers similarly stunning views, but the

in the
know

Pet Pathos

About 500 yards from San Francisco National Cemetery, unobtrusively tucked beneath the US 101 overpass, is a small, picket-fenced graveyard. The **Presidio Pet Cemetery,** or Station 16 as it was designated by the military, is the final resting place of 200 military pets, buried between the 1950s and as recently as 1998, though the cemetery officially closed for burials when the military moved out of the Presidio in 1994.

Among the overgrown graves, simple wooden markers and elaborate marble headstones bear occasionally silly, heartfelt epitaphs. "Trouble. He was no trouble," reads one; "Mr. Bird, a Canary," reads another. Between them lies "The Unknown Pet."

The fake flowers, beads, and other trinkets that litter the ground in homage to these departed animals convey the endurance of memory more humanly than do many of the remembrances of the National Cemetery. As the handpainted sign will remind you ("please show respect whatever reason you may be here"), these animals were buried out of love, so please be courteous when you walk amongst their graves. Skipper, Bullet, Muffin Witty, and Macaroni Heart may have become fertilizer for the pines that shade their graves, but they have not been forgotten.

martinis and Harvey Wallbangers ain't free. The ascent of a **Powell Street cable car,** which climbs through busy Chinatown en route to the waterfront and Nob Hill, is slow but equally scenic. The cable car crawls at a stately 9½ mph, but the line to board the cars is even more plodding. Be prepared for an hour-long wait, or wake up early—the shortest lines are generally before 9am and after 9pm. (Cable car routes and fees, p. 37.)

GALLERIES

▉ Martin Lawrence: *366 Geary St., between Powell and Mason St. ☎956-0345. Open M-Th 9am-8pm, F-Sa 9am-10pm, Su 10am-7pm.* **Hang Gallery:** *556 Sutter St., between Powell and Mason St. ☎434-4264; www.hangart.com. Open M-Sa 10am-6pm, Su noon-5pm.* **sf black & white:** *619 Post St., at Taylor St. ☎929-9424. Open daily 9am-9pm.* **Academy of Art Gallery:** *688 Sutter St., near Mason St. ☎274-2200.* **Academy of Art College:** *410 Bush St., between Kearny St. and Grant Ave. ☎274-8680. Additional locations: 625 Sutter St. ☎274-2229 and 79 New Montgomery St. ☎274-2292. Both locations open daily 9am-5pm but because some of the galleries are attached to the school building, if students are milling around, it may be possible to get in later.*

Post and Sutter St. (especially the block between Mason and Powell St.) are both lined with galleries catering to serious collectors and casual browsers alike. It's easy to spend a whole morning ducking in and out of the lavish galleries; moving from young, up-and-coming artists to legends like Warhol is as easy as stepping from door to door. Staff members are friendly, knowledgeable, and willing to talk.

The **Martin Lawrence Gallery** is a two-story space that houses America's largest collection of work by painter Marc Chagall, as well as a number of pieces by Keith Haring, Andy Warhol, and Pablo Picasso. The gallery would feel like a very intimate modern art museum were it not for the $2 million price tags on some of the works. **Hang** is a sleek, urban gallery, housed in a cozy chrome warehouse in which the works *hang* from the exposed beams in the ceiling. The Hang Annex, located directly across the street on the 2nd floor of 567 Sutter, tends to display solo shows for a month or so while the original Hang changes its art every few days. Both galleries specialize in the rental of paintings and sculpture "by emerging artists for emerging collectors." If you're more partial to classical photography, the newly opened **sf black & white gallery** transforms a spare urban space into a backdrop for its collection of simple and elegant black and white images of San Francisco. The owners are in the process of transforming the back room into a chic bar called "The Darkroom" where patrons will be served over an extended lightboard topped with slides. An original photograph goes for as low as $30. **The Academy of Art College** offers four galleries that showcase virtuoso student work on a monthly basis. Get 'em while they're young. Also inquire about **"First Thursday,"** a gallery-coordinated spree of receptions that take place, you guessed it, on the first Thursday of each month. Many of the galleries in the area stay open late to allow viewers to amble in, sip wine, and check out burgeoning new artists from 5:30-7:30pm. The crowds usually assemble at one of the several galleries on Geary St. and continue in a procession of gazing and ruminating throughout the neighborhood.

GOLDEN GATE BRIDGE & THE PRESIDIO

⟶ *NEIGHBORHOOD QUICKFIND:* **Discover,** *p. 10.*

see map p. 78

GOLDEN GATE BRIDGE

When Captain John Fremont coined the term "Golden Gate" in 1846, he meant to name the harbor entrance to the San Francisco Bay after the mythical Golden Horn port of Constantinople. In 1937, however, the colorful name became permanently associated with Joseph Strauss's copper-hued engineering masterpiece—the Golden Gate Bridge. Built for only $35 million, the bridge stretches across 1¼ mi. of ocean, its towers looming 65 stories above the Bay. It can sway up to 27 ft. in each direction during high winds. On sunny days, hundreds of people take the 30min. walk across the bridge. The views from the bridge are amazing, especially from the Vista Point in Marin County just after the bridge. To see the bridge itself, it's best to get a bit farther away: Fort Point and Fort Baker in the Presidio, Land's End in Lincoln Park, Mt. Livermore on Angel Island, and Hawk Hill off Conzelman Rd. in the Marin Headlands all offer spectacular views of the Golden Gate on clear days.

BAKER BEACH

⟶ *Off Lincoln Blvd. and El Camino del Mar, near 25th Ave. Take MUNI bus #29 ("Presidio," not "California and 25th") or* **PresidiGo shuttle.** *Also right off the* **coastal trail.** *Parking is available but limited and tends to fill up quickly on sunny days. Park authorities are increasingly tough on illegal parking.*

Is there a better way to spend a summer day than by catching some rays and enjoying a picnic on a long, sandy beach with a spectacular view of the Golden Gate Bridge? Yes, there is: doing it naked. While Baker Beach offers little in the way of surfable waves or inviting waters, it recently garnered second place in the *Guardian*'s 29th annual poll of the best places to get wet and naked in Northern California. The southernmost portion of the beach fills up with pasty, bathing suit-clad sunseekers while tanner, less inhibited souls (mostly men) sun themselves *au naturel* farther up the beach. Enjoy the view but stay close to the shore: the chilly water is great for barefoot—or barebody—strolls along the dunes, but the undertow is very dangerous. For those less willing to brave the windy shores, there are plenty of picnic areas with restrooms and grills on the southern tip of the beach.

PRESIDIO

When Spanish settlers forged their way up the San Francisco peninsula from Baja California in 1769, they established *presidios*, or military outposts, along the way. San Francisco's Presidio, the northernmost point of Spanish territory in North America, was dedicated in 1776. The settlement stayed in Spanish hands for only 45 years before the deed was passed to Mexico when it won its independence from Spain. In 1848, the United States took over the Presidio as part of the Treaty of Guadalupe Hidalgo that ended the Mexican-American War. Gold fever stimulated expansion of the outpost and, eventually, the Presidio gained particular importance during WWII after the attack on Pearl Harbor. Crissy Field's Intelligence School and the Letterman Army Hospital became leaders in their respective fields during the war.

Today, the Presidio is part of the **Golden Gate National Recreation Area (GGNRA),** run by the National Park Service in conjunction with the Presidio Trust. The Presidio

The Presidio

Pacific Ocean

San Francisco Bay

Golden Gate Bridge

Fort Point

Coastal Defense Batteries

Coastal Bluffs Overlook

Battery Crosby

Battery Dynamite

Battery Chamberlin

Baker Beach

China Beach

SEA CLIFF

El Camino del Mar

Sea Cliff Ave.

25th Ave.

26th Ave.

Lincoln Blvd.

Coastal Trail

Anza Trail

Wedemeyer St. Housing

Pershing Dr.

Washington Blvd.

World War II Memorial

Battery McKinnon-Stotsenburg

Rob Hill

Compton Rd.

Public Health Service Hospital

Battery Caulfield Rd.

Lobos Creek

Mountain Lake

Park Presidio Blvd.

5th Ave.

6th Ave.

7th Ave.

Presidio Golf Course

Presidio Hill (382')

Officers' Family Housing

Park Presidio Blvd.

San Francisco National Cemetery

Chapel

Infantry Terr.

Officers' Club

Graham St.

Montgomery St.

Sheridan Ave.

Parade Ground

Funston Ave.

Main Post

Visitor Center

Lincoln Blvd.

Arguello Blvd.

Moraga Ave.

Barnard Ave.

El Polin Spring

Ecology Trail

Inspiration Point

Arguello Blvd. Gate

W. Pacific Ave.

Washington St.

Sacramento St.

California St.

Clay St.

Maple St.

Spruce St.

Locust St.

Laurel St.

Walnut St.

Presidio Blvd.

Presidio Blvd. Gate

Lyon St.

Broadway

Pacific Ave.

Jackson St.

Washington Blvd.

Sacramento St.

Vallejo St.

Green St.

Union St.

Filbert St.

Greenwich St.

Lombard St.

Chestnut St.

Francisco St.

Bay St.

North Point St.

Beach St.

Jefferson St.

Marina Blvd.

Palace of Fine Arts

Exploratorium

Doyle Dr.

Gorgas Ave.

Halleck St.

Letterman Complex

Letterman Dr.

Lombard St.

Presidio Blvd.

Baker St.

Lyon St.

Broderick St.

Richardson St.

Crissy Field

Golden Gate Promenade

Commissary

Military Intelligence School

Battery Blaney

Crissy Field Ave.

Mason St.

Crissy Field Overlook

Long Ave.

Torpedo Wharf

Aircraft Hangars

Pilot's Quarters

Battery East

Marine Dr.

Lincoln Blvd.

Merchant Rd.

Toll Plaza

Ralston Ave.

Storey Ave.

Fort Winfield Scott

Battery Amistad Rd.

Ruckman Ave.

Stables

Cavalry Barracks

School

Pet Cemetery

McDowell Ave.

Post Chapel

Kobbe Ave.

Officers' Row

Lincoln Blvd.

Upton Ave.

Paul Goode Field

Julius Kahn Playground

MacArthur Ave.

Portola St.

Quarry Rd.

Pacific Ave.

Walking Path

500 yards

500 meters

0

1

2

3

4

A B C D E F G

Pacific Ocean

Trust is raising funds to make the park self-sufficient by 2013 and coordinating the ongoing renovation and modernization of roads, buildings, and trails in the park.

MAIN POST

⚑ Visitors Center: *102 Montgomery St. ☎ 561-4323; www.nps.gov/psrf. Open daily 9am-5pm.*
The once-grand barracks that make up Main Post are now a semi-historic playground for the San Francisco Film Society and any other non-profit agency willing to fork over funds for a lease. Remnants of the original Spanish settlement are on view in the Officer's Club, one of the many historic buildings that surround the 1776 Parade Ground. The William Penn Mott, Jr. Visitors Center offers free maps, glossy viewbooks, and pocket walking tour guides that explain the park's history.

SAN FRANCISCO NATIONAL CEMETERY

⚑ *Just off Lincoln Blvd. in the center of the Presidio. ☎ 650-589-7737.*
This 28 acre cemetery, which houses the graves of over 30,000 soldiers and their families, was the first national cemetery on the West Coast. The 450 soldiers of the all-black Buffalo Soldier regiments of the US Army as well as Pauline Cushman Fryer, the Union's most famous female spy, are buried here. Maps and registers are available inside the entrance gate.

TRAILS

Miles of paths for hiking and biking, most with relatively moderate grades, crisscross the rest of the park. For **hiking,** the **Coastal Trail** near Lobos Creek, in the southwest corner of the park, is accessible from Baker Beach and from Merchant Rd. on the western side of Highway 101. **Bikers** starting from the southeast corner of the park can zip down tree-lined **West Pacific Avenue,** which separates the Presidio Golf Course and the Richmond; the road curves around **Mountain Lake** and heads northward to Washington St. and **Rob Hill,** the park's only campsite (information ☎ 561-5444). The best **jogging** trail is the 3 mi. **Golden Gate Promenade,** a flat, paved stretch of road along the Bay. Picnickers should avoid munching on the golf course or in residential areas—it's not allowed—and instead try **El Polin Spring,** off the **Ecology Trail** in the southeast corner of the park. The women of the Ohlone tribe, the first inhabitants of the Presidio, used to drink the water here during the full moon believing that it would bring them a large and happy family. For a sylvan, biker- and walker-friendly tour of the whole park, the recently completed **Bay Area Ridge Trail** will give you a 3 mi. stretch of fresh pavement following the ridge line from Arguello Gate in the southern Presidio all the way up to the Golden Gate Bridge.

The artists and outlaws of an East Bay area known as the **Albany Bulb** have attracted a passionate following in the past four years. Vagrants living in the area have created an open-air gallery, studio, and home out of a trash-dump abandoned in the 1980s.

When the area became recognized as part of the Golden Gate Fields State Park in 1999, officials evicted the large homeless population living there. However, many artists continue to squat there in innovative lodgings, such as huts woven from fennel. Their work—including clay and styrofoam carvings, wooden sculptures, and rusting junk metal—reflect what one artist describes as a "visual ecological history of the post-industrial debris, gradually decaying."

Recent plans to redevelop the area into a park and soccer fields have sparked fierce debate. The artists and their followers want the Bulb to remain one of the few unregulated areas left in the Bay Area. In the summer of 2002, however, the council voted that the Bulb should be off-limits to most of the artists because of their works' often sexually explicit content. The final deciding vote on the new park plan will be taken in December 2003. Follow the debate on www.albanyletitbe.org.

Peace Pagoda

Wave Organ

Pacific Heights

LINCOLN PARK

see map p. 341

⚐ NEIGHBORHOOD QUICKFIND: Discover, p. 11.

▓ CALIFORNIA PALACE OF THE LEGION OF HONOR

⚐ California Palace of the Legion of Honor: ☎ 863-3330; www.legionofhonor.org. Open Tu-Su 9:30am-5pm. Adults $8, seniors $6, under 17 $5, under 12 free. $2 discount with MUNI transfer; Tu is free. Admission included in San Francisco CityPass (p. 92). Wheelchair-accessible. **Holocaust Memorial:** Free to the public.

In the middle of Lincoln Park, between the golf course (which was once a cemetery) and the **Land's End** wilderness, sits a magnificent enclave of European proportions and aspirations. The California Palace of the Legion of Honor was built in 1924 after one of San Francisco's leading ladies, Mrs. Alma Spreckels, fell in love with the temporary "French Pavilion" built on Golden Gate Park for the Panama International Exhibition. The pavilion was a replica of the *Palais de la Legion d'Honneur* on Paris' Left Bank, and Spreckels was determined to build one of equal stature. A copy of Rodin's *Thinker* beckons visitors into the grand courtyard, where a little glass pyramid recalls another Paris treasure, the Louvre. A thorough catalogue of great masters, from Rubens to Dalí (including the largest collection of Rodin sculptures outside Paris) hangs inside. Other draws include a pneumatically operated 4500-pipe organ, played in free weekly recitals (Sa-Su 4pm), and a gilded ceiling from a 15th-century *palacio* in Toledo, Spain. Free tours given on Sa in a different language (either French, Spanish, or Italian) each week. Just outside the Palace, a Holocaust Memorial offers a sobering reminder of one of history's darkest moments. The memorial depicts the Holocaust as a mass of emaciated victims with a single, hopeful survivor looking out through a barbed-wire fence to the beauty of the Pacific.

CAMERA OBSCURA

⚐ ☎ 750-0415. Open daily 11am-sunset, weather permitting—you can't see anything in fog. $2.

On the observation deck of the Cliff House, the Camera Obscura kiosk sets the mood with holographic wall mountings and trancey "ocean music." Meanwhile, a periscope-like mirrored lens on its roof rotates and reflects light from outside into a "dark room" and onto a concave viewing plate, magnifying the already stunning ocean vistas and nearby Seal Rocks by 700%. The draw comes from the novelty of witnessing Leonardo da Vinci's precursor to the modern camera, not from the actual view it produces. Closed for renovations until summer 2004.

SUTRO BATHS

🚩 *Just north of Cliff House on Point Lobos Ave.*

Opened with great fanfare in 1896, the Sutro Baths consisted of seven luxuriously heated pools that could accommodate up to 10,000 swimmers. Unfortunately though, after the excitement surrounding the $1,000,000 indoor pools died down, the pools rarely held even close to that many. In the 30s and 40s, various combinations of pools and skating rinks failed to keep the operation afloat, and the buildings were finally abandoned after a fire gutted them in 1966. Now they serve mostly as a reminder of the elegance (and perhaps decadence) of turn-of-the century SF.

SUTRO HEIGHTS PARK

🚩 *Up the hill from the intersection of Pt. Lobos and 48th Ave., east of the Cliff House.*

More secluded than the better known parks in the city, Sutro Heights offers unparalleled views of San Francisco and the surrounding watery expanses. A lion-guarded gate recalls the day when the hill was home to millionaire and one-time San Francisco mayor Adolph Sutro's private estate. The plentiful benches and quiet nooks make this one of the city's perfect places for an intimate picnic. Exercise caution if you find yourself in the park at night, especially if traveling alone.

TRAILS

🚩 **Coastal Trail:** *begins at the intersection of Pt. Lobos and 48th Ave. Free and open to the public.* **El Camino del Mar:** *begins at the intersection of Pt. Lobos and Sea Rock Dr. Free and open to the public.*

The **Coastal Trail** loops around the interior of Lincoln Park for a scenic and sometimes taxing coastal hike. The entrance to the trail is not particularly well marked, so be careful not to mistakenly tackle a considerably more extreme—and dangerous—cliffside jaunt. The path leads first into the abandoned army post of **Fort Miley.** Near the parking lot and picnic tables rests the **USS San Francisco Memorial.** The *USS SF* sustained 45 direct hits (which started 25 fires) in the battle of Guadalcanal on November 12-13th, 1942. Nearly 100 sailors died in the clash, but the ship went on to fight in 10 more battles.

Fort Point

Presidio Cemetery

Golden Gate Bridge

The Coastal Trail continues for a 3 mi. hike into **Land's End,** the area of Lincoln Park famous for its views of the Golden Gate Bridge and "sunken ships" that signal treacherous waters below. Dense pine and cypress trees, colorful flowers, and an array of cheerful fauna line the rocky coastline. Except for the occasionally harsh winds and warning signs, the trail is a few talking animals and an original score short of a Disney film paradise. Biking is permitted on the trail, although parts contain stairs and bumpy terrain that suit mountain bikes best. At Land's End, onlookers have the option of hiking an extra 6 mi. into the Presidio and on to the arches of Golden Gate Bridge.

Golden Gate Park

🌼 GARDENS & GROVES

Conservatory of Flowers, **33**
De Leveuga Dell, **31**
Garden of Fragrance, **23**
Heroes Grove, **16**
Japanese Cherry Orchard, **18**
Japanese Tea Garden, **19**
Moon Viewing Garden, **21**
National AIDS Memorial
  Grove, **31**
Primitive Plant Garden, **20**
Queen Wilhelmina Tulip
  Garden, **2**
Rhododendron Dell, **29**
Rose Garden, **15**
Shakespeare Garden, **26**
Strybing Arboretum &
  Botanical Gardens, **22**

🌸 ACTIVITIES

Archery Field, **3**
Athletics Field Reservations
  Office, **13**
Boat & Bicycle Rentals, **11**
Bocce Ball, **5**
Children's Playground &
  Carousel, **36**
Dog Running Areas, **9, 30 & 37**
Dog Training Area, **4**
Fly-casting Pools, **8**
Golden Gate Park Stables, **7**
Handball & Raquetball, **28**
Horseshoe Pits, **38**
Lawn Bowling, **32 & 35**
Parcourse, **10**
Senior Citizens' Exercise
  Course, **6**
Tennis Courts, **34**

● SIGHTS

Beach Chalet & Visitor's Center, **1**
California Academy of Sciences,
  Steinhart Aquarium,
  Morrison Planetarium, **27**
Chinese Pavillion, **14**
M. H. de Young Museum
  (Closed for renovation until
  2005), **17**
Pioneer Log Cabin, **12**
Russell Library of Horticulture, **24**
San Francisco County Fair
  Building, **25**

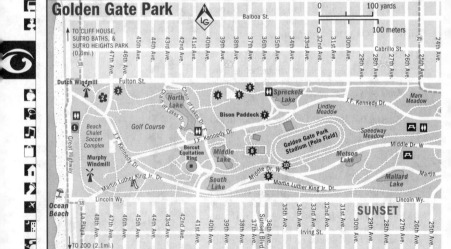

Golden Gate Park

For hikers and bikers who aren't so inclined, the brisker (and mercifully flatter) walk along **El Camino del Mar** originates close to the Coastal Trail but runs further in from the shore. Along the trail enjoy the forested views and a stop at the Legion of Honor before finishing "The Path of the Sea" at China Beach. In all, this makes for a 1½ mi. afternoon stroll that will leave you with enough energy for a night on the town.

CHINA BEACH

◪ *On the eastern edge of Lincoln Park at the end of Seacliff Ave.*

Tucked into the walls of the steep cliffs, the beach here is small and intimate (but only PG-13 intimate: the free public beach stays closed sunset to sunrise). Swimming is dangerous because of the wildly unpredictable surf, and the waters are frigid. Grassy space lies just beyond the sand, perfect for frolicking or picnicking.

GOLDEN GATE PARK

◪ *NEIGHBORHOOD QUICKFIND:* **Discover**, *p. 12;* **Entertainment (sports and recreation)**, *p. 173.*

see map p. 82-83

◪ CALIFORNIA ACADEMY OF SCIENCES

◪ *East of Stow Lake, near 9th Ave.* ☎ *750-7145; www.calacademy.org. Open June-Aug. daily 9am-6pm; Sept.-May 10am-5pm. Adults $8.50; students, seniors, and ages 12-17 $5.50; ages 4-11 $2. Extended hours (open until 8:45pm) and free entrance 1st W of each month. $2.50 discount for bicycle riders; indoor bike parking available. Discounts also available with MUNI pass or transfer slip.* **Aquarium:** *Shark feedings M-W and F-Su 10:30am, 12:30, 2:30, and 4:30pm. Open ocean fish feedings 1:30pm. Penguin feeding daily 11:30am and 4pm. Admission included in CityPass (p. 92).* **Planetarium:** *Sky shows M-F 2pm, with additional summer showings. Adults $2.50; students, seniors, and ages 6-17 $1.25.* **Academy Cafe:** *Offers soups, salads, sandwiches, pizzas, burgers, and beverages. Open daily 10am-4pm.*

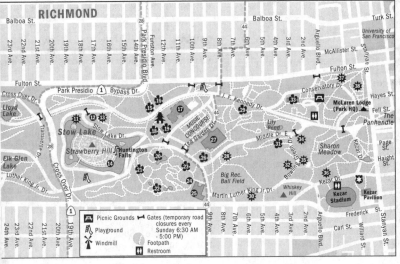

Some of the most significant performance art of the past thirty years has been based on walking. Steve Paxton, the dancer and choreographer best known for developing contact improvisation, was a member of the Judson Dance Theater in New York, the center of avant-garde dance in the United States in the 1960s. In his 1967 *Satisfyin' Lover*, Paxton invited members of the audience to walk across the stage, one at a time. Fat, thin, young, old, black, and white bodies strode, ambled, and shuffled across the flat space. Paxton and the other artists of Judson were interested in using everyday movements like walking, running, and sitting in their choreography in order to get away from the narrow set of highly theatrical movements of concert dance—the leap, the pose, the *pas de deux*. Moreover, these choreographers, especially the nascent feminist choreographers of Judson, Yvonne Rainer, Lucinda Childs and Trisha Brown among them, rejected the image of 'the dancer's body'—the lithe, tall, willowy form central to ballet. By featuring trained and untrained dancers together, Judson choreographers hoped to inspire everyone to find their inner dancer. What Paxton and his cohorts did not anticipate was how thoroughly walking conveyed self-expression. Expecting to see tasklike and neutral movement, they were startled to find that walking actually seethes with deeply personal signatures. In this literally pedestrian movement, character and personality are revealed with every step.

This insight then led to a series of performances in the 70s and 80s in which walking was central. Indeed, twenty years on, walking had become charged with an emotional and psychological density that made it seem capable of both joining and severing the human relation to landscape and architecture; walking promised a cartography of one's most intimate emotional and historical pathways. In 1988, the performance artists Marina Abramović and Ulay walked for three months covering 1,200 miles of the Great Wall of China. When they initially decided to perform this piece, in 1981, they thought they would walk the wall together and marry at the end. But in the seven years it took to complete the complicated negotiations with Chinese authorities, their purpose had changed. Starting out at opposite ends of the Great Wall, Abramović and Ulay met in the middle to say goodbye to their twelve-year personal and professional collaborations. As they charted the landscape, they also chronicled separate memories of their relationship, thus deftly showing the ways in which we often map our personal histories across the landscape of our environment.

So too when traveling: one traverses a new terrain and often stumbles into unexpected memories. This corner looks like the one where I first fell in love; this hill was in the film I saw last night. When we walk in a city with alert eyes, we often find architectural ghosts that prompt surprising emotions. The entwining of space and time at the core of walking helps give density to our travels. Or as the superb French dancer, Sylvie Guillem, put it, "Life's emotions are basically merely steps."

The compression of history into space is one of the great treats of the US city; some of its most potent effects can be felt in the smallest stones of a sidewalk intersection. All that human and vehicular traffic stalled in space and compressed, briefly, in the traffic light halt and flow is given density by the history of innumerable previous crossings. But even more dramatically one can feel time bearing down on space when one struggles to climb one of San Francisco's breathtaking hills.

According to the San Francisco archivist, the city has 42 hills ranging from 200 to 938 feet. These are serious climbs. But quite apart from these 42 hills, San Francisco is dotted with slopes, gradual upgrades, and challenging crests. Walking here requires focus on the physical aspects of breathing and climbing, but this very focus also allows for a deeper contemplation than the more mundane trip to the corner store. San Francisco, in short, is an ideal city to consider and reconsider the potent fusions between thinking, walking, and making art.

Some of the steepest hills will leave you breathless and sore-kneed. But others simply astonish in their capacity to hold secrets. Two of my favorite walks, one carefully designed and one haphazardly groomed by nature and city history, are the labyrinth at Grace Cathedral and the beach walk at the Cliff House and Sutro Baths. The labyrinth sits in the courtyard of Grace Cathedral; it is 400 feet wide and it takes about thirty minutes to walk in and out of at a leisurely pace. Constructed in 1995, it is the first permanent labyrinth built in the United States. A short trolley car ride up the hill from Union Square, the labyrinth looks rather unprepossessing when first seen. But once you begin your journey, its secrets will become delightfully clear. Each step becomes a metaphor for the values of persistence, for the inevitability of confusion and unknowingness, and for the virtues of endurance. The San Francisco labyrinth has more hair-pin turns than most and these rather tight crossings makes one especially aware of how often we turn and twist in indecision and uncertainty. But as one walks such psychological knots and snarls flatten out. Walking becomes in this labyrinth a kind of kneading of the dense matter of unknowingness. One step after the other a kind of direction emerges, even if it remains only a rehearsal, a kind of silent audition for other paths still to be discovered.

The remains of the Sutro Baths, originally opened in 1896, are in a spectacular setting: the ocean before them, the bay to the right of the hill's bluff. Sutro, a wealthy engineer and railroad developer, designed the baths with enormous crowds in mind. Adjacent to a museum and amphitheater with 3,700 seats, the ruins of the baths now are largely deserted and peaceful. As you walk down the main hill, there is a small opening to your left. This is called Seal's Rock Cave. Entering it one is arrested by the sound of the sea hitting deep rock. It takes about five minutes to walk from one end to the other and there are two gorgeous hollows that refract the color of the ocean in a hushed and cool light. Coming back out into the sun, the remains of the Sutro Baths seem to hold San Francisco's ongoing history of utopic dreaming and harsher reality. The baths eventually went out of fashion, and after an unsuccessful transformation into an ice rink, out of business in 1964. The remains of the baths situated as they are on the threshold of land and sea also pivot between the past and the future. Walking across these stone ghosts help us braid these two strands of our lives together and remind us of the mixture of dream and reality humming between all our strides.

Grace Church, 1100 California St., at Taylor; wheelchair-accessible (p. 74). Cliff House (p. 137) and Sutro Baths (p. 81), at the intersection of Great Highway and Merrie St. The Golden Gate National Recreation Area, a division of the National Park Service, maintains the site.

848 Community Space, 848 Divisadero St., between Fulton and McAllister St. near the Upper Haight offers contact improvisation classes and jams (p. 169).

Peggy Phelan is the Ann O'Day Maples Chair in the Arts at Stanford University. She is the author of Unmarked: The Politics of Performance (1993) and Mourning Sex: Performing Public Memories (1997) and the co-editor of Art and Feminism (2001).

The Gospel Truth

Charismatic, liberal, and dedicated to empowering the community, Rev. Cecil Williams, Minister of Liberation, leads a congregation of nearly 10,000 at the **Glide Memorial United Methodist Church** in the Tenderloin.

Hundreds of San Franciscans from diverse political, ethnic, economic, and social backgrounds (sometimes joined by famous followers like Oprah, Maya Angelou, and Bill Cosby) come every Sunday for thunderous, transformational celebrations, complete with a world-famous Gospel choir.

Williams's famous unorthodox practices date back to jazz services and hippie happenings in the 1960s, and the fateful day when he took down the sanctuary's cross. He disliked the cross's status as a symbol of death and exclusivity.

Glide has a policy of unconditional acceptance that insists that all members of the community should have a chance to better themselves. That belief translates into 39 programs ranging from job skills and computer training to HIV/AIDS health services, making Glide the most comprehensive non-profit provider of human services in the city. (☎771-6300; www.glide.org. 330 Ellis St. at Taylor St. Celebrations Su 9, 11am.)

The Academy of Sciences is definitely worth the trip, particularly if you have any children in tow. The Academy houses several smaller museums specializing in different fields of science: the Steinhart Aquarium, the Morrison Planetarium, and the Natural History Museum. The Steinhart Aquarium is home to members of over 600 aquatic species. Head through the entrance and across the Fountain Courtyard to enter a world of sharks, penguins, and all things water-happy and slimy. If you choose to, you can get up close and personal with that slimy goodness in the touching pool. The Morrison Planetarium recreates the heavens above with impressive sky shows. The remainder of the Academy is considered the Natural History Museum. In the Space and Earth Hall, you can learn how the earth rotates and see a piece of moonrock. The Earthquake room explains all about those famous shakes around the Bay Area, and the Earthquake Theater allows visitors to experience a little rock 'n' roll in person. More zaniness lurks down the corridor, where the Far Side of Science gallery pays tribute to writer Gary Larsen.

HISTORICAL WALKING TOURS

🏠 ☎ 263-0991; www.sfparks.org.

Park volunteers will guide you around the highlights of the park on a variety of free, themed walking tours. Walk windmill to windmill, explore the Japanese tea garden, or scale Strawberry Hill. Call for meeting points and times of specific tours.

QUEEN WILHELMINA TULIP GARDEN

🏠 Northwest corner of the park.

The **Dutch Windmill,** once the muscle behind the park's irrigation system, has turned its last turn. The outdated but renovated old powerhouse (102 ft. from sail to sail) is now the purely ornamental centerpiece of the cheery **Queen Wilhelmina Tulip Garden,** which bursts forth with 10,000 bulbs of color in early spring and late summer.

BEACH CHALET AND GOLDEN GATE PARK VISITORS CENTER

🏠 *Visitors Center:* ☎ 751-2766. Open daily 9am-7pm. *Restaurant:* ☎ 386-8439. Bottled beer $4.50. Open Su-Th 9am-11pm, F-Sa 9am-midnight. AmEx/MC/V.

The Beach Chalet, a Spanish-Colonial-style villa built in 1925, sits on the western edge of the park on the Great Hwy., south of Fulton St. During the Great Depression the Works Progress Administration (WPA), developed in the late 1930s to fund artists, enlisted the French-born artist Lucien Labaudt to design frescoes for the Chalet's walls. The elaborate paintings of 1930s San Francisco were completed just in time for WWII, when the building was used as an army outpost. The walls were restored for the chalet's reopening in 1996, and the building now serves as the official Visitors Center for Golden Gate Park. For the beer-loving beach-goer, the **Beach Chalet Restaurant** on the 2nd floor houses a microbrewery.

SPRECKELS LAKE AND NEARBY

Spreckels Lake, on John F. Kennedy Dr., is populated by crowds of turtles that pile onto a big rock to sun themselves. The multi-national collection of gardens and museums in Golden Gate Park would not be complete without something distinctly Californian...like **a herd of bison!** A dozen of the shaggy beasts loll about in a spacious paddock just west of Spreckels—thankfully contained within a 6 ft. fence.

Fort Mason

STRYBING ARBORETUM AND BOTANICAL GARDENS

◪ *On Lincoln Way at 9th Ave. ☎661-1316; www.strybing.org. Open M-F 8am-4:30pm, Sa-Su 10am-5pm.* **Free guided tours:** *From Strybing Store M-F 1:30pm, Sa-Su 10:30am and 1:30pm; from North Entrance W, F, Su 2pm.* **Classes and workshops:** *Practical landscaping, botanical drawing, and more.*

The Gardens are home to over 7,500 species of plants, including collections from Chile, New Zealand, and the tropical New World Cloud Forests. Check out the **Primitive Plant Garden** near the Friends Gate in the northern part of the Arboretum. On the eastern side, near the Strybing Store and Russel Library of Horticulture, is the **Garden of Fragrance,** designed especially for the visually impaired—labels are in Braille and the plants are chosen specifically for their textures and scents. On the western side is the spacious **Moon Viewing Garden,** perfect for celestial gazing.

Exploratorium

SHAKESPEARE GARDEN

◪ *At the intersection of Martin Luther King Jr. Dr., Middle Drive East, and 9th Ave. Open in summer daily dawn-dusk; off-season Tu-Su dawn-dusk. Free.*

The Shakespeare Garden contains almost every flower and plant ever mentioned by the Bard. Stroll across the lawns seeking hyancinths and rue, or ponder the poetics of the relevant quotations inscribed on back-wall plaques.

JAPANESE TEA GARDEN

◪ ☎752-4227. *Open in summer daily 8:30am-6pm; in winter 8:30am-5pm. Adults $3.50, seniors and ages 6-12 $1.25. Free for all in summer 8:30-9:30am and 5-6pm and in winter 8:30-9:30am and 4-5pm. Half-price admission on the 1st W of the month.*

Fisherman's Wharf

Created for the 1894 Mid-Winter Exposition, the Tea Garden is the oldest Japanese-style garden in the US. It houses a serene collection of dark wooden buildings, small pools, graceful footbridges, carefully pruned trees, and lush plants. Renamed the Oriental Tea Garden during WWII, the garden has at many times served as a sort of diplomatic symbol between the US and Japan. In 1953, donations from Japanese schoolchildren funded a 9000 lb. Lantern of Peace that was given as a token of friendship to the new generation of Americans. Meditate on the meaning of camaraderie in front of Buddha, the oldest statue in the park (cast in 1790), or snack on tea and cookies ($2.50) and watch the giant carp circle the central pond. The 🖼 **Japanese Cherry Orchard** at Lincoln Way and South Dr., near the elegant Japanese Tea Garden, blooms lavishly the first week of April.

Alcatraz

NATIONAL AIDS MEMORIAL GROVE

🚩 *Grove: ☎ 750-8340; www.aidsmemorial.org. Northeast corner of the park, near John F. Kennedy Dr. Tours Th 9:30am-12:30pm and by special arrangement. Tours start at the Main Portal of the Grove, near the corner of Middle Dr. East and Bowling Green Dr. Free.*

Just south of Lily Pond, near the intersection of Middle Dr. East and Bowling Green Dr., the National AIDS Memorial Grove rests among the flowering dogwoods and giant redwoods of **De Laveaga Dell.** Created in 1991 by an environmental and social justice organization and given national status by President Clinton and Congress in 1996, the grove has become a site for remembrance and renewal, at once somber and also rejuvenating. **Volunteers welcome** to help garden for the AIDS memorial the 3rd Sa of each month (reservation required for groups of five and over).

Grace Cathedral

STOW LAKE AND NEARBY

Cross the lake via one of two stone bridges and settle down on the island of **Strawberry Hill**—the place to perch for a view of the city below. The **Rhododendron Dell,** between the Academy of Sciences and JFK Dr., honors park designer John McLaren with a splendid profusion of his favorite flower. The 850 varieties bloom during the first weeks of spring. The **Chinese Pavilion,** given by the people of Taipei as a symbol of friendship, is also a must-see. A perfect view of **Huntington Falls,** the waterfall of Stow Lake, can be seen from the pavilion's wildly decorated multi-colored interior.

CONSERVATORY OF FLOWERS

🚩 *Near the northeast corner of the park. ☎ 750-5105; www.conservatoryofflowers.org. The Conservatory is currently being restored and is* **scheduled to reopen soon after summer 2003.**

Ghirardelli Square

Despite its sandy past, the soil of Golden Gate Park is rich enough today to support a wealth of flowers, particularly in spring and summer. The Conservatory of Flowers, a 12,000 sq. ft. Victorian-style greenhouse erected in 1878, was closed in 1995 when severe storms and 100mph winds destroyed thousands of glass panes and many precious species of flora. Currently undergoing seismic upgrades and rehabilitation, the Conservatory is set to open with a wealth of new exhibitions. The six climate chambers will include wax palms, gingers, and coffee in the Lowland Tropics, orchids in the Highland Tropics, and carnivorous flora in the Aquatic Plants gallery. The **Conservatory Valley**, much like London's Kew Gardens, is almost unbelievably perfect—not a bloom is out of place in this display of botanic symmetry.

Frank Lloyd Wright Building

FINANCIAL DISTRICT & THE EMBARCADERO

🔲 *NEIGHBORHOOD QUICKFIND:* **Discover**, *p. 12;* **Food & Drink**, *p. 112;* **Accommodations**, *p. 182.*

THE TRANSAMERICA PYRAMID

🔲 *600 Montgomery St., between. Clay and Washington St.*

The leading lady of the city's skyline, this distinctive office building is allegedly directly centered on the Golden Dragon Ley line between Easter Island and Stonehenge. Planned to allow as much light as possible to shine on the streets below, and co-opted by one of the leading architectural firms in the country, the building earned disdain from design purists and retroactive reverence from city planners. Unless you're an employee, tight security means there is no chance of a top-floor view. The lobby is currently undergoing renovation to modernize a virtual viewing lounge in the Washington St. entrance so you can peer down on the masses from ground-level. From 1850-1950, the pyramid was an important meeting place for many radical thinkers and writers. This site was where Sun Yat-Sen envisioned the first Chinese revolution and the overthrow of the last Chinese dynasty. The pyramid now serves as the headquarters for the Transamerica Corporation.

Embarcadero Plaza

JUSTIN HERMAN PLAZA

🔲 *At the foot of Market St. and the Embarcadero.*

When not overrun by skateboarders, the Plaza is home to bands and rallyists who sometimes provide lunch-hour entertainment. One free concert performed by U2 in November of 1987 resulted in the arrest of the self-proclaimed "rockstar with a

Sutro Baths

City Hall

Cable Car Powerhouse and Museum

Yerba Buena

heart" Bono for spray-painting "Stop the Traffic—Rock and Roll" on the fountain. Recently, the plaza has been the starting point for **Critical Mass,** a pro-bicyclist ride that takes place after 5pm on the last Friday evening of every month (p. 91). If you are around on a hot day, walk through the inviting mist of the **Vaillancourt Fountain** to cool off.

FERRY BUILDING

◪ *At the foot of Market St. and the Embarcadero.*

Dubbed "a famous city's most famous landmark" by Herb Caen, this 660 ft. waterfront edifice has lost a bit of grandeur over the years as bigger and better buildings have developed in the Embarcadero and stolen the spotlight. A. Page Brown designed the elegant port with repeated archways and Corinthian columns to recall grand Roman aqueducts, but he never saw his vision completed—he was thrown from a horse and killed before construction started in 1898. At its peak, the port served 22 million passengers a year. Today, commuters walk through to catch ferries to Marin and East Bay. The current large empty space is due to a major renovation project that will transform the Ferry Building into a covered marketplace with restaurants and local produce vendors.

FARMER'S MARKET

◪ *Ferry Plaza, at Embarcadero and Green. Sa 8am-2pm, Tu 10am-2pm, Th 3-7pm, Su 8am-2pm.*

Buy fresh produce from local family-run and organic farms. In peak season (April-November) over 100 vendors gather each week; between December and March the selection is much more limited.

CIVIC CENTER

◪ *NEIGHBORHOOD QUICKFIND:* **Discover,** *p. 13;* **Food & Drink,** *p. 124;* **Accommodations,** *p. 196.*

see map p. 345

The culturally-minded Civic Center is a spectacle to behold, though only a select few of the buildings allow curious tourists to wander their halls. The **Bill Graham Civic Auditorium,** 99 Grove St., between Larkin and Polk St., though the site of many large conventions and the occasional concert (Elvis '57, Lauryn Hill '98) is not open to the public. Neither is San Francisco's **State Building,** 350 McAllister St. The San Francisco Public Library offers free public **tours** of the Civic Center, which leave daily at 11:45am from the Pioneer Monument on Fulton St. in front of the library.

SAN FRANCISCO CITY HALL

🏛 *1 Dr. Carlton B. Goodlett Pl., at Van Ness Ave.* ☎ *554-4000. Open M-F 8am-5pm.* **Docent tours:** ☎ *554-7491. 1hr. tours depart Tu-F 10am, noon, and 2pm from main floor near Van Ness entrance. Free.*

Referred to as "The Crown Jewel" of American Classical architecture, City Hall reigns supreme over the Civic Center with a dome to rival St. Paul's cathedral and an area of over 500,000 sq. ft. In 1978, twinkie assassin Dan White, murdered Mayor George Moscone and City Supervisor Harvey Milk on this spot (p. 56). Damaged in the 1989 earthquake, the building recently underwent a remodeling campaign that made it the world's largest structure with base-isolated foundations.

UNITED NATIONS PLAZA AND SAN FRANCISCO PUBLIC LIBRARY

🏛 **Library:** *100 Larkin St., at Grove St. Main entrance on Grove St.* ☎ *557-4400. Open M 10am-6pm, Tu-Th 9am-8pm, F noon-6pm, Sa 10am-6pm, Su noon-5pm.* **Tours:** *Civic Center tours leave daily 11:45am from the Pioneer Monument on Fulton St. in front of the library.* **Farmer's Market:** *W and Su 5:30am-5:30pm.*

The **United Nations Plaza** houses the area's pigeons and itinerants, as well as one of the city's **farmer's markets.** The main branch of the **San Francisco Public Library** faces the plaza. Opened in 1996, the state-of-the-art facility features an excellent video library, the nation's first gay-and-lesbian archives, and a small rooftop garden. It also hosts free tours of the Civic Center and the entire city. The former library sits beside the new one, and as of Jan. 2003 became the new home of the **Asian Art Museum,** which is relocating from Golden Gate Park.

SAN FRANCISCO ASIAN ART MUSEUM

🏛 *200 Larkin St.* ☎ *581-3500. Open Tu-W and F-Su 10am-5pm, Th 10am-9pm. Adults $10, seniors $7, college students and ages 13-17 $6, under 12 free. After 5pm on Th admission $5. AmEx/D/MC/V.*

Relocated to the San Francisco Public Library as of January 2003, the Asian Art Museum is an outstanding collection of over 15,000 pieces that reflect on the culture and history of different Asian civilizations. The museum focuses on the development of Buddhism, trade and cultural exchange, and local beliefs and customs. Exhibits include Indonesian puppetry, stone sculptures of India, Chinese jade collections, and Japanese scrolls.

LOUISE M. DAVIES SYMPHONY HALL AND WAR MEMORIAL OPERA HOUSE

🏛 **Symphony Hall:** *201 Van Ness Ave.* ☎ *552-8000; tickets* ☎ *431-5400. Open M-F 9am-5pm.* **Opera House:** *301 Van Ness Ave., between Grove and McAllister St.* **Opera Box Office:** *199 Grove St.* ☎ *864-3330. Open M-Sa 10am-6pm and in Opera House 2hr. before show.*

The Local LEGEND

A Critical Mess?

The first time you lose your temper in SF very well may be over traffic. Plan your route poorly and you'll likely find yourself spending an hour on the Bay Bridge. Get caught in traffic on the last Friday of the month, and you may run into Critical Mass (CM).

"The Commuter Clot" was started in 1992 to both celebrate cyclist lifestyle and to protest a lack of public amenities for bikers. Now, CM is a monthly "organized coincidence" of 500 or more bicyclists taking to the streets for a commute en masse. For many participants, the trek is a demonstrative reminder to others that life without cars is possible and a social gathering for biking enthusiasts; to others, it's a highly political statement about oil companies and the right to public space.

Not everyone supports the bikers' actions as high-minded, though. The cyclists don't acknowledge traffic laws, claiming they were formulated only with cars in mind. In 1997, over 100 bicyclists were arrested during a ride, and newspapers were flooded with letters condemning Critical Mass as chaos. CM has persisted, though, and although many of their goals remain unattained as of its 10th anniversary, many seem satisfied with the new global sense of biker community—CM now exists in dozens of cities.

91

Museum Quickfind

If you're planning a museum binge, consider a **CityPass**, which covers admission to (and lets you skip lines at) the San Francisco Museum of Modern Art (p. 94), Blue and Gold Fleet Cruise (p. 109), the Exploratorium (p. 68), the Palace of the Legion of Honor (p. 80), California Academy of Sciences (p. 83), and the Steinhart Aquarium (p. 83). It also acts as a MUNI and cable car 7-day passport (p. 40). Passes (available at any of the attractions or www.citypass.com) are valid for either 7 or 9 days. They cost $36 (ages 5-17 $28), which amounts to about a 50% discount off admission fees.

Art Museums:

California Palace of the Legion of Honor (p. 80)

Museo Italo Americano (p. 70)

Museum of Craft and Folk Art (p. 69)

North Beach Museum (p. 71)

San Francisco Art Institute (p. 73)

SFMOMA (p. 94)

Cultural Museums:

African-American History and Cultural Society Museum (p. 70)

Chinese Historical Society of America (p. 72)

Randall Museum (p. 98)

Pacific Heritage Museum (p. 94)

Performance Art Library and Museum (p. 92)

(cont'd on next pg.)

The seating in the $33 million glass-and-brass **Louise M. Davies Symphony Hall** was designed to give all audience members a close-up view of performers. In addition, the building's striking architectural elements provide stunning visuals and intense acoustics. The **San Francisco Symphony,** which plays here, is equally esteemed (p. 166). The recently renovated **War Memorial Opera House** hosts the well-regarded **San Francisco Opera Company** (p. 166) and the **San Francisco Ballet** (p. 166).

VETERAN'S BUILDING

🔢 *On Van Ness Ave., between Grove and McAllister St.* **Herbst Theatre Box Office:** ☎392-4400. *Open M-F 9:30am-5pm, Sa 10am-4pm.* **PALM:** ☎255-4800; *www.sfpalm.org. Open W-F 11am-5pm, Sa 1-5pm. Free. Reservations to guarantee research access is recommended.* **Gallery:** ☎554-6080. *Open W-Sa noon-5:30pm. Free.* **Tours:** ☎552-8338. *Depart M 10am-2pm, every hour on the hour from Symphony Hall, Grove St. entrance. Adults $5, students and seniors $3.*

The Veteran's Building is home to a host of museums and cultural activities. **Herbst Theatre,** on the first floor, hosts solo singers, ensembles, and lecturers. The **Performance Art Library and Museum (PALM),** on the fourth floor, features over two million items related to the performing arts, such as costumes, playbills, books, and photos. The **SF Art Commission Gallery,** in Room 172, exhibits works by artists from all over the nation. **Performing Arts Visit Tours** lead tours of Davies Symphony Hall, the War Memorial Opera House, and Herbst Theatre.

HAYES VALLEY

🔢 *NEIGHBORHOOD QUICKFIND:* **Discover,** *p. 14;* **Food & Drink,** *p. 126;* **Nightlife,** *p. 149;* **Accommodations,** *p. 196.*

POLANCO

see map p. 345

🔢 *393 Hayes St. at Gough St.* ☎252-5753; *www.polancogallery.com. Open Tu-Sa 11am-7pm, Su 1-6pm. AmEx/D/MC/V.*

"A Gallery of Mexican Arts," Polanco is the only art space of its kind. The gallery features antique and religious art, vintage and contemporary folk craft, and contemporary fine arts.

OCTAVIA'S HAZE GALLERY

🔢 *498 Hayes St. at Octavia St.* ☎255-6818; *www.octaviashaze.com. Open W-Su noon-6pm. D/MC/V.*

Octavia's Haze features one-of-a-kind hand-blown glass creations from Bay Area, Seattle, and Italian artists. The gallery also has a modest collection of contemporary art and frequently changing new exhibits.

DUDLEY PERKINS COMPANY

🟥 *66 Page St., between Gough and Van Ness St.* ☎ *703-9494; www.dpchd.com. Open M-F 8am-6pm, Sa 9am-7pm. Free.*

For something completely different, take a walk outside Hayes Valley to the 89-year-old Dudley Perkins Company, the oldest motorcycle shop in San Francisco and the third oldest Harley-Davidson dealership in the world. The shiny shop displays and sells all sorts of biking memorabilia, including engine models from all the Harleys produced over the years.

TENDERLOIN

see map p. 345

🟥 *NEIGHBORHOOD QUICKFIND:* **Discover,** *p. 14;* **Food & Drink,** *p. 127;* **Nightlife,** *p. 150;* **Accommodations,** *p. 197.*

509 CULTURAL CENTER/LUGGAGE STORE GALLERY

🟥 *509 Cultural Center: 509 Ellis St., near 6th St.* ☎ *440-5090. Luggage Store: 1007 Market St., near Leavenworth St.* ☎ *255-5971; www.luggagestoregallery.org. Exhibits open for viewing W-Sa noon-5pm.*

Founded by a group of Tenderloin artists and residents in the late 80s, the 509 Center and the Luggage Store Gallery (two venues for the same group) have tried to create an arts presence within the area to support and promote up-and- coming neighborhood artists (starting with programs for middle-schoolers). Regular events at the Luggage Store include sewing parties (literally, people bring clothes to mend as they hang out) on the 15th of every month and Thursday improvisational music concerts (8pm; $6-10 suggested donation, no one refused for lack of funds). Next door to the 509 Cultural Center, **Cohen Alley** houses a third venue for the community's creative talent and serves, in the words of one activist, as a "model for other inner city reclamation projects." For $1 a year, the City leases the once derelict alley to the Luggage Store, whose vibrant murals and ornately sculpted gate have transformed the dead-end space

Museums Cont'd.

Science Museums:

California Academy of Science (p. 83)

Exploratorium (p. 68)

Ones-of-a-kind:

Cable Car Powerhouse and Museum (p. 74)

Dudley Perkins Company (p. 93)

Ripley's Believe It Or Not Museum (p. 67)

Wax Museum (p. 67)

Gallery Spaces:

509 Cultural Center/Luggage Store (p. 93)

Academy of Art College Gallery (p. 95)

Art Institute of California: SF (p. 94)

Canvas Cafe/Gallery (p. 105)

The Coffee Gallery (p. 70)

Diego Rivera Gallery and Walter and McBean Galleries (p. 73)

Galería La Raza (p. 103)

Hang Gallery (p. 76)

Martin Lawrence Gallery (p. 76)

Octavia's Haze (p. 92)

Peter Lik Gallery (p. 68)

Polanco (p. 92)

Public Art Space (p. 95)

SF Art Commission Gallery (p. 92)

sf black & white gallery (p. 76)

Xanadu Gallery (p. 75)

Yerba Buena Center for the Arts (p. 94)

Bernal Heights

into a lively artistic showcase for free performances, gallery showings, and workshops. If you find yourself in the area in October, check out the free, three-day "In the Street" theater festival.

THE ART INSTITUTE OF CALIFORNIA: SAN FRANCISCO

🚩 1170 Market St. at UN Plaza, near 8th St. ☎865-0198; www.aicasf.edu. Open M-Th 8am-8pm, F 8am-5pm, Sa 10am-4pm.

This small lobby/gallery displays student projects in fashion, photography, painting and graphic design. The place is great for a brief viewing, but don't expect to find a multitude of works—it does not hold more than fifteen pieces.

Mission Dolores Park

SOUTH OF MARKET AREA (SOMA)

🚩 NEIGHBORHOOD QUICKFIND: **Discover**, p. 15; **Food & Drink**, p. 127; **Nightlife**, p. 151; **Accommodations**, p. 198.

see map p. 347

🖼 SAN FRANCISCO MUSEUM OF MODERN ART (SFMOMA)

🚩 151 3rd St., between Mission and Howard St. ☎357-4000; www.sfmoma.org. Open Sept. 3-May 24 M-Tu and F-Su 11am-5:45pm, Th 11am-8:45pm. Open May 25-Sept. 2 M-Tu and F-Su 10am-6pm, Th 10am-9pm. Adults $10, over 62 $7, students with valid ID $6, under 13 free. Th 6-9pm half-price. Free 1st Tu of each month. Four free gallery tours per day, 2 additional tours during the late hours on Th. Admission included in CityPass (p. 92).

Fascinating for its architecture as well as for the art it contains, this black and gray marble-trimmed museum houses five spacious floors of art, with emphasis on design, photography, and audiovisuals. Its contemporary European and American collections are impressive—SFMOMA has the most 20th-century art this side of New York, including impressive collections of Warhol, Johns, Rauschenberg, and Stella. The museum, indeed, has one of Marcel Duchamp's famous urinals, an example of "readymade" art. SFMOMA is a must-see for any appreciator of modern art.

YERBA BUENA CENTER FOR THE ARTS

🚩 701 Mission St., at 3rd St. ☎978-2787; www.yerba-buenaarts.org. Open Tu-Su 11am-6pm. Adults $6, free 1st Tu of month; seniors and students $3, free every Th. Free tours with admission Th 5pm and Sa 4pm.

Alamo Square

The center runs an excellent theater and gallery space that emphasizes performance, film, viewer involvement, and local multicultural work— essentially anything that can be considered "adventurous art." It is surrounded by the **Yerba Buena Rooftop Gardens,** an oasis of foliage and gurgling fountains in a predominantly concrete neighborhood.

ZEUM

🖪 *221 4th St., at Howard St. ☎ 777-2800; www.zeum.org. Open in summer Tu-Su 11am-5pm, off-season W-Su 11am-5pm. Adults $7, students and seniors $6, ages 4-18 $5, under 4 free.* **Carousel:** *open daily 11am-6pm. $2 for 2 rides.*

Within the gardens but a sight unto itself, this completely interactive "art and technology center" is aimed primarily at children and teenagers. Besides studios for arts and crafts, claymation, and karaoke, Zeum also has a music performance space and an ice skating and bowling center. The best draw, however, is the **carousel,** built in 1906 and reopened after a 25-year hiatus.

PUBLIC ART SPACE

🖪 *101 2nd St., at Mission St. Open M-F 8am-6pm.*

In the glass and chrome **Public Art Space,** a huge open lobby showcases oversized sculpture and paintings. With its enormous windows and ceiling-scraper trees to protect people-watchers from the drizzle, this is *the* place for an artistically inspired rainy day picnic.

ACADEMY OF ART COLLEGE GALLERY

🖪 *79 New Montgomery St., at Mission St. ☎ 274-2292 or 800-544-2787; www.academyart.edu. Open M-F 9am-5pm.*

A "best in show" of student works chosen as stand-outs, now on sale. The gallery primarily showcases fine art and sculpture, but also includes periodic exhibits on film, fashion, photography, and computer design.

PACIFIC HEIGHTS & JAPANTOWN

🖪 *NEIGHBORHOOD QUICKFIND:* **Discover,** *p. 15;* **Food & Drink,** *p. 129;* **Accommodations,** *p. 198.*

see map p. 348

Shake It Up

On April 18, 1906, the Great Quake struck the infant metropolis of San Francisco with a magnitude of 8.25 on the Richter scale. The collision of tectonic plates 30 mi. beneath the ocean bed triggered the shifting of billions of tons of rock, effectively levelling much of San Francisco. The rip in the Earth's surface tore a gash down the coastline that was named the San Andreas fault.

The Bay Area has since prepared itself for and feared a second earthquake of similar magnitude. These fears were realized in Oct. 1989, during a World Series game between cross-Bay rivals Oakland Athletics and San Francisco Giants. The Loma Prieta quake measured a 7.1 on the Richter scale. While it was not as devastating as the Great Quake, it did cause the collapse of the Nimitz Freeway and part of the upper deck of the Bay Bridge, as well as $3 billion in damage to the city and surrounding areas.

Again, the blame rested on the precarious Marin County's Point Reyes. The most sizeable piece of California located on the North Pacific plate, Pt. Reyes is slowly moving north. Geologists calculate a 70% probability that another earthquake of at least 6.0 magnitude will strike.

You can see where two fence posts were ripped apart in the Great Quake on the **Earthquake Trail** (p. 242).

Mission Murals

Mission Dolores

At the Zoo

PACIFIC HEIGHTS

SAINT DOMINIC'S ROMAN CATHOLIC CHURCH

🚩 *2390 Bush St., at Steiner St. Open M-Sa 6:30am-5:30pm, Su 7:30am-9pm. Mass M-F 6:30, 8am, and 5:30pm; Sa 8am and 5:30pm; Su 7:30, 9:30, 11:30am, 1:30, 5:30, and 9pm candlelight service.*

Churchgoers and architecture buffs alike will appreciate St. Dominic's towering altar that is carved in the shape of Jesus and the 12 apostles. With its imposing gray stone and Gothic-style architecture, St. Dominic's is a must-see, especially its renowned shrine of St. Jude—who died a martyr preaching and converting many to Christianity—skirted by candles and intricately carved oak.

ALTA PLAZA

🚩 *Bound by Jackson, Scott, Steiner, and Clay St.*

If you have any breath left after the steep climb up to the Alta Plaza, the views will snatch it right away. Gaze downhill for a panoramic view of downtown San Fran and Twin Peaks, or uphill along Pierce Street to catch a spectacular glimpse of the Bay. Sunbathe on the grassy slopes or swing like a carefree kid in the playground; this is a great place to spend the afternoon or pack a picnic (p. 128).

JAPANTOWN (NIHONMACHI)

FUJI SHIATSU AND KABUKI SPRINGS AND SPA

🚩 *Shiatsu: 1721 Buchanan Mall., between Post and Sutter St. ☎ 346-4484. Morning $41, afternoon $44. Springs and Spa: 1750 Geary Blvd. ☎ 922-6000; www.kabukisprings.com. M-F before 5pm $15, after 5pm and Sa-Su $18. Open 10am-10pm; men only M, Th, Sa; women only Su, W, F; co-ed (clothing required) Tu.*

After a rigorous day of hiking the city's hills, reward your weary muscles with an massage at Fuji Shiatsu or a leisurely rest in the Kabuki Hot Springs' bathhouse with sauna and steamroom. Combine with a seaweed wrap, or *Reiki* treatment (additional $75) to heal, rejuvenate, and restore energy balance.

SOTO ZEN MISSION SOKOJI BUDDHIST TEMPLE

🚩 *1691 Laguna St., at Sutter St. ☎ 346-7540. Public Zazen services Su 8am. Arrive 15min. early.*

It is in the five churches of this area that the Japantown community comes alive. Many families no longer living in the area return for services. Join members of the Soto Zen Mission Buddhist Temple for Zazen services that include meditation, temple cleaning, and tea. Since 1934, the Sokoji Congregation has offered viewers zen with its meditative spirituality and sublime architecture.

PEACE PAGODA

⏷ *Japan Center, between the Kintetsu and Miyako entrances.*

Designed by Tokyo architect Yoshiro Taniguchi, the five-tiered Peace Pagoda, a gift to the community from the Japanese government in 1968, once sat amid cherry trees and a reflecting pool. It is currently in the midst of a slow restoration process to convert the surrounding paved lot into an inviting centerpiece for the Japan Center.

Japanese Tea Garden

JAPANESE CULTURAL AND COMMUNITY CENTER

⏷ *1840 Sutter St., near Buchanan Mall.* ☎ *567-5505; www.jcccnc.org. Open M-F 9am-10pm, Sa-Su 9am-6pm.*

If the Japan Center begins to seem like any other mall in the Western hemisphere, check out what's going on at the Japanese Cultural and Community Center of Northern California (JCCCNC). With art exhibitions, writing workshops, film screenings, discussion groups, and summer camps for kids, this is a great place to connect with the community and learn about Japanese-American history.

HAIGHT-ASHBURY

see map p. 349

⏷ NEIGHBORHOOD QUICKFIND: **Discover,** p. 16; **Food & Drink,** p. 130; **Nightlife,** p. 154; **Accommodations,** p. 198.

PARKS

⏷ *Hill Habitat Restoration:* ☎ *554-9604*

Buena Vista Park, which runs along Haight St. between Central and Baker St. and continues south, resembles a dense jungle. The lush and exotic flora provide a haven for those who want to do their own thing and an unofficial crash pad for San Francisco skaters. **Alamo Square** lies northeast of the Haight at Hayes St., between Steiner and Scott St. On the Steiner St. side, across Alamo Square's gentle grassy slope, a string of beautiful and brightly colored Victorian homes known as the **Painted Ladies**—subject of a thousand postcards—glows against the back-

Dutch Windmill

Palace of the Legion of Honor

from the
road

Reimagining a City

I loved the idea of San Francisco long before I ever stepped foot on its soil. As my plane was landing at SFO, I looked around and realized it was 2am. I couldn't see anything. But I still knew I would love it once I *could* see it. This was the city that had fostered some of the greatest social movements in America, a city that throughout its history refused to conform to the status quo and allowed its citizens to be pioneers. Specifically, I wanted to explore the Haight-Ashbury neighborhood where, in my opinion, the last generation of great social rebels had settled. I knew not to expect the famed 1967 Summer of Love reenacted for my personal benefit, but I wasn't quite prepared for what I found.

The Haight is primarily a shopping area now. It has dozens of eateries, boutiques, and tourist traps. A big mural of Janis, Jimi, and Jerry is one of the few reminders of the area's role in history, and it has been updated to include Tupac. I knew it would be different than in the sixties but I was...confused. Where was the energy that had inspired the music, art, and political devotion of the sixties?

(cont'd next pg.)

drop of the metropolitan skyline. Below the Haight, near the **Randall Museum,** lies the sparse **Corona Heights Park.** While the park appears to consist primarily of a large rocky hill with tufts of bedraggled grass, its view of the city (when fogless) is spectacular. The greenless gap is actually purposeful—park managers are restoring the grounds to their native vegetation. To help in the restoration (you tree-hugging types) join in the public "Hill Habitat Restoration" program the last Saturday of every month from 10am-noon (See **Alternatives to Tourism,** p. 301).

FORMER CRIBS

The former homes of several countercultural legends continue to attract visitors, even though new residents inhabit the cribs. From the corner of Haight and Ashbury St., walk up Ashbury St. to #710, just south of Waller St., to check out the house occupied by the **Grateful Dead** when they were still the Warlocks (p. 56). Look across the street for the **Hell's Angels'** house. If you walk back to Haight St., go right three blocks, and make a left on Lyon St., you can check out **Janis Joplin's** old abode, 122 Lyon St., between Page and Oak St. Cross the Panhandle, continue three blocks to Fulton St., turn right, and wander seven blocks toward the park to see where the Manson "family" planned murder and mayhem at the **Charles Manson** mansion, 2400 Fulton St., at Willard St.

SAN FRANCISCO ZEN CENTER

🚩 *300 Page St., at Laguna St.* ☎ *863-3136.* **Office:** *Open M-F 9:30am-12:30pm and 1:30-5pm, Sa 9am-noon.* **Bookstore:** *Open M-F 1:30-5:30pm, M-Th 6:30-7:30pm, Sa 11am-1pm.* **Library:** *Open Tu-F 1:30-5pm.*

Appropriately removed from the havoc of the Haight, the Zen Center offers a peaceful retreat. Call for information on any of the multitude of classes they offer here. The temple is called Beginner's Mind Temple so don't worry if you don't even know where to begin looking for your *chi.* The best option for most beginners is the Saturday morning program which includes a mediation lecture at 8:45am followed by other activities and lunch ($6). Or just visit the bookstore and the library.

RANDALL MUSEUM

🚩 *199 Museum Way, at the bottom of Corona Heights Park, off Roosevelt Way. Take bus #37 up 14th St.* ☎ *554-9600; www.randallmuseum.org. Open Tu-Sa 10am-5pm. Free.*

The Randall Museum caters mainly to children through hands-on workshops that aim to integrate nature, culture, art, and science, with permanent exhibits on earthquakes and live animals, and rotating lobby exhibits, too. The Randall Theater hosts concerts, films, and lectures. Saturdays are family drop-in days when you can meet the animals (11:15am), throw yourself a ceramic pot (10am), or take any number of classes offered in the afternoon. Call or check the website for general info and details on classes and prices.

MURALS

By no means as magnificent as the murals marking the Mission, the Haight does yield a scattered few. Of particular note: the HIV awareness *Positive Visibility* mural at Haight and Scott St.; the larger-than-life Marley, Hendrix, and Garcia portraits at Haight St. and Central Ave.; and the *Evolutionary Rainbow* at Haight and Cole St.

CASTRO

▇ *NEIGHBORHOOD QUICKFIND:*
Discover, *p. 17;* **Food & Drink,** *p. 132;* **Nightlife,** *p. 155;* **Accommodations,** *p. 199.*

see map p. 350

Rainbow flags hoisted high, out and proud lesbian, gay, bisexual, and transgender (LGBT) folk find comfort and fun on the streets of the Castro. The concept, as well as the reality, of an all-queer neighborhood draws queer tourists and their friends from around the world, carrying the already absolutely fabulous Castro scene over-the-top. Those out and about are the main attraction on the picture-perfect streets, where seeing and being seen is practically a full-time occupation.

BROWSING

Stores throughout the area cater to gay mecca pilgrims, with everything from rainbow flags and pride-wear to the latest in LGBT books, dance music, and trinkets of the more unmentionable variety. Many local shops, especially on the wildly colorful **Castro Street,** also double as novelty museums. Discover just how anatomically correct Gay Billy is at **Does Your Father Know?,** a one-stop kitsch-and-camp overdose (p. 187), or find the perfect card to ask just that at **Does Your Mother Know?** (p. 188). To read up on gay history and culture, enlighten yourself at **A Different Light Bookstore** (p. 179), or head to **Worn Out West** for vintage, leather, and western pizzazz (p. 183).

(cont'd from previous pg.)

Where were the other people who came because they loved what the Haight stood for? Where were all the clothes that I could afford?

As I wandered around, I talked to the street's people and I began to figure it out. The energy was there, it was just different now. It was more subtle, more underground, but still palpable if you look in the right places. Venture to the far reaches of the Upper Haight to see the community of young backpackers, moving through the country just for the trip, with no definite destination. Walk through the area and notice that there is not a single Starbucks or McDonald's—the community has banded together to keep big chains out of their streets. Go to Amoeba Music for the free concerts. Or simply hang out in Buena Vista Park and people-watch.

Though the Haight may no longer be the hotbed of youth unrest and cultural rebellion that it was forty years ago, after a few hours hanging around these environs, you can tell that the people here still do things their own way and don't really care what anyone else thinks about it. The tourists and the transients come and go, but the free spirited independence of the Haight endures.

—Caitlin Casey

The Golden Hydrant

At 5:16am on April 18th, 1906, a 48-second shudder shook the city awake and stopped the massive clock on the face of the Ferry Building. Edifices twisted to splinters, and the city burst into flames. The fire department worked to stop the blaze, but dry cisterns and ruptured water mains prevented any real progress. The fire reduced 28,000 buildings to rubble, and was set to consume the Mission Dolores, arguably the city's most historic building, when a hydrant on the corner of 20th and Church St. miraculously continued to function. Firefighters contained the blaze and saved the church.

Today, to prevent future disasters, the city's system of hydrants is color coded for easy identification. Small white hydrants are connected to a high-pressure, independent system. Blue hydrants are connected to a tank on Jones St. on Nob Hill, with enough pressure to fight fires 150 ft. above sea level. Red hydrants are connected to a high-power tank on Ashbury St. If another earthquake were to rupture all these, there is still a system of 150 cisterns located at key intersections of the city, each with at least 75,000 gallons of water. The most prized hydrant, though, is the one that saved the Mission—every year on April 18th, it is given a fresh coat of gold paint.

WALKING TOURS

🗹 ☎ 550-8110; trvrhailey@aol.com. Tours Tu-Sa 10am. $40; lunch included. Email or phone reservations required.

For a guided tour of the Castro (one that includes sights other than those strolling around in cut-off shorts), check out **Cruisin' the Castro.** Trevor Hailey, a resident since 1972, is consistently recognized as one of San Fran's top tour leaders. Her 4hr. walking tour covers Castro life and history from the Gold Rush to the present.

OTHER SIGHTS

The steeply sloped areas to the south and west of Castro Village tend to be residential. The vibrantly painted old **Victorians** here are worth wandering for—Collingwood and Noe St. both have their share. For strokably toned calf muscles, Castro St.'s commercial luster gives way to gorgeous 19th-century embellishment past 19th St. and up toward Liberty St. Or get architecture without the walk, and look for the faux-baroque **Castro Theatre,** 429 Castro St. (p. 170)—not that you could miss it.

NOE VALLEY

see map p. 350

🗹 NEIGHBORHOOD QUICKFIND: **Discover,** p. 18; **Food & Drink,** p. 133; **Nightlife,** p. 158; **Accommodations,** p. 201.

The very residential Noe Valley lacks actual "sights" of note, but it's such a pretty neighborhood that it's worth spending a relaxing hour or two strolling along the quiet streets. Historic buildings blanket the valley—many can be seen on Jersey St., between 24th and 25th St., starting at the **Noe Valley Library,** 451 Jersey St., between Castro and Diamond St. and continuing around the block, down Castro and 24th St. and along Diamond St. (☎ 695-5095.) Noe Valley is also one of the few neighborhoods in San Francisco that still contains examples of **stick cottages**—houses ornately decorated with flat pieces of wood around the doors and windows to highlight the architecture. Most stick cottages date to before 1906 and thus, most were destroyed in the Great Earthquake. However, a few that have survived the century lie directly across from the library. Three **Queen Annes** sit in a row at 408, 410, and 412 Jersey St. **Victorian** buildings are everywhere, but for a few treasures, check out 345, 365, and 367 Jersey St. Maneuver past baby strollers and leashed dogs to get at the numerous flower, beauty, and children's stores. Several specialty stores sell everything from mystery novels to personalized chocolate boxes. If your feet need a rest, head over to Douglass and 26th St. to the **Douglass Playground.** Picnic benches, restrooms, a grassy lawn, and plenty of slides and swings make for a perfect rest stop. Despite the ever-rising prices in window displays, the shopping district, which centers on a few blocks of 24th St., resists posh pretensions and retains a neighborhood feel. Watching over Noe Valley are the **Twin Peaks,** the two mountains that offer arguably the best views in the city, and **West Portal,** the largely residential neighborhood.

TWIN PEAKS

Between Portola Dr., Clarendon Ave., and Market St. From Noe Valley take MUNI bus #48 to Diamond Heights, then #37 to the top. From elsewhere in the city take MUNI bus K, L, or M to Forest Hills, then MUNI bus #36. For a scenic route by car, bike, or foot, take 17th St. to Masonic Ave. to Clarendon Ave. Then head up Twin Peaks Blvd. to the end. Starting in Noe Valley, take the back route up Clipper St. to Burnett Ave. Stay on Burnett until you reach Twin Peaks Blvd. and bear left onto it.

Tourist hub by day, lovebird locale by night—the look/make-out point atop Twin Peaks offers what many consider to be **the best views of the city.** On rare fogless nights, the views at 922 ft. are particularly sublime; at all times of day, even in summer, the winds are intense and the temperature much chillier than in the valleys below. Local lore maintains that either the peaks were once a married Native American couple parted by the Great Spirit during a vicious squabble or that the mountains are actually the transformed daughters of a Native American chief. The Spanish opted for the more voluptuous interpretation and referred to the peaks as "Los Pechos de la Choca" (the Breasts of the Indian Maiden). Ultimately the name was settled on the far less steamy "Twin Peaks," which seemed like a bland title until David Lynch got TV audiences asking who killed Laura Palmer. Don't be deceived, though: this is *not* the same Twin Peaks. Still, this Twin Peaks has its own endangered resident: the **Mission Blue Butterfly.** Most bus tours in the city stop here, but you can reach the summit on your own by taking MUNI bus #36 or by driving toward the hulking three-masted radio tower, known by some as the Great Satan, where a pair of red warning lights blink ominously. Significantly south of the peaks stands **Mt. Davidson,** the highest spot in San Francisco at 938 ft.

SF Traffic

Seal Rock

The Presidio

WEST PORTAL

🔀 *West Portal refers to the west side of the hill, from which the MUNI bus emerges; take MUNI buses L, K, M to the West Portal stop.*

Described by its neighborhood committee as a bit of tranquility within a cosmopolitan environment, West Portal offers residents and tourists who are dedicated enough to make the trek a return to the simple life—small quiet streets, manicured lawns and gardens, and chirping birds. West Portal's pulsing heart—and the only place worth a traveler's time—is the strip of **retail shops** along West Portal Avenue, with the MUNI bus line cutting right down the middle. While West Portal is not necessarily worth a trip on its own, if you're in the neighborhood—perhaps at the nearby SF Zoo—it's definitely worth stopping in for a bite to eat and a taste of Americana. (*Let's Go* does not recommend going on Monday when most shops on West Portal Ave. are closed).

MISSION

🔀 NEIGHBORHOOD QUICKFIND: **Discover**, p. 18; **Food & Drink**, p. 135; **Nightlife**, p. 158; **Accommodations**, p. 202.

MISIÓN DE LOS DOLORES (MISSION DOLORES)

🔀 *3321 16th St., at 16th and Dolores St. ☎621-8203. Open May-Oct. daily 9am-4:30pm; Nov.-Apr. 9am-4pm. Adults $3, ages 5-12 $2. **Mass:** in English M-F 7:30, 9am; Sa 7:30, 9am, 5pm; Su 8, 10am. In Spanish Su noon.*

see map p. 352

Established over two centuries ago and located in the old heart of San Francisco, the Mission Dolores is thought to be the city's oldest building. Founded in 1776 by Father Junípero Serra, it was originally named in honor of St. Francis of Assisi. Later, due to its proximity to the Laguna de Nuestra Señora de los Dolores (Lagoon of Our Lady of Sorrows), the mission became universally known as *Misión de los Dolores*. Bougainvillea, poppies, and birds-of-paradise bloom in its cemetery, which was featured in Alfred Hitchcock's 1958 film *Vertigo*.

MISSION MURALS

A walk east or west along 24th St., weaving in and out of the side streets, reveals the Mission's magnificent murals. Simply walking up and down Mission St. will yield a taste as well, but the concentration is definitely on 24th. Continuing the long Mexican mural tradition brought to fame by Diego Rivera and José Orozco, the Mission murals have been a source of pride for Chicano artists, schoolchildren, and community members since the 1980s. Standouts include the more political murals of Balmy Alley, off 24th St. between Harrison and Folsom St.; a three-building tribute to guitar god Carlos Santana at 22nd St. and Van Ness Ave. (*Inspire to Aspire*, M. Rios, C. Gonzales, J. Mayorca, 1987); the face of St. Peter's Church at 24th and Florida St. (*500 Years of Resistance*, Isaias Mata, 1993); and the urban living center on 19th St. between Valencia and Guerrero St.

PRECITA EYES MURAL ARTS AND VISITOR CENTER

🔀 *Two locations: 2981 24th St. at Harrison St. ☎285-2287; and 348 Precita Ave. ☎285-2311; www.precitaeyes.org. Open M and W-Th 10am-5pm and 7-9pm, Tu and F 10am-5pm, Sa 10am-4pm, Su 11am-4pm. **Mural Walks:** leave from the 24th St. Center Sa-Su 11am and 1:30pm. Adults $12, students $8, seniors $5, under 18 $2. MC/V.*

Begun as a community mural workshop in 1977, Precita Eyes is one of three community mural organizations in the country. Precita's mural artists continue to paint around the neighborhood, creating and changing murals throughout the year. Precita also offers **Mission Mural Walks,** a six-block tour covering over 75 murals, with a talk on the history of community mural art.

CITY GUIDES

☎ 557-4266; www.sfcityguides.org. Free.

Sponsored by the San Francisco Public Library system, City Guides leads free tours of the Mission murals in summer. **Mural tours** meet at Precita and Harrison St., behind Flynn Elementary School, on the first and third Saturdays of each month at 11am. City Guides also offers more general **historical tours** of the Mission. Mission Dolores Neighborhood Tours meet at the gold fire hydrant (p. 100) on the southeast corner of Church and 20th St., on the first and third Sundays of each month at noon.

GALERÍA DE LA RAZA

2857 24th St., between Bryant and Florida St. ☎ 826-8009; www.galeriadelaraza.org. Usually open W-Sa noon-6pm. Call to confirm hours. Free. **Store:** Open Tu-Sa noon-6pm. MC/V.

The gallery celebrates international Chicano and Latino artists with exhibitions and parties. Attached to the gallery is **Studio 24,** a space where Chicano and Latino artists sell artwork, crafts, and jewelry.

MISSION CULTURAL CENTER FOR LATINO ARTS (MCCLA)

2868 Mission St., between 24th and 25th St. ☎ 821-1155; www.missionculturalcenter.org. Open M-F 10am-5:30pm, Sa 10am-5pm.

One of the most active cultural centers in the city, MCCLA offers a variety of programs for community members and visitors, including film series, plays, exhibitions, and a multicultural arts program for kids. Whether you want to view the artwork of queer Latino artists or help plan **Carnaval** (the Mission's insanely fun cultural celebration, p. 24), MCCLA is the place to go. Be sure to check their website for schedule information.

OTHER SIGHTS

16th St. is perhaps the most pulsing, pluralistic, personality-filled boulevard in all of San Francisco; people-watching possibilities make it a sight unto itself. **Mission Dolores Park,** which stretches from 18th to 20th St. between Church and Dolores St., is prime hang-out turf for residents of the Mission, the Castro, and Noe Valleys. **Osento,** 955 Valencia St., between 20th and 21st St., is a Japanese-style bathhouse for ladies, with wet and dry saunas, a jacuzzi, an outdoor dipping pool, sundecks, and a meditation room. (☎ 282-6333. Open daily 1pm-1am.

Colt Tower

SF Art Institute

Grant Street

Escaping the Rock

In 1936 Alcatraz became a maximum security federal prison, an ominous symbol of the government's determination to control crime and its perpetrators. In *Escape From Alcatraz*, the warden tells Clint Eastwood that "if you disobey the rules of society, they send you to prison; if you disobey the rules in prison, they send you to us." A walk through the prison's drafty corridors and a glance at the cramped steel cells easily convinces visitors that few things could be worse. The inmates agreed.

Between 1934 and 1963 when Alcatraz shut down, 36 men tried to escape from the Rock on 14 separate occasions. Of those 36, only five remain unaccounted for. The frigid water of the Bay and its notoriously strong currents have led to the official presumption that these five men drowned. The only escapee known to have survived the swim was recaptured shortly after escaping.

The most ingenious and compelling escape was engineered on June 11th, 1962 by Frank Morris and the Anglin brothers, who fashioned papier-mâché likenesses of their heads, fooling the guards long enough to allow the men to creep out of their cells through enlarged air vents into a service tunnel. They walked along the cell-block roof and lowered themselves into the water along a stovepipe. Neither they nor their homemade flotation devices were ever found.

Last admission at midnight. 14+. $10-20, senior discount, over 70 free. One hour massage $60-80. No credit cards.)

BERNAL HEIGHTS

◪ *NEIGHBORHOOD QUICKFIND:*
Discover, *p. 19;* ***Food & Drink,*** *p. 136;* ***Nightlife,*** *p. 160.*

Mostly residential, Bernal Heights lures visitors from the rest of the city to the steep and windy **Bernal Heights Park,** whose summit is one of the tallest vistas around. The Boulevard around the park is a favorite spot for runners and dog-walkers. Visitors should exercise caution at night around the park since roads are curvy and isolated. From Cortland Ave., walk two blocks uphill to reach it. Shops, cafes and restaurants brimming with local atmosphere lurk behind the bland facades of Cortland Ave.

see map p. 352

POTRERO HILL

◪ *NEIGHBORHOOD QUICKFIND:*
Discover, *p. 19;* ***Food & Drink,*** *p. 137;* ***Nightlife,*** *p. 160.*

SECOND CROOKEDEST STREET IN THE WORLD

see map p. 353

◪ *Between 20th and 22nd St., running down Potrero Hill.*

Tortuous **Vermont St.** offers a less manicured view than its Lombard St. cousin, but its six turns are more menacingly tight than Lombard's eight—a fun secret well kept by Potrero thrill-seekers that offers one hell of a heart-racing car ride down.

SAN FRANCISCO CENTER FOR THE BOOK

◪ *300 De Haro St. at 16th St.* ☎ *565-0545; www.sfcb.org. Open M-F 10am-5pm. Arrange free tours in advance.*

This production and educational space brings people together by bringing books together. Regular classes in binding, printing, and restoring range from a couple of weeks ($120) to a couple of hours ($50), drawing in artists as well as amateurs. Free lectures and "slams," rotating exhibits, and a new Vend-A-Book vending machine that sells books printed in-house ($1) foster artistic enthusiasm for printmaking.

CALIFORNIA COLLEGE OF ARTS

 1111 Eighth St. at 16th and Wisconsin St. ☎ 703-9500; www.ccac-art.edu. Open Tu and F 11am-8pm, W-Th and Sa 11am-6pm. Free.

The impressive Logan Gallery space showcases locally, nationally, and internationally renowned contemporary artists working in cutting edge mediums. Unfortunately, the college is closed to the public during summer but is definitely worth a look from Sept.-June.

RICHMOND

*NEIGHBORHOOD QUICKFIND: **Discover,** p. 20; **Food & Drink,** p. 139; **Nightlife,** p. 160; **Accommodations,** p. 202.*

The Chinese restaurant and Irish pub are the Richmond's claims to fame. Although not a tourist mecca, the Richmond has a sizable student and 20-something population, which infuses enough energy into this comparatively bland neighborhood to make it a fun destination for dinner and drinks.

see map p. 341

PLACES OF WORSHIP

*Temple Emanu-El: 2 Lake St., at Arguello Blvd. ☎ 751-2535. Open M-F 9am-5pm. Docent-lead tours M-F 1-3pm. Shabbat services F 5:30pm and Sa 10:30am. **St. John's Presbyterian Church:** 25 Lake St., at Arguello Blvd. ☎ 751-1626. Services Su 10am. **Holy Virgin Cathedral:** 6210 Geary Blvd., at 26th Ave. ☎ 221-3255. Services daily 8am and 6pm. Long sleeves, pants, and shoes required for all, head coverings for women as well.*

Religious building connoisseurs are spoilt for choice in this eclectic neighborhood. The Jewish Reform **Temple Emanu-El,** with its towering terra cotta-tiled dome, is a stunning Levantine structure. The temple opens from a shady courtyard, complete with fountain and columned arcades. Or seek refuge among the soaring dark wood beams and stained glass windows of **St. John's.** Besides the beautiful architecture, its claim to fame is a cameo in the movie *So I Married an Axe Murderer.* Glittering gold leaf and majestic mosaics decorate the **Holy Virgin Cathedral** in Outer Richmond. A daily prayer service is the only way to view the Russian Orthodox church's ornate interior; its five onion domes, though, can be viewed from outside.

UNIVERSITY OF SAN FRANCISCO

St. Ignatius: 650 Parker Ave., at Fulton St. ☎ 422-2188; www.stignatiussf.org. Open daily 8:30am-5pm. Mass scheduled M-F 8am and noon; Sa 8am, 2, and 5pm; Su 8, 9:30, 11am, and 4pm.

The **Lone Mountain Campus** is on a hill just East of Inner Richmond, at Stanyan St. and Masonic Ave. A climb up Turk St. brings you to the immaculate grounds of the Jesuit university, founded in 1855. The centerpiece of USF is **St. Ignatius Church,** a grand, elaborately decorated building with stunning shrines, altars, and stained glass.

SUNSET

*NEIGHBORHOOD QUICKFIND: **Discover,** p. 20; **Food & Drink,** p. 140; **Nightlife,** p. 161.*

THE CANVAS CAFE/GALLERY

1200 9th Ave. (☎ 504-0060; www.thecanvasgallery.com), at Lincoln. Live music Th-Sa 8pm. Free parking in rear. Open Su-Th 8am-midnight, F-Sa 8am-2am.

see map p. 341

A rare gem of gentrification, the Canvas is a hit as a cafe, bar, gallery, and live music venue. An ever-changing collection of quality contemporary artwork adorns the walls. Musicians, from independent singer-songwriters to celtic rock bands, perform four nights per week. Poetry readings and

The Writing on the Walls

When the doors of the Immigration Station on Angel Island opened, on January 21, 1910, hundreds began to pour into the "Ellis Island of the West." The majority of these immigrants were Chinese—175,000 over the years that the station was in operation.

Discrimination against the Chinese was prevalent throughout the country during this time. It was even condoned by laws such as the 1882 Chinese Exclusion Act, which forbade most Chinese immigrants from entering the country. Many were denied entry even to the immigration center. The "lucky" few who made it through faced another nightmare as they became inmates, sometimes detained as long as two years awaiting the verdict of their immigration applications. Poor sanitary conditions and intense questioning sessions made the long waits excruciating.

During their stays, some detainees expressed their sentiments by writing or carving poetry into the walls of the barracks where they were locked in. In the poems, they described their memories of home, the voyage over, and their anger and suffering. While many of the poems have faded or been destroyed over the years, some are still boldly evident. Together they create a haunting reminder of times not so distant.

wine tastings are also regular features. Check the website for exhibition schedule and featured artists. Go to enjoy a super selection of edibles, wines, and atmosphere.

OCEAN BEACH

◪ *NEIGHBORHOOD QUICK-FIND: Discover, p. 20; Transportation: p. 20.*

see map p. 341

Though swimming is permitted at Ocean Beach,-there are no lifeguards and **swimming here is dangerous.** Diehard surfers brave the treacherous currents, strong undertow, and 40-60 degree water for the best waves in San Francisco. September through March is surfing season here, with the best weather in November and December. Waves break at different points up and down the beach, so a reliable surf-watching post doesn't quite exist—just follow the wet suits. Be aware, though, that better, more dependable, and safer waves exist 15 minutes south at Lindamar Beach in Pacifica. Restaurants and markets line the Outer Richmond and Sunset just a few streets east of the beach. Check out the sandwiches ($5-7) and the surfer scene at **Fredy's Ocean Beach Deli,** 734 La Playa, at Balboa St. (☎221-2031. Open M-Sa 8:30am-6pm, Su 10am-4:30pm. AmEx/MC/V.)

ZOO, LAKE MERCED, FORT FUNSTON & STERN GROVE

◪ *NEIGHBORHOOD QUICK-FIND: Discover, p. 21; Food & Drink, p. 141.*

SAN FRANCISCO ZOO

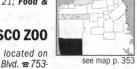

◪ *The entrance is located on Zoo Rd., off Skyline Blvd. ☎753-7080; www.sfzoo.org. Open* see map p. 353 *daily 10am-5pm. Adults $10, seniors and ages 12-17 $7, ages 3-11 $4, under 2 free. Discount for San Francisco residents. 1st W of each month free. $1 discount with MUNI transfer pass.*

Deep in the wilds of the western flank of the Great Peninsula lies the San Francisco Zoo, the native habitat of a mythical and much-feared animal—the *Kindergartner.* Though reared in small, familial environments, the *Kindergartner* travels these parts in large packs, shrieking and playing in a whirlwind of erratic and bullyish antics. Six-year-old males and females of the

species can be viewed at the swingsets, near the cotton candy booths, and at these other zoo locations: colorful **Rainbow Landing,** where the little devils feed nectar to Australian lorikeets; **Lion House,** and **Penguin Island,** right next to the elephant exhibit; **Koala Crossing,** site of a recent zoo heist (though the purloined koalas were eventually returned without a scratch); **Gorilla World,** one of the largest of its kind; and the revered **Primate Discovery Center,** where legions of rare and endangered monkeys and apes romp in treetop playgrounds. Zookeepers lead daily explanatory sessions at these and other animal exhibits. Recently unveiled additions include a shining new entrance and the long-awaited **Lemur Forest.** Continuing developments will bring the **African Savanna** and **Great Ape Forest** in 2004-2005. For a *kindergartner*-less visit, take an adults-only 🖼**Valentine's Day Sex Tour** (p. 31).

LAKE MERCED

🚩 *The entrance is on Harding Rd., off Skyline Blvd.* **Fishing and Boating:** ☎681-3310. *Rentals $10-15 per hr., $30-45 per half-day. Open for activities daily 6:30am-7pm.*

Lake Merced is a vaguely C-shaped freshwater lake among the lush reeds and occasional birdlife of **Harding Park** (best known for its golf course). Though the hum of traffic from the nearby highways can be heard, sandy patches on the water and the bike paths surrounding the lake are peaceful places to escape from city hubbub. The paths are popular with joggers and in-line skaters. Inside the main entrance and to the right, **Lake Merced Fishing and Boating** rents kayaks and canoes and sells fishing licenses and equipment. No activities are allowed after dark, but the gate remains open M-F until 11pm and Sa-Su until 1am. The dirt path and bridge over the northern part of the lake are nice spots for munching, chatting, and singing Simon & Garfunkel songs.

FORT FUNSTON

🚩 *The main entrance is on Skyline Blvd, about 1½ mi. south of the intersection with John Muir Dr., with an additional entrance at the intersection. Pedestrians may also enter at the northern tip of the park, where a trail meets Ocean Beach and the Great Hwy.* **Public Transportation:** *MUNI bus #18 stops along Lake Merced on John Muir Dr. From the bus stop, walk north along John Muir Dr. to the junction with Skyline Blvd., or follow Skyline Blvd. south to the main entrance.* **Driving:** *The easiest point of entry is off Skyline Blvd. which can be reached from the north via the Great Highway and Rte. 1. Limited parking is at Skyline Blvd. and John Muir Dr.* **Tandem Gliders:** ☎310-6602. *Reserve 1wk. in advance. From $215 cash, $225 check.*

With a rather unspectacular military history, Fort Funston is the last remnant of dunes that extended nearly to Haight-Ashbury. A **Golden Gate National Recreation Area (GGNRA),** this windy wilderness is popular with dog-walkers, bird-watchers, and hang-gliders. Several trails wind along the dunes and meet up with the **Coastal Trail** that reaches all the way to Presidio. The paths near the north have the least canine chaos. Near dog-restricted areas, you'll find the restored habitat of the rare South American **bank swallow.** To see some dare-devil human swallow-imitation, the **observation deck,** near the main entrance, provides a birds-eye view of hang gliders. If you feel inspired, **Pacific Tandem Gliders** offers tandem flights, allowing first-timers a 20min. taste of the flying fix.

STERN GROVE

The opening of the Trocadero Hotel in 1892 brought excitement and frolicking to Stern Grove. When Prohibition closed the hotel, architect William Gladstone Merchant kept entertainment alive, creating a playground and open-air concert locale. The **Trocadero** still stands, remodeled but with original pieces intact. Adjacent **Pine Lake Park** offers beautiful hiking under minty-scented eucalyptus trees, as well as lawn bowling and croquet courts, putting greens, tennis courts, horseshoe pits, a playground, and barbecue pits.

■ AMPHITHEATER

⊠ *At 19th Ave. and Sloat Blvd. ☎ 252-6252; www.sterngrove.com. Free concerts from mid-June to mid-Aug.*

Stern Grove's main attraction is its natural amphitheater. The tall eucalyptus trees on one side of the grove create a natural soundboard, resulting in astonishing outdoor acoustics. A little landscaping and some support from Mrs. Stern have made Stern Grove the venue for a summer-long **concert series.** Every Sunday at 2pm, families, pierced people, and Banana Republic come together for the free concerts. The music spans the globe in composition and style. Common performers include the San Francisco Ballet, and other symphony, jazz, Spanish, and opera ensembles. Performers are generally well-known, so don't miss out, and arrive early to claim a spot.

IN THE BAY

■ ALCATRAZ

⊠ *ISLAND QUICKFIND: **Discover,** p. 21; **Contact,** ☎ 556-0560; www.nps.gov/alcatraz; **Transportation,** p. 21.*

see map p. 336

Mention Alcatraz, and most people think of hardened criminals and daring escapes. In its 29 years as a maximum-security federal penitentiary, Alcatraz did encounter a menacing cast of characters: Al "Scarface" Capone, George "Machine Gun" Kelly, and Robert "The Birdman" Stroud, among others. There were 14 separate escape attempts—some desperate, defiant bolts for freedom, others carefully calculated and innovative. On the Rock, the award-winning cell-house audio tour takes you back to the infamous days of Alcatraz. Listen to the screaming gulls and booming foghorn, and watch the palm trees blowing in the wind outside. From the dining-room window view the glittering hubbub of San Francisco life, and experience some of the isolation that plagued the prison's inmates. But there is more to the history of Alcatraz than gangsters and their antics. A **Park Ranger guided tour** can take you around the island, and through its 200 years of occupation: from a hunting and fishing ground for Native Americans, to a Civil War defensive outpost, to a military prison, a federal prison, and finally a birthplace of the movement for Native American civil rights. Now part of the **Golden Gate National Recreation Area,** Alcatraz is home to diverse plants and birdlife. The Agave Trail footpath lets you explore these habitats (open Sept.-Jan.). For general orientation, the dockside theater gives a 13min. video of the Rock's history and resources. Next door is the bookstore, offering videos, audiotapes, books, and gifts to round out the Alcatraz experience. Check the website for occasional book-signings by former prisoners, guards, and residents.

ANGEL ISLAND

⊠ *ISLAND QUICKFIND: **Discover,** p. 21; **Contact,** www.angelisland.org;*

⊠ Camp Info, *Reservations ☎ 800-444-7275; www.park-net.com. 7-night max. stay. Max. 8 people per campsite. Check-in 2pm. Check-out noon. $7 per night ❷. **Visitor Center,** ☎ 435-3522. Open Apr.-Oct. 10am-5pm. **Bike Rental,** near the docks at Ayala Cove. $10 per hr.; $30 per day. Tandems $15 per hr.; $50 per day. Child trailers $5 per hr.; $15 per day. Helmets free with rental. Open M-F 10am-3pm, Sa-Su 10am-4pm. MC/V.*

Picturesque **Angel Island State Park** sits in the middle of San Francisco Bay. A 20min. ferry ride from San Francisco or Marin brings you to rolling hills, biking and hiking trails, and sprawling picnic grounds. The island is a heavenly escape from the bustle of the city, except for those sunny weekends when all of San Francisco shows up. In addition to great views, the island harbors some rich history. For over 2,000 years, Coastal Miwok tribes native to Marin County paddled here to hunt and fish. Spaniard Juan Manuel de Ayala "discovered" the island and gave his name to the sheltered cove he established as a harbor. The Mexicans used Angel Island to rear cattle until 1859, when it was taken over by the US Army. The forts left by the Army have housed a Civil War encampment, a Spanish-American War quarantine station, a missile site, and an immigration station. From 1910 to 1940, Angel Island served as a holding site for immigrants, mostly Chinese. During WWII, the station was used as a POW camp.

Public grills that dot the lawn in front of the **Visitor Center** at Ayala Cove. On weekends and summer weekdays, this area fills up with families; but if the screeching of small children is precisely what you're trying to escape, serenity is only a hike away. Just behind the picnic grounds, the Visitor Center has exhibits and free 20min. orientation videos about the history and activities of the island. Adjacent to the center, the **Park Ranger Station** offers tours, including of the Immigration Station, Camp Reynolds, and Fort McDowell. For a leisurely island circuit, the one hour **Tram Tour** (p. 20) hits all major historic sites and provides some decent views. With a bit of legwork, the bike and hike trails allow some escape from the masses and reward with stunning panoramas. **Bikes** can be brought on the ferry or rented near the docks at Ayala Cove. Bikers are allowed only on the perimeter road and the steeper fire road. The perimeter road balances exhausting uphills with exhilarating downhills. Hikers can choose several trails to the 781 ft. summit of Mt. Livermore. If the exertion leaves you famished, a **dock-side cafe** serves coffee, soft drinks, alcohol, snacks ($3-4), sandwiches, and ice cream ($2-3). Maps at the gift shop are available for $1.

If a daytrip isn't enough, you can **camp** at one of the nine eco-friendly hike-in sites. All sites have running water, pit toilets, BBQ, table, and food-lockers. No wood fires allowed; bring charcoal or a stove.

food by neighborhood:

Food & Drink

Fine dining is here for the taking. San Francisco's diverse, multicultural population has infused local cuisine with tastes and trends taken from Chinese, Mexican, Indian, Italian, Vietnamese, French, and Peruvian cuisine (to mention only a few). Cheap and abundant holes-in-the-wall serve burritos or dim sum as satisfying and delicious as those produced in the most upscale kitchens. Vegetarians will never be stuck eating the garnish off the plates of meat-eating friends; even burger joints almost always have a "garden" option, because on the West Coast, vegetarianism stopped being a "fad" 30 years ago. Fresh, local, organic ingredients make for delicious dishes, and California's fertile valleys keep up the supply year-round—even exotic fruits and vegetables thrive in the mild weather. To accompany your meal, the Napa and Sonoma Valleys churn out wines that compete with those of Europe, and local microbrews are carried alongside the bigger names in almost all bars and cafes. Whatever your craving, some San Francisco restaurant is waiting to serve you. Visitors often associate ethnic foods with specific neighborhoods but are often pleasantly surprised to realize that great sushi can be found easily in the Mission or great tapas in Japantown. For those who occasionally like to cook for themselves, neighborhood grocery markets are highlighted in the introduction to each neighborhood in the **Food** section. Check out our **Nightlife** chapter too, since many cafes and bars serve good eats as well.

FOOD BY TYPE

AFRICAN
Axum Cafe (131)	LH ❶
Cafe Ethiopia (136)	MI ❷
Bissap Baobab (136)	MI ❷

AMERICAN& DINERS
▨ Pat's Café (116)	FW ❶
Perry's (118)	MA ❸
▨ Home Plate (117)	MA ❷
Pluto's (117)	MA ❶
Bob's Broiler Restuarant (122)	NH ❶
Lori's Diner (123)	US ❶
Moishe's Pippic (126)	HV ❶
Café Bosse (128)	SoMa ❶
▨ Welcome Home (132)	CA ❸
Orphan Andy's (133)	CA ❷
Miss Millie's (134)	NV ❷
Cliff House (137)	RI ❸

BAKERIES
Italian French Baking Co. (119)	NB ❶
▨ Golden Gate Bakery (120)	CH ❶
Schubert's Bakery (139)	RI ❶
▨ Arizmendi Bakery (140)	SU ❶
Sheng Hea Bakery and Cafe (140)	SU ❶
Ambrosia Bakery (141)	LM ❶

BREAKFAST
Mama's (119)	NB ❷
▨ Café Bean (123)	US ❶
▨ Moonlight Café (137)	BH ❶
Kate's Kitchen (131)	LH ❶
Sweet Inspiration (132)	CA ❷
Bagdad Cafe (133)	CA ❷
▨ Savor (133)	NV ❷

BRUNCH
▨ Liberty Café (137)	BH ❷
▨ Dottie's True Blue Café (122)	US ❶
Equinox (124)	FDE ❺
Max's Opera Café (125)	CC ❸
Momi Toby's Revolution Café, Art (126)	HV ❶
▨ Squat and Gobble (131)	UH ❶
Chatz (138)	PO ❶
Trio Café (129)	PH ❷

BURGERS
Barney's Gourmet Hamburgers (134)	NV ❶
Sparky's (133)	CA ❷

CAFES, TEA & COFFEE
▨ It's Tops Coffee Shop (126)	NV ❶
▨ Lovejoy's Antiques & Tea Shop	NV ❷
Caffe Espresso (123)	US ❶
The Castro Cheesery (133)	CA ❶
Cafe XO (135)	NV ❶
Progressive Grounds Coffee H. (137)	BH ❶

CALIFORNIA CUISINE
Bell Tower (121)	NH ❷
▨ Cafe Venue (124)	FDE ❷
▨ California Culinary Academy (127)	TE ❺
foreign cinema (135)	MI ❻
Q (139)	RI ❷
▨ Home (132)	CA ❸

CHINESE
▨ Brandy Ho's (119)	NB ❷
▨ Chef Jia (120)	CH ❶
Hing Lung (120)	CH ❶
Yong Kee (121)	CH ❶
City View Restaurant (120)	CH ❷
Kay Cheung's Restaurant (120)	CH ❶
▨ House of Nanking (120)	CH ❷
▨ Eliza's (138)	PO ❶
Lee Hou Restaurant (139)	RI ❶
Taiwan Restaurant (139)	RI ❷
Taipei Restaurant (141)	LM ❷

DESSERT
La Nouvelle Patisserie (117)	MA ❶
Café Gelato Classico (119)	NB ❶
Stella Pasticceria e Caffé (119)	NB ❶
Citizen Cake (126)	HV ❸
Tango Gelato (129)	PH ❶
Swensen's (122)	RH ❶
Isabella's Ice Cream (134)	NV ❶
Bombay Ice Creamery (135)	MI ❶
Mitchell's Ice Cream (135)	MI ❶

FRENCH AND CREPERIES
Café Bastille (124)	FDE ❹
Café Claude (124)	FDE ❷
▨ Peasant Pies (133)	NV ❶
Frijtz (126)	HV ❶
The Butler and the Chef Cafe (128)	SoMa ❶
Ti Couz (136)	MI ❷
Crepevine (140)	SU ❷
Crepes A-Go-Go (118)	MA ❶
The Crêpe House (121)	NH ❸
Patisserie Café (128)	SoMa ❷
Genki Crepes & Mini Mart (139)	RI ❶

BH bernal heights **CA** castro **CC** civic center **CH** chinatown **FDE** financial district & the embarcadero **FW** fisherman's wharf **HV** hayes valley **LH** lower haight-ashbury **LM** lake merced, stern grove, & sf state **MA** marina, fort mason, & cow hollow **MI** mission **NB** north beach **NH** nob hill **JT** japantown **NV** noe valley **PH** pacific heights **RH** russian hlll **PO** potrero hill **RI** richmond **SoMa** south of market **SU** sunset **TE** tenderloin **UH** upper haight-ashbury **US** union square

GERMAN
Suppenkuche (126)   HV ❸

GROCERY STORE/MEAT MARKET
North Point Centre Safeway (116)   FW
Cost Plus World Market (116)   FW
Marina Safeway (117)   MA
Real Food Company (117)   MA
Napoli Market (118)   NB
Rossi Supermarket (118)   NB
Search Light Market (121)   RH
Real Food Company (121)   RH
Cala Foods (121)   NH
McAllister's Market and Deli (127)   TE
Rainbow Grovery (127)   SoMa
Trader Joe's (127)   SoMa
Mayflower Market (129)   PH
Mollie Stone's (129)   PH
Super Mira Japanese Foods (129)   JT
Haight Street Market (130)   UH
Real Food Company (133)   NV
24th St. Cheese Co. (133)   NV
The Good Life Grocery (136)   BH
Klein's Deli (137)   PO
The Good Life Grocery (137)   PO
New May Wah Supermarket (139)   RI
Gastronom Deli and Bakery (139)   RI ❶

HAWAIIAN
Kaleo Cafe (140)   SU ❶

INDIAN AND PAKISTANI
Tandoori Mahal (120)   CH ❸
Mela Tandoori (123)   US ❷
🔲 Taj Mahal (127)   TE ❶

INDONESIAN
Indonesia Restaurant (123)   US ❷

ITALIAN
🔲 L'Osteria del Forno (119)   NB ❷
The Stinking Rose (119)   NB ❹
ASodini's Trattoria (119)   NB ❹
🔲 Mario's Bohemian Cigar, Café (119)   NB ❷
Steps of Rome (119)   NB ❸
Pane e Vino (118)   MA ❹
Caffé Centro (128)   SoMa ❷
Vino e Cucina Trattoria (128)   SoMa ❷
Pasta Pomodoro (132)   CA ❷
Caffe Ponte Vecchio (136)   MI ❷
Café Abo (135) l   MI❶
Aperto (138)   PO ❸

JAPANESE
Enoshima Sushi and Teriyaki (117)   MA ❶

Sanraku (123)   US ❷
Sushigroove (121)   RH ❶
Mifune (130)   JT ❷
🔲 Isobune (129)   JT ❶
On The Bridge (130)   JT ❷
Juban (130)   JT ❸
Umeko (130)   JT ❹
Deep Sushi (134)   NV ❷
We Be Sushi (136)   MI ❶
Moki's (137)   BH ❶
Kitaro (139)   RI ❷
Yum Yum Fish (141)   SU ❷
Hotei (140)   SU ❷

KOREAN
Hahn's Hibachi (134)   NV ❶

MEDITERRANEAN
Café Mediterraneo (124)   FDE ❷
Zuni (126)   HV ❹
La Méditerranée (129)   PH ❷
🔲 La Mediterranee (132)   CA ❷

MEXICAN
🔲 La Canasta (117)   MA ❶
🔲 Rico's (121)   RH ❶
Sotano Grill (123)   US ❶
Taqueria Castillo (127)   TE ❶
Sweet Heat (131)   UH ❶
🔲 Taqueria El Farolito (135)   MI ❶
Balompié (136)   MI ❶
Pancho Villa Taqueria (136)   MI ❶

MIDDLE EASTERN
Krivaar Café (124)   FDE ❶
Blue Front Café (131)   UH ❶
Amira (136)   MI ❷
Yumma's Mediterranean Grill (140)   SU ❶

PAN-ASIAN
Zao (118)   MA ❷
Ponzu (123)   US ❸
Citrus Club (131)   UH ❶
🔲 Nirvana (132)   CA ❷

PIZZA
🔲 Pizza Orgasmica (115)   MA ❶
Pizza Inferno (129)   PH ❷
Extreme Pizza (129)   SoMa ❶
Marcello's (133)   CA ❶
Goat Hill Pizza (126)   PH ❶

SANDWICHES
🔲 Marina Submarine (117)   MA ❶
The Grove (117)   MA ❶

BH bernal heights **CA** castro **CC** civic center **CH** chinatown **FDE** financial district & the embarcadero **FW** fisherman's wharf **HV** hayes valley **LH** lower haight-ashbury **LM** lake merced, stern grove, & sf state **MA** marina, fort mason, & cow hollow **MI** mission **NB** north beach **NH** nob hill **JT** japantown **NV** noe valley **PH** pacific heights **RH** russian hlll **PO** potrero hill **RI** richmond **SoMa** south of market **SU** sunset **TE** tenderloin **UH** upper haight-ashbury **US** union square

BH bernal heights CA castro CC civic center CH chinatown FDE financial district & the embarcadero FW fisherman's wharf HV hayes valley LH lower haight-ashbury LM lake merced, stern grove, & sf state MA marina, fort mason, & cow hollow MI mission NB north beach NH nob hill NI nihonmachi (japantown) NV noe valley PH pacific heights RH russian hill RI richmond SoMa south of market SU sunset TE tenderloin UH upper haight-ashbury US union square

FISHERMAN'S WHARF

see map p. 338

🔼 *NEIGHBORHOOD QUICKFIND:* ***Discover***, *p. 7;* ***Sights***, *p. 65.*

Pier 39 and Fisherman's Wharf are overflowing with opportunities to refuel, but because they are tourist central, most eateries are fairly expensive for average food. The true budget traveler may choose to pick up a picnic from the **North Point Centre Safeway**, 350 Bay St. (☎781-4374. Open daily 6am-midnight), and check out the cheap Ghirardelli bars and huge wine selection ($5-15) at **Cost Plus World Market**, 2552 Taylor St. (☎928-6200. Open M-Sa 10am-9pm, Su 10am-8pm). For those who can resist chowder and sourdough bread bowls, walking a few blocks inland offers appetizing options that are a bit cheaper.

▨ **Pat's Café**, 2330 Taylor St. (☎776-8735), between Chestnut and Francisco St. One of a string of breakfast joints, Pat's stands out from the crowd, not just because of its bright yellow building, but also for its huge, delicious, home-cooked portions. Burgers, sandwiches, and big breakfast plates ($4-7). Open daily 7:30am-2pm. No credit cards. ❶

McCormick and Kuleto's, 900 North Point St. (☎929-1730), in Ghirardelli Sq. Can't leave the wharf without trying crabcakes or clam chowder, but skeptical about the vendors on the piers? This stylish seafood restaurant offers a comprehensive menu and a spectacular view of Aquatic Park. Most entrees $10-25, brick-oven pizzas $7.50-10.50. Open daily 11:30am-11pm. AmEx/D/MC/V. ❸

Bob's Sushi, 393 Bay St. (☎693-9218), at Mason St. Just three blocks inland from the wharf, Bob's offers sushi at moderate prices (from $3). Dinner combos: 2 entrees for $10.95, or 3 for $12.95. Open daily 11am-2:30pm and 5-10pm. AmEx/D/MC/V. ❷

MARINA, FORT MASON & COW HOLLOW

🔳 *NEIGHBORHOOD QUICKFIND:* **Discover,** *p. 7;* **Sights,** *p. 68;* **Night-life,** *p. 144;* **Accommodations,** *p. 191.*

see map p. 338

The **Real Food Company,** 3060 Fillmore St., on the corner of Filbert St. Sample sweet juices and nibble on nuts at this organically-oriented grocery store. The fruit is fresher and the prices are right. (☎567-6900. Open daily 8am-9pm. MC/V). **Marina Safeway,** 15 Marina Blvd., between Laguna and Buchanan St., is legendary as a spot to pick up more than just groceries. (☎563-4946. Open 24hr. AmEx/D/MC/V).

🔳 **Marina Submarine,** 2299 Union St. (☎921-3990), at Steiner St. in **Cow Hollow.** Often a long (but worthwhile) wait for superlative subs that satisfy in several sizes ($4-8). The sandwich-maker is a delightful spectacle, and your sub will taste better after you've viewed its creation. The art of the avocado is perfected at this unassuming spot (try the avocado and sprouts). Open M-F 10am-6:30pm, Sa 11am-4:30pm, Su 11am-3:30pm. No credit cards. ❶

🔳 **La Canasta,** 3006 Buchanan St. (☎474-2627), near Union St. in **Cow Hollow.** Hard-working cooks at this tiny kitchen give you their best tacos, burritos, and ensaladas. The Mexican food is fresh and cooked in healthy oils. Soups fashioned on the spot. All food is take-out only. Almost everything on the menu under $5. Open daily 11am-10pm. AmEx/D/MC/V. ❶

🔳 **Home Plate,** 2774 Lombard St. (☎922-4663), off Pierce St. in the **Marina.** Hard-to-beat, hearty breakfast, brunch, and lunch (most items under $8). Friendly service and scones with homemade strawberry-apple jam with every meal. Don't be turned off by the weak lighting or out-of-the-way location. This place is a neighborhood gem. Open M-Su 7am-4pm. MC/V. ❷

Greens, Bldg. A (☎771-6222), in **Fort Mason.** A somewhat expensive establishment, Greens provides the Fort Mason area with a gourmet restaurant and an excellent view of the water. Vegetables and fish only, cooked into delicious dishes such as Sri Lankan Curry ($18.75), Eggplant Gratin, and Cannellini Bean Soup ($5). **Greens-to-go counter** crowded at lunch. Open lunch Tu-Sa noon-2:30pm; afternoon menu 2:30pm; Su brunch 10:30am-2pm; dinner M-Sa 5:30-9pm; Greens-to-go M-Th 8am-8pm, F-Sa 8am-5pm, Su 9am-4pm. D/MC/V. ❸

The Grove, 2250 Chestnut St. (☎474-4843), at Avilla St. in **Fort Mason.** Wide and comfortable seating adds to the laid-back atmosphere of The Grove, a restaurant serving everything from Apple and Gorgonzola Toast ($4.75) to the classic Reuben ($8.00). Full espresso and coffee bar as well as wireless Internet combined with unfinished wooden seats give The Grove an unusual ambience. Open M-F 7am-11pm, Sa-Su 8am-11pm. AmEx/D/MC/V. ❶

La Nouvelle Patisserie, 2184 Union St. (☎ 931-7655), at Fillmore in **Cow Hollow.** This pastry boutique flaunts tastefully artistic desserts that meet the tongue's expectations. Sandwiches and sweets make a pricey meal, but one petite treat is a sound investment. Try the Matigny or Napoleon (all $2-5). Open M-Th 7am-8pm, F-Sa 7am-11pm. AmEx/D/MC/V. ❶

Enoshima Sushi and Teriyaki, 2280 Chestnut St. (☎563-0162), at Scott St. in the **Marina.** Great service and a wide variety of sushi. Lunch box special (2-item combo plus miso soup and rice $5.95; M-F 11am-2:30pm). Eat there or get take-out and wander to the water for a stunning view. Open M-Th 11:30am-10:30pm, F-Sa 11:30am-10:30pm. AmEx/D/MC/V. ❶

Pluto's, 3258 Scott St. (☎775-8867), off Chestnut St. in the **Marina.** Pluto's specializes in food done your way—pick your own ingredients and pay low prices for fresh fast food. Specializes in (large) salads, but also offers meats and poultry, veggies, and spuds (all $3-6). Open M-F 11am-10pm, Sa-Su 9:30am-10pm. MC/V. ❶

Pizza Orgasmica, 3157 Fillmore St. (☎931-5300), at Greenwich St. in **Cow Hollow.** "We never fake it," says the sign. Pizzas are not quite as exciting as their namesake positions ("menage a trois" and "doggy style"), but bring as much of a smile as more traditional positions and pizzas do. Don't miss the daily all-you-can-eat special ($5.50; 11am-4pm). Slices $2-3.50, pies $10-23. Open Su-W 11am-midnight, Th-Sa 11am-2:30am. AmEx/D/MC/V. ❶

NO WORK ALL PLAY

Feeling Crabby?

SF is known for its subversive art and cultural festivals; the month of February, though, is reserved for the Dungeness Crab. The month-long **San Francisco Crab Festival** (www.sfvisitor.org/crab) sprawls from Fisherman's Wharf to Union Square during the peak of the crab season. Each year, over two million pounds of crabmeat are imported from the Central California Fishery.

The festivities include the Wine & Spirits Focus, a weekend in which chefs from elite spots such as Hawthorne Lane, Rubicon, and Greens host tastings of their crab delicacies and choice wines. The Crab & Wine Marketplace offers tastings, demonstrations, and activities for crustacean connoisseurs. Throughout February, local businesses on the Wharf offer great crab deals and specials.

Volunteers are often welcomed for setup, maintenance, and information staffing. Contact the San Francisco Convention & Visitors Bureau (☎283-0106) for more information. In 2004, San Francisco will again **salute the crab** for the month of February, this time with a classic car show in a supporting role. The Wine & Spirits Focus and the classic car show will take place Feb. 13-6 at Pier 45 from 9am-6pm. The Crab & Wine Marketplace will take place Feb. 28-29 at Fort Mason from 11am-6pm.

Pano e Vino, 3011 Steiner St., (☎346-2111), off Union St. in **Cow Hollow.** Small, neighborhood trattoria serving classic Italian cuisine. Watch as the chef prepares your pasta ($10-16) or entree ($18-24). Try the *stuffes branzino* (stuffed fish). A good option for bit of a splurge. Open M-Th 11:30am-2:30pm and 5-10pm, F-Sa 11:30am-10:30pm, Su 5-9:30pm. AmEx/MC/V. ❹

Crepes A-Go-Go, 2165 Union St., (☎928-1919), off of Fillmore St. in **Cow Hollow.** Great crepes, sweet or savory, made before your eyes ($2.50-6). Counter service and small seating area. Open M-Th 8am-10pm, F-Sa 8am-midnight, Su 8am-9pm. MC/V. ❶

Zao, 2031 Chestnut St. (☎928-3088), between Steiner and Fillmore St. in the **Marina.** "The way of the noodle is long and narrow." Ponder this and other cryptic thoughts over the noodle dishes—many vegetarian—that hail from all over the Asian world (about $7-9). Finish off each meal with a Mystic Fish Fortune. Su-Th 11am-10pm, F-Sa 11am-11pm. MC/V. ❶

Perry's, 1944 Union St. (☎922-9022), between Buchanan and Laguna St. in **Cow Hollow.** This classic NY-style saloon puts more emphasis on dining than on drinking. Popular with different age groups, but generally frequented by an older, tamer crowd. Customers especially praise the cheeseburgers (about $10; sandwiches from $9-13; entrees $14-22). Open for breakfast. Kitchen closes 2hr. before bar. Open Su-F 9am-midnight, Sa 9am-1am. AmEx/D/MC/V. ❸

NORTH BEACH

🇫 *NEIGHBORHOOD QUICKFIND:* **Discover,** *p. 8;* **Sights,** *p. 70;* **Nightlife,** *p. 144;* **Accommodations,** *p. 193.*

see map p. 339

In North Beach, tourism and California cuisine merged with the taste of Little Italy, yielding unique, *delizioso* tastes that blend old and new. For Italian foods, try **Napoli Market,** 1756 Stockton Ave., between Greenwich and Filbert St. (☎362-5655. Open M-F 8:30am-9:30pm, Su 8am-9pm. AmEx/D/MC/V). Find large-scale grocery shopping at **Rossi Supermarket,** 627 Vallejo St., near Columbus Ave. (☎986-1068. Open M-Th 8am-9pm, F-Sa 8am-10pm, Su 8am-8pm. AmEx/D/MC/V). The **Nature Stop,** 1336 Grant Ave., between Green and Vallejo St., offers a vegetarian deli (sandwiches $3.50-5), smoothies ($2.50-4), and extensive dried fruit and nuts, as well as basic groceries. (☎398-3810. Open M-F 9am-9pm, Sa-Su 10am-9pm. AmEx/D/MC/V).

L'Osteria del Forno, 519 Columbus Ave. (☎982-1124), between Green and Union St. Acclaimed Italian roasted and cold foods, plus homemade breads. The tiny dining room is crowded but romantic. Terrific thin-crust pizzas (slices $2.50-3.75, whole pizzas $10-17) and focaccia sandwiches ($5-6.50) abound. Salads and antipasti ($4.50-8.50) and entrees ($7-15). Open Su-M and W-Th 11:30am-10pm, F-Sa 11:30am-10:30pm. No credit cards. ❷

Mario's Bohemian Cigar Store Cafe, 566 Columbus Ave. (☎362-0536), at Union St. on the corner of Washington Sq. The Beats frequented this laid-back cafe; these days, locals drop by to have coffee ($1.25-3.25) and drinks (wine from $4, beer from $3). A great place to hang out and grab some first-rate grub (hot focaccia sandwiches $4.25-8; pizza $7-9; pasta $8.25). Open M-Th and Su 10am-11pm, F-Sa 10am-midnight. MC/V. ❷

Brandy Ho's Hunan Food, 217 Columbus Ave. (☎788-7527; www.brandy-hoshunan.com), at Pacific St. Heat-seeking diners lock on target, where the lines blur between Chinatown and North Beach. This Hunan food is *spicy*. Heed the chef's suggestions, like the Three Delicacies (toss-fried scallops and shrimp; $11.50), and feast in the classy dining room. Average meal $10-11. Lunch specials $5-6 (M-F 11:30am-3pm). Open M-Th and Su 11:30am-11pm, F-Sa 11:30am-midnight. AmEx/D/MC/V. ❷

Sodini's Trattoria, 510 Green St. (☎291-0499), at Grant Ave. In the heart of North Beach, Sodini's has been serving authentic homestyle Italian food since 1906. Pasta $10-15; pizzas $10.50-23.50; entrees $15-20. Bar open daily 5-11pm. Open daily 5-10pm. MC/V. ❹

Mama's, 1701 Stockton St. (☎362-6421), at Filbert St. on the corner of Washington Sq. Mama's yummy breakfast is served all day (omelettes $6-10, french toast $6.50-9), so try to avoid the long weekend brunch lines. Sandwiches ($7-9), salads ($5-9), and other vegetarian-friendly lunch dishes served 11:30am-3pm. Open Tu-Su 8am-3pm. No credit cards. ❷

Gelato Classico, 576 Union St. (☎391-6667), near Stockton St. Ice cream just can't compete with smooth, creamy gelato. Try sweet spumoni or classic tiramisu, or coppimista. Small $2.75; medium $3.50; large $4.25. Open daily noon-10pm. No credit cards. ❶

North Beach Pizza, 1499 Grant St. (☎433-2444; www.northbeachpizza.com), at Union St. Heralded as San Francisco's best pizza by *SF Weekly*. Dark red booths make for a good old-fashioned pizza parlor experience. Small pizzas from $8.60; medium from $10.95; large from $20.95. Lunch special daily 11am-4pm; individual 8-in. for $3.95. Slices $2-3 after 5pm. Take-out and free delivery. Open M-Th and Su 11am-1am, F-Sa 11am-3am. AmEx/D/MC/V. Additional location: 1310 Grant St. near Vallejo St. ❷

Steps of Rome, 348 Columbus Ave. (☎397-0435), between Vallejo St. and Broadway. Oh-so-suave waiters expertly flirt for tips in this busy, brightly painted cafe. Big menu with lots of vegetarian options. Focaccia sandwiches $5-7; antipasto appetizers $7-10; pasta $7-10; entrees $12-16. Italian beers $4. Sidewalk seating available. 21+ after 6pm. Open M-Th and Su 9am-2am, F-Sa 9am-3am. No credit cards. ❸

The Stinking Rose, 325 Columbus Ave. (☎781-7673), between Vallejo and Broadway. The world's longest garlic braid hangs in this restaurant, which boasts "We season our garlic with food." "Vampire" (garlic-free) fare available, but what's the point? Appetizers $5-10; pastas $10-15; entrees $14-22; garlic ice cream $4. Open daily 11am-11pm. AmEx/D/MC/V. ❹

Italian French Baking Co., 1501 Grant Ave. (☎421-3796), at Union St. Provides nearly every restaurant in the area (as well as hungry SF civilians) with baked goods of all kinds, including breads, baguettes, and biscotti ($1-6). Oversized coconut macaroons for just $1. Although you'd never guess it from the innocent facade, the basement was the chosen locale for the murder scene in *Basic Instinct* and scenes from several mobster movies. Open M-F and Su 6am-6pm, Sa 6am-7pm. No credit cards. ❶

Stella Pasticceria e Caffé, 446 Columbus Ave. (☎986-2914), between Green and Vallejo St. This family-run establishment serves traditional Italian pastries ($3-6) and coffee ($1.40-2.70). Tip: the sacripantina is their specialty. *Deliziosa!* Open M-W 7:30am-7pm, Th 7:30am-10pm, F-Sa 7:30am-midnight, Su 8:30am-6pm. AmEx/D/MC/V. ❶

119

Have Sum Dim Sum

Dim Sum ("little bits of the heart") are the foods traditionally eaten at Cantonese or Southern Chinese *yum cha* ("drink tea") eateries. This heavenly dining experience involves various small dishes eaten in the morning or early afternoon, typically on Sundays, in mass quantities.

Waiters and waitresses push carts laden with all sorts of Chinese finger foods (from dumplings to chicken feet). Dumplings and buns are steamed; rolls and squares are deep fried. When they stop at your table, point to whatever looks good (or use the handy mini-menu below). The waiter will stamp a card to charge you by dish.

Cha Siu Bao: Steamed BBQ pork buns.

Haar Gao: Steamed shrimp dumplings.

Dan Taat: Tiny tart shells filled with sweet egg custard.

Siu Mai: Shrimp and pork in a fancy dumpling "basket."

Walteep: The classic steamed pork dumplings.

Dou Sha Bao: Steamed rolls filled with sweet red bean paste.

Loh Bak Goh: Mashed turnip patty. Don't knock it 'til you've tried it.

Fun Gwor: Chicken and mushroom dumplings.

CHINATOWN

⑦ NEIGHBORHOOD QUICKFIND: **Discover,** p. 9; **Sights,** p. 71; **Nightlife,** p. 146; **Accommodations,** p. 193.

see map p. 339

House of Nanking, 919 Kearny St. (☎421-1429), near Columbus Ave. Ample, high-quality portions conspicuously offset a low-key setting and a low-key check in this famous Chinatown institution. Most entrees under $8. Many regulars trust their server to select their meal, usually resulting in a three-course feast of varied flavors and styles for a reasonable price. Open M-F 11am-10pm, Sa noon-10pm, Su noon-9:30pm. MC/V. ❷

Golden Gate Bakery, 1029 Grant Ave. (☎781-2627). This tiny bakery's moon cakes, noodle puffs, and vanilla cream buns (all $.75-1.50) draw long lines of tourists and locals. Open daily 8am-8pm. No credit cards. ❶

Chef Jia, 925 Kearny St. (☎398-1626), at Pacific St. Just next door to Nanking, Chef Jia's espouses a similar principle: lots of good, cheap food in a small, informal space. Yummy lunch specials (all under $5) served 11:30am-4pm (try the spicy string beans with yams) and evening rice plate specials from 4-10pm (all $4.80). Entrees $6-7. Open daily 11:30am-10pm. No credit cards. ❶

City View Restaurant, 662 Commercial St. (☎398-2838), between Kearny and Montgomery St. City View is where Chinatown entrees meet Financial District prices. More expensive than average dim sum ($2.30-4.20 a plate), but classier too. Open M-F 11am-2:30pm, Sa-Su 10am-2:30pm. AmEx/MC/V. ❷

Tandoori Mahal, 941 Kearny St. (☎951-0505), at Columbus Ave. This quiet South Asian restaurant in an area dominated by oft-crowded East Asian eateries. A variety of veggie options (mushroom *mattar* $8) in a tasteful environment. All-you-can-eat lunch buffet $8 (M-F 11:30am-2:30pm). Entrees $8-13. Open M-F 11:30am-2:30pm and 5-10:30pm, Sa 12:15-11:30pm, Su 12:15-10:30pm. AmEx/D/MC/V. ❸

Hing Lung, 674 Broadway (☎398-8838), between Grant Ave. and Stockton St. Famous for its steamed rice porridge ($2.50), wonton soup, and great specials ($2 meals M-F 3pm-6pm and Th-Sa 10pm-1am), this larger-than-average eatery has a reputation for being packed with locals all day. Entrees $3-6. Open daily 8am-1am. MC/V. ❶

Kay Cheung's Restaurant, 615 Jackson St. (☎989-6838), at Kearny St. Patrons line up on weekends to sample some of the best dumplings

Chinatown has to offer. The shrimp dumplings are a must-eat. Tasty seafood entrees straight from the tank ($4-7.50). Dim sum ($2.15 per plate) served 9am-2pm. Open daily 9:30am-9pm. MC/V. ❶

Yong Kee, 732 Jackson St. (☎986-3759), at Ross Alley. A small space and caravan of carts make this a perfect place to take out (no tables). Sweet egg tarts and other Chinese dessert treats. Generous portions ($0.50-2 per plate) but little-to-no English. Just point and feast. Open daily 7am-6pm. No credit cards. ❶

NOB HILL & RUSSIAN HILL

🚩 *NEIGHBORHOOD QUICKFIND: **Discover**, p. 9; **Sights**, p. 73; **Nightlife**, p. 147; **Accommodations**, p. 194.*

see map p. 342

Your stomach will thank you for braving the steep hills of this snug residential area. **Polk St.** and **Hyde St.** teem with small neighborhood eateries that satisfy all cravings and price brackets, from pizza to pâté. Numerous markets occupy the corners not conquered by restaurants. For corner-market shopping, visit **Search Light Market,** 1964 Hyde St., at Union St. in Russian Hill (☎673-1010. Open M-F 7am-10pm, Sa-Su 8am-10pm. AmEx/D/MC/V), or its organically-grown equivalent, **Real Food Company,** 2140 Polk St., between Broadway and Vallejo St. in Russian Hill. (☎673-7420. Open daily 9am-9pm.) You can also find major chain **Cala Foods** at California and Hyde St. in Nob Hill. (☎776-3650. Open 24 hr. AmEx/D/MC/V).

🌆 **Rico's,** 943 Columbus Ave. (☎928-5404), between Taylor and Lombard St. in **Russian Hill.** An unpretentious, cafeteria-style restaurant that proves that even in San Francisco, there is no need to pay an arm and a leg for wharf-size snacks. Choose from over a dozen enormous specialty burritos ($3.50-6), sandwiches ($5.50), and quesadillas ($7). Open daily 10am-10pm. AmEx/MC/V. ❶

The Crêpe House, 1755 Polk St. (☎441-2421), at Washington St. in **Nob Hill.** Eggplant, chicken pesto, and nutella all find $5-7 lodging in this rustic coffeehouse-style establishment. Good selection of salads ($6-8) and sandwiches ($6.25) High-speed Internet access available ($10 per hr.). Open Su-Th 7:30am-9:30pm, F-Sa 7:30am-10:30pm. No credit cards. ❶

Zarzuela, 2000 Hyde St. (☎346-0800), at Union St. in **Russian Hill.** Authentic Spanish homestyle cooking with exceptional fish specialities, tapas ($6), and an upscale setting make the 20-30min. wait on the weekends and the climb up the hill worth it. Entrees $8-9 for small portions, $11-14 for large. Open Tu-Th 5:30-10pm, F-Sa 5:30-10:30pm. D/MC/V. ❷

Sushigroove, 1916 Hyde St. (☎440-1905), between Union and Green St. in **Russian Hill.** Only sushi-lovers need reserve. Without a full kitchen, this chic, inexpensive sushi-*sake* joint (most sushi and *maki* $3-7) serves up a lot of rolls (many vegetarian) but nothing that has seen the inside of an oven. Valet parking ($10) available on Polk St. Reservations highly recommended for weekend nights. Open Su-Th 6-10pm, F-Sa 6-10:30pm. AmEx/DC/MC/V. ❶

Bell Tower, 1900 Polk St. (☎567-9596), at Jackson St. in **Nob Hill.** A bright and casually upscale restaurant replete with classy window-side tables and carved wooden bar. A relaxed atmosphere, $6-8 appetizers that include choices like pistachio-crusted baked brie with pomegranate or classics like quesadillas, and $8-15 entrees prove that exploring Californian cuisine doesn't have to leave you starving. Vegetarian friendly. Sa-Su brunch 10:30am-2pm. Lunch served until 2pm, dinner 5:30pm-midnight. Open M-F 11am-2am. AmEx/MC/V. ❷

Lemongrass, 2348 Polk St. (☎346-1818 or 929-1183; www.lemongrasssf.com), between Green and Union St. in **Russian Hill.** Candlelight and coconut milk accent plentiful meat and tofu dishes ($6-8), where first-daters and families come for affordably upscale Thai. Open Su-Th 11am-10pm, F-Sa 11am-10:30pm. Reservations recommended F-Sa. AmEx/MC/V. ❶

Sourdough Bread

Fisherman

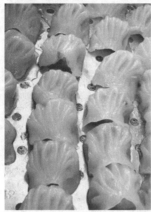
Dim Sum

Polker's American Cafe, 2226 Polk St. (☎885-1000), between Green and Vallejo St. in **Russian Hill.** Don't let the classy decor mislead you—Polker's is really just an upscale diner with solid, if slightly pricey breakfasts ($6-8) and famous "gourmet" hamburgers ($7). Breakfast served until 2pm. Open daily 8am-11pm. MC/V. ❶

The Golden Turtle, 2211 Van Ness Ave. (☎441-4419), at Vallejo St. in **Russian Hill.** Fabulous Vietnamese restaurant serves mind-blowing entrees ($10-15), like the "Look Luck" cubed filet mignon ($12), amid intricately carved walls. Ample options for "the vegetarian gourmet." Reservations recommended on weekends. Open Tu-Su 5-11pm. AmEx/D/MC/V. ❸

Bob's Broiler Restaurant, 1601 Polk St. (☎474-6161), at Sacramento St. in **Nob Hill.** Bob's diner has occupied this corner in Nob Hill for over 50 years, as have most of its loyal patrons. Many of them return day after day for the cheap all-day breakfasts (under $6) or the daily specials that move away from traditional diner food (steaks $12, chicken pasta $9). Open daily 7am-10pm. MC/V. ❶

Swensen's, 1909 Hyde St. (☎775-6818), at Union St. in **Russian Hill.** The original of over 200 Swensen's ice cream shops in the US, opened in 1948. Since then, the Swensen daughters held on to the first store until just a few years ago. All ice cream (except fat-free and sugar-free flavors) is made on site and their milkshakes ($3.25) and cones ($1.85) maintain that old-fashioned, rich taste. Open Su-Th noon-10pm, F-Sa noon-11pm. No credit cards. ❶

UNION SQUARE

see map p. 343

🔽 *NEIGHBORHOOD QUICKFIND:* ***Discover,*** *p. 10;* ***Sights,*** *p. 80;* ***Nightlife,*** *p. 148;* ***Accommodations,*** *p. 194.*

While not as ubiquitous as in nearby Chinatown or North Beach, satisfying, inexpensive hot food does exist in the primarily high-end Union Square, provided you're willing to move away from the main shopping thoroughfares to some of the quieter side streets.

🌂 **Dottie's True Blue Café,** 522 Jones St. (☎885-2767), between Geary and O'Farrell St. The French toast tastes so delicately rich because all bread is baked on site, all day long. Hearty portions, quirky variations like chicken-apple sausage, and the long list of specials (3 or 4 are always vegetarian) often inspire a long line extending outside during breakfast and lunch hours, so arrive early or be prepared to wait. Breakfast runs about $6 per entree and lunch runs about $7. Open Th-M 7:30am-3pm. D/MC/V. ❶

✍ **Café Bean,** 800 Sutter St. (☎923-9539). Upon entering Bianca and Peter's cozy Café Bean, you can immediately tell that it's a family-owned eatery. Family pictures, postcards, and drawings cover the tables and counters, providing viewing material as you wait for your meal. All-day breakfasts like steaming eggs and toast ($4) and Dutch pancakes ($4) or hearty lunch fare like huge barbecue turkey sandwiches ($6.50) make Café Bean attractive to tourists, business people, and wayward hipsters. Internet connection ($3 for 20 minutes). Open M-Sa 6am-7pm, Su 6am-5pm. MC/V. ❶

Caffe Espresso, 462 Powell St. (☎395-8585), near Bush St. This spacious cafe decorated with old fashioned French cabaret posters adds a touch of urbane, European charm to the corner of Powell and Bush St. At $7.25 for the express lunch (small salad, soup, and a half sandwich) or $6.50 for the fresh seafood chowder, Caffe Espresso is a perfect place to sit outside and sip espresso ($1.25) as you watch sloping cable cars amble up Powell St. Open Su-Th 6:30am-10pm, F-Sa 6:30am-10:30pm. MC/V. ❶

Mela Tandoori, 417 O'Farrell St. (☎447-4041), between Jones and Taylor St. Don't be misled by Mela's rather unassuming exterior. A traditional clay oven infuses barbecue meats with a delicious sweet spiciness as authentic as the vibrant wall murals and hand-crafted silver ceilings imported from India. Mood lighting, an indoor fountain, and naan-a-plenty transform chicken tandoori ($9) into an affordably romantic sample of the Indian subcontinent. Extensive vegetarian options ($5.95). Open M-Sa 11:30am-2:30pm and 5:30-10:30pm, Su 1-9:30pm. AmEx/D/MC. ❷

Sotano Grill, 550 Powell St. (☎989-7131), near Bush St. Enormous fajitas ($8.50-10.50) with guitar music and vegetarian tortilla bowls. Free chips and homemade salsa with soup (black bean, $4) or margaritas ($4.50) make this convivial fiesta a worthwhile stop. Happy Hour daily 4-7pm. Live music W-Sa evenings. Open daily 11am-1am. AmEx/D/MC/V. ❶

Ponzu, 401 Taylor St. (☎775-7979), at O'Farrell St. The dark-hued, curving spaces scream "Chic!," as your wallet might be shouting "Ouch!," but the self-described "contemporary Asian cuisine" is popular, tasty, and worth it. Mongolian lamb ($16) and beef short ribs with green apple ($15) leave little room for veggies, but just enough for dessert. Chocolate dim sum for 2 ($12). Feng Shui Happy Hour (M-F 5-7pm) features $3 drinks and appetizers. Open for breakfast M-F 7-10am, Sa-Su 8-11am; dinner Su-Th 5pm-midnight, F-Sa 5pm-11pm; bar opens at 4:30pm. DJ spins house music Sa 8pm-midnight. AmEx/D/MC/V. ❸

Indonesia Restaurant, 678-680 Post St. (☎474-4026), at Jones St. The straightforward name tells it like it is—this humble space serves delicious Indonesian fare. *Satays* ($7-8), meat entrees ($7-9), and many veggie dishes ($6-8). Open daily 11:30am-10pm. AmEx/MC/V. ❷

Sanraku, 704 Sutter St. (☎771-0803; www.sanraku.com), near Taylor St. Comparatively expensive (2 pieces of sushi $3-6), Sanraku still has a super sushi lunch combo: 12 pieces, miso soup, and salad for $7.75. The large sushi selection, vegetarian options, and ample seating in three rooms make it great for group outings. Open M-F 11am-10pm, Sa-Su 4-10pm. AmEx/D/MC/V. ❷

Lori's Diner, 149 Powell St. (☎677-9999), at O'Farrell St. Elvis is most certainly not dead—he's working as a short-order cook at Lori's. Waitresses in period costumes careen by Gomer Pyle gas pumps with stacked burger plates and huge omelettes ($6-8). Not the best place for a vegetarian friendly meal. Neon, vinyl, and a teal Chrysler round out the decor. Open Su-F 6am-11pm, Sa 6am-midnight. Additional locations: 336 Mason St. (☎392-8646), at Geary St. Open 24hr. 500 Sutter St. (☎891-1950), at Powell St. Open Su-F 6am-11pm, Sa 6am-midnight. AmEx/D/MC/V. ❶

FINANCIAL DISTRICT & THE EMBARCADERO

🔁 *NEIGHBORHOOD QUICKFIND:* **Discover,** p. 13; **Nightlife,** p. 149; **Accommodations,** p. 195.

see map p. 344

In the financial district, eateries are everywhere and cater to the full range of budgets. Corner cafes vend Mediterranean grub at rock-bottom prices. Pedestrian side streets, nestled between banks, are packed with pavement bistros. Sit-down restaurants serve *haut cuisine* with a liberal portion of ambience, though you may need an MBA (or a well-to-do sugar daddy) to afford more than an appetizer.

🍽 **Cafe Venue,** 721 Market St. (☎546-1144), between 3rd and 4th St. Oh, to be a decadent San Franciscan, washing down roasted eggplant on sourdough ($4.50) with a wheatgrass "shot" ($1) to energize for an afternoon of Union Square shopping. The people-watching patio juxtaposes Market Street's bustle, and a similarly diverse menu offers pasta ($6), smoothies ($3), and even spirits in a conspicuously affordable venue. Open M-F 7am-7pm, Sa 8am-5:30pm, Su 11am-5:30pm. No credit cards. ❷

Café Bastille, 22 Belden Pl. (☎986-5673), between Pine and Bush St., and Kearny and Montgomery St. In this strip of pricey pavement cafes, Bastille stands out for its quality food and carefree atmosphere. The tasty lunch menu ranges from $8-11 and includes French favorites like crepes ($8.50). The dinner menu ($16.50-18) is filled with light French offerings like steak with wild mushroom pudding ($18.50), mussels and frites ($13), and a heavenly chocolate almond dessert crepe ($5). Open 11:30am-10pm. AmEx/D/MC/V. ❹

Café Mediterraneo, 357 Kearny St. (☎397-5850), at Bush St. Oven-baked pizzas and lunch-sized pizzettas ($5-8) with lots of tasty toppings. Lunch combo includes pizzetta, house salad, and soda ($6.85). Open M-Th 9am-9pm. AmEx/D/MC/V. ❷

Café Claude, 7 Claude Ln., (☎392-3515), off Bush and Kearney St. The ambience will make you think you're on the Champs-Elysees (*croque-monsieur* $7), but so will the prices. Live jazz (no cover) F-Sa evenings, outdoor seating, and French waiters—the best of the Old World hidden in an alley in the New. Open M-Sa 11:30am-11pm. AmEx/D/MC/V. ❷

Krivaar Café, 475 Pine St. (☎781-0894), between Kearny and Montgomery St. Middle Eastern and Greek specialties that are tasty and marvelously cheap. Mammoth Wowee Plate ($5.75) includes falafel, dolma, pita, and over 4 types of salad. Pita sandwiches $1.25-5. Squeeze in at a tiny table or take grub to go. Open M-F 6am-5pm. No credit cards . ❶

Equinox, 5 Embarcadero Ctr., Hyatt Regency Hotel, 20th floor, (☎788-1234), at Drumm St. Take the express elevator on the Atrium level with the Equinox sign above. This extravagant restaurant offers a 360-degree panorama of the city and Bay, while you feast on the finest cuisine. Su champagne brunch ($35) includes omelets, French toast, salads, salmon or chicken entree, and dessert. Daily dinner options range from pasta ($25) to lobster ($39) with a delicious selection of appetizers ($6-12) and desserts ($7-13). Open daily 6-10pm; Su brunch 10am-2pm. AmEx/D/MC/V. ❺

Banana Leaf Cafe, 321 Kearny St. (☎981-9399), between Pine and Bush St. Not the cleanest restaurant in town, but the Banana Leaf serves up intensely aromatic Thai cuisine with superb prices. Curries, rice plates, and noodles ($6.50-7.50), some with tofu options. Delivery available for minimum order $10. Open 10:30am-9pm. AmEx/D/MC/V. ❶

CIVIC CENTER

🔁 *NEIGHBORHOOD QUICKFIND:* **Discover,** p. 13; **Sights,** p. 90; **Accommodations,** p. 196.

This home to opera, musicals, and movies has fewer restaurants than would be expected. The Opera Plaza, Van Ness Ave., and McAllister St. have a sprinkling of appetizing eateries hidden amongst fast-food chains. Nearby Hayes Valley has some popular pre-opera offerings as well.

see map p. 345

Ananda Fuara, 1298 Market St. (☎621-1994), at Larkin St. With a serene sky blue interior and a traditionally dressed waitstaff, this vegetarian cafe with vegan tendencies offers creative combinations of super-fresh ingredients—terrific smoothies ($3.25) and great sandwiches like the BBQ tofu burger ($5.75). The most popular dish and house specialty is the "neatloaf" (with mashed potatoes and gravy, $10.50; in a sandwich, $6.75.) A delicious selection of vegan cakes, pies, and cookies ($1-2.50). Open M-Tu and Th-Sa 8am-8pm, W 8am-3pm, occasional Su brunch; call for dates. No credit cards. ❷

Lalita Thai Restaurant and Bar, 96 McAllister St. (☎552-5744), at Leavenworth St. Mood lighting, an elaborate water-lily mural, and a touch of plastic foliage give this elegant Thai restaurant an Alice-In-Wonderland, feasting-with-the-frogs feel. Daily and weekly lunch specials $7.25. Most dinner entrees $10.95, with veggie options. Try the Twisted Thai Iced Tea ($5). Beer $3, cocktails $5-8. Reservations recommended. Open M-F 11am-10pm, Sa 11:30am-10pm. AmEx/D/MC/V with $8 min. ❷

Millennium, 580 Geary St. in Savoy Hotel (☎345-3400), at Larkin St. Though the award-winning menu is vegan, Millennium is an entirely tie-dye-free area and the first restaurant in the US to feature an all-organic wine list. Feast on gourmet cuisine in a romantic, candle-lit, soft-jazz setting. Entrees, like the Szechuan Eggplant Crêpe, range from $12.95-18.95 and gather global influences. Reservations recommended. Open daily 5-9pm. MC/V. ❸

Max's Opera Café, 601 Van Ness Ave. (☎771-7300), in the Opera Plaza. The doors open, and faster than you can say "Figaro, Figaro, Figaro," it's packed. Max's prepares New York deli-style foods in a New York hustle-bustle atmosphere. Specializes in huge salads and sandwiches ($9-12) with common favorites that include hot pastrami ($7.50) and roast beef sandwiches ($7.50). Entrees run on the expensive side, ranging from $12-20. Decadent deserts include the Tiramisu Cheesecake ($3.95). Open Su-Tu 11:30am-10pm, W-Th 11:30am-11pm, F-Sa 11:30am-11:30pm. AmEx/D/MC/V. ❸

Thai Bar-B-Q, 730 Van Ness Ave. (☎441-1640), between Eddy and Turk St. With quick service, sizable portions, and super combo deals, Thai Bar-B-Q could be mistaken for one of many nearby fast-food joints. Yet great quality, natural decor and a relaxed atmosphere make it a much better pick. Lunch and dinner combos $6.50; noodles $5.95-6.95. Most entrees ($6-9) come with salad and rice. Open M-F 11:30am-2:30pm and 4:30-9:30pm, Sa 4:30-9:30pm. MC/V with $15 min. ❷

The Stinking Rose

The Cliff House

Farmer's Market

HAYES VALLEY

⌐ NEIGHBORHOOD QUICKFIND: **Discover,** p. 14; **Sights,** p. 92; **Nightlife,** p. 149; **Accommodations,** p. 196.

Though the art galleries and designer stores are the main attraction, Hayes Valley's restaurants and cafes give them a run for their money, serving specialized ethnic foods, from schnitzels to *genackte Leber* (chopped liver).

see map p. 345

☒ It's Tops Coffee Shop, 1801 Market St. (☎715-6868), at Octavia St. With a soda fountain, an old-school counter, orange booths, and a doo-wop sound track, this 1952 establishment has been around since its nostalgic decor was just plain cool. Breakfast $4.50-9; burgers $6-8; fountain drinks $2.50-5. Some vegetables, but remember, red meat was considered healthy in the 50s. Open M and W-F 8am-3pm and 8pm-3am, Tu 8am-3pm, Sa 8am-3am, Su 8am-11pm. MC/V. ❶

Frjtz, 579 Hayes St. (☎864-7654), at Laguna St. Artsy Belgian coffeehouse makes fantastic *frites* (with choice of dips, $3-4.50) and hosts hip DJs M, W 7-9pm, and Sa evenings starting at 4:30pm (sometimes F at 8pm). Progressive rotating art shows and an oasis of an outdoor patio. Crêpes ($4-7.25), sandwiches ($6-7.25), and big salads ($5.75-7) all named after artists, from Michelangelo to Magritte. Open M-Th 9am-10pm, F 9am-midnight, Sa 9am-midnight, Su 10am-9pm. AmEx/D/MC/V. ❶

Momi Toby's Revolution Café and Art Bar, 528 Laguna St. (☎626-1508), between Hayes and Fell St. Someone once said that the Intellectual Revolution was aided by the cultural decision to make coffee, rather than beer, the daytime drink of choice. In artsy Hayes Valley, the Intellectual Revolution is here. Good but light menu ($4-8). Happy Hour daily 5-7pm (beers $3.50, wines $5-6). Open M-F 7:30am-10pm, Sa-Su 8am-10pm. No credit cards. ❶

Moishe's Pippic, 425-A Hayes St. (☎431-2440), between Gough and Octavia St. A good old kosher-style Jewish deli, with loads of hot dogs, corned beef, pastrami, and chopped liver, and of course, *matzoh* ball soup. Sandwiches $5.50-8. Open M-F 8am-4pm, Sa 9am-4pm. No credit cards. ❶

Powell's Place, 511 Hayes St. (☎863-1404), at Octavia St. Soul food that'll put some meat on your bones. Founded by the gospel radio and TV star Emmit Powell, the restaurant is best known for its award-winning fried chicken and sweet potato pie. Dinner combos $8-11. Breakfast ($4-7.50) M-Sa 9am-3pm, Su 9am-noon. Take-out and delivery available. Open daily 9am-11pm. AmEx/D/MC/V. ❷

Citizen Cake, 399 Grove St. (☎861-2228), at Gough St. It's not just cake, it's art: sugar twisted and contorted into edible sculptures too magnificent to eat. Almost. Desserts $5-9. Homemade ice creams and sorbets $2 per scoop. Cookies, cakes, and tarts-to-go $1-5. Full meals, too; "contemporary seasonal American" entrees $15-19. Reservations recommended. Open Tu-F 7am-10pm, Sa-Su 9am-10pm. AmEx/MC/V. ❸

Suppenkuche, 601 Hayes St. (☎252-9289), at Laguna St. A sparse German beer hall with a noteworthy selection of beers (½L $5). Act like a good Lutheran monk and enjoy a *Wiener Schnitzel vom Schwein mit Bratkartoffeln und grünem Salat* (breaded and sauteed porkloin with roasted potatoes and green salad, $16) or any other authentic entree ($8.50-17.50) from a bench at small, communal wood tables. A few vegetarian options. Open M-F 5-10pm, Su brunch 10am-2:30pm and 5-10pm. AmEx/D/MC/V. ❸

Zuni, 1658 Market St. (☎552-2522), at Rose St. between Gough and Franklin St. Regional French, Italian, and Mediterranean cuisine with a Californian twist and a focus on local organic foods. May be a splurge, but heralded as one of the best dining experiences in town. Quite a scene—everyone from the rich and famous to struggling artists. Lunch $9.50-35; dinner $12-35. The $35 roast chicken serves two. Reservations recommended. Open Tu-Sa 11:30am-midnight, Su 11am-11pm. AmEx/MC/V. ❹

TENDERLOIN

🔎 *NEIGHBORHOOD QUICKFIND: **Discover**, p. 14; **Sights**, p. 93; **Nightlife**, p. 150; **Accommodations**, p. 197.*

see map p. 345

The Tenderloin's reputation as a sketchy neighborhood in no way carries over to its eateries. In fact, the Tenderloin is fast becoming the hottest thing in quality affordable food in San Francisco. With options from old-fashioned to gourmet, the area is an excellent place to grab a bite, and, as many locals will tell you, the only affordable way to dine in style. You can also stock up for home or the park at any of the Tenderloin's corner markets, including **McAllister's Market and Deli**, 136 McAllister St., near Market St., with its impressive convenience store carrying basic groceries and household products, hot deli sandwiches, Middle Eastern food, beer, and wine. (☎861-5315. Open daily 9am-10pm. AmEx/MC/V).

🍴 **The California Culinary Academy**, 625 Polk St. (☎292-8229 or 800-229-2433), at Turk St. Built in 1912 as a German cultural center, then turned into a theater in the 1940s, the building now houses classrooms for 600 culinary students and the affordably upscale Caremé. The bustling kitchen and dining room are separated by a glass wall so you can watch the student chefs work as you enjoy the delicious fruits of their training. Tu-W three-course lunch ($14) and dinners ($24); Th lunch buffet ($20) and French Buffet dinner ($30); F Grande Buffet ($36). Under 12 half-price for all meals. Open Tu-F 11:30am-1pm and 6-8pm. AmEx/D/MC/V. ❺

🍴 **Tommy's Joynt**, 1101 Geary Blvd. (☎775-4216; www.tommysjoynt.com), at Van Ness Ave. A delicious hybrid of a saloon, school cafeteria, and slaughterhouse. Guzzle monster meat sandwiches ($4.45) or carnivorous daily specials ($4.25-6.65) at a plastic-cloth covered bench, with animal heads and sports memorabilia hanging overhead. Great selection of domestic and imported beers ($2 glass, $8 pitcher). Open daily 11am-2am. ATM inside. No credit cards. ❶

🍴 **Taj Mahal**, 398 Eddy St. (☎922-9055), at Leavenworth St. The low-key ambience (complete with sports-broadcasting big screen TV) and cheap prices (entrees $4-7.50) are classic Tenderloin; the delectable curries and vegetarian specialties are classic Tandoori. Try the Afghani naan stuffed with raisins, nuts, cheese, and cherries ($3.75). Don't miss the unbeatable all-you-can-eat lunch buffet ($4.95) M-F until 3pm and Sa until 4pm. Open M-F 11am-11:30pm, Sa 11:30am-11:30pm, Su noon-11:30pm. D/MC/V. ❶

Osha Thai Noodle Café, 696 Geary St. (☎673-2368), at Leavenworth St. This place is worth a detour into the Tenderloin. Large menu with tons of meat, noodle, and veggie specialities like lemon curry ($9) as well as old favorites like pad thai ($7). The big booths, late hours and relatively safe location make this a perfect place for late-night munching. Open Su-Th 11am-1am, F-Sa 11am-3am. AmEx/D/MC/V. ❶

Taqueria Castillo, 86 McAllister St. (☎431-1092), at Leavenworth St. The food is fast, but with flavorful dishes and decor, fast food it ain't. Tacos ($2.25), BBQ steak marinated in Sangria, and burritos ($4.50-5.50) also come with sauteed vegetables and healthy brown rice. Open daily 9am-9pm. No credit cards. ❶

SOUTH OF MARKET AREA (SOMA)

🔎 *NEIGHBORHOOD QUICKFIND: **Discover**, p. 15; **Sights**, p. 94; **Nightlife**, p. 151; **Accommodations**, p. 198.*

see map p. 347

Hidden amid the industrial hum of SoMa are some of the city's best restaurants, dishing up yummy cuisines in diverse settings. The area is home to two wonderful health food stores. **Rainbow Grocery**, 1745 Folsom St., at 13th St., is a worker-owned cooperative. Rainbow carries a huge selection of groceries, all vegetarian,

Pack a Picnic!

Some of the cheapest food can be contained in a well-packed bag and some of the best locations to dine can be found on a hilltop or at a park. To make a picnic as cheap as possible, skip the take-out and head for a grocery store or corner market, listed at the top of each neighborhood food section.

On a rainy day, pick up Italian bread and salami at **Napoli Market** (p. 118) in **North Beach** and take it up to the **San Francisco Art Institute** (p. 73) for a sheltered picnic.

In **Pacific Heights**, buy a bottle of wine and some fine sandwich fixings from **Mayflower Market** (p. 129) and climb to **Alta Plaza** (p. 96).

On a windy day, cruise through **Marina Safeway** (p. 117) and then wander over to the **Marina Green** (p. 68) for kite watching and lunching.

Stop into any of the numerous corner markets on **Nob Hill** like **Cala Foods** (p. 121) for goodies to munch on at **Huntington Park** in the shadow of Grace Cathedral (p. 74).

Swing by the **Real Food Company** (p. 133) in **Noe Valley** for healthy eats on your way up to **Twin Peaks** (p. 101) where the great views will more than make up for the lack of grass.

and most organic, and inexpensive bulk food from pasta and cereal to sugar and spices. Foods are bought from local producers when possible. (☎863-0620. Open daily 9am-9pm. D/MC/V.) **Trader Joe's**, 555 9th St., at Bryant St., is a chain supermarket with standard groceries and specialty imports. (☎863-1292. Open daily 9am-9pm. D/MC/V.)

Patisserie Café, 1155 Folsom St. (☎703-0557; patisseriecafe.com; chefmohamed@yahoo.com), between 7th and 8th St. This small cafe captures the artsy yet industrial feel of SoMa—a converted warehouse decorated with experimental art by local artists. You can get a cheap breakfast (bagel and egg $3.50), a reasonable lunch (gourmet sandwiches $7), or a decadent dinner from a very small menu (appetizers around $6, entrees $15). Open M-W 8am-5pm, Th 8am-4pm and 6:30-10pm, F 8am-4pm, 6:30pm-midnight. D/MC/V. ❷

Cafe Bosse, 1599 Howard St. (☎864-2446), at 12th St. Bright, shiny, and quick, Bosse provides restaurant quality meals with cafeteria-style decor: burgers, breakfast omelettes, and lunch specials (all about $6-7). Philly cheesesteak or lots of veggie and salad options, too. Open M-F 7am-4pm. AmEx/D/MC/V. ❶

The Butler and the Chef Cafe, 155A South Park Ave. (☎896-2075; www.thebutlerandthechef.com), between Bryant, Brannan, 2nd, and 3rd St. Pierre serves breakfast crepes ($3-7), delicious *croque-monsieur* or baguette sandwiches (from $6), and a huge assortment of wine ($4) in a stellar reproduction of a Parisian street cafe, complete with a mini-gallery displaying local photographers. Open M 7:30am-6pm, Tu-Sa 7:30am-9:30pm. MC/V. ❶

Basil, 1175 Folsom St. (☎552-8999; www.basilthai.com), near 8th St. A light-filled airy decor sets the mood for delectably classy Thai with a dash of spice. Curries and entrees "from the grill" or "from the wok" (lunch $7-9, dinner $9-12) include wine-sauteed "drunken tofu" and piquant "mussels inferno." Open M-Th 11:30am-2:45pm and 5-10pm, F 11:30am-2:45pm and 5-10:30pm, Sa 5-10:30pm, Su 5-9:30pm. AmEx/MC/V. ❸

Vino e Cucina Trattoria, 489 3rd St. (☎543-6962), at Bryant St. Look for the big tomato. Large portions, friendly staff, and lots of fresh Tuscan bread make this family-owned romantic nook one of the most affordable sit-down restaurants in the area. Pastas ($10-12), pizzas ($9-10), and panini ($7) with lots of veggie options. Wines from $5. Open M-F 11am-2:30pm and 5:30-10pm, Sa 5:30-10pm. AmEx/MC/V. ❷

Caffè Centro, 102 South Park Ave. (☎882-1500; www.caffecentro.com), between Bryant, Brannan, 2nd, and 3rd St. Dine in (style) with panini ($2.75 for half) and loads of coffee or order to-go and picnic in the serene park across the street. Open M-F 7am-5pm, Sa 8:30am-5pm. AmEx/D/MC/V. ❶

Extreme Pizza, 1052 Folsom St. (☎701-9000), between 6th and 7th St. Not your average pizza place. Over 20 specialty pizzas like the all-meat "Everest" ($5.95 for an individual pie) or the "Yard Sale," topped with "everything in the house" ($6.45). Lot of subs, salads, and calzones too. Full bar. Open daily 11:30am-midnight. AmEx/D/MC/V. ❶

PACIFIC HEIGHTS & JAPANTOWN

🚩 *NEIGHBORHOOD QUICKFIND: **Discover,** p. 15; **Sights,** p. 95; **Accommodations,** p. 198.*

see map p. 348

PACIFIC HEIGHTS

Fillmore St., which runs through the center of Pacific Heights, offers an eclectic mix of eateries ranging from everyday pizzerias to elegant boulangeries. For a cost-conscious, veggie-friendly alternative, stop by a grocery store and pack a picnic: **Mayflower Market,** 2498 Fillmore St., at Jackson St. (☎346-1700. Open M-F 6:30am-9:30pm, Sa-Su 8am-9pm) boasts a great wine selection ($6-20), and **Mollie Stone's Market,** 2335 California St. (☎567-4902. Open daily 8am-10pm) offer wide selections of fresh produce.

🍴 **Pizza Inferno,** 1800 Fillmore St. (☎775-1800), at Sutter St. The multicolor paint job and wild interior make this pizza parlor trendier than you might expect. Daily lunch specials (11:30am-2:00pm) include a slice of mouth-watering, fresh-baked pizza, large salad, and soda (starting at $6.50). Happy Hour daily 4-6:30pm and 10-11pm with pitchers of beer ($11) and 2-for-1 pizzas. Open daily 11:30am-11pm. AmEx/D/MC/V. ❷

La Méditerranée, 2210 Fillmore St. (☎921-2956), between Sacramento and Clay St. Narrow, colorful, and bustling, La Méditerranée feels like a street in southern Europe. Lunch specials (served until 5pm, about $6.50) and entrees ($7-9) are light, Mediterranean-inspired with a home-cooked taste. Filled phyllo dough ($7.50-9) and quiche of the day ($7) are both must-tries. Open Su-Th 11am-10pm, F-Sa 11am-11pm. AmEx/MC/V. ❷

Tango Gelato, 2015 Fillmore St. (☎ 346-3692), at Pine St. This newly opened gelataria combines tangy ices with tango for an entertaining and refreshing dessert. Free demonstrations by Bay area tango dancers on the 3rd Su of every month. At any time, enjoy the wide range of tongue-tingling gelato and fruity sorbeto, shakes, smoothies, and espresso. Small cup $2.50; large $4.75. Open Su-Th noon-10pm, F-Sa noon-11pm. No credit cards. ❶

2001 Thai Stick, 2001 Fillmore St. (☎885-6100), at Pine St. Marble floors and a wooden interior ensure an elegant Thai meal for surprisingly reasonable prices. Lunch special $5-6. Vegetarian and noodle dishes $7.50-8.75; curries $7.50-11. Open daily 11am-10pm. AmEx/D/DC/JCB/MC/V. ❷

Trio Cafe, 1870 Fillmore St. (☎563-2248), at Bush St. Simply decorated by modern art on white walls, this elegant cafe is a great stop for coffee or lunch. Breakfast $4-6; sandwiches $5-7. Open Tu-Sa 8am-5pm, Su 9am-5pm. MC/V. ❷

JAPANTOWN

Slightly above average sushi is the staple of Japantown dining. Restaurants cluster in the Japan Center and across Post St. in the Buchanan Mall. Or if you think sushi is easy enough to make at home, try **Super Mira Japanese Foods,** 1790 Sutter St., at Buchanan St. (☎921-6529. Open M-Sa 9:30am-7pm, Su 11am-6pm. MC/V).

🍴 **Isobune,** 1737 Post St. (☎563-1030), in the Kintetsu Bldg., upper level. Swipe sumptuous sushi as it sails by your moat-side seat in America's first sushi boat restaurant. Menu includes hot items, vegetarian entrees, sushi, and take-out. Color-coded plates correspond to item prices ($1.50-$3.75). Beer $2.75-3; sake $3-5.50; wine $3-5. Open daily 11:30am-10pm. MC/V. ❶

Sweet Sourdough

Vendors and bakeries throughout the city brandish San Francisco's famous sourdough bread—well-known brands include Boudin, Parisian, and Colombo. Sourdough bread's tangy taste and chewy texture come from special yeast cultures used in the bread's sponge.

Bread aficionados may want to try making sourdough at home. Although you can buy dried "sourdough starters," the only real way to make sourdough is to use a fresh yeast culture. If you plan on being a repeat sourdough baker, make a little extra sponge. Before making the dough, put ¼ cup of the sponge in a glass jar with 1 tbsp. flour and water. Tightly sealed in the refrigerator, this starter should stay alive for up to a month. Each time you bake bread you should also make a new starter.

Sponge: Mix together ¼ cup sourdough starter, ½ cup warm (not hot) water, and ½ cup bread flour. Mix until sponge reaches a batter consistency. Cover with a cloth and let stand at room temperature (70-80°F) 4-12hr. Mix in 1 cup bread flour and 1 cup warm water, and let sit another 4-12hr.

Dough: Combine 1½ cups sponge, 2 cups bread flour, ¾ tsp. Salt. Mix well, then knead for about 10min. Let the dough rise in an oiled bowl covered with plastic until it doubles in size (about 1hr.). Punch it down, and then let rise again until it's almost double (3-4hr.). Bake 1hr. at 400°F.

Mifune, 1737 Post St. (☎922-0337), in the Kintetsu Bldg., upper level. Excellent and much-loved noodle restaurant with minimalist wooden booths and stark red walls. Choices include *udon* (heavy flour noodles) or *soba* (slender buckwheat noodles). Hot noodles from $4.50; cold noodles from $5.25; sake from $2.80. Open M-F and Su 11am-9:30pm, Sa 11am-10pm. AmEx/MC/V. ❷

On The Bridge, 1581 Webster St. (☎922-7765), on the bridge connecting the Kinetsu and Kinokuniya Bldgs. *Yoshoku*—a food fad from Japan—alters Western cuisine to suit Japanese tastes. Join the animated illustrations of Japanese kids in this quirky cafe, offering 38 types of curry, 42 types of spaghetti, and hamburgers. Entrees $6-10. $15 minimum for credit cards. Open daily 11:30am-10pm. MC/V. ❷

Juban, in the Kinokuniya Bldg. (☎776-5822). Literally "10th" in Japanese, Juban is named after the Yakiniku-style restaurants in the 10th district of Azabu in Tokyo, famous for its hearty meats. Continue the fine tradition of Japanese barbecue—grill meats ($6-8) and vegetables at your table. Enjoy dinner combinations of beef, seafood, and chicken ($17-27), or tasty soup and rice bowls ($6-8). Open M-F 11:30am-2pm and 5-10pm, Sa-Su 11:30am-10pm. AmEx/MC/V. ❸

Umeko, 1675 Post St. (☎776-1491), in the Miyako Bldg., upper level. All-you-can-eat Japanese seafood buffet, boasting over 20 kinds of sushi, teriyaki chicken dishes, fresh lobster, and Asian-inspired ice cream. Lunch $12.95 (children under 5 $6.95); dinner $18.95 (children under 5 $9.95). Open Su-Th 11:30am-3:00pm and 5-9:30pm, F-Sa 11:30am-3pm and 5-10pm. AmEx/MC/V. ❹

Sophie's Crepes, 1581 Webster St. (☎929-7732), in the Kinokuniya Bldg., upper level. Walk through the **Japan Center** (p. 189) and virtually every group of teens is munching on delicious crepes. Made from the owner's secret crepe mixture and stuffed with fruits, Nutella, or gelato, take-out crepes are as big a hit in Japantown as they are in Japan. Savory crepes $2.95-4.95; sweet crepes $2.45-5.70; gelato $3-4; sundaes $4-5. Open Su and Tu-Th 11am-9pm, F-Sa 11am-10pm. No credit cards. ❶

HAIGHT-ASHBURY

🔁 NEIGHBORHOOD QUICKFIND: **Discover,** p. 16; **Sights,** p. 97; **Nightlife,** p. 154; **Accommodations,** p. 198.

Haight-Ashbury is lined with dozens of small, affordable cafes that serve up anything you crave

see map p. 349

from American breakfasts **(Kate's Kitchen)** to Ethiopian **(Axum Cafe)** to a half-dozen Mexican, crepe, pizza, and noodle places, especially in the **Upper Haight**. In addition, there are several grocery stores along and near Haight St. For organic foods, try **Haight St. Market,** 1530 Haight St., which has a large selection of produce, juices, and vitamins. (☎255-0643. Open M-Sa 7am-9pm, Su 7am-8:30pm. AmEx/D/MC/V.)

UPPER HAIGHT

🔲 **Squat and Gobble,** 1428 Haight St. (☎864-8484; www.squatandgobble.com), between Ashbury St. and Masonic Ave. This popular, light-filled cafe offers enormous omelettes ($5.50-7.25) and equally colossal crepes ($4.50-7.75). Lots of salads, sandwiches, and vegetarian options, too. Additional locations: 237 Fillmore St. (☎487-0551), in the **Lower Haight** and 3600 16th St. (☎552-2125), in the **Castro.** Open 8am-10pm daily. MC/V. ❶

Blue Front Café, 1430 Haight St. (☎252-5917; www.bluefrontcafe.com), between Ashbury St. and Masonic Ave. This eat-in or take-out cafe caters to everyone and anyone. Technically a Middle Eastern restaurant, the huge wraps ($6.45-7.25, the chicken Mediterranean is the house specialty), omelettes ($7.25), salads ($5-7.25), and deli sandwiches ($4.95-5.95) that dominate the menu move well beyond hummus and falafel. Down one of the cheapest beers in the city ($1.50) or ginseng chai ($2.50) with your lunch. 10% discount with student ID. Open Su-Th 7:30am-10pm, F-Sa 7:30am-11pm. MC/V. ❶

Citrus Club, 1790 Haight St. (☎387-6366). This pan-Asian noodle house offers up popular noodle dishes from your favorite Thai, Vietnamese, Chinese, Japanese, and Indonesian cuisines. Heavy oils are replaced with citrus oil making the food healthier without losing the flavor. The most expensive entree on the menu—the highly recommended Garlic Shrimp and Shiitake Mushroom with rice noodles—is only $7.95. Plenty of veggie options. What's more, there's a bar! Try the Sake Margaritas. Open Su and Tu-Th 11:30am-10pm, F-Sa 11:30am-11pm. MC/V. ❶

Sweet Heat, 1725 Haight St. (☎387-8845), between Shrader and Cole St. Living up to its motto "Healthy Mexican Food to Die For," Sweet Heat takes standard dishes like burritos, quesadillas, and tacos and adds a dash of California cuisine through creative ingredients. For example, the crab quesadilla with ginger chutney ($5.95) and calamari burrito ($6.95) are favorites. You can also get it the traditional way. Exotic fruits spice up the menu, accentuating the margaritas and extensive tequila selection. Happy Hour M-F 4-6pm with $2 draft beers, sangria, and $3 house margaritas. Open Su-Th 11:30am-10pm, F-Sa 11:30am-11pm. AmEx/MC/V. ❶

LOWER HAIGHT

Kate's Kitchen, 471 Haight St. (☎626-3984), near Fillmore St. Start your day off right with one of the best breakfasts in the neighborhood (served all day). It's often packed, so you'll need to sign up on a waiting list outside. Try the "French Toast Orgy," with fruit, yogurt, granola, and honey ($5.25) or, if you're in the mood for lunch, the sandwiches are big and come with enormous sides ($5-6.50). Open M 9am-2:45pm, Tu-F 8am-2:45pm, Sa-Su 8:30am-3:45pm. Lunch served after 11am. No credit cards. ❶

Estela's Fresh Sandwiches, 250 Fillmore St. (☎864-1850), between Haight and Waller St. Massive fresh sandwiches in this tiny nook. Order one off the menu of over 30 options ($5.50-6.75) or build your own ($5.50). Check out the "Big Sherm," filled with turkey, roast beef, smoked gouda, pepperocini, and more. Veggie options, too. Open daily 10am-6pm, or whenever they run out of bread. MC/V. ❶

Axum Cafe, 698 Haight St. (☎252-7912), at Pierce St. Enjoy spicy, fun-to-eat-with-your-hands food in this small, sunshine yellow cafe. One of the few and the proud restaurants where vegetarian entrees dominate the menu. Meat dishes $7.50-8.50. Vegetarian dishes $5-7. Open M-F 5-10:30pm, Sa-Su 1-10:30pm. D/MC/V. ❶

Memphis Minnie's, 576 Haight St. (☎864-7675), at Steiner St. Self-proclaimed home of "swine dining," Minnie's is the place to park for pork. The Memphis sweet smoked pork (2-3 people, $9-20) sandwich ($6.25), Texas big beef ribs ($11), and meats by the pound draw big meat-loving crowds with even bigger appetites. For a fusion of tastes, try some sake with your BBQ. Open Th-Sa 11am-10pm, Su 11am-9pm. AmEx/D/MC/V. ❶

◪ *NEIGHBORHOOD QUICKFIND:* **Discover,** *p. 17;* **Sights,** *p. 99;* **Nightlife,** *p. 155;* **Accommodations,** *p. 199.*

Slightly posh diners and cafes dominate the Castro's culinary offerings, where little is as cheap as in the nearby Mission. But quality munchies that cost less than Streisand tickets do exist. Head away from Castro St. along Market St., toward Noe and Sanchez St. for generally cheaper options. Try **Harvest,** 2285 Market St., a "ranch market" with hummus, organic produce ($5-10 per lb.), and cruisey outdoor benches. (☎626-0805. Open daily 8:30am-11pm. AmEx/MC/V.) The Castro is also one of the best places in the city for good 24hr. food, as evidenced by the grocery behemoth **Safeway,** 2020 Market St., at Church St. border. (☎861-7660. Open 24hr. D/MC/V.)

see map p. 350

▨ **Home,** 2100 Market St. (☎503-0333), at 14th and Church St. Red-hued living room, patio fireplace, and one hot family bring unpretentious sophistication to this house-warming. Inventively Californian take on meat and veggie dishes (Sausalito watercress salad with jicama, peaches, and citrus vinaigrette $6) varies seasonally according to the chef's preferences. Entrees $8-13. Early-bird special includes three-course dinner with a glass of wine (Su-Th 5-6pm $12). "Flip-Flop" cocktail party 2-6pm, and dinner 5:30-10pm. Backyard bar open daily 5pm for $5 cocktails like "The Homeboy." Open M-Th 5:30-10pm, F-Sa 5:30-11pm, and Su brunch 10:30am-3pm ($11). AmEx/MC/V. ❸

▨ **Welcome Home,** 464 Castro St. (☎626-3600), across from the Castro Theatre. If grandma were a drag queen, this would be her kitchen. The crepe paper and Coke bottles, antique ovens and pride flags, fried chicken and milkshakes have brought an all-American and decidedly queer comfort to the Castro for 26 years. Dinners $7-10. Banana split $4.95. W all-you-can-eat spaghetti and salad $9. Open daily 8am-4pm. No credit cards. ❷

▨ **Nirvana,** 544 Castro St. (☎861-2226), between 18th and 19th St. A gorgeous waitstaff, heavenly Thai entrees ($7-12), a plethora of vegetarian options (sauteed, satayed vegetables in Buddha's Garden $11), and specialty drinks like the nirvana coloda ($7-8) all help you reach apotheosis in a simple, swanky setting. Open M-Th 4:30-10pm, F 2-10:30pm, Sa 11:30am-10:30pm, Su noon-10pm. D/MC/V. ❷

▨ **La Méditerranée,** 288 Noe St. (☎431-7210), at 16th and Market St. The copper-top tables, lush greenery, and dominant blue hues in this cool spot are like a warm Middle Eastern breeze. A filling phyllo dough combination plate ($9) is as refreshing as the varied colors. If you're with a group, try the Mediterranean Meza (for 2 or more; $12 per person) and feast on a sampling of appetizers (average $4) and entrees (average $9) from the menu. The tasty chocolate mousse is a must ($4.50). Open Su-Th 11am-10pm, F-Sa 11am-11pm. AmEx/D/MC/V. Additional location: 2210 Fillmore St. (☎921-2956), in **Pacific Heights.** ❷

Café Flore, 2298 Market St. (☎621-8579), at 16th and Noe St. A rainforest concretized in post-modern street-side form? A sublime, chrome-hued, industrialized greenhouse? No, just a killer cafe with lots of plants. The crostini salad ($5.75) is nice under the sun on the patio. Healthy sandwiches ($5.75-7.25) served until 10pm. Breakfast served daily until 3pm. Open Su-Th 7am-10:30pm, F-Sa 7am-11pm. No credit cards. ❷

Sweet Inspiration, 2239 Market St. (☎621-8664), between Noe and Sanchez St. Additional location: 2123 Fillmore St. in **Pacific Heights**. Black forest cake, bread pudding, lemon meringue pie. You won't mind working out or paying up for these deliciously well-proportioned hunks ($6). This popular cafe also serves breakfast (Market St. breakfast plate: two eggs, chicken-apple sausage, hash browns, and toast, $8) and lunch daily 8am-3pm. DSL Internet access for $10 per hr. or $2.50 per 15min. Open M-Th 7am-11:30pm, F 7am-12:30am, Sa 8am-12:30am, Su 8am-11:30pm. No credit cards. ❷

Pasta Pomodoro, 2304 Market St. (☎558-8123; www.pastapomodoro.com), between Castro and Noe St. Of all the upscale guppie eateries in the area, Pomodoro's high-quality Italian summer fare is the most affordable, and the hot waitstaff makes the food worth every penny.

Entrees range from $7-10 and include pasta primavera ($7), shrimp scampi ($10), chicken parmigiana ($9), and selected wines (about $5.50 per glass). Multiple locations throughout the Bay Area. Open M-Sa 11am-11pm, Su 11am-10:30pm. AmEx/MC/V. ❷

Bagdad Cafe, 2295 Market St. (☎621-4434), at 16th and Noe St. Bagdad's giant windows facing a busy intersection make this Castro institution a popular place to, uh...people-watch. Extensive all-day breakfast menu includes "The Glu teus" (4 scrambled egg whites, dry toast, fruit, and cottage cheese; $9.35). Try the hot turkey pastrami sandwich with mashed potatoes ($9) for dinner or, for you vegetarian queens out there, the steamed fresh vegetables with brown rice and sweet rice vinegar ($6.25). Open 24hr. No credit cards. ❷

Marcello's, 420 Castro St. (☎863-3900), across from the Castro Theatre. No-frills joint serves locally adored pizza with a list of toppings as long as your...leg. Slices $2-3; whole pizzas $10-23. Beer $2. Open Su-Th 11am-1am, F-Sa 11am-2am. No credit cards. ❶

The Castro Cheesery, 427 Castro St. (☎552-6676 or 888-528-2349), next to the Castro Theatre. Ken and his kin keep this tiny treasure stocked full of gourmet coffee (around $6.50 per lb.) and cheeses ($5-14 per lb.). Perfect place to grab a quick cup of caffeine to give you enough energy for a wild night in the Castro. Famous for their cheddars and awesome ice-blended mochas. Take-out only. Open M-Sa 8am-10pm, Su 9am-8pm. AmEx/D/MC/V. ❶

Sparky's, 242 Church St. (☎626-8666), at 14th and Market St. A trendy, mellow sophistication fills the Castro niche for better-than-average all-night eats. Sparky burger with fries ($6.25), NY steak sandwich ($9.25), turkey club ($7.25), and sun-dried tomato pasta ($7.25) are common favorites. Open 24hr. D/MC/V. ❷

Orphan Andy's, 3991A 17th St. (☎864-9795), at Castro and Market St. Andy's has been serving midnight burgers for years. A hot-spot to grab a bite to eat after a night at the bars or before hitting the infamous after-hours clubs. Red vinyl booths and a vintage jukebox heavy on 50s and 60s girl groups like the Supremes create an atmosphere of calming familiarity. Burgers ($6-7), tuna melt ($6.75), huge milkshakes ($4.70), and loads more diner eats, including all-day (and all-night) breakfast. For a midnight snack try the double fudge chocolate cake ($3.65). Open 24hr. AmEx/MC/V. ❷

NOE VALLEY

🄽 *NEIGHBORHOOD QUICKFIND:* **Discover,** *p. 18;* **Sights,** *p. 100;* **Nightlife,** *p. 158;* **Accommodations,** *p. 201.*

Excellent cafes, ethnic restaurants, and specialty food stores are scattered on 24th St. and down Church St. **The Real Food Company,** 3939 24th St., is great for fresh fruits and veggies. (☎282-9500. Open daily 9am-8:30pm. AmEx/MC.) **24th St. Cheese Co.,** 3893 24th St., stocks 400 varieties for real cheesemongers and offers fondu rentals. (☎821-6658. Open M-F 10am-7pm, Sa 10am-6pm, Su 10am-5pm. MC/ V.)

see map p. 350

🄼 **Lovejoy's Tea Room,** 1351 Church St. (☎648-5895), at Clipper St. near 24th St. Victorian divans and delightful individually-designed pots of Yorkshire Gold or Black Currant tea enhance a popular experience in an antique British living room. Traditional English fare: High Tea ($14) includes a bottomless pot of tea, 2 sandwiches from the seemingly endless selection, spring greens, a scone, and a shortbread biscuit with preserves and double Devon cream. Heartier, cheaper sausage rolls or shepherd's pie (each $8) are just as delectable. Individual pots of tea $4; scones $5; tea sandwiches $2.50; petits-fours $2. $7.50 min. per person. Reservations recommended. Open Tu-Su 11am-6pm, F 11am-7pm. MC/V. ❷

🄼 **Peasant Pies,** 4108 24th St. (☎642-1316; www.peasantpies.com), near Castro St. These portable pies, a traditional French peasant staple, make the perfect lunch or snack. Eat in the small cafe and people-watch or grab your pie to go. Low-fat vegan crusts, with fillings ranging from veggie to seafood and poultry to desserts. Two pies make a meal for $4.25; single pie $2.50, after 7:30pm $1.50. Open daily 10am-7pm. No credit cards. ❶

The Local LEGEND

The San Francisco Treat

Charlie DeDomenico immigrated to the US in 1890 and headed west immediately upon hearing that San Francisco's streets were paved with gold. He brought his bride, Maria Ferrigno, over from Italy a few years later. Her family sold its pasta factory in Salerno to join the youngsters. In 1912, Maria convinced DeDomenico to set up a pasta factory, Gragnano Products, in the Mission district.

Sometime in the 1930s, a neighbor introduced the DeDomenico family to an Armenian-style rice pilaf, which quickly became a favorite. In 1958, Charlie and Maria's son Vince mixed a dry chicken soup with rice and vermicelli, and Rice-a-Roni got a simmering start.

In the 1960s, Rice-a-Roni became known to households across the US as "The San Francisco Treat," thanks to a hugely successful advertisement campaign that showed cable cars sporting huge Rice-a-Roni billboards traveling up and down San Francisco's steep streets to the catchy "sautee and simmer" jingle. Updated versions of the same ad still play today.

Savor, 3913 24th St. (☎282-0344), between Sanchez St. and Noe St. Bountiful breakfasts ($8-10) served all day, tremendous salads ($9), and creative sandwiches on homemade breads ($8-9). But crêpes are the specialty. Savory ($8-10) or sweet ($5.25), they draw a crowd, especially on weekends. Open Su-Th 8am-10pm, F-Sa 8am-11pm. MC/V. ❷

Barney's Gourmet Hamburgers, 4138 24th St. (☎282-7770; www.barneyshamburgers.com), between Castro and Diamond St. Much more than your average burger joint, Barney's is consistently honored by San Franciscans for having the best burgers and fries in the city. Endless menu of burgers—beef, chicken, turkey, garden, tofu, or portabello—and loaded salads (all $6-8). Open M-Th 11am-9:30pm, F-Sa 11am-10pm, Su 11am-9pm. MC/V. ❶

Miss Millie's, 4123 24th St. (☎285-5598), near Castro St. "Creative American cuisine" served in what feels like your favorite aunt's rustic country kitchen. Great place for brunch, with fun twists on country favorites including lemon ricotta pancakes with blueberry compote ($10) and mango bread ($3.90). Slightly pricey for breakfast, but Millie makes it worth the splurge. Entrees $9-13. Open for dinner Tu-Th 6-9:30pm, F-Sa until 10pm. Open for brunch Sa-Su 9am-2pm. MC/V. ❷

Alcatraces, 4042 24th St. (☎401-7668), between Castro and Noe St. On a street filled with eateries, this Cajun/Creole restaurant stands out for its eclectic decor—masks and beads predominantly—as well as its food. A bit more expensive (lunch entrees around $10) but where else are you going to find an alligator po'boy in the middle of the city? Live music at the "Blues Brunch" Su noon-3pm. Open for lunch M-Sa 11:30am-3pm; dinner M-Th 5:30-10pm, F-Sa 5:30-10:30pm, Su 5:30-9pm. MC/V.❷

Deep Sushi, 1740 Church St. (☎970-3337; www.deepsushi-sf.com), between 29th and 30th St. Creative ingredients and gravity-defying presentations make this chic spot worth the extra few blocks down Church St. Superior quality *nigiri, maki,* and *sashimi* ($3.50-10). Open M-Sa 6-11pm. MC/V. ❷

Isabella's Ice Cream, 1300 Castro St. (☎648-4256), at 24th St. An old-fashioned ice cream parlor serving new favorites. Make-your-own s'mores platter (6 s'mores $8) and fondue (chocolate or cheese $15) are favorites. With the panini/soup/salad combo, Isabella's is also a perfect lunch spot. Open Su-Th 11am-10pm, F-Sa 11am-11pm. No credit cards. ❶

Hahn's Hibachi, 1305 Castro St. (☎642-8151; www.hahnshibachi.com), between 24th and Jersey St. Mellow, red-lit Korean BBQ with a huge menu of sandwiches, kebabs, and ribs as well as more traditional fare like *chopchae* (rice noodles mixed with meat) and *tempura* (all $8-12). Open daily 11am-11pm. MC/V. ❶

Cafe XO, 1799 Church St. (☎826-3535; www.caf-exo.com), at 30th St. A standard coffee shop in front, but the back of XO makes it worth a stop. A plush blue couch, two armchairs, a fireplace, and bookshelves transform this space into the living room you always wished you had. Lots of cakes, cookies, and muffins ($1.50) and a wide selection of coffee ($1.45-2.50), teas ($2-3), and fruit smoothies ($3.75). DSL $3 per 20min., $7 per hr. Free wireless Internet with purchase and own laptop. Open M-Sa 6am-7pm, Su 7am-7pm. MC/V. ●

MISSION

◪ *NEIGHBORHOOD QUICKFIND:* **Discover,** *p. 18;* **Sights,** *p. 102;* **Nightlife,** *p. 158;* **Accommodations,** *p. 202.*

see map p. 352

The Mission is famous for its delicious, authentic Central American and Mexican specialties, but the area is home to other excellent, ethnically diverse, and delightfully dirt-cheap cuisine as well, including Indian, Japanese, and Arabic. Several restaurants even strive for all-organic menus while maintaining reasonable prices.

◪ **Café Abo,** 3369 Mission St. (☎821-6275), near 30th St., directly across from the Safeway. A bizarre fusion of art gallery, island resort, political activism, and Yoda paraphernalia, Café Abo still manages to dish up some of the best sandwiches ($8-9) and mouth-watering miniature pizzas ($5-6) in the city. Soup, salad ($4-8), and pasta ($8-9) available as well. Loosely Italian-inspired and organic whenever possible. It's deep in the Mission, and worth the extra walk. Open M-F 7:30am-4pm and 6pm-10pm, Sa 8am-4pm. No credit cards. ●

◪ **Taquería El Farolito,** 2779 Mission St. (☎824-7877), at 24th St. The spot for cheap and authentic Mexican food—chow down as Latin beats blast through this fast-food joint. After any kind of evening activity in the Mission, El Farolito is a great late-night fix. Tacos $1.75. Open Su-Th 10am-3am, F-Sa 10am-4am. No credit cards. ●

Mitchell's Ice Cream, 688 San Jose Ave. (☎648-2300), at 29th St. Scooping ice cream for San Francisco hordes since the 1950s, Mitchell's litany of awards and superlatives is almost as long as its list of flavors. There is no seating, so take your cantaloupe, *buko* (baby coconut), *ube* (yam), or avocado ice cream outside. Open daily 11am-11pm. No credit cards. ●

Bombay Ice Creamery, 548 Valencia St. (☎431-1103), at 16th St. It's not just the ice cream, but also the food that merits a visit to Bombay. Mango *kulfi* ($2.50; get it with rose water and sweet rice noodles—trust us). Try the date and almond ice cream—it

the BIG $plurge

foreign cinema

foreign cinema, a secluded restaurant in the heart of the **Mission,** takes the dinner and movie narrative to a literal and delicious high. Prices are a bit high for the Mediterranean-influenced cuisine, but the quality of the food is worth the expense for a nice evening out.

From tango and rose endive Caesar salad to Spanish sweet paprika roast chicken and quail, the menu is delectable *and* delicate. The kitchen-masters, though not the original chefs, have trained at the *Zuni Cafe* and *Chez Panisse.*

Like the Mission, foreign cinema emphasizes both local and international flavor, with a worldly wine list, farmer's market-fresh organic vegetables, and a regular raw oyster bar, the best of the *fruits de mer,* from the northwest.

Remember that entertainment is included in each entree: daily in summer, beginning at dusk, a classic foreign film is projected on a wall in the restaurant. Summer 2003 brought *The Italian Job, Crouching Tiger, Hidden Dragon, Beauty and the Beast,* and *All About My Mother.* Films screen for one week, with two projections most nights. No taxis necessary.

(2543 Mission St. ☎415-648-7600; www.foreigncinema.com. Open Tu-Sa 6-10pm, F-Sa 6-11pm, Su 11am-9pm with brunch.)

is to die for. The *bhel* (a puffed rice dish; $3.50) and the *dhai puris* ($3.50) are both delicious Indian Chaat fast food. Slightly larger dishes reach the $6 range. Attached to an Indian bazaar that sells groceries and clothes. Open Tu-Su 11am-8pm. MC/V. ❶

We Be Sushi, 538 Valencia St. (☎565-0749), at 16th St. Serving "sushi like mom used to make," this little Japanese jewel proves that all kinds of good, cheap food abound in the Mission. Rolls $1.80-2.75 for 2-of-a-kind. The lunch special is unreal: soup, rice, *maki* roll, and 4 pieces of *nigiri* sushi for $6. And the early-bird special (5-7pm) is good too: soup, salad, rice, roll, and 5 pieces of *nigiri* for $8. Open Su-Th 11:45am-10pm, F-Sa 11:30am-11pm. Additional location: 1071 Valencia St. (☎826-0607). AmEx/MC/V. ❶

Amira, 590 Valencia St. (☎621-6213). Couch seating lines the walls and elegant belly-dancing performers shake their bodies and wave their scarves at this pan-Arabian restaurant. The relaxed atmosphere makes up for the somewhat pricey entrees (couscous with meat $10-14). Open Su and Tu-Th 5-10:30pm, F-Sa 5-11:30pm. AmEx/D/MC/V. ❷

Caffe Ponte Vecchio, 1136 Valencia St. (☎206-9677), between 22nd and 23rd St. Small and intimate, Old-World friendly staff, and good Italian food. Most entrees under $13 despite $13 per person minimum. Open M-Sa 6-10pm. MC/V. ❷

Cafe Ethiopia, 878 Valencia St. (☎285-2728), just north of 20th St. Large portions of Ethiopian food characterize this pleasant cafe. Be sure to try honey wine ($3.75 per glass). Ample vegetarian options. Everything on menu $4-8. Open W-M 11:30am-9:30pm. MC/V. ❶

Ti Couz, 3108 16th St. (☎252-7373), at Valencia St. Almost too many varieties of traditional savory ($2-6.50) and sweet ($2.50-5.50) crepes, plus dozens of tempting toppings. Be prepared to wait up to an hour on weekends; grab a drink from the bar while you chill. What's more, Ti Couz becomes a cocktail and oyster bar at night. No reservations. Open M-W 11am-11pm, Th-F 11am-midnight, Sa 10am-midnight, Su 10am-11pm. MC/V. ❷

Pancho Villa Taquería, 3071 16th St. (☎864-8840), between Mission and Valencia St. Don't let the cafeteria-style dining fool you—each piece of your meal has been carefully prepared with the best ingredients. Pancho Villa's cuisine appeals to the more Americanized, California Mexican appetite. Splurge for Tequila Prawns ($10) or save on a simple quesadilla ($1.35). Open daily 10am-midnight. MC/V. ❷

Herbivore, 983 Valencia St. (☎826-5657), at 21st St. All vegan, all the time. Displays fresh-off-the-vine produce as decor. Pleasant outdoor patio. A range of ethnic influences: grilled *seitan* $6.95; pad thai $6.25; lasagna with tofu ricotta $8.95. Open Su-Th 11am-10pm, F-Sa 11am-11pm. MC/V. ❶

Charanga, 2351 Mission St. (☎282-1813), just north of 20th St. Huge portions of tapas ($5.25-13) and some of the tastiest sangria in the Mission. Try the classic, but delicious *maduros.* Wood decor and friendly staff. Open Tu-W 5:30-10pm, Th-Sa 5:30-11pm. MC/V. ❷

Balompié, 3349 18th St. (☎648-9199), just west of Capp St. The authentic Salvadorian cuisine dispells the misconception that the Mission is mainly Mexican-Hispanic. *Pupusas* $1.50. Everything else on the menu $5-12. Combo plate with all three specialties, $6.95. Open M-F 8am-9:30pm, Sa-Su 8:30am-9:30pm. MC/V. ❶

Bissap Baobab, 2323 Mission St. (☎826-9287), just south of 19th St. Lots of vegetables, chicken, or fish. Vegetarian friendly. Most entrees under $10. Open Tu-Su 6-10pm. Bar open Tu-Th and Su until midnight, F-Sa until 2am. MC/V. ❷

BERNAL HEIGHTS

▸ NEIGHBORHOOD QUICKFIND: **Discover,** p. 19; **Sights,** p. 104; **Night-life,** p. 160.

Cortland Ave. is the commercial heart of Bernal Heights, and a handful of quality eateries line the street. There are also restaurants around Precita Park. For shopping try **The Good Life Grocery,** 448 Cortland Ave., with tasty supplies for a Bernal Heights Park picnic. Most food is organic and somewhat expensive. (☎648-3221. Open M-Sa 8am-9pm, Su 8am-8pm.)

see map p. 352

🍴 **Moonlight Cafe,** 634 Cortland Ave. (☎647-6448), at Anderson St. Breakfast ($3-5.75) and crêpe ($4-6.50) heaven. Bright, relaxed atmosphere and low prices. Large vegetarian selection. Sandwiches $4-5.45; crêpes $4-6; burgers $5-6. Coffee drinks $1-2.50. Take-out available. Open M-F 6:30am-6pm, Sa-Su 7am-5pm. No credit cards. ❶

🍴 **Liberty Cafe,** 410 Cortland Ave. (☎695-8777), between Bennington and Andover St. Quality food and terrific weekend brunch in an upscale French farmhouse-style setting. Menu changes monthly, but their signature pot pies (vegetarian or chicken, $10) are a sure bet. The cottage and patio in the back double as a breakfast bakery (Tu-Su 7:30am-2pm) and as a wine bar (Th-Sa 5:30-9pm). Entrees $6-15. Open for lunch Tu-F 11:30am-3pm; brunch Sa-Su 10am-2pm; dinner Tu-Th 5:30-9pm and F-Su 5:30-9:30pm. No credit cards. ❷

Progressive Grounds Coffee House, 400 Cortland Ave. (☎282-6233), at Bennington. Locals sip smoothies and espresso drinks on roomy, cushion-covered benches or in the secluded, leafy backyard patio. Delicious hot and cold sandwiches ($4.50-7), salads ($4-5), hummus ($5.50), ice cream, and sweet treats. Coffee, espresso, and mocha drinks ($1.50-3). Large smoothies with inventive flavors like nanaberry and berry buster ($4). Open M-F 6:30am-7pm, Sa-Su 7:30am-7pm. No credit cards. ❶

Moki's, 830 Cortland Ave. (☎647-6448), at Gates. Award-winning sushi in a Pacific-grill style restaurant. *Maki* $3-4.25. Famous for its speciality *nigri*, from $5.50. Open daily 5:30-10:30pm. AmEx/D/MC/V. ❶

POTRERO HILL

🔖 *NEIGHBORHOOD QUICKFIND:*
Discover, p. 19; **Sights,** p. 104; **Nightlife,** p. 160.

Small and secluded, Potrero clusters its comparatively few eateries within a two-block radius of the popular **18th** and **Connecticut St.**

see map p. 353

intersection. The **Good Life Grocery,** 524 20th St., supplies the health-conscious with cheeses, granola, and organically grown produce. (☎282-9204. Open M-Sa 8am-8pm, Su 8:30am-7pm. D/MC/V). **Klein's Deli,** 501 Connecticut St., serves select meats to go and a fun variety of made-to-order sandwiches named after famous women ($4-6). (☎821-9149. Open M-F 7am-7pm, Sa 7:30am-7pm, Su 8am-5:30pm. AmEx/MC/V).

🍴 **Farley's,** 1315 18th St. (☎648-1545). The quintessential Potrero Hill hangout for young, non-pretentious urbanites looking to down a cheap latte

the BIG $plurge

Cliff House

At the northern tip of Ocean Beach in **Lincoln Park** sits a monument from San Francisco's early days. The Cliff House, built in 1909, is the third building with that name to occupy the spot—the previous two burned down.

The original Cliff House was built in 1863 and played host to three US presidents, the Hearsts, and other members of the American aristocracy. Adolph Sutro purchased it in 1881 and built a railroad to bring the public to see his gem, but it burned down on Christmas Day 13 years later. Sutro rebuilt the Cliff House in 1896 in the style of a French château, with huge spires, eight stories, and an observation tower. His masterpiece survived the 1906 earthquake but burned in another disastrous fire a year later.

Adolph and his wife Kama eventually had a daughter, Emma, who rebuilt the Cliff House in a neoclassical style. Massive renovation efforts (to be completed by summer 2004)—and the allure of untapped tourist dollars—have begun to restore the complex to its original glory, while the ever-growing restaurant inside affords a stately view to tourists who can afford a stately check (sandwich $11, omelets $10). (*☎386-3330. Open daily 9am-3:30pm and 4:30-10pm. AmEx/D/MC/V.*)

ON THE MENU

Italian Pastries

Sweets are an integral part of Italian cultural and religious celebrations; there are a mind-boggling number of different varieties. Some North Beach standards include:

sfogliatelle: a flaky "clam shell" pastry filled with cheese, semolina flour, and citron fruit, mixed with eggs and sugar with a faint cinnamon/orange flavor.

neapolitan: alternating layers of flaky pastry puff and pastry cream topped with buttercream frosting and chocolate swirl.

biscotti: a twice-baked, hard anise-flavored cookie.

regina: crunchy tea-biscuits covered with sesame seeds.

zuccherati: a cinnamon sweet bread covered with sesame seeds (also known as "passa tempo").

amaretti: traditional soft, chewy almond macaroons, either plain, topped with candied cherries, or pignoli nuts.

tiramisu: cake soaked with espresso and coffee liqueur, topped with mascarpone cheese and cocoa.

mustaccioli: diamond-shaped chocolate allspice treats, either plain or stuffed with a fig and nut filling, covered with chocolate frosting.

strufoli: small round fried dough balls drizzled with honey and colorful sprinkles.

POTRERO HILL

see map p. 353

⯈ *NEIGHBORHOOD QUICKFIND:* **Discover,** p. 19; **Sights,** p. 104; **Nightlife,** p. 160.

Small and secluded, Potrero clusters its comparatively few eateries within a two-block radius of the popular **18th** and **Connecticut St.** intersection. The **Good Life Grocery,** 524 20th St., supplies the health-conscious with cheeses, granola, and organically grown produce. (☎282-9204. Open M-Sa 8am-8pm, Su 8:30am-7pm. D/MC/V). **Klein's Deli,** 501 Connecticut St., serves select meats to go and a fun variety of made-to-order sandwiches named after famous women ($4-6). (☎821-9149. Open M-F 7am-7pm, Sa 7:30am-7pm, Su 8am-5:30pm. AmEx/MC/V).

▧ **Farley's,** 1315 18th St. (☎648-1545). The quintessential Potrero Hill hangout for young, non-pretentious urbanites looking to down a cheap latte (all drinks $1.50-2.50) over a board game or a magazine from the extensive newsstand in the back. Local artists display their work and the community events board advertises volunteer opportunities and upcoming exhibitions. Impressive dessert bar and cookies all about $1.50. Open M-F 6:30am-10pm, Sa-Su 8am-10pm. No credit cards. ❶

▧ **Eliza's,** 1457 18th St. (☎648-9999), between Connecticut and Missouri St. Upscale art deco decor and affordable Hunan and Mandarin eats with a California twist make this a favorite with locals. Entrees $6.50-10. People-watch from the picture windows in front while enjoying the famed Sunflower Beef ($8.25), spicy eggplant ($9.15), or ample lunch specials ($4.50). Eliza's sometimes lacks a host, so on busy evenings be sure to sign up for a table on the pad provided. Open M-F 11am-3pm and 5-9:45pm, Sa-Su 11am-9:45pm. MC/V. ❶

Goat Hill Pizza, 300 Connecticut St. (☎641-1440), at 18th St. Locals' favorite hang-out for the meatiest (or veggiest) sourdough crusted pizzas (10-inch pie around $12.50, 16-inch $20), pastas ($7-11), and sandwiches ($6). All-you-can-eat pizza and salad M after 5pm ($9). Open Su-Th 11:30am-10:30pm, F-Sa 11:30am-11pm. AmEx/D/DC/MC/V. ❶

Thanya and Salee's Thai Cuisine, 1469 18th St. (☎647-6469), at Connecticut St. Friendly service, good food, and a central location make this a perfect spot to grab a bite. The lunch menu is one of the most

RICHMOND

⚐ NEIGHBORHOOD QUICKFIND: **Discover,** p. 20; **Nightlife,** p. 160; **Accommodations,** p. 202.

The variety of international restaurants and markets is one of the main attractions of the Richmond. The area is home to some of the city's most highly-regarded Chinese, Thai, Burmese, Cambodian, Japanese, Italian, Russian, Korean, and Vietnamese cuisine—all at prices tough to beat. Clement Street, between 2nd and 12th Ave., has the widest variety of restaurants, in addition

see map p. 341

to gritty Chinese bakeries. The **New May Wah Supermarket,** 525-547 Clement St., at 7th Ave., is a jostling bargain barn of produce, dried fish bits, candy, and packet curiosities. (☎668-2583. Open daily 8am-7:30pm. MC/V.)

Lee Hou Restaurant, 332 Clement St. (☎668-8070), at 5th Ave. Some of the best dim sum New Chinatown has to offer. Huge round tables and 2 floors of seating accommodate the demand. The fact that this place never seems to close helps too. Service is basic, but come for the food. Thirteen pieces of dim sum $8. Lunch $4-10. Open Su-Th 8am-1am, F-Sa 8am-2am. MC/V. ❶

Le Soleil, 133 Clement St. (☎668-4848), between 2nd and 3rd Ave. Serves Vietnamese food at prices so low they rival Chinatown's best. Huge vegetarian selection and nothing on the menu cracks $8. Lunch and dinner menus available. Entrees average $5-7; imported beers $3.50 per glass. Open Su-Th 11am-10pm, F-Sa 11am-10:30pm. MC/V. ❶

Taiwan Restaurant, 445 Clement St. (☎387-1789), at 6th Ave. If you can handle the salmon pink interior and bare walls, then this veggie-friendly spot might be worth the stylized Northern Chinese cuisine. Vegetarian specials $4.25-5; seafood entrees $5-8; rice and noodle dishes $4. Lunch specials $3.50. M-F 11am-4pm, dim sum daily 10am-4pm. Open M-F 11am-9:30pm, Sa-Su 10am-10:30pm. MC/V. ❷

Q, 225 Clement St. (☎752-2249), between 3rd and 4th Ave. Strings of lights, transparent tables with fun toys inside, and an ever-changing Cali cuisine menu. Lunch entrees and salads (M-F 11:30am-3pm) and weekend brunch (Sa-Su 10am-3pm) $6.50-9. Dinner gets pricey (entrees $10-12), but portions are big and good. Open M-F 11:30am-3pm and 5-11pm, Sa 10am-11pm, Su 10am-10pm. AmEx/MC/V. ❷

Kitaro, 5723 Geary Blvd. (☎386-2777), between 21st and 22nd Ave. Fantastic sushi at some of the best prices in town. No frills and no reservations, but the food is worth the wait. Most sushi $2 per roll. Lunch combo $6-9; dinner entrees $8-12. Open M-Th 11:30am-10:10pm, F-Sa 11:30am-10:20pm, Su 11:30am-9:50pm. D/MC/V. ❷

Schubert's Bakery, 521 Clement St. (☎752-1580), between 6th and 7th Ave. Baking up a storm since 1911. If you can't make it over to North Beach for your sweet goodies, this place will satisfy—fruit tarts, cookies, and freshly-baked bread ($2.50-3.50). Cookies $5 per ½ lb. Open M-F 7am-6:30pm, Sa 7am-6pm, Su 9am-5pm. AmEx/MC/V. ❶

Gastronom Russian Deli and Bakery, 5801 Geary Blvd. (☎387-4211), at 22nd St. This small deli is a center for the San Francisco Russian community, and offers a mixture of Russian meats, candies, groceries, vodkas, and free weekly Russian newspapers. Premium Russian Vodka ($15-30 per bottle), fresh meats ($7-10 per lb.), and tasty desserts and breads ($2-4). Open daily 9am-9pm. D/MC/V. ❶

Genki Crepes & Mini Mart, 330 Clement St. (☎379-6414; www.genkicrepes.com), between 4th and 5th St. This small treasure is both a superb mini-mart and hotspot to grab some of the best tasting crepes on the go. Huge ice cream crêpes ($3.75). If not in a dessert mood, try the savory crêpes with salmon, tuna, spinach, and turkey ($4.15). Large tapioca drinks and milk shakes ($2.75-3.50). Open M 2-10:30pm, Tu-Th and Su 10:30am-10pm, F-Sa 10:30am-11:30pm. No credit cards. ❶

SUNSET

see map p. 341

◪ NEIGHBORHOOD QUICKFIND: **Discover,** p. 20; **Sights,** p. 105; **Nightlife,** p. 161.

Inner Sunset has the best culinary variety and value in the city. Best of all, few tourists make their way out here. Most restaurants are along Irving St.—American food, cafes, and bakeries primarily between 7th and 10th, and Asian restaurants and bakeries between 19th and 25th. If eating in, grab fresh fruit and groceries at **22nd & Irving Market,** 2101 Irving St., at 22nd. (☎681-5212. Open M-Sa 7am-6:30pm, Su 7:30am-6pm. AmEx/D/MC/V.)

▨ **Arizmendi Bakery,** 1331 9th Ave. (☎556-3117; www.arizmendibakery.org), between Irving and Judah St. Praised to be one of the best in the city, this small bakery has a variety of delicious baked goods from fresh breadsticks to tasty cheese rolls. Divine gourmet pizza, with daily recipes such as roasted fennel, garlic oil, and lemon juice ($2 slice, $7 half, $14 whole). Mouth-watering loaves on a weekly schedule and delicious breakfast goodies. Even better, this is a worker-owned co-op, so you can eat your fill without feeding corporate fatcats. Open Tu-F 7am-7pm, Sa 8am-7pm, Su 8am-4pm. ❶

▨ **Cafe,** 1200 9th Ave. (☎504-0060; www.thecanvasgallery.com), at Lincoln Ave. Filled with pale wood, simple glass tables, comfy sofas, and a young artsy crowd, this gallery cafe is a virtual cultural center to enjoy great art and food. Some of the biggest, best salads in the city, sandwiches, and favorite entrees from mac-and-cheese to eggplant parmesan (most $6-8). Wine $4-6 per glass; beer $4 per glass. Happy Hour M-F 4-7pm. Live music Tu-Sa 8pm. Free parking in rear. Open Su-Th 8am-midnight, F-Sa 8am-2am. AmEx/D/MC/V. ❷

Hotei, 1290 9th Ave. (☎753-6045; www.hoteisf.com), between Judah and Irving St. Claims to have the top Japanese noodle cuisine in the city, with a variety of creative sushi entrees like rainbow rolls, rock 'n' rolls, and dragon rolls. Entrees come with rice, salad, and soup ($8-13). Sushi deluxe with soup of the day ($12-15), rice specials ($6.45), and tempura plates ($6). Open M and W-Su 11:30am-10pm. AmEx/MC/V. ❷

Yumma's Mediterranean Grill, 721 Irving St. (☎682-0762), between 8th and 9th Ave. Small, bright restaurant dishes out quality Middle Eastern food. Grab a falafel ($4), chicken shawarma ($5), or beef shish kebab ($6) and head out back to the patio. Open daily 11am-10pm. AmEx/D/MC/V. ❶

Crepevine, 624 Irving St. (☎681-5858), between 7th and 8th Ave. Crêpes a cliche? Not here. Crepevine's vast menu includes Cali-style sweet and savory crêpes ($6-8), all sorts of egg concoctions ($4), french toast ($5), pasta ($7-8), pancakes, sandwiches ($7-8) and salads ($5-7). Kids' menu ($2.95 and under) with breakfast served all day. Additional location 216 Church St. (☎431-4646). Open M-Th and Su 7:30am-11pm, F-Sa 7:30am-midnight. ATM inside. No credit cards. ❷

Kaleo Café, 1340 Irving St. (☎753-2460), at 15th. A favorite student study-haunt, this neighborhood oasis serves coffee and food Hawaiian style. Exotic sodas ($1.75), specialty mochas ($3-4), and teriyaki chicken bowls ($4.50) add to the usual cafe grub. The indoor waterfall, comfy chairs, and soothing Hawaiian tunes will tempt you to linger. Weekly entertainment includes free beginning ukulele classes (M 7:30-8:30pm), karaoke (F 8-10pm), and live Hawaiian music (Sa 7:30-10pm). Open M-Th 7am-9pm, F 7:30am-11pm, Sa 8am-11pm, Su 9am-8pm. No credit cards. ❶

Sheng Kee Bakery and Cafe, 1941 Irving St. (☎753-1111), between 20th and 21st St. Feast your eyes on these buns. Immaculate Chinese bakery serves mouth-watering pastries, buns, cookies, and breads from 75¢. Tasty and cheap sandwiches include tuna rolls ($1), turkey and cheese rolls ($1.35), and ham or roast beef croissants ($2.25). Desserts with inventive flavors such as pineapple, custard, mocha chocolate, and green tea. Freshly baked loaves include white, taro, wheat, and raisin walnut ($2.50-4). Open daily 7am-7:30pm. No credit cards. ❶

Yum Yum Fish, 2181 Irving St. (☎556-6433), at 23rd Ave. A feast in a fish market, Yum Yum's serves famously fresh and low-cost sushi. Take out or squish in at a small table and enjoy your meal under the watchful gaze of the market's marine deceased. Variety of fish in the market including catfish ($6 per lb.), tuna ($14 per lb.), and salmon ($18 per lb.). Sushi (from $1.20 per piece) and affordable combos ($8-10) available. Open Tu-Su 10:30am-7:30pm. D/MC/V. ❷

NEAR ZOO, LAKE MERCED, FORT FUNSTON & STERN GROVE

◪ *NEIGHBORHOOD QUICKFIND:* **Discover,** *p. 21;* **Sights,** *p. 106.*

Food and drink in the area are located in Parkside, on the northwestern side of Stern Grove, and in Lakeside Village and West Portal, on the northeastern side of Stern Grove. West Portal Ave., running along the eastern edge of Stern Grove, has a sprinkling of cafes and some tasty neighborhood restaurants.

see map p. 341

Ambrosia Bakery, 2605 Ocean Ave. (☎334-5305), near 19th Ave. in nearby Lakeside Village. Pastries fit for the gods (from $1.50), an espresso bar (from $1.25 per cup), and great sandwiches (from $4.25). Open M-F 6am-6pm, Sa 7am-6pm, Su 8am-2pm. MC/V. ❶

Taipei Restaurant, 2666 Ocean Ave. (☎753-3338), at 19th Ave. in nearby Lakeside Village. This garish Chinese restaurant has a massive menu that includes dim sum Sa-Su. Lunch and dinner menus available. Lunch entrees from $6, dinner entrees from $8. No MSG. Open Tu-Su 11:30am-9:30pm. AmEx/D/MC/V. ❷

Jitra, 2545 Ocean Ave. (☎585-7251), near Junipero Serra Blvd. in nearby Lakeside Village. An impressive selection of reasonably-priced Thai dishes with varying degrees of spiciness. Lunch and dinner menus available with plenty of veggie options. Known for its great Thai Noodle ($6.50). Lunch entrees average $6, dinner entrees $6.50. Open daily 11:30am-3pm and Tu-Su 5-9:30pm. MC/V with $10 min. ❷

Nightlife

Nightlife in San Francisco is as varied as the city's personal ads. Everyone from "shy first-timer" to "bearded strap daddy" to "pre-op transsexual top" can find a place to go on a Saturday (or Tuesday) night. The spots in each neighborhood are sub-divided into bars and pubs, clubs, and cafes, but these lines can get pretty blurred after dark. Every other bar calls itself a cafe, every second cafe is a club, and half the clubs in town declare themselves to be lounges. Although San Francisco in many ways invented the American "gay bar" and a number of venues carry decades-long legacies, nightlife in the city is generally quite mixed; the listings in this section will thus use the label "gay bar" sparingly. Don't fret—there are 10,000 night spots in the city, and you're sure to find something that suits your fancy. If the spots listed below don't inspire you, check out the nightlife listings in *S.F. Weekly*, the *Guardian*, and *Metropolitan* or go online—www.sanfrancisco.citysearch.com is one of the best sites for general reviews of San Francisco nightlife. Get dolled-up (keep in mind it's San Francisco, though, so not *that* dolled up), grab a honey and remember, the **legal drinking age in California is 21 and bouncers and bartenders take that very seriously**—unfortunately, spots for underagers, though existent, are very limited.

MARINA, FORT MASON & COW HOLLOW

see map p. 338

⊠ NEIGHBORHOOD QUICKFIND: **Discover**, p. 7; **Sights**, p. 68; **Food & Drink**, p. 117; **Accommodations**, p. 191.

BARS AND PUBS

⊠ Matrix Fillmore, 3138 Fillmore St. (☎563-4180), between Filbert and Greenwhich St. in **Cow Hollow**. Playfully hidden behind one-way viewing glass, the club is easy to miss—but missing it is a mistake. Voted one of the best night clubs in the city, Matrix Fillmore features an art deco fireplace, upscale lounge, and large flatscreen TVs (even in the bathrooms). Cutting-edge "down-tempo lounge music" and an unparalleled drink list ($5-10). Wines sold at retail. Light appetizers $4-12. Open M-Su 5:30pm-2am. AmEx/MC/V.

⊠ Comet Club, 3111 Fillmore St. (☎567-5589), at Filbert St. in the **Marina**. This dark red lounge attracts mobs of late-night scenesters. This is *the* place to be Th-Sa nights after 10pm, when the clientele is young and high-energy and the DJ spins classic 70s and 80s house, funk, and groove. $3 cover on F-Sa is well worth it. Or if you're in a laid-back mood, Happy Hour daily until 8:30pm (beer and mixed drinks $2.50; martinis $2.50 Tu-W, $3.50 Th-Su). "Smart attire" required after 9pm on weekends. Open Su and Tu-W 7pm-2am, Th-Sa 5:30pm-2am. AmEx/D/MC/V.

Gravity, 3251 Scott St. (☎776-1928), near Chestnut St. in the **Marina**. Behind the deep red velvet curtains is a hip lounge that's a favorite among the young trendsetters in the area. House, funk, and Top 40 DJs pack the place on F and Sa nights. Tiled walls, oversized booths, and a small dance floor. Cover around $10. Open W-Sa 7pm-2am. MC/V.

Hi-Fi Lounge, 2125 Lombard St. (☎345-8663; www.maximumproductions.com), at Fillmore St. in the **Marina**. SoMa-style (a lil' more clubby, a lil' more NY warehouse district) with a blue vinyl bar, white booths, and a Mondrian-influenced light wall. W and Sa particularly big nights. Different nights feature different house music. F hip-hop theme. Open W 9pm-2am, Th 8pm-2am, F-Sa 9pm-2am. MC/V.

Bus Stop, 1901 Union St. (☎567-6905), at Laguna St. in **Cow Hollow**. Giants and A's fans alike can feed their addictions at this popular neighborhood sports bar open since 1900. Multiple TV screens. Happy Hour M-F 4pm-6pm (drinks half price). Open M-F 10am-2am, Sa-Su 9am-2am. AmEx/D/MC/V.

Balboa Cafe, 3199 Fillmore St. (☎921-3944), at Greenwich St. in **Cow Hollow**. The swankiest of singles bars, where you can hobnob with 30-something socialites. Since its 1913 opening, Balboa Cafe hasn't changed much; bartenders still use the original Bloody Mary mix and chefs cook the original Balboa burgers on baguettes. Mostly "regulars" fill the crowd, but there is space at the long bar for splurging visitors (drinks around $10). Wood paneling and cushy seating. Kitchen closes Su-W 10pm, Th-Sa 11pm. Open daily 11:30am-2am. AmEx/MC/V.

Bar None, 1980 Union St. (☎409-4469), at Buchanan St. in **Cow Hollow**. Huge underground sports bar and neighborhood hot-spot with the usual raucous fun of weekday night beer-drinking ($4-5). Happy Hour M-F 4-8pm, buy first pint get second for $1. Full menu includes appetizers and sandwiches under $7 available M-Th until 10 pm, F-Sa until 11pm. Open M-F 3pm-2am, Sa-Su noon-2am. AmEx/D/MC/V.

NORTH BEACH

see map p. 339

⊠ NEIGHBORHOOD QUICKFIND: **Discover**, p. 8; **Sights**, p. 70; **Food & Drink**, p. 118; **Accommodations**, p. 193.

BARS AND PUBS

⊠ San Francisco Brewing Company, 155 Columbus Ave. (☎434-3344; www.sfbrewing.com), between Pacific Ave. and Jackson St. Beer brewed on the premises in a delightful stained-glass and wood-paneled setting. Sidewalk seating for a perfect combination of drinking and viewing the city vibes on Columbus Ave. Pints $4; pitchers $13. 2 Happy Hours daily, 4-6pm and midnight-1am: 1/2 pints $1; pitchers $7.75. Live jazz M 8-11:30pm. Kitchen closes about 10pm. Open M-Sa 11:30am-1:45am, Su noon-1:45am. AmEx/MC/V.

15 Romolo, 15 Romolo Pl. (☎398-1359), off Broadway between Columbus Ave. and Kearny St. Tucked in an alley behind the Hungry i strip club (p. 145), this spacious dark wood and velvet lounge is far hipper and more low-key than one would imagine, given its brash neighbor. An oasis for your favorite obscure drinks. Drinks $4-6. Open M-F 5:30pm-2am, Sa-Su 7:30pm-2am. MC/V.

Spec's Adler Museum, 12 Saroyan Pl. (☎421-4112), in a little alley off Columbus Ave. between Broadway and Pacific Ave. Memorabilia packs every inch of the walls, floor, and ceiling in this cozy, woodsy bar. Start your scavenger hunt by finding a gold toilet plunger, a walrus penis-bone, a human skull, and bottles of Anchor Steam. Figure drawing classes Su 1-4pm ($13). Go figure. Music jams often erupt out front, as well. Open daily 5pm-2am. No credit cards.

Savoy Tivoli, 1434 Grant Ave. (☎362-7023), between Green and Union St. A popular nighttime yuppster hangout, Savoy Tivoli is reminiscent of a European cafe, but two huge bars and a pool room help foster a somewhat more low-key, hopping bar ambience. Beer $3-4; other drinks $4.50-6. See and be seen on the covered front patio. Open W-F 5pm-2am, Sa 3pm-2am. No credit cards.

CLUBS

Velvet Lounge, 443 Broadway (☎788-0228), between Kearny and Montgomery St. Decked-out 20- and 30-somethings pack this club and thump along to top 40, hip-hop, and house. The main room features house, hip-hop, and funk on F nights, and 70s, 80s, 90s, house, and hip-hop on Sa. F occasional live cover bands. No sneakers, torn/faded jeans, or athletic wear. Cover usually ($10). Open Th-Sa 9pm-2am.

Royale, 1326 Grant Ave. (☎433-4247), between Green and Vallejo St. A small, dimly lit, deep blue club that's got local R&B DJs spinning Tu-Sa. Mainstream on weekends, more underground during the week. Packed to the brim on F and Sa night; the door often closes at 11pm. Happy Hour 7-9pm with specials on beer and well drinks ($3). Cover $3-5 after 10pm. Su nights Royale turns into a much more mellow neighborhood bar. Open Su-W 7pm-2am, Th-Sa 5pm-2am. AmEx/MC/V.

Broadway Studios, 435 Broadway (☎291-0333; www.broadwaystudios.com), between Kearny St. and Montgomery Ave. Live music and DJs. Swing every Tu ($15) and Argentine Tango every second and fourth Su ($12). Tango and swing nights include beginner instruction at 7pm, intermediate instruction at 8pm, and social dancing from 9pm-midnight. There is a bar and restaurant, as well. San Fran Songwriter's Showcase W nights featuring local bands. F-Sa the club is booked to promoters and private parties, so themes and cover charges change. No credit cards.

Hungry i, 542 Broadway (☎362-7763), between Columbus Ave. and Kearny St. Legendary comedian Lenny Bruce was first busted for obscenity while performing at this once-bohemian nightspot in October of 1961. His San Francisco arrest and trial, the first of the 19 arrests and several trials that led to his premature death in 1966, became a lengthy First Amendment battle that ultimately ended in his acquittal. Bruce's supposedly dirty words would be a pleasant addition to the live strip shows featured nightly at the Hungry i these days. 2-drink minimum. Men $10; "ladies" free. Open daily 6pm-2am. AmEx/MC/V.

CAFES

Vesuvio Café, 255 Columbus Ave. (☎362-3370), next to Jack Kerouac Alley. Jack and his friends started their days over pints at Vesuvio, which established itself as a center for the beatnik revolution of the 50s. The wooden, tiled, and stained-glass bar with an upstairs balcony remains a great place to drink with a friend (9 beers on tap). Draught beers $4.25, bottled $3.50, pitchers $9-12. Happy Hour M-Th 3-7pm: drinks $1 off, pitchers and bottles of wine $3 off. Open daily 6am-2am. No credit cards.

Beyond City Lights

Back in the 50s, these dharma bums sipped, sloshed, and scatted around a remarkably small section of North Beach. Not one hangout is more than five minutes from another, which makes for the perfect cafe and pub-crawl. So grab your dog-eared copy of The Portable Beat Reader, a fistful of greenbacks (almost every place is cash-only) and drink deep of literary history.

The Lost & Found Saloon, 1353 Grant Ave. (☎458-8980), between Green and Vallejo St. A shabby blue velvet and wood bar whose past lives include Miss Smith's Tea Room, where the Beats flocked for poetry and bebop, and the Coffee Gallery, where a young Janis Joplin got her start. Performances nightly. Cover $5. Open daily noon-2am. No credit cards.

Gino & Carlo, 548 Green St. (☎421-0896). Boho goes sportsbar. Gone are yesterday's poetry readings, but you can still rack up a 50¢ pool game 'neath a signed portrait of Sinatra and some plasticky Coors signs. Open daily 6am-2am.

Mario's Bohemian Cigar Store Cafe (p. 119). Lookee here! One of the few Beat haunts that actually serves food. Hot foccacia sandwiches ($7) and good Washington Sq. people-watching. Open daily 10am-10pm.

Tosca (p. 146). All honeyed wood, vinyl-record jukebox and sparkly red booths—the quintessential 1940s Italian cocktail lounge. Ferlinghetti still drinks here! Open Tu-Su 5pm-2am.

(cont'd next pg.)

Caffè Trieste, 601 Vallejo St. (☎392-6739), at Grant Ave. Though every bar in North Beach claims to be a Beat haunt, this is the genuine article. While Vesuvio's is where the gang got trashed, Trieste remained their more mellow living room. The leftovers still hang out in the front. It hasn't changed much since then—a few new photos of famous patrons on the walls, but the jukebox still plays opera, and it's still the cornerstone of North Beach's remaining Italian community. Live Italian pop and opera concerts every Sa 1:45-6pm (since 1973) alone are worth a stop here. Espresso drinks $1.50-3.25; bottles of beer $2-3; glasses of wine $2.25-3.75. Open M-Sa 10am-6pm. No credit cards.

Tosca Cafe, 242 Columbus Ave. (☎986-9651), between Broadway and Pacific St. Although this cafe first opened in the 1930s, the assemblage of beautiful people lolling about the grand bar and lounging in red vinyl booths more closely resembles a late-1950s Fellini scene. Regular coffee drinks around $2 (but *Let's Go* recommends the House Cappucino with a dose of brandy included, $4), other drinks $3.50-5. Open daily 5pm-2am. No credit cards.

CHINATOWN

NEIGHBORHOOD QUICKFIND: ***Discover,*** *p. 9;* ***Sights,*** *p. 71;* ***Food & Drink,*** *p. 120;* ***Accommodations,*** *p. 193.*

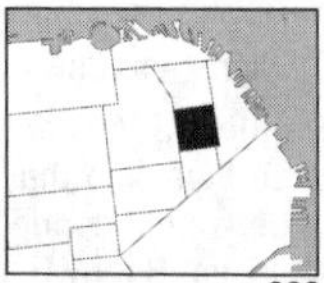

see map p. 339

Chinatown's nightlife is peopled primarily by tourists and late-night diners; shops close around 10pm, and the once-bustling neighborhood goes to sleep. Nonetheless, the area's limited offerings can be good places to get a drink after a chaotic day or a fun and cheap detour from North Beach's more happenin' spots.

BARS AND PUBS

Blind Tiger, 787 Broadway (☎788-4020; www.blindtigersf.com), at Powell St. Named after the Prohibition custom of displaying a stuffed tiger to identify an establishment as a speakeasy to thirsty patrons, Blind Tiger is outfitted in a high Mandarin style. This upscale lounge and dance floor lives up to the implied China-America fusion as a young crowd sips specialty cocktails ($5-6) and visits the sake bar amid Chinese wall hangings. Resident DJs spin house and R&B. 21+. Cover varies after 10pm. Open Th-Sa 8pm-2am. MC/V.

Li Po Cocktail Lounge, 916 Grant Ave. (☎982-0072), between Jackson and Washington St. The curved counter and plentiful cushioned seating offer a comfortable vantage point from which to take in the huge alcove with a golden statue of Buddha behind the bar. Sparsely populated during the day, but weekends see some serious partyers, with a DJ spinning on Th. Daytimes tend to cater to thirsty tourists, but the nighttime crowd is primarily locals. Beers $3, well drinks $3.75. Open daily 2pm-2am. No credit cards.

Buddha Lounge, 901 Grant Ave. (☎362-1792), at Washington St. A pretty standard neighborhood bar mixes Chinatown locals and tourists for affordable, low-key carousing. Beer $2.75-3.50. Well drinks $3.75. 21+. Open M-Sa 11:30am-2am, Su 2pm-9pm. No credit cards.

NOB HILL & RUSSIAN HILL

◪ *NEIGHBORHOOD QUICKFIND:*
Discover, p. 9; Sights, p. 73;
Food & Drink, p. 121; Accom-
modations, p. 194.

see map p. 342

BARS AND PUBS

▨ **The Bigfoot Lodge,** 1750 Polk St. (☎440-2355), between Clay and Washington St. in **Nob Hill.** Campy bear heads, a gigantic Big Foot, and bartenders uniformed as scouts keep up more of an image than does the easy-going crowd in this log cabin retreat. Beer $3.50-4.50, cocktails around $5. Happy Hour daily from opening until 8pm. Open M-F 3pm-2am, Sa-Su noon-2am. AmEx/D/MC/V.

▨ **Lush Lounge,** 1092 Post St. (☎771-2022), at Polk St. in **Nob Hill.** Some of the best bartenders in the city shake their cocktails as an eclectically upscale crowd begs for more. $4 speciality drinks, a steady stream of ABBA and Madonna, and the best chocolate martinis in the city make this place a must-see, even if you can't snag one of the few tables. Happy Hour 4-9pm. Open M-Tu 5pm-2am, W-Su 4pm-2am. No credit cards.

▨ **Café Royale,** 800 Post St. (☎441-4099), at Leavenworth St. in **Nob Hill.** "Lemondrop" *sake* cocktails and fresh sandwiches ($7.50) served until closing make this the right setting for jazz, pool, and 19th-century burgundy couch seating. DJs spin some nights for a mixed crowd. Happy Hour M-F 3-7pm. Brunch Su 11am-5pm features omelettes and chicken-apple sausage ($5-7). Open Su 11am-midnight, M-Th 4pm-midnight, F-Sa 4pm-2am. MC/V.

Royal Oak, 2201 Polk St. (☎928-2303), at Vallejo St. in **Russian Hill.** Though the decor is a bizarre cross between a Victorian drawing room and a rainforest bar complete with enormous ferns and red velvet couches, Royal Oak still manages to cater to the just-out-of-college 20-year-olds who miss the good ol' fraternity days. A big place but make sure to get there early on weekends to get a seat. Beer $4, cocktails $5. Open daily 11pm-2am. No credit cards.

(cont'd from previous pg.)

Enrico's Sidewalk Cafe, 504 Broadway (982-6223), past Kearny St. Slick black granite bar that has served mojitos and polished jazz to the well heeled for the past 40 years. No Beat could afford to drink on the chichi terrace today unless his latest book was selling really, really well. Live jazz nightly. Open Su-Th 11am-10pm, F-Sa 11am-11pm.

Spec's Adler Museum (p. 145). A dimly lit bar chockablock with Merchant Marine and Old West memorabilia—Dylan's on the jukebox, a taxedermied mongoose guards the bathroom and the barkeep's slicing slabs of cheese for hungry poets. Is it any wonder Herb Caen coined the term "beatnik" here? Come early if you want a seat.

Jazz at Pearl's (p. 165). A jazz den of flesh-colored tablecloths and flickering candles. Monday nights here host the city's only regular bop jazz sessions.

Saloon (p. 165). As worn and comfortable as an old pair of Levi's. The city's oldest bar (est. 1886), it survived the fire of 1906 because local firemen diverted water to save it while the rest of the neighborhood burned.

The beat also goes on at:

Vesuvio Cafe (p. 145).

Club Fugazi (p. 168).

Cafe Trieste (p. 146).

and, of course, **City Lights Bookstore** (p. 177).

— **Stephanie Smith**

Tonga Room, 950 Mason St. (☎772-5278), in the Fairmont Hotel in **Nob Hill.** Go down 2 floors to level "T." It "Takes Two to Mango" ($8.50), but one—tourist or local—can have fun at this enormous tiki (and fabulously tacky) bar featuring "bamboo" trees, palm frond huts, and gigantic fruity drinks ($8-11). A band performs recent covers on a floating stage in an artificial lagoon while tropical storms roll in every 30min. with simulated thunder, lightning, and rain. During Happy Hour (M-F 5-7pm) drinks are "only" $3-7 with an all-you-can-eat Polynesian buffet ($7). Open Su-Th 5-11:45pm, F-Sa 5pm-12:45am. AmEx/D/MC/V.

The Cinch, 1723 Polk St. (☎776-4162), between Washington and Clay St. A gay bar with a Southwestern theme? Ride 'em, cowboy! This casual, neighborhood bar offers something a little different from the venues of the Castro—men in chaps. Well, maybe not, but it does have a large heated patio, pool tables, jukeboxes, and pinball machines. Beer $4, cocktails $3.50. Happy Hour M 4pm-closing, Tu-Th 4-8pm. Open daily 6am-2am. No credit cards.

Hyde Out, 1068 Hyde St. (☎441-1914), at California St. in **Nob Hill.** A friendly neighborhood bar with a great "street scene view." Grab some pretzels, find a seat upstairs, and watch people struggle up the hill as you kick back with one of 30 draft beers ($4). Open daily 11am-2am. No credit cards.

Bohemia Bar, 1624 California St. (☎474-6968), between Van Ness and Polk St. in **Nob Hill.** A cross between a warehouse and a Chuck E. Cheese's for professional youth. Downstairs has pool, foosball, a dance floor, a fireplace, and live DJs, while the 3000 sq. ft. upper story houses pinball, ping-pong, jukeboxes, and a scattering of leather couches. Happy Hour M-Th all night, F-Sa 6-9pm (beer $3). Open Tu-Sa 6pm-2am. No credit cards.

CLUBS

N Touch SF, 1548 Polk St. (☎441-8413; www.ntouchsf.com), between California and Sacramento St. in **Nob Hill.** A small dance club packed with male bodies bopping to techno pop alongside some seriously toned go-go boys in San Fran's longest-running and most popular Asian gay bar and nightclub. W ladies night "Club Flow." Happy Hour daily 3-8:30pm. Cover after 9pm F $2, Sa $3. 21+. Open daily 3pm-2am. No credit cards.

UNION SQUARE

see map p. 343

🔏 *NEIGHBORHOOD QUICKFIND:* **Discover,** p. 10; **Sights,** p. 80; **Food & Drink,** p. 122; **Accommodations,** p. 194.

BARS AND PUBS

Lefty O'Doul's, 333 Geary St. (☎982-8900), between Mason and Powell St. Named after iconic baseball hero Frank "Lefty" O'Doul, this colossal Irish tavern is like 3 smaller bars in one: a piano lounge, a vast bar and buffet (entrees $7, sandwiches $5) with booths and sit-down tables, and a sports bar in the back. Come for the drinks (most $4) and the nightly piano sing-along. Open daily 7am–2am; kitchen closes at midnight. MC/V.

Gold Dust Lounge, 247 Powell St. (☎397-1695), between Geary and O'Farrell St. Opened around 1905, this old burlesque house and speakeasy still exhibits traces of its past in the red velour couches and the hole in the ceiling that used to hold the dancers' pole. Rock n' roll trio, Johnny Z and the Cameros, plays here every night from 8:30pm-1:30am. Drinks go up a dollar (from $3.75) when the band starts to play. Daytime specials include champagne, Irish coffee, and margaritas ($2.75) anytime before 8:30pm. 21+. No Cover. Open daily 6am-2am. No credit cards.

Tunnel Top, 601 Bush St (☎986-8900), at Powell St. This slightly cramped two-story bar appeals to a diverse clientele. Everyone—from students relaxing with a beer ($4-5) on the calmer lower floor to the couples drinking mojitos ($6) and salsa-ing on the second floor—stops at the Tunnel Top eventually. Every night features a different style of music (from M jazz to F electro-clash). 21+. No cover. M-Sa 5pm-2am. No credit cards.

The Red Room, 827 Sutter St. (☎346-7666), at Jones St. Melodic vibes and urban chic hypnotize upwardly mobile post-grads and professionals as they lounge on scarlet couches and demurely sip cosmos ($7)–recently voted the best in the city. The all-female bartending staff are fast and friendly and make killer specialty drinks. Don't try to be cute—just wear black. Intimate and casual early, packed after 11pm. Open M-Sa 5pm-2am, Su 6pm-2am. MC/V.

CLUBS

Ruby Skye, 420 Mason St. (☎693-0777; www.rubyskye.com), between Post and Geary St. Explore your rhythm at the restored 1896 Stage Door Theater (stained-glass windows intact) with a million other downtown clubbers and a million-and-one out-of-town partiers. You may look inadequate compared to the jaw-dropping go-go dancers, but so will everyone else despite the dress code ("fashionable attire" required, no jeans F-Sa). Dependable house DJs. Drinks from $5. Cover W-Th $10, F-Sa $20. 21+. Open W-Sa 7pm-3am. AmEx/D/MC/V.

FINANCIAL DISTRICT

⌖ *NEIGHBORHOOD QUICKFIND:*
Discover, *p. 13;* ***Food & Drink,*** *p. 124;* ***Accommodations,*** *p. 195.*

BARS AND PUBS

see map p. 344

▨ The Irish Bank, 10 Mark Lane (☎788-7152), just off Bush St., between Grant and Kearny St. An authentic Irish bar, with an award-winning scotch list, super pub-grub and a friendly staff that creates a homey atmosphere. Caters to a mixed crowd of tourists, unwinding suits, and ex-pats. Visit on Sunday to share a cracking ploughman's lunch ($7) and a pint ($3-4) with people from the old-country. Open daily 11:30am-1:30am. AmEx/MC/V.

HAYES VALLEY

⌖ *NEIGHBORHOOD QUICKFIND:*
Discover, *p. 14;* ***Sights,*** *p. 92;* ***Food & Drink,*** *p. 126;* ***Accommodations,*** *p. 196.*

BARS AND PUBS

see map p. 345

▨ Place Pigalle, 520 Hayes St. (☎552-2671), between Octavia and Laguna St. After a long day at work, the designers, boutique owners, and artists of Hayes St. close shop and relax on vintage velvet sofas at this

the BIG $plurge

The Redwood Room

The ten Ian Schrager hotels worldwide are internationally renowned for incredible luxury and style at relatively affordable rates (as low as $195). The Clift, in SF's fashionable Union Square, features original works by Salvador Dalí and Phillipe Stark displayed in a lush lobby, partly designed by Ralph Lauren. If you choose not to splurge to sleep on Egyptian sheets, though, you can still enjoy the Clift's famed Redwood Room bar.

Added to the original Clift Hotel in 1934, the Redwood Room nightclub quickly rose to the pinnacle of SF grandeur and style. When Schrager took over the hotel in 1996, he kept the structure of the bar, but transformed its ambience from hunting lodge to something more Surrealist. Carved from a single redwood tree, the space remains elegant and definitely worth stopping by, even if you can only afford one drink (beers $8, cocktails $11-18). Note the bar, created from one 40ft. piece of carved Venetian glass and the five plasma screens rotating art displays. There are only twelve tables, so arrive early and sport your most stylish outfit, especially on weekends.

(Clift Hotel, 495 Geary St., near Taylor St. ☎775-4700 or 800-652-5438. Open daily 5pm-2am.)

big, dark, airy bar. Weekend nights the wine flows freely, the music blares, and crowds of 20- and 30-somethings with bohemian sensibilities pack the place beyond capacity. Occasional DJs and a rotating art exhibit liven up the back room. Happy Hour daily 4-7pm (beer, house wines $2.75). Open daily 4pm-2am. AmEx/MC/V.

Hayes and Vine, 377 Hayes St. (☎626-5301), between Franklin and Gough St. A perfectly elegant wine bar without a pillow out of place. This favorite for symphony-goers also attracts local merchants. Nibble on a cheese plate ($6-15) or dab some caviar on a cracker, and sip from a selection of over 800 bottles of wine (tastings $2.50-10; glasses $5-20). Open M-Th 5pm-midnight, F-Sa 5pm-1am, Su 4-9pm. MC/V.

Marlena's, 488 Hayes St. (☎864-6672), at Octavia St. Mellow neighborhood bar by day, extravagant drag queen venue by night. Easily and often converted into pool bar, piano bar, or DJ club atmosphere, too. Drag shows most weekends. Open M-F noon-2am, Sa-Su 10am-2am. No credit cards.

TENDERLOIN

see map p. 345

🔲 *NEIGHBORHOOD QUICKFIND: Discover, p. 14; Sights, p. 93; Food & Drink, p. 93; Accommodations, p. 197.*

The Tenderloin, while home to some great nighttime fun, can also be extremely dangerous. **Do not walk alone here at night, especially in the rectangle formed by Ellis St., Van Ness Ave., Taylor St., and Golden Gate Ave., or on Market St. between 5th and 8th St.**

BARS AND PUBS

Bambuddha Lounge, 601 Eddy St. (☎771-3547), between Larkin and Polk St. Classy chic permeates this South Beach-style lounge. Lots of outdoor seating, enormous bed-like couches, and nightly DJs (house on weekends, more mellow mood music during the week) make this one of San Francisco's newest hotspots. A definite must-see, even if the drinks are a little pricier than most other bars in the area (cocktails $6-9). AmEx/MC/V.

Edinburgh Castle, 950 Geary St. (☎885-4074), at Polk St. Lads and lassies drink Tennant's, Guinness, and eat fish & chips at this watering hole. Non-image-conscious crowd unwinds with $4 beer and occasionally with local bands F-Sa. Lots of interesting literary-themed parties like Big Brother Night and readings by young, new writers. Cover only on nights with events. Happy Hour 5-7pm. Open daily 5pm-2am. MC/V.

Jezebel's Joint, 510 Larkin St. (☎345-9832; www.jezebelsjoint.com), near Turk St. This once famous transvestite bar now appeals to a much more rock-and-roll crowd. The music changes nightly in the downstairs dance floor but if you're not feeling the 70s rock or goth beats, you can always migrate upstairs to the pool room or the lounge and its velvet couches. Beer $4, cocktails $4-5. Try the blue and red concoctions that come from the ceiling ($3). Check the website for theme parties. Happy Hour 7-9pm daily. Open M-Sa 7pm-2am. No credit cards.

Hollywood Billiards, 61 Golden Gate Ave. (☎252-9643), between Taylor and Jones St. A buzzing sign and more "provocative" neighbors conceal this enormous second-floor pool hall—the oldest in SF. Dozens of tables, friendly bartenders, and specials (2-for-1 tables Tu, half-price for students Th) keep locals and tourists coming back for good drinks (cocktails $4, beer $3.25) and pool. 21+. Tables $4 per person per hr. M-Th, $6 per person per hr. F-Su. Open daily 5pm-2am. AmEx/MC/V.

CLUBS

Polly Esther's, 181 Eddy St. (☎885-1977; www.pollyesthers.com), between Taylor and Mason St. Savor the anachronism of this touristy retro dig where Le Freak plays as you sip "Brady Punch" cocktails ($7) under a velvet Top Gun painting. Downstairs **Culture Club** spins 80s. Cover F $10, Sa $12-15. No cover Th or before 9pm. Open Th 9pm-3am, F-Sa 8pm-4am. MC/V.

Diva's, 1081 Post St. (☎928-6006; www.divassf.com), at Polk St. Billed as San Francisco's only full-time transgender nightclub, this bar's layout is as diverse as its clientele (men, women, and everyone between and around flock to Diva's on weekends). Take in the scene on the three floors of dancing, pool tables, and plush couches, or sit back and enjoy a good, old-fashioned drag show (F-Sa 12:30am). Cover $10, ladies free before 11pm. Happy Hour M-F 5-7pm. Open daily 6am-2am. No credit cards.

SOUTH OF MARKET AREA (SOMA)

🔢 *NEIGHBORHOOD QUICKFIND:*
***Discover,** p. 15; **Sights,** p. 94;*
***Food & Drink,** p. 127; **Accom-**
***modations,** p. 198.*

BARS AND PUBS

see map p. 347

🔲 **Hotel Utah Saloon,** 500 4th St. (☎546-6300; www.the-hotelutahsaloon.com), at Bryant St. Excellent and unpretentious saloon—with an original Belgian Bar from 1908—and one of the friendliest crowds around. More than your average bar food, including veggie options and build your own burger (from $7). Downstairs stage hosts live bluegrass, rock, alternative, country, or any combination nightly and one of the best open mics in the city on M (shows begin 8pm). Beer $3.75. Show cover $3-7. 21+. Open M-F 11:30am-2am, Sa-Su 6pm-2am. MC/V.

Julie's Supper Club and Lounge, 1123 Folsom St. (☎861-0707; juliessupperclub.com), near 7th St. Always a good time at this revamped old supper club, now maintaining an air somewhere between SoMa chic and 50s camp. Entrees $14-19. Happy Hour Tu-F 5-7:30pm with free appetizers. Open for drinks Tu-Th 5pm-midnight, F-Sa 5pm-2am; for dinner Tu-W 5:30-10:30pm, Th 5:30-11pm, F-Sa 5:30-11:30pm. AmEx/MC/V.

Butter, 354 11th St. (☎863-5964; www.smoothas-butter.com), between Folsom and Harrison St. Equal parts garage, trailer park, and bar, "two turntables and a microwave" energize Butter's innovatively campy parody of white trash. Serves up "Trailer Punch" and other specialty drinks ($6) with hearty, dirt-cheap meals like Spaghettios ($3), French Bread pizza ($4) and Ding-Dongs ($1) served from the back window of an actual 50s trailer. Satire gets serious W nights when a homely crowd shows up for classic rock and WWF. Open W-Sa 5pm-2am. AmEx/D/MC/V.

Wish Lounge, 1539 Folsom St (☎278-9474), between 11th and 12th St. Plush leather couches and deep red lighting make this new SoMa hotspot a must for the young and hip. But underneath the uber-cool decor, the laid-back crowd, the good drinks (cocktails $4-5, beer $4), and the very hot and fast bartenders help Wish achieve that delicate balance between chic and actually fun. Open M-F 5pm-2am, Sa 7pm-2am. AmEx/MC/V.

Acid Test

In Basel, Switzerland in 1938 scientist Albert Hoffman synthesized a compound called lysergic acid diethylamide (LSD) during a series of experiments to find a cure for the common headache. When it failed testing on animals, he discarded it. Five years later Hoffman accidentally ingested a sample through his finger, and became aware of its effect on human perception.

LSD was hailed as a new wonder drug, said to cure psychosis and alcoholism. In the early 1950s, the CIA adopted LSD as part of Operation MK-ULTRA, a series of Cold War mind control experiments. By the end of the 60s, the drug had been tested on some 1,500 military personnel in a series of ethically shady operations, and psychologists had tested its therapeutic value on 40,000 people. Writers Ken Kesey, Allen Ginsberg, and the Grateful Dead's Robert Hunter were first exposed to acid as subjects in government experiments.

In October 1966, the unpredictable drug was made illegal in CA, but had already become integrated into the San Francisco countercultural lifestyle. Kesey's Merry Pranksters had been hosting public Acid Tests for almost a year across the Bay Area.

Once a secret weapon of the military-industrial complex and a potential panacea of the mental health industry, acid became an ingredient in much of the youth culture of the time, juicing up anti-war rallies and love-ins across the Bay and the country.

in recent news

Zoning Out

The 50s had the Beats in North Beach. The 60s had the hippies in the Haight. For decades, San Francisco has fostered small enclaves of bohemian artists and musicians. The area known as South of Market, or SoMa, emerged as the latest incarnation of fringe lifestyle in the 80s. For years, SoMa was predominantly a light industry area with auto repair shops, manufacturing plants, and empty lots with virtually no residential life. In the 80s, artists began to seize on low rents, eclectic housing, and the secluded geography. Instead of a community of coffeehouses and neighborhood bars, these musicians embraced the dance scene of the time and opened clubs—large, loud, electronica clubs where people danced all night and stumbled into the streets at dawn. For the last twenty years, SoMa has been renowned for these clubs.

Things have begun to change in the last few years. In 1988, in an effort to support the artists, the city rezoned SoMa to allow for affordable work/live units (lofts that include art studios) for anyone who considered himself an artist. For years, the spaces were inhabited by low-income artists who helped push the music and art scene of SF into the 90s.

With the 90s, though, came the tech boom, which brought (cont'd next pg.)

12th@Folsom, 1582 Folsom St. (☎626-1985), at 12th St. Two Happy Hours (4:30-6:30pm and 9:30pm-2am), an enormous menu of bar favorites as well as pastas, salads, and sandwiches (all around $6-9) and a laid back atmosphere make this new bar/restaurant a perfect spot for pre-club drinks or late night munching (food served until closing). Beer $4. Cocktails $5-7. DJs on some F-Sa. Open daily 9:30am-2am. AmEx/D/MC/V.

Cassidy's Irish Pub, 1145 Folsom St. (☎241-9990), between 7th and 8th St. Situated between a number of hostels, this unpretentious pub caters to a relaxed, beer-drinking crowd of travelers and young professionals. Two pool tables, a jukebox with a totally random selection of music, and 30 beers on tap ($3-4.50) make Cassidy's an unusual and appreciated option in an area dominated by more upscale bars and clubs. Open daily 2pm-2am. MC/V.

Buzz9, 139 8th St. (☎255-8783), at Minna St. Different flavors mix well in the chic blue-lit splendor. Awesome entrees ($9-17) and an extremely impressive breakfast menu for a bar. Downstairs The Underground Lounge, once a hot 1920s speakeasy, now houses electronic DJs and live acid jazz performed for an eclectic audience. Cocktails $6-8. Open for breakfast M-F 8-11am, brunch Su 11am-3pm, lunch M-F 11am-3pm and dinner M-W 5-9pm, Th-Sa 5-10pm, Su 5-8pm. The Underground Lounge open W-F 7pm-2am, Sa 8pm-2am; $5 cover after 9pm. AmEx/MC/V.

Hole in the Wall Saloon, 289 8th St. (☎431-4695, www.holeinthewallsaloon.com), near Folsom St. Known for its good music and rowdy clientele, this is one of the most famous legendary gay leather bars in the area. Lots of bald heads, moustaches, vests, and hairy bottoms. Happy Hour M-F 4-7pm, 50¢ off all drinks. Open daily noon-2am. No credit cards.

Infusion Bar and Restaurant, 555 2nd St. (☎543-2282), between Bryant and Brannan St. Laid back but upscale after-work destination. Perfect for sampling flavorful sourdough flatbread and California-inspired dishes (small plates $8-11, large plates $14-18), or schmoozing with a peach or cucumber cosmo ($6.50) from an ever-changing list of fruit-infused vodka creations. Open M-F 11am-9pm. AmEx/MC/V.

CLUBS

⊠ 111 Minna, 111 Minna St. (☎974-1719; www.111minnagallery.com), at 2nd St. "Art and Leisure" at this funky up-and-comer's art gallery by day, hipster lounge-y groove-spot by night. Cocktails and beer $3-10. Open M-Tu noon-10pm, W noon-11pm, Th-F noon-2am, Sa 10pm-2am, Su 9pm-2am. Cover $5-15 for bands and progressive house DJs. AmEx/D/MC/V.

The EndUp, 401 6th St. (☎357-0827; www.theendup.com), at Harrison St. A San Francisco institution—complete with outdoor garden and patio—where everyone eventually ends up. DJs spin progressive house for the mostly straight KitKat Th, the pretty-boy Fag F (which are known for redefining the word "fabulous"; if you retain your shirt, you may feel out of place), and the blissful hetero-homo mix during popular all-day Sa-Su parties. Sa morning "Otherwhirled" party goes from 6am-noon. Infamous Su 'T' Dance (27 years strong) 6am-8pm. For those who still need a little more EndUp, try Devotion 8pm-4am Su. Check the website for special event nights. Cover $5-15. Open Th 10:30pm-4 am, F 10pm-4am, Sa 6am-noon and 10pm-4am and Su 6am-4am. No credit cards.

Asia SF, 201 9th St. (☎255-2742; www.asiasf.com), at Howard St. Expensive Cal-Asian-fusion eats served by fabulous gender "illusionists." Each waitress takes a break every half hour to perform in an audience-rousing runway show through the bamboo and lantern decorated dining area. Entrees $10-20; $25 minimum per person. Reservations a must. Open daily 5-10pm for dinner. A more affordable downstairs club, "Dragon's Belly" open F-Sa 10:30pm-3am, with varying cover charge. AmEx/D/MC/V.

The Stud, 399 9th St. (☎252-7883; www.studsf.com), at Harrison St. This legendary bar and club (a 35-year-old stallion) recreates itself every night of the week: go Tu for the wild and wacky midnight drag and transgender shows known as "Trannyshack," Th for Reform School boy-cruising party, F for a mixed straight-gay dance party with some of the most fun DJs in town spinning rock, pop, old-school, electronic, and everything in between, Sa for Sugar's free, delicious eye-candy. Crowd is mostly gay male. Cover $5-9. Open M, W, F, and Su 5pm-2am, Tu 5pm-3am, Th and Sa 5pm-4am. No credit cards.

Up and Down Club, 1151 Folsom St. (☎626-2388; www.updownsf.com), between 7th and 8th St. This aptly named 2-level club is actually two bars in one. The downstairs is geared toward an international fusion restaurant during the day and dancing at night, while the upstairs feels more like a bar than a club. DJs on the two floors spin different genres but hip-hop, house, and funk are common. Check out the W Hump Night—no cover and $3 drinks help you over humpday. Open M-F 11am-3pm for lunch and low-key mingling and Tu-Su 9pm-2am for drinks and dancing. Cover F-Sa $5-8. D/MC/V.

Club Six, 60 6th St. (☎863-1221; www.clubsix1.com), near Mission St. A large, comfy upstairs for chilling and a more raging downstairs for flailing limbs. The schedule and DJs change every weekend but Club Six is known for its consistently good music in six different dance areas, late hours, and young crowds. Great place to hang out or groove on weekends. Beer $5, cocktails $6. Cover $5-10. Open Th 9pm-2am, F-Sa 9pm-4am. No credit cards.

(cont'd from previous pg.)

hordes of young professionals to the city looking for hip places to settle. SoMa seemed perfect. The work/live units began to sell for as much as $500,000 and condos sprang up all over the neighborhood (the artists had refused to impose guidelines on who should be considered an artist in 1988). A previously ignored noise-level stipulation of the 1988 rezoning was resurrected by new residents who had to be awake at 6am, not to stumble home, but to go to work. Noise complaints became common (legendary club 1015 Folsom received nineteen in a period of six months) and clubs began to lose their licenses. By 1999, almost all after-hours clubs in SOMA had been shut down. Despite newly sound-proofed buildings, posted warning signs, and greatly reduced hours, most clubs in the area are still struggling to keep their doors open and their licenses current against a community that claims as much a right to live (and sleep) there as anyone else.

Many long-term residents of the area invested in the club scene have bonded together in grassroots organizations such as the San Francisco Late Night Coalition (www.sflnc.org). Now that many residents have vacated following the collapse of the dot-com boom, the issue has again changed shape. The debate continues to rage in newspaper editorials and community forums as San Francisco tries to negotiate between its traditional support of artistic diversity and an increasingly professional and mobile citizenry.

Rave Reviews

Some say it's chaos, some say it's ecstasy. Probably both, the rave scene in San Francisco is at the forefront of the subcultural phenomenon in the US. Every weekend (if not every night), thousands of party-goers arrive at inconspicuous warehouses where trance, jungle, and other electronic musical genres pulse and bodies gyrate under flashing lights. Armed with water bottles, glow sticks, and glitter, ravers dance until dawn while rotating DJs ensure that the energy and spirits remain high. With few burly bouncers to turn near-toddlers or potential troublemakers away, raves welcome almost everyone in to party, as long as they buy a ticket and can find the place.

Locating a rave used to be like completing a James Bond mission; at a certain time you would have to call a phone number that would then disclose the secret address of an abandoned warehouse. Today the melodrama has been replaced by a more user-friendly system, thanks to a growing network of web sites and email lists:

www.hyperreal.org

www.sfraves.org

www.ravelinks.com/calendars/sanfran.html

www.groovethemovie.com

The scene has further emerged from the underground into the mainstream through recent movies like Groove, which depicts an authentic San Francisco rave with local DJs including the legendary DJ John Digweed.

Liquid, 2925 16th St. (☎431-8889), between Mission St. and South Van Ness Ave. Hard-core dancers and a mixed late-night crowd fill this one room club to listen to some of the hottest DJs spin trip-hop, house, and heavy jungle beats. Cover $3-5. Open M-Sa 9pm-3am. MC/V.

Ten 15 Folsom, 1015 Folsom St. (☎431-1200; www.1015.com), near 6th St. Schizophrenic dance cavern where mind-blowing DJs spin disco, deep house, and acid jazz. Famous for its hypnotic sound and lights, this adult playground parties to the extreme: multiple levels, inflated cover (up to $20), and late hours. Dress code Sa. Open F 9:30pm-7am, Sa 10pm-7am. Su 10pm-5:30am. MC/V.

HAIGHT-ASHBURY

☒ NEIGHBORHOOD QUICKFIND: **Discover,** p. 16; **Sights,** p. 97; **Food & Drink,** p. 130; **Accommodations,** p. 198.

see map p. 349

BARS AND PUBS

Noc Noc, 557 Haight St. (☎861-5811), between Steiner and Fillmore St. in the **Lower Haight.** Cavernous, colorful chaos, padded floor seating, and a DJ spinning hip-hop, jazz, and rock. Micros, imports, bottled Belgians, and some *sake.* Happy Hour daily until 7pm, all pints $2.50. Magic Hour Tarot Readings M 7-10pm. Open daily 5pm-2am. MC/V.

Mad Dog in the Fog, 530 Haight St. (☎626-7279, soccer broadcast hotline ☎442-7994), near Fillmore St. in the **Lower Haight.** Soccer is everything at this British expat bar. Key matches shown live via satellite no matter what bloody time it is—don't miss the spectacle of 50 drunken expats screaming at the telly at 7am. Pints $3.75 until 7pm. Beer specials daily ($2-3). Pub grub with a couple of twists. Bangers and mash $5. Breakfast all day—try the "Greedy Bastard" ($6.50). High-stakes pub-quiz trivia M and Th 9pm with specialized quizzes on Tu (*The Simpsons* is a favorite). DJs or live music F nights and acoustic W. Open M-F 11:30am-2am, Sa-Su 10am-2am. No credit cards.

Toronado, 547 Haight St. (☎863-2276), west of Fillmore St. in the **Lower Haight.** Simple, unpretentious bar worth noting for its amazing draft selection: 46 beers on tap (most $3.50). 60+ Belgian bottles ($4-20). A great afternoon and nighttime hangout with chill music. Happy Hour until 6pm with $1 off most beers. Open daily 11:30am-2am. No credit cards.

Martin Macks, 1568 Haight St. (☎864-0124; www.maddog.citysearch.com), between Ashbury and Clayton St. in the **Upper Haight.** Guinness, Guinness, and more Guinness, plus a little footsie. If Gaelic soccer is being played and televised somewhere in the world, it's being shown here (even if it's 6am). All other times, old-fashioned American sports dominate the 10 screens. Hearty pub food like lamb stew ($7.25) and traditional Irish breakfast ($8; served daily until 9:30pm). Happy Hour M-F 3-6pm. Check website for schedules. Cover only if a big game is on, but then it can be up to $20. Open daily 10am-2am. AmEx/D/MC/V.

CLUBS

Nickie's BBQ, 460 Haight St. (☎621-6508; www.nickies.com), east of Fillmore St. in the **Lower Haight.** After many incarnations (including a brothel where Nickie worked), this venue has evolved into one of the chillest, friendliest small clubs in the city. Great dancing and diverse crowd. Live DJ M-Sa nights with various themes, including Grateful Dead M, world music T, reggae W, and an eclectic mix of funk, hip-hop, and dance music Th-Sa. Cover $5. Open daily 9pm-2am. No credit cards.

The Top, 424 Haight St. (☎864-7386), at Fillmore St. in the **Lower Haight.** Host to some of the finest house DJs in San Francisco. A definite must for turntable loyalists. Su, W, and F House and M Hip Hop are huge. Drum and bass Tu and Sa. Plenty of cushy benches and strong drinks ($4.50) to keep you dancing. Happy Hour until 10pm, $1 off drinks. 21+. Cover $5 after 10pm. Open daily 7pm-2am. No credit cards.

Milk, 1840 Haight St. (☎387-6455), just west of Stanyan St., across from Amoeba, in the **Upper Haight.** Dance club featuring mainly house and hip-hop, with just a little breakbeat and Caribbean influence thrown in to make it interesting. Nothing too crazy or electronic, just the good dance beats to get the young crowd onto the big dance floor. 21+. Weekend cover $5-10. Open M-Th 7pm-2am, F-Sa noon-2am. AmEx/D/MC/V.

CAFES

Café International, 508 Haight St. (☎552-7390; www.cafeinternational.com), west of Fillmore St. in the **Lower Haight.** Hang with local artists and psychics as you sip your java (or beer) and chill to live music. Or take your coffee and sit in one of the few truly green outdoor patios in San Francisco. F nights are devoted to spoken word artists (8pm-midnight) while live jazz brightens Su afternoons at 4pm. Monthly art exhibits. Salads, sandwiches, and Middle Eastern cuisine $5-7. Coffee menu $1.25-2.50. Opens when the spirits move them and closes when everyone wants to go home, generally Tu-Th 8am-10pm, F-Su 8am-midnight. Check website for music schedule. No credit cards.

The Horseshoe Café, 566 Haight St. (☎626-8852), between Steiner and Fillmore St. in the **Lower Haight.** Big-screen TV, movie, and music video projections in the back set the mood in this uncluttered and easygoing coffee/sandwich shop, DSL Internet access ($7 per hr.), and plenty of space to read, write, or ruminate over chai iced tea ($2.25), a root beer float ($1), or cookies (50¢). Open daily 6am-midnight. No credit cards.

CASTRO

◪ *NEIGHBORHOOD QUICKFIND:* ***Discover,*** *p. 17;* ***Sights,*** *p. 99;* ***Food & Drink,*** *p. 132;* ***Accommodations,*** *p. 199.*

The Castro makes up for its paltry selection of good dance spots with an impressive array of well-stocked bars. Famous for a fly-dropping concentration of gorgeous gay men (and the rare lesbian), Castro nightlife generally falls into four categories. There are the younger (or strikingly well-preserved) S&M (that's see-and-model, of course) clubs, where

see map p. 350

pretty boys shrewdly exercise their flirtation across the dance floor; the friendlier neighborhood bars catering to a slightly older crowd; the predominantly straight strongholds; and, of course, the dark, seedy dens of sexual promiscuity (not listed—just look for a black door and buzzing sign).

LGB

Rainbow Delirium

Probably no city could live up to the queer utopian visions that many harbor for dear San Francisco. Nevertheless, it does offer a variety of nightlife options that could be overwhelming for even the most seasoned gay partier. With flags flanking a significant stretch of Market St. and adorning establishments of all types, the massive summer Pride celebration, and the almost mythical allure of the Castro, it may be difficult to avoid slipping into a rainbow-induced delirium.

Take a deep breath, and remember that SF has some of the country's best nightlife, in *and* outside the Castro. So choose wisely, ask locals for advice on finding the right "scene," and don't get too caught up with looking for the word "gay" in these listings. Let SF have its way with you.

Still, some general guidelines: the **Castro** is a safe place to begin (p. 155), especially for bars. **Bar on Castro, SF Badlands,** and **The Pilsner Inn** tend to attract younger crowds. **Moby Dick** and **Twin Peaks** will lead you to the neighborhood stalwarts.

(cont'd next pg.)

BARS AND PUBS

The Bar on Castro, 456 Castro St. (☎626-7220), between Market and 18th St. A refreshingly urbane Castro staple with dark plush couches perfect for eyeing the stylish young crowd, scoping the techno-raging dance floor, or watching Queer as Folk on Su. Happy Hour M-F 3-8pm (beer $2.25). Su beer $1.75. Open M-F 4pm-2am, Sa-Su noon-2am. No credit cards.

The Pilsner Inn, 225 Church St. (☎621-7058), between 14th and 15th St. It's like a big, gay frat house: new pledges play pool and pinball around the bar, while seasoned alumni hang out and smoke on the backyard patio. It's also one of the best mixed places to grab a relaxed drink in the Castro. Beer $3-4.50. Open daily 10am-2am. No credit cards.

Transfer, 198 Church St. (☎861-7499), at 14th St. Predominantly a neighborhood bar, Transfer brings a few newcomers and a wide age-range of returning patrons. Bartenders are friendly and happy to share stories with new Castro visitors. Pool and pinball available for entertainment if the barebreasted men on coasters aren't enough stimulation. Open M-F noon-2am, Sa-Su 6am-2am. No credit cards.

Moby Dick, 4049 18th St. (no public phone) at Hartford St. This standard Castro 30-something bar brims with locals staring into the deep abyss of the large barside aquarium and asking that age-old question: "Are goldfish gay?" Su Beer Bust (Foster's and all domestics $1.50) swarms with stories from the bar's softball team. Happy Hour daily 4-8pm, with $2.25 ale. 2-for-1 frozen drinks all night $5. Open M-F 2pm-2am, Sa-Su 10am-2am. No credit cards.

The Edge, 4149 18th St. (☎863-4027), at Hartford St. Rock music and trance-y house attract some of the younger-at-heart bar-goers in the area. Popular special events include the monthly basket contest, which allows men with no functional knowledge of wicker manipulation to display their "baskets" on stage (1st Th of the month). Happy Hour M-F noon-7pm, domestic beers $2.25. W-Su margaritas $2.25. Domestic beers $2.75-3.25. Open daily noon-2am.

Twin Peaks, 401 Castro St. (☎864-9470), at Market St. The wide-open picture windows were extremely radical for a gay bar (because you can peek in as well as out) when Twin Peaks opened over 20 years ago. It's like reliving your less coherent 60s "visions"—friendly, gay, white-bearded sages perch atop neon pillowed couches surrounded by equally fluorescent balloons and more youthful onlookers from the upstairs balcony. Domestic drafts $2. Cocktails from $3. Open daily noon-2am. No credit cards.

Lucky 13, 2140 Market St. (☎487-1313), between Church and Sanchez St. Laid-back, with a hetero, punk-rock vibe. Pool, pinball, and a crowded balcony. Good selection of scotch and 28 beers on tap, not one of them named Bud, Miller, or Coors (pints $3.50, before 8pm $2.50). Pint of goldfish crackers $1.25. Open M-Th 4pm-2am, F-Su 2pm-2am.

CLUBS

☒ **SF Badlands,** 4121 18th St. (☎626-9320), near Castro St. Strutting past the sea of boys at the bar, the Castro's prettiest faces and bodies cruise a futuristic blue-and-chrome dance floor, where Madonna, George Michael, and Janet Jackson—all in enthralling teleprojection—make SF Badlands just as amazing as its heart-stealing Dupont Circle twin. Cover F-Sa $2. Open daily 2pm-2am. No credit cards.

The Café, 2367 Market St. (☎861-3846), between 17th and 18th St. The Café is chill in the afternoon with pool and pinball, but come evening, it morphs into speaker-pumping, house- and pop-remix bliss, when the dance floor, balcony, and patio crowds rotate in a constant game of see-and-be-seen. Repeat *Guardian* awards for best gay bar. $2 cover some nights. Open M-F 2pm-2am, Sa-Su 12:30pm-2am. No credit cards.

CAFES

☒ **Spike's,** 4117 19th St. (☎626-5573; www.spikescoffee.com), between Castro and Collingwood St. Candy ($6-9 per lb.), sweets, and dog-friendly treats at this juice and coffee joint merit walking with Fido away from the center of Castro Village. Neighborly Spike's place is also one of the few cafes with indoor and outdoor seating. Wash down a tasty hot apple turnover ($1.50) with mocha, hot chocolate, or iced coffee ($1.50-2.50). Open daily 6:30am-8pm. AmEx/MC/V.

☒ **Café du Nord,** 2170 Market St. (☎861-5016), between Church and Sanchez St. Takes you back in time to a red velvet club with speakeasy ambience. Excellent live music nightly—from pop and groove to garage rock. Local favorites include vintage jazz, blues, and R&B. Special weekly events include the popular Monday Night Hoot, a showcase of local singing and songwriting talent. Dinner served from 5:30-11pm. Favorites include Du Nord's Newly Famous Gourmet Burger (6.50), and Pesto Pizza (6.25). Other entrees are on the expensive side, ranging from $10-17. Happy Hour 6-7:30pm with swank $2.50 martinis, Manhattans, and cosmos. 21+. Cover $5-10 after 8:30pm. Open daily 6pm-2am. No credit cards.

Morning Due Cafe, 3698 17th St. (☎621-7156), at Church St., is a peaceful, grrly book spot with turquoise tables and all the free newspapers you could ever want. Big tea and vegan cookie selection, with great hot apple cider ($1.75) and mocha ($2.50). Lunch offerings include sandwiches ($4), quiche with green salad ($5.50), and croissants ($2). Wireless Internet access $2.50 per 30min. with own laptop. Open daily 7am-8pm. ATM available inside. No credit cards.

LGB

(cont'd from previous pg.)

If you're looking to dance all night, you'll inevitably wind up in **SoMa** (p. 151). **The EndUp** is a popular after-hours hotspot. Similarly, **SoMa** may be the place to go to fill your Leather & Levis craving (p. 184).

Queer women may want to explore SoMa and the Mission. **The Lexington** (p. 158) is an SF classic. **Wild Side West** in **Bernal Heights** claims to be the oldest lesbian bar in SF (p. 160).

If you're **under 21,** you're basically out of luck in this city. Cruising the streets for sketchy bouncers (or absent ones) may seem like a good option, but some of the cafes in the city can be just as stimulating as that bar that looks so fun. One friendly option, though, is **Club Faith,** 715 Harrison St., at 3rd St. in **SoMa,** whose cover may be a bit high, but at least they let you in for the progressive house and hip-hop. (☎905-4100; www.clubfaithsf.com. 18+. Cover $12. Open Th 9:30pm-2:30am.)

Hotspots open and close their doors quickly in SF. Look around and hit the web (*San Francisco Bay Guardian,* www.sfbg.com; and www.citysearch.com are good places to start) for the latest advice.

NOE VALLEY

see map p. 350

◪ NEIGHBORHOOD QUICKFIND: **Discover**, p. 18; **Sights**, p. 100; **Food & Drink**, p. 133; **Accommodations**, p. 201.

BARS AND PUBS

◪ **The Dubliner,** 3838 24th St. (☎826-2279), between Church and Sanchez St. A grand pub with no pretensions: lots of Guinness, 11 screens broadcasting sports, and a back-slapping friendly crowd. Smoking-friendly patio in the front where you can get drinks served through a window. Pints $4. Open M-F 1pm-2am, Sa-Su 11am-2am, when NFL is on 9am-2am. AmEx/D/MC/V.

Valley Tavern, 4054 24th St. (☎285-0674), between Noe and Castro St. Despite its standard name, this newly renovated bar manages to avoid the cramped, stuffy feeling of traditional pubs. Check out the back alcove where they hide the good stuff—the jukebox, Golden Tee, and a small pool table. No food served, but at night you can order from **Alcatraces,** (p. 134), the Creole restaurant next door. Open M-Th 2pm-2am, F-Sa 1pm-2am. AmEx/MC/V.

Bliss Bar, 4026 24th St. (☎826-6200; www.blissbarsf.com), at Noe St. In an area full of pubs and bars, this stylish neighborhood lounge is definitely the best place to get a martini. Live DJ spins more for ambience than for dancing W-Sa 9pm-2am. Beer $4; cocktails $6-8. Happy Hour daily 4:30-7:30pm; martinis $3. Open daily 4:30pm-2am. MC/V.

Noe's Bar and Grill, 1199 Church St. (☎282-4007), at 24th St. A sports bar with 6 TVs, video games and a pizza place next door that delivers to your table (pizza, sandwiches, and burgers $5-7). Pints $3-4. Open M-F 10am-2am, Sa-Su 8am-2am. No credit cards.

The Peaks, 1316 Castro St. (☎826-0100), at 24th St. Simple bar whose main concessions to decor are Nascar posters and a pool table. Friendly staff, cheap drinks (cocktails $3, beer $2.50-3.50) and an outdoor patio, however, make this a great place to get a beer and unwind after a long day. Open M-F 8am-2am, Sa-Su 6am-2am. No credit cards.

MISSION

see map p. 352

◪ NEIGHBORHOOD QUICKFIND: **Discover**, p. 18; **Sights**, p. 102; **Food & Drink**, p. 135; **Accommodations**, p. 202.

BARS AND PUBS

◪ **Hush Hush,** 496 14th St. (☎241-9944), at Guerrero St. You'll feel hip when you find Hush Hush, since this spot is too hot to need a sign; look for the blue awning with 496 in white letters. Large leather booths, pool, and local DJs spinning almost every night have everyone whispering about this place. Generally Latin, hip-hop, or electronica, but they do mix it up quite a bit. MC Battle 1st Tu of every month. Smile Su with Rock DJs. Open daily 6pm-2am. No credit cards.

The Lexington Club, 3464 19th St. (☎863-2052), at Lexington St. The only bar in San Francisco that is all lesbian, all the time. Jukebox plays all the grrly favorites. Though there's not much room for dancing, bar-goers sometimes spill out into the streets. Tarot Tu with Jessica. Happy Hour M-F 3-7pm. Open daily 3pm-2am. No credit cards.

The Attic, 3336 24th St. (☎643-3376), between Bartlett and Mission St. Squeeze into the barely lit booths in back once you squeeze past the bar, hopefully before (or after?) someone squeezes you. Romantic and hip M nights, with jazz, trip-hop, and occasional bands. Th-Sa rock and hip-hop DJs bring in a more mixed crowd. Happy Hour M-F 5-7:30pm. Beers $3-3.75; Happy Hour drafts $2.50. Open daily 5pm-2am. No credit cards.

The Argus, 3187 Mission St. (☎824-1447). With only a delicate peacock feather gracing the sign for this intimate bar, you'll confirm your place among the elite when you slip past the doors. Hear live music as you sip your drink, and each Su enjoy a game of pool courtesy of Argus. Open M-Sa 4pm-2am, Su 5pm-2am. No credit cards.

Esta Noche, 3079 16th St. (☎861-5757), at Valencia St. Where the Mission meets the Castro. The city's premier gay Latino bar hosts regular shows, both on stage and off. The bar is quite popular and space is tight on weekends. Domestic bottles and drafts $2.25. Happy Hour daily 4-9pm. Cover F-Su $5-10. Open Su-Th 1pm-2am, F-Sa 1pm-2am. No credit cards.

Skylark, 3086 16th St. (☎861-9294), at Valencia St. Young professionals mix with urban hipsters and a few old-school Mission locals in this loungy bar. DJs mix almost every night, and a spontaneously erupting dance floor often spills over into the narrower bar area. Come later for dancing and earlier for lounging in the golden booths. Happy Hour 5-8pm. Open Su 6pm-2am, M-W 7pm-2am, Th-Sa 5pm-2am. No credit cards.

CLUBS

Liquid, 2925 16th St. (☎431-8889), at South Van Ness Ave. Nightly mix usually includes trip-hop and hip-hop, but mainly house. Young but mature and mellow crowd fills the small space. Meet a cutie and practice those long-forgotten backseat skills; all of Liquid's couches are car seats. 21+. Cover $4-5. Open daily 9pm-3am (one of the area's only after-hours spots). No credit cards.

Odeon Bar, 3223 Mission St. (☎550-6994; www.odeonbar.com), south of César Chavez St. Fun and quirky artists' hangout in the deep Mission. Offbeat and off the beaten path. Nightly events, like "Ask Dr. How" W, and Card Trick Sa. Inquire here about the Burning Man festival; this is one of its San Fran hubs. If it gets too crowded, climb the ladder and cage yourself in "jail" above the club. *Let's Go* recommends knowing what drink you want to order before you advance toward the bar. Open daily 4pm-2am. Accepts "every credit card that's neither expired nor stolen."

amnesia, 853 Valencia St. (☎970-8336). Supporting a strong local community and following of DJ music, amnesia brings serious shows to an appreciative audience. Great selection of Belgian beers ($2-12) poured for you by sleek and casual bartenders (who sometimes double as performers). Open daily 6pm-2am. No credit cards.

El Rio, 3158 Mission St. (282-3325), between César Chavez and Valencia St. A classy, mixed club with a strict ID policy, El Rio is worth the wait until you're 21. Stylish lighting and decor, large outdoor patio, and well-groomed bartenders. Come to Salsa Su, including a dance lesson and patio barbecue. F 5-7pm free oysters on the half-shell. Drinks $4-10. Occasional cover $5-8. Open M-Th 5pm-2am, F-Su 3pm-2am. No credit cards.

Make Out Room, 3225 22nd St. (☎647-2888), between Mission and Valencia St. Equipped with namesake-designed booths. The bar is a live music venue, promoting local bands on M and Su nights. DJs take over the rest of the week, while bar-goers kick back and shoot some pool. Cover $6. Open daily 6pm-2am. No credit cards.

The Elbo Room, 647 Valencia St. (☎552-7788; www.elbo.com), between 17th and 18th St. Clothing is skimpy on the crowded dance floor. Cool off downstairs with pool, PacMan, huge TVs, and $3.25-3.50 pints. Live music Tu-Sa. Rockabilly W. Reggae DJs Sa. Happy Hour daily 5-9pm; $1 off. 21+. Cover $5-10. Open daily 5pm-2am. No credit cards.

CAFES

⚑ Café Macondo, 5159 16th St. (☎431-7516), at Valencia St. Macondo is all that a coffeehouse should be. Mismatched comfy old furniture to sink into and shelves of books for those who forgot their own. Sandwiches $4.25-5; salads $3.75-6; dinner entrees $5-6.50. Coffee and drinks $1.25-2.75. Open M-F 10am-10pm, Sa 11am-10pm. No credit cards.

Qué Tal Coffeehouse, 1005 Guerrero St. (☎282-8855), at 22nd St. Clean and airy with a welcoming staff and decor, Qué Tal is a favorite among locals. The prices are a sweet deal too: coffee drinks $1-3.50; sandwiches $5; soups $2.50-3.65. A towering wall of tea options. Open M-F 7am-8pm, Sa-Su 8am-8pm. No credit cards.

Muddy's, 1304 Valencia St. (☎647-7994), at 24th St. An open space with a mix of people, Muddy's is one of those cute little coffeehouses found all over the Mission. Bagels, tea, and pastries as well as coffee drinks ($1-3). Internet access available ($7 per hr.). Open M-F 6am-11pm, Sa-Su 7am-midnight. No credit cards.

BERNAL HEIGHTS

see map p. 352

▶ *NEIGHBORHOOD QUICKFIND: **Discover**, p. 19; **Sights**, p. 104; **Food & Drink**, p. 136.*

BARS AND PUBS

Wild Side West, 424 Cortland Ave. (☎647-3099), at Wool St. The oldest lesbian bar in SF is a neighborhood favorite for women and men alike. There's pool, a cool jukebox, cheap beer ($2.50-3.50), and a friendly atmosphere. The hidden highlight is a junkyard jungle with benches, fountains, and scrap-art statues in back. Open daily 1pm-2am. No credit cards.

POTRERO HILL

see map p. 353

▶ *NEIGHBORHOOD QUICKFIND: **Discover**, p. 19; **Sights**, p. 104; **Food & Drink**, p. 137.*

BARS AND PUBS

Lingba Lounge, 1469 18th St. (☎355-0001), at Connecticut St. After dinner at Thanya and Salee's Thai Cuisine, head over to their lounge whose name translates into "crazy monkey." This theme is reflected in the decor (jungle/tiki/rainforest chic), its artwork (wall-sized mural of frolicking monkeys), and its drinks (the house speciality is a Bowl of Monkeys—a scorpion bowl with even more zing, $21). The young crowd, specialty drinks ($6-7), and occasional DJ make this a necessary stop if you're in the area. Open daily 5pm-2am. AmEx/D/MC/V.

Thee Parkside, 1600 17th St. (☎503-0393, www.theeparkside.com), at Wisconsin St. Younger, relaxed crowd comes to unwind with live music W-Su and maybe grab a quick bite from the bar menu of "Southern Specialities" (fried chicken, $12). Outdoor patio with ping-pong table and lots of seating. Free oyster BBQ Su 5pm. Beer $3-4, cocktails $4-7. Happy Hour M-F 4-7pm; $2 beer. Cover $5-7 F-Sa, varies on weeknights. Open daily 4pm-2am. AmEx/D/MC/V.

Connecticut Yankee, 100 Connecticut St. (☎552-4440). Miss New England? Get your fill of the Sox, Bruins, and Pats at this classic tavern. Signed pictures of Ted Williams complement $4 Sam Adams, and 5 TVs broadcast sports from the other coast (and during slow days, table tennis tournaments). Live music on weekends, heated patio, and big burgers ($7.50) and salads ($7-9). M-F 11am-2am, Sa-Su 10am-2am. MC/V.

RICHMOND

see map p. 341

▶ *NEIGHBORHOOD QUICKFIND: **Discover**, p. 20; **Food & Drink**, p. 139; **Accommodations**, p. 202.*

BARS AND PUBS

▨ The Last Day Saloon, 406 Clement St. (show info ☎387-6343, bar 387-6344) at 4th Ave. A game room and bar in one, with 2 pool tables, darts, and foosball. Satellite TV for sports events. Live music—from rock to roots to hip-hop to funk—Tu-Sa around 9pm (cover usually $4-10). Domestic bottles $2.75, imports $3.75. Happy Hour M-F 2-6pm with bud drafts ($2), well drinks ($2), and complimentary snacks. All-day weekly drink specials $3. Open M-F 2pm-2am, Sa-Su noon-2am. No credit cards.

Pat O' Shea's Mad Hatter, 3848 Geary Blvd. (☎752-3148), between 3rd and 4th Ave. You can't resist a pub whose motto is "We cheat tourists and drunks!" TVs, pool tables, pinball machines, and the friendliest bar staff around make this place a local and student favorite, especially when football season rolls around. American football, that is. Happy Hour daily 4-7pm with 2 for 1 pitchers and $1 off draft beer and well drinks. Kitchen open M-Tu 4-10pm, W-Sa 11:30am-10pm, Su 11:30am-4pm. Open daily 10am-2am; AmEx/D/MC/V.

The Plough and the Stars, 116 Clement St. (☎751-1122), at 2nd Ave. In the land of Irish pubs, this place, with accents so thick you'll feel like you're in County Derry, is the real deal. Irish music Tu-Su nights, includes *seisiun,* step-dancing, and bluegrass. Happy Hour M-F 4-7pm $1 off draft. Bottled beers $2.75, drafts $4. Open daily 4pm-2am. AmEx/D/MC/V.

Trad'r Sam, 6150 Geary Blvd., (☎221-0773), at 26th Ave. Don't let the unassuming (almost downright shady) exterior deter you. This neighborhood spot dons a Polynesian get-up. Locals drown their South Pacific sorrows in large exotic cocktails ($5-6), and young 20-somethings flock here for after-dark antics. The cramped atmosphere does not stop customers from dancing or lounging on one of many comfy couches. Open daily 10:30am-2am. No credit cards.

SUNSET

🔀 *NEIGHBORHOOD QUICKFIND:* **Discover,** *p. 20;* **Sights,** *p. 105;* **Food & Drink,** *p. 140.*

BARS AND PUBS

🔲 **Yancy's Saloon,** 734 Irving St. (☎665-6551), at 9th Ave. With San Francisco Giants banners everywhere in sight, this bar is a haven for local sports fans. A big comfy saloon, with old velvet couches, hanging plants, TVs, and dartboards. Huge beer selection ($3-5). Happy Hour M-F 4-6pm.

see map p. 341

Various daily drink specials and shots ($2.75-3). Open M-Sa 4pm-2am, Su noon-2am.

Little Shamrock, 807 Lincoln Way (☎661-0060), at 9th Ave. This dark, jostling bar has been serving ale to the Sunset for over a century. From the old men propping up the bar, to the students playing darts, to the middle-aged couples watching sports on the TV, this is a real neighborhood haunt. Beer ($3-4); wines ($4 per glass), Irish coffee ($4). Open M-Th 3pm-2am, F 2pm-2am, Sa-Su 1pm-2am.

Entertainment

MUSIC

The live music scene in San Fran is a vibrant mix of class and brass, funk and punk, hippies and hip-hop, and everything in between. Wailing guitars and scratchy voices still fill the halls of San Francisco's most famous rock clubs, where several stars in the classic rock pantheon got their starts. If you're in a mellow mood, low-profile, funked-up soul seems to draw today's pimped-out booty shakers, while the San Francisco Symphony, with Michael Tilson Thomas as music director, reaches world-class status.

The distinction between bars, clubs, and live music venues is hazy in San Francisco. Almost all bars will occasionally have bands, and small venues often host rock and hip-hop shows. Start looking for the latest live music listings in *S.F. Weekly* and *The Guardian*. Hardcore audiophiles might also snag a copy of *Bay Area Music (BAM)* (**Publications,** p. 49). Many of the bars and a few of the clubs listed in **Nightlife** feature regular live bands at various times. *The List* is a calendar of rock and rock-like gigs all over Northern California (http://jon.luini.com/thelist.txt). Often the best way to get a pulse of the music scene is just to keep your eyes and ears open on the streets.

ENTERTAINMENT BY NEIGHBORHOOD

MARINA, FT. MASON, COW HOLLOW

Magic Theatre (167)	theater
Cowell Theater (168)	theater
Bayfront Theater (168)	theater

NORTH BEACH

Jazz at Pearl's (165)	jazz
Saloon (165)	blues
Bannam Place Theater (168)	theater
Club Fugazi (168)	theater

NOB HILL & RUSSIAN HILL

▨ Red Devil Lounge (164)	rock
Bimbo's 365 Club (164)	rock
The Lumière (170)	movies

UNION SQUARE

Biscuits & Blues (166)	blues
Blue Lamp (166)	blues
Geary Theater (168)	theater

FINANCIAL DISTRICT

The Punchline (170)	comedy

CIVIC CENTER

Louise M. Davies Symphony Hall (166)	class.
War Memorial Opera House (166)	class.
San Francisco Ballet (166)	dance
Herbst Theatre (167)	class.
The Orpheum (168)	theater
Golden Gate Theater (168)	theater
Curran Theater (168)	theater

HAYES VALLEY

▨ Alonzo King's L. Cont. Ballet (171)	dance

TENDERLOIN

Exit Theater (168)	theater

SOUTH OF MARKET AREA (SOMA)

Slim's (164)	rock

PACIFIC HEIGHTS & JAPANTOWN

Boom Boom Room (166)	blues
The Fillmore (165)	rock

HAIGHT-ASHBURY

▨ Amoeba Music (165)	rock
▨ Justice League (167)	hip-hop
Storyville (167)	hip-hop
848 Community Space (169)	theater
Red Vic Movie House (170)	movies

CASTRO

▨ Café du Nord (165)	rock
▨ Castro Theatre (170)	movies

MISSION

The Marsh (169)	theater
Intersection for the Arts (169)	theater
Theatre Rhinoceros (169)	theater
Oberlin Dance Company (171)	dance
▨ Roxie (170)	movies
Dancer's Group (171)	dance

POTRERO HILL

▨ Bottom of the Hill (165)	rock

SUNSET

California Contemp. Dancers (171)	dance

ROCK

▨ **Red Devil Lounge,** 1695 Polk St. (☎921-1695), at Clay St. in **Nob Hill.** A two-story wrought iron and red leather showcase for not-yet-famous local bands every night. "Strong Island Iced Tea" ($7) and plenty of beer ($4) guarantee that the twenty-something crowd is hopping regardless of who's playing. M night "Viv and a movie" offers a multimedia celebration of local artists and bands, artwork on the walls, and a series of short movies by filmmakers for $10. Cover $3-10 after 9:30pm every other night. Open M-Sa 7pm-2am. AmEx/MC/V.

Bimbo's 365 Club, 1025 Columbus Ave. (☎474-0365; www.bimbos365club.com; tickets www.tickets.com or www.ticketweb.com), at Chestnut St. in **Russian Hill.** Keeping the party going since 1931. Named after its founder, the club began as a speakeasy where Rita Hayworth got her start. With two-level seating and a huge dance floor, Bimbo's now hosts prestigious acts from swing to indie rock. Two-drink minimum. Tickets around $15. Doors open around 8pm; concerts start at 9pm. Box office open M-F 10am-4pm. MC/V.

Slim's, 333 11th St. (☎522-0333; www.slims-sf.com), between Folsom and Harrison St., in **SoMa.** Slim's low-key bar, food, and dedication to bringing blues, R&B, jazz, Cajun, and some alternative to San Francisco make this venue a perennial favorite among music lovers. All ages. Tickets $10-25, cheaper in advance. Box office open M-F 10:30am-6pm. MC/V.

The Fillmore, 1805 Geary Blvd. (☎346-6000; www.thefillmore.com), at Fillmore St. in **Japantown.** Bands that would pack stadiums in other cities are often eager to play at the truly legendary Fillmore, the foundation of San Francisco's music and cultural scene in the 60s. Grand, brightly lit, and filled with anecdotal and nostalgic wall-hangings. All ages. Tickets $15-40. Call for hours. Wheelchair-accessible. AmEx/MC/V.

▨ **Amoeba Music,** 1855 Haight St. (☎831-1200; www.amoebamusic.com), just east of Stanyan St. in the **Upper Haight.** Free weekly concerts of all types in this enormous warehouse of a store. Some fairly well-known acts. Also features weekly in-house DJ series called Mandala F 7-10pm. Check website for listings. Open M-Sa 10:30am-10pm, Su 11am-9pm.

▨ **Café du Nord,** 2170 Market St. (☎861-5016), between Church and Sanchez St. in the **Castro.** Takes you back in time to a red velvet club with speakeasy ambiance. Excellent live music nightly—from pop and groove to garage rock. Local favorites include vintage jazz, blues, and R&B. Special weekly events include the popular Monday Night Hoot, a showcase of local singing and songwriting talent. Happy Hour daily until 7:30pm with swank $2.50 martinis, Manhattans, and cosmos. Cover $5-10 after 8:30pm. 21+. Open Su-Tu 6pm-2am, W-Sa 4pm-2am.

▨ **Bottom of the Hill,** 1233 17th St. (☎626-4455; 24hr. info 621-4455; www.bottomofthehill.com), between Missouri and Texas St. in **Potrero Hill.** A big bar or an intimate rock club depending on how you think of it, this space hosts three bands—some local, some bigger names—nightly. Come for the live music or the Su afternoon all-you-can-eat barbecues (most Su, $5-10), but make sure you come. Happy Hour F 3pm-7pm, $1 beers. 21+. Cover most nights, $5-12. Open M-Th 8:30pm-2am, F 3pm-2am, Sa 8:30pm-2am, Su hours vary. MC/V.

BLUES & JAZZ

Jazz at Pearl's, 256 Columbus Ave. (☎291-8255), at Broadway in **North Beach.** Traditional jazz combos in a comfortable setting for a casual crowd, young and old alike. Beer $4, well drinks $5, light menu $4-9. 21+. No cover, but a 2-drink minimum. Open M-Sa 8:30pm-2am.

Saloon, 1232 Grant Ave. (☎989-7666), between Columbus Ave. and Vallejo St. in **North Beach.** The oldest bar in San Francisco (established in 1861), which still looks like, well, a saloon. Home to live rock and blues bands nightly (M-F 9:30pm-1:30am, Sa-Su 4-8pm and 9:30pm-1:30am). Beer $3-4, well drinks $3. Cover F-Sa $3-5; 1-drink min. other nights. Open daily noon-2am. No credit cards.

SF Jazz Festival

From the International Gay and Lesbian Film Festival to the Fringe Festival, SF hosts an impressive number of annual avant-garde artistic forums. One of particular notoriety is the **San Francisco Jazz Festival,** an annual two-week autumn celebration. Like many SF festivals, the Jazz Festival was originally a local, community-based event. Now, described by the *London Observer* as "probably the best jazz festival in the world," the event has become a gathering space for legends, rising stars, eager novices, and curious listeners alike.

Recently, SF JAZZ founded a new seasonal forum for avant-garde jazz. The **SF Modern JAZZ Collective** will stem from a newly-formed group of artists including Joshua Redman, Miguel Zenón, Joshua Roseman, Renee Rosnes, Brian Blade, and Bobby Hutcherson. The group will hold an annual multi-week residency in San Francisco during which they will workshop new compositions by the band-members themselves, perform in concert, and lead educational events. In addition, they will work with new arrangements of seminal pieces from modern jazz history, focusing on a different composer each year. The first season in Spring of 2004 will emphasize the work of Ornette Coleman.

Visit www.sfjazz.com for more information.

Jazz Festival saxophonist

SF Art Institute

Washington Square

Boom Boom Room, 1601 Fillmore St. (☎673-8000; www.boomboomblues.com), at Geary St., near **Japantown.** Once owned by John Lee Hooker, praised as one of the greatest bluesmen of all time, Boom Boom Room is known as the city's home to "blues and boogie, funk, and bumpin' jazz" and features live music nightly, often with big-name acts. This place is leading the revival of the 50s Fillmore Jazz scene with style. Cover: M-Tu $3, W-Th $5, F-Sa $10, Su $4, varies by act. Open daily 4pm-2am.

Blue Lamp, 561 Geary St. (☎885-1464; www.bluelamp.com), at Taylor St., in **Union Sq**. Lots of local bands (including the owners) perform nightly at 9:30pm in a range of styles at this friendly and comfortable venue. Rock usually dominates the weekends, while weekdays see a lot of folk jams. Su nights boast one of the city's longest running open blues jams, and M nights feature an acoustic open mic for undiscovered performers. Drinks average $4. 21+. Cover usually $5-6 on weekends. Open daily 3pm-2am. No credit cards.

Biscuits & Blues, 401 Mason St. (☎292-2583; www.biscuitsandbluessf.com), at Geary St., in **Union Sq.** "Dedicated to the preservation of hot biscuits and cool blues," this unpretentious basement joint will make you feel downright Southern with fried chicken and, of course, biscuits. Live, kickin' blues every night. Entrees $11-15 (smoked turkey and chicken jambalaya with rice and piquante is a must-have). Drinks $3-7. Happy Hour Su-F 5-7pm with cheap snacks ($2-4) and drink specials. All ages. Cover varies with act. Open M-F 5pm-11:30pm, Sa-Su 5pm-1am. AmEx/D/MC/V.

CLASSICAL

Louise M. Davies Symphony Hall, 201 Van Ness Ave. (☎431-5400), near the **Civic Center,** houses the **San Francisco Symphony** in an impressive if controversial structure (p. 91). The cheapest seats are on the center terrace, directly above the orchestra—the acoustics are slightly off, but you get an excellent (and rare) head-on view of the conductor (and the rest of the audience). Prices vary with performance. Open M-F 9am-5pm.

War Memorial Opera House, 301 Van Ness Ave. Open for tickets 2hr. before each show. Box office, 199 Grove St. Open M-Sa 10am-6pm. **San Francisco Opera** (☎864-3330; www.sfopera.com). Tickets start at $23. Standing-room-only tickets ($10, cash only) available from 10am on day of performance.

San Francisco Ballet (☎865-2000; www.sfballet.org), shares the War Memorial Opera House with the San Francisco Opera (p. 13). Box office in the Opera House. Open M-Sa noon-6pm. Phones open M-F 10am-4pm. Tickets start at $30. Same-day discounts available for students, seniors, and military from $10-20 anytime after noon on performance date. 2 discount tickets per ID.

Herbst Theatre, 401 Van Ness Ave. (☎392-4400), near the **Civic Center,** provides a plush setting for a year-round schedule of classical soloists, quartets, and smaller symphonies, plus occasional lectures by renowned authors, artists, and other intellectuals. Box office open M-F 9:30am-5pm, Sa 10am-4pm.

HIP-HOP

🎐 **Justice League,** 628 Divisadero St. (☎440-0409, info 289-2038), at Hayes St. in the **Lower Haight.** Live hip-hop is hard to find in San Francisco, but the Justice League fights ever onward for a good beat. Excellent variety of artists. M 10pm Club Dred, reggae and dub. W 10pm Bang Bang, soul night. 21+. Cover $5-25, usually $10-14. Usually open daily 9pm-2am. Tickets at www.ticketweb.com, **Red Top Clothing,** 1472 Haight (☎552-6494), and **Open Mind Music** (☎621-2244), at Divisadero and Page St.

Storyville, 1751 Fulton St. (☎441-1751; www.storyvillesf.com), between Masonic and Central Ave. in the **Upper Haight.** The introduction of reggae, soul, funk, hip-hop, and a turntable have added diversity and bigger crowds to this primarily jazz club. Kitchen serves California Creole cuisine; entrees $6-10. 21+. Cover $5-10. Open Th-Sa 7pm-2am. AmEx/MC/V.

THEATER

Downtown, **Mason St.** and **Geary St.** constitute "**Theater Row,**" the city's prime place for theatrical entertainment. **Fort Mason,** near Fisherman's Wharf, is also a popular area. For the latest on shows, check local listings in the city's many free magazines and newspapers. **TIX Bay Area,** located in a kiosk in **Union Sq.** on the corner of Geary and Powell St., is a Ticketmaster outlet with tickets for almost all shows and concerts in the city as well as information about city tours and MUNI passes. Assure yourself a seat in advance or try for cash-only, half-price tickets on the day of the show. (☎433-7827; www.theaterbayarea.org. Open Tu-Th 11am-6pm, F-Sa 11am-7pm, Su 11am-3pm. MC/V).

Magic Theatre, Bldg. D, 3rd fl.(☎441-8822; www.magictheatre.org), in **Fort Mason** (use Fort Mason Center entrance). Sam Shepard served as playwright-in-residence at the Magic Theatre from 1975 to 1985. Today, the theater stages exclusively premiere shows. In 2004, the theater will premier Mamet's play on the Faust legend. W-Th $22-32, F-Su $27-37. Senior and student rush tickets (available 30min. before the show, $10). Shows start at 8 or 8:30pm. Su matinees start at 2:30pm ($15), reduced cost for previews ($17). Call for exact times. Box office open Tu-Sa noon-5pm. AmEx/D/MC/V.

the local story

A Performer's City

Diana, a Mask Italia (p. 185) employee and performance artist, shares her take on the SF scene.

My friends and I have a performance collective; we're all working-class professionals with degrees in our areas. Artists here are turning to the cabaret format for performing arts as a way to get exposure. There are a lot of unemployed artists willing to work for free, since there isn't a lot of funding in San Francisco. There is support, but not funding. If any of my colleagues can get paid to perform, that's a wonderful thing.

The Mission has been an artistic center with underground performers and activists working out of the area. I don't want to say it's "radical" and give off the wrong connotation, but I'll say it anyway. It's an ethnically diverse neighborhood...a lot of Mexican and Central American immigrants, you know, working-class individuals who have lived here for decades. With the dot-com explosion, the area got more gentrified with upper-class folk trying to challenge the neighborhood's cultural tone. But now that it's busted, younger artists have come here and, of course, the people who have always lived here are still here. The scene is still as diverse as ever and has a strong desire to express itself.

Castro Theatre

Red Vic Movie House

Herbst Theatre

Cowell Theater, Herbst Pavilion (☎345-7575; www.fortmason.org), in **Fort Mason** (use Fort Mason Center entrance). A rentable space that hosts a variety of multimedia art events such as film, dance, and theater performances. It also boasts a fabulous view of the bay. Prices and showtimes are determined by the group renting the facility. Check website for event details. AmEx/MC/V.

Bayfront Theater, Bldg. B, 3rd fl. (☎474-8935, www.improv.org), in **Fort Mason** (use the Fort Mason Center entrance). Home of the BATS (Bay Area Theater Sports) Center for Improvisational theater. Offers high-quality improvisational comedy shows (tickets $7-15) and workshops. Stop by for information on theater happenings in the city. Main show 8pm, late night show 10:30pm. Check online for calendar and listings. Call for reservations.

Bannam Place Theater, 50 Bannam Pl. (☎986-4607; www.fugitivetheatre.com), between Union and Green St. in **North Beach.** Tucked in a tiny alley, Bannam hosts a variety of shows, mainly plays and one-man bands. Tickets $12-20; available at door. Call for shows and showtimes. No credit cards.

Club Fugazi, 678 Green St. (☎421-4222; www.beachblanketbabylon.com), between Columbus Ave. and Powell St. in **North Beach.** Cabaret-style *Beach Blanket Babylon* is a long-running SF classic. Now in its 30th year! Tickets $25-70. 21+ except Su 3pm. Shows W-Th 8pm, F-Sa 7 and 10pm, Su 3 and 7pm. Box office open M-Sa 10am-6pm, Su noon-6pm. MC/V.

Geary Theater, 415 Geary St. (☎749-2228; www.act-sfbay.org), at Mason St. in **Union Sq.** Home to the renowned American Conservatory Theater, the jewel in SF's theatrical crown. The elegant theater's gilded ceiling and columns make it a show-stealer in its own right. Wheelchair-accessible. Tickets $11-61 (cheaper for previews and on weekdays). Half-price student, teacher, and senior discounts available two hours before showtime with ID. Box office open Tu-Su noon-6pm. AmEx/MC/V.

The Orpheum, 1192 Market St., at Hyde St. near the **Civic Center.** Box Office (☎512-7770), 6th St. at Market St. This famous San Francisco landmark hosts the big Broadway shows. Past shows include *Phantom of the Opera, Chicago,* and *The Graduate.* BART entrance in front of theater. Wheelchair-accessible. Two sister theaters in the area host smaller shows: **Golden Gate Theatre,** 1 Taylor St., and **Curran Theatre,** 445 Geary St. Individual show times and ticket prices vary. AmEx/D/MC/V.

Exit Theater, 156 Eddy St. (☎931-1094, box office 673-5944; www.theexit.org), between Mason and Taylor St. in the **Tenderloin.** Additional location:

277 Taylor St. between Eddy and Ellis St. Two locations and 3 stages produce independent and experimental theater for a youthful, urban audience. Special events like Classic Absurdity Theater Festival in February; sassy DIVAfest, two weeks in May devoted to "theater of a female persuasion"; and the big daddy of national indie theater—the San Francisco Fringe Festival showcasing 250 performances over 12 days in September—all make their mark at the Exit Theater. Exit Cafe at Eddy St. location opens 1hr. before showtime for drinks and light bistro fare. Tickets $12-20, $8 and under for SF Fringe. No credit cards.

848 Community Space, 848 Divisadero St. (☎922-2385; www.848.com), between Fulton and McAllister St. near the **Upper Haight.** Basically a glorified living room, the 848 is a community performance/rehearsal/gallery/educational space that tries to do a little of everything. Comedy troupes, one-man shows, one-act plays, and music dominate the calendar but everything from night-long tribal rituals to live erotica readings have taken place here. Check the website for listings. M yoga $12; Tu night contact improv classes ($8) and jams ($3). Shows free-$15. No credit cards.

City Lights Bookstore

Intersection for the Arts, 446 Valencia St. (☎626-2787, box office 626-3311; www.theintersection.org), between 15th and 16th St. Another of the **Mission's** thriving theater and arts spaces, Intersection is known primarily for its innovative play productions (many put on by Campo Santo, the resident theater company). A gallery of local artists' work is also in the building. Also hosts monthly jazz and literary series. Tickets $9-15. Box office open daily 9am-5pm. MC/V in advance; cash only at the door.

The Marsh, 1062 Valencia St. (☎826-5750), between 21st and 22nd St. in the **Mission.** Small space houses fresh and new performance art. Offerings include playwriting workshops, staged reading series, and a fabulous set of classes for kids called "The Growing Stage." Tickets $6-30. Discount tickets for M night works-in-progress. Previews half-price. Volunteer as an usher and see the shows for free. Call for schedules and prices (9am-5pm). MC/V.

Jazz Festival bassist

Theatre Rhinoceros, 2926 16th St. (box office ☎861-5079; www.therhino.org), at South Van Ness Ave. in the **Mission.** The oldest queer theater in the world, the Rhino has been an innovator in the SF arts community since 1977. The theater emphasizes playwriting by and for the gay/lesbian/bisexual/transgender community, with its own production company. Box office opens 1hr. before shows. Tickets $10-30. Discounts for students, seniors, disabled, and groups of 10+. Box office open Tu-Su 1-6pm. No wheelchair access. D/MC/V.

Nightlife

Strippers of the World Unite!

While some might be tempted to pity or condemn women dancing nude on tables, some SF dancers are smiling as they co-opt club traditions and take matters into their own hands.

In 1995 Lusty Lady Theater workers became the first and only strip club in the US to unionize, joining the Service Employees International Union. Now, the employees have taken over the entire establishment and become the first cooperatively-owned strip joint in the country.

Members of the co-op come from a spectrum of backgrounds; one is a lawyer, some left high school before finishing, several are in graduate school, and a few have doctoral degrees. The club retains its peep-show style entertainment, where dancers are separated from club-goers by transparent casing.

About 60 dancers and support staff had joined the cooperative when it opened under self-management in June 2003. More will likely join as the business grows.

For those interested, Julia Query's award-winning documentary *Live Nude Girls Unite!* (2000; www.livenudegirl-sunite.com) investigates the club's unionization. Query was one of the dancers involved in the unionization effort.

(1033 Kearny St. in **North Beach** ☎391-3991. 18+. Free admission. Open daily 24hr.)

COMEDY

The Punchline, 444 Battery St. (☎397-7573, box office 397-4337; www.punchlinecomedyclub.com). between Clay and Washington St. in the **Financial District.** Big-league comedy, full-service bar, and dinner menu. Su features SF Comedy Showcase with famous and up-and-coming acts. The Punchline has featured Robin Williams, Drew Carey, Dana Carvey, and Rosie O'Donnell. Wheelchair-accessible. 18+. Cover $5-15 with 2 drink min. Shows Su-Th 9pm, F-Sa 9 and 11pm. Doors open at 7:30pm for 9pm shows, 10:45pm for 11pm shows. Tickets available online at www.ticketweb.com and from 1-6pm at the box office.

MOVIES

For a complete listing of features and locations, check the weekly papers or call **MovieFone** (☎777-FILM). Keep in mind that San Francisco movie theaters, even the massive AMC-1000, have nowhere near enough parking.

The Lumière, 1572 California St. (showtimes ☎267-4983, box office 885-3201; www.landmarktheatres.com), between Larkin and Polk St. in **Nob Hill.** Indie, foreign, and art films. Adults $9; seniors, children, and 1st show each day $5.75 (before 6pm). AmEx/MC/V.

Red Vic Movie House, 1727 Haight St., (recorded info ☎668-3994, direct contact 668-8999; www.redvicmoviehouse.com), between Cole and Shrader St. in **Upper Haight.** The Red Vic Movie House is a collectively-owned and volunteer-run theater. Couch-like seating and organic goodies. Foreign, student, and offbeat Hollywood films, second run indies, and first run obscure documentaries. Tickets $6.50, 2pm matinees $4. Phone recording gives an insightful and amusing commentary on the current feature. Check the website for calendar. No credit cards.

Castro Theatre, 429 Castro St. (☎621-6350, automated 621-6120; www.thecastrotheatre.com), near Market St. in the **Castro.** This landmark 1922 movie palace has live organ music before evening showings. Eclectic films, festivals, and double features. Far from silent—a bawdy, catty crowd turns many a movie into *The Rocky Horror Picture Show.* Highlights include the Sing-along Sound of Music, for those who believe Julie Andrews would be better with chest hair. Adults $8, seniors and under 12 $5. Advance tickets at www.ticketweb.com. Matinees W and Sa-Su $5. Box office opens 1hr. before 1st show. No credit cards.

Roxie, 3117 16th St. (☎863-1087; www.roxie.com), off Valencia St. in the **Mission.** This trendy movie house shows sharp indie films and fashionably foolish retro classics, plus a late-night series of truly disturbing European gore flicks. Try to walk with a companion at night. Adults $8, seniors and under 13 $4. Bargain matinees: 1st show W and Sa-Su $5, seniors and kids free. Discount pass (good for 5 shows) $22. No credit cards.

DANCE

SPECTATOR

San Francisco Ballet (☎865-2000; www.sfballet.org) shares the War Memorial Opera House with the San Francisco Opera (p. 166). Tickets start at $30; available online or by phone M-Sa noon-6pm. Discounted standing-room-only tickets are available at the Opera House 2hr. before performances.

▨ **Alonzo King's Lines Contemporary Ballet** (☎863-3360; www.linesballet.org), in **Hayes Valley.** Dancers combine elegant classical moves with athletic flair to the music of great living jazz and world music composers. Springtime shows are performed at the Yerba Buena Center for the Arts (p. 94). Tickets $15-25.

Dancer's Group, 3252A 19th St. (☎920-9181; www.dancersgroup.org), at Shotwell St., in the **Mission.** Dedicated to promoting cultural dance and original works. Open M-F 10am-4pm.

▨ **Oberlin Dance Company,** 3153 17th St. (☎863-9834; www.odctheater.org), between South Van Ness and Folsom St. in the **Mission.** Mainly dance, but occasional theater space with gallery attached. With 2-6 shows a week, there's always something going on. Tickets $10-20 dollars, but occasional 2-for-1 and "pay what you can" nights. $1 parking across the street. Box office open W-Sa 2-5pm. AmEx/MC/V.

California Contemporary Dancers, 530 Moraga St. (☎753-6066; www.ccdancers.org), in the **Sunset.** The all-woman modern dance company was founded in 1990 by Yasmen Sorab Mehta and brings together the best of widely diverse dance and musical traditions to create exciting, innovative performances. They play at venues throughout the city; call or check their web site for ticket and showtime information.

San Francisco Dance Center, below.

PARTICIPANT

Dance Group Studio Theater, 3252a 19th St. (☎920-9181; www.dancersgroup.org), at Shotwell. A non-profit group that advocates dance in the Bay area. Check their website for listings of classes and summer workshops throughout San Francisco. The group also offers a rehearsal space that can be reserved 9am-10pm daily ($8 per hr.) Call for details.

The Local LEGEND

Bill Graham

The 60s changed the way many Americans thought about race, war, sex, and, of course, music. One man stands out as a pioneer in era—Bill Graham. Graham entered the scene as the manager of the **San Francisco Mime Troupe,** a small improv group devoted to raising political awareness through art. In 1965, the Mime Troupe came under legal fire, and Graham organized his first concert—a fundraiser in the legendary Fillmore concert hall. The Fillmore had been a 30s dance hall, a 40s roller rink, and a 50s stage for young artists such as James Brown and Tina Turner. Soon, it would become the hub of the countercultural music scene.

Graham began drawing the biggest names in music to the Fillmore. After clashes with authorities, he got a permit and the Fillmore became *the* spot for up-and-coming artists. Jefferson Airplane, Jimi Hendrix, the Grateful Dead, the Who, and Buffalo Springfield all graced the Fillmore stage. Most importantly, perhaps, Graham made a community space out of the hall—he catered holiday meals for his "family" of friends, creating a community of viewers, musicians, and promoters alike.

In 1968, Graham moved his party to a bigger venue. The legendary theater still sits at Geary and Fillmore, hosting young, independent artists and audiences.

Colit Tower

Working the turntables

Jazz Festival guitarist

Shawl-Anderson, 2704 Alcatraz Ave. (☎510-654-5921; www.shawl-anderson.org), at College Ave. in **Berkeley** . AC Transit #51. 6 blocks North of Rockridge BART station. Instruction in jazz, modern, and ballet. Ask for Mr. Savage's jazz class for a physically and mentally intense experience; not for the faint of heart nor the out-of-shape. Drop-in $12 per class. No credit cards.

San Francisco Dance Center, 26 7th St. (☎863-3040; www.sfdancecenter.org/dance), at Market St. Besides supporting a professional company, the Dance Center offers 100 classes per week, mostly ballet and modern, with a mix of flamenco, salsa, and hip-hop. Drop-in $11 per class.

Rhythm & Motion, 1133 Mission St. (☎621-0643; www.rhythmandmotion.com), at 8th St., specializes in technique in jazz, rhythm, tap, salsa, hip-hop, modern, and yoga. Also has dance-based workout programs and movement classes. Drop-in $11 per class.

RECREATION AND SPORTS

SPECTATOR

3COM Park, (☎tickets 656-4900). By car: take US 101 8 miles south to the Candlestick Park exit. Via public transportation, take MUNI bus #9X (Sutter and Sansome), 28X (Funston and California), or 47X (California and Van Ness) Ballpark Express Line. Home to the five-time NFL Super Bowl champion **49ers** (☎468-2249; www.sf49ers.com) and former grounds for the SF Giants, 3Com (aka Candlestick Park) sits as close to the ocean as a ballpark can, resulting in trademarks gusts that led to one of the lowest homerun averages in the NBL back when it was also the Giant's turf.

Pacific Bell Park, 24 Willie Mays Plaza (☎972-2000; tickets 888-464-2468), in SoMa near the ocean off Townsend St. By care: take Hyde St. to 8th St.; turn left on Bryant St. and right on 4th St. The parking lot is directly ahead. Via public transportation take the Metro Ballpark Service beginning at the Balboa Park station (via M-Ocean View route) or the West Portal Station. MUNI buses #10, 15, 30, 45, and 47 all stop within one block of the park. The new Pac Bell park, home to the NBL **Giants** (www.sfgiants.com) is the first privately funded ballpark since Dodgers Stadium opened in 1962. Cheer "splash hits"—balls that find their way into the Pacific—with the knowledge that no taxes were collected to fund this afternoon of old-fashioned fun. AmEx/D/MC/V.

Oakland Coliseum, home of the Oakland Raiders (NFL) and Oakland A's (NBL), (p. 228).

Coliseum Arena, home of the Golden State Warriors (NBA), (p. 228).

PARTICIPANT

IN GOLDEN GATE PARK

Athletic Fields Reservation Office, in Pioneer Log Cabin (☎831-5510), near Stow Lake. The **Beach Chalet soccer complex** at the western edge of the park, the **Big Rec. ball field** off 7th Ave., the **Polo Field** in GGP Stadium, and **Kezar Stadium** in the southeast corner of the city were all designed for sports use, and can be reserved ahead of time through the Athletic Fields Reservation Office. Although most of these fields are reserved every week by organized ground-sports leagues, if you make the rounds you may find an "organized" pickup game. Unreserved parties are often bumped off fields. Open M-F 9am-5pm, Sa 9am-noon.

Golden Gate Park Stables (☎668-7360; fax 666-0421; www.goldengateparkstables.com), John F. Kennedy Dr., opposite 36th Ave. There are 20 mi. of bridle trails for horseback riding in Golden Gate Park. The Park Stables offers lessons in dressage, as well as equitation, jumping, and western riding. They lead 1hr. guided trail rides through the park, pony rides for kids 1-5 yrs. old, lead-rein lessons for kids 6-8 yrs. old, and weekly private and group lessons.

Mary B. Connolly Children's Playground, opposite Kezar Stadium. Built in 1888, the playground was the first one in a public park. Today it is complete with gymnastic equipment, lots of things to climb, and a carousel. See p. 68.

Baseball, Hardball (☎753-7022); softball (☎753-7024). The Big Rec. Ball Field, just north of 7th Ave., houses two hardball fields, while two softball fields are located at Kezar Dr. and Waller St. (Mother's Meadow) and on John F. Kennedy Dr. just south of 24th St. (Speedway Meadow).

Basketball, courts located on the Panhandle. No reservations required.

Biking (☎753-0257), rental near Stow Lake. Biking (and inline skating) are best on Sundays, when certain roads are closed to traffic and parties of dancing bladers gather at the Rose Garden near the museum complex. There are also about 4 mi. of multi-purpose paved paths available every day for bike and blade use. The smooth race track at the Polo Fields, opposite 35th Ave., is great for biking and skating. Or for a longer ride, the 7½ mi. path that stretches from the tip of the Panhandle through the park, along Ocean Beach to Lake Merced in the southwestern part of the city, is also enjoyable. Open M-F 9am-7pm, Sa-Su 10am-6pm. Driver's license deposit required. Mountain bikes $8; cruisers $7; surreys $15. Additional bike and blade rental, see **Service Directory** (p. 312).

Boating (☎752-0347), rental on Stow Lake. Though boating is allowed on Stow Lake, there are no private launching ramps. The boathouse rents rowboats, pedal boats, and motorboats. Dogs allowed only on rowboats. Open M-F 10am-4pm, weather permitting. Rentals per hr.: rowboats $13, pedal boats $17. Deposit $1. No credit cards.

Fly-casting (☎386-2630), pools are adjacent to Angler's Lodge, opposite the Bison Paddock. Operated Sa only. No equipment provided. No reservations required.

Golf (☎751-8987), opposite 47th St. Golden Gate Park's nine-hole course requires no reservations. Green fees M-F $10, Sa-Su $13; clubs $6. Open daily 6:30am-8pm.

Handball, two indoor and two outdoor courts located just north of the "Big Rec." baseball field opposite 7th Ave. No equipment provided. No reservations required.

Horseshoe (☎668-7360), courts located off Conservatory Dr. at the northwestern edge of the park. No equipment provided. No reservations required. Call for info on lessons.

Jogging and (Dog)walking, can be done on the intricate, looping dirt trails that run through almost every corner of the park. Trails are happily complemented by the parcourse at the Polo Field and the senior citizens' exercise course behind the Senior Center at 36th Ave. and Fulton St. Off-leash dog running is allowed in four sections of Golden Gate Park: the southeast section bounded by Lincoln Way, Martin Luther King, Jr. Dr., 2nd, and 7th Ave.;

the northeast section at Stanyan and Grove St.; the south central area bounded by Martin Luther King, Jr. Dr., Middle Dr., 34th, and 38th Ave.; and lastly, the fenced dog-training area near 38th and Fulton St.

Model yachting, on Spreckels Lake opposite 36th Ave. The park also hosts a regatta on weekends. No equipment provided. No reservations required.

Pentanque/Bocce Ball, courts located opposite 38th Ave. just north of the Bison Paddock. No equipment provided. No reservations required.

Playgrounds, located on the Panhandle, at 47th St. and Lincoln Way, on Martin Luther King, Jr. Dr. east of 19th Ave., and on Fulton St. near 10th Ave.

Tennis (reservations ☎753-7031), courts across from the conservatory. The park's 21 tennis courts are maintained year-round. Group and private lessons are available.

IN THE CITY

PARKS

The following parks and recreation centers are run by the **San Francisco Recreation and Parks Department** (☎831-2700; parks.sfgov.org). All have **tennis, basketball,** and **baseball** facilities; additional sports facilities, such as soccer fields and volleyball courts, are specified. Hours and restrictions vary widely; call ahead whenever possible. In all cases, bring your own equipment.

Eureka Valley Recreation Center, 100 Collingwood St. (☎695-5012), in the **Castro.** Soccer, badminton, softball, and volleyball.

Moscone Recreation Center, 1800 Chestnut St. (☎292-2003), in the **Marina.**

Hayward Playground, 1016 Laguna St. (☎292-2018), near the **Civic Center.** Soccer.

Dolores Park, 19th and Dolores St. (☎554-9529), in the **Mission.** Soccer, jogging trail, and tennis courts.

South of Market Recreation Center, 270 6th St. (☎554-9532), at Folsom St. in **SoMa.** Volleyball, badminton, and jogging trail.

The Bay Area Outdoor Adventure Club (☎954-7190; www.sfoac.com) plans adrenaline-pumping weekend getaways and daytrips, from kayaking and skiing to cave-crawling and hang gliding. Email lana@best.com to get on the free email info list. The website carries additional information on Bay-area **extreme sports**.

GYMS, ROCK CLIMBING, YOGA, AND GOLF

Every neighborhood has dozens of private gyms and fitness centers that often compete for members and might offer 24hr. access. Most will offer a free day or week's membership and may even waive initial fees or extend introductory rates. Expect to pay around $65 per month for a basic gym. Adding extras like steam and sauna will raise you another $20 per month.

Unfortunately, climbing *au naturel* (in the rough, not the buff) doesn't exist in metropolitan San Francisco. The closest quality bouldering and climbing is at **Indian Rock** in the Berkeley Hills and **Turtle Rock** in Marin near Tiburon. Both **Mt. Tam** and **Mickey's Beach** in Marin offer basic climbs, while slightly bigger ones are at **Castle Rock** and the **Pinnacles.** For serious fun, however, some serious driving is required: **Yosemite,** the **Sierras,** and **Joshua Tree** are all frequent destinations for SF's climbing community. For information on these climbs and more, check out **Bay Area Bouldering** or http://totalescape.com/active/camp/rock.html.

Mission Cliffs, 2295 Harrison St. (☎550-0515; www.mission-cliffs.com), at 19th St. The only rock gym in SF is also the only rock gym you'll ever need. Excellent, mammoth 50 ft. lead walls and dual-level bouldering dens. Room for 60 top ropes, plus a full weight room, locker rooms, safety classes, private lessons, and kids' clinics. Membership rates available. Non-member day passes: M-F 3-10pm and Sa-Su 10am-6pm $18, M-F 6:30am-3pm $10. One-month pass $100. Ten visit pass $180. Open M-F 6:30am-10pm, Sa-Su 10am-6pm.

Funky Door Yoga, 186 Second St. (☎673-8659; www.funkydoor.com), at Howard. Additional locations: 1334 Polk St. at Pine and 1749 Waller St. at Stanyan in San Francisco; 2567 Shattuck Ave. in Berkeley. Turn on the heat with some Bikram yoga. $10 drop-in for students, $15 for adults. Monthly passes available.

It's Yoga, 848 Folsom St. (☎543-1970; www.itsyoga.com), specializes in Ashtanga yoga, with 15 beginner classes per week. $15 drop-in rate. Free Sa class for first-timers. Hours depend on location.

Presidio Golf Course, 300 Finley Rd. (☎561-4661; www.presidiogolf.com). 18 holes.

Lincoln Park Golf Course, 34th and Clement St. (☎221-9911). 18 holes.

Golden Gate Park Golf Course (☎751-8987). 9 holes.

Harding Park Golf Course (☎661-1865), on Harding Blvd. near **Lake Merced.** 18 holes.

INSIDE

Shopping

Let's face it: in a city as chic as San Francisco, if you're looking to go *couture*, you'll need to cash in the trust fund or bust out the plastic. For those without the *cojones* to spend! Spend! SPEND!, window shopping is a safe and often satisfying option, especially in those specialty (fun!) stores that pride themselves on quirky over-the-topness. Establishments are categorized by type of store and then organized by neighborhood.

BOOKSTORES

Great Overland Bookstore Company, 2848 Webster St. (☎351-1538) in **Cow Hollow.** Originally a Sausalito establishment, Great Overland expanded to the big city, bringing San Fran dwellers a selection of rare, out-of-print, California history books and other more common titles. Jazz and world music play for your browsing enjoyment. Paperbacks around $7, but left-handers will find even better deals in the middle of August when the left-handed owner gives leftys an extra 20% off for National Left-Hander's Week. Open daily 11am-7pm. AmEx/D/MC/V.

Book Bay Bookstore, Bldg. C., 1st fl. (☎771-1076), in **Fort Mason Center.** Sells donated books at stupendously low prices (paperbacks $2-6, hardbacks $5-8). Profits benefit the public library. Great selection of vintage pulp novels and a wide variety of other books including a few pricey collectibles. Open daily 11am-5pm. D/MC/V.

▧ **City Lights Bookstore,** 261 Columbus Ave. (☎362-8193), near Broadway in **North Beach.** This Beat generation landmark (p. 70), famous for promoting banned books in the 1950s and 60s, has a wide selection of fiction, poetry, art, and, of course, Beat literature. Founder and owner Lawrence Ferlinghetti is still committed to publishing and publicizing the work of new authors. Open daily 10am-midnight. AmEx/D/MC/V.

Acorn Books, 1436 Polk St. (☎563-1736; www.acornbooks.com), between California and Pine St. in **Nob Hill.** A gigantic, well-organized selection of used hardcovers and paperbacks at 40-50% off original prices. Extensive San Francisco history, art, 1st edition, and out-of-print rarities ($2-20,000), including Victorian-era board games and a Webster's Dictionary from 1828. Perfect for browsing. Open M-Sa 10:30am-8pm, Su noon-7pm. AmEx/D/MC/V.

Fields Book Store, 1419 Polk St. (☎673-2027; www.fieldsbooks.com), at California St. in **Nob Hill.** Dedicated to the education and spiritual enlightenment of its customers for over 70 years, Fields specializes in new, used, and rare books on Eastern and Western spiritual traditions—from Miss Cleo to the Kabbalah. Open Tu-F 11am-8pm, Sa-Su 11am-6pm. D/MC/V.

Café de la Presse, 469 Bush St. (☎398-2680), at Grant Ave. **Union Sq.'s** *très grande* collection of international media includes novels, newspapers, and magazines from both American coasts as well as Europe. For those with European time and money, the sophisticated restaurant offers your favorite Italian espresso or French wine (1 egg $5.95, sandwiches $10-12) to sip while you peruse a periodical. Open daily 7am-10pm. AmEx/D/MC/V.

Psychic Eye Bookshop, 301 Fell St. (☎863-9997; www.pebooks.com), at Gough St. in **Hayes Valley.** This SF branch of the west coast new age store serves all of your occult needs. Self-help, religion, and philosophy books, as well as astrology charts and an enormous selection of metaphysical merchandise. Psychic readings available in store (15-20min. $20). Reasonably priced "Tarot for Dummies" and astrology classes offered ($10-15). Open M-Sa 10am-10pm, Su 11am-7pm. AmEx/D/MC/V.

Kayo Books, 814 Post St. (☎749-0554, www.kayobooks.com), at Leavenworth St. in the **Tenderloin.** Two floors of sex, violence, and mystery! No, it's not a shady brothel, but a pulp fiction dreamworld, complete with seductive original illustrations from the 60s, and at $3-7 for most books, retro prices to match. Open W-Su 11am-6pm. AmEx/D/MC/V.

The Magazine, 920 Larkin St. (☎441-7737), at Geary St. in the **Tenderloin.** This specialty shop is almost like two stores in one. The front half is devoted to collectible posters and magazines—everything from old theater reviews to Maxim—while the back section is dedicated to gently "pre-owned" porn magazines, videos, and DVDs from as far back as the 50s. An interesting selection ranging from $3-15 in both sections. Open Tu-Sa noon-7pm. AmEx/D/MC/V.

European Book Company, 925 Larkin St. (☎474-0626; www.europeanbook.com), near Geary St. in the **Tenderloin.** This primarily French and German bookstore also stocks Dutch travel guides, Germanophone dictionaries, and baby's first Spanish storybooks. Novels are a little more expensive than in your friendly neighborhood corporate giant (around $10) but anything that's been sitting on the shelf for a while automatically gets discounted. Open M 11am-4pm, Th-Sa 11am-5pm. MC/V.

Kinokuniya Bookstores, 151 Webster St. (☎567-7626), in the Kinokuniya Bldg. in **Japantown.** Proud home to "everything from comics to Confucius." The vast collection of books, music, and videos in English and a variety of Asian languages highlights Japanese and Asian issues, lifestyles, and culture. Open daily 10:30am-8pm. AmEx/D/MC/V.

Bound Together Anarchist Bookstore, 1369 Haight St. (☎431-8355; www.boundtogether.org), just east of Masonic Ave. in the **Upper Haight.** Surprisingly orderly stacks of subversive books, political pamphlets, and underground 'zines at this volunteer-staffed collective. Bound Together also sells accessories (t-shirts, pins, patches, CDs) so that you can proudly display your beliefs (or anti-beliefs) and help support the store. Open daily "approximately" 11:30am-7:30pm. No credit cards.

Comix Experience, 305 Divisadero St. (☎863-9258; www.comixexperience.com), at Page St. in the **Lower Haight.** Classy comic book store with chatty staff and excellent selection that appeals to collectors and the just-curious alike. Specializes in graphic novels as well, but don't go in asking for Pokemon. Open M-Sa 11am-7pm, Su noon-5pm. AmEx/D/MC/V.

Booksmith, 1644 Haight St. (☎863-8688), between Clayton and Cole St. in the **Upper Haight.** An independent, local institution for 26 years, offering impressive sections on counterculture, San Francisco, eastern philosophy, and children's books. Free in-store author readings weekly. Open M-Sa 10am-9pm, Su 10am-6pm. AmEx/MC/V.

178

Forever After Books, 1475 Haight St. (☎431-8299), between Ashbury and Masonic St. in the **Upper Haight**. If you thought the Redwoods were ancient, traipse through this primitive forest of used books. Perfect for browsing, but if you are looking for something specific, be warned that it may appear disorganized. Ask the staff. They know where everything is. Specializes in obscure non-fiction, particularly history, religion, psychology, holistic health, and true crime. Open daily approximately 11am-8pm. AmEx/MC/V.

A Different Light Bookstore, 489 Castro St. (☎431-0891), near 18th St. in the **Castro.** All queer, all the time, with more-than-plentiful special interest subdivisions, including poetry, travel, and of course, transsexual Asian firefighters. Also the ultimate resource for free Bay Area mags, a popular community bulletin board, and free monthly readings by notable queer authors. Open daily 10am-10pm. AmEx/D/MC/V.

Phoenix Books and Music, 3850 24th St. (☎821-3477; www.dogearedbooks.com), at Vicksburg St. between Church and Sanchez St. in **Noe Valley.** New, remainder, and used books and CDs. Extensive fiction and children's sections, great bargains on hardcovers (most $4-15), and a friendly and knowledgeable staff. Sister stores: **Red Hill Books,** 401 Cortland St. (☎648-5331) and **Dog Eared Books,** 900 Valencia St. (☎282-1901), at Valencia St. All open M-Sa 10am-10pm, Su 10am-8pm. AmEx/D/MC/V.

The San Francisco Mystery Bookstore, 4175 24th St. (☎282-7444; www.sfmystery-books.com), between Castro and Diamond St. in **Noe Valley.** Hard-to-find first editions and out of print mysteries as well as the newest from today's writers. True crime and mystery puzzle books for the amateur sleuth. Frequent book signings. Open M-Th 11am-6pm, F-Su 11am-8pm. AmEx/D/MC/V.

Christopher's Books, 1400 18th St. (☎255-8802), at Missouri St. in **Potrero Hill.** This neighborhood bookstore's selection, hand-selected by the owner, is diverse. In addition to the old and new classics, strong travel, children's, and cooking sections reflect the family feel of the store. Open daily 10am-10pm. MC/V.

Needles and Pens, 482 14th St. (☎255-1534; www.needles-pens.com), near Guerrero St. in the **Mission.** Selling 'zines of all sorts, Needles and Pens is a unique store of high caliber. If you've never heard of a "zine," stop by for an important education. A small selection of handmade clothes on rack as well. 'Zines $1-5. Open Th-Su noon-7pm. No credit cards.

Modern Times Bookstore, 888 Valencia St. (☎282-9246; www.moderntimesbook-store.com), between 19th and 20th St. in the **Mission.** A collective bookstore, focusing on progressive world politics and literature. Extensive sexuality/gender, Spanish language, and *la raza* labor studies sections. A fine selection of indie girl-zines and earnest poetry. Speakers and readings in-house, as well as shelves of fliers and pamphlets on Mission and SF happenings. Open M-Sa 10am-9pm, Su 11am-6pm. AmEx/MC/V.

La Casa del Libro, 973 Valencia St. (☎285-1399), between 20th and 21st St. in the **Mission.** Spanish literature, newspapers, and political goods fill this tiny store. Dictionaries and instruction books as well. La Casa can special order any book in Spanish. Customer service available in English. Open M-F 9:30am-6pm, Sa 10am-6pm, Su noon-5pm. AmEx/MC/V.

Borderland Books, 866 Valencia St. (☎824-8203 or 888 893-4008), in the **Mission.** Housing an extensive inventory of science fiction, Borderland Books has been named the best fantasy/sci-fi bookstore in San Francisco. Selection includes new and used sci-fi, fantasy, and horror. Small press titles abound. Author events spring up occasionally. A hairless cat keeps guard of the store. Open daily noon-8pm. MC/V.

Green Apple Music and Books, 506 Clement St. (☎382-2272), at 6th Ave. in **Richmond.** In a city teeming with impressive independent book stores, Green Apple's enormous collection of used books stands out as one of the best. Green Apple's popularity gives it a chaotic marketplace feel—no quiet, comfy-armchair perusing here. The main store covers everything from cooking to transportation; find fiction and a small but significant DVD and used CD section in the **Annex,** 2 doors down at 520 Clement St. Open M-Th and Su 10am-10:30pm, F-Sa 10am-11:30pm. Annex closes 15 min. earlier. MC/V.

Chelsea Books, 637 Irving St. (☎566-0507), between 7th and 8th Ave., in the **Sunset.** Don't be deterred by the size. Chelsea Books may be small, but it has quality collections of vintage children's, cookery, history, literature, drama, art, and Western Americana. Prices range, but average pocket literature ($3), paperback ($5), hardcover ($9), and a small collection of discount books outside ($1-2). A comfy armchair allows you to try before you buy. Open Su-Th 11am-10pm, F-Sa 11am-11pm. MC/V.

Berkeley

Henna

Maiden Lane

MUSIC & INSTRUMENTS

101 Basement, 513 Green St. (☎392-6368), near Grant Ave. in **North Beach.** Grant St. location stocks high-end jazz, R&B, and soul, with new arrivals daily (records $5-45; cassettes $5-6). At Green St., find the basement, crammed with 50,000 rock records ($5), a sizable classical collection, and second-hand instruments, record needles, cartridges, and turntables. Additional location: 1414 Grant Ave. (☎392-6369), near Green St. Both open Su-Th 11am-8pm, F-Sa 11am-10pm. MC/V.

Clarion Music Center, 816 Sacramento St. (☎391-1317; www.clarionmusic.com), at Waverly Pl. in **Chinatown.** A must-see for music lovers. Explore the gongs, harps, violins, Chinese drums, and didgeridoos that line the walls as you listen to the owner play his flute. Lessons for the unusual instruments offered in the basement for $36 per hr. Open M-F 11am-6pm, Sa 9am-5pm. AmEx/D/MC/V.

BPM Records, 573 Hayes St. (☎487-8680), between Octavia and Laguna St. in **Hayes Valley.** What to some may look like a sparse selection of CDs and vinyls to the eyes of a DJ is a bountiful array of "underground kultcha." Listen to any record in the store, if you can decide which one to pick up. Open M-Sa 11am-8pm, Su 11am-7pm. AmEx/D/MC/V.

🎵 **Amoeba Music,** 1855 Haight St. (☎831-1200; www.amoebamusic.com), between Shrader and Stanyan St. in the **Upper Haight.** *Rolling Stone* dubbed this the best record store in the world. Three times as big as its parent in Berkeley (p. 221), the Haight St. Amoeba stocks an amazing selection of used CDs, plus new music and a parade of vintage concert posters. The store doubles as a venue for free concerts by some big names and a weekly in-house DJ series (**Entertainment,** p. 165). Check website for details. Open M-Sa 10:30am-10pm, Su 11am-9pm. D/MC/V.

Open Mind Music, 342 Divisadero St. (☎621-2244; www.openmindmusic.com), at Page St. in the **Lower Haight.** Insane quantities of new and used vinyl and a fair number of collectibles: dance, down tempo, new hip-hop, experimental, lounge music, and, yes, even Zeppelin. 5 listening stations to sample before you buy. Serving vinylheads since 1994. Open M-Sa 11am-9pm, Su noon-8pm. MC/V.

Recycled Records, 1377 Haight St. (☎626-4075), between Masonic and Central Ave. in the **Upper Haight.** RR fights the good fight for the preservation of analog sound. Vinyl is king here, but CDs and some DVDs are infiltrating this vast collection of rock, jazz, funk, blues, and soundtracks ($3-15). Open M-F 10am-8pm, Sa 10am-9pm, Su 11am-7pm. AmEx/MC/V.

Medium Rare Records, 2310 Market St. (☎255-7273), between Castro and Noe St. in the **Castro.** Showtunes, lounge music, and the standard divas make up this small but irreplaceable CD selection. Signatures from Sharon McKnight, et al., supervise Dean Martin, disco, and the latest Pride dance remixes. Open M-Sa noon-7pm, Su noon-6pm. AmEx/D/MC/V.

Streetlight Records, 3979 24th St. (☎282-3550), between Noe St. and Sanchez St. in Noe Valley. Good selection of used vinyl, 7-inches, CDs, and tapes (all roughly $10-40), as well as all the new stuff you would find in any music store. A decent DVD and VHS selection, too. Open M-Sa 10am-10pm, Su 10:30am-9pm. AmEx/D/DC/MC/V. Additional location: 2350 Market St. (☎282-8000) in the **Castro.** Open M-Sa 11am-9pm, Su 11am-8pm.

Aquarius Records, 1055 Valencia St. (☎647-2272), at 21st St. in the **Mission.** Tiny store known worldwide for obscure selection of all genres of music and a staff to guide you when you don't know where to start: Japanese Rock or 60s psychedelics? Its real specialties are drum & bass, indie, and imports from all over the globe. New and used. Great vinyl section, too. Ask about local group recordings and performances. Open M-W 10am-9pm, Th-Su 10am-10pm. AmEx/D/MC/V.

Ritmo Latino, 2401 Mission St. (☎824-8556), at 20th St. in the **Mission.** If your love for Latin music extends beyond Shakira, Ritmo's huge selection will captivate you. Salsa, *norteños, románticas,* rock, even concert tickets (Ticketmaster outlet). Open M-Th and Su 10am-9:30pm, F-Sa 10am-10:30pm. D/MC/V.

CLOTHING AND SHOES

Rabat, 2080 Chestnut St. (☎929-8869), at Steiner St. in the **Marina.** Hip clothing, shoes, and accessories. Apparel is fresh from the runway, as are the prices (jackets $500). The permanent sale rack may make this a worthwhile stop (pants $80), but window shopping might be a more savvy option. Open M-F 10:30am-6:30pm, Su 11am-5:30pm. AmEx/D/MC/V.

a b fits, 1519 Grant Ave. (☎982-5726), between Filbert and Union St. in **North Beach.** Designer jeans ($60-475), for the millionaire disguised as a budget traveler, and casual women's wear ($20-500). Open Tu-Sa 11am-6:30pm, Su noon-6pm. AmEx/D/MC/V.

Manifesto, 514 Octavia St. (☎431-4778), just north of Hayes St. in **Hayes Valley.** Local designer makes 1950s-inspired clothes for men and women. The retro-looking dresses and shirts are well cut, reasonably priced ($65-150), and more flattering than many of their authentic cousins. Open Tu-F 11am-7pm, Sa 11am-6pm, Su noon-5pm. AmEx/MC/V.

Bulo, 418 Hayes St. (☎255-4939), between Gough and Octavia St. in **Hayes Valley.** One of SF's most stylish and unusual collections of shoes. Expensive ($99-450), but look for great sales. Men's shoes across the street at 437-A Hayes St. (☎864-3244). Additional location: 3040 Filmore St. (☎614-9959), at Union St. in **Cow Hollow.** Open M-Sa 11am-7pm, Su noon-6pm. AmEx/D/MC/V.

Minnie Wilde, 519 Laguna St. (☎863-9453; www.minniewilde.com), between Hayes and Fell St. in **Hayes Valley.** Fresh, fun women's clothing by local designers. The clothing is eclectic in style and uniform in (high) quality. Open Tu-Sa noon-7pm, Su noon-5pm. MC/V.

Alla Prima, 539 Hayes St. (☎864-8180), between Octavia and Laguna St. in **Hayes Valley.** An airy boutique of booty-ful high-end European lingerie and swimwear ($15-150). Additional location: 1420 Grant Ave. (☎397-4077), in **North Beach.** Open M-Sa 11am-7pm, Su noon-5pm. AmEx/D/MC/V.

Piedmont Boutique, 1452 Haight St. (☎864-8075; www.piedmontsf.com) between Masonic Ave. and Ashbury St., in the **Upper Haight.** Look for the enormous legs dangling over the door. If you've always dreamed of being a Vegas showgirl, this over-the-top-emporium will supply the wardrobe. Feathers, headdresses, sequins, abundant accessories, spandex clubwear, and custom-made costumes of any kind. On the pricey side but check out the sale racks for great deals. Open daily 11am-7pm. AmEx/D/MC/V.

in the know

501 Blue Blood

Prague's not the only city where an old pair of 501s is worth more than a used car. **Vintage Levi's** collectors sift through San Francisco's thrift shops in hot pursuit of those finer details that turn denim into diamonds. A few telltale signs mark the precious Levi's produced before a major 1960s design overhaul. Look for red stitching on the inside legs and the number "2" underneath the top button snap. Next, check for a little red tag on the back pocket—before 1961, the brand name was spelled with a capital E (LEVI'S, rather than "LeVI'S," as it appears today).

These rarities can cost $100-1800, depending on condition and shade (dark indigo is worth more). To join the vintage-collecting elite, track down a pair of Levi's made in the 1940s, when the company (in a show of wartime patriotism) saved materials by painting, not sewing, the trademark outside stitches. If you don't have any luck in your search, you can always fake it—Levi's is putting out a new "Vintage Revival" line, complete with the red lines, "2," and big E. But be warned: you won't fool SF's Leather and Levi's community p. 184.

THRIFT AND VINTAGE

M, 1425 Grant St., between Green and Union St. in **North Beach.** A small store crammed with vintage clothes of the female variety, mostly $25-40 per piece. Homemade beanies and crochet hats $20-45. Open daily 9:30am "until whenever everyone feels like going home." AmEx/MC/V.

Old Vogue, 1412 Grant Ave. (☎392-1522), between Green and Union St. in **North Beach.** Small boutique for mostly men, but also women with moderately priced vintage and classics (shirts $25, pants from $35, dresses from $25). Upstairs houses a large selection of organized piles of Levi's 501s, most for $25. Open Su-Tu 11am-6pm, W 11am-8pm, Th-Sa 11am-10pm. AmEx/D/MC/V.

Rosalie's New Look, 782 Columbus Ave. (☎397-6246), near Greenwich St. in **North Beach.** Higher prices, but oh, what clothes! Sequins, furs, and high heels for the diva within, though wondrous wigs ($40-200) are their specialty. Open M-Sa 9am-5pm, Su 1-5pm. AmEx/D/MC/V.

🐾 **Departures From the Past,** 2028 Fillmore St. (☎885-3377), at Pine St. in **Pacific Heights.** Extraordinary collection of genuine vintage clothing for men and women. Unearth a flashy-colored tuxedo shirt ($15), wild collared shirt ($20), or trendy skirt ($15-20) from the collection. Particularly impressive range of lingerie (if second-hand lingerie doesn't make you itch). Tons of wacky accessories including, but not limited to, costume jewelry, sunglasses, hats, gloves, and bow ties. Open M-Sa 11am-7pm, Su noon-6pm. AmEx/MC/V.

American Rag, 1305 Van Ness Ave. (☎474-5214), at Fern St. in **Pacific Heights.** A California vintage clothing institution. Shopaholics will adore big-name retro styles up front while bargain-hunters will be tempted by plentiful racks of vintage in the back. Even thrift prices aren't great (most pants, skirts, and jeans $30-45) but the selection is staggering. Open M-Sa 10am-9pm, Su 10am-7pm. AmEx/MC/V.

Crossroads Trading Co., 1901 Fillmore St. (☎775-8885), at Bush St. in **Pacific Heights**. Truly a crossroads in the shopping world: come here to buy, sell, and trade new and used clothes, shoes, and accessories. Vast selection at very reasonable prices. Blue jeans average $13. Look out for name-brand gems. Additional location: 2231 Market St. in the **Castro.** Open M-Th 11am-7pm, F-Sa 11am-8pm, Su noon-7pm. MC/V.

🐾 **Buffalo Exchange,** 1555 Haight St. (☎431-7737; www.buffaloexchange.com), between Clayton and Ashbury St. in the **Upper Haight.** One of those rare thrift stores that actually allows you to be thrifty and get high-quality clothes, shoes, and accessories. Almost everything under $20. Additional locations: 1800 Polk St. (☎346-5726) in **Nob Hill** and 2585 Telegraph Ave. (☎510-644-9202) in **Berkeley**. Open Su-Th 11am-7pm, F-Sa 11am-8pm. MC/V.

Wasteland, 1660 Haight St. (☎863-3150), in the **Upper Haight.** The formidable facade and elaborate window displays, as well as pulsing music, are enough to entice any vintage fanatic. Probably the best-known thrift store in the Haight, Wasteland features a massive selection including used duds intermingled with vintage designer goodies and lots of one-of-a-kinds in a hip, rock n' roll environment. Open M-Sa 11am-8pm, Su noon-7pm. AmEx/MC/V.

Goodwill, 1700 Haight St. (☎387-1192), at Cole St., in the **Upper Haight.** Though they may not be as obvious as in the trendier stores along the street, good bargains on cool things are buried in the racks and racks of ever-popular Levi's ($7-11) and shelves and shelves of everything else: shoes, housewares, books, linens, and oddities. All incredibly cheap. Open M-Sa 10am-8pm, Su 11am-8pm. AmEx/D/MC/V.

Vintage Clothing

Worn Out West, 582 Castro St. (☎431-6020), between 18th and 19th St. in the **Castro.** The place to dream of cowboys, Indians, and all the other Village People. Stocked with an extensive collection of vintage, leather, uniforms, toys, and a big selection of cowboy boots, hats, and army fatigues. Butt-less chaps, too. Fitting rooms beneath the cow skull, partner. Open Su-M, F noon-7pm, Tu-Th 3-7pm, Sa 11am-7pm. D/MC/V.

Guys and Dolls, 3798 24th St. (☎285-7174), between Church and Dolores St. in **Noe Valley.** Mainly vintage clothes and accessories for men and women, many of the 50s bowling shirt and print dress variety. Good selection of vintage bags, costume jewelry, and Hawaiian shirts. Open M-F 11am-7pm, Sa 11am-6pm, Su noon-6pm. AmEx/D/MC/V.

Pipe Dreams

Clothes Contact, 473 Valencia St. (☎621-3212), just north of 16th St in the **Mission.** "Vintage by the Pound." All clothing sold by weight ($8 per lb.); no single item over $25, 99¢ rack out front. Open M-Sa 11am-7pm, Su noon-6pm. AmEx/D/MC/V.

Community Thrift Store, 623 Valencia St. (☎861-4910), between 17th and 18th St. in the **Mission.** This non-profit shop is where to come for all the random things: furniture, purses, kiddie thrift clothes, books. Check out the furnishings if you are hanging around SF for a bit—napkins, placemats, and dishes galore for 50¢. Even cooler though: donators select from over 200 charities where they want the money from their sold items to go. Open daily 10am-6:30pm. Donations 10am-5pm. AmEx/D/MC/V.

Union Square

183

Leather & Levi's

The Leather and Levi's community originally grew out of a 1950s working class gay male culture and is characterized by black leather and denim attire.

In 1962, San Francisco's first all-leather bar, Why Not, opened in the Tenderloin; the following year, Tool Box opened in SoMa. When Detour followed in SoMa in 1965, the neighborhood (specifically Folsom St.) established itself as the center of the Leather and Levi's community. Since the 1960s, the Leather and Levi's community has extended to include lesbians, bisexuals, and most recently, a growing number of heterosexuals.

While the community is quite welcoming to newcomers, as a whole, it tries to avoid becoming a gawking-ground for people (usually tourists) who are fascinated by the group's novelty.

Most Leather and Levi's bars require appropriate dress—the leather must be black, the denim must be Levi's. In some cases, full cowboy gear and latex suits are also acceptable.

The uninitiated are, however, welcome to find out what it's all about in September at the unforgettable Folsom Street Fair (p. 10).

SPORTS AND OUTDOORS

Leland Fly Fishing Outfitters, 463 Bush St. (☎781-3474), between Grant Ave. and Kearny St. in **Union Sq.** Grab your rod and stock up on woolly buggers, hot bulls, and humpy reds. This store offers lures, gear, advice, and excursions for fly-fishing enthusiasts and lots of goofy and practical products (like sturdy raincoats) for the average customer. Open M-F 10am-6pm, Sa 11am-4pm. AmEx/MC/V.

See Jane Run, 3870 24th St. (☎401-8338; www.seejanerunsports.com), between Sanchez and Church St. in **Noe Valley.** Excellent quality and selection of athletic clothes and gear for women, especially for swimming and running. Store sponsors several community runs and athletic events, including a 5K FunRun every Su at 10am. Open M-F 11am-7pm, Sa 10am-6pm, Su 11am-5pm. AmEx/MC/V.

ART SUPPLIES AND STATIONERY

Waxen Moon, 1814 Polk St. (☎359-1936; www.waxenmoon.com), between Washington and Jackson St. in **Nob Hill.** Make your candle and burn it too! A candle studio where you can create your own from hundreds of candles and holders for $10; includes scent, color, wicking, studio time (about 20min. to make, 30min. to harden), and instruction. Private parties and specialty classes available. Reservations recommended but unnecessary on most days. Open M-Th noon-8pm, F noon-10pm, Sa-Su 10:30am-6pm. AmEx/D/MC/V.

The Art Store, 1414 Van Ness Ave. (☎441-6075; www.artstore.com), between Bush and Pine St. in **Nob Hill.** *The* emporium for paints, brushes, colored pencils, posterboard, framing, and portfolios at warehouse prices. Stop by weekend afternoons (1-4pm) for free demonstrations on fun at-home projects. Students receive 10% off with ID. Free parking for artists available at Bush St. Open M-F 9am-8pm, Sa 9am-7pm, Su 11am-6pm. AmEx/D/MC/V.

Flax, 1699 Market St. (☎552-2355), between Gough and Octavia St. just south of **Hayes Valley.** Behind the already impressive exterior, this enormous warehouse of art supplies is dazzling eye-candy for the artistically inclined. Their paper collection will give you a new appreciation for paper-making as an art form. Open M-Sa 9:30am-6pm, Su 11am-5pm. AmEx/D/MC/V.

Mendel's Far Out Fabrics, 1556 Haight St. (☎621-1287; www.mendels.com), between Clayton and Ashbury St. in the **Upper Haight.** One of the oldest stores on Haight St., stocked with art supplies, stationery, and an enormous selection of far-out fabrics ($5-30 per yard). Nice staff of artists who are more than happy to guide you in a project or just help navigate the fabric room. Open M-F 10am-5:50pm, Sa 10am-5:20pm, Su noon-4:50pm. D/MC/V.

CRAFT STORES

🎭 **Mask Italia, Inc.,** 2176 Chestnut St. (☎409-4743; www.maskitalia.com), off Pierce St. in the **Marina.** Mask Italia imports authentic Venetian masks perfect for the sophisticated interior decorator, the cache collector, or the moneyed masquerader. Even if you don't plan on purchasing, the masks are a great sight. Prices start at $20 and quickly increase. Open daily 11am-6pm. AmEx/D/MC/V.

Canton Bazaar, 616 Grant Ave. (☎362-5750; cantonbazaar@aol.com), between Sacramento and California St. in **Chinatown.** Variety, variety, variety. This three-level store is definitely tailored toward tourist demand and houses an incredible array of trinkets and treasures, from beaded Chinese slippers ($4) to a genuine, hand-carved ivory tusk ($60,000), or erotic pottery. But don't worry, if you can't find the Bazaar, most every shop in the area has similar wares to choose from. Free Chinatown maps downstairs. Open daily 10am-10pm. AmEx/D/MC/V.

The Wok Shop, 718 Grant Ave. (☎989-3797, www.wokshop.com), between Sacramento and Clay St. in **Chinatown.** Though this small shop caters mostly to serious chefs and restaurant owners, it has everything even the most amateur cook could need to make a mean stir-fry–from cookbooks ($6) to cleavers ($10) to, of course, a huge array of woks (about $15). Open daily 10am-6pm. AmEx/D/MC/V.

The African Outlet, 524 Octavia St. (☎864-3576), just north of Hayes St. in **Hayes Valley.** "The coolest and hardest store in the nation," where behind the beaded curtain, shelves overflow with statues, textiles, and eye-catching cargo from all over Africa. Open M-Sa 10am-8pm, Su noon-6:30pm. AmEx/D/MC/V.

Worldwares, 336 Hayes St. (☎487-9030), between Gough and Franklin St. in **Hayes Valley.** This international melange of leather books, wooden picture frames, colorful silk pillows, wicker furniture, and scented candles exemplifies the neighborhood's unique range of ethnic and artistic crafts for the home. Open M-Sa 11am-6pm, Su noon-5pm. AmEx/D/MC/V.

Evelyn's, 381 Hayes St. (☎255-1815; www.evelynantique.com), between Gough and Franklin St. in **Hayes Valley.** Don't be fooled by the small scale of the first room—the shop seems to go on forever and is full of interesting baskets, statues, and Chinese antique furniture from the 17th-19th centuries. Open M-Sa 10:30am-6:30pm. AmEx/MC/V.

Global Exchange, 4018 24th St. (☎648-8068; www.globalexchange.org) in **Noe Valley.** An upscale boutique with a conscience: all of its world-wide imports—from Nepali coats ($50) to hand-painted South African candles ($12) and kids clothes ($20)—are made under Fair Trade conditions, a portion of the profits go to global charities. Open Su-F 11am-7pm, Sa 10am-7pm. AmEx/MC/V.

Terra Mia, 1314 Castro St. (☎642-9911; www.terramia.net), at 24th St., in **Noe Valley.** Enliven plain pieces of pottery with your personal touch. Flat charge for the pottery (from $9) and all-day studio fee (adults $10; children $4 plus $1 for clear glaze). Community-supportive: W bring in 3 cans of food as a donation and studio charge is waived. 2-for-1 adult discount on studio time F-Sa 4-8pm–perfect for dates. Private party rates available. Open M-Sa 11am-8pm, Su 11am-6pm. MC/V.

SPECIALTY STORES

House of Magic, 2025 Chestnut St. (☎346-2218), near Fillmore St. in the **Marina.** A colorful jungle of magic tricks, gags, wigs, and low-brow laughs. It's comforting to find a place still selling the same old fart-noisemakers after 40 years in business. Whoopie cushions and "who farted?" clocks galore. Open M-Sa 10am-7pm, Su 11am-4pm. AmEx/D/MC/V.

Secret Flower Garden, 2164 Union St. (☎346-1001), between Webster and Fillmore St. in **Cow Hollow.** The Secret reveals itself in the depths of this narrow plant-spotted haven. Step in for a breath of fresh flowers and a rest for aching feet. The garden out back is delightfully shady, letting in just enough sun to keep shoulders warm. Trickles from a tiny fountain decorate the sound of breeze-brushed bamboo, and the small shelter inside is a perfect space to engage in conversation. Buy a flower or two ($1-$20) to follow in Scott Mackenzie's footsteps. Open M-Sa 8am-6pm, Su 10am-5pm. AmEx/D/MC/V.

Gity Joon's, 1828 Union St. (☎292-7388; www.gittyjoon.com), off Octavia St. in **Cow Hollow.** Take a refreshing spiritual break and admire religious art and artifacts from over 37 countries. Whether you purchase or not, wander into the Serenity Garden and drink tea amidst bright flowers and statues. Gity also offers one-time classes in Feng-Shui, but they fill up quickly so call ahead! Open M-Sa noon-7pm, Su noon-6pm. MC/V.

🔲 **Imperial Tea Court,** 1411 Powell St. (☎788-6080 or 800-567-5898; www.imperial-teas.com), at Broadway in **Chinatown.** This oasis of serenity is a must for tea lovers. Exotic scents of green, black, oolong, and rare herbal teas waft about this little shop's soothing earthen tones and singing rainbow finches. If you have the time, enjoy an elegantly presented tea service (formal $8 per person per tea, informal $3 per person per tea). Otherwise, all tea is available for sale though some of it is very pricey (up to $1000 a pound for the rarest types). Open M and W-Su 11am-6:30pm. MC/V.

Yau Hing Co, 831 Grant Ave (☎989-0620, fax 956-8818; www.yhteas.com) between Clay and Washington St in **Chinatown.** This store actually serves a dual purpose in the neighborhood. First, it is a bustling tea shop, offering such aromatic treats as dragon pearl jasmine tea for as little as $5 per oz. Second, it acts as one of the areas pharmacies for traditional Chinese herbalists and doctors. Though they won't give you their most potent herbs without a prescription, sibling owners Alice and Peter can definitely find something among their wares to put the bounce back in any weary traveler's step. MC/V.

China Town Kites, 717 Grant Ave. (☎989-5182; www.chinatownkite.com), between Sacramento and Clay St. in **Chinatown.** Tiny shop filled with goodies for all ages, from bird kites and cartoon characters ($10-20) to windchimes ($5-50) and 80 ft. Chinese dragon kites ($300). Open daily 10am-9pm. AmEx/MC/V.

Pet Central, 660 Broadway (☎399-0164), at Grant Ave. in **Chinatown.** Forget the Zoo and the Aquarium—visit these 3 staggering floors of pets and the products that make them happy. Though their speciality is fish (bring in your own aquatic companion to trade, if you'd like), there are enough lovebirds, puppies, iguanas, eels, and chinchillas to fill another Ark. Open daily 10am-7pm. AmEx/D/MC/V.

Chan's Trains and Hobbies, 2450 Van Ness Ave. (☎885-2899; www.chanstrains.com), at Union St. in **Russian Hill.** Take your Lionel in for a tune-up, or trade it in for a new one at the shop. Specializes in helping collectors find rare models, but the knowledgeable and friendly Mr. Chan welcomes train, ship, plane, and military model novices as well. Open M-Sa 10am-6pm, Su noon-5pm. MC/V.

Kar'ikter, 418 Sutter St. (☎434-1120; www.karikter.com), between Powell and Stockton St. in **Union Sq.** This pricey boutique dedicates itself to "European characters." A Tin Tin wall hanging runs $300, but his books are generally more inexpensive ($15) and offer delight in nearly thirty titles. Despite the focus on Babar, the Little Prince, and Tin Tin, the cartoons at Kar'ikter aren't just for kids, and the store's curiously colorful puzzles and gadgets attract kitsch-collectors of all ages. Open M-Sa 10am-7pm, Su 11am-5pm. MC/V.

Monkee Bizzness, 275 Gough St. (☎864-7788), between Fell and Oak St. in **Hayes Valley.** Straight up *and* twisted toys (with an emphasis on the twisted), abounding with "pop culture foo." Everything from chocolate bandages to "Handy Hindu" finger puppets in this tiny shop. Open M-Sa noon-7pm, Su noon-6pm. AmEx/D/MC/V.

Pipe Dreams, 1376 Haight St. (☎431-3553), between Central and Masonic Ave. in the **Upper Haight.** The oldest of the Haight's innumerable head shops, and the one with the nicest staff, although they'll get feisty if you call them "hippies." Glass pipes from $7 with the best setting you back up to $1,000. Books on hemp, posters, and other accessories. Merchandise is, of course, intended for legal use only, so shopping here comes with its very own set of vocabulary restrictions—patrons must not use the taboo words posted outside the store. Must be 18+ to enter. Open M-Sa 10am-7:50pm, Su 11am-6:50pm. AmEx/D/MC/V.

Costumes on Haight, 735 Haight St. (☎621-1356; www.costumesonhaight.com), between Scott and Pierce St. in **Lower Haight.** A carnival of costumes for all occasions. Sale or rental. Also vintage clothes and club-wear sections for playing dress-up or for actually dressing up. Open M-Sa 11am-7pm, Su noon-6pm. AmEx/D/MC/V.

⚑ Under One Roof, 549 Castro St. (☎503-2300; www.underoneroof.org), between 18th and 19th St. in the **Castro.** More sophisticated than your average kitsch shop, Under One Roof donates 100% of the profit from every sale—be it an AbFab magnet, scented bath oil, or a Pride holiday ornament—to organizations working to fight AIDS. Sign-up and orientation are simple for those looking to join the all-volunteer staff that has helped raise over $9 million to date. Open M-Sa 10am-8pm, Su 11am-7pm. AmEx/D/MC/V.

⚑ Does Your Father Know?, 548 Castro St. (☎241-9865), between 18th and 19th St. in the **Castro.** Your dad told you not to waste your money on touristy trinkets. Now you can show him you didn't listen *and* you're queer! DYFK is stocked with Castro's finest kitschy, trivial junk, from Judy Garland figurines to glow-in-the-dark vibrators and boxes of penis pasta. Open M-Th 9:30am-10pm, F-Sa 9:30am-11pm, Su 10am-9pm. AmEx/D/MC/V.

⚑ Otsu, 3253 16th St. (☎255-7900; www.veganmart.com), in the **Mission.** The only vegan boutique west of Maryland. Otsu carries beautiful shoes, bags, books, belts, cards, comics, music, and other handmade oddities created by local artists. For the animal lover and hipster alike. The products are well made, well designed, and not nearly as expensive as one might imagine. Open W-Su noon-7pm, M-Tu by appointment. MC/V.

The Scarlet Sage & Herb Co., 1173 Valencia St. (☎821-0997), at 23rd St. in the **Mission.** Zen paradise. An entire wall of glass jars filled with every (legal) herb imaginable. Books, vitamins, oils, and anything else needed in your search for nirvana, holistic health, or a cure for the common cold. The staff is helpful without being irritatingly new-agey. Tarot card readings available Th and F 2-4pm. Open daily 11am-6:30pm. AmEx/D/MC/V.

X-21, 890 Valencia St. (☎647-4211), just north of 20th St. in the **Mission**. Take a look at the delightfully larger-than-life Lego Man. Mid-20th century furnishings and one-of-a-kind items for sale and prop rental...or just an afternoon of window shopping. Servicing budgets from $5-5,000, X-21 will ship anywhere in the world. Open M-Th noon-6pm, F-Su noon-7pm. D/MC/V.

Just for Fun, 3982 24th St. (☎285-4068) in **Noe Valley.** Vast and varied toy/knickknack/ stationery store that caters to both kids and adults. You are as likely to find engraved flasks and watches, as board games ($15) and bobbleheads ($12). **Scribbledoodles** (www.justfor-fun.invitations.com), shares the address and phone number, and offers custom printing and invitations. Open M-F 9am-8pm, Sa 9am-7pm, Su 10am-6pm. AmEx/D/MC/V.

Le Video, 1231 9th Ave. (☎566-3606; www.levideo.com), between Irving and Lincoln in **Richmond.** San Francisco's premier video rental store has 2 floors and over 87,000 videos. Whatever you're into, you'll find it here—rare and foreign films from Egypt to Jamaica, and 2 aisles devoted entirely to the BBC. A smaller but equally diverse selection of new and used videos for sale starting at $4.99. Open daily 10am-11pm. AmEx/MC/V.

Collage Gallery, 1345 18th St. (☎282-4401), between Missouri and Texas St. in **Potrero Hill.** An ever-changing collage of affordable to upscale art, jewelry, and housewares unites kitsch and cool. Open receptions four to five Th nights a year feature work from the store's primarily Potrero artists. Classes in collage-creating ($35) offered every few weeks. Call ahead for openings. Open Tu-W and Sa noon-6pm, Th-F noon-8pm, and Su noon-5pm. MC/V.

The Arch, 99 Missouri St. (☎433-2724), in **Potrero Hill.** An entire warehouse-sized space filled with an odd combination of kitschy gift items (backscratcher, anyone?) in one half and very serious and well-stocked art and architectural design supplies in the other. The canine-loving management urges you to bring Rover in for a special treat. Open M-F 9am-6pm, Sa noon-5pm. AmEx/D/MC/V.

POSTCARDS

Tilt, 507 Columbus St. (☎788-5566), between Green and Union St., in **North Beach,** provides wonderful chaos for those with an attention deficit. From Americana memorabilia to Hindu statuettes, fridge magnets, old license plates, a wall full of obscure, originally printed postcards (85¢ each, cheaper if you buy more), and almost everything in between. Check out their jewelry shop next door (509 Columbus St.) filled with sterling silver jewelry and pricey stone accessories. Open daily noon-midnight. MC/V.

Does Your Mother Know?, 4079 18th St. (☎864-3160), near Castro St. in the **Castro.** Although card shops like this cover the area, this one takes the prize for most provocative name. What better way to tell Mom than with hard-core porn? More subtle and hilarious options also available. Open M-Th 9:30am-10pm, F-Sa 9:30am-11pm, Su 9:30am-9pm. AmEx/D/MC/V.

I'M TOO SEXY

Chadwicks of London, 2068 Chestnut St. (☎775-3423), near Steiner St. in the **Marina.** An "intimate apparel" shop, Chadwicks offers everything from full-butt-coverage underpants to dental floss g-strings. Cheerful service offered to those looking to outfit a partner with a gift. Open M-F 11am-7pm, Sa 10:30am-6pm, Su noon-6pm. AmEx/D/MC/V.

🖾 **Good Vibrations,** 1210 Valencia St. (☎974-8980; www.goodvibes.com), at 23rd St. in the **Mission.** The well known erotica cooperative for enthusiastic do-it-yourselfers (see their "Make Your Own Dildo" kit). The woman-owned and -operated sex store is so tasteful (flavored condoms and more) you could almost take your parents there. Try out "Tester" bottles of lube or observe the progression from wooden cranks to C-cell batteries in a small, but informative display of vibrator evolution dating back to 1910! Excellent collection of instructional books, including the invaluable *Good Vibrations Guide to the G-Spot.* Vibrators from $15-100+. 18+ to enter. Open Su-W noon-7pm, Th-Sa 11am-8pm. AmEx/D/MC/V. Additional locations: 1620 Polk St. (☎345-0400), at Sacramento St. in **Pacific Heights** and 2504 San Pablo Ave. (☎510-841-8987), in **Berkeley.**

Stormy Leather, 1158 Howard St. (☎626-1672; www.stormyleather.com) between 7th and 8th St. in **SoMa.** One of the country's biggest women's fetishwear boutiques. Leather, vinyl, latex, various fetters, whips, shoes, corsets, and toys. Most garments $80-300 but some run as low as $10. Small men's selection upholds the friendly store's "pansexual" theme, as do BDSM classes for all levels of interest ($20 per person; call to schedule) and free gallery receptions for well-known fetish photographers. Open daily noon-7pm. AmEx/MC/V.

Mr. S. Leather, 310 7th St. (☎863-7764 or ☎800-746-7677; www.mr-s-leather.com), between Folsom and Harrison St. in **SoMa.** Selections range from $2 cock-rings to 500 types of dildos to a $2,900 flying sleep sack/bondage suit. A huge variety of men's leather clothes and a helpful staff have made Mr. S a shopping mecca for the leather community for the last decade. Sister store **Madame S,** 321 7th., across the street, specializes in leather and latex "hâute fetish couture." (☎863-9447; www.madame-s.com). Mr. S. open daily 11am-7pm. Madame S open W-Su noon-7pm. AmEx/D/MC/V.

Worn Out West, p. 183.

CANDY SHOPS

🖾 **XOX Truffles,** 754 Columbus Ave. (☎421-4814; www.xoxtruffles.com), between Filbert and Greenwich St in **North Beach.** Unbelievably good truffles in 26 flavors handmade by JeanMarc Gorce, one of San Fran's most famous French chefs. 10 liqueur, 10 non-liqueur, and 6 soy vegan. 75¢ each; 1lb. (80 pieces!) $20. Free truffle with coffee drinks ($1-2.75). Open M-Sa 9am-6pm. AmEx/D/MC/V.

See's, 1519 Polk St. (☎775-7049; www.sees.com), near California St. in **Nob Hill.** Visit the oldest surviving See's store for a taste of "California's Famous Old-Time Candies." Chocolicious variety of homemade sweets since 1921. Come in for a 🖾 **free sample** of butter cream, walk out with a 1lb. box for $12. Open M-Sa 10am-5:30pm, Su 11am-4pm. AmEx/D/MC/V. Additional locations downtown: 754 Clement St. (☎752-0953); 542 Market St. (☎362-1593); 846 Market St. (☎434-2771).

Chocolate Covered Sweets & Gifts, 3977 24th St. (☎641-8123), between Sanchez and Noe St. in **Noe Valley.** Chocolates handpicked from the owner's fifty favorite chocolate retailers in the world ($2-4) in awesome packaging. Wrap them up in N'Sync, Wonder Woman, or Elvis lunchboxes ($10)—or have a box made just for you: they will print cyanotypes (blue photo-images) onto tin boxes and finish the edges with Japanese "washi paper" in the same blue tones, all for around $25. Open daily around 11am-7pm. AmEx/MC/V.

TATTOOS AND PIERCINGS

California law states that **you must be 18 years old** to get a tattoo. Generally, minors need an adult present for piercing.

Lyle Tuttle's Tattoo Art Studio, 841 Columbus Ave. (☎775-4991), in **North Beach.** Lyle Tuttle opened his modern, clean tattoo studio in the 1960s, permanently decorating the skins of Janis Joplin, Joan Baez, and Cher. While the eminently professional Tuttle, age 71, himself covered in tattoos from head to foot, no longer tattoos behind the bar, his proteges continue the tradition, amidst a small but impressive collection of tattoo memorabilia—consider it an added bonus if you drop by when someone's under the needle behind the bar. Tattoos start at $60. Open daily noon-9pm. No credit cards.

Mom's Body Shop, 1408 Haight St. (☎864-6667), in the **Upper Haight.** This family-run establishment takes great pride in its craftsmanship, proclaiming their tattoos are just "like Mom's apple pie." Tons of design books and portfolios to help you finalize your decision, or work with your artist to develop something more original. Piercings from $10, plus the cost of the jewelry. Tattoos $120 per hr., min. $60. Appointments or walk-ins welcome. Must be 18+ with state identification. Open daily in summer noon-9pm; in winter noon-8pm. MC/V.

Black and Blue Tattoo, 381 Guerrero (☎626-0770), near 16th St. in the **Mission.** Entirely owned and operated by an eclectic group of women. Piercings and brandings as well as high-quality tattoos. Appointments recommended. Tattoos start around $50. Tattoos daily, piercing and scarification Su and M, branding F and Su-M. Open in summer daily noon-7pm; in winter M and W-Su noon-7pm. MC/V.

MALLS

Pier 39 (☎981-7437), two blocks east of **Fisherman's Wharf.** 110 specialty shops (open Su-Th 10am-9pm, F-Sa 10am-10pm), 11 bay-view restaurants (open Su-Th 11:30am-10pm, F-Sa 11:30am-11pm), sea lions, an arcade, street performers, ferry rides and tours ($5-$30), and even a double-decker Venetian carousel. Parking garage. 1hr. free parking before 6pm, 2hr. after 6pm.

San Francisco Shopping Centre (☎495-5656; www.westfield.com), on Market St. at 5th St., near **Union Sq.** This fairly typical American mall—J. Crew, Nordstrom, and Abercrombie & Fitch are all prominently placed—is worth noting for its proximity to Union Sq. and its six hypnotically curving escalators, the only ones of their kind in the world. Check out the Centre if nearby Gucci and Prada don't quite fit your budget but have left you with a craving to splurge. The Centre also features a food court. Open M-Sa 9:30am-8pm, Su 11am-6pm.

Japan Center (☎922-6776), along Geary and Post St. between Fillmore and Laguna St. The Japan Center's 3-block complex encompasses most of **Japantown.** The Kabuki 8 Theatres, the Kinokuniya Bldg., and the Kintetsu Mall are connected to the Miyako Mall and the Radisson Hotel by the Peace Plaza. The five sections of the mall include Japanese cafes, restaurants, music and clothing stores, art galleries, and shops. The Japan Center's offerings make it a good place to stock up on Sanrio, Sailor Moon, and sushi. Open daily 10am-midnight.

Stonestown Galleria, 19th Ave. and Winston Drive (☎759-2623; www.shopstonestown.com), between **Stern Grove** and the SF State University campus. This 2-story shopping mall caters more to spendthrift sophisticates than to students. 250 mall favorites and a grease-laden food court will satisfy mainstream shopping spree needs. Open M-Sa 10am-9pm, Su 11am-6pm. Hours of department stores and restaurants may vary.

Accommodations

For those who don't mind sharing a room with strangers, San Francisco's better **hostels,** an experience in themselves, can be homier, cheaper, and safer than many budget **hotels.** Book in advance if at all possible, but since many do not take reservations for the summer, you might have to just show up or call early (well before noon) on your day of arrival. Surprisingly affordable and comfortable hotels can be found in the city proper, especially in Union Sq. Travelers with cars should also consider the **Marin Headlands Hostel** (p. 234), a tranquil and beautiful spot just minutes from the city across the Golden Gate Bridge. Some hostels ask for a foreign passport as identification; American citizens are usually welcome but sometimes must prove they are not local residents through valid forms of identification such as a driver's licence or state identification.

MARINA, FORT MASON & COW HOLLOW

⚑ *NEIGHBORHOOD QUICKFIND: **Discover**, p. 7; **Sights**, p. 68; **Food & Drink**, p. 117; **Nightlife**, p. 144.*

You shouldn't have trouble finding a place to lay your head here; between the bohemian hostels in Fort Mason, the motels along Lombard St., and the posh B&B offerings in Cow Hollow, countless accommodations cater to all types of visitors.

see map p. 338

🛏 **Fort Mason Hostel (HI-AYH),** Bldg. #240 (☎ 771-7277; www.norcalhostels.org), in **Fort Mason,** entrance at the corner of Bay and Franklin St. past the administrative buildings. Beautiful surroundings give this 160-bed hostel a campground feel. Most rooms hold 6-10, but can accommodate more. Strictly enforced quiet hours and other rules, such as no smoking or alcohol. Movies, walking tours, dining room, bike storage. Huge, clean kitchen, cute cafe with vegetarian dinner ($3). Minor chores expected. Lockers (bring lock or rent for $4). Laundry (wash $1, dry $1). Parking. Reception 24hr. Check-in 2:30pm. Check-out 11am. No curfew, but lights-out at midnight. Book two weeks in advance for best chances of reservation, as there are few beds for walk-ins. IBN reservations available. Dorms $24.50. MC/V. ❶

ACCOMMODATIONS BY PRICE (SINGLE PER NIGHT)

UNDER $40 (❶)

⚑ Fort Mason Hostel (191)	FM
⚑ Green Tortoise Hostel (193)	NB
Pacific Tradewinds Hostel (193)	CH
YMCA Chinatown (193)	CH
⚑ Adelaide Hostel (194)	US
Hostel at Union Square (HI-AYH) (195)	US
New Central Hotel and Hostel (196)	CC
Central YMCA of San Francisco (197)	TE
⚑ HI-AYH Hostel SF-City Center (197)	TE
Interclub Globe Hostel (198)	SoMa
SoMa Inn (198)	SoMa
555 Haight (199)	HA
⚑ San Fran Int'l Guesthouse (202)	MI
Easy Goin' & Calif. Dreamin' Guest. (202)	MI

UNDER $80 (❷)

Motel Capri (192)	MA
⚑ Grant Plaza Hotel (193)	CH
Hotel Astoria (193)	CH
The San Remo Hotel (194)	RH
Harcourt Residence Club (194)	NH
⚑ Ansonia Abby Hotel (194)	US
Hotel Beresford Manor (195)	US
Grant Hotel (195)	US
The Biltmore (195)	US
Alisa Hotel (195)	FD
The Embassy Hotel (196)	CC
Edwardian San Francisco Hotel (196)	HV
Hayes Valley Inn (196)	HV
⚑ Hotel Essex (197)	TE

Hotel Metropolis (197)	TE
Metro Hotel (199)	HA
Red Coach Motor Lodge (197)	TE
San Francisco Zen Center (199)	HA
Herb'N Inn (199)	NH
24 Henry Street (201)	CA
Twin Peaks Hotel (201)	CA

UNDER $120 (❸)

Edward II Pub & Inn (192)	MA
Marina Inn (193)	MA
⚑ Golden Gate Hotel (194)	US
The Sheehan Hotel (195)	US
The Stratford Hotel (195)	US
THayes Valley Inn (196)	HV
⚑ The Phoenix (197)	TE
⚑ The Parker House (199)	CA
⚑ The Willows (200)	CA
Dolores Park Inn (200)	CA
Inn on Castro (200)	CA
Village House (200)	CA
Noe's Nest (201)	NV

$121-160 (❹)

⚑ Hotel Triton (195)	US
The Mosser Hotel (198)	SoMa
Flamingo Inn (198)	SoMa
⚑ The Queen Anne Hotel (198)	PH
The Red Victorian B&B and Art (198)	UH
The Seal Rock Inn (202)	RI

CA castro **CC** civic center **CH** chinatown **FD** financial district **FM** fort mason **HV** hayes valley **HA** haight-ashbury **MA** marina, fort mason, & cow hollow **MI** mission **NB** north beach **NH** nob hill **NV** noe valley **PH** pacific heights **RH** russian hill **RI** richmond **SoMa** south of market **TE** tenderloin **UH** upper haight-ashbury **US** union square

Edward II Inn & Pub, 3155 Scott St. (☎ 922-3000 or 800-473-2846; www.edwardii.com), at Lombard St. in the **Marina.** Quiet and private, this "English Country" inn is tastefully decorated and maintained. For otherworldly designs, ask for an "apartment suite" in the Inn. Free continental breakfast and sherry in the front lobby. Two-night min. stay on weekends for private baths and suites. Check-in 3pm. Check-out noon. Rooms with shared bath $82.50, private bath $115; suites with kitchens (some with jacuzzi) for up to 5 people $185-235. AmEx/D/MC/V. ❸

Motel Capri, 2015 Greenwich St. (☎346-4667), at Buchanan St. in the **Marina.** Not necessarily the most elegant place around, but it's cheap and clean, with private baths and all the amenities. Friendly and humorous service. Free parking. Reception 6:30am-12:30am. Check-in after 2pm. Check-out noon. Reservations recommended. Singles from $70; two double beds $80; three double beds and kitchen $160; winter rates $10 less. AmEx/D/MC/V. ❷

Marina Inn, 3110 Octavia St. (☎928-1000 or 800-274-1420; www.marinainn.com), at Lombard St. in the **Marina.** Despite bustling US 101 outside, the inside is quiet, comfortable, and simple. Free continental breakfast, afternoon sherry, and chocolates on your pillow. Check-in 2pm. Check-out noon. Reservations recommended. Doubles with private bath Mar.-Oct. $85-135, Nov.-Feb. $65-105, $10 more on weekends. AmEx/DC/MC/V. ❸

NORTH BEACH

🔲 *NEIGHBORHOOD QUICKFIND:* ***Discover,*** *p. 8;* ***Sights,*** *p. 70;* ***Food & Drink,*** *p. 118;* ***Nightlife,*** *p. 144.*

see map p. 339

🔲 **Green Tortoise Hostel,** 494 Broadway (☎834-1000; www.green-tortoise.com), off Columbus Ave., at Kearny St. A former brothel, ballroom, and apartment flat sprouted this super mellow and friendly pad geared toward a good time—backpackers of the world, unite! Get to know fellow travelers, and crash a keg party or special event in the Fior D'Italia ballroom (now a smoker, drinker, and pianist-friendly lounge). The new center of attention is the gray kitten Stinson, the friendly and adorable mascot of the hostel. 6 free computers and printing (up to 5 pages) with DSL Internet access. The hotel is next to the **Green Tortoise Adventure Travel** agency, which books backpacking bus tours around the southwest US, across the country, and in Baja, Alaska, Costa Rica, and Mexico (open M-F 9am-7pm, Sa-Su noon-6pm). Breakfast, occasional dinners, and kitchen access included. Storage lockers ($1 per day, though smaller free lockers are under every bed), laundry (wash $1.25, dry 75¢), and free sauna. Key deposit $20. 10-day max. stay. Reception 24hr. Check-in noon. Check-out 11am. Reservations recommended; call at noon your day of arrival for walk-in availability. 4-, 6-, and 8-bed dorms $19-22; private rooms $48-56. No credit cards. ❶

CHINATOWN

🔲 *NEIGHBORHOOD QUICKFIND:* ***Discover,*** *p. 9;* ***Sights,*** *p. 71;* ***Food & Drink,*** *p. 120;* ***Nightlife,*** *p. 146.*

see map p. 339

🔲 **Grant Plaza Hotel,** 465 Grant Ave. (☎434-3883 or 800-472-6899; www.grantplaza.com), at Pine St. Clean, modern furnishings, and friendly bilingual service complement a central location and budget prices. All rooms with private bath and satellite TV. Staff will arrange airport shuttles and guided tours for guests. Safe deposit $25. Lockers 50¢. F-Sa may require two-night min. stay. Singles $55-63; doubles $59-76; quads $79-109 (about $6 cheaper during off-season). AmEx/D/DC/MC/V. ❷

Pacific Tradewinds Hostel, 680 Sacramento St. (☎433-7970; www.hostels.com/pt), at Kearny St. Pacific Tradewinds' friendly staff and sardine-can intimacy serve as a sanctuary for solo travelers. Linens, laundry, free DSL, no curfew, and no lockout make this very small (only five rooms) hostel a good bargain, but be prepared—it's on the fourth floor of a building with no elevator. 2 week max. stay. Reception 8am-midnight. Reservations recommended. Single beds in dorm-style rooms $16-24; double beds $16-22 per person; no private rooms. AmEx/D/MC/V. ❶

YMCA Chinatown, 855 Sacramento St. (☎576-9622), between Grant Ave. and Stockton St. The ornate Chinese gate in the entrance contrasts the simple interior of this 30-room hotel. Pool and gym available to guests. No visitors allowed. Men over 18 only. Key deposit $5. The friendly staff works reception M-F 6:30am-10pm, Sa 9am-5pm, Su 9am-4pm. Check-out noon. No curfew. Singles $35-38, with bath $47; doubles $46. MC/V. ❶

Hotel Astoria, 510 Bush St. (☎434-8889; www.hotelastoria-sf.com), at Grant Ave. This large hotel is located right outside the busy gateway to Chinatown, and offers small, clean rooms with baths, TVs, and well appointed common lounges. Continental breakfast $2. Parking $20. Reception 24hr. Check-in 3pm. Check-out noon. Singles and doubles with shared hall bath $49; queen bed with bath $65; quads with two double beds $76-86. AmEx/D/MC/V. ❷

NOB HILL & RUSSIAN HILL

see map p. 342

NEIGHBORHOOD QUICKFIND: Discover, p. 9; Sights, p. 73; Food & Drink, p. 121; Nightlife, p. 147.

The San Remo Hotel, 2237 Mason St. (☎776-8688; www.sanremo-hotel.com), between Chestnut and Francisco St. in Russian Hill. Built in 1906, this old-fashioned hotel has rooms that are very small but elegantly furnished with antique armoires, bedposts, lamps, and complimentary (if random) backscratchers, but no telephones or TVs. The sparkling shared bathrooms with brass pull-chain toilets harken back to the end of the 19th-century. The hotel's pride and joy is the "penthouse," which offers a private garden, bathroom, and windowed rooftop room with a nice cityscape view ($175; reservations 2 months in advance). Friendly staff will book tours, bikes, cars, and airport shuttles. Free modem connections for those carrying their laptops. Laundry room (wash $1.50, dry $1). Check-in 2pm. Check-out 11am. Reservations recommended. Singles $55-85; doubles $65-95; triples $95. AmEx/MC/V. ❷

The Harcourt, 1105 Larkin St. (☎673-7721; fax 474-6729; www.harcourthotel.net), near Sutter St. in **Nob Hill.** Popular with students and those on longer stays, the Harcourt supplements decent rooms with convenient extras, including private phone, mailbox, and message service. Smoking permitted. Common TV room, dining room, and refrigerator. Laundry facilities. No max. stay; long-term residents get maid service and weekly towel change. 24hr. reception. Refundable reservation deposit $20. Singles $49, with private bath $59. Weekly rates $180, with private bath $225. ❷

UNION SQUARE

see map p. 343

⏹ *NEIGHBORHOOD QUICKFIND: **Discover**, p. 10; **Sights**, p. 80; **Food & Drink**, p. 122; **Nightlife**, p. 148.*

Union Square is chock full of hotels, especially expensive, intimidating, five-star temporary abodes. Still, there are a variety of options for the budget traveler. Reserve ahead if possible—the area is packed in the summer. If you're staying at an establishment to the west, toward the Tenderloin, see a room before you pay.

🏨 **Ansonia Abby Hotel,** 711 Post St. (☎673-2670 or 800-221-6470; fax 673-9217), between Jones and Leavenworth St. Quell the urge to say you've been undercharged, and keep this gloriously affordable secret to yourself. Free breakfast (daily 7-8:30am), dinner (M-Sa), overnight storage, and safety deposit; TV and minibar in every room; and access to DSL-equipped computer lab and wireless Internet on each floor. Laundry facilities. Check-out 11am. Singles $56-66; doubles $66, with bath $79. Cheap weekly rates (from $211) available Sept.-Apr. for Bay Area summer students. AmEx/MC/V. ❷

🏨 **Golden Gate Hotel,** 775 Bush St. (☎392-3702 or 800-835-1118; fax 392-6202; www.goldengatehotel.com), between Mason and Powell St. The amicable owners and their cat, Captain Nemo, invoke a warm, homey feel in this antique gem of a hotel. Wicker chairs, floral bedspreads, turn-of-the-century photographs lining the walls, and big bay windows make this one of the most comfortable B&Bs in the area. German, French, and Spanish spoken. Continental breakfast and afternoon tea (4-7pm) included. Garage parking $15 per day. Doubles with sink $85, with bath $115. AmEx/DC/MC/V. ❸

🏨 **Adelaide Hostel,** 5 Isadora Duncan Ln. (☎359-1915 or 877-359-1915; fax 359-1940; www.adelaidehostel.com), at the end of a little alley off Taylor St. between Geary and Post St. Welcoming hosts, common areas, and reasonable prices make this quiet 18-room oasis the perfect hostel in which to meet a bloke from Australia or a lass from Ireland. Steep stairs let you flex your Frisco calves. Those needing handicapped accessibility can arrange for nearby hotel accommodations at Adelaide's rates. All rooms have large windows, TV, and wash basin. Small shared hallway bathrooms. Fully equipped kitchen. Hostel offers shuttle to SFO airport each morning ($8). 24hr. reception. Check-out 11am. Recommended to reserve at least 10 days in advance. Oct. 16-May 14 dorms $20; singles and doubles from $55. May 15-Oct.15 dorms $24; singles and doubles from $65. AmEx/D/DC/MC/V. ●

🏨 **Hotel Triton,** 342 Grant Ave. (☎394-0500, reservations 800-433-6611; www.hotel-tritonsf.com), at Bush St. Not just a hotel, but an experience—a wonderfully surreal experience. Elegant and playful rooms, with bead-fringed curtains, plush carpets, TV, Internet, coffee pots, fax, and a minibar complete with rubber duck. Smoking, wired, and pet-friendly rooms available. Tarot reading, room-service, and in-room massage available. Mezzanine fitness room. Cookies at 3pm and free wine or beer 5-6pm daily in the lobby. Single $139, king bed $199. Look for deals on website—rates can drop as low as $109. AmEx/D/DC/MC/V. ❹

Hotel Beresford Manor, 860 Sutter St. (☎673-3330 or 800-533-6533; fax 474-0449; beresfordsfo@delphi.com), at Jones St. Two additional locations: Hotel Beresford at 635 Sutter St. (☎673-9900) and the Hotel Beresford Arms at 701 Post St. (☎673-2600). Of the 3 Beresford hotels in the area, the Manor's rooms with walk-in closets (available upon request) and carved wooden dressers offer the best in economical luxury. TV lounge, free Internet, and laundry facilities. Breakfast and dinner M-Sa; complimentary morning tea Su. Singles $60; doubles $70; triples $80. Shared bath $5 extra; private bath $15 extra. Students receive $5 discount. Weekly rates available. AmEx/D/MC/V. ❷

Grant Hotel, 753 Bush St. (☎421-7540 or 800-522-0979; fax 989-7719; www.granthotel.citysearch.com), between Mason and Powell St. An unassuming hotel that comes through where it counts—the rooms and private baths are spacious, simple, and clean; the location is practically unbeatable; and the price is right. Free Internet access. Cable TV. Wheelchair-accessible. Singles $55-70; doubles $60-85. AmEx/MC/V. ❷

Hostel at Union Square (HI-AYH), 312 Mason St. (☎788-5604; fax 788-3023; www.norcalhostels.org), between Geary and O'Farrell St. Tidy and unadorned rooms, basic TV, Internet access ($1 per 10min.), weekly listings of free walking tours, ballgame outings, and free movies to borrow from the hostel library. Quiet hours are from midnight-7am, but unlike many hostels, there is no curfew and no lockouts. $5 deposit for key. 3 wk. max. stay. Reserve in advance or show up around 8am. IBN reservations available. Wheelchair-accessible. Dorm-style triples and quads $22; non-members $25. Private rooms $60; non-members $66. Under 13 half-price with parent. JCB/MC/V. ●

The Biltmore, 735 Taylor St. (☎673-4277 or 888-290-5508; fax 673-0453; www.biltmoresf.com), between Bush and Sutter St. Recently remodeled, the Biltmore offers elegant rooms at very affordable rates. The hand-carved wooden elevator and richly upholstered lobby and lounge area add to the Old World charm of the building, while the great location, continental breakfast, and Internet access ($3 per 20min.) make it perfect for the busiest traveler. Singles $49; doubles from $59. MC/V. ❷

The Sheehan Hotel, 620 Sutter St. (☎775-6500 or 800-848-3271; fax 775-3271; www.sheehanhotel.com), at Mason St. Once part of a YMCA, the Sheehan, with its complimentary pool, exercise room, and continental breakfast is a good find for travelers aiming to fit in a workout during their stay. 3wk. max. stay. Check-in 3pm. Check-out 11am. Singles from $85; doubles from $95. AmEx/D/DC/MC/V. ❸

The Stratford Hotel, 242 Powell St. (☎397-7080 or 888-504-6835; fax 397-7087; www.hotelstratford.com), between Geary and O'Farrell St. Clean lines and soft tones bring a sense of peace to Union Sq. Private baths, TV, irons, and hairdryers in simple, cream-colored rooms. Breakfast included. Singles $79-129; doubles $89-139. AmEx/D/MC/V. ❸

FINANCIAL DISTRICT

NEIGHBORHOOD QUICKFIND: **Discover,** p. 13; **Food & Drink,** p. 124; **Nightlife,** p. 149.

Alisa Hotel, 447 Bush St. (☎956-3232; fax 956-0399). They claim that a stay will reward you with good luck—one can always hope. Small, simple hotel with clean, airy rooms. Each room is non-smoking and has a refrigerator, microwave, hairdryer, TV, and a telephone with

see map p. 344

two lines for computer networks. Private baths available. Coffee and tea served each morning. Reception 24hr. Make weekend reservations 2 wk. in advance. Must cancel reservations at least 48hr. in advance to not be charged for one night. Singles, doubles, twins $59-159. Corporate discounts available. AmEx/MC/V. ❷

CIVIC CENTER

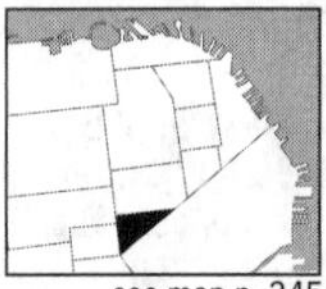

see map p. 345

NEIGHBORHOOD QUICKFIND: ***Discover,*** *p. 13;* ***Sights,*** *p. 90;* ***Food & Drink,*** *p. 124.*

The hazy territory between Civic Center and the Tenderloin is rife with hotels and motels. **Eddy St.** seems devoted to short-term housing, while vocal panhandlers, especially on Market St. between 6th and 10th St., make some visitors feel uncomfortable. Some accommodations are comfortable, pleasant, and great values. See what you're paying for first to avoid nasty surprises.

The Embassy Hotel, 610 Polk St. (☎673-1404 or ☎888-814-6835; fax 474-4188; www.embassyhotelsf.com), at Turk St. A rare find in Civic Center—respectable, affordable, and not too far into unpleasant territory. Rooms are neat and spare. Small, but classy espresso bar open M-F 6am-4pm near the hotel entrance. Adjoining bar, TV, Internet access, and telephones. Continental breakfast included. Free parking. Wheelchair-accessible. Singles $59-79; doubles $69-89. Higher summer rates. AmEx/D/MC/V. ❷

New Central Hotel and Hostel, 1412 Market St. (☎703-9988), between Van Ness Ave. and Polk St. This conventional, no-frills hostel is dim and austere, but clean. Facilities include lockers, TV room, kitchens, laundry, and free linens. Proof of travel required. 24hr. reception. Check-in anytime. Check-out 11am. Dorms $17 per night, $105 per week. Private room with shared bath $40, with private bath $52. AmEx/D/MC/V with $20 min. charge. ❶

HAYES VALLEY

see map p. 345

NEIGHBORHOOD QUICKFIND: ***Discover,*** *p. 14;* ***Sights,*** *p. 92;* ***Food & Drink,*** *p. 126;* ***Nightlife,*** *p. 149.*

Of the few places in or relatively near Hayes Valley, a European style seems to be the favorite design scheme, with pension room arrangements. For a wider array of choice, try Union Sq. or the Tenderloin.

Hayes Valley Inn, 417 Gough St. (☎431-9131 or 800-930-7999; www.hayesvalleyinn.com), just north of Hayes St. European charm means small, clean rooms and shared baths. Although you will get to know your neighbor, the rooms are well maintained and have cable TV, phone, and private sink and vanity. Some smoking and pet-friendly rooms. Continental breakfast. Check-in 3pm. Check-out 11am. Reservations recommended for summer and holidays. In summer singles $58; doubles $68-79; queens $78-89; queen turret $88-99. In winter singles $42; doubles $48-56; queens $54-61; queen turret $58-66. AmEx/MC/V. ❷

Edwardian San Francisco Hotel, 1668 Market St. (☎864-1271 or 888-864-8070; www.edwardiansfhotel.com), at Gough St. Convenient location gives easy access to Union Sq., the Civic Center, Hayes Valley, and MUNI. Burgundy rooms with TV and phone make for a simple yet pleasant stay. Bathrooms recently remodeled. 2-night min. stay on holidays. Check-in 2pm. Check-out 11:30am. Reservations recommended. Standard room with double bed $89-119; two-bedroom suite $149-189; European style 2- to 3-person suite with shared bath $79-99. AmEx/MC/V. ❷

TENDERLOIN

🔲 *NEIGHBORHOOD QUICKFIND: **Discover**, p. 14; **Sights**, p. 93; **Food & Drink**, p. 127; **Nightlife**, p. 150.*

There are tons of cheap hotels in the Tenderloin, but be sure you're staying somewhere safe and legitimate—many places in this area cater to hourly (or even, ahem, half-hourly) guests.

see map p. 345

🔳 **Phoenix Hotel,** 601 Eddy St. (☎776-1380 or 800-248-9466; www.thephoenixhotel.com), at Larkin St. Hip rooms decorated in a funky beach resort meets safari style and a gorgeous blue-and-white-tiled swimming pool (complete with cabanas and complimentary pool-side breakfast) make this throwback to the 50s an oasis in the urban Tenderloin. Free access to the popular Bambuddha Lounge (p. 150) next door. All rooms equipped with xylophones. Parking included. Doubles start at a pricey $139, but may go as low as $89-109 on a slow night. AmEx/D/MC/V. ❸

🔳 **HI-AYH Hostel San Francisco-City Center,** 685 Ellis St. (☎474-5721; www.norcalhostels.org), between Larkin and Hyde St. This converted hotel has private baths in every room and plentiful common space. Rooms themselves are simple but come with perks like cheap Internet access ($1 for 10min.), nightly movie screenings, and weekly listings of walking tours and pub crawls. Warm 24hr. reception in intimate and classy foyer. Best to call ahead for reservations. Dorms $22; non-members $25. Doubles $66; non-members $69. Check-in 3pm; check-out noon. D/MC/V. ❶

🔳 **Hotel Essex,** 684 Ellis St. (☎474-4664; fax 441-1800), between Larkin and Hyde St. The elegantly decorated European foyer foreshadows the rooms, which noticeably lack that sterile budget hotel feel. Rates vary from cheap to affordable depending on the night and who you are (students, Let's Go readers, and international clientele may get special deals). TV and discounted parking. Check-in and -out noon. Singles $49-79 (those with shared hall bath from $39); doubles $59-89. AmEx/MC/V. ❷

Central YMCA of San Francisco, 220 Golden Gate Ave. (☎345-6700; www.centralymcasf.org), at Leavenworth St. east of Hyde St. Opened in 1910, the Tenderloin Y houses 3 floors of hotel space—106 simple rooms, some with TV and private baths. Refuel in the elegant and affordable cafe with complimentary continental breakfast in preparation for the fitness facility's yoga workshops and cardio kickboxing (free). Pool, towels, lockers, laundry, mail facilities, and cheap parking. Key and remote deposit $20. Dorms $25; singles $40-50; doubles $50-60; triples $65-78. MC/V. ❶

Red Coach Motor Lodge, 700 Eddy St. (☎771-2100), between Van Ness Ave. and Polk St. An independent motel. Rooms are very spacious, immaculately kept, and simple. TV, private bath, free parking, and 24hr. reception. Singles $69-79, doubles $99-109. You must pay with a credit card so a valid ID is required at check-in. AmEx/D/MC/V. ❷

Hotel Metropolis, 25 Mason St. (☎775-4600 or 800-553-1900; www.hotelmetropolis.com), at Market St. A stylish alternative to the Hilton up the street, the elegant Metropolis is based on the 1927 sci-fi film of the same name, with spotless rooms and a futuristic feel. More expensive than some other hotels in the area, but a room here comes with more perks: Nintendo, weekend wine receptions in the mezzanine library (Th-Su 4-6pm), business center, Internet access, "holistic well-being center" with meditation classes and zen music, and a cardio workout room. Check-in 3pm, check-out noon. Rooms with 2 double beds or 1 queen bed start at $75; suites with connecting bedrooms and lounges $195-315. AmEx/D/MC/V. ❷

SOUTH OF MARKET AREA (SOMA)

🔁 NEIGHBORHOOD QUICKFIND: *Discover*, p. 15; *Sights*, p. 94; *Food & Drink*, p. 127; *Nightlife*, p. 151.

see map p. 347

The Mosser Hotel, 54 4th St. (☎986-4400 or 800-227-3804; www.themosser.com), between Market and Mission St. Built for the 1915 Pan-American Exposition and restored in 2002. Rooms, although on the small side, are stylishly decorated and have cable TV. Singles and doubles from $139; as low as $99 off-season or on a slow night. About half of the 166 rooms have shared granite bath $59-89. AmEx/D/MC/V. ❹

Flamingo Inn, 114 7th St. (☎621-0701 or 800-444-5818; www.renesonhotels.com), between Howard and Mission St. The least expensive of the 4 motels on 7th St., the Flamingo offers simple but immaculately clean and colorfully decorated rooms that feature Nintendo, cable TV, and movies. Continental breakfast included. Free parking and shuttle to Union Sq. Rooms $115-135. AmEx/D/MC/V. ❹

Interclub Globe Hostel, 10 Hallam Pl. (☎431-0540), off Folsom St. between 7th and 8th St. This vibrant hostel, packed with young travelers, takes safety seriously. A nice aquarium in the lobby lets you sleep with the fishes, while a rooftop terrace allow guests to catch a few rays in the day. 24 hr. Internet access $1 per minute. Happening common room has a pool table, microwave, and fridge. All rooms have private bath. Refundable key deposit $10. Refundable safe deposit (optional) $10. No curfew. Check-out noon. Passport required. Most rooms are spare 5-8 bed dorms for $19, 3 nights $50; private singles or doubles $50; reduced off-season rates. No credit cards. ❶

SoMa Inn, 1082 Folsom St. (☎863-7522; fax 558-8562), between 6th and 7th St. Clean, no-frills rooms on an industrial block of Folsom St. Shared hall bath. Kitchen and Internet access. Reception 24hr. Refundable key deposit $5. 8-bed dorms $17; singles $28; doubles $36; triples $66; quads $88. Weekly: dorms $99.50; singles $160; doubles $180; triples $330; quads $440. AmEx/D/MC/V. ❶

PACIFIC HEIGHTS

🔁 NEIGHBORHOOD QUICKFIND: *Discover*, p. 15; *Sights*, p. 95; *Food & Drink*, p. 129.

see map p. 348

🏨 **The Queen Anne Hotel,** 1590 Sutter St. (☎441-2828 or 800-227-3970; www.queenanne.com), at Octavia St. Each room in this beautiful mansion (actually a renovated girls' finishing school) is uniquely and elaborately decorated with furnishings from the 1890s. Breakfast, afternoon tea, and sherry served daily. Fireplaces, jacuzzis, and wheelchair-accessible rooms available. All rooms include spacious private bath and television. Moderate from $139; deluxe from $159; suites from $179. Look out for off-season specials for as little as $79 a night. AmEx/D/MC/V. ❹

HAIGHT-ASHBURY

see map p. 349

🔁 NEIGHBORHOOD QUICKFIND: *Discover*, p. 16; *Sights*, p. 97; *Food & Drink*, p. 130; *Nightlife*, p. 154.

Accommodations in the Haight are few and far between, but none are lacking in character. Whether you're searching for enlightenment or just yearning for a simple getaway, you'll find a place to match your taste. The trick will be getting a reservation. Prices are moderate, with single rooms starting around $80.

The Red Victorian Bed, Breakfast, and Art, 1665 Haight St. (☎864-1978; www.redvic.com), west of Belvedere St. in the **Upper Haight**. The "Summer of Love" lives on in this B&B and gallery of meditative art. Striving to create peace through tourism, guests come together at breakfast to meditate and chat. All 18 rooms are individually decorated by the owner, Sami Sunchid, to honor such themes as sunshine, redwoods, peacocks, and butterflies. Even the hall bathrooms have motifs. Breakfast included. Reception 9am-9pm. Check-in 3-9pm or by appointment. Check-out 11am. Reservations required (can be up to a month in advance during summer). Smaller rooms with hall baths from $79; midsize rooms about $96; bigger rooms from $110-200. Check website to see pictures of your room before you reserve. Discounts for stays longer than 3 days. AmEx/D/MC/V. ❹

Metro Hotel, 319 Divisadero St. (☎861-5364), between Oak and Page St. in the **Lower Haight.** Slightly removed from the hubbub, a simple, charming retreat with a sunny backyard garden. Private baths and TVs in all rooms. Though this place looks pretty standard from the outside, it wins definite hip points for being the favorite crash pad for many of the performers at the nearby Justice League as well as a number of professional sports teams. The "ballplayer/band room" sleeps six in 3 enormous beds on two levels. 28-day max. stay. Reception 7:30am-midnight. Check-out noon. Reserve well in advance. Singles $66; doubles $77; triples $120. AmEx/D/MC/V. ❷

555 Haight, 555 Haight St. (☎864-4646; www.easygoinghostel.com), between Steiner and Fillmore St. in the **Lower Haight.** As the web address implies, this place is as easygoing as they come. With free Internet, 3 fully stocked kitchens, a TV lounge, and a prime location in the middle of the safest and best part of the Haight, this hostel is a find for any traveler—hippie or not. Check-out noon. 54 beds divided into coed and single-sex dorm rooms $20; private rooms that house up to 3 people $44. AmEx/MC/V. ❶

San Francisco Zen Center, 300 Page St. (☎863-3136; www.sfzc.org), near Laguna St. in the **Lower Haight.** You don't have to be a fully committed Buddhist to find the meditative peace of mind (and affordable rooms) offered here appealing. Simple, light-filled single and double rooms range about $66-105 in a beautifully designed building complete with a stunning garden overlooking the city, meditation room, and library. Breakfast included. Weekly and monthly rates. Checks and cash preferred for payment, but credit card needed to reserve room. Cancellation fees are steep. For classes and programs, see **Sights, p. 98.** ❸

Herb'N Inn, 525 Ashbury St. (☎553-8542), off Haight St. Smack in the heart of the **Upper Haight**. Decorated with 60s memorabilia from the owners' own collection, this B&B feels more like a private home than a hotel. In fact, many of its guests are actually long-term residents—the inn offers daily, weekly, and monthly rates. Breakfast is served in the kitchen with a view of the garden. If there isn't room at this inn, they will often refer people to one of the other smaller, underground B&Bs in the area. Also, take the psychedelic 60s walking tour that is run out of the dining room. 2-night min. stay. Reception 24hr. Check-out noon. Some rooms with private baths. Reserve 6 months in advance. Doubles $75-85. MC/V. ❷

CASTRO

🗷 *NEIGHBORHOOD QUICKFIND:* **Discover,** *p. 17;* **Sights,** *p. 99;* **Food & Drink,** *p. 132;* **Nightlife,** *p. 155.*

Finding an available room in the Castro, during the summer and especially during Pride Week (June 26-27, 2004) and other queer festivals, is difficult. Act early and get reservations. Staying here is worth it. The area has good eats, cafes, and lots of late-night distractions without the fog and hubbub of downtown.

see map p. 350

🞨 **The Parker House,** 520 Church St. (☎621-3222 or 888-520-7275; fax 621-4139; www.parkerguesthouse.com), near 17th St. Serene and stylish. Regularly voted best LGB B&B in the city. A beautiful parlor, with dark wood paneling, grand piano, and flowers galore. Every room has cable and modem ports, but best of all, there are heavenly down comforters and a spa and steam room downstairs. Daily complimentary afternoon wine and breakfast included in a sunny porch-room overlooking rose gardens. Parkin.g $15 per day. 2-night min. stay on weekends, 4-night min. stay some holiday weekends. Check-in 3pm. Check-out noon. Reservations recommended. Rooms with shared bath from $119, with private bath from $139. Deluxe rooms and suites from $169-199. AmEx/D/MC/V. ❸

The Willows, 710 14th St. (☎431-4770; fax 431-5295; www.willowssf.com), near Church St. A friendly staff, handmade willow-branch furnishings, window gardens, and kimono bathrobes make for a little glen of queer happiness. Expanded continental breakfast (8-11am), evening cocktails, guest pantry with microwave and fridge, 8 sparkling hall baths, and washbasins in all 12 rooms. All rooms also come with cable TV, VCR, phone line with a data port, and mini-fridge. Reception 8am-8pm. Singles $100-140; doubles and suites $120-$160. AmEx/D/MC/V. ❸

Dolores Park Inn, 3621 17th St. (☎621-0482 or 553-6060; www.doloresparkinnbnb.com), between Church and Dolores St. "Darling," he wrote during breakfast, "plush, velvety elegance fills the 4 pleasantly secluded rooms here, as does the sweet scent of Burmese honeysuckle, which drifts up from the carriage house every evening." He resigned himself to the drawing room for afternoon tea but took no sugar—he was strong. Sitting by the window and the garden, he said to the others milling about: "One *must* vacation alone from time to time." 2-night min. stay. Singles fit for a romance novel $109-229; doubles $139-249. MC/V. ❸

Inn On Castro, 321 Castro St. (☎861-0321; www.innoncastro2.com), near Market St. Brightly refurbished Victorian exterior complements the cozy living room—the perfect place to enjoy a good book, the Inn's popular full breakfast, or a swig of brandy (compliments of the host). Full common kitchen opens onto a sun deck with a beautiful, sweeping view of the East Bay, while the immaculately clean, well-kept dining area and comfy common lounge are reminiscent of a compulsive friend's apartment. Gay-owned and -operated, but straight-friendly. Parking $15 per day. 2-night minimum stay over weekends, 3-night over holidays, 4-night over Gay holidays (Pride and Folsom St. Fair). Reception 7:30am-10:30pm. Singles $100-165; doubles $115-185; patio suite $185; apartments $135-185. AmEx/MC/V. ❸

Village House, 4080 18th St. (☎864-0994 or 800-864-5666; fax 864-0406; www.24henry.com), near Castro St. Under the same management as 24 Henry St., Village House offers a similarly elegant Victorian parlor with extended continental breakfast, along with 5 plush, internationally-themed rooms. Two rooms are bath en-suite, three share a bath. Free Internet access in the foyer. Singles and doubles with shared baths $75-119; during special events $119-149. Single or double occupancy same price. AmEx/MC/V. ❸

24 Henry Street, 24 Henry St. (☎864-5686 or 800-900-5686; fax 864-0406; www.24henry.com), between Noe and Sanchez St. The 5 rooms in this side-street Victorian have been refurbished nicely since surviving the 1906 earthquake and fires. All antique-adorned rooms (except the master bedroom) share a hall bath with an accommodating shower built for 2. Continental breakfast. Reservations recommended. 10th night free. Singles $65-119; doubles $85-119; during special events $89-179. AmEx/MC/V. ❷

Twin Peaks Hotel, 2160 Market St. (☎863-2909), near 15th St. The strikingly minimalist, single-bed rooms may frighten those with claustrophobia (or gigantic wardrobes), but cable TVs provide a welcome distraction. One of the most affordable stays in the Castro frees up cash for cocktails elsewhere. Key deposit $10. Reception 8am-10pm. Rooms with clean hall bath $45; private bath $59. Weekly rates available. MC/V. ❷

NOE VALLEY

🔲 *NEIGHBORHOOD QUICKFIND:* **Discover,** *p. 18;* **Sights,** *p. 100;* **Food & Drink,** *p. 133;* **Nightlife,** *p. 158.*

Noe Valley has only recently begun attracting visitors, and consequently, small B&Bs reign supreme. Most are simply one or two rooms in a home and tend to remain low-profile. Your best bet to discover their locations is to pick up a copy of the local paper, the *Noe Valley Voice* (available just about everywhere in Noe Valley or online at www.noevalleyvoice.com).

see map p. 350

Noe's Nest, 3973 23rd St. (☎821-0751; www.noesnest.com), between Noe and Sanchez St. Definitely feels like a home with all the family memorabilia—though maybe not your own, unless you have a taste for rather flamboyant decor, like enormous masks and Japanese kimonos. The 7 rooms—all with private bath, phone, cable TV, VCR, and modem ports—are

individually (and creatively) themed. Huge breakfast served in the kitchen, to which the guests have free access. Or enjoy some quiet time on the front patio or back garden next to the hot tub. Laundry service available. 2-night min. stay on weekends, 3-night min. during holidays. Reservations required. Room prices vary depending on size and time of year, but $119-179 is standard. Weekly rates available. AmEx/D/MC/V. ❸

MISSION

see map p. 352

ⁿ *NEIGHBORHOOD QUICKFIND:* **Discover,** *p. 18;* **Sights,** *p. 102;* **Food & Drink,** *p. 135;* **Nightlife,** *p. 158.*

As one of the youngest, hippest, and cheapest neighborhoods in San Francisco, the Mission might seem like the perfect place to stay. Be forewarned: you are likely to fail miserably in a search for short-term lodging. San Francisco's ridiculously tight housing market has turned almost everything called a "hotel" in Mission into a residence house and only a few savory spots offer daily rates.

San Francisco International Guesthouse, 2976 23rd St. (☎641-1411), at Harrison St. From downtown, take BART to 24th St., or the #16 bus to 23rd St. and walk east. No sign marks this beautiful Victorian; look for the blue house near the corner. If you can get a bed, this is the place to stay. Hardwood floors, wall tapestries, and house plants. Free coffee and foreign magazines. TV area, 2 kitchens (smoking and non-smoking), guest phones, and free Internet. 5-night min. stay. Getting in can be like escaping Alcatraz: the Guesthouse does not take reservations, is almost always full, and caters primarily to international visitors. All you can do is try calling. Dorm beds $15 ($13 if paid 25 days in advance, Oct. and June only); private doubles $30. Passport with international stamps "required." ❶

Easy Goin' Travel and California Dreamin' Guesthouse, 3145-47 Mission St. (☎552-8452; www.easygo.com), at Precita Ave. The super-friendly staff and excellent amenities more than make up for the slightly removed new location of this independent hostel. The old Haight St. location has retained a similar name, but no other association. 20 dorm-style beds are located in 4 rooms, and 10 private rooms have 2 double beds each. In-room TVs, kitchen, free coffee, TV lounge, laundry, Internet, bike rental, basic cable, pay phone, and travel services. $20 security and key deposit. 2-night min. Check-in noon. Check-out 11am. Reservations recommended. Dorm beds $18-19; private rooms $40-43. AmEx/D/MC/V with $1 surcharge. Additional location: Harrison and 7th. Check-in and booking through the Mission St. location; shuttle to Harrison and 7th St. provided. ❶

RICHMOND

see map p. 341

ⁿ *NEIGHBORHOOD QUICKFIND:* **Discover,** *p. 20;* **Food & Drink,** *p. 139;* **Nightlife,** *p. 160.*

Accommodation in this outlying residential neighborhood is scarce, though park-lovers looking for a quiet area may find the Richmond worth the trip.

The Seal Rock Inn, 545 Point Lobos Ave. (☎752-8000 or 888-732-5762; fax 752-6034; www.sealrockinn.com), at 48th Ave. opposite the Sutro Baths (p. 81). Though the area is remote, it's a quiet, attractive place to escape city chaos. Pastel houses with well-kept gardens run to the beach. Seal Rock's big, clean rooms are a great deal, especially for families. Pool and patio area. Free parking. One night's advance deposit required by check for weekends and late arrivals. Check-in 1pm. Check-out 11am. Singles $120-140; doubles $130-150; $10 per additional person, $5 per child. Reduced rates Sept.-May. AmEx/MC/V. ❹

LONG-TERM ACCOMMODATIONS

RESIDENCY PERMITS

Residency is the most common path to permanent immigration to the United States. A permanent resident can live and work in the US for as long as (s)he wishes and may eventually apply to become a naturalized US citizen. All residency and permanent immigration issues are controlled by the national **Bureau of Citizenship and Immigration Services** (☎ 800-375-5283, Forms Hotline 800-870-3676; www.bcis.gov). In order to apply for permanent residency, you must file **Form I-485** (Application to Register Permanent Residence), **Form G-325A** (Biographic Data Sheet), **Form I-693** (Medical Examination Sheet), **Form I-94,** and either **Form I-864** (Affidavit of Support) or **Form I-765** (Authorization for Employment). The filing fees for these forms total over $250. Call the hotline or see the website for all necessary forms. Permanent resident status is generally granted with the sponsorship of a family member or an employer. The **San Francisco BCIS Office,** 444 Washington St., provides services for immigration benefits. Call the main BCIS hotline for more information on the San Francisco office. (Open M-Tu and Th-F 7am-3pm, W 7am-2:30pm).

STUDENTS

If you are attending school in San Francisco, your institution of learning may have a special service to help you find on- or off-campus housing. In general, you will probably pay above-market rent and you may or may not have your own bedroom, but you have the benefit of being close to campus, and you don't have to pay a realtor's fee. School offices generally have long lists of other students looking for roommates and apartments with summer sublets.

RENTING AN APARTMENT OR A ROOM

Though apartments are more readily available now than during the dot-com boom, the improvement in rents has not been drastic enough for most apartment-hunters. The longer you stay and the more you are willing to pay, the better your chances will be of finding an apartment quickly. **Studio apartments** start at around $1000 per month. **One- and two-bedroom apartments** start at around $1200 per month. **Sharing an apartment** tends to make housing more affordable: you typically get a private bedroom and shared use of a living room and kitchen for $500-700 per month. Most landlords will ask for a **security deposit** and the **last month's rent** when you sign the lease. They will also ask for **references** from former landlords and may want to run a credit check. If this will be your first time renting, you may want to ask a parent or someone else to co-sign your lease, in effect lending you their credit history and references. The **cheapest** neighborhoods in SF are the Mission and the Western Addition. Some nearby southern suburbs, like the Excelsior and Brisbane, are also less expensive. Berkeley and Oakland also offer nearby housing, generally at more reasonable rents.

Students tend to cluster in Potrero Hill, the Sunset near SF State, the Mission, Haight-Ashbury, and Berkeley. **Gay-owned** and **-occupied** buildings abound in the Castro and can also be found in the Mission and SoMa. **Lesbian** households are most concentrated in the Mission and Bernal Heights. **Young professionals** in the city tend to live in the Marina, the Sunset, the Richmond, Noe Valley, Bernal Heights, and SoMa. **Dot-commers** persist in the southern parts of the city and along the Peninsula—in Colma, Daly City, Visitacion Valley, Ocean View, Brisbane, and Palo Alto.

APARTMENT- AND ROOMMATE-HUNTING RESOURCES

▨ **www.craigslist.org**. Started in San Francisco, Craig's list has become a national posting board for apartments, jobs, services, and some more discreet needs. You can search the hundreds of constantly updated lists for rental announcements or place your own ad for a room needed at no cost. Often the cheapest and easiest way to shop for apartments online. Be careful to check the legality of any rental or subletting options you consider.

▨ **www.apartmentstores.com.** Has a great range of apartments in all ranges, from studios to 4-bedrooms. The fee is $44.99 for a 30-day subscription. Included in the fee is a credit report that they will conduct so you can show it to potential landlords.

www.springstreet.com. Has a great list of affordable apartments that you can search and contact for free. Their listings include photographs and floor plans. Spring Street is one of the only free online search services; their listed apartments go like wildfire.

www.sfrenter.com. Their free service allows you to search their listings (they mainly feature roommate advertisements, but also list apartments) and post your own for free. It also offers a number of free tips and links for more renting help.

www.easyroommate.com. You can advertise for a room or roommate for free, but you need to pay a fee to access the apartments listed by others and to read emails sent to you by possible landlords. Basic services for as low as $19.99; 60-day membership $40.

Roommate Link, 610-A Cole St. (☎800-446-2887; www.roommatelink.com). In operation since 1975, Roommate Link is the oldest roommate referral service in SF and has absorbed several other agencies. They charge $30 per person for the first two months of your search; if they still haven't found you the right room by then, they'll keep looking for $10 per month until you are situated. Open M-F 10am-8pm, Sa 11am-6pm, Su 11am-4pm. MC/V.

Rental Solutions, 369 Hayes St. (http://rentalsolutions.com). Finds apartments throughout SF proper. Fill out an application online or in person. Expect to wait 2 weeks for an interview, and then 2 more weeks to find an apartment. They charge $30 plus 1 month's rent upon placement.

The Rental Source, 2013 16th St. (☎771-7685; http://therentalsource.com). Takes tenant applications online and in person. They charge a half-month's rent upon placement but it is free to view their listings and their roommate connection web board.

Rent Tech, 4054 18th St. (☎863-7368; www.renttech.com). Offers Internet and in-person services. $65 gets you online and walk-in access to their listings for 90 days; if within that time you don't find an apartment, they'll refund you a portion of your fee.

INSIDE

east bay **209**

berkeley **209** oakland **221**

marin county **229**

west marin: the roadtrip **229**
sausalito **244** mill valley **246**
san anselmo **247**

wine country **249**

napa valley **249** sonoma valley **257**

south of san francisco **260**

palo alto **260**
half moon bay, rte. 1 & greater san mateo **265**

lake tahoe & rte. 80 **272**

Daytripping

EAST BAY	HIGHLIGHTS	TRAVEL TIME
Berkeley	UC Berkeley, Telegraph Ave.	20-30 minutes
Oakland	live music, professional sports	20-30 minutes
MARIN COUNTY	**HIGHLIGHTS**	**TRAVEL TIME**
Marin Headlands	the roadtrip, great hikes	10-20 minutes
Marin Coast	the roadtrip, Muir Beach, Bolinas	50-70 minutes
Mt. Tamalpais and Muir Woods	redwoods, great trails, and hikes	30-40 minutes
Sausalito	great views, relaxing getaway	30-40 minutes
Mill Valley	mountain biking, picnic provisions	30-40 minutes
San Anselmo	laid back get-away	40-50 minutes
WINE COUNTRY	**HIGHLIGHTS**	**TRAVEL TIME**
Napa Valley	wine, wine, wine! (and some history)	60-90 minutes
Sonoma Valley	wine, wine, wine! (and hotsprings)	60-90 minutes
SOUTH OF SF	**HIGHLIGHTS**	**TRAVEL TIME**
Palo Alto	Stanford	40-60 minutes
Half Moon Bay and Rte. 1	the coast and great beaches	30-90 minutes
FARTHER AFIELD	**HIGHLIGHTS**	**TRAVEL TIME**
Lake Tahoe	Hiking, skiing, scenery, great roadtrip	3½-4 hours

San Francisco Bay Area

Pt. Reyes Station

Point Reyes National Seashore

Novato

SONOMA COUNTY

TO SONOMA (8mi.)

NAPA COUNTY

TO NAPA (3mi.)

TO SACRAMENTO (30mi.)

Napa-Sonoma Marsh Wildlife Area

Six Flags Marine World

San Pablo Bay

Vallejo

SOLANO COUNTY

MARIN COUNTY

Fairfax

San Anselmo

San Rafael

Richmond-San Rafael Bridge ($2 westbound)

Carquinez Bridge ($2 eastbound)

Crockett

Benicia

Benicia Bridge ($2 northbound)

Martinez

Bolinas
Stinson Beach

Mt. Tamalpais (2571ft.)

Larkspur

Mill Valley

Richmond

CONTRA COSTA COUNTY

Hercules

Muir Woods Nat'l Monument

Sausalito

El Cerrito

Wildcat Canyon Reg. Park

Briones Reg. Park

Pleasant Hill

Concord

Golden Gate Nat'l Rec. Area

Pt. Bonita

Marin Headlands

Angel Island

Albany

Tilden Reg. Park

Golden Gate Bridge ($5 southbound)

Alcatraz

Treasure Island

Berkeley

UC Berkeley

Walnut Creek

Mt. Diablo State Park

Pacific Ocean

San Francisco

Bay Bridge ($2 westbound)

Oakland

Redwood Reg. Park

San Leandro Reservoir

Danville

San Ramon

Daly City

Candlestick Park

Alameda

Pacifica

San Bruno Mtn. State Park

South San Francisco

Oakland Internat'l Airport

San Leandro

Anthony Chabot Reg. Park

Gray Whale Cove State Beach

San Bruno

San Francisco International Airport

San Francisco Bay

Castro Valley

Montara State Beach

Montara

Millbrae

Hayward

ALAMEDA COUNTY

TO (36mi.)

Burlingame

Half Moon Bay State Beach

San Mateo

San Mateo Bridge ($2 westbound)

Pleasanton

Belmont

Half Moon Bay

San Carlos
Redwood City

Dumbarton Bridge ($2 westbound)

Union City

Woodside

Menlo Park

Newark

Fremont

SAN MATEO COUNTY

Stanford University

Palo Alto

San Francisco Bay Nat'l Wildlife Refuge

Mission Peak Reg. Park

San Gregorio

Portola Valley

San Gregorio Beach

Los Altos Hills

Mountain View

Great America

Ed R. Levine County Park

Pescadero State Beach

Pescadero

Sunnyvale

Santa Clara

San Jose

SANTA CLARA COUNTY

The Silicon Valley

Cupertino

Pigeon Point

TO SANTA CRUZ (20mi.)

Año Nuevo State Reserve

Big Basin Redwoods State Park

Campbell

Los Gatos

TO LOS ANGELES (389mi.)

PACIFIC COAST HIGHWAY

SAN MATEO COUNTY COAST

Crystal Springs Reservoirs

Santa Cruz Mtns.

N
LG

0   10 mi
0   10 km

EAST BAY

Longer and older than its Golden Gate neighbor, the **Bay Bridge** carries the weight of San Francisco traffic east to **Oakland,** where freeways fan out in all directions. The urbanized port of Oakland sprawls north into **Berkeley,** an assertively post-hippie college town. The two towns have long shared an interest in political activism, reflected in wonderfully progressive and effective city government and policies. Berkeley, bookish and bizarre as ever, offers outstanding boutiques and cafes, while its sister city Oakland echoes with the sounds of a progressive blues and jazz scene.

BERKELEY

Famous as an intellectual center and a haven for iconoclasts, Berkeley continues to live up to its reputation. Although the peak of its political activism occurred in the 1960s and 70s—when students attended more protests than classes—**UC Berkeley** continues to cultivate consciousness and an intellectual atmosphere. The vitality of the population infuses the streets, which are strewn with hip cafes and top-notch bookstores, with a slightly psychotic vigor. **Telegraph Avenue,** with its street-corner soothsayers, hirsute hippies, and itinerant musicians, remains one of this town's main draws. Travelers looking to soak up all that Berkeley has to offer should also venture to the north and south of the UC Berkeley campus.

AREA CODE	Berkeley's area code is ☎510.

TRANSPORTATION

Freeway congestion can make driving in the Bay Area frustrating, especially during rush hours. Drivers fortunate enough to reach Berkeley despite the traffic will face congestion, numerous one-way streets, vexing concrete planters, and an earnest quest for a parking spot—the city's precious holy grail. If you're driving from SF, cross the Bay Bridge on **I-80,** take one of the four Berkeley exits. The **University Ave. exit** leads most directly to UC Berkeley and downtown. Reasonably priced public lots (most are $10-15 per day) let you ditch your car and explore on foot—the best way to see downtown and the college area.

Public Transportation: Berkeley TRiP, 2033 Center St. (☎644-POOL/7665), provides commuter-oriented information on public transportation, biking, carpooling, Segways, and other alternative rides. They also sell extended-use transit passes and maps. Open Tu-F noon-5:30pm. Satellite office at 2543 Channing Way, open M-F 9am-2pm. **Bay Area Rapid Transit (BART)** (☎465-2278; www.bart.gov. See **Once In,** p. 37) has 3 Berkeley stops. The Downtown Berkeley station, 2160 Shattuck Ave., at Center St., is close to the western edge of campus, while the North Berkeley station, at Delaware and Sacramento St., lies 4 blocks north of University Ave. To get to Southern Berkeley, take the BART to the Ashby stop at the corner of Ashby and Adeline St. (20-30min. to downtown SF, $2.65). **Alameda County (AC) Transit city buses** #15, 43, and 51 run from the Berkeley BART station to downtown Oakland on Martin Luther King, Jr. Way, Telegraph Ave., and Broadway, respectively (adults $1.50; seniors, disabled, and ages 5-12 75¢; under 5 free; 1hr. transfers 25¢). **Ride Share: Berkeley Ride Board,** 1st level of the student store in the Student Union. **KALX Radio, 90.7 FM** (☎642-5259), broadcasts a daily list of those needing or giving rides at 10am and 10pm. Call to put your request on the air for free.

Taxis: A1 Yellow Cab (☎644-2552) and **Berkeley Yellow Cab** (☎548-2561). Both 24hr.

Car Rental: Budget, 600 Gilman St. (☎800-763-2999), at 2nd St. Car prices vary each day. Unlimited mileage. Call for current prices. Must be 21; under 25 surcharge $20 per day. Open M-F 7am-6pm, Sa 7am-4pm, Su 9am-4pm. (Rental cars are often cheaper in San Francisco, p. 317.) AmEx/D/MC/V. Credit card acceptance varies by location.

ORIENTATION & PRACTICAL INFORMATION

Just across the Bay Bridge, northeast of San Francisco and just north of Oakland, resides the not-so-little Berkeley community famous for acting up and speaking out. The **Marina** rests on the western side of Berkeley while **Tilden Regional Park** climbs the sharp grades to the east. Undergraduates from **UC Berkeley** tend to do their thing on the campus's south side, while graduate students stick to the north. **Downtown Berkeley,** around the **BART station** at Shattuck Ave. and Center St., is where you'll find banks, public libraries, restaurants, and shops, while Addison St. is fast becoming the area's theater district. The magnetic heart of town, **Telegraph Ave.** runs south from the Student Union and is lined with bookstores, cafes, palm readers, and panhandlers. North of campus, the **Gourmet Ghetto** has some of California's finest dining in the area around Shattuck Ave. between Virginia and Rose St. Farther afield, **4th St.,** near the waterfront (take MUNI bus #51 bus west) and **Solano Ave.** to the northwest (take MUNI bus #15 north) are home to yummy eats and shops. The intersection at **College and Ashby Ave.** (take MUNI bus #51 south) also offers some delectable dining. Quality cafes, music stores, and specialty shops grace the **Rockridge** district on the border between Berkeley and Oakland (**Downtown Oakland,** p. 224).

Visitor Information: Berkeley Convention and Visitor Bureau, 2015 Center St. (☎549-8710), at Milvia St. Helpful maps, friendly service, up-to-date practical information, accommodation resources, tons of brochures. Open M-F 9am-5pm. **UC Berkeley Visitors Center,** 101 University Hall (☎642-5215), at the corner of University Ave. and Oxford St. Detailed maps and campus info. Guided campus tours depart from the center M-Sa 10am, Su 1pm. Open M-F 8:30am-4:30pm. **UC Berkeley Switchboard** (☎642-6000) can direct you to info on everything from community events to drug counseling. Open M-F 8am-5pm.

Gay and Lesbian Organizations: UC Berkeley Multicultural BLGA/Queer Resource Center, 305 Eshleman Hall (☎642-6942; http://queer.berkeley.edu), at Bancroft Way and Telegraph Ave. Open Sept.-May M-F 10am-9pm; June-Aug. by appointment only. **Pacific Center,** 2712 Telegraph Ave. (☎548-8283), at Derby St. Counseling and info on gay community events, housing, and clubs. Open M-F 10am-10pm, Sa noon-3pm, Su 6-9pm.

Emergency: ☎911. **Campus Emergency** from campus phones ☎9-911, or 642-3333.

Police: Berkeley Police ☎981-5900 (non-emergency). **Campus Police,** Sproul Hall basement (☎642-6760). Open 24hr.

Berkeley

● SIGHTS
Berkeley Art Museum, **14**
First Church of Christ
  Scientist, **18**
Lawrence Hall of
  Science, **4**
Takara Sake USA Inc., **6**

🍴 FOOD & DRINK
Ann's Soup
  Kitchen, **29**
The Blue Nile, **31**
Café Intermezzo, **27**
Chaat Café, **8**

César, **3**
Holy Land, **21**
The Juice Bar
  Collective, **2**
La Mediterranee, **20**
Long Life Noodle
  Co., **34**
Long Life Vegi
  House, **11**
Mario's La Fiesta, **28**
Naan 'N' Curry, **25**
O Chamé, **5**
Razan's Kitchen, **35**
Yogurt Park, **23**

🍺 NIGHTLIFE
924 Gilman, **1**
Blakes, **26**
Café Milano, **24**
Caffè Strada, **17**
Far Leaves Tea, **22**
Jupiter, **33**
Mediterraneum
  Café, **30**
Shattuck Down
  Low, **36**
Triple Rock
  Brewery, **9**

★ ENTERTAINMENT
Berkeley Repertory
  Theater, **10**
Hertz and Morrison
  Halls, **13**
Julia Morgan Center
  for Arts, **19**
Pacific Film
  Archive, **16**
Zellerbach
  Playhouse, **15**

🛏 ACCOMMODATIONS
Capri Motel, **7**
UC Berkeley Summer
  Visitor Housing, **12**
YMCA, **32**

Berkeley

Tilden Regional Park

Grizzly Peak Blvd.
Golf Course Dr.
TO MINIATURE TRAIN
Centennial Rd.

TO MAIN ENTRANCES OF TILDEN PARK

TO BOTANICAL GARDENS
N. Canyon Rd. Centennial Rd.
Canyon Rd.
Cyclotron Rd.
Stadium Rimway
Strawberry Creek Rd.

La Loma Ave.
Highland

Berkeley Rose Garden

Claremont Canyon Regional Reserve

Claremont Hotel

Inset 2

Shattuck Ave.
Center St.
Allston Wy.
Kittredge St.
Bancroft Wy.

BERKELEY

Clark Kerr Campus (Univ. of Calif.)

Panoramic Wy.

Prospect St.
Warring St.
Piedmont Ave.

Forest Ave.
Garber St.
Russell St.
Prince St.

College Ave.
Benvenue Ave.
Stuart St.

Greek Theater

Gayley Rd.

Le Conte St.
Ridge Rd.
Hearst Ave.

University of California

Euclid St.
Scenic St.

Arch St.
Spruce St.
Oxford St.

Rose St.
Henry St.

GOURMET GHETTO

TO INDIAN ROCK & BODEGA'S BOOKS

Milvia St.

Martin Luther King Jr. Wy.

Vine St.
Grant St.

Carlota Ave.
Monterey Ave.
Hopkins St.
Ordway St.
Acton St.

NORTH BERKELEY

Rose St.

Lincoln St.

Francisco St.
Delaware St.

Berkeley Wy.
University Ave.
Addison Wy.
McGee Ave.
Bancroft Wy.
California St.

Sacramento St.

Acton St.

DOWNTOWN

Shattuck Ave.
Center St.

see inset 2

Bowditch
Hillegass Ave.
Derby Ave.
Dana St.

People's Park

Sproul Pl.
Bancroft
Durant Ave.

Telegraph Ave.

ROCKRIDGE

Regent St.
Woolsey St.

Ashby Ave.
Prince St.

Ellsworth St.
Fulton St.

Shattuck Ave.

Haste St.
Milvia St.

Martin Luther King Jr. Wy.

Grant St.

Dwight Wy.
Blake St.
Parker St.
Carleton St.
Derby St.
Ward St.
Stuart St.
Oregon St.
Russell St.
Julia St.

Adeline St.

ASHBY

Sacramento St.

San Pablo Park

Ashby Ave.

Carlotta Ave.
Santa Fe Ave.
Curtis St.

Evelyn Ave.
Talbot Ave.
Cornell Ave.
Stannage Ave.
Kains Ave.

Cedar St.
Virginia St.
Chestnut St.

Bonar St.
Browning St.
Curtis St.

Parker Wy.
Carleton St.
Grayson St.
Heinz Ave.

Harrison St.
Gilman St.
Camelia St.
Page St.
Jones St.

San Pablo Ave.
10th St.
9th St.
8th St.
7th St.
6th St.
5th St.
4th St.
3rd St.
2nd St.

Bancroft Wy.
Channing Wy.
Dwight Wy.

Greyhound Depot
Addison St.
Allston Wy.

Amtrak Station

East Shore Highway
West Frontage Rd.

Golden Gate Fields

San Francisco Bay

TO CESAR E. CHAVEZ PARK

Berkeley Marina

Marina Blvd.

Aquatic Park

Ped Bridge

500 yards
500 meters

Inset 1

UC Berkeley

Bancroft Wy.
Durant Ave.
Channing Wy.
Haste St.
Dwight Wy.

People's Park

Telegraph Ave.

211

Medical Services: Berkeley Free Clinic, 2339 Durant Ave. (☎800-625-4642 or 548-2570; www.berkeleyfreeclinic.org/home.html), at Dana St. 2 blocks west of Telegraph Ave. Call for hours of service; the best times to talk to a real person are M-F 3am-9pm, Sa 8am-5pm, Su 5-8pm. **STD Clinic and HIV/AIDS Testing:** ☎644-0425. **Dental:** ☎548-2745. **Counseling:** ☎548-2744. **Berkeley Dept. of Health & Human Services,** 830 University Ave. (☎981-5350), at 6th St. Medical help on a sliding payment scale. Specialty clinics vary from day to day, so call ahead. Open M-F 8am-5pm. **Berkeley Women's Health Center,** 2908 Ellsworth St. (☎843-6194), 1 block west of Telegraph Ave. Open M and F 8am-noon and 1-5pm, Tu-Th 9am-1pm and 2-6pm.

Internet Access: UC Computer, 2569 Telegraph Ave. (☎649-6089; www.transbay.net). $3 per 15min., $5 per 30min., $7 per hr. Open M-F 10am-6pm. **Berkeley Espresso,** 1900 Shattuck Ave. (☎848-9576). Free wireless Internet access with purchase (bring your own laptop). Open daily 6am-11pm. No credit cards.

Post Office: 2000 Allston Way (☎649-3155), at Milvia St. Open M-F 9am-5pm, Sa 10am-2pm. **Postal code:** 94704.

ACCOMMODATIONS

There are surprisingly few cheap accommodations in Berkeley. The **Berkeley-Oakland Bed and Breakfast Network** (☎547-6380; www.bbonline.com/ca/berkeley-oakland) coordinates some great East Bay B&Bs with a range of rates (singles $50-150; doubles $60-150; twins $85-150). Although the motels are technically within walking distance of the BART stations, Downtown Berkeley, UC, and other prime attractions, they are much more accessible with a car. No-frills motels line University Ave. between Shattuck and Sacramento St., while the ritzier joints are downtown, especially on Durant Ave.

UC Berkeley Summer Visitor Housing, (☎642-4108; www.housing.berkeley.edu). Visitors are housed in Stern Hall, 2700 Hearst Ave., at Highland St. Simple college dorm rooms minus the Grateful Dead posters. Easy accessibility and great location make this a good deal. Shared baths. Free Internet access, local phone calls, games, and TV room. Parking ($6 per day), laundry (wash $1.35), meals, and photocopying available. Open June to mid-Aug. Apply online for a reservation request. Singles $53; doubles $68; 7th night free. Availability limited by season due to construction. ❷

YMCA, 2001 Allston Way (☎848-6800), at Milvia St. The Ritz it ain't, but adequate rooms in the co-ed hotel portion of this YMCA make it worthwhile, especially if you find yourself without other options. Shared bath. Use of pool and fitness facilities included. Communal kitchen, computer room (with Internet), and TV lounge. Pay phones in hall. 10-night max. stay; special applications available for longer stays. Reception daily 8am-9:30pm. No curfew. Must be 18+ with ID. Singles $39; doubles $49; triples $59. MC/V. ❷

Capri Motel, 1512 University Ave. (☎845-7090), at Sacramento St. Clean, tasteful rooms with cable TV, A/C, and fridge. Must be 18+ with ID. Singles and doubles from $85 (independently owned, so prices tend to vary). AmEx/D/MC/V. ❸

FOOD & DRINK

Blending a bit of hipster hippie sensibility with posh pretention, Berkeley's **Gourmet Ghetto**—at Shattuck Ave. and Cedar St.—is the famous birthplace of Californian cuisine. When chef Alice Waters opened *Chez Panisse* in 1971, she introduced the nation to the joys of goat cheese and polenta. Budget traveler beware: in this ghetto, "gourmet" often equals big bucks for skimpy servings. With thousands of starving students, the area is also home to pizza joints and hamburger stands, though the ghetto mentality may spruce menu items up a bit ("I'll have a slice of cheese-less alfalfa pizza"). The north end of **Telegraph Ave.** caters to student appetites and wallets with late-night offerings of all varieties along **Durant Ave.** If you don't eat meat (or Berkeley has inspired you to give it up), you're in luck because Berkeley does greens like nowhere else, and a growing number of international establishments are helping to diversify the area. **Solano Ave.** to the north is great for Asian cuisine while **4th St.** has more upscale eats. If you have access to a kitchen or simply like your veggies raw, stop by the **farmer's markets** (cash only) run by the Ecology Center (☎548-3333). Markets sprout up Sa at Center St. and Martin Luther King, Jr. Way (10am-2pm), Tu at Derby St. and Martin Luther King, Jr. Way (summer 2-7pm; off-season 2-6pm), and you'll find a summer-only market at Shattuck and Cedar (May-Oct. Th 2-6pm).

DOWNTOWN AND COLLEGE AREA

Yogurt Park, 2433 Durant Ave. (☎549-2198; 549-0570 for daily list of yogurt flavors), just west of Telegraph Ave. An icon of Berkeley gastronomic life. Yogurt $1.75-2.20; additional toppings 65¢. Huge portions. Open daily 10am-midnight. No credit cards. ❶

Razan's Kitchen, 2119 Kittredge St. (☎486-0449). Serving an eclectic group of foods including (but not limited to) international wraps, burritos, meat, veggies, and juices, this **all organic** restaurant is a great pick for those hungry for environmentally-friendly food. Even the ketchup is organic! Sandwiches $5-10. Juice $2-4. Open daily 10am-10pm. AmEx/D/MC/V.

Chaat Café, 1902 University Ave. (☎845-1431), at Martin Luther King, Jr. Way. Berkeley has very large Indian population and consequently countless restaurants cooking from the subcontinent. Chaat Café is among the cheapest and the best. Appetizers $3-6; entrees and wraps $4-6; curries $6-10; lunch specials $5-6. Open daily 11:30am-9:30pm. MC/V. ❶

Long Life Vegi House, 2129 University Ave. (☎845-6072), between Shattuck Ave. and Walnut St. Vast menu with countless vegetable and "vegetarian meat" options. Huge portions; most entrees $6-9. Friendly, prompt service. No MSG. Daily lunch specials ($4) served from 11:30am-3pm include an entree, spring roll, soup, and brown rice. Open Su-Th 11:30am-10pm, F-Sa 11:30am-10:30pm. AmEx/D/MC/V. ❶

Long Life Noodle Co. and Jook Joint, 2261 Shattuck St. (☎548-8083), at Kittredge St. You name the noodle, they've got it: Japanese, Chinese, Korean, Thai, Vietnamese noodles, *udon*, ramen, egg, and *soba*. Wok-tossed dishes, soups, and noodles ($6-9, large portions). Sake and interesting specialty drinks too; try the "Cool" Cucumber Juice ($2.50) or the Mango Martini ($5). Open Su-Th 11:30am-9:30pm, F-Sa 11:30am-10:30pm. MC/V. ❶

TELEGRAPH AVENUE

Café Intermezzo, 2442 Telegraph Ave. (☎849-4592), at Haste St. This veggie-lover's paradise serves heaping salads with homemade dressing, huge sandwiches on freshly baked bread, and tasty soups—all at delicious prices. Even the most famished will find sal(ad)vation here (meat options available). Sandwiches $4.99; salads $3.50-6.75; combo $5.50. Espresso bar opens at 8:30am. Kitchen open daily 10am-10pm. No credit cards. ❶

The Blue Nile, 2525 Telegraph Ave. (☎540-6777), between Blake and Dwight St. Waitresses in traditional gowns serve huge portions of Ethiopian food in a lavish setting. Eat *injera* bread with your fingers while sipping *mes* (honey wine $2). Variety of vegetarian dishes (lentils happily abound). Open Tu-Su 5-10pm. Reservations recommended on weekends. MC/V. ❷

Naan 'N' Curry, 2366 Telegraph Ave. (☎843-6226). Recently spawned from a location in the Tenderloin, Naan 'N' Curry thrives on restaurant-packed Telegraph Ave. because of its tasty, ample, and cheap offerings. Menu carries curry dishes almost exclusively, but includes some Tandoori options for those who can't take the heat. All dishes $4-10. Crowded around lunchtime. Open M-Th noon-midnight, F-Su noon-2am. No credit cards. ❷

Ann's Soup Kitchen, 2494 Telegraph Ave. (☎548-8885), at Dwight St. The crowded dining area proves that this place is a campus favorite. Two eggs and toast or hearty home fries $3 (all breakfast items under $5). Fresh-squeezed juice is their best deal, ringing up at only $1.35. Lunch is equally affordable (sandwiches under $5). Open M and W-F 8am-6pm, Tu 8am-3pm, Sa-Su 8am-5pm. No credit cards. ❶

Mario's La Fiesta, 2444 Telegraph Ave. (☎848-2588), at Haste St. Gritty and great Mexican food since 1959. Friendly service and hearty burritos are a real deal for only $1.80-4.85. Enjoy a large meal with one of several dinner combos ($6.70-11.10), and throw in a beer for only a few bucks more. Open daily 10:30am-10:30pm. No credit cards. ❶

Pack a Picnic!

Often sunnier than its neighbor across the Bay, Berkeley is an ideal place to plop down for a picnic. What better way to take in the Berkeley scene than lolling on a grassy knoll with bread and wine in hand? Campus conveniently sprawls across acres of grass, dotted with benches and covered areas, so stock up at a store or deli listed below and enjoy! Inspiration Pt. in Tilden Park (p. 216) also provides an excellent location for some outdoor dining.

Berkeley Bowl, 2020 Oregon St. (☎843-6929), near Adeline St. The Bowl is chock full with fresh produce, seafood, and bread. Open M-Sa 9am-8pm, Su 10am-6pm. AmEx/D/MC/V.

Cheese Board, 1504 Shattuck Ave. (☎549-3183), between Cedar and Vine St. Gourmet cheese shop and bakery and cafe. Bakery and cheese shop open M 7am-1pm, Tu-F 7am-6pm, Sa 8:30am-5pm. No credit cards.

Monterey Foods, 1550 Hopkins St. (☎526-6042). Local produce, some of it organic, affordable wines, and crusty bread. Open M-F 9am-7pm; Sa 8:30am-6pm. No credit cards.

Éclair Pastries, 2565 Telegraph Ave. (☎848-4221), at Blake St. Top off your picnic with meringues or Florentines ($1). Open M-F 6:30am-7pm, Su 6:30am-5:30pm. MC/V.

NORTH OF CEDAR STREET

The Juice Bar Collective, 2114 Vine St. (☎548-8473), just east of Shattuck Ave. This tiny juice co-op, known originally for its great tasting orange, carrot, and grapefruit juice, has expanded its repertoire to include fresh smoothies ($3), sandwiches ($4.50-5), cookie-treats ($2), soups ($2), and entrees ($2-5). Most items are vegetarian though they roast an organic turkey daily. Fresh ginger soda is delightful. Open M-Sa 10am-4:30pm. No credit cards. ❶

César, 1515 Shattuck Ave. (☎883-0222), just south of Vine St. A great place for wining and dining, with savory tapas ($3-12), *bocadillos* (a small sandwich on french bread, $5-7), desserts ($4-5), and an impressive list of spirits. Open, airy, European feel. Open daily noon-midnight; kitchen closes Su-Th 11pm, F-Sa 11:30pm. No reservations. MC/V, AmEx. ❷

SOUTH OF DWIGHT AVE.

Holy Land, 2965 College Ave. (☎665-1672), just south of Ashby Ave. Fantastic Falafel $4.95; Schuperlative Schwarmma $5.75. Pitas $5-6. Lunches $7.95; dinner after 4pm $15-20. Open M-F, Su 11am-9pm. MC/V. ❶

La Mediterranee, 2936 College Ave. (☎540-7773; www.cafelamed.com), just north of Ashby Ave. Warm and cool all at the same time. The refreshingly calm Mediterranean atmosphere (replete with a roofed terrace, mosaic walls, tiled tables, and fern foliage) enhances the Middle Eastern cuisine (all dishes under $10, served with soup or salad). *Anoush Ella* (May it be sweet!). Open M-Th 10am-10pm, F-Sa 10am-11pm, Su 10am-9:30pm. AmEx/MC/V. ❷

WEST BERKELEY/4TH STREET

O Chamé, 1830 4th St. (☎841-8783), between Virginia and Hearst St. Innovative Japanese fusion cooking in a tranquil setting. Become one with a bowl of *soba* or *udon* noodles and get tipsy while sipping *sake* ($5). Appetizers $5-12 (try the white corn and green onion pancake). Entrees and soups $9.50-20. Open for lunch M-Sa 11:30am-3pm; dinner 5:30-9:30pm. AmEx/MC/V. ❷

SIGHTS

You haven't really visited Berkeley until you've strolled the first five or so blocks of **Telegraph Ave.,** which runs south from Sproul Plaza as far as downtown Oakland. The action is close to the university, where Telegraph Ave. is lined with a motley assortment of cafes, bookstores, and used clothing and record stores. Businesses come and go at the whims of the marketplace, but the scene—a rowdy jumble of 60s and 90s counterculture—persists. Vendors push tie-dye, Tarot readings, and jewelry; the homeless and disenfranchised hustle for change; and characters looking like Old Testament prophets carry on hyper-dimensional conversations, transmitting knowledge and meditations accrued from years of Berkeley experience.

Berkeley's active presses, which can be found in corner boxes and at cafes, are invaluable for an up-to-date list of happenings around town, including the latest goings-on in San Francisco. Look in bookstores and bins for the free weekly *East Bay Express* (www.eastbayexpress.com), filled with theater, film, and concert listings. If you can find a recent edition of *Resource*, the guide given to new Berkeley students, grab it (try the Visitors Center at 101 University Hall). The *Daily Californian* (www.dailycal.org), which publishes on Tuesdays and Fridays in the summer and daily during the academic year, carries university news and features.

█ FIRST CHURCH OF CHRIST SCIENTIST. Built in 1910, architect Bernard Maybeck's (credited with transforming SF into the "Athens of the west") masterpiece is a conglomeration of Gothic, Renaissance, Classical, Japanese, Mediterranean, and industrial architectural styles located just east of People's Park. *(2526 Dwight St., at Bowditch St. ☎ 845-7199. Open during services W 8pm and Su 11am; tours at noon on the 1st Su of each month.)*

TAKARA SAKE USA INC. Learn the history and science of *sake* making, and sample 15 different varieties of *sake*. The friendly and knowledgeable hosts will not laugh in your face when you wobble out the door, another pitiful victim of Japan's merciless fire-water. *Kam Pai* (Cheers!). The museum, video, and tastings are all free. Tasting takes about half an hour, so arrive before 5:30pm if you plan to partake. *(708 Addison St., just west of 4th St. Take the #51 bus to 4th St. and walk down to Addison St. ☎ 540-8250; www.takarasake.com. Open daily noon-6pm. MC/V.)*

UC BERKELEY

In 1868, the private College of California and the public Agricultural, Mining, and Mechanical Arts College united as the **University of California.** The stunning 178 acre university was the first of the nine University of California campuses, so by seniority it has sole right to the nickname "Cal." With over 30,000 students and 1,350 full professors, the University is especially active when classes are in session, from late August to mid-May. If you'd like to sit in on some classes, track down a course catalog and schedule of classes at the campus bookstore or online (www.berkeley.edu). The campus is bound on the south by Bancroft Way, on the west by Oxford St., on the north by Hearst Ave., and on the east by **Tilden Park.** Remodeling often occurs during academic downtime, so watch for closings due to structural changes or "seismic corrections." Maps of campus are posted everywhere; the **Visitors Center** (p. 210) hands out campus maps (10¢) and also offers free tours.

█ BERKELEY ART MUSEUM. BAM is most respected for its collection of 20th-century American and Asian art and Hofmann Collection in particular. Rotating exhibitions showcase experimental work. Also associated with **The Pacific Film Archive**. *(2626 Bancroft Way, at College Ave. ☎ 642-0808; www.bampfa.berkeley.edu. Open W-Su 11am-7pm. Adults $8; students, seniors, disabled, and ages 12-17 $5. Free first Th of each month.)*

SPROUL PLAZA. In October 1964, students protested the arrest of one of their own who had been distributing civil rights pamphlets in the plaza, galvanizing a series of confrontations that lasted several years. Mario Savio, a student and member of the widely influential Free Speech Movement, famously addressed a crowd from the steps of the plaza, arguing for students' rights to free expression and assembly. Savio was eventually jailed and expelled from school, but in 1997 the plaza steps were named in his honor. A popular social (and activist) hangout during the school year.

SATHER TOWER. Sather Tower, better known as the **Campanile** (roughly Italian for "bell tower"), a 1914 monument to Berkeley benefactor Jane Krom Sather, is the third tallest free-standing clocktower in the world (at 307 ft.). For a great view, ride to its observation level (M-F 10am-4pm, $2; tip-top is not wheelchair-accessible). 61-bell **carillon** plays during the school year weekdays at 7:10am, noon, and 6pm, and gives a 45min. concert on Sundays at 2pm.

LAWRENCE HALL OF SCIENCE. High atop the eucalyptus-covered hills east of the main campus is one of the finest science museums in the Bay Area. Ever-changing exhibits stress hands-on science activities catering to children but fun for all ages. The courtyard offers a life-size model whale, a stunning view of the bay, and stargazing workshops on clear Saturday evenings. Visit the Planetarium for its "Constellations Tonight" show and be sure to check out the outdoor "Forces That Shape The Bay" exhibit. *(On Centennial Dr. Take bus #8 or 65 from the Berkeley BART station and keep your transfer for $2 off admission. Once there, use the University shuttle (50¢; ☎ 642-5149), or brace yourself for the long, steep walk. ☎ 642-5132; www.lawrencehallofscience.org. Open daily 10am-5pm. Adults $8; students, seniors, and ages 5-18 $6; ages 3-4 $4.)*

HEARST GREEK THEATRE. This impressive marble structure, donated by William Randolph and Phoebe Hearst in 1903, is modeled after the classical amphitheater in Epidaurus, Greece and seats up to 8,200 people. Big-name acts play to big crowds, especially during the summer. Be sure to bring sunscreen for summer performances. *(On the northeast side of main campus at Gayley Rd. ☎ 642- 9988.)*

BOTANICAL GARDENS. The Botanical Gardens contain over 13,000 varieties of plant life from around the world, including a huge number of rare and endangered plants, that thrive in Berkeley's Mediterranean-like climate. Agatha Christie supposedly came here to examine a rare poisonous plant whose deadly powers she later put to use in a mystery novel. If you take the time to come up to the Gardens, also visit the **Stephen Mather Redwood Grove** across the street. *Let's Go* recommends catching the 🖱University shuttle (50¢; ☎ 642-5149), because the walk is long. *(200 Centennial Dr., in Strawberry Canyon, midway between the UC Stadium and Lawrence Hall of Science. From I-80, take University to its end at Oxford. Turn right. Right on Hearst. Right on Galey. Left on Stadium Rimway. Left on Centennial. Parking is past the garden (50¢ per hr.) ☎ 643-2755; www.mip.berkeley.edu/garden. Open daily 9am-5pm except major holidays and the 1st Tuesday of each month. Open until 8pm Memorial Day through Labor Day. Adults $3, seniors $2, ages 3-18 $1. Free on Th. AmEx/D/MC/V.)*

PARKS AND RECREATION

🖱**BERKELEY ROSE GARDEN.** Built by the Works Projects Administration in the Depression era, the garden spills from one terrace to another in a vast semicircular amphitheater. Roses are pruned in January in preparation for Mother's Day (May 9, 2004), when the garden is at its glorious peak. Flowers aside, it is a great place to watch the sunset. *(North of campus, walk or drive up Euclid Ave. to Bayview Pl. Or take the #65 bus up Euclid Ave. Enter on Euclid. Open May-Sept. dawn-dusk.)*

PEOPLE'S PARK. Berkeley's biggest confrontation between the People and the Man was not fought over Freedom of Speech or the war in Vietnam, but over a muddy vacant lot. In April 1969, students, hippies, and radicals christened the patch of university-owned land **"People's Park,"** tearing up pavement and laying down sod to establish, in the words of the *Berkeley Barb*, "a cultural, political freak out and rap center for the Western world." When the university moved to evict squatters and build a parking garage, resistance stiffened. Governor Ronald "trickle-down" Reagan sent in 2,000 troops, and the conflict ended with helicopters dropping tear gas on students in Sproul Plaza, one bystander shot dead by police, and a 17-day National Guard occupation of Berkeley. The park's grassy existence represents a small victory over the establishment, though that's sometimes hard to remember on a sunny Saturday afternoon when kids play sports or a cold Monday night when homeless huddle in the bushes. A mural on Haste St. at Telegraph Ave. depicts the park's history, from protesters to panhandlers. *(East of Telegraph Ave. between Dwight and Haste St.)*

TILDEN REGIONAL PARK AND WILDCAT CANYON. In the pine and eucalyptus forests east of the city lies the beautiful anchor of the East Bay park system—**Tilden Regional Park.** Hiking, biking, running, and riding trails criss-cross the park and provide impressive views of the Bay Area. The **ridgeline trail** makes for an especially spectacular bike ride. For those looking to frolic without getting all sweaty, a 19th-century carousel inside the park is a fun option. Also inside the park, **Lake Anza's** small, sandy beach is a popular swimming spot during the hottest summer days (but not the place to go for a quiet, romantic skinny dip, as Lake Anza tends to attract children). At the north end of the park, the **Environmental Education Center** offers exhibits and naturalist-led programs. **Grizzly Peak** and **Inspiration Point** provides breathtaking panoramas of the entire Bay Area and is a good starting points for hiking and running in the park. **Wildcat Canyon** is a less developed park than Tilden, with gorgeous hiking (though no biking) through grassy meadows and densely wooded canyons. *(Tilden: East of the city. By car or bicycle, take Spruce St. to Grizzly Peak Blvd. to Canon Ave. AC Transit buses #7 and 8 run from the Berkeley BART station to the entrance at Grizzly Peak Blvd. and Golf Course Dr. ☎ 635-0135. Open daily dawn-dusk. Lake: ☎ 843-2137. Open in summer 11am-6pm. Adults $3, seniors and children $2. Trail maps free. Education Center: ☎ 525-2233. Open Tu-Su 10am-5pm. Free. Wildcat Canyon: Adjacent to Tilden Park. Open daily dawn-dusk.)*

INDIAN ROCK. The basalt face of **Indian Rock** challenges thrill-junkies with short but demanding climbs. For the vertically challenged, easy side steps lead to an impressive view of the Headlands. *(At the north end of Shattuck Ave., past the traffic circle. Open daily dawn-dusk.)*

BERKELEY MARINA & CESAR CHAVEZ PARK. This quiet, serene park might be out of the way for those doing Berkeley by foot. If you can get there, take a fishing pole out onto the 3,000 ft. **Historic Berkeley Marina** public fishing pier to catch some crabs, halibut, or bass, or just the sunset. Enjoy a stroll, a bike ride, a game of frisbee, or a plain old picnic in **Cesar Chavez Park's** 90 rolling acres. The breeze is best by the water. The park hosts a well-regarded annual Kite Festival at the end of July. *(Take bus #51 west, all the way down University Ave. If you're walking or biking, go all the way to the end of Addison St. and over the overpass. Pier open daily dawn-dusk.)*

NIGHTLIFE

Because Berkeley is so close to SF proper, when hard-core clubbers need to bump-bump-and-grind, they just take the bridge. What Berkeley does offer is an unrivaled array of casual brew-pubs and brainy cafes. Crowded at almost any hour of the night or day, they serve as surrogate libraries, living rooms, and lecture theaters; espresso drinks and microbrews loosen the tongues of an already talkative city. Many bars have some great live music offerings, as well.

from the road

The Soul of Berkeley

Having spent one summer in Berkeley, I was familiar with the communal spirit that infuses its air. But it wasn't until I came as a writer that I found just how much Berkeley residents really care for one another.

On my first day in the city I stopped ritually at one of the best bookstores in Berkeley. I was purchasing a tiny, but expensive art book by one of my favorite drawers, Yoshitoma Nara, when the cashier said to me "Fortunately, art books are not one of my vices." I asked him what, in that case, were some of his vices. "Oh tequila. And pot, but I grow my own so that doesn't cost me." I told him I was new to town. He chuckled, handing me my book, and told me to come back in a few days.

Two days later, I stopped in the store out of curiosity. The same guy was there, and when we made eye contact I announced that I was going to browse the fourth floor. A few minutes later, the cashier appeared and asked, "Are you the person who said she was new to town?" I nodded my head, yes, and he extended a cookie and an envelope marked "Welcome!" containing a smokable item. Cherry pie has been pushed aside, and Berkeley is raising the standards for community.

217

STIMULANTS

 Far Leaves Tea, 2979 College Ave. (☎665-9409; www.farleaves.com), just south of Ashby Ave. Meditative tea shop offering a vast selection of teas (with an emphasis on traditional Chinese and Taiwanese green and oolong blends). Teas range from $1.25-6. Brew your own while you sit on green pillows (or chairs if you need them), breathe, and sip with a book, a friend, or your own reflections. Also offers Chinese tea ceremony classes. Open daily 11am-9pm. MC/V.

Mediterraneum Café, 2475 Telegraph Ave. (☎549-1128), north of Dwight Way. For a taste of "old Berkeley," visit "the Med"—a landmark more popular with residents than students. Spacious upstairs and downstairs, black-and-white checkered floors, art on the walls. A nice place to get some work done, with inspiration provided by the ghosts of Berkeley past (Alan Ginsburg wrote his epic poem "Howl" at "the Med".) Latte $1.95. Fresh smoothies $2.95. Cheap breakfast and sandwich items under $3. Desserts $1-2. Open M-F 7am-11:30pm, Sa-Su 7:30am-11:30pm. No credit cards.

Caffè Strada, 2300 College Ave. (☎843-5282), at Bancroft Way. The glittering jewel of the caffeine-fueled intellectual scene. Go to be seen, discuss philosophy, or just enjoy the beautiful outdoor terrace. Small latte $1.95. Most drinks under $2.50. Try the *Strada Bianca*, white hot chocolate ($1.90). Open daily 6:30am-midnight. No credit cards.

Café Milano, 2522 Bancroft Way (☎644-3100), east of Telegraph Ave. High wood-beam ceilings equipped with opening sun roof, 10 ft. windows, and interior foliage make Milano one of Telegraph's top contenders. Along with Strada, Milano is a common meeting space for Berkeley students. Latte $2. Open M-F 7am-10pm, Sa-Su 8am-10pm. No credit cards.

DEPRESSANTS

 Jupiter, 2181 Shattuck Ave. (☎843-8277), near the BART station. Stained glass, church pews, and elaborate Gothic-patterned paneling that you'll only see if the place is empty. And we promise you, it won't be. Live music in the spacious beer garden (winter W-Su, rest of the year Tu-Sa). Th night "Beat Down" offers trance and hip-hop, accompanied by psychedelic projections on a massive brick wall. Su nights catch indie shorts projections. Terrific pizza to boot (9-inch pie $8). No cover. Open M-Th 11:30am-1am, F 11:30am-2am, Sa noon-2am, Su midnight. MC/V.

Blakes, 2367 Telegraph Ave. (☎848-0886), at Durant Ave. A jam-packed and unabashed meat market, but at least the cuts are premium. The pint-sized upstairs has a loud sports bar feel, while the middle floor is mellow with more seating. In the basement, kick it to the loud beats of local bands. Some shows 18+. Beverages from $2.50. Appetizers $2-5. Meals $4-8. Happy Hour daily 4-7pm. Drink specials 9pm-midnight. Cover $3-7. Open M-F 11:30am-2am, Sa noon-2am, Su noon-1am. AmEx/D/MC/V.

Triple Rock Brewery, 1920 Shattuck Ave. (☎843-2739; www.triplerock.com), north of Berkeley Way. Boisterous and friendly, the Rock was the first (and to many remains the best) of Berkeley's many brewpubs. Long and ever-changing menu of original ales, stouts, and porters (made 2-3 times a week, through their hands-on 7-barrel process). Award-winning Red Rock Ale $3.25. Shuffleboard table in back supports those not sober enough to stand. Open Su-W 11:30am-midnight, Th-Sa 11:30am-1am (later, if busy). Rooftop garden closes at 9pm, kitchen closes Su-W 10:30pm, Th-Sa midnight. MC/V.

924 Gilman, 924 Gilman St. (☎524-8180, 24hr. info 525-9926), at 8th St. This all-ages club is a legendary staple of California punk that has helped bands like Green Day, Operation Ivy, and Crimpshrine gain following. Join the crowd and colored hair for a crazy show. Local, national, and international acts rock this joint, although major labels are strictly taboo. Most shows start at 8pm. Cover $5 with $2 membership card (good for 1 year, sold at the door).

Shattuck Down Low, 2284 Shattuck Ave. (☎548-1159; www.shattuckdownlow.com), at Bancroft Way. Recently opened, this sleek and sexy dance club lounge is for the young Berkeley hipster who doesn't want to have to BART it to SF for a cool clubbing scene. Very eclectic mix of music—always loud, most often live. M live reading, Tu Karaoke, and W salsa and dance lessons. Th DJ spins funk, soul, and hip-hop. F-Sa live music, Su reggae. Once a month

Brazilian party and frequent Cuban and funk jam bands. Check website for calendar. Average drink $4.50-5. Food served W-Su 8pm until late. 21+. Casual dress code. Occasional cover. Open Tu-Sa 8pm-2am. Su-M 9pm-2am. AmEx/MC/V.

ENTERTAINMENT

ON CAMPUS

Zellerbach Playhouse, near the corner of Bancroft Way and Dana St. Shared by professional dance and theater companies and student ensembles alike, Zellerbach is a community favorite. Summertime shows usually consist of musicals and romantic comedies. Tickets during the academic year $6-12; summer shows $5-10, students and seniors $3-6. Contact CAL Performances for tickets.

CAL Performances (☎642-9988; www.calperformances.berkeley.edu), at the north corner of Zellerbach Hall . Information and tickets for concerts, plays, and movies available here. Open M-F 10am-5:30pm, Sa 10am-2pm. AmEx/MC/V.

Hertz and Morrison Halls (☎642-0527), on campus, between Bowditch St. and College Ave. The Berkeley music department hosts noon concerts, with music by Berkeley's best student and faculty performers, including the African Music Ensemble, the Berkeley Contemporary Chamber Players, the Javanese Gamelan, and the 1991 Grammy-nominated University Chamber Chorus. During the academic year, catch free W (and some F) afternoon concerts at 125 Morrison Hall and at 104 Morrison Hall, Berkeley's music department. For ticketed performances contact CAL Performances (p. 219).

CAL Athletics, 2233 Fulton St., first fl. (☎800-462-3277). PAC-10 athletics at its best. Ticket office staffed M-F 8:30am-4:30pm. AmEx/D/MC/V.

OFF CAMPUS

▨ **Pacific Film Archive,** 2575 Bancroft Way (☎642-1124; www.bampfa.berkeley.edu/pfa), near Bowditch St. With a new facility and a huge collection of archived foreign and independent films, the PFA is a great place to catch any number of underground, experimental, and hard-to-find flicks. Tickets $5. Ticket office open M-F 11am-5pm. AmEx/D/MC/V.

▨ **Berkeley Repertory Theater,** 2025 Addison St. (☎845-4700; www.berkeleyrep.org). The best-known and arguably finest theater in the area, with an eclectic repertoire of classics and unknowns. Half-price tickets may be available Tu-F on the day of the show—line up at the box office at noon. Rush tickets for students and seniors 30min. before show. $20 advance tickets for anyone under 30 except Sa night. Box office open Tu-Su noon-7pm. AmEx/D/MC/V.

The Local LEGEND

The Mad Bookseller

The walls of Serendipity Books (p. 220) are lined with extraordinary first edition Faulkners and rare radio-plays by Beckett. The floors are filled with even more: heaps of overflow and unshelved books make the store a klutz's nightmare. Indeed, when you walk through the doors of Serendipity you are bound to trip, but will most likely stumble into a literary treasure as you fall.

Most would call it "disorganized," or "untidy" if being polite; however you say it, Peter B. Howard's antiquarian bookstore is no less than the biblioreality of a carefully plotted map of genius in his head.

For this bookseller, book-browsing is neither random nor haphazard, but a "Serendipitous" occasion. The discovery of the first-printed copy of your favorite Bukowski poem (which is not in the poetry section but on a table under a photograph of Ginsberg) isn't merely luck within chaos, but an event carefully catalyzed by Peter's crafty system: he knows where everything is, even if you don't.

Peter B. Howard is the owner of **Serendipity Books** in Berkeley, California. Serendipity's website reads, "If you're in Berkeley, California, feel free to come in and browse. We are usually friendly." Don't be nervous, and don't miss Peter or his store.

Biking

UC Berkeley

Julia Morgan Center for Arts, 2640 College Ave. (☎845-8542; tickets 925-798-1300; www.juliamorgan.org), at Derby St., shares space with a preschool and yoga center in a beautiful building that was once a church. Its namesake and designer was the 1st female architect in California. Noted for its graceful mix of materials, this building was Morgan's first commission; she later built Hearst Castle. The theater hosts diverse performances including the **Berkeley Opera.** Open M-Sa 10am-6pm, Su noon-5pm.

SHOPPING

Telegraph Ave. is an excellent source for books, music, and secondhand clothing, along with homemade tie-dye, jewelry, and pipes. If you are willing to walk or drive a few miles off Telegraph, you will be rewarded with some of Berkeley's best bookstores and sex shops. Chain stores seem conspicuously misplaced in this happy land of independent and locally-supported stores.

BOOKSTORES

🖾 **Serendipity Books,** 1201 University Ave. (☎841-7455). This dusty and awe-inspiring collection earns Serendipity nation-wide respect in the antiquarian book industry. Peter Howard, the owner, is a sage and legend. Ask him for suggestions on where to browse in his enormous store. Stay as long as you can. Open M-Sa 9am-5pm. AmEx/D/MC/V.

🖾 **Moe's Books,** 2476 Telegraph Ave. (☎849-2087; www.moesbooks.com), between Dwight and Haste St. This hip little spot was featured in *The Graduate* and has 4 well-arranged floors of secondhand knowledge, as well as new books at a 10% discount and a nice selection of art and antiquarian books on the 4th floor. Open daily 10am-11pm. AmEx/D/MC/V.

Boadecia's Books, 398 Colusa Ave. (☎559-9184; www.bookpride.com). Independent, friendly, and feminist. Lesbian-owned bookstore features LGBT, women's, and progressive books and videos, from Chabonian fiction to Foucauldian theory. Book discussion groups, author events, and workshops. Open Su-M 11am-6pm, Tu-F noon-8pm, Sa 11am-8pm. AmEx/D/MC/V.

Shambhala Booksellers, 2482 Telegraph Ave. (☎848-8443), at Dwight St. next door to Moe's. Shambhala is the place to go for a new deck of Tarot cards and a few books on the Kaballah, Tibetan Buddhism, Wicca, and the Zohar. Open daily 11am-8pm. AmEx/D/MC/V.

Comic Relief, 2138 University Ave. (☎843-5002). Holy biceps, Batman! At Comic Relief you can read about and buy merchandise featuring men who run around in tight, brightly colored spandex. Open Oct. to mid-June Su-Tu 11am-7pm, W-Sa 11am-9pm; mid-June to Sept. M-Sa 11am-9pm, Su 11am-7pm. AmEx/D/MC/V.

MUSIC

Amoeba Music, 2455 Telegraph Ave. (☎549-1125; www.amoebamusic.com), near Haste St. The champion of the buy-sell-trade scene. Go crazy in the warehouse-sized store with tons of new and used CDs, including a popular collection of music and mutterings by Telegraph Ave's least coherent residents. Open M-Sa 10:30am-10pm, Su 11am-9pm. D/MC/V.

Rasputin, 2401 Telegraph Ave. (☎800-350-8700; www.rasputinmusic.com). Browse the budget used records and CDs and find obscure jazz imports, indie rock albums, or Latin and international cuts. New California underground hip-hop artists make their way into the Rasputin's stocks as well. Opened in 1971, Rasputin now has several locations in the Bay-area, but Berkeley boasts the original. Open M and W-Th 10:30am-10pm, Tu 10am-10pm, F 10:30am-11pm, Sa 10am-11pm, Su 11am-10pm.

SPECIALTY SHOPS

✪ Good Vibrations, Berkeley boasts the second location of this renowned woman-run sex store cooperative. See p. 188 for listing info.

Zebra, 2467 Telegraph Ave. (☎649-8002, www.mrzebra.com). Tattoos here, from a true artist, will cost you, but they will be clean and safe (if a bit painful). Piercings and leather goods to boot. Open daily 10am-8pm. AmEx/D/MC/V.

Wicked, 2431 Telegraph Ave. (☎883-1055), near Channing Way. Despite its high prices and designer labels, Wicked takes a crack at counterculture feel with its in-store pipe shop (tattoo parlor unfortunately recently closed). Open M-Sa 11am-9pm, Su 11am-8pm. AmEx/D/MC/V.

OAKLAND

Led by mayor and one-time US presidential hopeful Jerry Brown, the city of Oakland launched a public relations campaign to promote the lower prices and warmer weather across the bay from San Francisco. Indeed, newcomers to the Bay Area too easily forget that Oakland, with 400,000 people, 81 languages, and considerable land mass, is a thriving city in its own right. Although historically less economically blessed than its neighbors, Oakland has maintained a commercial center and some beautiful residential neighborhoods. Travelers often fail to incorporate Oakland into their perspective of the Bay Area, even though a nice afternoon downtown, a gourmet dinner in Rockridge, and a legendary live music scene are just a short car or BART ride away.

AREA CODE	Oakland's area code is ☎510.

TRANSPORTATION

If you have access to wheels, they'll be worthwhile here; Oakland's attractions are spread out, and nighttime fun runs later than the BART. Drivers can take **I-80** from San Francisco across the Bay Bridge to **I-580** and connect with Oakland **I-980 South**, which has downtown exits at 12th St. and 19th St. Get traffic updates from **TravInfo** (☎817-1717).

Public Transportation: Bay Area Rapid Transit (BART: ☎465-2278; www.bart.gov) is the most convenient way to travel from San Francisco to and within Oakland. BART runs from downtown San Francisco to Oakland's stations at **Lake Merritt** (Dublin/Pleasanton or Fremont trains), **12th St.** (Richmond or Pittsburg/Bay Point trains), **19th St.** (Richmond or Pittsburg/Bay Point trains), **Rockridge** (Pittsburg/Bay Point trains), and **Coliseum** (Dublin/ Pleasanton or Fremont trains). **Alameda County (AC) Transit** (☎817-1717, ext. 1111; www.actransit.org). Adults $1.35; seniors, disabled, and ages 5-12 65¢; under 5 free. 1hr. transfers 25¢. **Transbay** routes to San Francisco (adults $2.75; seniors, disabled, and ages 5-12 $1.35). All AC buses are wheelchair-accessible and equipped with bike racks. **Greyhound,** 2103 San Pablo Ave. (station info ☎834-3213, schedules and reservations 800-231-2222). **Buses** depart daily to: **L.A.** (adults $45, roundtrip $82; 8hr.); **Sacramento** (adults $13, roundtrip $21; 1½hr.); **Santa Cruz** (adults $12, roundtrip $22; 2.5hr.). Seniors and children receive discounted tickets; call for rates. **As always, be careful at night.**

Ferries: Alameda/Oakland Ferry (☎522-3300; www.eastbayferry.com). Purchase tickets on board. Ferries run between Oakland, Alameda, the SF Ferry Building, and Pier 41/Fisherman's Wharf. Adults $5, round-trip $10; seniors and disabled $3, $6; children 5-12 $2.25, $4.50; under 5 free. Free AC and MUNI transfers; MUNI transfers must be validated on ferry.

Taxis: A1 Yellow Cab (☎843-1111). 24hr.

ORIENTATION & PRACTICAL INFORMATION

The scarcity of noteworthy sights and cheap and safe accommodations make Oakland a better daytrip than vacation destination. Oakland's main artery is **Broadway.** Broadway runs northeast, under the Nimitz Fwy. (I-880) at 5th St., and separates **Old Oakland** (to the west) from **Chinatown** (to the east). The **city center** is at 13th St. and Broadway, but the greater downtown area occupies all of **Lake Merritt,** including Lakeside Park on the north side and the Lake Merritt Channel on the south side. North-south addresses are numbered to match the east-west cross streets; for example, 1355 Broadway is between 13th and 14th St. To get to **Jack London Sq.** and the waterfront from the 12th St. BART stop, just head down Broadway away from the hills. North of downtown, past some of Oakland's poorest areas, are a few Berkeleyesque neighborhoods with boutiques, grocers, and restaurants. **Rockridge** (take Broadway north off 580), with its well-kept lawns (and residents), lies toward Berkeley and is accessible from downtown Oakland by BART or AC Transit bus #51.

Visitor Information: Oakland Visitors Information Bureau, 475 14th St., Suite 120 (☎839-9000), between Broadway and Clay St. Free maps of the city and brochures. Open M-F 8:30am-5pm. **Port of Oakland Information Booths** (24hr. info ☎814-6000; www.jacklondonsquare.com), on Broadway in Jack London Sq. under the Barnes & Noble bookstore. Info focuses on waterfront sights. Also at Oakland International Airport. Open M-Su 9am-4pm.

Police: 455 7th St. (☎238-3481).

Emergency: ☎911.

Medical Services: Highland Hospital, 1411 E. 31st St. (☎437-4800), at Beaumont Ave. 24hr. emergency care.

Pharmacy: Leo's Day and Night Pharmacy, 1776 19th St. (☎839-7900), at Broadway. Open M-F 9am-6:30pm.

Post Office: Main Office, 1675 7th St. at Peralta St. Open M 6:30am-midnight, Tu-Th 8:30am-midnight, F 8:30am-11pm. **Postal code:** 94615

ACCOMMODATIONS

Although Oakland is full of motels, few downtown are safe, clean, or economical compared to those in San Francisco and Berkeley. Motels clustered along W. MacArthur Blvd. near the MacArthur BART station are around $45 per night for a room with private bath. Ask to see the room before checking in. Commercial inns and hotels, (cleaner and safer, but bland) are also clustered around Broadway at Jack London Sq. Try one of the beautiful and affordable B&Bs sprouting up in the northern part of the city. For more information, contact the **Berkeley-Oakland Bed and Breakfast Network** (www.bbonline.com/ca/berkeley-oakland).

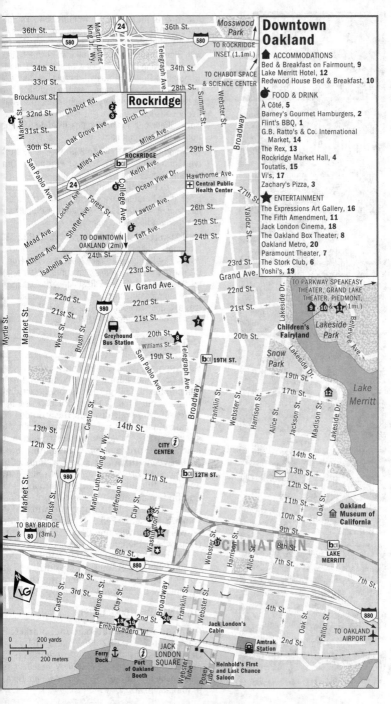

Downtown Oakland

🏠 ACCOMMODATIONS

Bed & Breakfast on Fairmount, **9**
Lake Merritt Hotel, **12**
Redwood House Bed & Breakfast, **10**

🍴 FOOD & DRINK

À Côté, **5**
Barney's Gourmet Hamburgers, **2**
Flint's BBQ, **1**
G.B. Ratto's & Co. International Market, **14**
The Rex, **13**
Rockridge Market Hall, **4**
Toutatis, **15**
Vi's, **17**
Zachary's Pizza, **3**

⭐ ENTERTAINMENT

The Expressions Art Gallery, **16**
The Fifth Amendment, **11**
Jack London Cinema, **18**
The Oakland Box Theater, **8**
Oakland Metro, **20**
Paramount Theater, **7**
The Stork Club, **6**
Yoshi's, **19**

223

LGB

Queer in Oakland

If you're in search of any kind of concentrated queer community or nightlife, stay in San Francisco. However, Oakland does add some important and fun elements to the community. **The Black Gay Lesbian Transgender Bisexual Same Gender Loving Organization** sponsors events and assures queer representation at the June Black Pride celebration. Oakland is also home to a gay and lesbian running club, the East Bay Frontrunners (☎873 0300; eastbayfrontrunners.org), who invite newcomers to their 30-45min. runs Saturday mornings at 9am. Email ebfr@aol.com for the starting location.

Oakland's oldest gay bar is the ☑White Horse Inn, in North Oakland on Telegraph. It's an easygoing place with a disco ball. W old-school music, no cover. Th no cover with student ID. F-Sa free drink coupon with student ID. (6551 Telegraph Ave. ☎652-3820. Open M-Tu 3pm-2am, W-Su 1pm-2am).

Just outside of Oakland in Walnut Creek, **Club 1220** offers nightly themes for a lively young gay and lesbian crowd. (1220 Pine St. ☎925-938-4550; www.club1220.com. Open daily 4pm-2am).

A Bed & Breakfast on Fairmount, 640 Fairmo Ave. (☎653-7726; www.bbonline.com/ca/f mount), in **Piedmont.** Large, beautiful Victorian ho with 3 charming, airy rooms, all with private bath. served in living room with view of the sunset and Tamalpais. Huge, homestyle breakfast, made w ingredients from its organic vegetable garden, ser in the sunny conservatory. 2-night min., 2-week m Every consecutive 7th night is free. Check-in a 3pm. Check-out 11am. Singles from $85; doub from $95. No credit cards. ❸

Redwood House B&B, 4244 39th Ave. (☎530-68 tyler_don@yahoo.com), east of **Piedmont.** Orn Victorian house brimming with antiques. Lush hot plants, tufted silks, marble surfaces, and stair glass detail around every corner. Master suite w jacuzzi is a steal at $121; smaller but equally lux ous rooms $100. No credit cards. ❸

Lake Merritt Hotel, 1800 Madison St. (☎832-230 A bit more expensive, though still moderately priced its swank offerings. Centrally located in the Finan District (the hotel often fills with corporate types), v great views of Lake Merritt. Restaurant downstairs. F ervations recommended. Wheelchair-accessible. S gles and doubles from $179; suites $219-289. Alw 40% off on weekends. AmEx/MC/V. ❺

FOOD & DRINK

For the most part, downtown Oakland resta rants are about eating (not dining), and Ame can staples like burger joints, breakfast dine and barbecue shacks abound. However, in t increasingly upscale districts, the attitude of C ifornia cuisine has made a few inroads. Mo gourmet cafes, mostly open for breakfast a lunch, have sprung up on Washington and C St. between 7th and 12th St. Oakland's **Chi town,** west of Broadway around 9th St., featu a host of dim sum restaurants, Vietnamese a Cambodian cuisine, and Asian markets. Ev Friday from 8am to 2pm, the **Old Oakla Farmer's Market** (☎745-7100) takes over 9th between Broadway and Clay St., offering fre fruits, vegetables, and some of the best bak goods in the Golden State. A similar mark (☎800-949-3276) takes over a corner of Ja London Sq. on Broadway, near the waterfro on Sundays from 10am to 2pm.

DOWNTOWN OAKLAND

G.B. Ratto's & Co. International Market, 8 Washington St. (☎832-6503), is a 104 year- Oakland institution with more ingredients th ready-to-eats, except for the speedy, excellent sa wich counter ($3.50-6.75). Open M-F 9am-6pm, 9:30am-5pm. MC/V. ❶

Toutatis, 719 Washington St. (☎465-6984), was the Celtic god of fertility, war, and wealth. In Gaul his worshipers fed their grumbly Druid tummies with the same hearty *galettes* and crêpes offered here ($2.25-7.75). Open M 11:30am-2pm, Tu-Th 11:30am-2pm and 6-9pm, F 11:30am-2pm and 6-10pm, Sa 10am-2pm and 6-10pm, Su 10am-2pm. MC/V. ❶

The Rex, 827 Washington St. (☎767 3131). A bar and restaurant that's perfect as an after-work hangout. Friendly staff warms up the warehouse setting. Minestrone and calamari whet the appetite for burgers and steaks. Appetizers $5-10, dinner $10-18. Happy Hour 4-6pm. Open 11am-9:30pm M-Sa. AmEx/D/MC/V.

NORTH OAKLAND AND ROCKRIDGE

■ **Zachary's Pizza,** 5801 College Ave. (☎655-6385), at Oak Grove Ave. Loyal fans will tell you Zachary's makes the best pizza in the Bay, zealots say west of Chicago, extremists insist it's the best in the world. *Let's Go* will say that it is quite flavorful, lacks grease, and is pretty damn good. Eat in or take out, but be prepared to wait either way. Pizzas $7-24.50. Slices $2.50-2.75. Open Su-Th 11am-10pm, F-Sa 11am-10:30pm. No credit cards. ❶

Barney's Gourmet Hamburgers, 5819 College Ave. (☎601-0444). "Gourmet" could be pushing it. But of the 57 types of beef, garden, tofu, portabello, and poultry burgers served ($5-7), at least 1 has your name on it. Also try the award-winning fries. Open M-Th 11am-9:30pm, F 11am-10pm, Sa 11am-10pm, Su 11am-9pm. No credit cards. ❶

À Côté, 5478 College Ave. (☎655-6469). Critics rave about the small, vaguely French-inspired menu and dark velvet decor. Reasonably priced considering its hot-spot buzz. Entrees $7-14. Open Tu 5:30-10pm, W 5:30-11pm, Th 11:30am-2pm and 5:30-11pm, F-Sa 11:30am-2pm and 5:30pm-midnight, Su 11:30am-2pm. ❷

The Rockridge Market Hall, 5655 College Ave. (☎655-7748), at Keith St., houses an array of gourmet shops, goods, and take-out. **Market Hall Bakery** makes heavenly sourdough, walnut, and focaccia goodies. (☎428-2662. Breads $3.40, pastries $1.50-3). The **Pasta Shop** (☎547-4005) sells fresh *gnocchi, rigatoni, creste di gallo,* and pre-prepared take-out ($6-10 per lb.). Open M-F 7am-8pm, Sa-Su 8am-7pm. MC/V. ❶

NORTHWEST OAKLAND

■ **Flint's BBQ,** 3114 San Pablo Ave. (☎652-9605), south of 32nd St. No side dishes, no appetizers...hell, no tables or chairs either. A serious BBQ joint in a serious neighborhood. Heaping take-out only portions of soul-food style pork ribs, beef ribs, beef links, and chicken ($9-10). Sandwiches $7.50. *Not* a vegetarian option. Open daily 11am-11pm. No credit cards. ❷

Oakland's Avant Garde

Tucked away under the veneer of suburbia is an underground and emerging culture of cutting edge, experimental, performance, installation, and avant garde art. Here are a couple places to check out, if that's your thing.

Oakland Box Theater houses a well-equipped theater space and art gallery and is getting increasing support from the city to perpetuate its commitment to "the spirit of experimentation, multicultural collaboration and community building through the celebration of life, art and cosmos." Check the website for listings. *(1928 Telegraph Ave., just south of 20th St. ☎451-1932; www.oaklandbox.com).*

The Oakland Metro, was spawned by the Oakland Opera Theater with the vision of creating an affordable, intimate performance space. *(201 Broadway, near Jack London Sq. ☎763-1146; www.oaklandmetro.org.)*

The Expressions Art Gallery, offers incredible displays with a focus on installation art. *(512 8th St., at Washington St. ☎451-6646. Open noon-8pm).*

CHINATOWN

Vi's, 724 Webster St. (☎835-8375), just south of 8th St. Wonderful Vietnamese cuisine in a tasteful setting. At Vi's you get an upscale atmosphere without going broke: all menu items between $4.75-6.75. Open M-W and F-Su 9am-8:30pm. No credit cards. ❶

SIGHTS

Haunted by **Gertrude Stein's** withering observation that "there is no there there," Oakland's tourist literature wages a war of attrition against its former resident, assuring visitors that City Square is "always there for you" and "there is shopping there." Free walking tours of the city highlight the *thereness* of downtown's best sights, including Roslyn Mazzilli's sculpture in City Square's upper plaza, defiantly entitled "There!" (☎238-3234; www.oaklandnet.com. Reservations recommended.) For a somewhat more militant view of the city, take the **Black Panther Legacy Tour.** Former party chief-of-staff David Hillard guides visitors through a first-hand account of the events, locations, and personalities that defined the Party. Reservations required. (☎986-0660; www.blackpanthertours.com. Tickets $25. Regularly scheduled tour leaves last Saturday of the month from the West Oakland Library, 18th and Adeline St. .)

JACK LONDON SQUARE. Oakland's one come-on to the tourist industry is this eight-block commercial district named for its native son, author of *White Fang* and *The Call of the Wild.* Ferries from San Francisco arrive at this sunny wharf, making it a nice first stop on your way to other Oakland outings. A replica of ⬛**Jack London's Cabin,** near Webster St., which stands where the author's home did during his 1890s prospecting days, is open mid-May to mid-September for $2. Next to the cabin, the small, wooden **Heinold's First and Last Chance Saloon** has barely changed since London's days, except, presumably, for the addition of the London-themed mural. The same gaslight still burns, and the sunken floor and bar from '06 have never been fixed. Service is proud and friendly. *(Cabin: Along the waterfront. Take Broadway south. Event info ☎814-6000. Saloon: 56 Jack London Sq., at the foot of Webster St. ☎839-6761; www.firstandlastchance.com. Open M noon-10pm, Tu-Th noon-midnight, F-Sa noon-2am, Su 11am-10pm. $4 pints, $4 cocktails. No credit cards.)*

OAKLAND MUSEUM OF CALIFORNIA. The three garden-topped levels of Bauhaus-inspired poured concrete at the Oakland Museum of California showcase the collections of three established area museums, brought together in 1969 to reflect the collective artistic, historical, and environmental legacy of California and Oakland. The cultural and political forces that shaped several centuries of California dreaming are well documented and displayed in the **Cowell Hall of History.** The Hall of California Ecology on the first floor recreates the state's eight biotic zones, and the Gallery of California Art includes photography by Edward Weston, Ansel Adams, and Dorothea Lange, paintings by Richard Diebenkorn, and a bevy of varied modern works. Rotating exhibits, with a more modern flair, change every few months. *(1000 Oak St., on the southwestern side of the lake. From the Lake Merritt BART station, walk 1 block north on Oak St. toward the hills. ☎238-2200 or 888-625-6873; www.museumca.org. Open W-Sa 10am-5pm, Su noon-5pm, 1st F of each month until 9pm. Adults $6; seniors, students, and 6-18 $4; under 6 free. 2nd Su of each month free.)*

CHABOT SPACE AND SCIENCE CENTER. Like a space station in the East Oakland Hills, the amazing Smithsonian-sponsored, three-year-old **Chabot Space and Science Center** offers stargazing both indoors at the **Planetarium** and outdoors with high-powered telescopes, daily screenings in the **Tien MegaDome Theater,** and interactive exhibits in various science and computer labs. *(Space and Science Center: 10000 Skyline Blvd, at Skyline Blvd., in Joaquin Miller Park in the Oakland Hills. ☎336-7300; www.chabotspace.org. Open Sept. 2-June 18 Tu-Su 10am-3pm; June 17-Sept. 1 Su noon-5pm, Tu-Th 10am-5pm, F-Sa 10am-7:30pm. $11; students, seniors, and ages 4-12 $8; under 3 free. Planetarium and Tien MegaDome Theater: Open same hours as Science Center plus F-Sa 7:30-9pm. $6 for each; students, seniors, and ages 4-12 $5; under 3 free. Double and triple venue prices also available.)*

LAKE MERRITT. Lake Merritt was dammed off from the San Francisco Bay in 1869, and now provides a place for sailing, biking, and jogging—not to mention political protest. Activity revolves around **Lakeside Park,** which encompasses a stately gazebo, picnic facilities, and the nation's oldest urban bird sanctuary, where ducks, geese, and pigeons do their best Hitchcock impersonations. Every 4th Sunday of the month, **Lake Merritt Joggers and Striders** hold 5, 10, and 15K races around the lake. The **Lake Merritt Boating Center** rents canoes and rowboats ($6 per hr.), kayaks ($8 per hr.), pedalboats ($8 per hr.), and sailboats ($6-8 per hr.), and leads tour boats. *(Park:* ☎ 238-7275. Parking $2. **Lake:** ☎ 238-2196. $10 deposit for boat rentals. Rentals 50% off for seniors and disabled. Open June-Sept. M-F 9am-6pm, Sa-Su 10am-6pm; Oct. daily 10:30am-5pm, Nov.-Feb. M-F 10:30am-3:30pm, Sa-Su 10:30am-4pm; Mar.-May M-F 10:30am-4pm, Sa-Su 10:30am-5pm. **Boating Center:** 568 Bellevue Ave. ☎ 238-2196; www.oaklandnet.com/parks/programs/boating.asp. Lake tours Sa-Su. Adults $1.50, children and seniors 75¢.)*

CHILDREN'S FAIRYLAND. Generations of Oakland children have enjoyed Children's Fairyland, a cluster of disproportionate gingerbread houses, trippy overgrown mushrooms, and an acclaimed puppet theater at the northeastern edge of Lake Merritt. Buy a Magic Key for $2 to listen to muffled fairy tale recordings at each stop along the way. *(At Grand Ave. and Bellevue, at the northwest tip of Lake Merritt. ☎ 238-6876; www.fairyland.org. Open mid-Apr. to mid-June W-Su 10am-4pm; mid-June to Aug. M-F 10am-4pm, Sa-Su 10am-5pm; Sept.-Oct. W-Su 10am-4pm; Nov. to mid-Apr. F-Su 10am-4pm. **Puppet shows:** 11am, 2, 4pm. $6. Adults must be accompanied by a child and vice versa. MC/V).*

PARAMOUNT THEATER. The **Paramount Theater** hosts not only movies and big-name acts, but also occasional tours of its venerable Art Deco interior. Lovingly restored to its 1931 grandeur, the theater shows classic films on weekends accompanied by the mighty Wurlitzer organ, vintage newsreels, and a cartoon. Showtime is usually 8pm; come early to explore the theater or to have a cocktail at the bar. *(2025 Broadway, at 21st St. ☎ 465-6400; www.paramounttheater.com. **Films:** $5-7. **Music:** Box office open Tu-F noon-6pm, Sa noon-5pm, and 2hr. before performances. **Tours:** ☎ 893-2300. $1. 1st and 3rd Sa each month 10am. Guided tours begin at Box Office entrance on 21st St. and last 2hr).*

NIGHTLIFE & ENTERTAINMENT

The **live music scene** is one of the best reasons to venture to Oakland. Whether it's West Coast blues, Oaktown hip-hop, or progressive jazz, Oakland's music venues are unsurpassed. Because many artists lack institutional representation, check posters and local papers for shows. *Urban View*, the free, Wednesday weekly and the daily *Oakland Tribune* (50¢, Su $1.25) are good resources and available in boxes throughout the city. If you want to be on the cutting edge of this fast-paced scene, rely on a bit of research and tips from locals (and keep your fingers crossed!).

MUSIC

▨ **The Fifth Amendment,** 3255 Lakeshore Ave. (☎832-3242), at Lake Park Ave. Not the most famous, but one of the best. Jazz and blues musicians take the stage in this downtown club, where there's never a cover or drink minimum and the crowd is serious about its music. 21+. Shows Th-Su, usually at 9pm. Open W-M 4pm-2am. MC/V.

▨ **Yoshi's,** 510 Embarcadero W. (☎238-9200; www.yoshis.com), in Jack London Sq. An upscale institution bringing together world-class sushi and world-class jazz. Big names command cover prices; tickets sometimes sell out but are often available at the door. 1-drink minimum. Local musician nights (usually M) $8-10. Family discount Su matinee: adult (with child) $10, child $5. Half-price student and senior tickets for selected shows. Cover usually $20-25. Shows M-Sa 8, 10pm; Su 2, 8pm. Box office open daily 10:30am-11pm. Lunch M-F 11:30am-2pm, Sa-Su noon-2:30pm; dinner Su-Th 5:30-9:30pm, F-Sa 5:30-10pm. Sushi bar open Su-M until 10:30pm, Tu-Sa until 11pm. AmEx/D/MC/V.

The Stork Club, 2330 Telegraph Ave. (☎444-6174), at 23rd St. This laid-back country and western bar by day becomes a raging rock venue by night. What's more, Stork offers kitschy

Christmas decor year-round (ho! ho! ho!). Indie rock, punk, and underground Tu-Sa around 9:30pm. Open mic Su 9pm with "Girl George." No cover but 2-drink min. 21+. Cover normally from $5. Open Tu-Su 4pm-2am. No credit cards.

Koncepts Cultural Gallery (☎451-5231; www.oaklandculturalarts.org), is not a venue but an organization that hosts some of the most groundbreaking progressive jazz sessions. Call for locations, artists, and performance schedules. Cover $5-25.

Paramount Theater (Sights, p. 227).

THEATER, FINE ARTS & MOVIES

▓ **Parkway Speakeasy Theater,** 1834 Park Blvd. (☎834-1506; www.picturepubpizza.com), 1 mi. west off Park Blvd. exit 580. Accessible by AC transit buses #13, 14, 15, 40, and 43. Another groovy place to see a movie, this 2nd-run theater has lounge seating—couches, chairs, and tables—where you can order pizza ($3-3.50 per slice), pasta, sandwiches, and wine or beer by the pitcher ($8) or pint ($4) right at your seat. Keep an eye open for special Thrillville features, movies undoubtedly enhanced by inebriation. Tickets $5. 21+ enforced. *Rocky Horror Picture Show* F midnight ($5). 17+. Weekend matinees $3, all ages.

Oakland East Bay Symphony (☎444-0801; www.oebs.org) and the **Oakland Ballet** (☎893-2300, box office ☎286-8914; www.oaklandballet.org) share the stage with the Paramount Theater (p. 227). Throughout the year, the Symphony performs 6 F classical concerts. Symphony tickets $15-55. The ballet, committed to providing equal opportunity to minority talent, performs several programs, including a not-so-traditional *Nutcracker Sweetie*. Ballet tickets $8-45. Box office open Tu-F noon-6pm, Sa noon-5pm, and 2hr. before all shows.

Grand Lake Theater, 3200 Grand Lake Ave. (☎452-3446; www.rrfilms.com). This classic theater features Wurlitzer organ music before F and Sa evening shows and all the latest, hottest movies. Adults $8.50; children, seniors, and matinees $5.50.

Jack London Cinema, 100 Washington St. (☎433 1325), at Embarcadero. No frills 1st-run theater. Adults $8.75; children, seniors, and matinees $5.75.

SEASONAL EVENTS

▓**Midnight Mass,** 3010 Geary Blvd., at the Bridge Theatre, presents a series of summer midnight Sa screenings of campy classic films. Services, which include a pre-show spectacle, are officiated by Peaches Christ and sidekick Martiny, who offer an unpredictable and unparalleled viewing experience (☎267-4893; www.peacheschrist.com). Lake Merritt's Lakeside Park hosts several festivals over the summer. In June, the **Festival at the Lake** (☎286-1061), sponsored by the city, takes over Oakland with a long weekend of international foods, crafts, and nonstop music. On Father's Day Sunday (June 13 in 2004), **Juneteenth** (☎238-7765) commemorates the anniversary of the Emancipation Proclamation and black history and culture with parades, soul food, blues, and R&B. In past years, Lake Merritt has also hosted **Fuck the Police Day,** a free beach and barbecue party in late June to protest police treatment of young blacks. The park also has **free Shakespeare performances** in summer. (☎415-422-2222 or 800-978-7529; www.sfshakes.org).

SPORTS

Oakland Coliseum, 7000 Coliseum Way (☎569-2121), at the intersection of Nimitz Fwy. (I-880) and Hegenberger Rd. Home to baseball's Oakland Athletics (A's) (tickets ☎762-BALL/2255; http://oakland.athletics.mlb.com. Open M-F 10am-6pm, Sa 10am-4pm) and football's oft-transplanted Oakland Raiders (tickets ☎762-2277; www.raiders.com.). The Coliseum has its own BART station and is a much cozier place than frigid 3Com/Candlestick Park in San Francisco. Adjacent to the Coliseum, the **Coliseum Arena** is home to basketball's Golden State Warriors (tickets ☎888-GSW-HOOP/479-4667; www.nba.com/warriors). Check team websites for schedules and ticket prices.

California Canoe & Kayak, 409 Water St. (☎ 893-7833 or 800-366-9804; www.calkayak.com), in Jack London Sq. Forget watching sports. Rent a variety of paddling equipment and take a class or a 1-14 day adventure trip. Boat rentals daily 10am-5pm, last boat leaves 4pm. $15-25 per hr., $50-60 per day. Basic day-long sea kayaking or canoe class $109. Open M-Th 10am-6pm, F-Sa 10am-7pm, Su 10am-5pm.

MARIN COUNTY

Just across the Golden Gate Bridge, the jacuzzi of the bay—Marin (muh-RIN) County—bubbles over with enthusiastic (some might say dogmatic) residents who help the area strike a nice balance between upscale chic and counterculture nostalgia. If the new VW Beetle were sold nowhere but here, Volkswagen still might reap a tidy profit. Marin is strikingly beautiful, politically liberal, and visibly wealthy. The locals might seem a bit smug, but protective scowls give way to pleasant smiles when visitors appreciate the land and care for it as their own. The cathedral stillness of ancient redwoods, sweet-smell of eucalyptus (though not a native species), brilliant wildflowers, high bluffs, and crashing surf along Rte. 1 are ample justification for civic pride and earnest preservation concerns.

If you have a car or bike, Marin's pleasure spots lend themselves to the perfect city-escaping **roadtrip.** A web of trails negotiates the state and national parks and watershed land, welcoming mountain bikers and hikers in search of day- or week-long adventures. On the eastern side of the county, pleasant **Sausalito, Mill Valley,** and San Rafael line US 101; **San Anselmo,** Fairfax, and San Jose are also easily accessible. Each town can be a solitary weekend get-away or one destination of a roadtrip.

WEST MARIN: THE ROADTRIP

The sights and stops in the suggested roadtrip are listed roughly south to north from the Marin Headlands up the coast to Point Reyes Station. Renting a car (**Car Rental,** p. 312) and stocking up on grub will be worthwhile as most places of interest are close together but not well-connected by public transportation. If your roadtrip veers toward East Marin, similar information for Sausalito, Mill Valley, and San Rafael can be found at the end of this chapter. Happy trails!

| **AREA CODE** | Marin County's area code is ☎ 415. |

TRANSPORTATION

The Marin peninsula lies at the northern end of the San Francisco Bay and is connected to the city by **US 101** via the **Golden Gate Bridge.** US 101 extends north inland to Santa Rosa and Sonoma County, while **Rte. 1** winds north along the Pacific coast. The **Richmond-San Rafael Bridge** connects Marin to the East Bay via **I-580. Gas** is scarce and expensive in West Marin, so fill up in town before you head out for the coast. If you start running low in West Marin, head toward Point Reyes Station where you'll find one of few gas stations in the area. Drivers should exercise caution in West Marin, where roads are narrow, sinuous, and perched on the edges of cliffs.

Public Transportation: Golden Gate Transit (☎ 455-2000, in SF 923-2000; www.goldengate.org; phones operated M-F 7am-7pm, Sa-Su 8am-6pm), provides bus service between San Francisco and Marin County via the Golden Gate Bridge, as well as local service in Marin. Within Marin County, bus #63 runs on the weekends from Marin City through Sausalito, Mount Tamalpais State Park, and Stinson Beach (adults $4.75, seniors and disabled $2.40, under 18 $3.65, under 6 free). Bus #65 goes from San Rafael to Samuel P. Taylor Park and Point Reyes Station on weekends (adults $3.30, seniors and disabled $1.65, under 6 free). **West Marin Stagecoach** (☎ 526-3239; www.marin-stagecoach.org; phones operated daily 8am-5pm), now provides **weekday service** connecting West Marin communities to the rest of

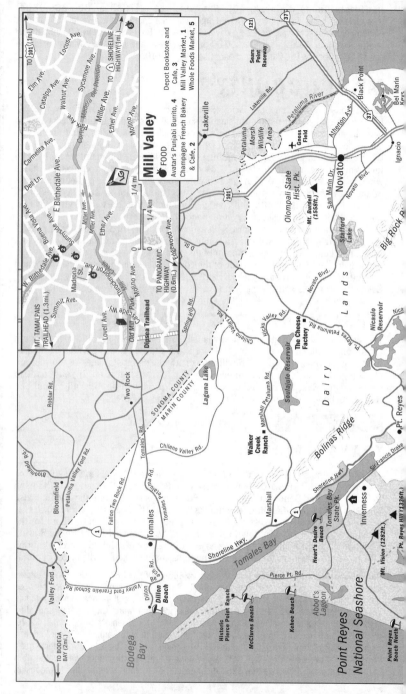

Mill Valley

● FOOD

Avatar's Punjabi Burrito, **4**
Champagne French Bakery & Cafe, **2**
Depot Bookstore and Cafe, **3**
Mill Valley Market, **1**
Whole Foods Market, **5**

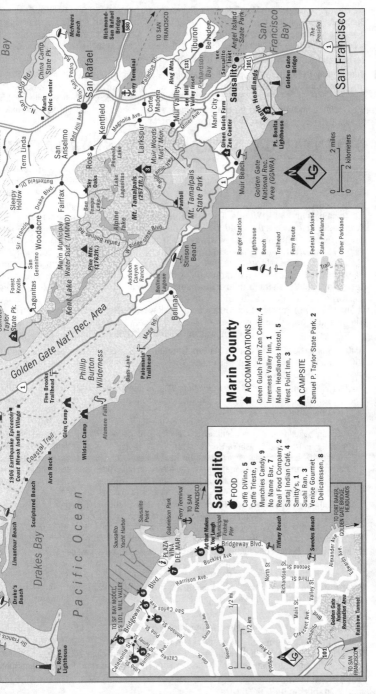

Marin County

▲ ACCOMMODATIONS

Green Gulch Farm Zen Center, **4**
Inverness Valley Inn, **1**
Marin Headlands Hostel, **5**
West Point Inn, **3**

▲ CAMPSITE

Samuel P. Taylor State Park, **2**

Map Legend

- Ranger Station
- Lighthouse
- Beach
- Trailhead
- Ferry Route
- Trail
- Federal Parkland
- State Parkland
- Other Parkland

Sausalito

● FOOD

Caffè DiVino, **5**
Caffè Trieste, **6**
Munchies Candy, **9**
No Name Bar, **7**
Real Food Company, **2**
Sartaj Indian Café, **4**
Smitty's, **3**
Sushi Ran, **3**
Venice Gourmet
Delicatessen, **8**

the county. Stops include: Muir Beach, Pt. Reyes Station, Samuel P. Taylor Park, and Stinson Beach. Anyone can flag the bus to pull over or drop off between scheduled stops, provided there is a safe place. Free Golden Gate Transit transfers. Call or check the website for specific schedules and more detailed routes. $1.50 each way; seniors, disabled, and under 18 75¢.

Taxis: Belaire Cab Co. (☎388-1234). Open 24hr. MC/V.

Bike Rental: Cycle Analysis, out of a hitch-up in the empty, grassy lot at 4th and Main St. off Hwy. 1 in **Point Reyes Station** (☎663-9164; www.cyclepointreyes.com). Cycle Analysis rents unsuspended bikes ($30), front-suspension mountain bikes ($35), and child trailers ($25-30). Helmets included. Also provides emergency repairs and offer advice for self-guided tours. Open F-Su 10am-5pm, M-Th by appointment. MC/V.

ORIENTATION & PRACTICAL INFORMATION

National seashore and park land constitute most of West Marin. Hwy. 1 splits from US 101 north of Sausalito and runs up the Pacific Coast through Muir Beach, Stinson Beach, Olema, Inverness, and Pt. Reyes. About 4 mi. north of where Hwy. 1 splits from US 101, the Panoramic Highway branches off Hwy. 1 and winds its way up to **Mt. Tamalpais** and Muir Woods. The **Marin Headlands** sit 10 mi. from downtown San Francisco, just across the Golden Gate Bridge. Beaches and coastal wonders line Hwy. 1, which runs along the Marin coast from Marin City and continues north. Slightly inland, Mt. Tamalpais is about 15 mi. northwest of San Francisco; the state park encompasses a large area just inside the coast from Muir Beach to around Stinson Beach. Muir Woods stands about 5 mi. west of US 101 on Hwy. 1. The **Pt. Reyes National Seashore,** a near-island surrounded by close to 100 mi. of isolated coastline, is a wilderness of pine forests, chaparral ridges, and grassy flatlands, about 15 mi. northwest of San Francisco. **Pt. Reyes Station** sits about 2 mi. north of Olema and about 20 mi. northwest of San Francisco. Check out the individual sights listings for sights in or near each area and detailed driving directions.

Visitor Information: Marin County Visitors Bureau, 1013 Larkspur Landing Circle (☎499-5000; www.visitmarin.org), off the Sir Francis Drake Blvd. Exit from US 101, near the ferry terminal. Open M-F 9am-5pm.

Park Visitor Information: Marin Headlands Visitors Center, Bldg. 948, Fort Barry (☎331-1540), at Bunker and Field Rd. Talk to the helpful staff about hiking and biking in the park, and pick up maps, trail advice, and permits for free campsites. The center is also a museum and a store with artifacts, exhibits on the history of the Headlands, and models of military buildings and equipment. Open daily 9:30am-4:30pm. Wheelchair-accessible.

Point Reyes National Seashore Headquarters (also referred to as **Bear Valley Visitor Center;** ☎464-5100; www.nps.gov/pore), on Bear Valley Rd., ½ mi. west of Olema. Rangers distribute camping permits, maps, and sage advice on trails, tides, and weather conditions, and lead guided hikes. The headquarters house excellent exhibits on the cultural and natural history of Pt. Reyes. Open M-F 9am-5pm, Sa-Su and holidays 8am-5pm.

Pan Toll Ranger's Station, 801 Panoramic Hwy. (☎388-2070), in Mt. Tamalpais State Park, about 2½ mi. inland from Stinson Beach. Operates Mt. Tam's campgrounds and trails. Rangers offer suggestions and explain restrictions on the trails. Bus #63 stops on the weekends (about 8 times daily) at the Ranger's Station.

Muir Woods National Monument Visitors Center (☎388-2596; www.nps.gov/muwo), near the entrance to Muir Woods. Muir Woods trail map $1 (free download on website). Great selection of hiking, biking, and driving maps of Marin and Mt. Tam. Open daily 9am-6pm.

Library: Stinson Beach Library, 3521 Shoreline Hwy. (☎868-0252). Free Internet access. Open M 10am-1pm, Tu 1-5pm and 6-9pm, F 10am-1pm and 2-6pm, Sa 10am-1pm.

Emergency: ☎911.

Police: ☎258-4610 in San Anselmo. **Marin County Sheriff:** ☎479-2311.

Medical Services: Marin General Hospital and Community Clinic, 250 Bon Air Rd. (☎925-7000, clinic ☎461-7400), in **Greenbrae,** off the US 101 San Anselmo exit. 24hr. emergency care. Clinic open for appointment only M and Th 8am-7pm, W 9am-7pm, Tu and F 8am-5pm.

Post Offices: In Stinson Beach: 15 Calle Del Mar, at Shoreline Hwy. Open M-F 8:30am-5pm. **Postal code:** 94970.

OUTDOOR EQUIPMENT TIPS

A hike through the Bay Area's beautiful landscape offers an affordable and exhilarating travel experience unlike any other. Before heading out, consider the following tips:

Footwear: Your feet are the most important component of your hike experience. Care for them. Appropriate hiking footwear provides stability and support for your feet and ankles while protecting them from the abuses of the environment. Mid-weight hiking boots are a good all-around choice, but appropriate footwear may range from running shoes to heavyweight boots depending on the hiking environment and necessary support. Stability over uneven ground is enhanced by a stiffer sole and higher ankle collar.

Keep in mind that a good fit is the most important feature—your toes should not hit the front of your shoe when you're going downhill, your heel should be locked in place, and there should be a minimum of extra space around your foot. When lacing, leave the laces over the top of your foot loose but tie them tightly across the ankle to lock the heel. All-leather footwear lasts longer, has good natural water resistance, and will mold to your feet over time. Synthetic materials or fabric/leather combinations are lighter and cheaper, but not as durable. Some boots use Gore-Tex, making them totally waterproof (but less breathable). Expect to pay $100-200 for a good pair of hiking boots.

Blisters are almost always caused by friction due to repetitive foot movement (slippage) inside the shoe. Buying footwear that fits properly and taking a minimum of 1-2 weeks to break them in will make a huge difference. If the heel is blistering, try tightening the laces across the ankle to keep the heel in place. Damp feet blister more easily—avoid moisture-retaining cotton socks and try a fast-wicking synthetic liner if your feet tend to sweat. If you notice a blister developing, stop immediately and apply adhesive padding (such as moleskin) over the problem spot.

The Basics: A map of the area and a simple compass are critical. Carry at least one liter of water (two liters preferable) and drink regularly to avoid cramps and other effects of dehydration. Also, bring along a small knife and sunscreen.

Survival: Always be prepared for the unexpected night out. Carry waterproof matches, a headlamp/flashlight, extra clothes, and extra food. A whistle is a powerful distress signal and can save your life. Always hike with at least a basic First Aid Kit.

Pack: The best packs will have a padded waist belt that allows you to carry weight on your hips and lower body rather than your shoulders. For dayhikes, a pack with a capacity of 1-2,000 cubic inches (16-32 liters) is recommended.

Clothing: Go synthetic. Cotton absorbs a lot of moisture and dries slowly, leaving a wet layer next to your skin which conducts heat away from your body, greatly increasing the risk of hypothermia, especially in cool, windy conditions. Denim is the worst. Nylon and polyester absorb little moisture, and dry extremely fast.

Rain Gear: Waterproof/non-breathable rain gear is generally the best way to go. While it does not breathe and traps your sweat next to your body (sticky, sticky), they are cheap—you should be able to find a jacket for $25-50. Fully waterproof nylon jackets will have an impervious coating inside and all the seams will be taped. A poncho, the bare bones option, costs very little (less than $20), is lightweight and compact, but will not keep you dry in a heavy downpour. Waterproof/breathable rain gear is impervious to liquid water, but allows water vapor (sweat) to pass through and thus keeps you more comfortable. Note that in hot, humid conditions, waterproof/breathable jackets don't work. Gore-Tex is considered the best waterproof/breathable barrier, but there are a variety of similar products. Expect to pay a lot for these comforts ($100-300+).

Other Tips: Hiking time can be estimated using the following guidelines. A reasonably fit individual can expect to travel 2-3 mi. (3-5km) per hour over level ground and descents, 1-2 mi. (2-3km) per hour on gradual climbs, and only about 1 mile (1.6km)—or 750-1,000 feet (200-300 meters) of elevation—per hour on the steepest ascents. Last but not least, always remember to have fun!

Matt Heid was a Researcher-Writer for Let's Go: Alaska and Western Canada 1993, Let's Go: Europe 1995, *and* Let's Go: New Zealand 1998. *He is the author of* 101 Hikes in Northern California *and* Camping and Backpacking the San Francisco Bay Area *(Wilderness Press).*

ACCOMMODATIONS AND CAMPGROUNDS

If you find yourself driving through West Marin with neither a hostel reservation nor the gumption to camp out in the woods, stop by the **West Marin Network,** 11431 Hwy. 1 at Mesa Rd., in the Old Creamery Building in Port Reyes Station. Bobbi, a sweet old lady and veritable guesthouse guru, helps travelers locate B&Bs, inns, and private cottages to suit personalized needs and wallets. (☎663-9543. Open approx. M-F 9am-6pm, Sa noon-4pm). The establishments below are listed roughly south to north.

HOSTELS AND INNS

📷 **West Point Inn** (info ☎388-9955, reservations ☎646-0702), on Mt. Tamalpais, 2 mi. up Stage Rd. Park at the Pan Toll Ranger Station ($4) and hike or bike up. Not the lap of luxury, but one hell of an experience. This turn-of-the-century inn was built in 1904 and hasn't changed much since. Propane-generated heat, light, and refrigeration. No other electricity around. That's right, city-folk, no TVs, computers, fax machines, or even private bathrooms. 35-person capacity. 7 private rooms. 5 private cabins. Well-equipped, shared kitchen. $30, under 18 $15, under 5 free. Bring your own linens, sleeping bags, food, and flashlight, but not your pets. Reservations required. Sa vacancies are rare. Closed Su and M nights. Call for handicap arrangements. If you want to visit, but not for the night, West Point offers a pancake breakfast on the 3rd Su of the month May-Oct. 9am-1pm. Adults $6, children $5. Sells granola bars and beverages to those who make the trek. ❶

📷 **Green Gulch Farm Zen Center,** 1601 Shoreline Hwy. (☎383-3134; www.sfzc.org). If your hostel just isn't enlightened enough, Green Gulch's guest student program allows serious students of Zen to stay at the center for $45 per night for a minimum of 3 days and up to 6 weeks. Students are expected to work with the community and to take part in *zazen* and *sutra* chanting throughout the day. Not-so-serious students can come for the tranquility. Singles $75-90; doubles $125-140; prices include 3 vegetarian meals per day. (Classes and programs, p. 235). ❸

Marin Headlands Hostel (HI-AYH), Bldg. 941 on Rosenstock (☎331-2777 or 800-909-4776; www.headlandshostel.homestead.com), up the hill from the Visitors Center and next to the Headlands Center for the Arts. Two spacious and immaculate Victorian houses, with 100 beds, a game room, kitchens, and common rooms. Internet 10¢ per min. Linen $1; towels 50¢. Laundry $1.50. Key deposit $10. 15 nights per yr. max. stay. Check-in 3:30-10:30pm. Check-out 10am. Lockout 10am-3:30pm. Reservations with credit card recommended 2 months in advance for private rooms and weekends. Dorms $18, under 17 (with parent) $9. Private rooms for 2 or more people $54. D/MC/V. ❶

Inverness Valley Inn, 13275 Sir Francis Drake Blvd. (☎669-7250), in **Pt. Reyes.** Drive up Sir Francis Drake Blvd., the inn is on the left immediately before Heart's Desire Beach, as the road begins to turn inland away from the bay. For bigger budgets, the Inverness Valley Inn offers queen-sized beds, full bathrooms, gas fireplaces, 15 lush acres, 2 tennis courts, and a pool and hot tub. Doubles $115 during week, $130 on weekends ($15 cheaper Nov. 1-Apr. 30); $20 per extra bed. MC/V. ❷

CAMPGROUNDS

The Headlands (☎331-1540; www.nps.gov/goga/camping/index.htm), offers 3 small walk-in campgrounds with 11 primitive campsites for individual backpackers and small groups. Picnic tables and chemical toilets are available in the backpack camps. Bring your own water and camp stove. No fires allowed. No pets either. Showers and kitchen ($2 each) at Headlands Hostel (p. 234). Free outdoor cold showers at Rodeo Beach. 3-day max. stay per site; 9-day max. stay per yr. Reserve up to 90 days in advance. For all campgrounds, individual sites are free with a permit that can be obtained at the Headlands Visitors Center (p. 232). ❶

Haypress Backpack Camp, in Tennessee Valley in the north end of the Headlands, ¾ mi. from Tennessee Valley parking lot. 5 sites, each of which holds 4 people with 2 tents. Max. 3 sites per group.

Hawkcamp, in Gerbode Valley. The most remote camp site in the Headlands can be reached via a difficult 3.5 mi. hike up the Bobcat Trail or a 3 mi. hike up the Marincello or Miwok Trails from Tennessee Valley. 3 sites accommodate 4 people each.

Bicentennial Camp, 100 yd. from Battery Wallace parking area, is the most accessible of the primitive campgrounds. Each of 3 sites accommodates up to 2 people with 1 tent. Water is available at the Visitors Center, 1 mi. away.

Kirby Cove (reservations ☎800-365-2267), off Conzelman Rd. west of the Golden Gate Bridge, is in the **Marin Headlands,** but is not administered by the Visitors Center. Accessible by car, it consists of 4 campsites in a grove of cypress and eucalyptus trees on the shores of the bay, with fire rings and pit toilets. Each site can accommodate 10 people. Kirby Cove is designed for larger groups—singles would get more for their money by checking into the Headlands hostel. Bring your own water. No pets. 3-day max. stay per person per season; 1 weekend reservation per group per yr. Open Apr. 1-Oct. 31. $25 per night for campsite. ❶

Point Reyes National Seashore (☎663-8054; www.nps.gov/pore; open for reservations M-F 9am-2pm, walk-in 9am-5pm) has walk-in and boat-in camping only. Two camps are coastal and 2 are inland—some have exquisite views of the ocean and surrounding hills. Charcoal grills, non-potable running water, and pit toilets. 4-night max. stay. Reservations recommended. Sites for 1-6 people $12. Boat-in camping at Tomales Bay; call or check web page for info. Pick up permits at Point Reyes National Seashore Headquarters (p. 235). MC/V. ❶

Samuel P. Taylor State Park, P.O. Box 251 (☎488-9897; www.parks.ca.gov; Reserve America ☎800-444-7275; www.park-net.com), on Sir Francis Drake Blvd., 15 mi. west of San Rafael in **Lagunitas.** Family campground in a lush setting beneath stately, second-growth redwoods. Often crowded on weekends. Sites are cool and shady, though not always quiet. Running water, flush toilets, and free hot showers. Day-use parking $4. 7-night max. stay. Checkout noon. Reservations recommended for weekends. Sites $15, seniors $13. no reservations for hiker and biker sites; 2-night max. stay. $2 per person. ❶

SIGHTS

MARIN HEADLANDS

◪ *Driving from San Francisco, cross the Golden Gate Bridge, take the Alexander Ave. exit, and follow the road as it loops back to Conzelman Rd. and the Headlands. Driving from points north, take the 2nd Sausalito exit (the last one before the bridge). Turn left at the 1st road and follow signs into the Golden Gate Recreation Area and to the Marin Headlands Visitors Center.*

The fog-shrouded hills just west of the Golden Gate Bridge constitute the Marin Headlands. These windswept ridges, precipitous cliffs, and hidden sandy beaches offer superb hiking and biking within minutes of downtown. For instant gratification, drive up to any of the look-out spots and pose for your own postcard-perfect shot of the Golden Gate Bridge and the city skyline, or take a short walk out to Point Bonita. If you intend to do some more serious hiking or biking, choose one of the coastal trails that provide easy access to dark sand beaches and dramatic cliffs of basalt greenstone. Either way, bring a jacket in case of sudden wind, rain, or fog.

BATTERY SPENCER AND NIKE MISSILE SITES

◪ *Battery Spencer: On Conzelman Rd. just west of US 101. **NIKE Missile Site:** On Field Rd., at Fort Berry and Fort Cronkite. ☎331-1453. Open W-F and 1st Su of the month 12:30-3:30pm.*

Formerly a military installation charged with defending the San Francisco harbor, the Headlands are dotted with abandoned machine gun nests, missile sites, and soldiers' quarters dating from the Spanish-American War. Thousands of troops were stationed here during WWII to defend the Bay Area from potential attacks by the Japanese. Battery Spencer offers one of the best vistas of the city skyline and the Golden Gate Bridge, especially around sunset on a clear day. Farther into the park, the 90 NIKE (named for the Greek goddess of victory) Missile Sites were constructed in the early 1950s during the Korean War and remained active for 20 years. The missiles were capable of destroying planes moving at three times the speed of sound. For pamphlets on the area's wartime activities, stop by the Visitors Center.

Building a Sport

Because the systematic paving of roads is a relatively recent occurrence, people have been riding bikes "off-road" for as long as they have been riding bikes. But mountain biking (the extreme, knee-shattering sport) was born in Marin County in the early 70s, when a group of hotshot road racers headed out to Mt. Tamalpais's rocky fire roads.

Gary Fisher, Charlie Kelly, Joe Breeze, and others rode 30s bikes with fat balloon tires and coaster brakes that handled the rough terrain better than their fancy road bikes. Eventually, someone made the fateful claim, "I'm fastest," a challenge less subtle than the mountains they traveled.

In October 1976, the first Repack race was held on northern Mt. Tamalpais, down a steep, winding 2 mi. course with a 1,300 ft. drop. By the course's end, all the grease in the bike's coasters had vaporized, and the racers had finished trailing a plume of smoke. After each race, the brakes needed to be re-packed with grease (hence the race's name).

Enthusiasts came together yearly at Repack, trading ideas to improve the sport and their equipment. Fisher added derailleur gears and Breeze built the first modern frame. In 1979, Fisher, Kelly, and Tom Ritchey collaborated to create Mountain-Bikes, the first exclusively off-road bike company.

POINT BONITA

Lighthouse: 1 mi. from Visitors Center, ½ mi. from nearest parking. Open Sa-M 12:30-3:30pm. Guided walks Sa-M 12:30pm. Free. No dogs or bikes through tunnel.

Even if you're not interested in spending time hiking, the short walk down to Point Bonita is well worth a stop. The well-preserved little lighthouse at the end of the point really doesn't seem up to the job of guarding the whole San Francisco Bay, but it has done so valiantly with the same glass lens since 1855. The lens was actually lowered in 1877 in order to duck below the Bay's relentless fog. At the end of a narrow, knife-like ridge lined with purple wildflowers, the lighthouse is accessible via a short tunnel through the rock and a miniature suspension bridge. Even when the lighthouse is closed, the pleasant walk provides gorgeous views on sunny days; on the more common foggy days, there's a slightly mysterious feel. Regardless of visibility or time of year, strong winds make Point Bonita a chilly spot where you probably won't want to be caught without a jacket (or two).

HIKING AND BIKING

For any hiking or biking, a good map is a must; stop by the Visitors Center at Bunker and Field Rd. (p. 232) for trail routes, recommendations, camping information, and free maps. The 1 mi. **Lagoon Trail** walk from the Visitors Center down to sheltered **Rodeo Beach**, a favorite of cormorants and pelicans, is easy and pleasant. The 2 mi. **Tennessee Valley Trail**, a perennial favorite perfect for inexperienced hikers, bikers, and families (but not pets), is a fairly level trail that begins at the beach at the end of Tennessee Valley Rd. (off Hwy. 1). A popular 4.5 mi., pet-friendly hike begins at the Visitors Center and goes north along the **Miwok Trail;** it then heads left onto the **Wolf Ridge Trail,** which leads you past **Hill 88** and rejoins the **Coastal Trail** along the beach and follows the **Lagoon Trail** back to the Visitors Center. A more strenuous 6 mi. trip takes you along the Miwok Trail to the **Bobcat Trail,** around **Gerbody Valley,** and back to the Miwok Trail. All of these trails come near beautiful **Rodeo Lagoon,** just south of the Visitors Center. For the more sea-faring sort, the **Coastal Trail** allows hikers to hug the coastline and take in all the beauty that Hwy. 1, banished from the Headlands, misses. The trail runs along Muir Beach and Pirates Cove, down to Rodeo Beach, and around Rodeo Lagoon. **Bikes** are permitted on Miwok and Bobcat Trails, but not on Wolf Ridge or Lagoon. A popular 7 mi. bike loop offers views of both the East Bay and the Pacific by heading up Bobcat Trail (elevation 600 ft.), across Marincello Trail, up Old Springs Trail (elevation 650 ft.), and back down along Miwok.

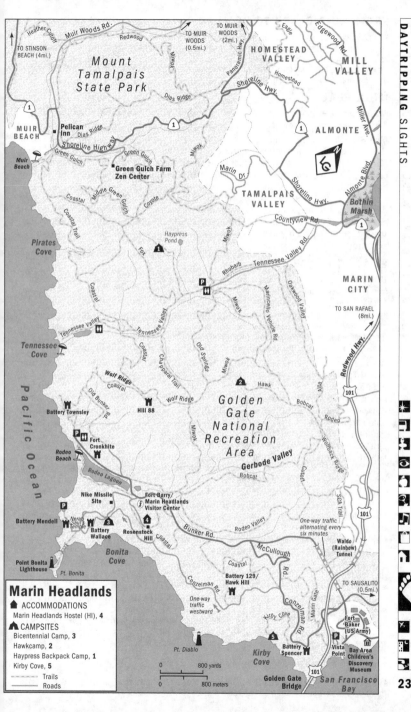

Mount Tamalpais State Park

TO STINSON BEACH (4mi.)

Heather Cutoff

Muir Woods Rd.

Redwood

TO MUIR WOODS (0.5mi.)

TO MUIR WOODS (2mi.)

Eagle

Edgewood Rd.

HOMESTEAD VALLEY

MILL VALLEY

Miwok

Panoramic Hwy.

Shoreline Hwy.

Dias Ridge

Homestead

ALMONTE

MUIR BEACH

Pelican Inn

Dias Ridge

Shoreline Highway

Green Gulch

Muir Beach

Green Gulch Farm Zen Center

Middle Green Gulch

Coyote

Miwok

Marin Dr.

Shoreline Hwy.

Almonte Blvd.

Miller Ave.

TAMALPAIS VALLEY

Bothin Marsh

Countyview Rd.

Coastal Trail

Coastal

Fox

Haypress Pond

1

Rhubarb

Tennessee Valley Rd.

Marincello Vehicle Rd.

Oakwood Valley

MARIN CITY

Pirates Cove

P

TO SAN RAFAEL (8mi.)

Redwood Hwy.

Tennessee Valley

Miwok

Tennessee Cove

Chaparral Trail

Old Springs

Miwok

Hawk

2

Bobcat

101

Pacific Ocean

Wolf Ridge

Coastal

Old Bunker Rd.

Wolf Ridge

Hill 88

Miwok

Golden Gate National Recreation Area

Bobcat

Rodeo

Wolfback Ridge

Battery Townsley

P

Fort Cronkhite

Gerbode Valley

Rodeo Beach

Rodeo Lagoon

Bobcat

Gulch

Nike Missile Site

Fort Barry/ Marin Headlands Visitor Center

One-way traffic alternating every six minutes

SCA Trail

101

Battery Mendell

P

Nearai Sau Temple

3

Battery Wallace

Rosenstock Hill

Bunker Rd.

Rodeo Valley

Coastal

Waldo (Rainbow) Tunnel

Point Bonita Lighthouse

Pt. Bonita

Bonita Cove

Coastal

McCullough Rd.

TO SAUSALITO (0.5mi.)

Marin Headlands

🏕 ACCOMMODATIONS
Marin Headlands Hostel (HI), **4**

⛺ CAMPSITES
Bicentennial Camp, **3**
Hawkcamp, **2**
Haypress Backpack Camp, **1**
Kirby Cove, **5**

Trails
Roads

One-way traffic westward

Conzelman Rd.

Battery 129/ Hawk Hill

Pt. Diablo

Kirby Cove

Conzelman Rd.

Marin Gate

Fort Baker (US Army)

P

Vista Point

Bay Area Children's Discovery Museum

0   800 yards

0   800 meters

5

Battery Spencer

Kirby Cove

Golden Gate Bridge

San Francisco Bay

101

FROM MUIR BEACH TO BOLINAS BAY

▐ *To approach the Marin coast from the south, take US 101 to Hwy. 1 in Marin City or Mill Valley. To approach the Marin coast from the north, follow US 101 past Mill Valley. The San Anselmo Exit leads straight onto Sir Francis Drake Blvd., which continues all the way to Olema, where it meets up with Hwy. 1; the Downtown San Rafael exit lets out onto 3rd St., which runs through San Rafael and then into Sir Francis Drake Blvd.*

MUIR BEACH

▐ **Information:** ☎ *388-2596, guest student manager 455-4968.* **Green Gulch Farm Zen Center:** *1601 Shoreline Hwy.* ☎ *383-3134; www.sfzc.org.*

Muir Beach is a semi-circular cove sans lifeguard. A smidgen further north is the **Muir Beach Overlook,** which offers splendid panoramic coastal views. Just inland from Muir Beach is the **Green Gulch Farm Zen Center,** a Buddhist community, retreat, and organic farm. Visitors are free to explore the tranquil grounds and gardens, and on Sunday mornings the public is welcome at meditation (9:25am), followed by a lecture on Zen Buddhism (10:15am) and tea. Sunday parking $5, free when 3+ people carpool. Would-be Zen masters are asked to wear dark, loose-fitting clothing for *zazen* meditation. If eating is more your thing, check out the Gulch-run **Greens Restaurant** (p. 117). And if you need a place to lay your head, the Zen Center also offers accommodations (p. 234).

STINSON BEACH

▐ **Information:** ☎ *868-0942.* **Local weather and surf forecasts:** *www.stinsonbeachonline.com.* **Live Water:** *3450 Shoreline Hwy.* ☎ *868-0333. Open daily 10am-5pm; in summer 10am-6:30pm.* *AmEx/D/MC/V.* ▓ *Mount Tamalpais and muir woods*

▐ *From US 101, take the Hwy. 1 North exit and follow Hwy. 1 for 3½ mi. until you reach the Panoramic Hwy. Continue on the Panoramic Hwy. for 5¼ mi. to reach the Ranger Station and Pan Toll Rd.* **State Park:** ☎ *388-2070; www.mttam.net. Open daily in summer 8am-9pm; rest of the year 9am-8pm. Free. Parking $0-4.* **Astronomy Program:** ☎ *455-5370; www.mttam.net.*

If you make one daytrip outside of San Francisco, it should take you to beautiful **Mount Tamalpais State Park** (tam-ull-PIE-us), resting between the upscale towns of East Marin and the rocky bluffs of West Marin. Tamalpais is believed to be a combination of two Miwok words, meaning "coast mountain." The 6300-acre park, one of the oldest and most popular in the California State Park System, has miles of hilly, challenging trails on and around the 2571 ft. high Mt. Tam, the highest peak in the county (and the original "mountain" in "mountain bike," p. 236). On a clear day, you can gaze from Mt. Tam across all of the San Francisco shoreline, the Farallon Islands, the Golden Gate Bridge, and the nooks and crannies of the East Bay, including redwood groves, ridges, and oak woodlands. Between 1896 and 1930, the park was also home to "the crookedest railroad in the world," an 8¼ mi. railroad that curved a dizzying 281 times on its way up to the peak. Train passengers then hopped into "gravity cars, the world's longest roller-coaster ride"—which in the early 1900s meant brake-equipped carts pushed along tracks straight down the side of the mountain and into Muir Woods. Even if you're not looking to hike, Mt. Tam is worth a visit: enjoy a roller-coaster drive up the steep and windy Panoramic Highway.

Mt. Tamalpais has a variety of picnic areas for day travelers and campers. The **Bootjack Picnic Area,** on the Panoramic Highway ¼ mi. east of Pan Toll, offers tables, grills, drinking water, bathrooms, and free parking. The **East Peak Summit** is home to a Visitors Center, refreshment stand, picnic tables (no barbecues allowed), and bathrooms. The **Mountain Theater** is known throughout the area for its Mountain Play, staged every summer since 1913. The natural 3750-seat amphitheater houses many special events as well. Mt. Tam also offers an annual **Astronomy Program,** a series of free lectures held in the Mountain Theater followed by telescope observation in the Rock Spring Parking Area.

TRAILS

▐ **Pan Toll Ranger Station:** *801 Panoramic Hwy., about 2½ mi. inland from Stinson Beach. Open in summer 8am-9pm; rest of the year 10am-5pm.*

Mt. Tam has over 50 mi. of trails, suitable for a variety of fitness levels. If you want to check out the view but aren't up for the climb, you can drive up the mountain and stop at vista points along the way. The bubbling waterfall on **Cataract Trail** (2 mi.) and the **Gardner Lookout** on Mt. Tam's east peak are worthy destinations. The **Bootjack Trail** (1 mi.) up to the Mountain Theater offers breathtaking views. The **Steep Ravine Trail** (3 mi.) heads to the beach, and the **Matt Davis Trail** (3 mi.) winds itself up toward the peak (connect with **Fern Creek Trail** to make it all the way to the top). Although Mt. Tam is the home of the mountain bike, cyclists who go off designated trails and fire roads risk incurring the wrath of eco-happy Marin hikers. Signs posted at parking lots and picnic areas give maps with mileage. The **Pan Toll Ranger Station** sells maps ($1) and can offer suggestions for loops of various length and difficulty.

MUIR WOODS

◪ National Monument: *Just inside entrance.* ☎388-2595. *Open daily 9am-dusk. $3, under 17 free. (Hikers have been known to avoid the $3 charge by hiking in 2 mi. from the Pan Toll Ranger Station, which is also the best way to reach Muir Woods by public transport.) Parking lot closes at 8pm, though the trails are still accessible. Parking difficult; try before 10am or after 4pm for best bet.* **Visitors Center:** ☎388-7368; www.nps.gov/muwo. **Full Moon Hike** *and* **Solstice Events:** *reservations* ☎388-2596.

Muir Woods National Monument is a 560-acre stand of old growth coastal redwoods. California coastal redwoods are the tallest and among the oldest living organisms on earth (try 6000-12,000 years on for size), but the tallest tree in Muir Woods (ironically pronounced "mere woods") reaches only 260 ft., a full 100 ft. shorter than those farther north. Nonetheless, the magically dark and still Muir Woods exude a rare beauty and serenity. It's no wonder that in a galaxy far, far away, the Ewoks battled in a forest remarkably familiar to residents of Marin (scenes from *Return of the Jedi* were filmed in Muir Woods.) Spared from logging by the steep sides of Redwood Canyon, these centuries-old redwoods are massive and shrouded in silence. To solidify the protection of the lands along Redwood Creek, in 1905 California Congressman William Kent and his wife Elizabeth purchased 295 acres of land for $45,000 and donated it to the federal government. Kent requested that the lands be named after conservationist John Muir.

Just inside the entrance is the **Muir Woods National Monument Visitors Center.** A trail map and suggestions for hikes are posted on signs just inside the entrance to Muir Woods, and a very good selection of Marin County hiking and biking maps ($0-10) are available in the Visitors Center. Picnicking and camping in Muir Woods is prohibited—head elsewhere in Mt. Tamalpais State Park for sites or stop by the snack bar and gift shop on your way in or out for a quick bite. The level trails along the canyon floor are paved, lined with wooden fences, and usually filled with tourists—who actually come in handy for a change, accentuating the unbelievable height of the redwoods. A hike up the canyon's sides will soon take you away from the hubbub and bring you face-to-face with the wildlife scarce on the forest floor. Birds, insects, and animals make their homes in the forest, although the thick canopy greatly affects what grows in the woods. It also affects the temperature—while it may be 80-90°F around Mt. Tam, temperatures in Muir Woods rarely rise above 70°F. So if you're planning a daytrip to the woods, heed the mantra of Bay Area residents everywhere: dress in layers, layers, and more layers. The park offers free monthly **Full Moon Hikes** as well as special **Solstice Events** every summer and winter.

POINT REYES NATIONAL SEASHORE

◪ *Hwy. 1 provides direct access to the park from the north or south; Sir Francis Drake Blvd. comes west from US 101 just south of San Rafael.* **Park Headquarters:** *Just west of Olema on Bear Valley Rd.* ☎464-5100; www.nps.gov/pore. *Open M-F 9am-5pm, Sa-Su 8am-5pm.* **Visitors Center:** *Open M-F 9am-5pm, Sa-Su 8am-5pm.* **Ranch:** ☎464-5169. *Open daily 9am-4:30pm.*

Five million years ago, Pt. Reyes National Seashore was a suburb of Los Angeles, but it hitched a ride on the submerged Pacific Plate and has been creeping northward along the San Andreas Fault ever since. In summer, colorful wildflowers attract crowds of gawking tourists, but with hundreds of miles of amazing trails, it's quite

Muir Woods and Mt. Tamalpais

▲ CAMPSITE
Rocky Point - Steep Ravine, 1

- - - Trail
- · - · Fire Road
—— Paved Roads
—— Old Railroads (now trails)
········ Park/Water District Boundary

TO SIR FRANCIS DRAKE BLVD. (1.5mi.)

KENTFIELD

ROSS

Crown Rd.

Goodhill Rd.

Indian Rd.

Lagunitas Rd.

Bill Williams Tr.

Gertrude Ord Tr.

Phoenix Lake

Worn S. Fire Rd.

Yolanda Tr.

Shaver Grade

Concrete Pipe Rd.

Fish Gulch

Fish Grade

Eldridge Grade Rd.

Madrone Tr.

Pumpkin Tr.

Lagunitas Rd.

Pilot Knob Tr.

Pilot Knob (1187ft.) ▲

Lakeview Rd.

Marin Line Rd.

Southern

Lake Lagunitas

Berry Tr.

Lagunitas Fire Tr.

Collier Spring Tr.

Marin Municipal Water District

Eldridge Grade Rd.

Inspiration Point ■

East Peak (2571ft.) ▲

Verna Dunshee

P ℹ

Fern Creek Tr.

North Side Tr.

Middle Peak ▲

Old Railroad Grade Rd.

Lower North Side

Upper North Side

International

Old Railroad Grade

Hoo-Koo-E-Koo

Temelpa Tr.

Indian Rd.

Southern Marin Line Rd.

Mount Tamalpais

West Peak (2560ft.) ▲

Miller

Arturo

Mount Tamalpais State Park

Bon Tempe Lake

Bon Tempe Sunnyside Tr.

Bon Tempe Shadyside Tr.

Rocky Ridge Rd.

Rock Spring - Lagunitas

Lagoon Rd.

Azalea Flat

Azalea Meadow Tr.

Potrero Meadows

Kent Tr.

Lagunitas

Alpine Lake

Sky Oaks Rd.

Hogan's Tree

Sky King Tr.

Hidden Lake

Kent Tr.

High Marsh

High Marsh Tr.

Old Stove Tr.

Laurel Dell

Hwy O'Brien Tr.

Cataract Tr.

Cataract Falls

Blake Canyon

Kent Tr.

Helen Markt Tr.

TO FAIRFAX (8mi.)

Fairfax-Bolinas Rd.

TO BOLINAS (15mi.)

Dam

TO DOWNTOWN
MILL VALLEY (1.5mi.)

MILL VALLEY

Cypress Tr.

Cascade Dr.

Edgewood Ave.

Tenderfoot Tr.

Old Pipeline Tr.

Panoramic Hwy.

Redwood Ct. Tr.

MARIN MUNICIPAL
WATER DIST.
PRIVATE LAND

Double
Bowknot

TO ① (1mi.)

MUIR WOODS NAT'L MONUMENT/
MT. TAMALPAIS STATE PARK

Ocean View Tr.

Dipsea Tr.

Sun Tr.

Mt. Tam. Tr.

Muir Woods Rd.

Gravity Car Grade Rd.

Mountain
Home Inn

Panoramic Tr.

Lost Tr.

Fern Creek Tr.

Hillside

Muir Woods
Visitor Center ℹ

Miwok Tr.

TO ① (4mi.)

Hoo-Koo-E-Koo

Mat Davis Tr.

Railroad Grade

Camp Eastwood Rd.

Sierra Tr.

Muir Woods
Nat'l Monument

Kent Canyon

Nora Tr.

West Point Inn

Bootjack Tr.

Ben Johnson Tr.

MUIR WOODS NAT'L MONUMENT

Deer Park Rd.

Dipsea Tr.

Panoramic Hwy.

Mat Davis Tr.

MT. TAMALPAIS STATE PARK

Old Stage Rd.

0   500 yards
0   500 meters

Rock Spring Tr.

TCC Tr.

Bootjack
Picnic Area

Alpine Tr.

Coastal Rd.

N
LG

E. Ridgecrest Blvd.

Mountain
Theater

Bootjack Tr.

Easy Grade Tr.

Old Mine Tr.

Pan Toll
Ranger Station ℹ

Old Mine

Benstein Tr.

Pantoll Rd.

Coastal Trail

Lone Tree
Spring

Mount Tamalpais
State Park

Simmons Tr.

Rock
Springs

Steep Ravine Tr.

Troop 80 Tr.

O'Rourke's
Bench

W. Ridgecrest Blvd.

Mat Davis Tr.

Panoramic Hwy.

Dipsea Tr.

Steep Ravine Tr.

Lone Tree Rd.

TO ① (18mi.)

101

Cataract Tr.

Coastal Trail

Coastal Tr.

MARIN MUNICIPAL WATER DIST.
MT. TAMALPAIS ST. PARK

Ballou
Point

TO STINSON BEACH (1.5mi.)

Willow Camp Rd.

MT. TAMALPAIS STATE PARK

Dipsea Tr.

Shoreline Hwy.

TO ①

Rocky
Point

1

STINSON
BEACH

Stinson
Beach

Redrock
Nude Beach

PACIFIC
OCEAN

possible to gaze in solitary bliss. The park headquarters are at the **Pt. Reyes National Seashore Headquarters,** also known as the **Bear Valley Visitors Center,** where rangers distribute camping permits and can suggest trails, drives, beaches, and picnic areas. A free detailed map of the hikes and their approximate lengths is available at the Visitors Center. Located behind the main building is the **Morgan Horse Ranch.** The first American breed of horse, the Morgans, are used by the park rangers on their patrols. The ranch provides exhibits and is open to the public.

TRAILS

In front of the Visitors Center is a half-mile trail that leads to **Kulo Loklo,** a simulated Native American Miwok village with self-guided exhibits describing the life and culture of the Coastal Miwok. In the summer on Sundays at 2pm, rangers give hour-long guided tours of the village, starting at the Visitors Center. The **Earthquake Trail,** beginning across the parking lot near the picnic area, is a ¾ mi. walk along the infamous San Andreas Fault Line that starts right at Bear Valley. It's an easy, paved walk, with several exhibits on the 1906 earthquake, including a fence that was ripped apart, the site where a cow was supposedly swallowed by the earth, and explanations of the geology involved. For longer hikes of countless varieties and combinations, start with the **Bear Valley Trail** (4 mi.), located behind the Visitors Center just past Morgan Horse Ranch. The trail branches off into several other hikes of various lengths, clearly marked throughout their course. Watch hawks glide overhead and lizards scurry by your feet as you cross meadows, scale mountains, and comb beaches.

BEACHES

🚩 *Blue Waters: 12938 Sir Francis Drake Blvd.* ☎ *669-2600; www.bwkayak.com. Rentals $30-70. Reservations recommended. Also offers tours and classes.* **Ken Patrick Visitors Center:** *On the beach.* ☎ *669-1250. Open in summer F-Tu 10am-5pm, rest of the year Sa-Su and holidays 10am-5pm.* **Drake's Cafe:** ☎ *669-1297. Open Th-M 10am-5pm. AmEx/MC/V.* **Lighthouse Visitors Center:** ☎ *669-1534. Open 10am-4:30pm. Free tours 2:30-4pm, weather permitting.*

Pt. Reyes National Seashore has several wonderful **beaches.** Lovely **Limantour Beach** lies at the end of Limantour Rd., 8 mi. west of the Visitors Center on Bear Valley Rd. The **Pt. Reyes Hostel** is at the bottom of a steep valley, 2 mi. from the end of Limantour Rd. Limantour and the other Pt. Reyes beaches boast high, grassy dunes and long stretches of sand, but strong ocean currents along the point make swimming very dangerous. Swimming is safest at **Heart's Desire Beach,** north of the Visitors Center on sheltered **Tomales Bay.** To reach the beach, take Sir Francis Drake Blvd., make a right at the turn-off for Tomales Bay State Park, and follow the signs. If swimming doesn't suit you, take to Tomales Bay in a **Blue Waters Kayak.** Several miles farther along Sir Francis Drake Blvd. is **Drake's Beach.** Sir Francis Drake, the English explorer and pirate, anchored just off shore in 1579. Learn more about the event at the **Ken Patrick Visitors Center,** which features an aquarium with local specimens. Next door, **Drake's Cafe** sells burgers, hot dogs, and snacks. The surrounding cliffs protect the area and make it good for sunbathing and picnicking. To reach the dramatic **Pt. Reyes Lighthouse** at the very tip of the point, follow Sir Francis Drake Blvd. to its end (30 mi. from the Visitors Center) and head right along the stairway to **Sea Lion Overlook**—migrating gray whales can be spotted from the overlook from December to February. The road is closed on weekends during the winter because of parking concerns; a $4 shuttle leaves hourly from Drake's Beach (call the Bear Valley Visitors Center for more info). Be prepared for heavy fog and strong winds on the Point year-round. The **Lighthouse Visitors Center** also has stair access to the lighthouse itself. Be forewarned: The Visitors Center is a half-mile walk from the parking lot and the lighthouse, a 300-step (read: 30 stories) walk down from there.

POINT REYES STATION

🚩 *Hwy. 1 leads right into and through the town from the north or south; Sir Francis Drake Blvd. comes west from US 101 just south of San Rafael.* **Station House** ❷: *11180 Hwy. 1.* ☎ *663-1515. Late supper served at the bar. Live entertainment F-Su evenings. Breakfast $5-8; lunch $6-14; din-*

ner $7-22. Open Su-Tu and Th-Sa 8am-10pm. D/MC/V. **Dance Palace:** *On the corner of 5th and B St.* ☎ *663-1075; www.svn.net/dance.* **Observatory:** *Mesa Rd. From the south, pick up Mesa Rd. from Horseshoe Hill Rd.; from the north, pick it up off Hwy. 1 in Pt. Reyes Station.* ☎ *868-9212; www.prbo.org. Open May1-Thanksgiving Tu-Su and in winter W, Sa, and Su 6hr. from sunrise.* **Saloon:** *11201 Hwy. 1.* ☎ *663-1661. 21+. DJ F, live music Sa with $4-5 cover. Open Su-Th 10:30am-midnight, F-Sa 10:30am-2am.*

Pt. Reyes Station is a nifty town with a population of about 350 (at least that's what the sign on the town line says). Following the Bolinas tradition, the sign has mysteriously been changed a few times, at one point simply reading "full." (The actual population is somewhere between 850 and 1,000.) Unlike Bolinas, however, the town enjoys a thriving tourist industry. Numerous B&Bs and restaurants have taken advantage of the excellent location at the edge of the national seashore, particularly along Francis Drake Blvd. Most visitors come to refuel, rest up, and then take off for a day in the wilderness. For a gourmet foray from your rustic ramblings try the **Station House Cafe's** Californian coastal cuisine (though their unusual variety of fresh foods makes for a delectably diverse menu). If you haven't had enough of the outdoors, ask to dine in their garden patio. If you do decide to stay in town longer, you'll have the opportunity to take advantage of the phenomenal community center, the **Dance Palace,** and its courses on everything from *capoeira* (a Brazilian martial art) to mystery novel-writing and kids' programs. It hosts numerous events, including jazz concerts, movies, plays, art exhibits, lectures, and much more. Pt. Reyes is a paradise for birdwatchers and mountain bikers (and doubly so for mountain-biking birdwatchers). For bird-watching info and occasional free tours, head over to the **Pt. Reyes Bird Observatory.** Or leave the birds alone and engage in a little people-watching at the **Old Western Saloon.** It's an old brothel from Pt. Reyes's days as a bustling railroad town. Though the prostitutes have moved on, it can get pretty raucous, especially on weekends (live music F-Sa evenings). Not too shabby for a small town of only, um, some indeterminate number of people.

SEASONAL EVENTS

Pt. Reyes National Seashore hosts annual **Native American Festivals** on the 3rd Saturday of April and July, featuring traditional dancing, crafts, and foods. Call the Visitors Center for more informa-

in recent news

Hands off the Parks!

The summer of 2003 greeted California with the worst budget crisis in the state's history. All state agencies were asked to cut their support budgets, and most did so significantly. Yet, matters have worsened in a stalemate between political parties struggling to pass their own budget proposals. Indications are that an additional $10 to 20 million will be cut from one of the most precious agencies, State Parks.

If such cuts are indeed implemented, it is likely that between 100 and 277 state parks in California will be forced to close, several from around the Bay Area.

A trend of disinvestment in the park system began in the 1990s, and seems to be continuing today, affecting small parks that do not generate high revenue. These parks provide affordable and accessible recreation for millions of Californians and visitors every year.

As visitors, one way to help protect the future of these parks is to make sure to pay park and parking lot fees (which may change unexpectedly), as these small fees amount to large sums throughout the year. Save the redwoods, and protect your camping grounds! Visit www.calparks.org.

243

tion. If you were making Michelangelo's David while other kids built flimsy castles, grab your pail and shovel and consider competing in the yearly Drake's Beach **Sand Sculpture Contest** on the Sunday of Labor Day weekend. Register at the Visitors Center at Drake's Beach. From June to October, a **Farmer's Market** is held at Toby's Feed Barn. (☎663-1075. Sa 9am-1pm.)

SAUSALITO

Originally a fishing center full of bars and bordellos, the city at Marin's extreme southeastern tip has long since traded its sea-dog days for retail boutiques and overpriced seafood restaurants. The palm trees and 14 ft. elephant statues of Plaza de Vina del Mar Park look out over a wonderful view of San Francisco Bay, making for a sunny, self-consciously Mediterraneanesque excursion. The sheer number and variety of quality art galleries in the small town make it worth checking out, regardless of the touristy feel.

TRANSPORTATION

Driving from San Francisco, take the **Alexander Ave.** exit just after the Golden Gate Bridge and follow Alexander Ave. for about 2½ mi. until it turns into the waterfront stretch of **Bridgeway Blvd.** From Muir Woods and other points north, take the **Sausalito** Bridgeway Blvd. exit off US 101, turn right on Bridgeway and follow it almost 3 mi. to the center of town.

Public Transportation: Golden Gate Transit (☎455-2000, in SF 923-2000; www.goldengate.org; phones operated daily 7am-7pm) provides bus service between San Francisco and Marin County via the Golden Gate Bridge, as well as local service in Marin. M-F buses #20 and 50 serve **Marin City** and **Sausalito** from **San Francisco's Transbay Terminal;** Sa-Su buses #10 and 25 will take you there (adults $2.65, seniors and disabled $1.30, under 18 $2, under 6 free). Within Marin County, bus #63 runs on the weekends from Marin City through Sausalito (adults $4.60, seniors and disabled $2.30, under 18 $3.45, under 6 free) There is also a free shuttle bus that runs through downtown Sausalito from the ferry landing to the Bay Model, post office, city hall, and back downtown.

Ferries: Golden Gate Ferry (☎455-2000; www.goldengate.org), runs from San Francisco's ferry terminal at the intersection of Embarcadero and Market St. on the eastern edge of the city to the Sausalito terminal (adults $5.60, seniors and disabled $4.20, under 6 free; AmEx/MC/V), and the Larkspur terminal at 101 E. Sir Francis Drake Blvd. (M-F adults $3.10, seniors and disabled $1.55, under 18 $2.35, under 6 free; Sa-Su adults $5.30, seniors and disabled $2.65, under 18 $3.95). No bike fees. Offices open M-F 6am-8pm, Sa-Su 7am-8pm. **Blue and Gold Fleet** (☎773-1188, tickets 705-5555; www.blueandgoldfleet.com) runs ferries from Pier 41 at Fisherman's Wharf to Sausalito and Tiburon (adults $6.75, under 5 free. AmEx/MC/V).

Taxis: Belaire Cab Co. (☎388-1234). Open 24hr. MC/V.

ORIENTATION & PRACTICAL INFORMATION

Sausalito lies 10 mi. north of San Francisco on the eastern side of Marin County. The short stretch of **Bridgeway Ave.** along the water is the city's main thoroughfare, and practically the only one on Visitors Center maps. Running parallel to Bridgeway after Johnson St., **Caledonia St.** offers charming and affordable restaurants but lacks the view of the Bay that touristy Bridgeway offers.

Visitor Information: Marin County Visitors Bureau, 1013 Larkspur Landing Circle (☎499-5000; www.visitmarin.org), off the Sir Francis Drake Blvd. Exit from US 101, near the ferry terminal. Open M-F 9am-5pm. There is also a visitors kiosk at the ferry landing that has maps and a few brochures.

Library: Sausalito Library, 420 Litho St. (☎289-4100, ext. 121), shares a building with Sausalito City Hall. Free **Internet** access. Open M-Th 10am-9pm, F-Sa 10am-5pm.

Laundromat: Water Works, 105 2nd St. (☎332-2632). Wash $2; dry 25¢ per 10min. Open M-F 7am-9pm, Sa-Su 8am-7pm.

Emergency: ☎911.

Police: ☎289-4170. **Marin County Sheriff:** ☎479-2311.

Post Office: 150 Harbor Dr., at Bridgeway Ave. Open M-Th 8:30am-5pm, F 8:30am-5:30pm. **Postal code:** 94965.

FOOD & DRINK

You can always stock up for the ferry ride home with organic produce from **Real Food Company,** 200 Caledonia St., at Turney St. (☎332-9640. Open daily 9am-8:30pm. AmEx/MC/V.) Though most of the restaurants along Bridgeway tend to be pricey, the **Venice Gourmet Delicatessen ❶,** 625 Bridgeway, serves easily sharable sandwiches ($6) and side dishes ($3-5) in a Mediterranean-style marketplace with waterside seating. (☎332-3544; www.venicegourmet.com. Open daily in summer 9am-7pm; in winter 9am-6pm.) For a sit-down lunch in town, try the grilled focaccia ($8) or salads ($7-8) at **Caffè Divino ❶,** 37A Caledonia St., at Johnson St. (☎331-9355. Open daily 6:30am-6pm. MC/V.) Another option down the street is **Sartaj Indian Café ❷,** 43 Caledonia St., where you can quash those *somas* cravings without breaking your budget. It's not gourmet, but the enormous meals with rice and salad for $9 are almost unbeatable. Sartaj also serves big, cheap breakfasts all day ($5 for Indian or American-style eggs). (☎332-7103. Open daily 6:30am-9:30pm. MC/V.) Locally popular **Sushi Ran ❷,** 107 Caledonia St., offers upscale Asian fare, including *sake* bar and vegetarian *maki*. Lunch specials, which include sushi or a cooked dish, soup, and salad for $11.50 are the budget travelers' best bet at this slightly pricier spot. (☎332-3620; www.sushiran.com. Open for lunch M-F 11:30am-2:30pm, and dinner M-Sa 5:30-11pm, Su 5:30-10:30pm. AmEx/MC/V.)

SIGHTS & SHOPPING

Afternoon shopping and gawking is absurdly ample along Bridgeway, whose galleries and upscale clothiers are intermingled with a few exceptional gems. The second and larger of the two **Mark Reuben Galleries** at 34 Princess St., close to Bridgeway sells glitzy black-and-whites of Judy Garland, reprints of battle shots from the Civil War, and lots of sports memorabilia. No original prints, but it offers San Fran history and hall-of-famers' autographs. (☎332-8815. Open daily 10:30am-5:30pm. AmEx/D/MC/V.) **Art That Makes You Laugh,** 607 Bridgeway Ave, showcases fine art with a definite sense of humor. The full-size prints and paintings make this one of the few galleries where laughing at the work is encouraged. (☎800-289-1354; www.leedyart.com. Open daily 10am-6 pm. AmEx/D/MC/V.) **Munchies,** 613 Bridgeway Ave., should be able to satisfy anyone's sweet tooth. Huge barrels of salt water taffy, assorted chocolates, and hard candies are available for $3.49 per ½ lb. or, for those with smaller cravings, sampling is welcomed. (☎331-3863. Open daily 10:30am-6:30pm. No credit cards.) Half a mile north of the town center is the **Bay Model and Marinship Museum,** 2100 Bridgeway. Turn off Bridgeway at Marinship to find the massive working model of San Francisco Bay. Built in the 1950s to test the ecological effects of proposals for damming the bay and other diabolical plans, the water-filled 1.5 acre model recreates tides and currents in great detail. A small exhibit catalogues Marin's days as a World War II ship-building headquarters, when the Marinship Co. recruited American workers from across the country to build 96 ships in record-breaking time. (☎332-1851. Open Tu-Sa 9am-4pm. Free. Wheelchair-accessible.)

NIGHTLIFE & ENTERTAINMENT

When nighttime falls, stop into the **No Name Bar,** 757 Bridgeway, an old time-looking saloon with a heated patio and live blues or jazz music every night at 8:30pm. (☎332-1392. Open daily 10am-2am. Cash only.) Or head to favorite local hangout **Smitty's,** 217 Caledonia St., for laid-back beer drinking ($4), pool at one of the four tables, and some of the area's best hot dogs ($1.50). (☎332-2637. Open daily 10am-2pm. MC/V.) **Caffe Trieste,** 1000 Bridgeway, is a Sausalito institution with a mostly local clientele and a wood-burning oven. It stays open late for gelato ($3), focaccia ($6), and live jazz on F-Sa. (☎332-7660. Open M-Th 6:30am-11pm, F 6:30am-midnight, Sa 7am-midnight, Su 7am-11pm. MC/V.)

MILL VALLEY

Although the logging industry of Marin County was masterminded in Mill Valley, this town of 13,600 residents, consisting of millionaires and mountain bikers (and millionaire mountain bikers), is now every bit as environmentally conscious as the rest of the county. Pretty and pricey Mill Valley was a haven for hippies and artists in the 60s and 70s. Today, its few remaining VW buses park beside Mercedes SUVs in driveways lined by 100 ft. redwoods.

TRANSPORTATION

The Marin peninsula lies at the northern end of the San Francisco Bay and is connected to the city by US 101 via the Golden Gate Bridge. US 101 extends north inland to Santa Rosa and Sonoma County, while Hwy. 1 winds north along the Pacific coast. The **Richmond-San Rafael Bridge** connects Marin to the East Bay via **I-580.** From US 101, take the **Rte. 131** exit toward **E. Blithedale Ave.** Follow Rte. 131 until it becomes E. Blithedale Ave., which will lead you directly into Mill Valley.

Public Transportation: Golden Gate Transit (☎455-2000; in SF ☎923-2000; www.goldengate.org; phones operated daily 7am-7pm), provides bus service between San Francisco and Marin County via the Golden Gate Bridge, as well as local service in Marin. From SF, take bus #10 northbound (multiple pick-ups along Mission St., Van Ness Ave., and Lombard St.) to either Miller and Sunnyside St. or E. Blithedale Ave. and Tower St. Bus #4 services same locations M-F during commuting hours. Adults $2.80, seniors and disabled $1.40, children $2.10.

Taxis: Belaire Cab Co. (☎388-1234). Open 24hrs. MC/V.

ORIENTATION & PRACTICAL INFORMATION

Mill Valley lies about 11 mi. north of San Francisco and 5 mi. east of Muir Woods, and is a 2 mi. hike from Mt. Tamalpais.

Visitor Information: Mill Valley Chamber of Commerce, 85 Throckmorton Ave. (☎388-9700; www.millvalley.org), next to the Depot Bookstore. A great place to go for hiking and biking info, and maps of the surrounding areas. Open M-F 10am-noon and 1-4pm.

Libraries: Mill Valley Public Library, 375 Throckmorton Ave. (☎389-4292), just behind Old Mill Park. Eleven free Internet terminals available. Weekly teen and children events, including reading programs. Open M-Th 10am-9pm, F noon-6pm, Sa 10am-5pm, Su 1pm-5pm.

Laundromats: Coin Laundry, 393 Miller Ave. Change machines. Wash $2; dry 25¢ per 10min. Wash, dry, fold service: in by 1pm, out by 6pm. Open 6am-11pm.

Emergency: ☎911.

Police: Marin County Sheriff ☎479-2311.

Post Office: 751 E. Blithedale Ave. Open M-F 8:30am-6pm, Sa 8:30am-2pm. **Postal code:** 94941

FOOD & DRINK

Given Mill Valley's proximity to Muir Woods, Muir Beach, and Mt. Tamalpais, it's a great place to grab picnic provisions pre-expedition. In the center of town, **Mill Valley Market ❷**, 12 Corte Madera Ave., has an acclaimed deli serving sandwiches to go, a selection of local produce, and a vast wine and liquor stock. (☎388-3222). On the outskirts of town, **Whole Foods ❷**, 414 Miller Ave., specializes in organic groceries (☎381-1200. Open daily 8am-8pm. MC/V.) For those looking to stay in town, Mill Valley offers a number of cafes where you can catch residents taking a breather mid-dogwalk, preaching 70s ideology, or downing an espresso between pilates class and picking up the kids. The old bus depot houses the popular **Depot Bookstore and Cafe ❶**, 87 Throckmorton Ave., which satisfies all caffeine, sandwich, salad, and breakfast needs. (☎383-2665; www.depotbookstore. Open daily 7am-7pm.) For a fantastic ethnic lunch or dinner, try **✦Avatar's Punjabi Burrito ❶**, 15 Madrona St. Take chickpeas, rice, chutney, yogurt, and spice. Add tofu and veggies or other things nice. Wrap in yummy Indian bread, and you have a delicious meal for $5.50-8.50. Rice plates and mango *lassi* also available. (☎381-8293. Open M-Sa 11am-8pm.) A number of more costly eateries line Throckmorton Ave. near its intersection with Miller Ave. Or try **Champagne French Bakery & Cafe ❶**, 41 Throckmorton Ave., a French-style bakery-cafe serving sandwiches, quiches, and delectable desserts. (☎380-0410.)

SIGHTS & SHOPPING

If the great outdoors aren't beckoning, indoor entertainment is available at the small movie theater on Throckmorton, or at the **Mill Valley Community Center,** 180 Camino Alto, at Blithedale. (☎383-1370. Open M-F 9am-5pm. Fitness Center available to adults $6, under age 18 $4, seniors over age 60 $5. Open M-Th 6:30am-9pm, F 6:30am-6:30pm, Sa 8am-5pm, Su 9:30pm-5pm.) Alongside the boutiques and design stores of Throckmorton and Miller Ave. are a couple of shops ranging from entertaining to downright bizarre. Leading the latter kind is **The Pleasure Principle,** 74 Throckmorton Ave. Claiming to keep the "radical rebel" spirit of the 60s alive, the store boasts floor-to-ceiling curiosities, from adult movies to dried alien lifeforms, and an intriguing collection of so-called "water pipes." (☎388-8588. Open daily noon-11pm.)

SAN ANSELMO

San Anselmo is a postcard-perfect slice of slightly-above-middle-class America. Streams with footbridges and tree-lined streets provide insulation from the nearby roar of the highway. Along with the pervading laid-back small town ambience is a prosperous city-style love of shopping and all its glories. Known for its bustling second-hand and vintage stores, the town is a favorite among fans of high-end kitsch. The main street, **San Anselmo Ave.,** brims with boutiques, specialty shops, and trendy eateries filled with families and weary consumers.

TRANSPORTATION, ORIENTATION & PRACTICAL INFORMATION

San Anselmo is about 14 mi. north of San Francisco, just south of Fairfax. From San Francisco, take U.S. 101 North to the San Anselmo exit, which turns into Sir Francis Drake Blvd. and will lead you into San Anselmo.

Public Transportation: Golden Gate Transit bus #20 stops at the corner of Center and Sir Francis Drake Blvd.

Taxis: Belaire Cab Co. (☎388-1234). Open 24hrs. MC/V.

Police: ☎485-3000. **Marin County Sheriff:** ☎479-2311

Post Office: 121 San Anselmo Ave. (☎453-0363). Open M-F 8:30am-5pm. **Postal code:** 94960. **247**

ACCOMMODATIONS

If you're looking to spend a night in San Anselmo, try **The San Anselmo Inn,** 339 San Anselmo Ave. (☎455-5366; www.sananselmoinn.com), a luxurious B&B in the heart of San Anselmo's main street. Big beds, a homey feel, and extra perks like Internet and cable make this cozy place a great deal. Extended continental breakfast included. Wine and appetizers served F-Sa 5:30-6:30pm. Parking available at nearby lot. Check-in 3pm; check-out 11am. Rooms start at $79, with private bath $99; two-room suite $179. MC/V. ❸

FOOD & DRINK

San Anselmo Ave. is full of quality sandwich shops as well as slightly more expensive sit-down restaurants. If you'd rather eat on the go, hit **Andronico's,** on Center Blvd. at Sir Francis Drake Blvd., a great grocery store providing "shopping the way it used to be" and freebies in the deli and to-go sections. (☎455-8194. Open daily 7am-10pm. AmEx/D/MC/V.) 🔳**Bubba's Diner ❷,** 566 San Anselmo Ave., is a local favorite that serves all the essentials like burgers and shakes and features daily specials. Sandwiches are about $8, but dinner is a little pricier at $13-15 per entree. (☎459-6862. Open M and W-F 9am-2pm and 5:30-9pm, Sa-Su 8am-2:30pm and 5:30-9:30pm. MC/V.) **Comforts ❷,** 335 San Anselmo Ave., delivers upscale deli counter delectables like pasta, chili, and salads at $3.50 per ½ lb. in addition to made-to-order hot and cold sandwiches ($6.50). (☎454-9840. Open M-F 6:30am-7:30pm, Sa 7:30am-7:30pm, Su 8:30am-3pm. Indoor and outdoor cafe tables available for seating M-F 8:30am-2:30pm, Su 8:30am-3pm. Deli open M-F 6:30am-7:30pm, Sa 7:30am-6:30pm, Su 8:30am-3pm. MC/V.) **Yahiro Sushi Bar and Restaurant ❷,** 69 Center Blvd., provides an affordable, classy non-sandwich option for dinner. Sushi ($3) and cooked entrees ($12). (☎459-1504. Open Tu-F 5:30-9:30pm, Sa-Su 5-9:30pm. MC/V.) **San Anselmo Coffee Roasters ❶,** 635 San Anselmo Ave., is the perfect place to go if you are looking for a decent cup of coffee or a great place to rest your feet. The gourmet brews are affordable ($1.50-3) and the back patio has two levels of seating surrounded by lush greenery. Scrumptious baked goods ($1.50) and smoothies ($3.50). (☎258-9549. Open M-F 6:30am-7pm, Sa-Su 7am-7pm. D/MC/V.)

SIGHTS & SHOPPING

Booksmith's, 615 San Anselmo Ave., is the oldest independent bookstore in Marin County, selling mostly new books but with a decent used section (most $6). (☎459-7323. Open daily 10am-10pm. MC/V.) **Heldfond Book Gallery,** 310 San Anselmo Ave., is an antiquarian bookseller, specializing in illustrated texts from the 14th-18th centuries (including children's texts). The store/gallery houses first editions of T.S Eliot's *The Wasteland,* Charles Dickens's *The Pickwick Papers,* and F.Scott Fitzgerald's *The Great Gatsby* ($30,000-45,000). (☎456-8194; www.heldfond.com. Open M-Sa 10:30am-5pm. AmEx/MC/V.) **The Vintage Flamingo,** 528 San Anselmo Ave., offers an eclectic mix of old and new, vintage and retro—hats galore, women's (and some men's) clothes, knickknacks, furniture, and, of course, the occasional flamingo. (☎721-7275. Open M-Sa 11:30am-5pm, Su noon-5pm. MC/V.) **SecondHandLand,** 703 San Anselmo Ave, is a cross between a second-hand store and a prop shop. Its contents range from wacky (a bathtub in the middle of the store) to just plain weird (a collection of mannequin heads), but is definitely worth checking out. There are some great deals on furniture and clothes if you're willing to pick through the piles. (☎793-2117. Usually open W-Su 11:30am-6pm.) **Doodlebugs,** 641 San Anselmo Ave., is an arts and crafts mecca for kids and adults. Paint a plate, throw a pot, mosaic a mirror, or take a class. The store is divided into gift shop/toy store in the back and a studio lined with choices of pottery to paint in front (pottery mostly $5-12, with some up to $100). (☎456-5989; www.doodlebug-marin.com. Open Su-W 10am-7pm, Th-Sa 10am-9pm. AmEx/D/MC/V.)

PARKS & RECREATION

Great weather year-round means that action in town centers around outdoors entertainment. In the summer, **Film Night in the Park** takes place in Creek Park between San Anselmo Ave. and Sir Francis Drake Blvd., right before Center Blvd. Shows are usually Friday and Saturday nights at about 8:30pm. Listings are posted above the gateway to the park off Sir Francis Drake Blvd., on the website (www.filmnight.org) and in the program, which you can pick up at the library. During the day, the area is also a nice place for a picnic under the redwoods. A bit farther north off Sir Francis Drake Blvd. is **San Anselmo Memorial Park,** with a baseball field, tennis courts, and the **Millennium Playground.** The largest and most impressive playground in the county, it includes forts, towers, slides, and loads of great hiding spots, and was built entirely by community volunteers and based on a plan generated by neighborhood families.

Next to the park is the **Log Cabin,** also called the American Legion Post 179. The cabin looks like something from the days of King Arthur, with an enormous fireplace, high-back chairs, and low chandeliers. It is a common meeting place for Boy Scout troops and often hosts major community bashes. Some say that three ghosts haunt the premises. Downstairs, a bar called **The Dugout,** decorated with military memorabilia, boasts a full bar, darts, and other games. (☎456-0834. Open to the public M, W, and F 6pm-1am. No credit cards.)

WINE COUNTRY

In the 1880s, Robert Louis Stevenson described Wine Country (the collective term for the Napa, Sonoma, and Russian River Valleys) as a place where "the stirring sunlight and the growing vines make a pleasant music for the mind, and the wine is poetry." Winery-hopping as a tourist art form, however, didn't emerge until the 70s, when the California wine industry secured a solid reputation in the world of fine wine, and many wineries began focusing energy toward hosting visitors at tours and tastings. Connoisseurs worldwide regard Napa and Sonoma vineyards highly, and even the least wine-savvy of daytrippers delight in sipping the samples and enjoying the similarly intoxicating landscape.

As most parts of Marin, Napa, and Sonoma Counties are within two hours of San Francisco by car, it might be wiser to make it a daytrip than to stay and endure the steep hotel prices. Wine country remains fairly inaccessible by public transportation, but its flat terrain, warm weather, and the short distances between wineries beckon cyclers. Stevenson and his bride once squatted in the abandoned Silverado mine when his budget couldn't stretch to include accommodations—if yours can't either, a quick daytrip will still allow enough time to sample the goods. A designated driver is probably a good idea, depending on your tastes.

AREA CODE	Wine Country's area code is ☎707.

NAPA VALLEY

Napa catapulted American wine into the big leagues in 1976, when a bottle of red from Napa's **Stag's Leap Vineyard** beat a bottle of critically acclaimed (and unfailingly French) Château Lafitte-Rothschild in a blind taste test in Paris. While not the oldest, and not necessarily the best, Napa Valley is certainly the best-known of America's wine-growing regions. Its golden hills, natural hot springs, and sunlight inspired Gold Rush millionaires to build luxury spas for vacationers in the 1850s. Indeed, it wasn't until the 1960s, when the now big-name wineries like Mondavi first opened, that the region was able to assert itself not as a spa retreat, but as Wine Country. Now firmly established as such, Napa draws a mostly older, well-to-do crowd, but in the midst of the tasting carnival there are plenty of young, budget-minded folks looking forward to their fill of chardonnay and their share of class.

LAKE CO.
NAPA CO.

Ida Clayton Rd.

Mt. St. Helena (4304ft.)
Robert Louis Stevenson State Park

TO GEYSERVILLE
Kellogg
128
Tubbs Ln.
TO CLEAR LAKE (28mi.)
29

Aetna Springs

N LG

Old Faithful Geyser

Cedar Rd.

1
2 Calistoga
Petrified Forest
3
Napa River
4
5
Petrified Forest Rd.

Bothe Napa State Park
29
128
6
7

8
St. Helena
Silverado Trail
Lake Hennessey
Chiles & Pope Valley Rd.
9
128
TO DAVIS

VINEYARDS

Bartholomew Park Winery, 35
Beaulieu Vineyards, 15
Benziger, 29
Beringer Vineyards, 8
Buena Vista, 36
Cakebread Cellars, 16
Carmenet, 30
Chateau St. Jean, 20
St. Clement Vineyards, 7
Cline Cellars, 43
Clos Du Val, 32
Clos Pegase, 4
Domaine Carneros, 40
Domaine Chandon, 28
Edgewood Estate Winery, 13
Goosecross Cellars, 25
Grgich Hills Cellar, 14
Gundlach-Bundschu, 39
Kenwood, 21

Kirkland Ranch, 42
Kunde, 22
Ledson Winery, 18
Nichelini Winery, 9
Niebaum-Coppola Winery, 17
Prager Port Works, 10
Ravenswood, 34
RMS Brandy Distillery, 41
Robert Mondavi La Famiglia, 24
Robert Mondavi Winery, 23
S. Anderson Vineyards, 26
Sebastiani Vineyards, 37
Stag's Leap Wine Cellars, 27
Sterling Vineyards, 3
Sutter Home Winery, 11
Trefethen Vineyards, 33
Wermuth Vineyards, 5
Valley of the Moon, 31
V. Sattui, 12

Calistoga Rd.
SONOMA CO.
NAPA CO.
Hood Mtn. Reg. Pk.
Valley of the Moon
12
Spring Lake
Oakmont
Annadel State Historic Park
Adobe Canyon Rd.
18
Sugarloaf Ridge State Park
19
Rustin Falls
Mt. St. John (2375ft.)

10
11 13 12
14
15 Rutherford
16
17 Wine Train
Dry Creek Rd.
23 Oakville Cross Rd.
24 Oakville
25 26
Silverado Trail
27
Soda Canyon Dr.
Sage Canyon Rd.
Napa River

20
21
22 Kenwood
Bennett Valley Rd.
Petaluma Hill Rd.
Sonoma Crane Cyn. Rd.
Mountain Rd.
29
Glen Ellen
30
Trinity Rd.
31
Mt. Veeder Rd.
Lokoya
Dry Creek Rd.
Redwood St.
Yountville
28 Wine Train
Napa Valley
29
32
33
Monticello Rd.

Jack London State Historic Park
Sonoma Development Ctr.
Eldridge
Mission Sonoma
12
Agua Caliente
Boyes Hot Springs
34
35 36
Carriger Rd.
Browns Valley Rd.
Trancas St.
Napa
121
Hagen Rd.
Coombsville Rd.

Sonoma State University
Penngrove
Adobe Rd.
38
101
Washington St.
El Verano
Sonoma State Historic Park
Napa St.
37
Sonoma
The Plaza
39
Broadway
Napa Rd.
Lovall Valley Rd.
Imola Ave.
Napa State Hospital

Petaluma
116
Stage Gulch Rd.
Arnold Dr.
Sonoma Valley
E 8th St.
Schellville
12 121
Rama Rd.
40
Cuttings Wharf Rd.
41
42
12
Jameson Cyn. Rd.
Lakeville Hwy.
Lakeville Rd.
121
43
Napa Sl.
Cuttings Wharf
Napa Co. Airport
29
Second
Skaggs Island
Napa-Sonoma Marshes Wildlife Area

ACCOMMODATIONS

Bothe-Napa Valley State Park, 6
Calistoga Inn and Brewery/ The Calistoga Village Inn & Spa, 2
Golden Haven Hot Springs Spa and Resort, 1
S.F.N./Petaluma KOA, 38
Sugarloaf Ridge State Park, 19

Boat Ramp

Lakeville
Sears Point Raceway
TO MARIN CO.
Sears Point Rd.
37
San Pablo Bay
37
Mare Island
Six Flags Marine World
VALLEJO
80

0   5 mi
0   5 km

The Wine Country: Sonoma & Napa Valleys

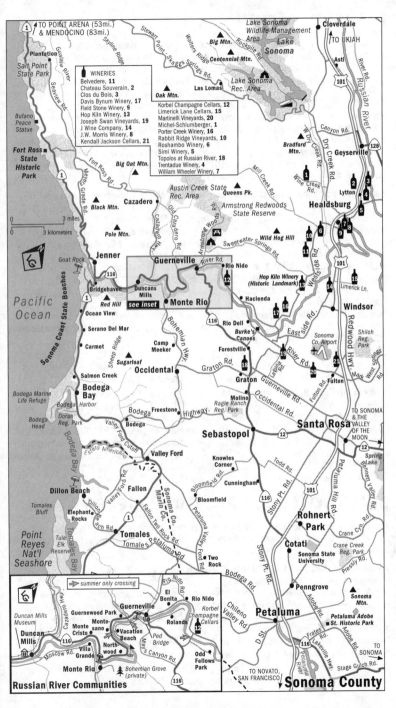

WINERIES
Belvedere, 11
Chateau Souverain, 2
Clos du Bois, 3
Davis Bynum Winery, 17
Field Stone Winery, 9
Hop Kiln Winery, 13
Joseph Swan Vineyards, 19
J Wine Company, 14
J.W. Morris Winery, 8
Kendall Jackson Cellars, 21

Korbel Champagne Cellars, 12
Limerick Lane Cellars, 15
Martinelli Vineyards, 20
Michel-Schlumberger, 1
Porter Creek Winery, 16
Rabbit Ridge Vineyards, 10
Roshambo Winery, 6
Simi Winery, 5
Topolos at Russian River, 18
Trentadue Winery, 4
William Wheeler Winery, 7

TRANSPORTATION

Scenic **Route 29 (Saint Helena Highway)** runs north from **Napa** through Napa Valley and the well-groomed villages of **Yountville** and **Saint Helena** (where it's called Main St.) to **Calistoga's** soothing spas. The relatively short distances between wineries can take unpleasantly long to cover on weekends when the roads crawl with visitors. The **Silverado Trail,** parallel to Rte. 29, is less crowded, but watch out for cyclists. Napa is 14 mi. east of Sonoma on **Route 12.** If you're planning a weekend trip from San Francisco, avoid Saturday mornings and Sunday afternoons; the roads are packed with like-minded people. Although harvest season in early September is the most exciting time to visit, winter weekdays are less packed and offer more personal attention. Most accommodations are also less expensive in the winter or offer specials. From San Francisco, take US 101 over the Golden Gate Bridge, then follow Rte. 37 east to catch Rte. 29, which runs north to Napa.

Public Transportation: Napa City Bus, or **Valley Intercity Neighborhood Express (VINE),** 1151 Pearl St. (☎800-696-6443 or 255-7631, TDD 226-9722), covers **Vallejo** (M-F 5:20am-8pm, Sa 6:15am-5:30pm, Su 11am-6pm; $1.50, students $1.10, seniors and disabled 75¢) and **Calistoga** (M-F 5:20am-8pm, Sa 6am-6:40pm, Su 9:30am-4:30pm; $2, students $1.45, seniors and disabled $1; free transfers). The nearest **Greyhound** station is in Vallejo, 1500 Lemon St. (☎643-7661 or 800-231-2222). A bus runs to **Napa** and Calistoga, but it's very slow—almost 3hr. from Vallejo to Calistoga—and does not stop near wineries. To: Napa (at the **Napa State Hospital,** 2100 Napa-Vallejo Hwy.; 12:30 and 5:25pm; $8.25 one-way, $15.25 round-trip) and **Calistoga** (5:25 and 8pm; $11.25 one-way, $21.25 round-trip). **Evans Airport Transport,** 4075 Solano Ave. (☎255-1559 or 944-2025), in Napa, runs daily shuttles from the **San Francisco** and **Oakland** airports via Vallejo to downtown Napa. Reservations required. To **Napa** ($29 one-way, children 12 and under $15) and **Vallejo** ($24 one-way, children 12 and under $15).

Car Rental: Budget, 407 Soscol Ave. (☎224-7846), in Napa. Cars $40 per day; under 25 surcharge $20 per day. Unlimited mileage. Must be at least 21 with credit card. Promotional specials often available; call Budget Reservation Center at ☎800-537-0700.

Bike Rental: ▓**St. Helena Cyclery,** 1156 Main St. (☎963-7736). Hybrid bikes $7 per hr., $30 per day; road bikes $15/$50; tandem bikes $20/$70. All bikes come with maps, helmet, lock, and picnic bag. Reservations recommended for road and tandem bikes. Open M-Sa 9:30am-5:30pm, Su 10am-5pm. **Getaway Adventures** (☎800-499-BIKE/2453, Calistoga office 942-0332, Petaluma office 763-3040; www.getawayadventures.com), behind the gas station at the corner of Rte. 29 and Lincoln Ave., in Calistoga. $9 per hr., $20 per half-day, $28 per day. 2hr. min. Also leads bike tours in Napa. Open M-Th 9:30am-5:30pm, F-Su 9:30am-6pm; open fewer hours in off-season, usually M and Th-Su 9:30am-5pm.

ORIENTATION & PRACTICAL INFORMATION

Yountville and **Saint Helena,** which lie between the relatively busy town of Napa and the soothing spas of **Calistoga,** are well-groomed little villages that each host several small restaurants and trendy shops.

Visitor Information: Napa Conference & Visitors Bureau, 1310 Town Ctr. (☎226-7459; www.napavalley.com/nvcvb.html). Very friendly staff. Free maps and info. Also sells the *Napa Valley Guidebook* ($6) with more comprehensive listings and fold-out maps. Ask about any specials during your visit (they come in daily) and pick up coupons from local businesses. Open daily 9am-5pm. **St. Helena Chamber of Commerce,** 1010A Main St. (☎963-4456), across from Taylor's Refresher (see p. 254). Eager to help. Open M-F 10am-5pm. **Calistoga Chamber of Commerce,** 1458 Lincoln Ave. (☎942-6333; www.calistogafun.com). Open M-F 10am-5pm, Sa 10am-4pm, Su 11am-3pm.

Winery Tours: Napa Valley Holidays (☎255-1050; www.napavalleyholidays.com). Afternoon tours $75 per person, $85 with round-trip transportation from San Francisco.

Police: In **Napa,** 1539 1st St. (☎253-4451). In **Calistoga,** 1235 Washington St. (☎942-2810).

Hospital: Queen of the Valley, 1000 Trancas St. (☎252-4411), in Napa.

Post Office: 1627 Trancas St. (☎255-0360), in Napa. Open M-F 8:30am-5pm. **Postal Code:** 94558.

ACCOMMODATIONS & CAMPGROUNDS

Rooms in Napa Valley can go quickly despite high prices; reserving ahead is best. Though Napa is close to the Bay Area and has the advantages of a city, smaller towns will prove more wallet-friendly. Calistoga is a good first choice; the quaint town is a short drive from many wineries and is close to Old Faithful Geyser, Petrified Forest, and Bothe-Napa State Park. It is also home to natural hot-spring spas. The least expensive alternative, as always, is camping, but be prepared for the intense heat which might drive you back to the air-conditioned civilization.

🖾 **Golden Haven Hot Springs Spa and Resort,** 1713 Lake St. (☎942-6793; www.goldenhaven.com), a few blocks from Lincoln Ave. in Calistoga. More of a nice motel than a resort. Large, well-decorated standard-issue rooms with TVs and phones. Rooms with king beds, kitchenettes, jacuzzis, and saunas also available. Mineral swimming pool and hot tub access. No children under 16. Weekends 2-night min. stay, holiday weekends 3-night min stay. Queen $79, with private sauna $145; king $95, with kitchenette $135, with private jacuzzi $185. Nov.-Mar. M-Th $69/$115/$75/$109/$145. ❺

🖾 **Calistoga Inn and Brewery,** 1250 Lincoln Ave. (☎942-4101; www.calistogainn.com), at the corner of Rte. 29 in Calistoga. 18 clean, simple, country inn double- and queen-sized rooms. Microbrewery and restaurant downstairs; the walk home from the pub is just a short stumble upstairs. Shared bathrooms. Restaurant and bar open 11:30am-11pm. Rooms Su-Th $75, F-Sa and holidays $100. ❹

The Calistoga Village Inn & Spa, 1880 Lincoln Ave. (☎942-0991), has clean, basic rooms with cable TV, phones, and private bath. Rooms with jacuzzi available. Heated mineral pools and hot tub, on-site spa, and restaurant. Doubles $79; queen $89, with sitting area $109, with kitchenette and hot tub $159; king with sitting area and Roman tub $139; 2 bedrooms $119. Nov.-Mar. M-Th rates are $10-20 less. 10% discount on spa treatments for guests. Ask about special packages for lodging, spa, and meals. ❹

Tasting 101

While European wines are often known by their region of origin, **California wines** are generally known by the type of grape from which they are made. California **white wines** include Chardonnay, Riesling, and Sauvignon Blanc; **reds** include Pinot Noir, Merlot, Cabernet Sauvignon; and Zinfandel, which is indigenous to California. **Blush or rosé wines** come from red grapes that have their skins removed during fermentation, leaving just a kiss of pink. **Dessert wines** such as Muscat, are made with grapes that have acquired the "noble rot" (botrytis) at the end of picking season, giving them an extra sweet flavor. When tasting, be sure to follow proper procedures. Always start with a white, moving from dry to sweet. Proceed through the reds, which range from lighter to more full-bodied, depending on tannin content. Ideally, you should cleanse your palate between wines with a biscuit, some fromage, or fruit.

Tasting proceeds thus: **stare, sniff, swirl, swallow.** You will probably encounter tasters who slurp their wine and make concerned faces, as though they're trying to cram the stuff up their noses with the back of their tongues. These are serious tasters who are aerating the wine into their mouths to better bring out the flavor. Key words to help you seem more astute during tasting sessions are: dry, sweet, buttery, light, crisp, fruity, balanced, rounded, subtle, rich, woody, and complex.

Bothe-Napa Valley State Park, 3801 Rte. 29 (☎942-4575, reservations 800-444-7275), north of St. Helena. The 50 quiet sites near Ritchey Creek Canyon often fill. Fairly rustic, though there are toilets, fire pits, and picnic tables at each site. Pool $2, under 17 free. Check-in 2pm. Picnic area day use $4. Hot showers 25¢ per 4min. Park open daily 8am-dusk. $16, seniors $10. ❶

FOOD & DRINK

Eating in Wine Country isn't cheap, but the food is usually worth it. Picnics are an inexpensive and romantic option—supplies can be bought at the numerous delis or Safeway stores in the area. Most wineries have shaded picnic grounds, often with excellent views, but most require patronage to use. The **Napa farmer's market,** at Pearl and West St., offers a sampling of the valley's non-alcoholic produce. (☎252-7142. Open daily 7:30am-noon.)

Taylor's Refresher, 933 Main St. (☎963-3486), on Rte. 29 across from the Merryvale Winery, in St. Helena. A roadside stand dishing up big burgers ($4.50-7) and truly phenomenal milkshakes ($4.60) since 1949. Outdoor seating only. Beer and wine served. Open daily 11am-9pm. ❷

First Squeeze Cafe & Juice Bar, 1126 First St. (☎224-6762), in Napa. Offers sandwiches, soups, salads, and smoothies. Try their most popular plate, *huevos rancheros* ($8), or grab a fresh smoothie ($4). Beer and wine available. Breakfast every day until 2pm. Free downtown delivery. Open M-F 7am-3pm, Sa-Su 8am-3pm. ❷

Calistoga Natural Foods and Juice Bar, 1426 Lincoln St. (☎942-5822), in Calistoga. One of a few natural foods stores in the area. Organic juices ($3-5), smoothies ($4.50), sandwiches ($4-6.25), and vegetarian specialties like the Cherry Wrapture ($6.50) and Yummus Hummus wrap ($6.50). Organic groceries also sold. Open M-Sa 9am-6pm. ❷

Armadellos, 1304 Main St. (☎963-8082), in St. Helena. Tasty, vegetarian-friendly Cali-Mexican dishes (mostly $6-13). Beer and wine available. Open Su-Th 11am-9pm, F-Sa 11am-10pm. ❷

WINERIES

There are more than 250 wineries in Napa County, nearly two-thirds of which line Rte. 29 and the Silverado Trail in Napa Valley, home of Wine Country's heavy-weights. Nationally recognized vineyards include Inglenook, Fetzer, and Mondavi. Some wineries have free tastings and some have free tours; all have large selections of bottled wine available for purchase at prices cheaper than in stores. Many wineries offer further reduced rates to visitors who purchase a tasting or become a club member. Style and atmosphere, from architecture down to visitor hospitality, vary from estate to estate; experiencing the larger touristy operations coupled with the smaller-name vineyards adds to the fun. No matter their marketing approach, the wineries listed below (from south to north) do card for underage drinkers; visitors must be 21+ to taste or purchase alcohol.

A good way to begin your Napa Valley experience is with a tour such as the ones offered at **Domaine Carneros** or **Beringer,** or a free tastings class, like the one on Saturday mornings at **Goosecross Cellars,** 1119 State Ln. (☎944-1986; open daily 11am-4pm), in Yountville. Many a well-educated lush has begun a successful career by going to wine school.

🏆 **Kirkland Ranch,** 1 Kirkland Ranch Rd. (☎254-9100), south of Napa off Rte. 29. Reminiscent of a ranch house, this family-operated winery has windows overlooking the production facilities. True to its Country Western style, the winery's walls are adorned with family pictures of cattle-herding cowboys. Tours by appointment. Tastings $5. US military personnel and veterans receive 30% off wine purchases.

Domaine Carneros, 1240 Duhig Rd. (☎257-0101), off Rte. 121 between Napa and Sonoma. Picturesque estate with an elegant terrace modeled after a French *château*. "Be prepared to feel like royalty" is their slogan. Owned by Champagne Taittinger and known for its sparkling wines. The free tour and film (daily every hr. 10:15am-4pm) is a great way to kick off a day of wine tasting. No tastings here, but wines by the glass $5-10 with complimentary *hors d'oeuvres.* Open daily 10am-5:30pm.

YOUNTVILLE & SURROUNDS

Clos Du Val Wine Company, Ltd., 5330 Silverado Trail (☎259-2225; www.closduval.com), north of Oak Knoll Rd., in Yountville. Small, stylish grounds. Tastings $5; price applicable toward wine purchase. Free tours by appointment. Open daily 10am-4:30pm.

Domaine Chandon, 1 California Dr. (☎944-2280 or 800-934-3975; www.chandon.com), in Yountville. Owned by Moët Chandon (the French makers of Dom Perignon), the winery produces 4-5 million bottles of sparkling wine annually. The sleek Visitors Center and manicured gardens evoke a Zen-like meditative spirit. French restaurant on site. 3 tastes for $9, by the glass $4.50-12. Open daily 10am-6pm.

Stag's Leap Wine Cellars, 5766 Silverado Trail (☎944-2020; www.cask23.com). "The tiny vineyard that beat Europe's best," reads the souvenir glass that comes with the portfolio or flights ($30) tasting. Call in advance to arrange a free 1hr. tour that includes a complimentary tasting. Open daily 10am-4pm.

OAKVILLE

Niebaum-Coppola Estate Winery, 1991 St. Helena Hwy. (☎968-1100). Famed film director Francis Ford Coppola and his wife bought the historic 1880 Inglenook Chateau and Niebaum vineyards in 1975. Restoring the estate to production capacity, Coppola also added a family history museum, including memorabilia from his films and his Oscar and Golden Globe statues (free access). $8.50 fee includes 4 tastes and commemorative glass. Regular tours ($20) given daily at 10:30am, 12:30, and 2:30pm; vineyard tours ($20) at 11am daily; Rubicon tours ($45) by reservation Su, Th, and Sa at 1pm. Open daily 10am-5pm.

Robert Mondavi Winery, 7801 Rte. 29 (☎963-9611 or 800-766-3284; www.robertmondavi-winery.com), 8 mi. north of Napa. Massive and touristy, with a beautiful mission-style visitors complex, 2 tasting rooms selling by the glass ($7), and the atmosphere of a luxury summer resort. Offers a variety of tours. The Vineyard and Winery tour takes place daily every hr. 10am-4pm. Reserve 1hr. in advance. Tour $10; includes 3 tastes and *hors d'oeuvres.* The other 6 tours are each given one day per week at 10am or 11am, some seasonally, and cost $30-95 per person. Open daily 9am-5pm.

ST. HELENA & CALISTOGA

Edgewood Estate Winery, 401 St. Helena Hwy. (☎963-7293), in St. Helena. Don't let the lack of cars and crowds outside deter you; a warm, attentive staff and five tastes for $4 can be found within this small, pretty lodge. Garden patio seating perfect for savoring wines by the glass. Open daily 11am-5:30pm.

V. Sattui, 1111 White Ln. (☎963-7774 or 800-799-2337; www.vsattui.com), at Rte. 29, in St. Helena. One of the few wineries in the valley that only sells at its winery. The family-owned operation has a gourmet cheese counter, meat shop, and bakery. Picnic area for customers. Free tastings. Open daily Mar.-Oct. 9am-6pm; Nov.-Feb. 9am-5pm.

Beringer Vineyards, 2000 Main St. (☎963-7115; www.beringer.com), off Rte. 29, in St. Helena. Huge Gothic Revival estate mobbed with tourists. Historic tours of Rhine House mansion every 30min.; includes tasting (10am-5pm; $5, under 21 free). To taste Beringer's better wines, try the reserve room on the 2nd floor of the mansion (samples cost 10% of the wine's price, about $2-10, and will be credited toward wine purchase). Open daily 10am-5pm.

SIGHTS & SHOPPING

Napa's gentle terrain makes for an excellent bike tour. The area is fairly flat, although small bike lanes, speeding cars, and blistering heat can make routes more challenging, especially after a few tastings. The 26 mi. **Silverado Trail** has a wider bike path than Rte. 29. ☙**St. Helena Cyclery,** 1156 Main St., rents bikes.

CALISTOGA. Calistoga is known as the "Hot Springs of the West." Sam Brannan, who first developed the area, meant to make the hot springs the "Saratoga of California," but he misspoke and promised instead to make them "The Calistoga of Saratina." Luckily, history has a soft spot for millionaires; Brannan's dream has come true and Calistoga is now a center for luxurious yet small-scale spas and resorts. His former cottage houses the **Sharpsteen Museum,** 1311 Washington St., which traces the town's development in exhibits designed by a Disney animator. *(Open daily 11am-4pm; in winter noon-4pm. Free.)*

Calistoga's luxuriant mud baths, massages, and mineral showers will feel even more welcome after a hard day of wine-tasting. Be sure to hydrate beforehand; alcohol-thinned blood and intense heat do not mix. A basic package consisting of a mud bath, mineral bath, eucalyptus steam, blanket wrap and 25min. massage costs around $80. Salt scrubs and facials are each about $50. The **Calistoga Village Inn & Spa** gives friendly service. *(☎942-0991. Mud bath treatment $45; 25min. massage $45; 25min. facial $49; ultimate 3hr. package of mud bath treatment, salt scrub, 55min. massage, and mini facial $185.)* For a less pretentious spa, try **Golden Haven.** *(☎942-6793. Mud bath treatment $65, 30min. massage $45, 30min. facial $45.)*

Cooler water is at **Lake Berryessa** *(☎966-2111)*, 20 mi. north of Napa off Hwy. 128, where swimming, sailing, and sunbathing are popular along its 169 mi. shoreline.

OLD FAITHFUL GEYSER OF CALIFORNIA. This steamy wonder should not be confused with its more famous namesake in Wyoming. The geyser regularly jets boiling water 60 ft. into the air; although it "erupts" about every 40min., weather conditions affect its cycle. The ticket vendor will tell you the estimated time of the next spurt. *(1299 Tubbs Ln. off Hwy. 128., 2 mi. outside Calistoga. ☎942-6463. Open daily 9am-6pm; in winter 9am-5pm. $6, seniors $5, ages 6-12 $2, disabled free.)*

MARINE WORLD. This 160-acre Vallejo attraction is an enormous zoo-oceanarium-theme park. It has animal shows and special attractions like the Lorikeet Aviary, the Butterfly Walk, and the Shark Experience. The park was recently purchased by Six Flags. *(Off Rte. 37, 10 mi. south of Napa. ☎643-6722. Vallejo is accessible from San Francisco by BART (☎510-465-2278) and the Blue and Gold fleet (☎415-705-5444). Open Mar.-Aug. Su-Th 10am-8pm, F-Sa 10am-9pm; Sept.-Oct. Su and F-Sa 10am-6pm. $34, seniors $25, ages 4-12 or under 48 inches $17. Parking $6.)*

OTHER SIGHTS. The Petrified Forest, 4100 Petrified Forest Rd., west of Calistoga, was formed over three million years ago when molten lava from a volcano eruption 7 mi. northeast of Mt. St. Helen covered a forested valley and preserved the trees. The quarter-mile trail is wheelchair-accessible. *(☎942-6667. Open daily 10am-6pm; winter 10am-5pm. Free.)* Experience an authentic Venetian gondola ride on Napa River with **Gondola Servizio Napa,** 540 Main St., inside Hatt Market. *(☎257-8495. 30min. private ride $55 per couple; $10 each additional person.)* **Napa Valley Wine Train,** 1275 McKinstry St., offers dining and drinking on board in the style of the early 1900s, traveling from Napa to St. Helena and back. *(☎253-2111 or 800-427-4124; www.winetrain.com. Train ride 3hr. M-F 11am and 6pm; Sa-Su 8:30am, 12:10, 5:30pm. Ticket and meal plans $35-90. Advance reservations and payments required.)*

SEASONAL EVENTS

The annual **Napa Valley Wine Festival,** in which around fifty vintners raise money for public education through dinners, tours, and rare vintage auctions, takes place in early November. Every weekend in February and March, the **Mustard Festival** *(☎259-9029; www.mustardfestival.org)* lines up different musical or theatrical presentations. **Napa Valley Fairgrounds** *(☎942-5111)* hosts a weekend fair in August, with wine tasting, music, juggling, rides, and a rodeo. In the summer, there are free afternoon concerts at **Music-in-the-Park,** downtown at the riverfront. Contact **Napa Parks and Recreation Office** *(☎257-9529)* for more info.

SONOMA VALLEY

Sprawling Sonoma Valley is a quieter alternative to Napa, but home to bigger wineries than the Russian River Valley. Many wineries are on winding side roads rather than a single thoroughfare, making for a more intimate wine-tasting experience. Sonoma Plaza is surrounded by art galleries, novelty shops, clothing stores, and Italian restaurants. Petaluma, west of the Sonoma Valley, has more budget-friendly lodgings than the expensive wine country.

TRANSPORTATION

From San Francisco, take **US 101 North** over the Golden Gate Bridge, then follow Rte. 37 E to Rte. 116 N, which turns into Rte. 121 N and crosses Rte. 12 N to Sonoma. Alternatively, follow US 101 N to Petaluma and cross over to Sonoma by Rte. 116. Driving time from San Francisco is about 1-1½hr. **Route 12** traverses the length of Sonoma Valley, from **Sonoma** through **Glen Ellen** to **Kenwood** in the north. The center of downtown Sonoma is **Sonoma Plaza,** which contains City Hall and the Visitors Center. **Broadway** dead ends at Napa St. in front of City Hall. Numbered streets run north-south. **Petaluma** lies to the west and is connected to Sonoma by **Route 116,** which becomes **Lakeville Street** in Petaluma.

Public Transportation: Buses: Sonoma County Transit (☎576-7433 or 800-345-7433; www.sctransit.com) serves the entire county. Bus #30 runs from **Sonoma** to **Santa Rosa** (daily every 1½hr. 6am-4pm; $2.05, students $1.70, seniors and disabled $1, under 6 free); buses #44 and #48 go to **Petaluma** (M-F; $1.75, students $1.45, seniors and disabled 85¢). A **SummerPass** allows unlimited summer rides for those under 18 ($20) and can be bought at the Safeway on Mendocino Ave. Within Sonoma, **county buses** stop when flagged down at bus stops (M-Su 8am-4:25pm; 95¢, students 75¢, seniors and disabled 45¢). **Golden Gate Transit** (☎541-2000 from Sonoma County or 415-923-2000 from San Francisco, TDD 257-4554) runs buses frequently between **San Francisco** and **Santa Rosa. Volunteer Wheels** (☎800-992-1006) offers door-to-door service for people with disabilities. Call for reservations. Open daily 8am-5pm.

Bike Rental: Sonoma Valley Cyclery, 20093 Broadway (☎935-3377), in Sonoma. Bikes $6 per hr., $25 per day; includes helmet. Open M-Sa 10am-6pm, Su 10am-4pm.

PRACTICAL INFORMATION

Visitor Information: Sonoma Valley Visitors Bureau, 453 E. 1st St. (☎996-1090; www.sonomavalley.com), in Sonoma Plaza. Maps $2. Open June-Oct. daily 9am-7pm; Nov.-May 9am-5pm. **Petaluma Visitors Program,** 800 Baywood Dr. (☎769-0429), at Lakeville St. Open May-Oct. M-F 9am-5:30pm, Sa-Su 10am-6pm; shorter weekend hours in the off-season. The free visitor's guide has listings of restaurants and activities.

Road Conditions: ☎817-1717.

Police: ☎778-4372 in Petaluma, ☎996-3602 in Sonoma.

Hospital: Petaluma Valley, 400 N. McDowell Blvd. (☎781-1111).

Post Office: Sonoma, 617 Broadway (☎996-9311), at Patten St. Open M-F 8:30am-5pm. **Petaluma,** 120 4th St. (☎769-5352). Open M-F 8:30am-5pm, Sa 10am-2pm. **Postal code:** 95476 (Sonoma), 94952 (Petaluma).

ACCOMMODATIONS AND CAMPGROUNDS

Pickings are pretty slim for lodging; rooms are scarce even on weekdays and generally start at $85. Less expensive motels cluster along **US 101** in Santa Rosa and Petaluma. Campers with cars should try the **Russian River Valley.**

Redwood Inn, 1670 Santa Rosa Ave. (☎545-0474), in Santa Rosa. A decent drive from Sonoma. Clean, comfortable rooms and suites with kitchenettes, cable TV, phones, and bath. Singles $55; doubles $65. $5 less in winter. AARP and AAA discounts. ❹

Sugarloaf Ridge State Park, 2605 Adobe Canyon Rd. (☎833-5712), off Rte. 12, north of Kenwood in the Mayacamas mountains. Arranged around a central meadow with flush toilets and running water (but no showers) are 49 sites with tables and fire rings. In summer and fall, take advantage of the sky-watching at Ferguson Observatory inside the park; see www.rfo.org for details. Reserve sites through ReserveAmerica (☎800-444-7275; www.reserveamerica.com). Sites $15, seniors $10; day use $4. No credit cards at the park, but ReserveAmerica accepts MC/V. ❶

San Francisco North/Petaluma KOA, 20 Rainsville Rd. (☎763-1492 or 800-992-2267; www.petalumakoa.com), in Petaluma off the Penngrove Exit. Suburban camp with 300 sites plus a recreation hall with activities, petting zoo, pool, store, laundry facilities, and jacuzzi. Many families. Hot showers. Check-in 1pm. Check-out 11am. 1-week max. tent stay. Reservations recommended. 2-person tent sites $31-35; each additional adult $5, child $3. RVs $38-41. Cabins (sleep 4; no linens) $55-60. ❸

FOOD & DRINK

Fresh produce is seasonally available directly from area farms or at roadside stands and farmer's markets. *Farm Trails* maps are free at the Sonoma Valley Visitors Bureau. Those in the area toward the end of the summer should ask about the ambrosial **crane melon,** a tasty hybrid of fruits grown only on the Crane Farm north of Petaluma. The **Sonoma Market,** 520 W. Napa St., in the Sonoma Valley Center, is an old-fashioned grocery store with deli sandwiches ($5-7) and very fresh produce. (☎996-0563. Open daily 6am-9pm.) The **Fruit Basket,** 18474 Sonoma Hwy., sells inexpensive fruit. (☎996-7433. Open daily 7am-7pm. No credit cards.) All things generic can be found at **Safeway,** 477 W. Napa St. (☎996-0633. Open 24hr.)

🏆 **Sonoma Cheese Factory,** 2 Spain St. (☎996-1931 or 800-535-2855; www.sonoma-jack.com), in Sonoma. Forget the wine for now—take a toothpick and skewer the free cheese samples. You can even watch the cheese-making process in the back room. Sandwiches ($4.50-5.50). Open daily 8:30am-5:30pm. ❷

Maya, 101 E. Napa St. (☎935-3500), at the corner of 1st St. E in Sonoma's Historic Town Square. Brings Yucatan spirit to Sonoma. The festive decor, mouth-watering food, and extensive wine and tequila menu are truly impressive. Entrees $10-20. Occasional live music in summer. Open daily 11am-11pm. ❸

Basque Boulangerie Cafe, 460 First St. E., (☎935-7687), in Sonoma Plaza. This little cafe is always packed; when you fight your way to the counter, you'll see why. Below the wall of freshly baked French breads is a counter filled with tarts, mini-gateaus, and pastries ($2-20). Delicious sandwiches $5.50 for lunch. With 24hr. advance notice they'll even arrange a box lunch ($10.50) for vineyard picnicking. Open daily 7am-6pm. ❸

Murphy's Irish Pub, 464 First St. E. (☎935-0660; www.sonomapub.com), tucked in an alleyway off Sonoma Plaza. A sign here reads, "God created whiskey to keep the Irish from ruling the world." Ponder the geopolitical ramifications over a grilled chicken sandwich ($7.50), fish 'n' chips ($6.25), or other popular pub grub. Extensive beer list. Live music on the outdoor patio almost every night (8pm). Open daily 11am-11pm. ❷

The Vasquez House, 414 First St. E. (☎938-0510), in El Paseo de Sonoma. Inconspicuously tucked behind touristy shops, this historic house hides a library and a minuscule tea room serving coffee, tea, and lemonade (75¢), along with freshly baked "indulgences" ($1). Open Su and W-Sa 1:30-4:30pm. No credit cards. ❶

WINERIES

Sonoma Valley's wineries, near Sonoma and Kenwood, are less touristy but just as elegant as Napa's. As an added bonus, there are more complimentary tastings of current vintages. Take a close look at the *Let's Go* map or bring an extra one along (they're all over the place and free), as there are few winery signs to guide you.

IN & AROUND SONOMA

Gundlach-Bundschu, 2000 Denmark St. (☎938-5277; www.gunbun.com), off 8th St. E. Established in 1858, this is the 2nd oldest winery in Sonoma and the oldest family-owned, family-run winery in the country. Fragrant wines and a setting of pronounced loveliness. In the summer it hosts outdoor events like the Mozart series. Free wine storage cave tours Sa-Su at noon, 1, 2, and 3pm. Free tastings daily 11am-4:30pm.

Buena Vista, 18000 Old Winery Rd. (☎938-1266; www.buenavistawinery.com). Take E. Napa St. from Sonoma Plaza and turn left on Old Winery Rd. The oldest winery in the valley. Famous stone buildings preserved just as Mr. Haraszthy built them in 1857 when he founded the California wine industry. Theater shows July-Sept. Historical presentation and guided tour daily 2pm. All other tours self-guided. Tastings ($5, including glass) daily 10am-5pm.

Ravenswood, 18701 Gehricke Rd. (☎938-1960 or 888-669-4679; www.ravenswood-wine.com), north of Sonoma. "Unwimpy" wines from a surprisingly light-hearted group that says "wine should also be fun." Price of tastings ($4) applicable to wine purchase and well worth it. Tours by appointment daily at 10:30am. Open daily 10am-4:30pm.

GLEN ELLEN

Benziger, 1833 London Ranch Rd. (☎935-4046 or 888-490-2379; www.benziger.com). This winery is known for its big, buttery, rich, and accessible wines. Tourists flock here for the acclaimed 45min. tram ride tour ($10, under 21 $5) through the vineyards, which runs in the summer M-F every hour 11:30am-3:30pm and Sa-Su every half-hour 11:30am-3:30pm. Self-guided tours lead from the parking lot through the vineyards and peacock aviary. Tastings of current vintage free, limited $5, reserves $10. With tram tour, free reserve tasting and 20% discount on purchases. Open daily 10am-5pm.

KENWOOD

Kunde, 10155 Sonoma Hwy. (☎833-5501; www.kunde.com), near Kenwood. The cave tours at Kunde offer respite from the sun. Known for its Chardonnays. Free tastings and cave tours hourly Su and F-Sa 11am-3pm, T-Th 11am. Open daily 10:30am-4:30pm.

Ledson Winery and Vineyards, 7335 Sonoma Hwy. (☎833-2330; www.ledson.com). A relatively new vineyard, known as a Merlot estate, that does not market its wines. Hosts free music concerts every summer weekend noon-4pm. BBQ meal $12. Home to many benefits and shows throughout the year. Tastings ($5) daily 10am-5pm.

Kenwood, 9592 Sonoma Hwy. (☎833-5891; www.kenwoodvineyards.com). One of a few wineries using organic grapes. Known for its Jack London Wolfe wine (they buy the grapes from the author's estate). Free tastings of current vintage, private reserves $5. Free 15min. tours daily 11:30am and 2:30pm. Open daily 10am-4:30pm.

SIGHTS

SONOMA STATE HISTORIC PARK. Within the park, an adobe church stands on the site of the **Mission San Francisco-Solano,** the northernmost and last of the 21 Franciscan missions. It marks the end of the El Camino Real, or the "Royal Road." Built in 1826 by Padre Jose Altimira, the mission has a fragment of the original California Republic flag, the rest of which was burned in the 1906 post-San Francisco earth-

quake fires. *(E. Spain and 1st St., in the northeast corner of town. ☎ 938-1519. Open daily 10am-5pm. $2, children under 17 free. Includes admission to Vallejo's Home, Sonoma Barracks, Petaluma Adobe, Bale Grist Mill, and Benicia Capital Historic State Park.)*

GENERAL VALLEJO'S HOME. The site is often referred to by its Latin name, *Lach-ryma Montis*, meaning "Tears of the Mountain." This "Yankee" home of the famed Mexican leader, who also was mayor of Sonoma and a California senator, is open for tours of the museum, pond, pavilions, and gardens. The grounds are graced with a serene picnic area designed in part by Vallejo and his wife. *(Located on W. Spain St. at Third St. ☎ 938-1519. Open daily 10am-5pm. $2, under 17 free.)*

JACK LONDON STATE PARK. Around the turn of the 20th century, hard-drinking and hard-living Jack London, author of *The Call of the Wild* and *White Fang*, bought 1400 acres here, determined to create his dream home. London's hopes were frustrated when the estate's main building, the Wolf House, was destroyed by arsonists in 1913. London died three years after the fire and is buried in the park, his grave marked by a volcanic boulder intended for the construction of his house. The nearby **House of Happy Walls,** built by London's widow in fond remembrance of him, is now a two-story museum devoted to the writer. The park's scenic half-mile **Beauty Ranch Trail** passes the lake, winery ruins, and quaint cottages. There are many longer trails that provide a greater challenge. Take **Lake Trail** (1 mi.) from the parking lot to the lake. There, follow **Mountain Trail** (½ mi.) to a lovely vista point. Continue on Mountain Trail all the way to the Park Summit (2½ mi.) or circle around Woodcutter's Meadow on the **Fallen Bridge Trail** (1¼ mi.) to return. *(Take Hwy. 12 4 mi. north from Sonoma to Arnold Ln. and follow signs. ☎ 938-5216. Park open daily 9:30am-7pm; in winter 9:30am-5pm. Museum open daily 10am-5pm.)* **Sonoma Cattle and Napa Valley Trail Rides** also amble through the fragrant forests. *(☎ 996-8566. 2hr. ride $55.)*

SEASONAL EVENTS

Sonoma Plaza hosts festivals and fairs nearly every summer weekend. **Kenwood** heats up **July 4** for the Kenwood Footrace, a tough 7½ mi. course through hills and vineyards. A chili cook-off and the **World Pillow Fighting Championships** continue the party. Eager contenders straddle a metal pipe over a mud pit and beat each other with wet pillows.

SOUTH OF SAN FRANCISCO

PALO ALTO

AREA CODE	Palo Alto's area code is ☎ 650.

Dominated by the 8000-acre Stanford University campus, Palo Alto offers pristine landscape and awe-inspiring architecture that have helped the university rise to international acclaim. Stanford's perfectly groomed grounds, tall palm trees, sparkling lake, and Spanish mission-style buildings show off the almost disturbingly picturesque side of the college in the west coast sun. The city that Stanford calls home is an equally manicured downtown strip of high quality restaurants, bookstores, and boutiques. Its nightlife caters to students and suburbanites, while weekday happy hours help silicon singles wind down.

TRANSPORTATION

Palo Alto is 35 mi. southeast of San Francisco, near the southern shore of the Bay. From the north, take **US 101 South** toward San Jose. Take the Oregon Expressway/Embarcadero Exit. Follow Embarcadero Rd. westbound, which will lead to the Stanford University campus. Alternatively, motorists from San Francisco can split off onto **Interstate 280 (Junípero Serra Highway)** for a slightly longer but more scenic route. Take I-280 south toward San Jose until the Page Mill Road Exit. You will travel several miles through an industrial park area and eventually hit the Stanford University Campus.

The **Palo Alto Transit Center,** on University Ave., serves local and regional buses and trains. (☎323-6105. Open M-F 5am-12:30pm.) A train-only depot lies on California Ave., 1¼ mi. south of the transit center. (☎326-3392. Open M-F 5:30am-12:30pm.) The transit center connects to points north via **San Mateo County buses** and to Stanford via the free **Marguerite Shuttle.**

Trains: CalTrain, 95 University Ave. (☎800-660-4287), at Alma St. Street-side stop at Stanford Stadium on Embarcadero Rd. To **San Francisco** ($4.50) and **San Jose** ($3). Half-price for seniors and disabled. Operates M-F 5am-midnight, departing 10 and 40min. past the hour (service on weekends is suspended pending construction).

Buses: SamTrans (☎800-660-4287). To downtown **San Francisco** ($3.50, under 17 $1.50) and **San Francisco International Airport** ($1.25). To reach Palo Alto from San Francisco, take **SamTrans** express bus KX from the Transbay Terminal in San Francisco to the Stanford Shopping Center. Operates daily 6am-10pm departing every 30min. on the hour.

Taxis: Yellow Cab (☎321-1234 or 800-595-1222). 24hr. $2.50 per mi.

Car Rental: Budget, 4230 El Camino Real (☎424-0684, reservations 800-527-0700; www.budget.com). From $39.99 per day. Unlimited mileage. Must be at least 21 with credit card. Under 25 surcharge $20 per day. Open M-Sa 7am-6pm, Su 9am-5pm.

Bike Rental: Campus Bike Shop, 551 Salvatierra Ln. (☎723-9300), across from Stanford Law School. A bike allows you to take advantage of Palo Alto's flat boulevards and rolling hills. $15 per day, $20 overnight, helmets $3 (under 18 free). Major credit card or $150-300 cash deposit. Open M-F 9am-5pm, Sa 9am-3pm.

ORIENTATION & PRACTICAL INFORMATION

The pristine lawns of residential Palo Alto are not easily distinguished from the stylized campus of Stanford University. Despite its name, **University Avenue,** the main thoroughfare off US 101, belongs much more to the town than to the college. Cars coming off US 101 onto University Ave. pass very briefly through **East Palo Alto,** a community incorporated in 1983 after Palo Alto and Menlo Park had already annexed most of their revenue-producing districts. East Palo Alto once had one of the highest violent crime rates in the nation. The town has cleaned up the area, and it has grown safer in recent years, but when you cross the city limits, you'll still find a striking contrast with the immaculate tree-lined lawns of Palo Alto.

Stanford University spreads out from the west end of University Ave. Abutting University Ave. and running northwest-southeast through town is **El Camino Real** (part of Rt. 82). From there, University Ave. turns into Palm Dr., which accesses the heart of Stanford's campus, the **Main Quad.**

Visitor Information: Palo Alto Chamber of Commerce, 122 Hamilton Ave. (☎324-3121), between Hude and Alta St. Open M-F 9am-5pm. **Stanford University Information Booth** (☎723-2560), across from Hoover Tower in Memorial Auditorium. Visitors can obtain parking passes, maps, and information about the university. Free student-led 1hr. **tours** depart daily 11am and 3:15pm. Open daily 8am-5pm.

Police: 275 Forest Ave. (☎329-2406, after hours 329-2413).

Internet Access: Palo Alto Main Library, 1213 Newell Rd. (☎329-2436). Open M-F 10am-9pm, Sa 10am-6pm, Su 1-5pm. **Downtown Branch,** 270 Forest Ave. (☎329-2641). Open Tu-F 11am-6pm. Free.

Post Office: Main Office, 2085 E. Bayshore Rd. (☎800-275-8777). Open M-F 8am-5pm. **Postal code:** 94303. **Hamilton Station,** 380 Hamilton Ave. (☎323-2650). **Postal code:** 94301.

ACCOMMODATIONS

Motels are plentiful along **El Camino Real,** but rates can be steep. Generally, rooms are cheaper farther away from Stanford. More reasonably priced accommodations may be found farther north toward Redwood City. Many Palo Alto motels cater to business travelers and are actually busier on weekdays than on weekends.

Coronet Motel, 2455 El Camino Real (☎326-1081), at California St. Clean, spacious rooms with big windows, cable TV, pool, telephone, private baths, and kitchenette. Under new management and cheap considering its proximity to Stanford. Check-out 11am. Singles $55; doubles $60. $5 charge per person for parties that exceed two people. Weekly rates available. AmEx/D/MC/V. ❷

Hidden Villa Ranch Hostel (HI-AYH), 26870 Moody Rd. (☎949-8648), about 10 mi. southwest of Palo Alto in the Los Altos Hills. The first hostel on the Pacific Coast (opened in 1937); functions as a working ranch and farm in a wilderness preserve. Recent renovations have completely rebuilt dorms and extended living, kitchen, and dining rooms. Heated cabins and 35 beds. Dorm, family, and private rooms available. Reception 8am-noon and 4-9:30pm. Reservations required for weekends and groups. Open Sept.-May. Dorms $15, non-members $18, children $7.50; private cabins $30-42. ❶

FOOD & DRINK

▨ **Café Borrone,** 1010 El Camino Real (☎327-0830), adjacent to Kepler's Books in Menlo Park. Bustling, brasserie-style cafe spills out onto a large patio. Heralded best cafe by the *Palo Alto Weekly,* Borrone serves freshly baked bread, sinful *gateaux* ($2-4), coffee drinks, Italian sodas, wine ($5-6 per glass), and beers ($3.75 per pint). Check the chalkboard for daily specials, or choose from an array of delicious salads ($3.75-8.75), sandwiches ($5.50-9.50), and quiches ($5.95). Open M-Th 8am-11pm, F-Sa 8am-midnight, Su 8am-5pm. AmEx/D/MC/V. ❷

▨ **Blue Chalk Cafe,** 630 Ramona St. (☎326-1020). Started for a project by a Stanford Business School student, this elegant restaurant became an instant hit with both students and Silicon-professionals. Intimate dining atmosphere perfect for dates. Lively pool and bar areas perfect for a night out. Free pool noon-4pm with lunch purchase. California cuisine includes shrimp and crabcakes ($9.25), grilled salmon, and steaks ($18.95). Popular appetizers include calamari ($9) and range from $8-10. Open for lunch M-F 11am-2:30pm and dinner M-Sa 5-10pm. Bar open M-Sa 11am-1:30am. Happy Hour M-F 3-7pm. AmEx/D/MC/V. ❷

Pluto's, 482 University Ave. (☎853-1556). Out-of-this-world cafeteria-style restaurant. Design your own salad from heaps of fresh fixings ($4.80) or choose from grilled meats and veggies to fill a sandwich ($5-6). The large selection of freshly baked desserts include s'mores, turnovers, and brownies ($1.65). Open M-Th 11am-10pm, F 11am-11pm, Sa 11:30am-11pm, Su 11:30am-10pm. AmEx/MC/V. ❶

Mango Café, 435 Hamilton Ave. (☎325-3229), 1 block east of University Ave. Reggae music and Caribbean cuisine. Seriously spicy Jamaican "jerked joints" ($6) and tropical smoothies ($3.50). Veggie options. Entrees range from $8-12, lunch specials from $5-10. Delicious bread pudding $3. Open M-Sa 11:30am-2:30pm and 6-10pm. AmEx/MC/V. ❷

Miyake, 140 University Ave. (☎323-9449). If you had to judge on decor alone, you'd never know this place was a sushi joint. Come to party on weekends when the chefs are barking orders, the waiters are screaming across the restaurant, and the tables are packed with students pounding sake bombs. Customers grab veggie rolls ($2) or local abalone ($2.50) off boats sailing in the moat around the bar. Open daily 11:30am-10pm. MC/V. ❷

Gelato Classico, 435 Emerson St. (☎327-1317). Join Stanford students for Italian ices and sorbets ($2.45-4.50), shakes, and sundaes ($4.50), and an espresso bar. Flavors include burgundy cherry, vanilla bean, chocolate chip, passion fruit, and raspberry. Huge banana splits for $6.50. Open M-Th 11am-10:30pm, F 11:30am-11pm, Sa noon-11pm, Su noon-9:30pm. Discount with any student ID. ATM available for 45¢. No credit cards. ❶

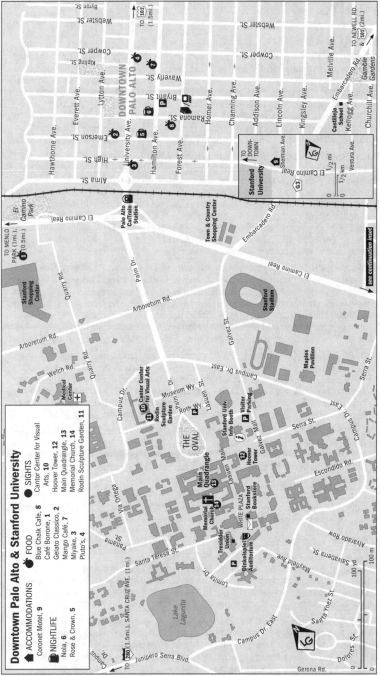

Downtown Palo Alto & Stanford University

◆ ACCOMMODATIONS
Coronet Motel, **9**

▮ NIGHTLIFE
Nola, **6**
Rose & Crown, **5**

● FOOD
Blue Chalk Cafe, **8**
Café Borrone, **1**
Gelato Classico, **2**
Mango Café, **7**
Miyake, **3**
Pluto's, **4**

● SIGHTS
Cantor Center for Visual Arts, **10**
Hoover Tower, **12**
Main Quadrangle, **13**
Memorial Church, **14**
Rodin Sculpture Garden, **11**

SIGHTS

STANFORD UNIVERSITY

Undoubtedly Palo Alto's main tourist attraction, the secular, co-educational **Stanford University** was founded in 1885 by railroad magnates Jane and Leland Stanford to honor their son, who died of typhoid at age 16. The Stanfords loved Spanish colonial mission architecture and collaborated with **Frederick Law Olmsted,** designer of New York City's Central Park, to create a red-tiled campus of uncompromising beauty. (UC Berkeley students sometimes refer to Stanford as "The World's Largest Taco Bell.") The beautiful school has produced such eminent conservatives as **Chief Justice William Rehnquist,** and the campus has been dubbed "a hotbed of social rest."

MAIN QUADRANGLE. Continually constructed and reconstructed between 1887 and 1991, the quad is the oldest part of campus and the site of most undergraduate classes. The walkways are dotted with diamond-shaped, gold-numbered stone tiles that mark the locations of time capsules collected by each year's graduating class. The quad serves as the home for numerous Stanford celebrations including opening convocation and graduation, as well as the "Full Moon on the Quad," a ceremony when the freshmen get kissed by seniors at midnight during the first full moon of the academic year. (Serra St., between Lasuen and Lomita Mall. Free tours at 11:15am and 3:15pm depart from Information Booth in Memorial Auditorium.)

MEMORIAL CHURCH. Memorial Church was built in the early 1900s by Jane Stanford in memory of her husband, the founder of the university. This non-denominational gold shrine has a beautiful display of stained glass windows and glittering mosaic walls similar to those of an Eastern Orthodox church. The church presents over 20,000 shades of color in the tiles, with 34 shades of pink alone in the cheeks of the 4 angels in the dome. (Just south of the Main Quad, at Escondido Mall and Duena. ☎ 723-3469; http://religiouslife.stanford.edu/memorial_church. Open M-F 8am-5pm. Free tours F 2pm.)

HOOVER TOWER. Completed in 1941 to celebrate the university's 50th anniversary, the tower is part of the Hoover Institution on War, Resolution, and Peace, a policy research center. The top tower is a carillon of 48 bells, and the tower's observation deck provides stunning views of campus, East Bay, and San Francisco. (East of the Main Quad, near Serra St., between Lasuen and Galvez Mall. ☎ 723-2053. Open daily 10am-4:30pm. Closed during finals and academic breaks. Adults $2, seniors and under 13 $1.)

IRIS AND B. GERALD CANTOR CENTER FOR VISUAL ARTS. The Visual Arts Center displays its eclectic collection of painting and sculpture for free. The center has 27 galleries, including highlights such as Renaissance paintings, Rodin sculptures, and a respectable modern art collection. (328 Lomita Dr., at Museum Way off Palm Dr. ☎ 723-4177. Open W and F-Su 11am-5pm, Th 11am-8pm.)

RODIN SCULPTURE GARDEN. The extensive garden contains a stunning bronze cast of *Gates of Hell,* among other larger figures. It's an ideal spot to enjoy a picnic lunch. (At Museum Way and Lomita Dr. ☎ 723-4177. Free tours Sa-Su 2pm.)

NIGHTLIFE

Palo Alto may not host the wild nightlife found in San Francisco, but it still has a few bars and hotspots that are great for sitting back and having a few beers. The upscale aspirations of Palo Alto force visitors to throw out a few extra bucks for the night, but welcome visitors, Stanford students, and Silicon Valley professionals alike.

🔳 **Nola,** 535 Ramona St. (☎328-2722). There is a fiesta everyday in this vibrant, super-popular bar. Colorful strings of lights and patio windows opening onto a cool, courtyard dining area create a hybrid Mediterranean-Mexican feel. Crowd of mostly young professionals. Late-night menu offers quesadillas ($7-9), crabcakes ($7), and gumbo ($7) to accompany your cocktails ($6-7). Open daily 5:30pm-2am.

Rose & Crown, 547 Emerson St. (☎327-7673). This low-key pub with an Ace jukebox is good for throwing darts or quietly nursing a Guinness. British bar menu includes fish and chips ($7-9), bangers and mash ($9), and ploughman's lunch ($7). Happy Hour M-F 4-6pm. 16 oz. draft beer $3. Weekly entertainment includes Su Jazz night (7:30pm) and M comedy showcase (9pm). Organize a team for Tu Quiz Night on general knowledge, sports, entertainment, and famous faces. Open M-F 11:30am-1:30am, Sa noon-1:30am, Su 1pm-1:30am.

Blue Chalk Cafe, See **Food** (p. 262).

ENTERTAINMENT

The Stanford-run *Palo Alto Daily* and local *Palo Alto Weekly* both contain listings of what's going on all over town. The free *Metro* and *Palo Alto Daily News*, available in downtown sidewalk boxes, also publish the local lowdown.

Dinkelspiel Auditorium (☎723-2448), at El Camino Real and Embarcadero. Called "the Dink" by locals, the auditorium holds classical concerts and other events coordinated through the Tressider Union ticket office (☎725-2787). Open M-F 10am-5pm, Sa noon-4pm.

Stanford Theater, 221 University Ave. (☎324-3700). Dedicated to Hollywood's "Golden Age." Devotes exhibition seasons to directors and stars, such as Billy Wilder and Cary Grant. The Wurlitzer organ plays before and after the 7:30pm show and accompanies silent films every W. Double features $6, seniors $4, under 18 $3.

The Lively Arts at Stanford (☎723-2551; http://livelyarts.stanford.edu), brings semi-big name concerts to Frost Amphitheater and Memorial Auditorium every year, usually at discount prices. The Memorial also hosts movies on Su in term-time. Adults $3, students $2.

Tresidder Memorial Union (events recording ☎723-0336, tickets 723-4317, info 723-4311; http://tickets.stanford.edu). Tickets for Stanford events. Open M-F 10am-5pm, Sa noon-4pm.

Stanford Department of Athletics (☎723-1021). Open M-F 9am-4pm.

SHOPPING

🎖 **Bell's Bookstore,** 536 Emerson St. (☎323-7822). Family-run since 1935, Bell's is a favorite among locals and Stanfordites. It's packed floor-to-ceiling with old, new, and rare books arranged by subject. Selection includes a large range of hardback and out-of-print texts. Open M-Th 9:30am-5:30pm, F 9:30am-9pm, Sa 9:30am-5pm. MC/V.

Stanford Bookstore, White Plaza (☎329-1217; www.stanfordbookstore.com), just behind the main quad. The main campus bookstore, complete with Barnes & Noble-style cafe. This is the place to stock up on your Stanford t-shirts and other insignia products. Open in winter M-F 7:45am-9pm, Sa 9am-6pm, Su 11am-6pm; in summer M-Th 8am-8pm, F 8am-7pm, Sa 9am-6pm, Su 11am-6pm. AmEx/D/MC/V.

Stanford Shopping Center (☎617-8585 or 800-772-9332; www.stanfordshop.com), between campus and El Camino Real. High-street designer clothes, department stores, speciality food shops, and restaurants line shady avenues. Doesn't cater to budget travelers, but its patio cafes are perfect for people-watching and its avenues great for window-shopping. Coveting is still free. Open M-F 10am-9pm, Sa 10am-7pm, Su 11am-6pm. Hours of department stores and restaurants may vary.

HALF MOON BAY, RTE. 1 & GREATER SAN MATEO

South of San Francisco, the Pacific Coast Highway **(Rte. 1)** stretches along the coast, dramatically winding its way through mountains and along cliffs. Under the cloaks of fog and night, Half Moon Bay (HMB), the largest beach hub on the coast, was once a premier spot for rumrunners and subsequent speakeasies in the 20s. Many locations still boast of their former romantic transgressions.

Simply driving 60 mi. or so down the coast, taking in the stunning views, makes for a spectacular daytrip. Spending the night in quiet Half Moon Bay, where the views are stunning and the fire-water is (thankfully) legal, allows more time to explore the isolated, sandy beaches scattered along this expanse of shore. Although the beaches are famous among the international surfer set for their waves (most notably "Mavericks," near Pillar Point Harbor), the water is usually too cold for swimming and the sands prove much more welcoming to picnickers, sunbathers, dogwalkers, and kite-fliers. Bikers should take advantage of the Coastal Trail, a paved 3 mi. path along the bluffs above the Half Moon Bay city beaches. Since Half Moon Bay maintains an intimate small-town feel, most establishments operate under a mantra of closing when the people stop coming; the times listed may be approximations.

The suburban sprawl of **Burlingame, San Mateo, Redwood City,** and **Silicon Valley** (the north tip of the valley is at the southernmost end of San Mateo) is, unlike Half Moon Bay, not necessarily worth an exclusive visit. If you do, however, find yourself swimming in suburbia instead of in the ocean, there are some sights to see.

AREA CODE	Half Moon Bay's area code is ☎650.

TRANSPORTATION

Driving the scenic route down PCH (Rte. 1, called Cabrillo Highway in San Mateo County), which winds along the coast from San Francisco to **Big Basin Redwoods State Park,** is arguably the only way to travel this area. Any other path is not nearly as beautiful nor worth your time (even if it is a bit shorter). If you are in such a hurry that a bit of extra time *is* worth giving up the best of California scenery, choose Rte. 92 which runs from US 101 in San Francisco straight into Half Moon Bay. Know, however, that the only views 92 has to offer are of strip malls and parking lots. Once in HMB, traveling by sneaker may lead to worn-out soles, as SamTrans services the area only somewhat successfully.

From Half Moon Bay, Rte. 92 reaches inland, while Rte. 84 will get you there from further south; I-280 and Rte. 101 both run roughly north to south. Once there, you'll find a smattering of farmland, majestic redwoods, and stretches of endless suburbs.

Public Transportation: San Mateo County Transit (SamTrans), 945 California Dr. (☎508-6455 or 800-660-4287; www.samtrans.com). Bus #17 and 294 service Half Moon Bay on a limited basis. #17 runs along the coast from El Granada to Half Moon Bay from 6am-5:30pm. #294 runs from Hillsdale to Linda Mar Park-and-Ride; San Mateo to Pacifica M-F from 5:30am-7:30pm, Sa-Su only from Linda Mar to Half Moon Bay. Bus route maps are available at CalTrain and BART stations; call for specific schedules. Adults $1.25, seniors and disabled 60¢, ages 5-17 75¢, under 5 free. Monthly pass $40, seniors and disabled $18, ages 5-17 $22.

Bike Rental: The Bike Works, 20 Stone Pine Ctr. (☎726-6708), off Main St. Friendly staff will set you up with a mountain bike ($7 per hr., $35 per day; helmet included). Open M-F 10am-6pm, Sa 10am-5pm, Su 11am-4pm. AmEx/MC/V.

ORIENTATION & PRACTICAL INFORMATION

From Rte. 1, turn away from the coast onto the Kelly Ave. ramp to reach Main St., Half Moon Bay's main strip, which harbors a handful of cafes, boutiques, and local art galleries. Rte. 92 intersects Main St. just north of the center of town. Taking Kelly Ave. toward the ocean brings you to the southernmost of Half Moon Bay's four dune-strewn beaches, all of which are connected by a paved path for walkers and bikers. More beach- and water-related sights lie north and south of Half Moon Bay proper.

Visitor Information: Half Moon Bay Coastside Chamber of Commerce and Visitors Bureau, 520 Kelly Ave. (☎726-8380). An amiable staff, lots of brochures, and local bus service maps sit in a Victorian house just east of Rte. 1. on Kelly Ave. Open M-F 9am-4pm. For weather conditions, tide information, and other Half Moon Bay happenings, visit www.half-moonbaychamber.org. **San Mateo County Convention and Visitors Bureau,** Seabreeze Plaza, 111 Anza Blvd., #410 (☎800-288-4748). Get off Rte. 101 at the Broadway exit, follow signs to Airport Blvd., take a left, and follow road around to Anza Blvd. Turn left; it's the mirrored building on your right, across the street from the Embassy Hotel. Near SFO, this sleek office offers info on the Central Coast and San Francisco area, including brochures and helpful maps. Open M-F 8:30am-5pm. **San Mateo County Parks and Recreation Department,** James V. Fitzgerald Marine Life Reserve, P.O. Box 451, Moss Beach (☎728-3584), off Rte. 1, 7 mi. north of Half Moon Bay. The department distributes information about exposed marine wildlife and other issues related to tidepooling. Open daily dawn-dusk.

Police: Half Moon Bay: 537 Kelly Ave. (☎726-8288). **San Mateo General Information:** ☎522-7710.

Emergency: ☎911.

Internet Access: Half Moon Bay Library, 620 Correas St. (☎726-2316), off Main St. Free Internet. Open M-W 10am-8pm, Th 1-8pm, F 10am-6pm, Sa 10am-5pm, Su 1-5pm.

Post Office: Half Moon Bay: 500 Stone Pine Rd., at Main St. Open M-F 8:30am-5pm, Sa 8:30am-noon. **Postal code:** 94019. **San Mateo:** 1630 S. Delaware St. Open M-F 8:30am-5pm, Sa 8:30am-12:30pm. **Postal code:** 94402.

ACCOMMODATIONS & CAMPGROUNDS

With twenty B&Bs, four motels, two hotels, a couple of hostels, a handful of campgrounds, and a Ritz Carlton, Half Moon Bay's accommodations cater to all income tax brackets. Besides this handful of *Let's Go* picks, there is a Holiday Inn Express for those who seek comfort and no-frills familiarity, and a smattering of beautiful campgrounds.

San Benito House, 356 Main St. (☎726-3425). Your money will be well spent on one of San Benito House's 12 airy, pristine rooms, each themed and impeccably decorated with antique furnishings. Most rooms have private baths with claw-footed bathtubs. Communal access to gleaming hall showers and a sauna. Continental breakfast included; guests receive 10% off at dinner Th-Su in the acclaimed restaurant downstairs. Try the delicious award-winning bread. Downstairs bar open daily 4pm-closing (usually around midnight). Check-in after 3pm. Check-out 11am. Reservations recommended. Rooms $75, with private bath $125, with living room suite $160. AmEx/MC/V. ❷

HI-AYH Pigeon Point Lighthouse Hostel, on Rte. 1 (☎879-0633), 6 mi. south of Pescadero. SamTrans will only take you to Pescadero, so bring a car, bike, or comfortable sneakers. Amazing views. 4 houses, each with a big, homey common room and fully equipped kitchen. 53 beds. Chores required. Amiable groundskeeper. Come during Apr. for spectacular whale-watching. $1 linen rental. Reception 7:30-10am and 4:30-9:30pm. Check-in 4:30pm. Check-out 10am. Lockout 10am-4:30pm. Curfew and quiet time 11pm. Reservations recommended. Phone reservations 5:30-10pm. Wheelchair-accessible. Dorms $15, non-members $18; extra $15 for 2-person room. MC/V. ❶

Francis State Beach Campground, 95 Kelly Ave. (☎726-8820), on Francis Beach at Half Moon Bay State Beach. 57 campsites (some exposed beachside) all with firepits and picnic tables. Park rangers often organize Sa campfires in peak season and sell firewood for the do-it-yourself types. Clean bathrooms. Hot showers 25¢ per 2min. 7-night max. stay in summer (June 1-Sept. 30); 15-night max. stay off-season. Check-out noon. Wheelchair-accessible (there's even a beach wheelchair available). No reservations. Day use of beach (open 8am-sunset) $4, seniors $3. Tent and RV sites $3, seniors $1. Hiker and biker sites $1 per person; max. stay 1 night. No credit cards. ❶

Costanoa, 2001 Rossi Rd. (☎879-1100, reservations ☎262-7848; www.costanoa.com), on the east side of Rte. 1, 25 mi. south of Half Moon Bay, between Pigeon Pt. and Año Nuevo. The Ritz Carlton of roughing it. If rugged ain't your style, but you still want to taste the great outdoors, Costanoa offers "the best of outdoor living in comfortable stylish surroundings." All accommodations include access to dry sauna and showers with heated floors. Guests also (includes heated mattress) $95-130; lodges $205-240. AmEx/D/MC/V. ❷

HI-AYH Point Montara Lighthouse Hostel (☎728-7177), on Lighthouse Point, at Rte. 1 and 16th St., 25 mi. south of San Francisco and 4 mi. north of Half Moon Bay. SamTrans #294 stops 1 block north of the hostel, though bus drivers will often drop you off at the lighthouse if you ask. Weary travelers will revel in this isolated 45-bed facility with 2 kitchens and serene surroundings. Ask for a room with a view of the coast. Laundry ($2 per load). Reception 7:30-10am and 4:30-9:30pm. Lockout 10am-4:30pm. Curfew 11pm (gate locks). Make reservations by phone well in advance for weekends, groups, and private rooms. Wheelchair-accessible. Members $17, non-members $20, children $12; $15 extra for private rooms. MC/V. ❶

FOOD & DRINK

Despite the area's remote feel, a surprising number of restaurants cater to hungry travelers. Those looking for late-night snacks or planning to picnic along the coast (a highly recommended option) can find a 24hr. **Safeway,** 70 N. Cabrillo Hwy., at the junction of Rte. 1 and 92. (☎726-1143. AmEx/D/MC/V.)

🍽 **3-Zero,** 8850 Cabrillo Hwy. (Hwy. 1) (☎728-1411; www.3-zero.com), at the Half Moon Bay Airport. Watch planes take off while you stay grounded with your hearty home style breakfast ($4-8). *HMB Review* has called it the "Best Breakfast on the Coast" for 7 consecutive years. Menu and owner come equipped with wit and charm. Also serves "launch" (lunch, $5.50-8). Visit website for discounts and coupons. Open daily 7am-3pm. MC/V. ❶

🍽 **Moon Juice,** Stone Pine Ctr. (☎712-1635), off Main St. Turn right off Rte. 92, head south on Main St., and Stone Pine Ctr. is on your left. Under new family management, this little juice and smoothie store will brighten your morning with a store-window cockatoo and softly-playing CNN. Come for lunch, dinner, or snacks. Be sure to get a dose of wheatgrass for a moon-like glow. Juices $1.50-6. AmEx/D/MC/V. ❶

The Flying Fish Grill (☎712-1125), at Main St. and Rte. 92, by Tom and Pete's Market. This small roadside cafe serves inexpensive, fresh local seafood. Famous fish tacos $3-4.35. Other oceanic offerings $7-14. Take-out available. Open Tu-Su 11:30am-8:30pm. MC/V. ❷

Half Moon Bay Brewing Co., 390 Capistrano Rd. (☎728-2739; www.hmbbrewingco.com), at the edge of Pillar Point Harbor in Princeton, half a mile from Mavericks. One of Half Moon Bay's singles hotspots. Fresh seafood $14-20; pub grub $8.50-13; and micro-brewed beers (pints $4.25). Indoor and outdoor ocean-view seating. Check out the Grateful Dead stained-glass window. Live music and dancing Su 4-8pm. Open daily 11:30am-closing (Su-Th around 9:30pm, F-Sa around 10pm, bar stays open 1hr. later). AmEx/D/MC/V. ❷

MCoffee, 522 Main St. (☎726-6241). After being established as "McCoffee's" for 17 years, MCoffee was sued by McDonald's for infringing upon its trademarked name. Settling out of court meant a little touchup paint over the first "c" on the store's sign. Come here for a snack that hasn't been deep-fried by 14-year-olds. Wireless Internet access. Sandwiches $5-6; coffee menu $1-3.50. Open M-F 6am-5pm, Sa 8am-6pm, Su 9am-6pm. AmEx/D/MC/V. ❶

DOWNTOWN SAN MATEO

Jeffrey's, 42 South B St. (☎348-8698). Somewhere between a dive and a nice family restaurant comes this hearty independent hamburger joint. Try an avocado burger ($5.50) or another pleasantly cheap menu item ($4.30-7). Open daily 11am-9pm. MC/V. ❶

Taqueria La Cumre, 28 North B St. (☎344-8989). This restaurant, which also has a San Francisco branch, has won the "best burrito" award in every major Bay Area magazine. Filling and tasty Mexican meals for under $8.50. Be prepared for long lines at lunchtime. Open Su-Th 11am-9pm, F-Sa 11am-10pm. MC/V. ❶

PESCADERO

Duarte's Tavern, 202 Stage Rd. (☎879-0464; www.duartestavern.com), at Pescadero Rd. As for restaurants in Pescadero, this is it (and has been since 1894). With a strong focus on local seafood and produce (very local), their menu extends through breakfast

($5.25-10), lunch (sandwiches $3.50-10, entrees $15.50-17.50), and dinner (surf or turf $16.50-22.50). Famed for their artichoke items and homemade olallieberry pies. Open daily 7am-9pm. AmEx/MC/V. ❸

LA HONDA

Apple Jack's, 8790 Rte. 84 (☎747-0331), at Entrada Way. Boasting a pool table, ping-pong, pinball, Pac Man, and the same creaky floorboards since 1879, this bar serves as both neighborhood hangout and town square since it is really all there is to La Honda. Though a true remnant of the Old West, they do know how to kick it—on F and Sa nights, live bands from rock to reggae bring down the house. Talk to the oldtimers at the bar who will gladly oblige you with tales of La Honda's bygone days. Beer $2.50. Open in summer M-F noon-2am, Sa-Su 10am-2am; in winter M-F 4pm-2am, Sa-Su 10am-2am. ❶

SIGHTS

Wide, sandy, and fairly deserted **state beaches** dot the coast along Cabrillo Highway (Rte. 1) in San Mateo County. Each state beach charges $2, a fare which covers admission to *all* state parks for the entire day—so hold onto your receipt if you get one. All beaches have parking lots and restrooms and are open daily 8am-sunset. Unless otherwise noted, leashed dogs are allowed on the beaches. Keep your eyes peeled for unmarked beaches along the coast; they're often breathtaking, crowdless spots with free parking. The water is too chilly for most swimmers, and surfers never venture out without full-body wetsuits. Rip currents and undertows are frequent, so be careful if you choose to brave the cold. The creeks near these beaches are often contaminated—signs will be posted at entrances to warn you, but simply staying out of them is generally a good idea. All coastal spots make for incredible sunsets, so take your pick.

GRAY WHALE COVE BEACH. This stunning (and startling) beach, shielded by high bluffs from the highway above, used to be one of the more popular *private* nude beaches in the Bay Area. Now legendary as the first "clothing-optional" (as they say in northern California) *state* beach, Gray Whale Cove offers some of the most gorgeous and not quite so gorgeous views on the coast. *(12 mi. south of San Francisco, in Devil's Slide—the curvy, cliffy stretch of Rte. 1 a few mi. south of Pacifica. You'll know it by the large parking lot on your left; it's the only one in the Slide—the beach is across the street. Take SamTrans bus #1L. Open daily 8am-sunset. $2.)*

HALF MOON BAY STATE BEACH. Lining the coast next to town, **Half Moon Bay State Beach** is actually composed of several smaller beaches strung together. The **Coastal Trail,** a paved path perfect for joggers, bikers, and dogwalkers, runs 3 mi. along all four beaches and then continues north. At the end of Kelly Ave., **Francis Beach** lies closest to town and is the southernmost of the four beaches. Although it's the least scenic of the bunch, it is the only one with a campsite (**Francis Beach State Campground,** p. 267), a guard station that operates year-round, and wheelchair-accessibility. To the north of Francis, the wider and prettier **Venice Beach** is down a flight of stairs at the end of a dirt road leading from Venice Blvd. off Rte. 1. **Dunes Beach** and **Roosevelt Beach** are down a short but steep trail at the end of Young Ave. off Rte. 1. Strong tides and undertows make swimming dangerous at the beaches, but they also create great waves and winds for board- and windsurfing—if you don't want to participate, just watching these sports can be an activity in itself. Windsurfers have to go a ways out to sea to catch the strong gusts because the half-moon shape of the bay protects the shores, making for wonderful picnicking and sunbathing options. *(The beach lines the coast right next to the town of Half Moon Bay. Francis Beach: ☎726-8820.)*

SAN GREGORIO AND POMPONIO STATE BEACHES. Of all of the beaches in the area, these are arguably the most picturesque—and often the most deserted. Walk to the southern end of San Gregorio to find little caves in the shore rocks. Between San Gregorio and Pomponio State Beaches, there allegedly rests a gorgeous, less frequented beach at the unmarked turnout at Marker 27.35 along Rte.

1. It's difficult to find without aid; keep an eye out for mysteriously vacant cars parked along the highway. *(San Gregorio: 8 mi. south of Half Moon Bay. Pomponio: 10 mi. south of Half Moon Bay. Both open daily 8am-sunset. $2.)*

PEBBLE BEACH AND PIGEON POINT. Though threatening signs attempt to discourage them from doing so, kids tend to pocket handfuls of tiny, smooth pebbles from **Pebble Beach.** Law-abiding parents have been known to mail the stolen stones back to the Half Moon Bay Visitors Center. A paved and level trail heads south from the parking lot along the bluffs; reaching the tidal pools below for exploration requires a bit of a climb down. **Pigeon Point,** 4 mi. south of Pebble Beach, takes its name from a hapless schooner that crashed into the rocky shore on its inaugural voyage in 1853. The point turns heads with its tidepools, 30 ft. plumes of surf, and 115 ft. operating lighthouse (the tallest on the West Coast), which houses 1008 glass prisms. The lighthouse is typically open for tours, but is currently scheduled to undergo structural renovation. The property is picturesque, nonetheless, and docents are often available F-Su 10:30am-4pm to show you around the grounds. Pigeon Point is also home to the hospitable **Pigeon Point Lighthouse Hostel** (p. 267). *(Pebble Beach: 19 mi. south of Half Moon Bay, 2 mi. south of Pescadero Rd. Open 8am-sunset. $2. Pigeon Point: 23 mi. south of Half Moon Bay, 6 mi. south of Pescadero Rd. Lighthouse and Point info ☎879-2120. Hostel: ☎879-0633.)*

AÑO NUEVO STATE RESERVE. This wildlife reserve has several hiking trails that offer views of Año Nuevo Island, the site of an abandoned lighthouse now taken over by birds, seals, and sea lions. Free hiking permits are available at the ranger station by the entrance and at the wheelchair-accessible Visitors Center (though seal-viewing permits are only issued up until 3:30pm). The Visitors Center also features real-time videos displaying the animal adventures out on the island. From mid-December to late March, the reserve is the mating place of the 15 ft., 4500 lb. **elephant seal.** Thousands of fat seals crowd the beach, and the males fight each other for dominance over a herd of females. To see this homosocial spectacle (if you're into that kind of thing), you must make reservations (preferably 8 weeks in advance) by calling ReserveAmerica (☎800-444-4445). Tickets go on sale November 15 and are generally sold out within a week or two (2½hr. guided tours $4). Before mid-August, you can still see the last of the "molters" and the young who have yet to find their sea legs. Don't get too close—they may be fat, but they're fast, and mothers are intolerant of strangers who appear to threaten their young. If they don't get you, the cops might; law requires staying 25 ft. away at all times. *(50 mi. south of San Francisco, 25 mi. south of Half Moon Bay, and 20 mi. north of Santa Cruz. Park information ☎879-0227. No pets. Open daily 8am-sunset. Visitors Center: open daily 8:30am-3:30pm. Parking $2; seniors $1.)*

HILLER AVIATION MUSEUM. For the airplane enthusiast, this impressively packed museum features flying machines from past and present, as well as imaginative renditions of future models. *(601 Skyway Rd. From San Francisco take US 101 south to Holly St./Redwood Shores Pkwy. exit. Go east onto Redwood Shores Pkwy., right onto Airport Rd., and right onto Skyway Rd. ☎654-0200. Open daily 10am-5pm. Adults $8, seniors and ages 8-17 $5, under 8 free. AmEx/MC/V.)*

PARKS AND TRAILS. **Memorial County Park** offers 65 mi. of redwood trails, open to hiking, horseback riding, and bicycling, stretching through its parks. The **Heritage Grove** spans 12 sq. mi. and has the oldest and largest redwood trees in the Santa Cruz Mountains. Among the many redwood parks, **Butano State Park** also stands out for its sweeping views of the Pacific Ocean. Its 3,200 acres offer 20 mi. of hiking and mountain biking trails off Pescadero Rd., 9 mi. east of Rte. 1. For those who prefer concrete, but still want scenic settings, the **Sawyer Camp Trail** stretches 10 mi. along the Crystal Springs Reservoir and is popular among local bicyclists, rollerbladers, joggers, and hikers. *(Memorial: Pescadero Rd. Go east from Rte. 1 to Cloverdale. ☎879-0212. Visitor Center open May-Sept. 10am-4pm. Heritage: Pescadero Rd. to Alpine, make a right. Butano: 5 mi. south of Pescadero. From the north, take Pescadero Rd. east from Rte. 1 to Cloverdale. From the south, take Gazos Creek from Rte. 1 to Cloverdale. ☎879-2040. Sawyer: 1801 Crystal Springs*

Rd. ☎589-4294. Closed on weekends. California State Parks do not discriminate against individuals with disabilities. Prior to arrival, visitors with disabilities who need assistance should contact ☎800-777-0369; www.parks.ca.gov.)

FILOLI ESTATE. If "old money" is your bag, check out this rare example of an early 1900s country estate, including a pristine Gregorian Revival House and a magnificent 16-acre garden. *(On Canada Road. From San Fran, take I-280 South to Edgewood Rd. West, turn right on Canada Rd. ☎364-8300; www.filoli.org. House and Garden tours Tu-Sa 10am-2:30pm. Closed Oct.-Feb. Adults $10, children 7-12 $1, under 7 free, students $5 with ID.)*

BURLINGAME MUSEUM OF PEZ MEMORABILIA. Admission to the largest public display of Pez Candy dispensers in the world is (thankfully) free. Enjoy the smaller (bite-sized, really) things in life at this once-in-a-lifetime stop. *(214 California Dr., between Burlingame and Howard Ave. Get off US 101 at Broadway Ave., head west, and turn left on California Dr. Also accessible by CalTran; get off at the Burlingame Station. ☎347-2301; www.burlingamepezmuseum.com. Open Tu-Sa 10am-6pm.)*

LA HONDA. A winding cross-peninsular trip down Rte. 84 will bring you to the little logging town in the redwoods where author Ken Kesey lived with his merry pranksters in the 1960s, before it got too small and they took off across the US in a psychedelic bus. The shady, scenic drive makes this detour worthwhile, even if you aren't familiar with Kesey's gang, but *Let's Go* recommends reading a copy of Tom Wolfe's *The Electric Kool-Aid Acid Test* before making the journey.

ENTERTAINMENT

Captain John's Fishing Trips (☎726-2913 or 800-391-8787), at Pillar Point Harbor in Princeton by the Sea. 7½hr. trips depart M-F 7:30am; check-in 6:30am. Adults $40, seniors and under 7 $35. Sa-Su all tickets (except special trips) $45. About $25 extra for a 1-day fishing license and gear. Special trips (Tu and F-Su) to the desolate Farallon Islands Wildlife Refuge and seasonal salmon fishing trips ($55). MC/V for the trip; no credit cards for license.

Sea Horse and Friendly Acres Ranch (☎726-2362; www.seahorserentals.com), 1 mi. north of Half Moon Bay on Rte. 1. Horses and ponies for unguided rides. No reservations. Ponies for children ages 1-5, horses for ages 5+. 1hr. trail ride $30. 1½hr. trail and beach ride $40. 2hr. trail and beach ride $50. 20min. pony ride $10. Lessons $45. Hired guides $20 per hr. Helmets $3. Early bird special (8-10am) $30 for 2hr. Open daily 8am-6pm.

Phipp's Country Store and Farm, 2700 Pescadero Rd. (☎879-0787). Turn off Rte. 1 onto Pescadero Rd., 17 mi. south of Half Moon Bay; the ranch is about 3 mi. down. Kids will enjoy olallieberry (oh-LA-la-behr-ee) gathering, a local pastime which originated about 25 years ago when the olallieberry was created by crossing a blackberry, a loganberry, and a youngberry. Mid-July yields the best berries. Gourmands will also revel in the abundance of fresh produce and herbs. $1 per lb. of strawberries, blackberries, olallieberries, or boysenberries. Entrance to animal stables and fields $3, ages 5-9 $1, seniors and infants free. Open May-Sept. daily 10am-6pm; Oct.-Apr. 10am-5pm. AmEx/D/MC/V.

Pescadero Marsh (☎879-2170), at Pescadero Rd. and Rte. 1. The marsh shelters such migratory birds as the elegant blue heron. Guided nature walks are often given on weekends. Call for specific departure times and locations.

SEASONAL EVENTS

On Columbus Day, Half Moon Bay hosts the nationally renowned **Great Pumpkin Weigh-Off** (Farm Bureau ☎726-4485). The following weekend, 300,000 people, 300 craft vendors, and an inordinate number of oversized pumpkins all come together for the **Half Moon Bay Art and Pumpkin Festival** on Main St. (☎726-9652. Sa-Su pancake breakfast 6am, fair 10am-5pm.) On the third Saturday of every month, flower vendors from around the Bay Area gather at the **Half Moon Bay Coastal Flower Market** to sell their wares at reduced prices. May-Sept. outdoors at Kelly and Main St.; Nov.-Apr. indoors at La Piazza on Main St. (☎712-9439. Open 9am-3pm.)

LAKE TAHOE & RTE. 80

Tahoe's natural beauty attracts outdoor fanatics from across the globe, and its burgeoning entertainment and hotel industries eagerly support their excursions. With a shoreline of 71 mi., thousands of acres of woods and trails, and dozens of surrounding mountains, Tahoe is known as one of the premier ski *and* outdoors locations in the country. In a town without an off-season, visitors can try their luck at everything from keno to kayaking. The centerpiece and the one constant in every experience remains Lake Tahoe, the highest alpine lake in North America. After the Bonanza Road was cut to reach California mines during the 19th-century Gold Rush, money started to pour into the Tahoe Basin. By the turn of the century, the lake was a haven for San Francisco's rich and famous. Now, everyone can enjoy Tahoe's pure blue waters, tall pines, and high-rise casinos silhouetted by the glow of the setting sun. An outdoor adventurer's dream in any season, Tahoe has miles of biking, hiking, and skiing trails, long stretches of golden beaches, and possibilities for almost every watersport imaginable, from canoeing to parasailing. The best hiking is in the **Desolation Wilderness,** but 200 mi. of excellent trails run throughout the Tahoe Basin. *Let's Go* recommends picking up a copy of Michael Sciealfa's *Trail Guide to the Lake Tahoe Basin* from the visitor's center. Only a 3½-4hr. drive from San Francisco, Tahoe is a worthwhile weekend excursion from the city.

| AREA CODE | Lake Tahoe's area code is ☎530. The Nevada side is ☎775. |

TRANSPORTATION

While essential during the trip to Tahoe, cars can be a bit of a headache once there. Parking around the lake is limited, though it's available in all campsites and several hotels. It's easiest to take shuttles to ski resorts, since lots become extremely crowded early, and you'll have to take a shuttle from the lot even if you *do* drive.

Trains: Amtrak (☎800-USA-RAIL/872-7245). Runs trains from San Francisco that stop at the Truckee Depot in downtown Truckee, which is along Rte. 80 north of the Lake (6½hr., 3 per day, $45-93).

Buses: Greyhound (☎800-231-2222). Buses stop at the Truckee Depot (5½hr., 5 per day, $37-39).

Public Transportation: Tahoe Area Regional Transport or **TART** (☎550-1212 or 800-736-6365; www.laketahoetransit.com). Connects the western and northern shores from Incline Village through Tahoe City to Meeks Bay, where it joins with South Lake Tahoe (STAGE) buses in the summer. Stops daily every hour or half hour 6:30am-6pm, depending on the route. Buses also run out to Truckee and Squaw Valley and back 5 times per day (7:30am-4:45pm). Adults one-way $1.25, disabled $1, under 5 free. All-day pass adults $3; child, senior, and disabled $2. Free night service.

Bike Rental: Cyclepaths Mtn. Bike Adventures, 1785 W. Lake Blvd. (☎800-780-BIKE/2453). Full service shop. Sales, rentals, tour packages, and shuttles. Mountain bike $6 per hr. or daily with front suspension $21; with full suspension $10-12 per hr. (min. 2 hr.) or daily $45. Open daily 9am-6pm. AmEx/D/MC/V.

Taxis: Checker Taxi (☎546-8844); Alpine Taxi (☎546-3232); Fast Taxi (☎583-6699).

Rental Cars: Avis (☎800-831-2847; www.avis.com); Enterprise (☎800-736-8222); Hertz (☎800-654-3131; www.hertz.com).

ORIENTATION & PRACTICAL INFORMATION

The perimeter of the large lake is accessible almost entirely by the TART and Tahoe Trolley. From San Francisco, automobiles enter the area on Rt. 80, the same highway that stretches across the country. Rt. 89 South drives past several good campsites before crossing Squaw Valley Rd., home to excellent ski slopes. It eventually hits Tahoe City, where gift shops and swanky restaurants concentrate. Continue South on Rt. 89 toward Emerald Bay for more campgrounds, some expensive restaurants, and access to Desolation Wilderness. Rt. 28 breaks off from Rt. 89 at Tahoe City and brings you through the city, northeastward, toward King's Beach.

Tourist Office: Tahoe North Visitors and Convention Bureau, 380 North Lake Hwy. (☎581-8716 or 800-462-5196; www.mytahoevacation.com), in Tahoe City. Staff is knowledgeable and publications are comprehensive and helpful. Transportation schedules, wildlife information, ski rates and times, park descriptions. Open M-F 9am-5pm, Sa-Su 9am-4pm. **North Lake Tahoe Resort Association Visitors Information Center,** 245 North Lake Blvd. (☎583-3494), in Tahoe City. Visitor information, maps, recreation, Western Union services. **Tahoe Guide,** (www.tahoeguide.com), complete Internet guide to North Lake Tahoe.

Laundromat: Big Tree Laundromat, Wash $1.50, dry 25¢, soap 50¢. Change machine available. Open daily 7am-7pm.

Road Conditions: California side (☎800-427-7623), Nevada side (☎775-793-1313).

Weather Information: (☎546-5253).

Emergency: ☎911

Police: Tahoe City: 2501 North Lake Blvd. (☎581-6330).

Internet Access: Vicky's Cyber Cafe, 255 North Lake Blvd., Suite #4 (☎581-5312; www.tahoecitycybercafe.com), located behind Watchdog Video. $3 for 15min., $10 for 1hr. Happy Hour 7-9am: 50% off. 2hr. limit. Open M-F 7am-6pm, Sa 9am-6pm. No credit cards.

Post Office: 950 North Lake Blvd., Tahoe City. **Postal code:** 96145.

ACCOMMODATIONS & CAMPGROUNDS

A vacation spot for the wealthy, as well as quintessentially middle-class families, individuals, and couples, Tahoe offers expensive and chic hotels in addition to a number of bed and breakfasts and many campsites. Check out **www.mytahoevacation.com** for a long list of options with a wide range of prices and amenities.

Sunnyside, 1850 West Lake Blvd. (☎583-7200 or 800-822-2SKI; www.sunnysideresort.com), located on West shore 2 mi. south of Tahoe City on Hwy 89. Sunnyside offers beautiful views of the lake from each of the 23 spacious rooms. Private decks and stylish serenity make this resort perfect for families, friends, and lovers. All rooms with cable TV and VCR. Lavish complimentary breakfast and afternoon teas. Reception 7:30am-9:30pm. Check-in 2pm; check-out 11am. Discount lift tickets available. Deluxe rooms (lake and garden view) $100-210; lakefront rooms (full lake view with balcony) $140-250; lakefront suites (full lake view with balcony, separate parlor, and wet bar) $175-$295. AmEx/D/MC/V. ❸

Sugar Pine Point State Park, Hwy. 89 (☎525-7982, reservations 800-444-7275), on the western shore of Lake Tahoe. From the North take 28 south, just past Tahoma. Parking and campsites on the right. With almost 2 mi. of lake front, several beaches, and natural access to the Desolation Wilderness Area, this campground is coveted. Clearly marked trails serve almost every part of the park. Day-use permits for entering Desolation Wilderness available at most Forest Service trailheads; day- and night-use permits from the South Lake Tahoe Forest Service Headquarters, Taylor Creek Visitor Center, or William Kent Campground. 157 campsites with table and stove. Restrooms with sinks and flush toilets. Shower facilities in summer. Ten group campsites. Reservations up to 8wk. in advance strongly advised during summer. $14 per night. Open year-round. AmEx/D/MC/V. Walk-in, no credit cards. ❶

Tahoe State Recreation Area (☎583-3074, reservations 800-444-7275; www.parks.ca.gov), Hwy. 28 on the North Shore of Lake Tahoe in Tahoe City. From the North take 28 east through most of Tahoe City, campground will be on the right. This campground makes up a bit for the lack of trails with its proximity to the lake. 36 units with swimming access, showers, water, and flush toilet. 8-person and 2-vehicle max. per site. Quiet hours 10pm-6am. Reservations up to seven months in advance. Walk-in first come first serve, cash or check only. Open summer only. $16 per night. AmEx/D/MC/V. ❶

FOOD & DRINK

Tahoe's best restaurants have planted themselves along the edge of the lake, resulting in a scattered dining scene. Whatever center there might be is certainly in Tahoe City, but some tasty breakfast and dinner menus lay outside that small strip. If you're a bit of a chef yourself head to **Safeway**, 850 North Lake Blvd. (☎583-2772. Open daily Sept.-June 6am-10pm, July-Aug. 6am-1am.) Alternatively, you could go *au naturel* at **New Moon Natural Foods**, 505 West Lake Blvd., just south of Tahoe City. (☎583-7426. Open M-Sa 9am-7pm, Su 10am-6pm.)

AUBURN

Ikeda, 13500 Lincoln Way. (☎885 4243; www.ikedas.com), off I-80 take Forest Hill or Bowman Rd. exits. About 2hr. from San Fran and 1½hr. from Tahoe, Ikeda is perfect for a midpoint stretch and snack. Started as a farm 50 years ago, Ikeda Market now sells goods made mostly from its own produce. Juicy peaches, award-winning pies (slice $3, whole $11-14), and top-notch burgers ($3.50) are delightful treats on the road. Open summer Sa-Th 8am-9pm, F 8am-10pm; winter M-Th 8am-7pm, F 8am-9pm, Sa-Su 8am-8pm. AmEx/D/MC/V. ❷

LAKE TAHOE

Java Stop, 521 North Lake Blvd. (☎581-4800), in **Tahoe City,** just off Rt. 89. Originally a coffee-stop, this hidden restaurant also brings the best fruit smoothies ($3-5), locally baked goods, and flatbread wraps to the Lake. With 7 brews, including some organic, Java Stop also salutes its heritage. ($3-5). Try the Granite Apple. Open daily 5:30am-5pm. D/MC/V. ❶

The Blue Agave, 425 North Lake Blvd. (☎583-8113), in **Tahoe City,** next to the Travelodge. Housed in the historic Tahoe Inn, this Mexican restaurant excels in flavor, presentation, and service. Down to its popular "Mexican Rice," Blue Agave makes mouths water. Try the veggie burrito ($8.95). Open 11:30am-10pm, bar until 1am. AmEx/D/MC/V. ❷

Sunnyside, 1850 West Lake Blvd. (☎583-7200), from the North turn south on 89, Sunnyside will be on the left. Lakeside seating in the summer is always bustling, but worth the wait. The more limited and bar-food oriented Mountain Grill menu is slightly less expensive than the Lakeside Dining menu, which includes shrimp martini ($10), prime choice steaks ($20-28), and angus burgers with gorgonzola ($10). Try the "world famous" Hula Pie ($6). Open M-Sa 11am-10pm, Su 10am-10pm. AmEx/D/MC/V. ❷

The Old Post Office Cafe, 5245 North Lake Blvd. (☎546-3205), in Carnelian Bay, from the North take 28 East past Tahoe City. Serving excellent breakfasts and lunches to a crowd of locals, this place serves as a reminder that Lake Tahoe is really still a rural area. Smiling waitresses emphasize the comfort in "comfort foods." Omelettes ($5-8) and potatoes, coffees and juices ($1.50). Open 6:30am-2pm daily, dinner menu Th-Su 5-9pm. AmEx/MC/V. ❶

NIGHTLIFE

Pierce Street Annex, 850 North Lake Blvd. (☎583-5800), in the Lighthouse Shopping Center. The most popular bar in town. The sole source of sustenance comes in liquid form. Free pool on Su, DJ W-Sa, locals night Th, so try to blend. Open daily 2pm-2am.

Naughty Dawg, 255 North Lake Blvd. (☎581-3294), across from the fire station. If you've brought your pet, park yourself here. On M beers start at $0.50 at 8pm and increase by $0.50 every 30min. until 10pm. Afterwards cool off with a mixed drink in a dawgy bowl. Open daily 11:30am-2am, kitchen 11:30am-11pm.

Pete and Peter's, 395 North Lake Blvd. (☎583-2400), in Tahoe City. One of the city's best and friendliest nightlife spots. Pete and Peter's is casual and conducive to conversation. Pool tables and space for impromptu dancing (mutually exclusive, or not?). Drafts $1.75, bottles $3. Open daily 11am-2am. No credit cards.

OUTDOOR ACTIVITIES

SKI RESORTS

Seven downhill ski resorts and seven cross-country resorts have long accommodated winter crowds, but the 1960 Winter Olympics at Squaw Valley put Tahoe on the world's map as a year-round outdoors treasure. **Squaw Valley** is still the largest and most popular resort. (☎583-6985; www.squaw.com). Less crowded **Sugar Bowl** also maintains excellent quality. (☎426-9000; www.sugarbowl.com). **Northstar-at-Tahoe** is great for families and more advanced skiers. (☎562-1010; www.skinorthstar.com). **Alpine Meadows** has a great mix of slopes. (☎583-4232; www.skialpine.com). Lift tickets in Tahoe range from $40-60 for adults and $0-30 for seniors.

OTHER ACTIVITIES

Tahoe City Kayak, 1355 North Lake Blvd. (☎581-4336; www.tahoecitykayak.com), in Tahoe City. Rentals (Single $50 per day, tandem $60 per day) must be transported by renter, but assistance is provided with car attachment. Three levels of classes on whitewater kayaking (full day any level $150, level 1 & 2 $250, half day $120). Tours of Emerald Bay ($95) and a popular Tahoe tour including brunch on the lake at Sunnyside ($65). Open early-Mar. to late-Sept. daily 9am-6pm. MC/V.

High Sierra Water Ski School, 1850 West Lake Blvd. (☎583 7417; www.highsierrawaterskiing.com), at Sunnyside Restaurant and Lodge. Waterski lessons: $60 per 30min., $100 per hr. $350 per half-day. Power boat rentals: 6 passenger $90 per hr., 9 passenger $100 per hr. Ski rental: $9 per 2hr., $10 per 3hr., $20 per 8hr. Wet suits available. MC/V.

Planning Your Trip

WHEN TO GO

Mark Twain once said, "The coldest winter I ever spent was a summer in San Francisco," a tidbit repeated by many locals in response to t-shirt-clad tourists complaining about the brisk weather. With the trademark fog blanketing the city most mornings, temperatures are significantly cooler than in inland suburbs, even those to the north (bring a jacket *and* a sweater). The upside is that winter temperatures barely dip below 50°F. Enjoy the outdoors with an umbrella from November to March. The sunniest parts of the city are the Mission District and Bernal Heights; the windiest are Ocean Beach and the Golden Gate Bridge. For a list of regional **festivals** and **national holidays,** see **Discover,** p. 31

US EMBASSIES AND CONSULATES ABROAD

For foreign consular services in SF, see **Once In,** p. 45.

Contact the nearest embassy or consulate to obtain information regarding visas and permits to the United States. The US State Department provides contact information for US diplomatic missions on the Internet at http://foia.state.gov/MMS/KOH/keyofficers.asp.

AUSTRALIA. Embassy and Consulate: Moonah Pl., Yarralumla (Canberra), ACT 2600 (☎02 6214 5600; fax 6214 5970; http://usembassy-australia.state.gov/consular). **Other Consulates:** MLC Centre, Level 59, 19-29 Martin Pl., **Sydney,** NSW 2000 (☎02 9373 9200; fax 9373 9184); 553 St. Kilda Rd., **Melbourne,** VIC 3004 (☎03 9526 5900; fax 9510 4646); 16 St. George's Terr., 13th fl., Perth, WA 6000 (☎08 9202 1224; fax 9231 9444).

CANADA. Embassy and Consulate: Consular Section, 490 Sussex Dr., **Ottawa,** P.O. Box 866, Station B, Ottawa, Ontario K1P 5T1(☎613-238-5335; fax 688-3081; www.usembassycanada.gov). **Other Consulates** (☎1-900-451-2778 or www.amcits.com): 615 Macleod Trail SE, Room 1000, **Calgary,** AB T2G 4T8 (☎403-266-8962; fax 264-6630); 1969 Upper Water St., Purdy's Wharf Tower II, Suite 904, **Halifax,** NS B3J 3R7 (☎902-429-2480; fax 423-6861); 1155 St. Alexandre, **Montréal,** QC H3B 1Z1 (mailing address: P.O. Box 65, Postal Station Desjardins, Montréal, QC H5B 1G1) (☎514-398-9695; fax 981-5059); 2 Place Terrasse Dufferin, behind Château Frontenac, B.P. 939, **Québec City,** QC G1R 4T9; 360 University Ave., **Toronto,** ON M5G 1S4 (☎418-692-2095; fax 692-2096); 1075 W. Pender St., Mezzanine (mailing address: 1095 W. Pender St., 21st fl., **Vancouver,** BC V6E 2M6) (☎604-685-4311; fax 685-7175).

IRELAND. Embassy and Consulate: 42 Elgin Rd., Ballsbridge, **Dublin** 4 (☎01 668 8777 or 668 7122; fax 668 9946; www.usembassy.ie).

NEW ZEALAND. Embassy and Consulate: 29 Fitzherbert Terr. (or P.O. Box 1190), Thorndon, **Wellington** (☎04 462 6000; fax 478 0490; usembassy.org.nz). **Other Consulate:** 23 Customs St., Citibank Building, 3rd fl., **Auckland** (☎09 303 2724; fax 366 0870.

SOUTH AFRICA. Embassy and Consulate: 877 Pretorius St., **Pretoria,** P.O. Box 9536, Pretoria 0001 (☎012 342 1048; fax 342-2244; usembassy.state.gov/pretoria). **Other Consulates:** Broadway Industries Center, Heerengracht, Foreshore, **Cape Town** (mailing address: P.O. Box 6773, Roggebaai, 8012; ☎021 342 1048; fax 342 2244); 303 West St., Old Mutual Building, 31st fl., **Durban** (☎031 305 7600; fax 305 7691); No. 1 River St., Killarney, **Johannesburg,** P.O. Box 1762, Houghton, 2041 (☎011 644 8000; fax 646 6916).

UK. Embassy and Consulate: 24 Grosvenor Sq., **London** W1A 1AE (☎020 7499 9000; fax 7495 5012; www.usembassy.org.uk). **Other Consulates**: Queen's House, 14 Queen St., Belfast, **N. Ireland** BT1 6EQ (☎028 9032 8239; fax 9024 8482); 3 Regent Terr., Edinburgh, **Scotland** EH7 5BW (☎013 1556 8315; fax 557 6023).

DOCUMENTS AND FORMALITIES

PASSPORTS

REQUIREMENTS. All foreign visitors except Canadians need valid passports to enter the United States and to re-enter their own country. The US does not allow entrance if the holder's passport expires in under six months; returning home with an expired passport is often illegal, and may result in a fine. Canadians need to show proof of citizenship, such as a citizenship card or birth certificate.

VISAS AND WORK PERMITS

VISAS

Citizens of South Africa and most other countries need a visa—a stamp, sticker, or insert in your passport specifying the purpose of your travel and the permitted duration of your stay—in addition to a valid passport for entrance to the US. See http://travel.state.gov/visa_services.html and www.unitedstatesvisas.gov for more information. To obtain a visa, contact a US embassy or consulate. Recent security measures have made the visa application process more rigorous, and therefore lengthy; apply well in advance of your travel date.

Canadian citizens do not need to obtain a visa for admission to the US. Citizens of Australia, New Zealand, and most European countries can waive US visas through the **Visa Waiver Program.** Visitors qualify if they are traveling only for business or pleasure (*not* work or study), are staying for fewer than **90 days,** have proof of intent to leave (e.g., a return plane ticket), possess an I-94W form, are traveling on particular carriers, and possess a machine readable passport from their country of citizenship. See http://travel.state.gov/vwp.html for more.

If you lose your I-94 form, you can replace it by filling out form I-102, although it's very unlikely that the form will be replaced within the time of your stay. The form is available at the nearest **Bureau of Citizenship and Immigration Services (BCIS)** office (www.bcis.gov), through the forms request line (☎800-870-3676), or online (www.bcis.gov/graphics/formsfee/forms/i-102.htm). **Visa extensions** are sometimes granted with a completed I-539 form; call the forms request line (☎800-870-3676) or get it online at www.immigration.gov/graphics/formsfee/forms/i-539.htm.

WORK PERMITS

Admission as a visitor does not include the right to work, which is authorized only by a work permit. Entering the US to study requires a special visa. For more information, see **Alternatives to Tourism**, p. 306.

IDENTIFICATION

When you travel, always carry two or more forms of identification on your person, including at least one photo ID; a passport combined with a driver's license or birth certificate is usually adequate. Never carry all your forms of ID together, and keep photocopies of them in your luggage and at home.

TEACHER, STUDENT & YOUTH IDENTIFICATION. The **International Student Identity Card (ISIC),** the most widely accepted form of student ID, provides discounts on some sights, accommodations, food, and transport; access to 24hr. emergency helpline (in North America call ☎877-370-ISIC; elsewhere call US collect ☎+1 715-345-0505); and insurance benefits for US cardholders. Applicants must be degree-seeking students of a secondary or post-secondary school and must be at least 12 years of age. Because of the proliferation of fake ISICs, some services (particularly airlines) require additional proof of student identity.

The **International Teacher Identity Card (ITIC)** offers teachers the same insurance coverage and similar discounts. For travelers who are under 26 years old but not students, the **International Youth Travel Card (IYTC)** offers many of the same benefits as the ISIC. Similarly, the **International Student Exchange ID Card (ISE)** provides discounts, medical benefits, and the ability to purchase student airfares.

Each of these cards costs US$22. ISIC and ITIC cards are valid for roughly one and a half academic years; IYTC cards are valid for one year from the date of issue. Many student travel agencies (see p. 288) issue the cards; for a list of issuing agencies, contact the International Student Travel Confederation (ISTC), Herengracht 479, 1017 BS Amsterdam, The Netherlands (☎+31 20 421 28 00; fax 421 28 10; www.istc.org).

CUSTOMS

ENTERING THE US

Upon entering the United States, international travelers must declare certain items from abroad and pay a duty on the value of those articles that exceeds the allowance established by the United States customs service, though tourists are unlikely to have anything to declare upon entering the US. You must be 21 years old to bring alcohol into the US (www.cbp.gov).

To protect its crops from fruit fly infestation, the state of California maintains strict controls on all fruits, vegetables, animals, and other farm products entering the state. You will be asked about these items when boarding an airplane for California. Your car may be searched at checkpoints stationed on all roads entering California.

MONEY

CURRENCY AND EXCHANGE

AUS$1 = US$0.64	US$1 = AUS$1.55
CDN$1 = US$0.71	US$1 = CDN$1.40
NZ$1 = US$0.58	US$1 = NZ$1.72
ZAR1 = US$0.13	US$1 = ZAR7.43
UK£1 = US$1.60	US$1 = UK£0.62
€1 = US$0.88	US$1 = €1.13

As a general rule, it's cheaper to convert money in the US than at home. However, you should bring enough US currency to last for the first 24-72hr. of a trip to avoid being penniless in case you have any problems with your credit card or traveler's checks, or if you arrive at a time when banks are closed.

When changing foreign currency in the US, try to go to banks that have at most a 5% margin between their buy and sell prices. Since you lose money with every transaction, **convert large sums** (unless the rate is unfavorable), **but no more than you'll need.**

If you use traveler's checks or bills, carry some in small denominations (the equivalent of $50 or less) for times when you are forced to exchange money at disadvantageous rates, but bring a range of denominations since charges may be levied per check cashed. Store your money in a variety of forms; ideally, you will at any given time be carrying some cash, an ATM and/or credit card, and some traveler's checks.

TRAVELER'S CHECKS

Traveler's checks are one of the safest and least troublesome means of carrying funds. American Express and Visa are the most widely recognized brands. Many banks and agencies sell them for a small commission. Check issuers provide refunds if the checks are lost or stolen, and many provide additional services, such as toll-free refund hotlines abroad, emergency message services, and stolen credit card assistance. They are readily accepted in San Francisco. Always carry emergency cash.

American Express: Checks available with commission at select banks and all AmEx offices. US residents can also purchase checks by phone (☎888-269-6669) or online (www.aexp.com). AAA (see p. 44) offers commission-free checks to its members. Checks available in US, Australian, British, Canadian, Japanese, and Euro currencies. *Cheques for Two* can be signed by either of 2 people traveling together. For purchase locations or more information contact AmEx's service centers: In the US and Canada ☎800-221-7282; in the UK ☎0800 521 313; in Australia ☎800 25 19 02; in New Zealand 0800 441 068; elsewhere US collect ☎+1 801-964-6665.

Visa: Checks available (generally with commission) at banks worldwide. For the location of the nearest office, call Visa's service centers: In the US ☎800-227-6811; in the UK ☎0800 89 50 78; elsewhere UK collect ☎+44 020 7937 8091. Checks available in US, British, Canadian, Japanese, and Euro currencies.

Travelex/Thomas Cook: In the US and Canada ☎800-287-7362; in the UK ☎0800 62 21 01; elsewhere call UK collect ☎+44 1733 31 89 50.

CREDIT, DEBIT & ATM CARDS

Where they are accepted, credit cards often offer superior exchange rates—up to 5% better than the retail rate used by banks and other currency exchange establishments. Credit cards may also offer services such as insurance or emergency help, and are sometimes required to reserve hotel rooms or rental cars. **MasterCard** and **Visa** are the most welcomed; **American Express** cards work at some ATMs and at AmEx offices and major airports.

The two major international money networks are **Cirrus** (to locate ATMs call ☎800-424-7787 or www.mastercard.com) and **Visa/PLUS** (to locate ATMs call ☎800-843-7587 or www.visa.com). Most ATMs charge a transaction fee that is paid to the bank that owns the ATM. For information on getting money from home, see **Once In,** p. 47.

COSTS

The cost of your trip will vary considerably, depending on how you travel and where you stay. The single biggest cost of your trip will probably be your round-trip **airfare** to San Francisco (p. 287). Before you go, spend some time calculating a reasonable per-day **budget** that will meet your needs.

STAYING ON A BUDGET. A bare-bones day in San Francisco (sleeping in hostels/guesthouses, buying food at supermarkets) would cost about US$30-45; a slightly more comfortable day (sleeping in hostels/guesthouses and the occasional budget hotel, eating one meal a day at a restaurant, going out at night) would run US$70-85; for a luxurious day, the sky's the limit. Also, don't forget to factor in emergency reserve funds (at least US$200) when planning how much money you'll need.

TIPS FOR SAVING MONEY. Some simpler ways include searching out opportunities for free entertainment (**museums** will typically be free about once a month, and San Francisco hosts many free open-air **concerts** and/or **cultural events**), splitting accommodation and food costs with other trustworthy fellow travelers, and buying food in supermarkets rather than eating out. Do your laundry in the sink (unless you're explicitly prohibited from doing so).

TAXES

Sales tax in California is the equivalent of the European Value-Added Tax. The sales tax rate on normal consumer goods varies by county from 7.25% to 8.5%; there are additional federal taxes on tobacco products and alcoholic beverages. Most grocery items in California are not taxed; clothing items, however, are. *Let's Go* does not usually include taxes in listed prices.

SAFETY & SECURITY

PERSONAL SAFETY

EXPLORING. Common sense and a little bit of thought will go a long way in helping you to avoid dangerous situations. Wherever possible, *Let's Go* warns of neighborhoods that should be avoided when traveling alone or at night. To avoid unwanted attention, try to blend in as much as possible. Familiarize yourself with your surroundings before setting out, and carry yourself with confidence. Check maps in shops and restaurants rather than on the street. If you are traveling alone, be sure someone at home knows your itinerary, and never admit that you're by yourself.

When walking at night, stick to busy, well-lit streets and avoid dark alleyways. If you feel uncomfortable, leave as quickly and directly as you can, but don't allow fear of the unknown to turn you into a hermit.

DRIVING. If you are using a **car,** learn local driving signals and wear a seat belt. Children under 40 lb. should ride only in specially-designed carseats, available for a small fee from most car rental agencies. For long drives in desolate areas, invest in a cellular phone and a roadside assistance program (see p. 44). **Sleeping in your car** is one of the most dangerous (and often illegal) ways to get your rest.

TERRORISM. In light of the September 11, 2001 terrorist attacks in the Eastern US, there is an elevated threat of further terrorist activities in the United States. Terrorists often target landmarks popular with tourists; however, the threat of an attack is generally not specific or great enough to warrant avoiding certain places or modes of transportation. Stay aware of developments in the news and watch for alerts from federal, state, and local law enforcement. Allow extra time for airport security and do not pack sharp objects in your carry-on luggage, as they will be confiscated.

TRAVEL ADVISORIES. The following government offices provide travel information and advisories by telephone, by fax, or via the web:

Australian Department of Foreign Affairs and Trade: ☎13 00 555135; fax 02 6261 1299; www.dfat.gov.au.

Canadian Department of Foreign Affairs and International Trade (DFAIT): In Canada and the US ☎800-267-8376, elsewhere ☎+1 613-944-4000; www.dfait-maeci.gc.ca. Call for their free booklet, *Bon Voyage...But.*

New Zealand Ministry of Foreign Affairs: ☎04 439 8000; fax 494 8506; www.mft.govt.nz/travel/index.html.

United Kingdom Foreign and Commonwealth Office: ☎020 7008 0232; fax 7008 0155; www.fco.gov.uk.

US Department of State: ☎202-647-5225, fax 202-647-3000; http://travel.state.gov. For *A Safe Trip Abroad,* call ☎202-512-1800.

FINANCIAL SECURITY

PROTECTING YOUR VALUABLES. There are a few steps you can take to minimize the financial risk associated with traveling. First, **bring as little with you as possible.** Second, buy a few combination **padlocks** to secure your belongings either in your pack or in a hostel or train station locker. Third, **carry as little cash as possible.** Keep your traveler's checks and ATM/credit cards in a **money belt**—not a "fanny pack"—along with your passport and ID cards. Fourth, **keep a small cash reserve separate from your primary stash.** This should be about US$50 sewn into or stored in the depths of your pack, along with your traveler's check numbers and important photocopies.

CON ARTISTS & PICKPOCKETS. In large cities **con artists** often work in groups, and children are among the most effective. **Never let your passport and your bags out of your sight.** Beware of **pickpockets** in crowds, especially on public transportation. Also, be alert in public telephone booths: If you must say your calling card number, do so very quietly; if you punch it in, make sure no one can look over your shoulder.

ACCOMMODATIONS & TRANSPORTATION. Never leave your belongings unattended; crime occurs in even the most demure-looking hostel or hotel. Bring your own **padlock** for hostel lockers.

Be particularly careful on **buses** and **trains;** horror stories abound about determined thieves who wait for travelers to fall asleep. Carry your backpack in front of you where you can see it. When traveling with others, sleep in alternate shifts. When alone, use good judgement in selecting a train compartment: never stay in an empty one, and use a lock to secure your pack to the luggage rack. Try to sleep on top bunks with your luggage stored above you (if not in bed with you), and keep important documents and other valuables on your person. If traveling by **car,** don't leave valuables (such as radios or luggage) in it while you are away.

DRUGS & ALCOHOL

In San Francisco, like the rest of the US, the **drinking age is 21** and strictly enforced. Avoid public drunkenness; it is illegal, and can jeopardize your safety. **Never drink and drive**—you risk your own life and those of others, and getting caught results in imprisonment and fines. It is illegal to have an open bottle of alcohol inside a car, even if you are not the driver and even if you are not drinking it.

The punishment for illegal **drug** possession ranges from a fine to imprisonment, depending on the type and amount. San Francisco allows medicinal marijuana use only with the possession of a medical cannabis user identification card, and it is still a federal offense to possess without a prescription. If you carry prescription drugs, it is vital to have a copy of the prescriptions. Cigarette purchasers must be at least 18 years old with photo ID.

HEALTH

BEFORE YOU GO

In your **passport,** write the names of any people you wish to be contacted in case of a medical emergency, and list any allergies or medical conditions. Matching a prescription to a foreign equivalent is not always easy, safe, or possible, so carry up-to-date, legible prescriptions or a statement from your doctor stating the medication's trade name, manufacturer, chemical name, and dosage. While traveling, be sure to keep all medication with you in your carry-on luggage.

IMMUNIZATIONS & MEDICAL PRECAUTIONS

Travelers over two years old should make sure that the following vaccines are up to date: MMR (for measles, mumps, and rubella); DTaP or Td (for diptheria, tetanus, and pertussis); OPV (for polio); HbCV (for haemophilus influenza B); HBV (for hepatitis B); and Varicella (for chickenpox, for those who are susceptible).

USEFUL ORGANIZATIONS & PUBLICATIONS

The US **Centers for Disease Control and Prevention** (☎877-FYI-TRIP/394-8747; fax 888-232-3299; www.cdc.gov/travel) maintains an international travelers' hotline and an informative website. The CDC's comprehensive booklet *Health Information for International Travel*, an annual rundown of disease, immunization, and general health advice, is free online or $29 via the Public Health Foundation (☎877-252-1200). Consult the appropriate government agency of your home country for consular information sheets on health, entry requirements, and other issues for various countries (see the listings in the box on **Travel Advisories,** p. 282).

ONCE IN SAN FRANCISCO

MEDICAL ASSISTANCE

In case of medical emergency, dial ☎**911** from any phone and an operator will send out an ambulance, fire, or police squad as needed. 911 calls are **free.** Emergency medical care is also readily available in San Francisco at any **emergency room** on a walk-in basis. If you do not have insurance, you will have to pay for emergency and other medical care (**Insurance,** p. 284). **Non-emergency** care is available at any hospital or doctor's office for a fee, or at the **Haight-Ashbury Free Clinic** free of charge (p. 314). Appointments are always required for non-emergency medical services.

ENVIRONMENTAL HAZARDS

Heat exhaustion and dehydration: Heat exhaustion can lead to fatigue, headaches, and wooziness. Avoid it by drinking plenty of fluids, and avoiding salty foods and dehydrating beverages (e.g. alcohol and caffeinated beverages). Continuous heat stress can eventually lead to heatstroke, characterized by a rising temperature, severe headache, and cessation of sweating. Victims should be cooled off with wet towels and taken to a doctor.

Earthquakes: Running the length of California, the San Andreas and other faults occasionally shake, rattle, and roll everything in sight. While most earthquakes are mild and harmless, stronger ones do occur in the state every few years. When you feel shaking, simply move away from any objects that could possibly fall on you. Indoors, duck underneath a desk or step underneath a doorway. In a car, pull over and wait for the quake to subside.

High altitude: Allow your body a couple of days to adjust to less oxygen before exerting yourself. Altitude sickness/acute mountain sickness (AMS) is characterized by headaches, loss of appetite, fatigue, dizziness, and confusion. Those suffering from AMS should stop ascending in all cases and seriously consider descending in altitude. Note that alcohol is more potent and UV rays are stronger at high elevations.

283

INSECT-BORNE DISEASES

Many diseases are transmitted by insects—mainly mosquitoes, fleas, ticks, and lice. Be aware of insects in wet or forested areas, especially while hiking and camping; wear long pants and long sleeves, tuck your pants into your socks, and use a mosquito net. Use insect repellents such as DEET and soak or spray your gear with permethrin (licensed in the US for use on clothing). **Ticks**—responsible for Lyme and other diseases—can be particularly dangerous in rural and forested regions of the Northeast, the Great Lakes, and the Pacific coast.

Lyme disease: A bacterial infection carried by ticks and marked by a circular bull's-eye rash of 2 in. or more. Later symptoms include fever, headache, fatigue, and aches and pains. Antibiotics are effective if administered early. Left untreated, Lyme can cause problems in joints, the heart, and the nervous system. If you find a tick attached to your skin, grasp the head with tweezers as close to your skin as possible and apply slow, steady traction. Removing a tick within 24 hours greatly reduces the risk of infection. Do not try to remove ticks by burning them or coating them with nail polish remover or petroleum jelly.

FOOD- & WATER-BORNE DISEASE

Prevention is the best cure, though virtually all tap water in California is chemically treated to be safe for drinking. Always wash your hands before eating.

Giardiasis: Transmitted through parasites (microbes, tapeworms, etc. in contaminated water and food) and acquired by drinking untreated water from streams or lakes. Symptoms include stomach cramps, bloating, fatigue, weight loss, flatulence, nausea, and diarrhea.

AIDS, HIV, STDS

For detailed information on **Acquired Immune Deficiency Syndrome (AIDS)** in San Francisco, call the **US Centers for Disease Control's** 24hr. hotline at ☎800-342-2437, or contact the **Joint United Nations Programme on HIV/AIDS (UNAIDS),** 20, ave. Appia, CH-1211 Geneva 27, Switzerland (☎+41 22 791 3666; www.unaids.org).

The Council on International Educational Exchange's pamphlet *Travel Safe: AIDS and International Travel* is posted on their web site (www.ciee.org/Isp/safety/travelsafe.htm), along with links to other online and phone resources. According to US law, HIV positive persons are not permitted to enter the US. However, HIV testing is conducted only for those who are planning to immigrate permanently. Travelers from areas with particularly high concentrations of HIV positive persons or those with AIDS may be required to provide more info when applying.

INSURANCE

Travel insurance generally covers four basic areas: medical/health problems, property loss, trip cancellation/interruption, and emergency evacuation. Although your regular insurance policies may extend to travel-related accidents, you may consider purchasing travel insurance if the cost of potential trip cancellation or emergency medical evacuation is greater than you can absorb. Prices for travel insurance purchased separately generally run about $40 per week for full coverage.

Medical insurance (especially university policies) often covers costs incurred abroad; check with your provider. **US Medicare** does not cover foreign travel, with the exception of travel to Canada and Mexico. **Canadians** are protected by their home province's health insurance plan for up to 90 days after leaving the country; check with the provincial Ministry of Health or Health Plan Headquarters for details. **Homeowners' insurance** (or your family's coverage) often covers theft during travel and loss of travel documents (passport, plane ticket, railpass, etc.) up to $500.

ISIC and **ITIC** (see p. 279) provide basic insurance benefits, including $100 per day of in-hospital sickness for up to 60 days, $3,000 of accident-related medical reimbursement, and $25,000 for emergency medical transport. Cardholders have access to a toll-free 24hr. helpline (run by **TravelGuard**) for medical, legal, and financial emergencies (US and Canada ☎877-370-4742. **American Express** (US ☎800-528-4800) grants some cardholders automatic car rental insurance (collision and theft, but not liability) and ground travel accident coverage of $100,000 on flight purchases made with the card.

INSURANCE PROVIDERS. STA (see p. 288) offers a range of plans that can supplement your basic coverage. Other private insurance providers in the US and Canada include: **Access America** (☎866-807-3982; www.accessamerica.com); **Berkely Group** (☎800-797-4514; www.berkely.com); **GlobalCare Insurance Services Inc.** (☎800-821-2488; www.globalcare-cocco.com); and **Travel Assistance International** (☎800-821-2828; www.travelassistance.com). Providers in the **UK** include **Columbus Direct** (☎020 7375 0011; www.columbusdirect.co.uk). In **Australia,** try **AFTA** (☎02 9264 3299; www.afta.com.au).

SMART TRAVEL

PACKING

CONVERTERS & ADAPTERS. In the US, electrical appliances are designed for 120V current. **Canadians,** who use 120V at home, will be able to use electrical appliances in the US with no problem. Visitors from the **U.K., Ireland, Australia, New Zealand** (who use 230V) as well as South Africa (who use 220-250V) won't need a converter, but will need an **adapter** to use anything electrical. In addition, they will need to purchase a **transformer** to convert the lower American voltage to the higher voltage required for most appliances; however, certain electrical devices may accept both 230V and 120V. For further details, visit http://kropla.com/electric.htm.

FIRST-AID KIT. For a basic first-aid kit, pack: bandages, pain reliever, antibiotic cream, a thermometer, a Swiss Army knife, tweezers, moleskin, decongestant, motion-sickness remedy, diarrhea or upset-stomach medication (Pepto Bismol or Imodium), an antihistamine, sunscreen, insect repellent, burn ointment, and a syringe for emergencies (get an explanatory letter from your doctor).

IMPORTANT DOCUMENTS. Don't forget your passport, traveler's checks, ATM and/or credit cards, adequate ID, and photocopies of all of the aforementioned in case these documents are lost or stolen. Also check that you have any of the following that might apply to you: a hosteling membership card (see p. 286), driver's license, travel insurance forms, and/or rail or bus pass (see p. 37).

ⅈ ESSENTIAL
INFORMATION

ENTERING THE US WITH HIV AND AIDS

The Immigration and Naturalization Service (INS) has authority over all non-US citizens entering the country. It wields the powers of exclusion (refusing entrance) and deportation (forcing departure). As a result, the INS is particularly relevant to travelers with HIV. Though being HIV positive is not sufficient grounds for deportation, the INS can deny you entrance to the US based on your HIV status, and it may be difficult to obtain a visa. Travelers who are HIV positive should fill out Form I-601, Application for Waiver of Excludability, available by calling ☎800-870-3676.

The INS does not test for HIV at all customs points, but it has the authority to do so. If you answer "yes" on the non-immigrant visa application to the question "Have you ever been afflicted with a communicable disease of significance of the public health?", they may stop you from entering the US.

In addition, INS officials may even stop you if you seem to be unhealthy or are carrying HIV or AIDS medication. Unfortunately, "looking gay" can be enough to motivate some officials to stop travelers at customs.

Travelers are not without rights. Knowing and asserting these rights can stop customs officials from abusing their authority. For more information, contact the **Immigration HIV Assistance Project,** Bar Association of San Francisco (☎782-8995).

ACCOMMODATIONS

HOSTELS

Hostels are generally laid out dorm-style, often with large single-sex rooms and bunk beds, although some also offer private rooms. They sometimes have kitchens for your use, bike or moped rentals, storage areas, transportation to airports, breakfast, and laundry facilities. There can be drawbacks: some hostels close during certain daytime "lockout" hours, have a curfew, don't accept reservations, impose a maximum stay, or, less frequently, require that you do chores. In San Francisco, a dorm bed in a hostel will average around $15-25 per night and a private room around $45-65. Many hostels require proof of foreign citizenship or international travel.

HOSTELLING INTERNATIONAL

Joining a youth hostel association in your own country (listed below) automatically grants you membership privileges in **Hostelling International (HI),** a federation of national hostelling associations. HI hostels are scattered throughout California and SF, and may accept reservations for a nominal fee via the **International Booking Network** (☎202-783-6161; www.hostelbooking.com). Two comprehensive hostelling websites are www.iyhf.org, which lists contact info for national associations, and www.hostels.com/us.ca.html, which has hostels in California and other resources.

Most HI hostels also honor **guest memberships**—you'll get a blank card with space for six validation stamps. Each night you'll pay a non-member supplement (one-sixth the membership fee) and earn one stamp; get six stamps, and you're a member. A new membership benefit is the Free Nites program, which allows hostelers to gain points toward free rooms. Most student travel agencies (see p. 288) sell HI cards, as do all of the hosteling organizations listed below. Prices listed below are valid for **one-year memberships** unless otherwise noted.

Hostelling International-American Youth Hostels (HI-AYH), 8401 Colesville Road, Suite 600, Silver Spring, MD, 20910 (☎301-495-1240; fax 495-6697; www.hiayh.org). US$28, over 55 US$18, under 18 free.

Hostelling International-Canada (HI-C), 205 Catherine St. #400, Ottawa, ON K2P 1C3 (☎613-237-7884; www.hihostels.ca). CDN$35, under 18 free.

An Óige (Irish Youth Hostel Association), 61 Mountjoy St., Dublin 7 (☎830 4555; fax 830 5808; www.irelandyha.org). €25, under 18 €10.50.

Youth Hostels Association of New Zealand (YHANZ), P.O. Box 436, 166 Moorhouse Ave., Level 1, Moorhouse City, Christchurch (☎03 379 9970; fax 365 4476; www.yha.org.nz). NZ$40, under 18 free.

Hostels Association of South Africa, 73 St. George's House, 3rd fl., Cape Town 8001 (☎021 424 2511; fax 424 4119; www.hisa.org.za). ZAR79, under 18 ZAR40.

Scottish Youth Hostels Association (SYHA), 7 Glebe Crescent, Stirling FK8 2JA (☎ 870 1 55 32 55; fax 871 3308 562; www.syha.org.uk). UK£6, under 18 £2.50.

Youth Hostels Association (England and Wales), Trevelyon House, Dimple Rd., Matlock, Derbyshire DE4 3YH, UK (☎01629 5962600; fax 01629 592702; www.yha.org.uk). UK£13.50, under 18 £6.75.

HI-AYH COUNCIL OFFICES IN THE BAY AREA

Golden Gate Council, 425 Divisadero St. #307, San Francisco 94117 (☎415-863-1444, travel center ☎415-701-1320; hiayh@norcalhostels.org).

Central California Council, P.O. Box 2538, Monterey 93942 (☎209-383-0686; hiayhccc@aol.com).

OTHER TYPES OF ACCOMMODATIONS

YMCAS & YWCAS

Young Men's Christian Association (YMCA) lodgings are usually cheaper than a hotel but more expensive than a hostel. Not all YMCA locations offer lodging; those that do are often located in urban downtowns. Many YMCAs accept women and families; some will not lodge those under 18 without parental permission. You can book online at Travel Y's International (www.travel-ys.com) for free.

YMCA of the USA, 101 North Wacker Drive, Chicago, IL 60606 USA(☎888-333-9622 or 800-872-9622; www.ymca.net). Provides a listing of the nearly 1000 Ys across the US and Canada. Offers info on prices, services available, telephone numbers, and addresses.

HOTELS & GUESTHOUSES

Hotel singles in SF generally cost about $35-75 per night, and doubles are $50-100. You'll typically have a private bathroom and shower, though some cheaper places may offer shared restrooms. Smaller **guesthouses** are often cheaper than hotels. Not all hotels take reservations, and few accept traveler's checks in a foreign currency.

BED & BREAKFASTS (B&BS)

For a cozy alternative to impersonal hotel rooms, B&Bs (private homes with rooms available to travelers) range from acceptable to sublime. Rooms in B&Bs generally cost $50-70 for a single and $70-90 for a double in SF, but on holidays or in expensive locations (such as Napa Valley), prices can soar to over $300. For more info on B&Bs, see **Bed & Breakfast Inns Online,** P.O. Box 829, Madison, TN 37116 (☎615-868-1946; www.bbonline.com), **InnFinder,** 6200 Gisholt Dr. #105, Madison, WI 53713 (☎608-285-6600; fax 285-6601; www.innfinder.com), or **InnSite** (www.innsite.com).

UNIVERSITY DORMS

Many **colleges and universities** open their residence halls to travelers when school is not in session; UC Berkeley, for example, offers summer visitor housing on a per night basis (for summer 2004, www.housing.berkeley.edu/conference/summervis). Getting a room may take a couple of phone calls and require advanced planning, but rates tend to be low, and many offer free local calls and Internet access.

KEEPING IN TOUCH

SENDING MAIL TO SAN FRANCISCO

Mark envelopes "air mail" or *"par avion,"* from abroad. In addition to the standard postage system whose rates are listed in **Once In** (p. 45), **Federal Express** (Australia ☎13 26 10; US and Canada ☎800-247-4747; New Zealand ☎0800 73 33 39; UK ☎0800 12 38 00; www.fedex.com) handles express mail services from most home countries to the United States, as well as within the country; for example, they can get a letter from New York to Los Angeles in 2 days for $9.95, and from London to New York in 2 days for UK£25.80.

GETTING TO SF

BY PLANE

When it comes to airfare, a little effort can save you a bundle. If your plans are flexible, courier fares are the cheapest. Tickets bought from consolidators and standby seating are also good deals, but last-minute specials, airfare wars, and charter flights often beat these fares. The key is to hunt around, be flexible, and ask persistently about discounts. Students, seniors, and those under 26 should never pay full price.

AIRFARES

Airfares to San Francisco peak between June and August and around holidays. Cheaper fares are often available in the winter (Dec.-Feb.). Mid-week (M-Th morning) round-trip flights run $40-50 cheaper than weekend flights. Traveling with an "open return" ticket can be pricier than fixing a return date at the time of purchase.

If San Francisco is only one stop on a more extensive globe-hop, consider a Round-the-World (RTW) ticket. Tickets usually include at least five stops and are valid for about a year; prices range $1200-5000. Try Northwest Airlines/KLM (☎800-447-4747; www.nwa.com) or Star Alliance, a consortium of 13 airlines including United Airlines (☎800-241-6522; www.united.com).

The following chart shows sample round-trip fares between SFO, San Fran's main airport, and various destinations. Be forewarned that airline prices change frequently; these are just guidelines.

ROUNDTRIP BETWEEN CALIFORNIA AND:	PRICE (IN US$)
Any North American destination	$200-650
UK and Ireland	$350-1100
Sydney, Australia	$900-1200
Auckland, New Zealand	$850-1200
Cape Town or Johannesburg	$950-1400

BUDGET & STUDENT TRAVEL AGENCIES

While knowledgeable agents can make your life easy and help you save, they may not spend the time to find you the lowest possible fare—they get paid on commission. Travelers holding **ISIC and IYTC cards** (see p. 279) qualify for big discounts from student travel agencies. Most flights from budget agencies are on major airlines, but in peak season some may sell seats on less reliable chartered aircraft.

USIT, 19-21 Aston Quay, Dublin 2 (☎01 602 1600; www.usitworld.com) Ireland's leading student/budget travel agency has 22 offices throughout Northern Ireland and the Republic of Ireland. Offers programs to work in North America.

CTS Travel, 30 Rathbone Pl., London W1T 1GQ, UK (☎020 7290 0630; www.ctstravel.co.uk). A British student travel agent with offices in 39 countries including the US, Empire State Building, 350 Fifth Ave., Suite 7813, .New York, NY 10118 (☎877-287-6665; www.ctstravelusa.com).

STA Travel, 7890 S. Hardy Dr., Ste. 110, Tempe AZ 85284, USA (24hr. ☎800-781-4040; www.sta-travel.com). A student and youth travel organization with over 150 offices worldwide (check their website for a listing of all their offices), including US offices in Boston, Chicago, L.A., New York, San Francisco, Seattle, and Washington, D.C. Ticket booking, travel insurance, railpasses, and more. In the UK, walk-in office 11 Goodge St., **London** W1T 2PF or call ☎0207-436-7779. In New Zealand, Shop 2B, 182 Queen St., **Auckland** (☎09 309 0458). In Australia, 366 Lygon St., **Carlton** Vic 3053 (☎03 9349 4344).

Travel CUTS (Canadian Universities Travel Services Limited), 187 College St., **Toronto,** ON M5T 1P7 (☎416-979-2406; fax 979-8167; www.travelcuts.com). Offices across Canada and the United States in Seattle, San Francisco, Los Angeles, New York and elsewhere. Also in the UK, 295-A Regent St., London W1B 2H9 (☎0207 255 2191).

COMMERCIAL AIRLINES

The commercial airlines' lowest regular offer is the **APEX** (Advance Purchase Excursion) fare, which provides confirmed reservations and allows "open-jaw" tickets. Generally, reservations must be made seven to 21 days ahead of departure, with seven- to 14-day minimum-stay and up to 90-day maximum-stay restrictions. These fares carry hefty cancellation and change penalties. Book peak-season APEX fares early; by May you will have a hard time getting your desired date. Use **Microsoft Expedia** (http://msn.expedia.com) or **Travelocity** (www.travelocity.com) to get an idea of the lowest published fares, then use the resources below to try to beat those fares.

AIR COURIER FLIGHTS

Those who travel light should consider courier flights. Couriers help transport cargo on international flights by using their checked luggage space for freight. Generally, couriers must travel with carry-ons only and deal with complex restrictions. Most flights are round-trip only, with short fixed-length stays (usually one week) and a limit of a one ticket per issue. Most of these flights also operate only out of major gateway cities: New York, Los Angeles, San Francisco, or Miami in the US; and Montreal, Toronto, or Vancouver in Canada. Generally, you must be over 21 (sometimes 18). In summer, the most popular destinations usually require about two weeks reservation (you can usually book up to two months ahead). Super-discounted fares are common for "last-minute" flights (three to 14 days ahead).

STANDBY FLIGHTS

Traveling standby requires considerable flexibility in arrival and departure dates and cities. Companies dealing in standby flights sell vouchers rather than tickets, along with the promise to get to your destination (or near your destination) within a certain window of time (typically 1-5 days). You may receive a monetary refund only if every available flight within your date range is full. Carefully read agreements with any company offering standby flights as tricky fine print can leave you in a lurch. To check on a company's service record in the US, call the Better Business Bureau (☎212-533-6200). It is difficult to receive refunds, and clients' vouchers will not be honored when an airline fails to receive payment in time.

TICKET CONSOLIDATORS

Ticket consolidators, or **"bucket shops,"** buy unsold tickets in bulk from commercial airlines and sell them at discounted rates. The best place to look is in the Sunday travel section of any major newspaper (such as the *New York Times*), where many bucket shops place tiny ads. Call quickly, as availability is typically extremely limited. Not all bucket shops are reliable, so insist on a receipt that gives full details of restrictions, refunds, and tickets, and pay by credit card (in spite of the 2-5% fee) so you can stop payment if you never receive your tickets. For more info, see www.travel-library.com/air-travel/consolidators.html.

TRAVELING FROM THE US & CANADA

Travel Avenue (☎800-333-3335; www.travelavenue.com) searches for best available published fares and then uses several consolidators to attempt to beat that fare. Other consolidators worth trying are **Interworld** (☎305-443-4929; fax 443-0351); **Rebel** (☎800-227-3235; travel@rebeltours.com; www.rebeltours.com); and **Travac** (☎800-872-8800; www.travac.com). Yet more consolidators on the web include the **Internet Travel Network** (www.itn.com); **Travel Information Services** (www.tiss.com); and **TravelHUB** (www.travelhub.com). Keep in mind that these are just suggestions to get you started in your research; *Let's Go* does not endorse any of these agencies. As always, be cautious, and research companies before you hand over your credit card number.

CHARTER FLIGHTS

Charters are flights a tour operator contracts with an airline to fly extra loads of passengers. Charter flights fly less frequently, make refunds particularly difficult, and are almost always fully booked. Schedules may also change or be cancelled at the last moment (as late as 48 hours before the trip), and check-in, boarding, and baggage claim are often much slower. However, they can also be cheaper.

    Discount clubs and **fare brokers** offer members savings on last-minute charter and tour deals. **Travelers Advantage**, Trumbull, CT, USA (☎877-259-2691; www.travelersadvantage.com; US$60 annual fee includes discounts and cheap flight directories) can provide more information.

BY BUS

Greyhound (☎800-231-2222; www.greyhound.com) is the only bus service that operates throughout the entire state. Reserve with a credit card over the phone at least 10 days in advance, and the ticket can be mailed anywhere in the US. Reservations available only up to 24hr. in advance or at the bus terminal. Schedule information is available at any Greyhound terminal or agency and on the website.

Advance purchase fares: Reserving space far ahead of time ensures a lower fare, but expect smaller discounts between June 5 and Sept. 15. Fares are often lower for 14-day, 7-day, or 3-day advance purchases. For 3-day advance purchase M-Th, 2 people ride for the price of 1 ticket. Call for up-to-date pricing or consult their web page.

Discounts on full fares: Senior citizens with a Greyhound Senior Club Card (10% off); children ages 2-11 (50% off); Student Advantage card holders (up to 15% off); disabled travelers and an attendant receive two tickets for the price of one; active and retired US military personnel and National Guard Reserves (10% off with valid ID); Veterans Administration affiliates (25% off with VA form 3068). With a ticket purchased 3 days in advance during the spring and summer months, a friend can travel along for free (with some exceptions).

Ameripass: ☎800-454-7277. Allows adults unlimited travel through the US. 7-day pass $229; 10-day pass $279; 15-day pass $349; 30-day pass $459, 45-day pass $519; 60-day pass $625. Student discounts available. Children's passes half-price. Before purchasing an Ameripass, total up the separate bus fares between towns to make sure that the pass is more economical or at least worth the flexibility it provides. For travelers from outside North America. **International:** ☎800-454-7277 for info. 7 days ($219), 10 ($269), 15 ($329), 30 ($439), 45 ($489), or 60 ($599). International Ameripasses not available at the terminal; can be purchased in foreign countries at Greyhound-affiliated agencies; telephone numbers are listed on the website. Passes can also be ordered at the website.

Adventurebus, 870 Market St. #416, San Francisco, CA 94102 (☎888-737-5263, outside the US ☎909-797-7366; www.adventurebus.com), runs fun-loving tours through cities, towns, and national parks in California and the southwestern US. Transportation in "extremely unconventional" buses, driven by knowledgeable guides, provides fun and like-minded company. Nine- to 16-day trips run from $300-700.

BY CAR

If you are driving into San Francisco **from the south,** approach the city directly on **US 101, I-280,** or **Rte. 1.** I-280 crosses US 101 in southern San Francisco, then continues through eastern Potrero Hill to end just southeast of SoMa. US 101 runs along the border of Potrero Hill and the Mission, then bears left through SoMa and becomes **Van Ness Ave.** Rte. 1 turns into **19th Ave.** around San Francisco State University and runs through the Sunset, Golden Gate Park, the Richmond, and the Presidio.

From the north, US 101 and Rte. 1 will bring you over the **Golden Gate Bridge** (southbound toll $3). Rte. 1 turns into **19th Ave.,** while US 101 turns into **Lombard St.** in the Marina. From there you have two options: taking a right on **Divisadero St.** and heading uphill and down will bring you to the **Haight** and the **Castro;** or, continuing on Lombard St., turning right on Van Ness Ave., and following it between Pacific Heights and Russian and Nob Hills will bring you to **Market St.** near the Civic Center.

From the east, I-5 to I-580 to I-80 runs across the **Bay Bridge** (westbound toll $2) into SoMa and then connects with US 101 just before it runs into Van Ness Ave.

AMERICAN AUTOMOBILE ASSOCIATION (AAA)

The high priest of California's vehicular pantheon. To join the automobile club, call 800-JOIN-AAA/564-6222, or go to www.aaa.com. Free trip-planning services, maps, and guidebooks, and 24hr. emergency road service in the US (☎800-AAA-HELP/222-4357). Offers free towing and commission-free American Express Traveler's Cheques, as well as discounts on Hertz car rental (5-20%), Amtrak tickets (10%), and various motel chains and theme parks. AAA has reciprocal agreements with the auto associations of many other countries, which often provide you with full benefits while in the US. Check with your auto association for details. Membership in the California branch costs $17 to join and $49 per year, plus $21 for each additional family member. Costs at other AAA branches vary slightly.

RENTING A CAR

Before leaving, make sure your car is in good condition and you have reliable maps. *Rand McNally's Road Atlas*, covering all of the US and Canada, is one of the best (available at bookstores and gas stations, $14; California state map $5). A compass and car manual can also be very useful. Always carry a spare tire and jack, jumper cables, extra oil, flares, a flashlight, and blankets.

While driving, be sure to **buckle up**—seat belts are required by law in California. The **speed limit** in California varies depending on the road on which you are traveling (some freeways have limits as high as 70mph, while residential areas are generally 25mph). Drivers should take necessary precautions against **carjacking,** which is a frequently committed crime in the state. Carjackers often prey on cars parked or stopped at red lights. Lock your doors and don't keep your purse in full view.

LICENSES

Visitors to California who are over 18 can drive with a valid license from their home state or country; however, some visitors may choose to get an **International Driver's Permit (IDP)** from their home automobile associations. Your IDP, valid for one year, must be issued in your country before you depart. An application usually needs to include one or two photos, a current local license, an additional form of identification, and a fee. Make sure to carry your home license at all times with your IDP.

CAR INSURANCE

Most credit cards cover standard insurance. If you rent, lease, or borrow a car, international travelers will need a **green card,** or **International Insurance Certificate,** to certify that you have liability insurance and that it applies abroad. Contact your nearest Automobile Association for more information. Green cards can be obtained at car rental agencies, or car dealers (for those leasing cars). For more information on car rentals in San Francisco, see the **Service Directory,** p. 312.

SPECIFIC CONCERNS

WOMEN TRAVELERS

If you feel unsafe anywhere as a woman, try to look as if you know where you're going and approach older women or couples for directions if you're lost or uncomfortable. Wearing a **wedding band** may help prevent unwanted overtures.

Your best answer to verbal harassment is no answer at all; feigning deafness, sitting motionless, and staring straight ahead at nothing in particular will do a world of good that reactions usually don't achieve. The extremely persistent can sometimes be dissuaded by a firm, loud, and very public "Go away!" Don't hesitate to seek out a police officer or a passerby if you are being harassed. Memorize the emergency numbers in places you visit, and consider carrying a key chain whistle.

For general information, contact the **National Organization for Women (NOW),** 733 15th St. NW, 2nd fl., Washington, D.C. 20005 (☎202-628-8669; www.now.org), which can refer travelers to rape crisis centers and counseling services.

TRAVELING ALONE

There are many benefits to traveling alone, including independence and greater interaction with locals. On the other hand, any solo traveler is a more vulnerable target of harassment and street theft. As a lone traveler, try not to stand out as a tourist; look confident, and be especially careful in deserted or very crowded areas. If questioned, never admit that you are traveling alone. Maintain regular contact with someone at home who knows your itinerary. For more tips, pick up *Traveling Solo* by Eleanor Berman (Globe Pequot Press, $18) or subscribe to **Connecting: Solo Travel Network,** 689 Park Road, Unit 6, Gibsons, BC V0N 1V7, Canada (☎604-886-9099; www.cstn.org; membership $35)

ELDERLY TRAVELERS

Senior citizens are eligible for a wide range of discounts on transportation, museums, movies, theaters, concerts, restaurants, and accommodations. The books *No Problem! Worldwise Tips for Mature Adventurers*, by Janice Kenyon (Orca Book Publishers; $16) and *Unbelievably Good Deals and Great Adventures That You Absolutely Can't Get Unless You're Over 50*, by Joan Rattner Heilman (NTC/Contemporary Publishing; $15) are both excellent resources. For more information, contact one of the following organizations:

Elderhostel, 11 Ave. de Lafayette, Boston, MA 02111 (☎877-426-8056; www.elderhostel.org). Organizes 1- to 4-week educational adventures for those 55+.

The Mature Traveler, P.O. Box 1543, Wildomar, CA 92595 (☎909-461-9598; www.thematuretraveler.com; subscription $30). Monthly newsletter with deals, discounts, tips, and travel packages for the senior traveler.

Walking the World, P.O. Box 1186, Fort Collins, CO 80522 (☎800-340-9255; www.walkingtheworld.com), runs walking-focused trips for travelers 50+. Trips run to destinations ranging from California to Iceland.

BISEXUAL, GAY, AND LESBIAN TRAVELERS

San Francisco has garnered a reputation as a **gay mecca.** For many, the center of the gay community is the Castro, while the lesbian community is spread between the Castro, the Mission, Bernal Heights, and the suburbs. The entire Bay Area is generally quite tolerant. Accommodations will usually have no problem with single-sex couples requesting rooms, and public displays of affection are usually safe, although you should exercise caution in more deserted areas.

Listed below are contact organizations, mail-order bookstores, and publishers which offer materials addressing some specific concerns. **Out and About** (www.planetout.com) offers a biweekly newsletter addressing travel concerns. For more local resources, see the **Service Directory: Gay/Lesbian Resources,** p. 314.

International Lesbian and Gay Association (ILGA), 81 rue Marché-au-Charbon, B-1000 Brussels, Belgium (☎+32 2 502 2471; www.ilga.org). Provides political information, such as homosexuality laws of individual countries.

Giovanni's Room, 1145 Pine St., Philadelphia, PA 19107, USA (☎215-923-2960; www.queerbooks.com). An international lesbian/feminist and gay bookstore with mail-order service (carries many of the publications listed below).

Gay's the Word, 66 Marchmont St., London WC1N 1AB, UK (☎+44 20 7278 7654; www.gaystheword.co.uk). The largest gay and lesbian bookshop in the UK, with both fiction and non-fiction titles. Mail-order service available.

TRAVELERS WITH DISABILITIES

Federal law dictates that all public buildings should be handicapped accessible, and recent building codes make disabled access more the norm than the exception. However, traveling with a disability still requires planning. Those with disabilities should inform airlines and hotels of their disabilities when making reservations; some time may be needed to prepare special accommodations.

Amtrak and major airlines will accommodate disabled passengers if notified 72 hours in advance. Hearing-impaired travelers may contact Amtrak using teletype printers (☎800-523-6590 or 800-654-5988). Greyhound buses will provide free travel for a companion; if you are alone, call Greyhound (☎800-752-4841) at least 48 hours, but no more than one week, before you leave. For information on transportation in individual US cities, contact the local chapter of the Easter Seals Society.

If you are planning to visit a park or attraction run by the National Park Service, obtain a free **Golden Access Passport,** which is available at all park entrances. The Passport entitles disabled travelers and their families to free park admission and provides a 50% discount on all campsite and parking fees. For further reading, check out *Resource Directory for the Disabled,* by Richard Neil Shrout ($45).

USEFUL ORGANIZATIONS

Mobility International USA (MIUSA), P.O. Box 10767, Eugene, OR 97440, USA (☎541-343-1284, voice and TDD; www.miusa.org). Provides a variety of books and other publications containing information for travelers with disabilities.

Society for Accessible Travel and Hospitality (SATH), 347 Fifth Ave., #610, New York, NY 10016, USA (☎212-447-7284; www.sath.org). An advocacy group that publishes free online travel information and the travel magazine *OPEN WORLD* (US$18, free for members). Annual membership US$45, students and seniors US$30.

TOUR AGENCIES

Directions Unlimited, 123 Green Ln., Bedford Hills, NY 10507 (☎800-533-5343). Books individual and group vacations for the physically disabled; not an info service.

The Guided Tour Inc., 7900 Old York Rd., #114B, Elkins Park, PA 19027 (☎800-783-5841; www.guidedtour.com). Organizes travel programs for persons with developmental and physical challenges in California and elsewhere in the United States.

MINORITY TRAVELERS

California is a multicultural state, but not always a harmonious one. Although "minority" groups are now the majority in California, anti-immigrant feeling persists in many areas, especially toward Mexican immigrants. Racial and ethnic minorities sometimes face blatant and, more often, subtle discrimination and/or harassment. Verbal harassment is now less common than unfair pricing, false info on accommodations, or inexcusably slow or unfriendly service at restaurants. Report individuals to a supervisor and establishments to the **Better Business Bureau** for the region (www.bbb.org, or call the operator for local listings); contact the police in extreme situations. *Let's Go* always welcomes reader input regarding discriminating establishments. Be aware that racial tensions do exist even in large, ostensibly progressive areas, and try to avoid confrontations.

TRAVELERS WITH CHILDREN

Family vacations often require that you slow your pace, and always require that you plan ahead. If you rent a car, make sure the rental company provides a car seat for younger children. **Be sure that your child carries some sort of ID** in case of an emergency of in case he or she gets lost. Tourist attractions, hotels, and restaurants often offer discounts for children. Children under two usually fly for 10% of the adult fare on overseas flights (this does not necessarily include a seat). International fares are usually discounted 25% for children two to 11. Some helpful resources include:

Adventuring with Children: An Inspirational Guide to World Travel and the Outdoors, Nan Jeffrey. Avalon House Publishing (US$15).

Backpacking with Babies and Small Children, Goldie Silverman. Wilderness Press ($10).

Gutsy Mamas: Travel Tips and Wisdom for Mothers on the Road, Marybeth Bond. Travelers' Tales, Inc. (US$8).

Have Kid, Will Travel: 101 Survival Strategies for Vacationing With Babies and Young Children, Claire and Lucille Tristram. Andrews McMeel Publishing ($9).

Kidding Around San Francisco, Bobi Martin. Avalon Travel Publishing ($8).

Trouble-Free Travel with Children, Vicki Lansky. Book Peddlers ($9).

DIETARY CONCERNS

Vegetarians should have a food fest in veggie-noshing, soy milk-guzzling California and in San Francisco in particular. *Let's Go* indicates vegetarian options in restaurant listings; other places to look for vegetarian and vegan cuisine are local health food stores, as well as natural food chains such as **Trader Joe's** and **Wild Oats**. The **North American Vegetarian Society**, P.O. Box 72, Dolgeville, NY 13329 (☎518-568-7970; www.navs-online.org), publishes info about vegetarian travel, including *Vegetarian Journal's Guide to Natural Food Restaurants in the US and Canada* ($12). You might also try the Vegetarian Resource Group's website, www.vrg.org/travel, or Jed Civic's *The Vegetarian Traveler: Where to Stay If You're Vegetarian, Vegan, Environmentally Sensitive.* (Larson Publishing; $16).

Travelers who keep kosher should contact synagogues in larger cities for information on kosher restaurants. Your own synagogue or college Hillel should have access to lists of Jewish institutions across the nation. You may also consult the

kosher restaurant database at www.shamash.org/kosher. A good resource is the *Jewish Travel Guide*, edited by Michael Zaidner (Vallentine Mitchell; $17). If you are strict in your observance, you may have to prepare your own food on the road.

OTHER RESOURCES

Listed below are bookstores, publishers, periodicals, and websites that can serve as jumping off points for your own research on a variety of concerns.

USEFUL PUBLICATIONS

San Francisco offers a variety of homegrown media. Brushing up on current events before you leave will undoubtedly make for a more informed trip. Try the *Chronicle* (www.sfchronicle.com), *SF Weekly* (www.sfweekly.com), the *Bay Guardian* (www.sfbg.com), and the *Bay Area Reporter*, a weekly queer newspaper (www.ebar.com).

TRAVEL BOOKSTORES & PUBLISHERS

Hunter Publishing, 470 W. Broadway, 2nd fl., South Boston, MA 02127 (☎617-269-0700; www.hunterpublishing.com). Has an extensive catalog of travel guides and diving and adventure travel books.

Rand McNally, P.O. Box 7600, Chicago, IL 60680 (☎847-329-8100; www.randmc-nally.com), publishes road atlases.

Adventurous Traveler Bookstore, P.O. Box 2221, Williston, VT 05495 (☎800-282-3963; www.adventuroustraveler.com).

Bon Voyage!, 2069 W. Bullard Ave., Fresno, CA 93711 (☎800-995-9716, from abroad 559-447-8441; www.bon-voyage-travel.com). They specialize in Europe but have titles pertaining to other regions as well. Free newsletter.

WWW

At the keyboard, you can make a hostel reservation, get advice on travel hotspots from fellow travelers, or find out how much your flight will cost. Listed here are budget travel sites to start off your surfing.

 WWW.LETSGO.COM Our website, www.letsgo.com, now includes introductory chapters from all our guides and a wealth of information on a monthly featured destination. As always, our website also has info about our books, a travel forum buzzing with stories and tips, and additional links that will help you make the most of a trip to San Francisco. In addition, all nine Let's Go City Guides are available for download on Palm OS PDAs.

THE ART OF BUDGET TRAVEL

How to See the World: www.artoftravel.com. A compendium of great travel tips, from cheap flights to self-defense to interacting with local culture.

Rec. Travel Library: www.travel-library.com. A fantastic set of links for general information and personal travelogues.

INFORMATION ON SAN FRANCISCO

Citysearch: www.bayarea.citysearch.com. Contains descriptions of just about everything there is in San Francisco.

Bay Guardian: www.sfbg.com. Current events and yearly Best of the Bay listings.

Atevo Travel: www.atevo.com/guides/destinations. Detailed introductions, travel tips, and suggested itineraries.

PlanetRider: www.planetrider.com. A subjective list of links to the "best" web sites covering the culture and tourist attractions of San Francisco.

Alternatives to Tourism

When we started out in 1961, about 1.7 million people in the world were traveling international-ly each year; in 2002, nearly 700 million trips were made, projected to be up to a billion by 2010. The dramatic rise in tourism has created an interdependence between the economies, environments, and cultures of many destinations and the tourists they host. In 2000 the San Francisco Convention & Visitors Bureau (SFCVB) reported that 142,700 visitors are in San Francisco on an average day, not too shabby for a city with a population of roughly 770,000. Tourism generates approximately $7.62 billion for the city annually and produces about 82,000 jobs. These statistics only provide a glimpse of how critical tourism and short-term stays are to daily life in San Francisco.

San Francisco is a city teeming with activism and awareness of both local and global issues. Activist communities range from student-based groups (like the legendary con-tingent at UC Berkeley) to neighborhood associations to city council campaigns. Here are a few hot topics to be addressed in the coming year: in late July 2003 President Bush declared his desire to promote legislation defining marriage as "between a man and a woman," a statement which many in the gay community in San Francisco (esti-mated at about one-sixth of the city) will presumably challenge. AIDS, often culturally disdained as a disease of the homosexual community, continues to be on the rise in San Francisco, with an estimated 17,838 cases of persons with HIV or AIDS living within the city . The AIDS foundation, one of the largest institutions in SF dedicated to AIDS prevention and education, estimates 1,084 new cases each year.

Finding affordable long-term accommodation in San Francisco has always been a challenge, and though rents have decreased somewhat since the economic downturn of 2001, they continue to plague residents and would-be residents of the city. The downturn has correspondingly had an effect on homelessness, with approximately 4,500 people living on the streets of SF, according to the Mayor's Office. Legislative initiatives such as "Care Not Cash" struggle through Congress with proposals to increase the availability of shelters and food services to the urban poor. In the meantime, numerous charitable and non-profit organizations labor diligently (if disjointedly) against poverty (see p. 301).

Environmentalism in San Fran is also an important activist concern. In a city where driving is discouraged, conservation is almost an economic necessity. A 2002 survey found that an astounding 93% of San Franciscans deem public transportation to be very important in their daily lives (MUNI survey). Citizens of SF are also willing to go the extra mile to keep their streets and neighborhoods clean. As a recent city clean-up campaign quips, "We are lucky to live in San Francisco" merging San Francisco's traditionally ecologically-minded population with an appeal to civic pride.

FIND THE PATH. To read more on a specific organization that is working to better its community, look for our **Giving Back** feature on the Tenderloin Playground and Recreation Center (p. 17).

Those looking to **volunteer** in San Francisco have many options. You can engage in projects whose goals extend from global to local, promoting world peace or encouraging neighborhood tolerance. Later in this section, we recommend organizations that can help you find the opportunities that best suit your interests, whether you're looking to pitch in for a day or a year.

Studying is another way to integrate yourself with the communities you visit. Full

---

Before handing your money over to any volunteer or study abroad program, make sure you know exactly what you're getting into. It's a good idea to get the name of **previous participants** and ask them about their experience, as some programs sound much better on paper than in reality. The **questions** below are a good place to start:

—Will you be the only person in the program? If not, what are the other participants like? How old are they? How much will you be expected to interact with them?

—Is room and board included? If so, what is the arrangement? Will you be expected to share a room? A bathroom? What are the meals like? Do they cater to any dietary restrictions?

—Is transportation included? Are there any additional expenses?

—How much free time will you have? Will you be able to travel around?

—What kind of safety network is set up? Will you still be covered by your home insurance? Does the program have an emergency plan?

---

of art galleries and museums, the San Francisco art and architecture schools are world-renowned. Home to a vibrant intellectual environment, San Fran caters to adults interested in continuing education. Many travelers also structure their trips by the work that they can do along the way—either odd jobs as they go, or full-time stints in cities where they plan to stay for some time. Though the IT bubble may have popped, short-term tech and clerical can still be found for the persistent.

For those who seek more active involvement, Earthwatch International, Operation Crossroads Africa, and Habitat for Humanity offer fulfilling volunteer opportunities all over the world. For more on volunteering, studying, and working in San Francisco and beyond, consult Let's Go's alternatives to tourism site, www.beyondtourism.com.

A NEW PHILOSOPHY OF TRAVEL

We at *Let's Go* have watched the growth of the 'ignorant tourist' stereotype with dismay, knowing that the majority of travelers care passionately about the state of the communities and environments they explore—but also knowing that even conscientious tourists can inadvertently damage natural wonders, rich cultures, and impoverished communities. We believe the philosophy of **sustainable travel** is among the most important travel tips we could impart to our readers, to help guide fellow backpackers and on-the-road philanthropists. By staying aware of the needs and troubles of local communities, today's travelers can be a powerful force in preserving and restoring this fragile world.

Working against the negative consequences of irresponsible tourism is much simpler than it might seem; it is often self-awareness, rather than self-sacrifice, that makes the biggest difference. Simply by trying to spend responsibly and conserve local resources, all travelers can positively impact the places they visit. Let's Go has partnered with **BEST** (**Business Enterprises for Sustainable Travel,** an affiliate of the Conference Board; see www.sustainabletravel.org), which recognizes businesses that operate based on the principles of sustainable travel. Below, they provide advice on how ordinary visitors can practice this philosophy in their daily travels, no matter where they are.

TIPS FOR CIVIC TRAVEL: HOW TO MAKE A DIFFERENCE

Travel by train when feasible. Rail travel requires only half the energy per passenger mile that planes do. On average, each of the 40,000 daily domestic air flights releases more than 1700 pounds of greenhouse gas emissions.

Use public mass transportation whenever possible; outside of cities, take advantage of group taxis or vans. Bicycles are an attractive way of seeing a community firsthand. And enjoy walking—purchase good maps of your destination and ask about on-foot touring opportunities.

When renting a car, ask whether fuel-efficient vehicles are available. Honda and Toyota produce cars that use hybrid engines powered by electricity and gasoline, thus reducing emissions of carbon dioxide. Ford Motor Company plans to introduce a hybrid fuel model by the end of 2004.

Reduce, reuse, recycle—use electronic tickets, recycle papers and bottles wherever possible, and avoid using containers made of styrofoam. Refillable water bottles and rechargable batteries both efficiently conserve expendable resources.

Be thoughtful in your purchases. Take care not to buy souvenir objects made from trees in old-growth or endangered forests, such as teak, or items made from endangered species, like ivory or tortoise jewelry. Ask whether products are made from renewable resources.

Buy from local enterprises, such as casual street vendors. In developing countries and low-income neighborhoods, many people depend on the "informal economy" to make a living.

Be on-the-road-philanthropists. If you are inspired by the natural environment of a destination or enriched by its culture, join in preserving their integrity by making a charitable contribution to a local organization.

Spread the word. Upon your return home, tell friends and colleagues about places to visit that will benefit greatly from their tourist dollars, and reward sustainable enterprises by recommending their services. Travelers can not only introduce friends to particular vendors but also to local causes and charities that they might choose to support when they travel.

Farmer's Market

Mission Dolores Park

Tai Chi

VOLUNTEERING

Though San Francisco is considered one of the wealthiest (and most expensive) cities in the United States, there is no shortage of organizations designed to benefit needs in the region. Volunteering can be an incredibly fulfilling experience, especially if you combine it with the thrill of traveling in a new place.

Most people who volunteer in San Francisco do so on a short-term basis, at organizations that make use of drop-in or once-a-week volunteers. More intensive volunteer services may charge you a fee to participate. These costs can be surprisingly hefty (although they frequently cover airfare and most, if not all, living expenses). Most people choose to go through a parent organization that takes care of logistical details and frequently provides a group environment and support system. There are two main types of organizations—religious and non-sectarian—although there are rarely restrictions on participation for either.

For those seeking immediate openings with non-profits in the Bay Area, an efficient place to begin your search is with the **Young, Non-Profit Professionals Network** (www.ynpn.org). Or, check postings on **www.nonprofitoyster.com.** Otherwise, see below for a listing of volunteer opportunities organized by issue.

ENVIRONMENTAL ACTIVISM

Rated as the most "green" city in the US, San Francisco offers a wealth of active and welcoming environmental organizations. The real challenge is not to be overwhelmed by the options. Be sure to shop around for the organization best tailored to your interests and try out **www.eco-jobs.com** for further openings.

Arc Ecology, 833 Market St., Suite 1104, San Francisco, CA 94103 (☎495-1789; fax 495-1787). A non-profit organization providing scientific and technical support to grassroots community-based organizations. Particularly concerned with the clean-up and utilization of former military property transitioning to the civilian sector.

Center for Urban Education about Sustainable Agriculture (CUESA), 2000 Van Ness Ave. Suite 512, San Francisco, CA 94109 (☎353-5650; www.ferry-plazafarmersmarket.com). Operates the Ferry Plaza's Farmer's market and sponsors educational programs on sustainable agriculture. Email info@cuesa.org for information on volunteer opportunities.

Earth Island Institute, 300 Broadway, Suite 28, San Francisco 94133-3312 (☎788-3666; www.earthisland.org). Operates as a support cooperative and centralized resource for independent projects on earth conservation, preservation, and restoration from protecting the whales to reducing pollution. Offers work, volunteer, and internship opportunities.

Earth Share of California, 49 Powell St. #510, San Francisco CA 94102 (☎ 800-368-1819 or 981-1999; www.earthshareca.org). Coordinates fundraising and environment-friendly volunteer activities for member groups' employees. Individuals may take advantage of Earth Share's directory for referrals to volunteer openings.

Greenaction for Health and Environmental Justice, One Hallidie Plaza, Suite 760, San Francisco, CA 94102 (☎ 248-5010; fax 248-5011). Sponsors campaigns from promoting sustainable energy to preserving sacred native American lands. Sends interns throughout the Bay Area and the San Joaquin Valley to tackle a vast range of projects.

Greenpeace USA, 702 H St. NW, Suite 300, Washington, DC 20001 (fax 561-258-2350; interns@wdc.greenpeace.org) One of the most well-known environmental organizations worldwide, the GP offers internships in Washington D.C. and a limited number in San Fran. Applicants should send a cover letter, resume, and short writing sample to Internship Program Director at the D.C. address.

Hill Habitat Restoration (☎554-9604), in Corona Heights Park in Haight-Ashbury. Help restore the grounds of the park from 10am-noon on the last Sa of the month (p. 97).

Pesticide Action Network of North America, 49 Powell St., Suite 500, San Francisco, CA 94102 (☎ 415-981-1771; www.panna.org). One of five regional centers worldwide, PANNA works to replace pesticide use with ecologically sound and socially just alternatives by linking local and international consumer, labor, and agriculture groups. Volunteer and college-credit internships available. Contact Angelica Barrera (☎981-6205)

Planet Drum Foundation, P.O. Box 31251, San Francisco, CA 94131. (☎285-6556; fax 285-6563; www.planetdrum.org; office open by appointment). Their Volunteer Network, comprised of over 450 Bay Area environmental groups, offers volunteer and internship opportunities for individuals, schools, and businesses. Check out their online Green City calendar for upcoming projects or call for a referral. Internships also available with the Foundation itself. Planet Drum also offers Green city tours of the Bay Area (2hr., fees negotiable).

Rainforest Action Network, 221 Pine St., Suite 500, San Francisco, CA 94104 (☎398-4404; www.ran.org). Dedicated to preserving rainforests worldwide, RAN offers 3-month internships in communications, campaigns, and development. Though no stipend is provided for the internship, RAN reimburses daily commuting costs (up to $7 per day). Contact Volunteer and Internship program at helpran@ran.org.

ECONOMIC JUSTICE

Since 2001 the disadvantaged in San Francisco have fallen on harder times. Unemployment has risen from 3.2 to 7 percent. Approximately 21% of children in San Francisco county live on or below the poverty line, a disproportionate number from minority families. Whether providing free health care, a hot plate of food, or just a friendly ear, community service organizations around San Fran are abundant and always looking for more helping hands.

Berkeley Free Clinic, 2339 Durant Avenue, Berkeley, 94704 (☎510-548-2570; www.berkeleyfreeclinic.org). Since 1969 this non-profit clinic has been providing free medical, dental, and counseling services to the public. Also sponsors a Gay Men's Health Collective. Volunteer in different health sectors, including Hepatitis prevention and HIV testing. Orientations 3rd Monday of every month at 7:30pm.

Coalition of Concerned Legal Professionals, 590 Leland Avenue, San Francisco, CA 94134 (☎587-4240) or 2107 Van Ness Ave, Suite 303, 94109 (☎614-0978). An all-volunteer, non-government funded association of attorneys, paralegals, law students, and others dedicated to serving the public interest. Offers on-the-job training.

Mission Mural

SF MoMA

City Lights Bookstore

Food First/Institute for Food and Development Policy, 398 60th St., Oakland, CA 94608 (☎510-654-4400; www.foodfirst.org). This non-profit think-tank produces books, reports, electronic media, and organizes interviews and workshops for activists and the public on world hunger. On-site internships in research, outreach, and publications require a 3-month commitment. Unique "virtual" internships allow volunteers to assist in translation, research, and editing from remote locations. Spanish, French, Portuguese and Italian speakers in demand. Contact Marilyn Borchardt, Development Director/Intern Coordinator at marbor@foodfirst.org

Food not Bombs, P.O. Box 40485, San Francisco, CA 94140 (☎675-9928; www.sffoodnotbombs.org). In protest against hunger, poverty, and militarization, FNB builds community by serving free vegetarian lunch and dinner to the public five days a week in the UN Plaza and Golden Gate Park. Volunteers always needed for transportation, cooking, serving, and cleaning. Meetings held weekly at The Coalition on Homelessness, 468 Turk St., Th 7:30-10pm.

San Francisco Senior Center, 481 O'Farrell St. (☎415-771-7950), between Jones and Taylor St.

Tenderloin Community Children's Center and Playground, 570 Ellis St., between Leavenworth and Hyde St. Though an official public park, it is open only to children 18 and under and their guardians. Built in 1995, the center staffs energetic volunteers who undergo a two-week screening process and provide the Tenderloin's 4,000 children with activities, sports, arts and crafts, and computer classes. See p. 17. Open M-F 10am-8:30pm, Sa 10am-6pm, Su noon-5pm.

Volunteer Center for the Bay Area, 1675 California St. (☎982-8999; www.vcsf.org), at Van Ness Ave. A registration clearinghouse for non-profit organizations, the center has a database of volunteer opportunities and counselors.

PEACE AND LOVE ON A GLOBAL SCALE

Yes, the ethic born of the 1960s is alive and well in many San Fran non-profits. Politically active (or "leftist" as some might say), these organizations are usually seeking help in public relations, fundraising, and research.

California Peace Action (☎510-849-2272; www.californiapeaceaction.org), in Berkeley. California's largest peace group, CPA works to reduce the threat posed by nuclear weapons, decrease US arms spending, and promote international cooperation. For more information on jobs, volunteering, and internships contact Kara Voss, kara@californiapeaceaction.org.

Global Exchange, 2017 Mission St., #303, San Francisco, CA 94110 (☎255-7296; www.globalexchange.org). A grassroots, international human rights organization dedicated to environmental, political, and social justice. 1-2 month internships are available in the fall, spring, and summer. Volunteers encouraged to call the office or email volunteers@globalexchange.org. to develop skills in language, computers, and public relations and organizing.

JustAct, Youth action for Global Justice, 333 Valencia St., Suite 325, San Francisco, CA 94103 (☎431-4204; www.justact.org). Founded by students in 1983 as non-profit organization promoting youth leadership and action for global justice. Facilitates trainings and workshops on globalization and organizes an internship referral service.

GAY, LESBIAN & WOMEN'S CONCERNS

Queer-friendly San Fran has a great deal to offer for the service-minded. Use these listings just as a starting point for your search.

Gay, Lesbian, Bisexual, Transgender Historical Society, 657 Mission St. #300, San Francisco, CA 94105 (☎777-5455; www.glbthistory.org) A non-profit, educational organization founded in 1985 to document the history and lives of LGBT people. Focuses on collecting and preserving the ephemera of GLBT communities in Northern California.

The San Francisco Lesbian, Gay, Bisexual and Transgender Community Center, 1800 Market St., San Francisco, CA 94102 (☎865-5555; info@sfcenter.org). Home to a dynamic range of organizations and activities that address the needs of LGBT individuals of every race, gender, age, and socioeconomic status. Largely volunteer-run, sponsors activities ranging from arts support services for families and friends of queers.

The Women's Refuge, P.O. Box 3298, Berkeley, CA 94703 (☎510-547-4663; www.thewomensrefuge.org). Provides temporary emergency shelter and transitional housing for homeless women and families. Support services includes counseling, HIV awareness, substance abuse, parenting, and computer training.

Under One Roof, 549 Castro St. (☎503-2300; www.underoneroof.org), between 18th and 19th St. in the **Castro.** Sign up to volunteer at this gift store that donates all of its profits to organizations fighting AIDS. See p. 187.

CULTURAL INSTITUTIONS

As diverse as the neighborhoods themselves, persons of every race, ethnicity, and faith can find community within the plethora of cultural groups in San Fran.

Archdiocese of SF, 1 Peter Yorke Way. (☎415-614-5500). Open M-F 8:30am-5pm.

Booker T. Washington Community Center, 800 Presidio Ave. (☎415-928-1430), between Post and Sutter St. Educational, cultural, and recreational programs. Open M-F 8am-5pm.

Chinese Cultural Center, 750 Kearny St., 3rd fl. (☎415-986-1822; c-c-c.org), at Washington St. in the Holiday Inn. Info on Chinese community events, cultural programs, and Chinatown walking tours. Open Tu-Su 10am-4pm.

Islamic Society of San Francisco, 20 Jones St. (☎415-863-7997), at Market St. Prayer daily at 12:15pm.

Italian American Community Services Agency, 678 Green St. (☎415-362-6423), between Columbus Ave. and Powell St. Open M-F 9am-noon and 1-5pm.

Japanese Cultural and Community Center of Northern California, 1840 Sutter St. (☎415-567-5505; www.jccnc.org), between Buchanan and Webster St. Open M-F 9am-10pm.

Jewish Community Federation of San Francisco, 121 Steuart St. (☎415-777-0411; www.sfjcf.org), between Mission and Howard St., near the Embarcadero. Umbrella organization for Jewish groups in the Bay Area. Open M-F 9am-5pm.

Mission Cultural Center for Latino Art, 2868 Mission St. (☎415-821-1155), between 24th and 25th St. Open M 9am-5pm, Tu-F 9am-7pm.

Yerba Buena Center

Glide Memorial Church

Bay Bridge

STUDYING

San Francisco harbors a range of educational opportunities—from hardcore academics to useful trades and creative arts. Programs range from basic language and culture courses to college-level classes, often for credit. Others are offer useful skills (e.g. cooking or tango lessons) as their sole rewards. To choose a program that best fits your needs, research all you can before making a decision—determine costs and duration, as well as what kind of students participate and potential accommodations.

A good place to search online for available programs (by location or degree) in San Francisco is **www.ussuniversities.com.**

DEGREE PROGRAMS

Most degree programs require that applications be submitted three to six months before classes begin. Admissions requirements and application procedures vary greatly. Most art schools require a portfolio. **Courses taken for credit** can be counted toward a degree if you are pursuing or plan to pursue one. **Extension classes** are taught at institutions offering formal degree programs but are open to the public. They are often taught by the same professors who teach in degree programs. Most course catalogs are available at public libraries, by mail, and on the web.

California College of Arts and Crafts, 1111 8th St. (☎703-9500 or 800-477-1278; www.ccac-art.edu/cgi-bin/dad), at the corner of Irwin at Wisconsin St. One of the few institutions in the country to offer degrees in crafts as well as arts. Acclaimed artists and craftspeople serve on the faculty.

San Francisco Institute of Architecture, 555 Howard St. (☎925-299-1325; www.sfia.net). Offers both non-credit and master's degree courses in history of architecture, urban ecology, and much more.

New College of California, 777 Valencia St. (☎437-3460; www.newcollege.edu). Offers undergraduate programs in the humanities and an array of master's programs.

San Francisco Art Institute, 800 Chestnut St. (☎771-7020; www.sanfranciscoart.edu), between Leavenworth and Jones St. Grants BFA and MFA degrees (p. 73).

San Francisco State University (SFSU), 1600 Holloway Ave. (☎338-1111; www.sfsu.edu). Offers undergraduate, master's, and special-certificate credit courses. CA residents pay about $600 per semester for part-time study, $900 for full-time; non-residents pay resident prices plus $282 per unit.

Stanford Continuing Studies, (☎650-725-2650; continuingstudies.stanford.edu), near Palo Alto. Tuition varies by course. Stanford also offers a Masters of Liberal Arts program, $1320 per seminar. Financial assistance available, see website for details.

University of California Berkeley, 110 Sproul Hall #5800 (☎510-642-3175; www.berkeley.edu). The shining star of the UC system, Berkeley is a public university with a world-class reputation—unfortunately, it's difficult to get in. Entrance is easier and tuition cheaper for CA residents. Admissions office open M-F 9am-noon and 1-4pm.

University of San Francisco, 2130 Fulton St., San Francisco, CA 94117 (☎422-5555; www.usfca.edu). Founded in 1855 as San Francisco's first university, this Jesuit institution offers a variety of study options, from undergraduate evening classes in professional studies ($650 per unit) to graduate and adult programs, ($855 per unit), and a credential program in education. Regional campuses located throughout the Bay Area.

STUDY VISAS

There are two non-immigrant visa categories for persons wishing to study in the United States. The "F" visa is for **academic studies,** while the "M" visa is for **nonacademic or vocational studies.** An applicant coming to the US to study **must be accepted for a full course of study** by an educational institution approved by the INS. The institution will send the applicant **Form I-20A-B,** a Certificate of Eligibility for Non-Immigrant **(F-1)** Student Status for Academic and Language Students. A nonacademic or vocational institution will send the student **Form I-20M-N,** a Certificate of Eligibility for Non-Immigrant **(M-1)** Student Status for Vocational Students. F-1 student visa applicants must also prove they have enough **readily available funds** to meet expenses for the first year of study, and that adequate funds will be available for each subsequent year of study. M-1 student visa applicants must demonstrate that sufficient funds are immediately available to pay all tuition and living costs for the entire period of intended stay.

Although visa applicants may apply at any US consular office abroad, it is usually easiest to qualify in their country of permanent residence. Applications must be accompanied by a nonrefundable $45 **application fee** and the following:

1) The application, **Form OF-156,** completed and signed. Blank forms are available without charge at all US consular offices.

2) A **passport** valid for travel to the United States and with a validity date at least 6 mo. beyond the applicant's intended period of stay in the United States.

3) One **photograph,** showing full face, without head covering, against a light background.

4) **Form I-20A-B** ("F" applicants) or **Form I-20M-N** ("M" applicants), obtained from the appropriate educational institution.

5) Evidence of sufficient **funds.**

NON-CREDIT COURSES

Non-credit courses are often a much less expensive option. While most are offered at universities, some are held at community centers and private businesses and stray from traditional academic subjects—options are endless. Most non-credit classes have no prerequisites and cost very little.

City College of San Francisco (CCSF), Phelan Campus, 50 Phelan Ave. (☎239-3000, admissions 239-3285; www.ccsf.org), with 8 other campus locations. Offers credit, non-credit, day, evening, and online classes in fields from business and cooking to sociology, BGLT studies, and aircraft maintenance. Credit courses $11 for CA residents; for non-residents $130 per semester unit plus $11 per class. Non-credit courses free.

Learning Annex, 291 Geary St. (☎788-5500; www.learningannex.com), near Powell St. The place for non-credit enrichment—everything from speed flirting and wine tasting to magazine writing and computer programming. Course catalogs often in boxes on busy street corners. Most courses $15-40, though some as much as $200.

San Francisco State University (SFSU), College of Extended Learning, 1600 Holloway Ave. (☎ 405-7700; www.cel.sfsu.edu). Offers a wide range of credit and non-credit courses for academic and personal enrichment. $50-550 per class.

University of California Berkeley Extension, 1995 University Ave. (☎ 512-642-4111; www.unex.berkeley.edu). An impressive range of credit and non-credit courses at 13 Bay Area locations (one in SF). Courses begin monthly and usually last 3 months ($250-600).

WORKING

VISA INFORMATION

Generally, a citizen of a foreign country who wishes to enter the United States must first obtain a **visa**—either a **non-immigrant** visa for a temporary stay or an **immigrant** visa for permanent residence. Visitors from most of Europe, Australia, and New Zealand can travel in the US for up to 90 days without a visa, although they may need to show a return plane ticket. Citizens of South Africa need a visa. The 90-day **"visitor"** visa is a non-immigrant visa to enter the United States temporarily, either for **business** (B-1) or for **pleasure** or **medical treatment** (B-2). Those planning to travel to the US for a different purpose—such as study or temporary work—must apply for specialized visas (see **Study and Work Visas,** below).

Travelers from certain eligible countries may be able to visit the US without a visa on the **Visa Waiver Pilot Program.** Currently, 29 countries participate in the program. Visitors entering via the Visa Waiver Pilot Program cannot work or study while in the US.

QUALIFYING FOR A VISA

Applicants for visitor visas must show that they do not intend to immigrate to the US by demonstrating that (1) the purpose of their trip is to enter the US for business, pleasure, or medical treatment; (2) they plan to remain for a specific, limited period of time; and (3) they have a residence outside the US as well as other binding ties that will insure their eventual return.

APPLYING FOR A VISITOR VISA

Potential visitors can technically apply for a visa at any US embassy or consulate abroad, but it is generally easiest to qualify for a visa in one's own country. The nonrefundable $45 **application fee** must be accompanied by a **Form OF-156,** completed and signed, a **passport** valid for travel to the United States and with an expiration date at least 6 months beyond the applicant's intended period of stay in the United States. And finally, **two photographs,** showing full face, without head covering, against a light background.

WORK VISAS

All foreigners planning to work in the U.S. are required to obtain a work visa. There are dozens of types of employment visas, most of which fit into two general categories: **Employment-Based Visas,** which are generally issued to skilled or highly educated workers who already have jobs in the States; and **Temporary Worker Visas,** which have fixed time limits and very specific job classifications. There are caps on both types of visas, so even if you qualify for one you may not get it. Don't make final travel arrangements or give up your job until a visa has been issued to you.

For more information on both student and work visas: **www.travel.state.gov.**

Finding a job in San Francisco can be amazingly easy or frighteningly hard. Legions of dot-commers swarmed the city in the 90s, generating tons of work for **computer**- and **design**-savvy professionals. As funding for these ventures is drying up, it's becoming more difficult to land a position in the "Internet gulch." It's relatively easy, though, with a resumé and experience, to find a position in retail or restaurants.

As with volunteering, work opportunities tend to fall into two categories. Some travelers seek long-term employment that will allow them to become invested in a new area, while other travelers seek short-term jobs to finance the next leg of their travels. Hitting the pavement and visiting businesses works well for retail jobs. Community boards at coffee shops and community centers can often be fruitful, though searching from a computer at home may yield greater results.

CAREER CENTERS

The **SF Public Library,** especially the main branch, Civic Center (☎ 557-4400; http:/ /sfpl4.sfpl.org/btdir/careers.html) is a good place to start a job search. The **Jobs & Careers Center** on the fourth floor has publications, plus a range of specialized magazines and non-circulating books on everything from writing resumés to changing careers.

International Co-operative Education, 15 Spiros Way, Menlo Park, CA, 94025, USA (☎ 650-323-4944; www.icemenlo.com). Finds summer jobs for students. Costs include a $200 application fee and a $600 placement fee.

University of San Francisco, (www.wcsfhr.ucsf.edu/jobs/). The University has an extensive job website for both long- and short-term career opportunities.

INTERNET RESOURCES

Putting the keywords "San Francisco" and "job" into any good **search engine** should turn up myriad listings. Here are a few that stand out:

http://jobstar.org. An excellent resource that connects you to all of the best Bay Area job banks, free of charge. You can search by area, by industry, or just in general.

www.craigslist.org. Find a job, an apartment, or even love on the Craig's infamous list.

www.opportunitynocs.org. Helps you search for positions at non-profit organizations, from environmental protection to political mobilization.

www.sfgate.com. A useful resource, with all *Chronicle* and *Examiner* classified listings.

www.jobhub.com. Distributes resumés for high-tech professionals in the Bay Area for free.

LONG-TERM WORK

If you're planning on spending a substantial amount of time (more than three months) working in San Francisco search for a job well in advance. International placement agencies are often the easiest way to find employment abroad, especially for teaching English. **Internships,** usually for college students, are a good way to segue into working abroad, although they are often unpaid or poorly paid (many say the experience, however, is well worth it). Be wary of advertisements or companies that claim the ability to get you a job abroad for a fee—often times the same listings are available online or in newspapers, or even out of date. Unfortunately, finding an internship in San Francisco can be just as hard as finding a paying gig. Nevertheless, here are some organizations and websites to get you started.

Similar to internships, apprenticeships are often the best way to get into a trade field. In the California Union Apprenticeship programs (www.calapprenticeship.org) you can learn anything from iron-working to pastry cooking hands-on, while taking a few classes through the Union. Some artists, such as potters and photographers, also take on apprentices. Local art schools are the best places to search for an internship with an artist.

INTERNET RESOURCES

■ **http://internships.wetfeet.com/home.asp.** A free search engine that connects students with internships in a variety of fields. Lots of opportunities in San Francisco.

www.careerbuilder.com. A free internship search engine that even carries listings for a few paid internships. Search by field (not just location) to maximize your options in SF.

www.opnetwork.org. Emphasizes information technology and multimedia internships for young people from disadvantaged backgrounds.

TEACHING ENGLISH

In almost all cases, you need at least a bachelors degree to be a full-fledged teacher, although college undergraduates can often get summer positions. Many schools require teachers to have a **Teaching English as a Foreign Language (TEFL)** certificate. Placement agencies or university fellowship programs are the best resources for finding teaching jobs in San Fran. The alternative is to make contacts directly with schools or just to try your luck once you get there. If you are going to try the latter, the best time of the year is several weeks before the start of the school year. The following organization can be helpful in placing teachers in the Bay Area.

Stanford University, English for Foreign Students Program, Linguistics Dept., Stanford University, Stanford, 94305-2150 (☎650-723-3636; www.stanford.edu/group/efs). Each summer Stanford hires around 30 outside instructors. Prospective applicants typically should have an MA in TESOL and at least three years teaching ESL in an academic setting. If the qualifications don't intimidate you, send your CV to efs@stanford.edu.

AU PAIR WORK

Au pairs are typically women, aged 18-27, who work as live-in nannies, caring for children and doing light housework in foreign countries in exchange for room, board, and a small spending allowance or stipend. Most former au pairs speak favorably of their experience, and the traveling it made possible. Drawbacks, however, often include long on-duty hours and somewhat mediocre pay (on average $150-250 per week). Much of the au pair experience really does depend on the family with which you're placed. The agencies below are a good starting point for looking for employment as an au pair.

Accord Cultural Exchange, 750 La Playa, San Francisco, CA 94121 (☎415-386-6203; www.cognitext.com/accord).

AuPair Care, 2226 Bush St., San Francisco, CA 94115

Childcare International, Ltd., Trafalgar House, Grenville Pl., London NW7 3SA, UK (☎+44 020 8906 3116; www.childint.co.uk).

InterExchange, 161 Sixth Ave., New York, NY 10013 (☎212-924-0446; www.interexchange.org).

4Nannies.com, Inc., 2 Pidgeon Hill Dr. #210, Potomac Falls, VA 20165 (☎800-810-2611; www.4nannies.com). Highly rated as a reliable referral agency for au pairs and nannies nationwide.

SHORT-TERM WORK

Traveling for long periods of time can get expensive; thus, many travelers try a hand at odd jobs for a few weeks at a time to make some extra cash to fund another month or two of touring. Work in custodial services and shopping centers is fairly easy to find, although for those without visas, tiptoeing around the Immigration and Naturalization Services can result in deportation upon discovery. Another popular option is to work several hours a day at a hostel in exchange for free or discounted board. Most often, these jobs are found by word of mouth. Many tourism-based establishments, due to the high turnover in the industry, are eager for help, even if only temporarily. *Let's Go* tries to list temporary jobs like these whenever possible; check out the list below for some of the available short-term jobs in popular destinations. Temporary employment (temp) agencies, abundant in the city, place clients in lucrative (though often mindless) jobs, often secretarial. At times, such jobs becomes permanent after a few weeks. Most will require a resumé, references, and a short diagnostic test to determine computer proficiency.

Taylor Grey, 90 New Montgomery St., 7th fl. (☎882-9866; www.taylorgrey.com), tends to reward transplants from well known colleges with better positions and higher pay.

ProStaff, 222 Front St. #700 (☎986-8500; www.prostaff.com), is also a well known agency.

Aba Staffing Inc., 690 Market St. (☎434-4222; www.abastaff.com). Finds jobs in San Francisco and Marin County. Additional location: 551 Foster City Blvd. (☎650-349-9200).

Advanced Employment Services, 760 Market St. Suite 458 (☎989-1188; www.advance-demployment.com). Offers placement in San Francisco and the greater Bay Area.

FOR FURTHER READING ON ALTERNATIVES TO TOURISM

Alternatives to the Peace Corps: A Directory of Third World and U.S. Volunteer Opportunities, by Joan Powell. Food First Books, 2000 (US$10).

How to Get a Job in Europe, by Sanborn and Matherly. Surrey Books, 1999 (US$22).

How to Live Your Dream of Volunteering Oversees, by Collins, DeZerega, and Heckscher. Penguin Books, 2002 (US$17).

International Directory of Voluntary Work, by Whetter and Pybus. Peterson's Guides and Vacation Work, 2000 (US$16).

International Jobs, by Kocher and Segal. Perseus Books, 1999 (US$18).

Work Abroad: The Complete Guide to Finding a Job Overseas, by Hubbs, Griffith, and Nolting. Transitions Abroad Publishing, 2000 (US$16).

Work Your Way Around the World, by Susan Griffith. Worldview Publishing Services, 2001 (US$18).

Invest Yourself: The Catalogue of Volunteer Opportunities, published by the Commission on Voluntary Service and Action (☎718-638-8487).

Service Directory

AIRLINES

American: ☎800-433-7300.
America West: ☎800-435-9282.
Continental: ☎800-525-0280.
Delta: ☎800-221-1212.
Northwest/KLM: ☎800-225-2525.
United: ☎800-241-6522.
US Airways: ☎800-428-4322.

AIRPORTS

Oakland International Airport: (☎510-577-4000; www.oaklandairport.com). Visitor Info Booth ☎510-563-2984. Open daily 8am-midnight.
San Francisco International Airport (SFO): (☎650-821-8211; www.flysfo.com). 4 public info booths in the terminals. Open daily 8am-1:30pm.

AIRPORT SHUTTLES

OAKLAND AIRPORT

A-1 Shuttle Services: ☎888-698-2663.
BayPorter Express: ☎877-467-1800; www.bayporter.com
City Express: ☎888-874-8885.
Luxor Shuttle: ☎510-562-7222.
Extensive list of shuttles: www.oaklandairport.com/shuttles.shtml

SAN FRANCISCO AIRPORT

Bay Shuttle: ☎415-564-3400.
Lorrie's Airport Shuttle: ☎415-334-9000.
Shuttle information: www.flysfo.com

BICYCLE AND SKATE RENTAL

Blazing Saddles, 1095 Columbus Ave. (☎415-202-8888), at Francisco St. Bikes $7 per hr., $28 per day; kids' bikes $20 per day. Open daily 8am-8pm. AmEx/MC/V.

Skates on Haight, 1818 Haight St. (☎415-752-8375). In-line skates $6 per hr., $24 per day; scooters $7/$28. Open M-F 11am-7pm, Sa-Su 10am-6pm. AmEx/D/MC/V.

Surrey Bikes and Blades in Golden Gate Park, 50 Stow Lake Dr. (☎415-668-6699), at Stow Boathouse. Bikes from $8 per hr., $25 per day; inline skates $7/$20. Open M-F 11am-dusk, Sa-Su 9am-7pm. No credit cards.

CAR RENTAL

A-One, 434 O'Farrell St. (☎415-771-3977), between Taylor and Jones St. $30 per day, 150 mi. included. Must be 21; $5 per day surcharge for drivers under 25. Open M-F 8am-6pm, Sa-Su 8am-5pm.

Budget, 321 Mason St. (☎800-527-0700), in Union Sq. Compacts from $30 per day. Must be 21; $20 surcharge per day for drivers under 25. Open M-F 6am-9pm, Sa 6:30am-7pm, Su 6:30am-9pm.

City, 1748 Folsom St. (☎877-861-1312), between Duboce St. and 14th St. Compacts from $29-35 per day, $160-170 per week. Small fee for unlimited mileage. Must be 21; $8 per day surcharge for drivers under 25. Open M-F 7:30am-6pm, Sa 9am-4pm. Additional location: 1433 Bush St. (☎866-359-1331), between Van Ness Ave. and Polk St.

Dollar, 364 O'Farrell St. (☎800-800-3665), opposite the Hilton Hotel. Compacts from $40 per day, $150-160 per week. Unlimited mileage. Must be 21; $20 per day surcharge for drivers under 25. Open daily 6am-8pm.

Enterprise, 222 Mission St. (in SF ☎800-736-8222, outside SF ☎800-325-8007). Compacts from $40 per day, $199 per week. Unlimited free mileage in CA; 150 mi. included per day outside CA, 25¢ per additional mi. Must be 21; $10 per day surcharge for drivers under 25. Several locations in SF; all branches open M-F 7:30am-6pm, weekend times vary.

Thrifty, 520 Mason St. (☎415-788-8111), at Post St. Compacts from $27 per day. Unlimited mileage. Must be 21; $25 per day surcharge for drivers under 25. Open daily 7am-7pm.

CHILDCARE

Children's Council of San Francisco, 445 Church St. (☎415-343-3300), provides referrals to all types of childcare providers throughout the city.

CONSULATES

Australia: 1 Bush St., #700 (☎415-536-1970), at Market St.

Canada: 555 Montgomery St. (☎415-834-3180; www.cdntrade.com). Open M-F 8:30am-4pm.

Colombia: 595 Market St. (☎415-495-7195), at Mission St.

Ireland: 44 Montgomery St. (☎415-392-4214), at Sutter St. Open M-F 9am-noon and 2-4pm.

India: 540 Arguello Blvd. (☎415-668-0662), one block west of 2nd St. Open daily 9am-5:15 pm.

Latin American: 870 Market St., between 5th and Powell St., in the Hallidie Plaza.

> **Ecuador:** Suite 858. ☎415-391-4148.
>
> **El Salvador:** Suite 721. ☎415-781-7924.
>
> **Guatemala:** 10th floor. ☎415-781-0118.
>
> **Peru:** Suite 482. ☎415-362-7136.
>
> **Venezuela:** Suite 665. ☎415-776-4941.

Norway: 20 California St., 6th floor. (☎415-986-0766), between Davis and Drumm St.

Sweden: 120 Montgomery St., Suite 2175. (☎415-788-2631), near Sheridan Ave. in the Presidio. Open M-F 9am-noon.

United Kingdom: 1 Sansome St., #850, (☎415-617-1300), at Market St.

Additional listings: www.cityinsights.com/sanfran/sfconsul.htm

CRISIS AND HELP LINES

AIDS Hotline, ☎800-342-2437.

Crisis Line for the Handicapped, ☎800-426-4263.

Drug Crisis Line, ☎415-362-3400.

Rape Crisis Center, ☎ 415-647-7273.

Suicide Prevention, ☎ 415-781-0500.

Youth Crisis Hotline, ☎ 800-448-4663

CULTURAL AND COMMUNITY CENTERS

Archdiocese of San Francisco, 9 Peter Yorke Wy. (☎ 415-614-5500). Open M-F 8:30am-5pm.

Booker T. Washington Community Center, 800 Presidio Ave. (☎ 415-928-6596), between Post and Sutter St. Educational, cultural, and recreational programs. Open M-F 8am-5pm.

Chinese Cultural Center, 750 Kearny St., 3rd fl. (☎ 415-986-1822; http://c-c-c.org), at Washington St. in the Holiday Inn. Info on Chinese community events, cultural programs, and Chinatown walking tours. Open Tu-Su 10am-4pm.

Islamic Society of San Francisco, 20 Jones St. (☎ 415-863-7997), at Market St. Prayer daily at 12:15pm.

Italian American Community Services Agency, 678 Green St. (☎ 415-362-6423), between Columbus Ave. and Powell St. Open M-F 9am-noon and 1-5pm.

Japanese Cultural and Community Center of Northern California, 1840 Sutter St. (☎ 415-567-5505; www.jccnc.org), between Buchanan and Webster St. Open M-F 9am-10pm.

Jewish Community Federation of San Francisco, 121 Steuart St. (☎ 415-777-0411; www.sfjcf.org), between Mission and Howard St. Umbrella organization for Jewish groups in the Bay Area. Open M-F 9am-5pm.

Mission Cultural Center for Latino Art, 2868 Mission St. (☎ 415-821-1155), between 24th and 25th St. Open M 9am-5pm, Tu-F 9am-7pm.

San Francisco Senior Center, 481 O'Farrell St. (☎ 415-71-7950), between Jones and Taylor St. Open M-Th 9am-4pm, F 9am-3:30pm, Sa-Su 10am-2pm.

CURRENCY EXCHANGE

American Express, 455 Market St. (☎ 415-536-2600; www.americanexpress.com). Open M-F 8:30am-5pm, Sa 9am-3:30pm.

Bank of America Foreign Currency Services, 1 Powell St. (☎ 415-953-5102), at Eddy St., near Market St. Open M-F 9am-6pm, Sa 9am-2pm.

Foreign Exchange Ltd., 429 Stockton St. (☎ 415-677-5100), near Sutter St. Open M-F 9am-5:30pm; Apr.-Sept. Sa 9:15-4:45pm.

Thomas Cook, 75 Geary St. (☎ 415-362-3452; www.us.thomascook.com). Open M-F 9am-5pm, Sa 10am-4pm.

DENTISTS

Dental Society Referral Service, ☎ 800-511-8663.

San Francisco Dental Office, 131 Steuart St., #323 (☎ 415-777-5115). 24hr. emergency service. Open for appointments M, Tu, and F 8am-4:40pm; W-Th 10:30am-6:30pm.

University of California Dental Clinic, 707 Parnassus Ave. (☎ 415-476-1891), at the UCSF Medical Center. Open M-F 8:30am-5pm.

DEPARTMENT OF MOTOR VEHICLES

San Francisco, 1377 Fell St. (☎ 800-777-0133; www.dmv.ca.gov). Open M-Tu 8am-5pm, W and F 9am-5pm, Th 8am-5pm.

DISABILITY RESOURCES

Berkeley Center For Independent Living, 2539 Telegraph Ave. (☎ 510-841-4776, TDD 510-848-3101; www.cilberkeley.org). Open M-F 9am-5pm.

Mayor's Council on Disabilities, 401 Van Ness Ave. #300 (☎ 415-554-6789, TTY/TDD 415-544-6799). Open M-F 8am-5pm.

Recreational Center for the Handicapped, 207 Skyline Blvd. (☎ 415-665-4100), at Herbst Rd. Open M-F 9am-5pm.

EMERGENCY

Emergency: ☎ 911.

Fire: ☎ 415-558-3200.

Police: ☎ 415-553-0123.

Poison: ☎ 800-876-4766.

ENTERTAINMENT

San Francisco Arts Monthly (www.artsmonthlysf.org). Comprehensive monthly listings of arts and cultural events in SF.

MovieFone (☎777-3456). Interactive recording with movies and movie theaters by name and location.

FINANCIAL SERVICES

American Express, 455 Market St. (☎415-536-2600; www.americanexpress.com). Open M-F 9am-5:30pm, Sa 10am-2pm. Additional locations: 311 9th Ave. (☎415-221-6760). Open M-F 9am-5pm. 1585 Sloat Blvd. (☎415-242-0277). Open M-F 9am-6pm, Sa 10am-5pm. Services vary by location.

GAY AND LESBIAN RESOURCES

Pacific Center for Human Growth, 2712 Telegraph Ave. (☎510-548-8283; www.pacificcenter.org), in Berkeley. Counseling and info on gay community events, housing, clubs, etc. Open M-F 10am-10pm, weekend hours vary.

Lyric, 127 Collingwood St. (☎415703-6150; www.lyric.org), at 18th St. A range of LGBT, 23-and-under, peer-based programs that stress youth leadership. Drop in resource center M-F 3-6pm.

HEALTH

GENERAL HEALTH

Chinatown Public Health Center, 1490 Mason St. (☎415-705-8500). Drop-in hours M-F 8:30am-11am, M 1-4pm. After-hours answering service for urgent care.

Downtown Medical, 450 Sutter St., #1723 (☎415-362-7177; www.downtownmedical.com). Open M 9:30am-4:30pm, Tu-W noon-5pm, F 9am-4:30pm.

Mission Health Center, 3850 17th St. (☎415-487-7500). Open M, W, F 7:45am-5pm, Tu 7:45am-9pm. After-hours doctor on call ☎510-286-2301.

Physician Referral Service (☎415-353-6566). Open M-F 9am-noon.

Traveler Medical Group, 490 Post St., #225 (☎415-981-1102). Open M-F 10am-6pm. 24hr. emergency operator.

SEXUAL HEALTH

AIDS Health Project, 1930 Market St. (☎415-476-3902). Open M-Th 8:30am-9pm, F 8:30am-6pm. Confidential testing line ☎415-502-8378.

National Abortion Federation Hotline (☎800-772-9100). Open M-F 8am-10pm, Sa-Su 9am-5pm (Eastern Standard Time).

Planned Parenthood of San Francisco, 815 Eddy St. (☎800-967-7526; www.ppgg.org). Open M 8am-8pm, Tu and Th 8am-5pm, W 9am-8pm, Sa 9am-2pm.

HOSPITALS

Central Public Health Center, 470 27th St. (☎415-271-4263), at Telegraph Ave. in Oakland. Make appointments far in advance. Open M-F 8-11:30am and 1-4pm.

Haight-Ashbury Free Medical Clinic, 558 Clayton St. (☎415-487-5632), at Haight St. Appointments only. Open M-Th 9am-9pm, F 1-5pm.

Lyon-Martin Women's Clinic, 1748 Market St., #201 (☎415-565-7667), at Octavia St. Open for drop-ins Th 1-3pm. Clinic hours: M-Tu and Th-F 8:30am-5pm, W 11am-7pm.

Saint Francis Memorial Hospital, 900 Hyde St. (☎415-353-6000). 24hr. emergency service.

San Francisco General Hospital, 1001 Potrero Ave. (☎415-206-8000), at 23rd St. Emergency room with 24hr. walk-in service.

INTERNET ACCESS

The Blue Danube, 306 Clement St. (☎415-221-9041), at 4th Ave. Internet access $3 per 20 min., $5 per 40 min., $7 per hr. Open daily 7am-9:30pm.

Samovar Tea Lounge, 498 Sanchez St. (☎415-626-4700), at 18th St. Free wireless access with purchase. Open M-F 7am-10:30pm, Sa-Su 8am-10pm.

CompUSA, 750 Market St. (☎415-391-9778). Free email access at computer kiosks downstairs. Open M-F 9am-8pm, Sa 10am-8pm, Su 11am-6pm.

Morning Due Café, 3698 17th St. (☎415-621-7156), at Church St. Free access with Surf and Sip membership ($20 per month). Open daily 7am-10pm.

Main Branch of the SF Library, 100 Larkin St. (☎415-557-4400), between Grove and Fulton St. A number of free Internet computers but get there early as they fill up fast. Open M 10am-6pm, Tu-Th 9am-8pm, F noon-6pm, Sa 10am-6pm, Su noon-5pm.

Additional listings: www.surfandsip.com

LAUNDROMATS

Doo Wash, 817 Columbus Ave. (☎415-885-1222), near Lombard St. in **North Beach.** Video games, pinball machines, pool table, and TV. Wash $1.50; dry $1. Open daily 7am-11pm, last load 9:30pm.

Launderland, 3800 24th St. (☎415-282-9839), at Church St. in **Noe Valley.** Wash $1.75; dry 50¢ per 10min. Open daily 7:30am-10:30pm.

Missing Sock Laundry, 1958 Hyde St. (☎415-673-5640), at Union St. in **Russian Hill.** Wash $1.50; dry 25¢ per 10min. Open daily 7am-11pm, last load 10pm.

Quality Wash & Dry, 1431 Haight St. (☎415-431-1330), near Masonic Ave. in the **Haight-Ashbury.** Small load wash $1.75; dry 25¢ per 8min. Open daily 7am-10pm, last wash 8:30pm.

Self-Service Laundromat, 600 Bush St. near Stockton St. in **Union Sq.** Wash $1.75; dry 25¢ per 10min. Open daily 7am-10pm, last load 9pm.

Star Wash, 392 Dolores St. (☎415-431-2443), at 17th St. in the **Mission.** Movies sometimes shown. Wash and fold $1.25 per lb. Wash $1.75-2.75; dry 25¢ per 8min. Open daily 7am-10pm, last wash 9pm.

Super Clean (☎415-431-8515), at the corner of 17th and Sanchez St. in the **Castro.** Wash $2-4.50; dry 25¢. Open M-Su 7am-10:30pm, last wash 9pm.

LEGAL SERVICES

La Raza Legal Center, 474 Valencia St., Suite 295 (☎415-575-3500), at 16 St.

Legal Services for Children, 1254 Market St., 3rd fl. ☎415-863-3762; www.lsc-sf.org.

Additional information: www.sfbar.org/lrs/general.html

LIBRARIES

San Francisco Public Library: www.sfpl4.sfpl.org

Main Branch, 100 Larkin St. (☎415-557-4400), between Grove and Fulton St. Open M 10am-6pm, Tu-Th 9am-8pm, F noon-6pm, Sa 10am-6pm, Su noon-5pm.

Chinatown Branch, 1135 Powell St. (☎415-335-2888), near Jackson St. Large selection of books in many different Asian languages, particularly Cantonese and Mandarin. Open M 1-9pm, W 10am-9pm, Th and Sa 10am-6pm, F 1-6pm, Su 1-5pm.

Eureka Valley/Harvey Milk Memorial, 3555 16th St. (☎415-554-5616), at Market St. Open M noon-6pm, Tu 10am-9pm, W noon-9pm, Th 10am-6pm, F-Sa1-6pm.

Marina, 1890 Chestnut St. (☎415-292-2150), near Webster St. Open M-Tu and Sa 10am-6pm, W-Th 1-9pm, F 1-6pm, Su 1-5pm.

Mission Branch, 300 Bartlett St. (☎415-355-2800), at 24th St. Spanish section. Open M 1-9pm, Tu-W 10am-9pm, Th and Sa 10am-6pm, F 1-6pm, Su 1-5pm.

Noe Valley/Sally Brunn, 451 Jersey St. (☎415-695-5095), near Castro St. Open Tu 10am-9pm, W 1-9pm, Th 10am-6pm, F 1-6pm, Sa noon-6pm.

North Beach, 2000 Mason St. (☎415-274-0270), at Columbus St. Open M noon-6pm, Tu 10am-9pm, W 1-9pm, Th 10am-6pm, F-Sa 1-6pm.

Presidio, 3150 Sacramento St. (☎415-355-2880), near Baker St. Open Tu 10am-9pm, W 1-9pm, Th and Sa 10am-6pm, F 1-6pm.

Richmond, 351 9th Ave. (☎415-666-7165, children's room ☎415-666-7021), near Clement St. Open M and Sa 10am-6pm, Tu-W 10am-9pm, Th 1-9pm, F 1-6pm, Su 1-5pm.

Sunset, 1305 18th Ave. (☎415-355-2808), at Irving St. Open M 1-9pm, Tu-W 10am-9pm, Th and Sa 10am-6pm, F 1-6pm, Su 1-5pm.

MAIL SERVICES

Copy Central, 705 Market St. (☎415-882-7377). UPS. Open M-F 9am-5pm.

Geary Rent-A-Box, 815 Geary St. (☎415-921-0355). Open M-F 9am-7pm.

Mail Box Plus, 1450 Sutter St. (☎415-928-8315). UPS and FedEx. Open M-F 10am-5pm, Sa 10:30am-3:30pm.

Mail Boxes Etc., 601 Van Ness Ave. (☎415-775-6644). UPS and FedEx. Open M-F 8am-6pm, Sa 9am-5pm.

UPS Letter Center, 1255 Post St. (☎800-742-5877). Open M-F 9am-5pm.

MINORITY RESOURCES

Cultural and Community Centers, p. 313.

PARKING GARAGES

Allright Parking, on Broadway, near Columbus Ave. $2 per 20min., max. $14. Open M-Tu 8am-10pm, W-Th 8am-11pm, F 8am-2am, Sa 10am-2am, Su 11am-10pm.

Chinatown North Beach Public Parking, on Kearny Ave., between Washington and Jackson St. $20 per day. After 4pm $8 flat rate, Sa-Su $10. Open M-F 7am-9pm, Sa-Su 9am-9pm. AmEx/D/MC/V.

Civic Center Garage, 355 McAllister St. (☎415-863-1537). $2 per hr. Open daily 6am-midnight.

Ellis-O'Farrell Garage, 123 O'Farrell St. (☎415-986-4800). $2 per hr.; 6am-6pm $22; 6pm-6am $6. Open Su-Th 5:30am-1am, F-Sa 5:30am-2am.

Embarcadero Center Garage (☎415-772-0670), in the Embarcadero Ctr. $1.75 per 20min., max. $27.50. Open 24hr.

5th and Mission Yerba Buena Garage, 833 Mission St. (☎415-982-8522; www.fifthandmission.com). $2 per hr. up to 5 hr., $3 per hr. up to 7hr., and $18 for 7-12hr., 12-24hr. $20. Open 24hr. AmEx/ MC/V.

Fisherman's Wharf Parking, 665 Beach St. (☎415-673-5197). $4.50 per hr., $12 max. 12hr. max. Open daily 8am-11pm.

Hilton Garage (☎415-771-1400, ask for garage), on Ellis St., between Mason and Taylor St. $10 per hr., max. $33. Open 24hr.

Portsmouth Sq. Garage, 733 Kearny St. (☎415-982-6353). $2 per hr. up to 4hr., $3-4 per hr. for each additional hr. Open 24hr.

Public Parking, on Green St., between Columbus and Powell Ave. $2 per 20min., $20 max. for 12hr.; after 6pm $15 flat rate. Parking attendant on duty 8:30am-1am.

Sutter-Stockton Garage (☎415-982-8370), at Sutter and Stockton St. $2 per hr. up to 5hr.; $13 for 6hr.; $16 for 7hr, $25 for 8 or more hr. Open 24hr.

Union Square Garage, 333 Post St. (☎415-397-0631). $1 per 30min.; $27 per day. Open 24hr.

Union Street Plaza Garage, 2001 Union St. (☎415-567-7357), at Buchanan St. $3 per 30min., $18 for 12hr., $25 for 24hr. Open M-Tu 7am-midnight, W-F 7am-2am, Sa 10am-2am, Su 10am-midnight.

POST OFFICES

24hr. automated service, connects to local Post Offices: ☎800-275-8777.

Bernal Heights Station, 45 29th St. Open M-F 8:30am-5pm. Postal code: 94110.

Chinatown Station, 867 Stockton St., at Clay St. Open M-F 9am-5:30pm, Sa 9am-4:30pm. Postal code: 94108.

Civic Center: Federal Building Station, 450 Golden Gate Ave., at Larkin St. Open M-F 8:30am-5pm. Postal code: 94102.

Geary Station, 5654 Geary Blvd., at 21st Ave. Open M-F 9am-5:30pm, Sa 9am-4:30pm. Postal code: 94121.

Haight-Ashbury: Clayton St. Station, 554 Clayton St., at Haight St. Open M-F 9am-5:30pm, Sa 9am-4pm. Postal code: 94117.

Marina Station, 2055 Lombard St., at Fillmore St. Open M-F 8:30am-5:30pm, Sa 9am-4:30pm. Postal code: 94123.

Nob Hill/Russian Hill: Pine St. Station, 1400 Pine St., at Larkin St. Open M-F 8am-5:30pm, Sa 8am-3pm. Postal code: 94109.

Noe Valley Station, 4083 24th St., at Castro St. Open M-F 8:30am-5pm, Sa 9am-4pm. Postal code: 94114.

North Beach Station, 2200 Powell St. Open M-F 9:30am-5:30pm, Sa 9:30am-1:30pm. Postal code: 94133.

Union Square Station, 170 O'Farrell St., at Stockton St., in the basement of Macy's. Open M-Sa 10am-5:30pm, Su 11am-5pm. Postal code: 94108.

RELIGIOUS RESOURCES

Cultural and Community Centers, p. 313.

ROAD CONDITIONS

CalTrans, ☎800-427-7623 within California; ☎916-445-7623 elsewhere.

TravInfo, ☎415-817-171; www.dot.ca.gov/hq/roadinfo

SURFBOARD RENTAL

Big Yank, 710 La Playa St. (☎415-666-1616; www.bigyank.com). Piles of surf and skate apparel. Board and suit rental $30 per day. Open M-Sa 9am-7pm, Su 10am-6pm.

TAXIS

SAN FRANCISCO

City Wide Dispatch: ☎415-920-0715.
Luxor Cab: ☎415-282-4141.
National Cab Company: ☎415-648-4444.
Town Taxi: ☎415-285-3800.
Yellow Cab: ☎415-626-2345.
Veteran's Cab: ☎415-552-1300.

OAKLAND

Friendly Cab: ☎510-536-3000.
Veteran's Cab: ☎510-533-1900.

TICKET SERVICES

Tickets.com (☎415-478-2277 or ☎800-225-2277). Open daily 8am-6pm.

TIX Bay Area (☎415-433-7827; www.theatrebayarea.org), on Powell St. between Post and Geary St. Tickets to concerts, clubs, plays, and sports. Half-price tickets often available on day of show (cash only; inquire in person) and on Sa. Carries travel passes and tourist info. Open Tu-Th 11am-6pm, F-Sa 11am-7pm, Su 11am-3pm.

TOURS

AIR TOURS

San Francisco Seaplane Tours, 242 Redwood Hwy. (☎415-332-4843 or 888-732-7526; www.seaplane.com), in Mill Valley. Flights over the city, Alcatraz, and the Golden Gate from $129 per person, departing from Pier 39 or Sausalito.

BAY TOURS

Blue and Gold Fleet, Pier 41 (info ☎415-773-1188, sales 705-5555; www.blueandgoldfleet.com). Bay cruises $20, seniors and ages 12-17 $15, ages 5-11 $11. Alcatraz departures every 30min. from 9:30am. Reservations recommended; check website for specials. Adults $11.50, seniors $9.75, ages 5-11 $8.25. Multilingual audio tours $4.50.

Red and White Fleet, Pier 43½ (info ☎415-673-2900, tickets/reservations ☎877-855-5506; www.redandwhite.com). 1hr. bay cruises. Motorcoach tours of Muir Woods, Wine Country, Yosemite, Monterey, and San Francisco.

WALKING TOURS

Flower Power Walking Tour (☎415-863-1621), 2½hr. tour of Haight-Ashbury Tu and Sa 9:30am. $15. Call for reservations.

Precita Eyes Mural Arts Center, 2981 24th St. (☎415-285-2287; www.precitaeyes.org). Mural tours of Mission and Bernal Heights on foot or by bike.

San Francisco Public Library: ☎557-4266; www.sfcityguides.org

Victorian Home Walk, 2226 15th St. (☎415-252-9485; www.victorianwalk.com). 2½hr. Apr.-Dec. daily 11am; Jan.-Mar. F-M 11am. $20.

SPECIALTY TOURS

Cable Car Charters, 2830 Geary Blvd. (☎415-922-2425; www.cablecars.citysearch.com).

California Nature Treks, 2562 Diamond St. (☎415-433-8735; www.naturetreks.com).

Citypass San Francisco, 1035 Barrow Ln. (☎707-253-1222; www.citypass.net). Can buy SF Citypass online, at SFMOMA in SoMa, Blue and Gold Fleet (p. 317), the Exploratorium in the Marina, or the SF Visitor's Info Center (below).

Supersightseeing Tours, 50 Quint St. (☎415-777-2288; www.supersightseeing.com).

317

VISITOR INFORMATION

California Welcome Center (☎415-956-3493), Pier 39 at the Great San Francisco Adventure. Open daily 9:30am-9pm.

Visitor Information Center, 900 Market St. (☎415-391-2000; 24hr. info recordings 391-2001; www.sfvisitor.org). Open M-F 9am-5pm, Sa-Su 9am-3pm; phones open M-F 8:30am-5pm.

WEATHER

National Weather Service, ☎650-364-7974.

WOMEN'S RESOURCES

Women's Building of the Bay Area (San Francisco Women's Center), 3543 18th St. (☎415-431-1180; www.womensbuilding.org), between Valencia and Guerrero St. Open daily 9am-5pm for info and referrals.

Index

Map Appendix

MAP LEGEND

Hospital	Zoo	Amusement Park
Police	Airport	Museum
Post Office	Bus Station	Hotel/Hostel
Tourist Office	Train Station	Camping
Bank	BART STATION	Food & Drink
Service	Ferry Landing	Beach
Site or Point of Interest	Church	Entertainment
Boat Ramp	Synagogue	Nightlife
Theater	Picnic Ground	Seals or Sea Lions
Library	Bunker/Fort	Internet Café
	Mountain	Winery

Garden
Gate or Entrance
Golf Course
Pedestrian Zone
Stairs
Cable Car Line
Subway Line
Bus Line
Ferry Line

The Let's Go compass always points NORTH

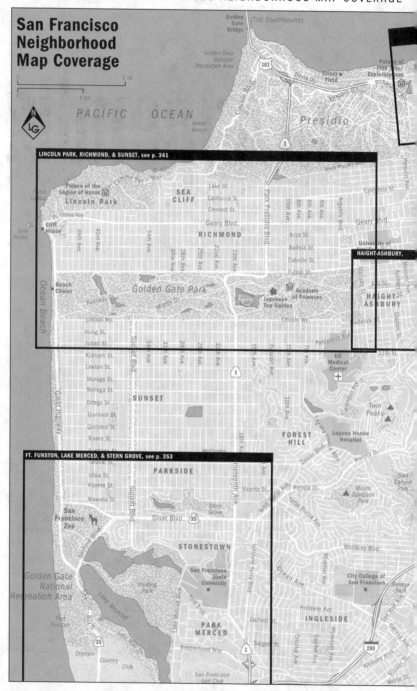

San Francisco Neighborhood Map Coverage

PACIFIC OCEAN

LINCOLN PARK, RICHMOND, & SUNSET, see p. 341

HAIGHT-ASHBURY,

FT. FUNSTON, LAKE MERCED, & STERN GROVE, see p. 353

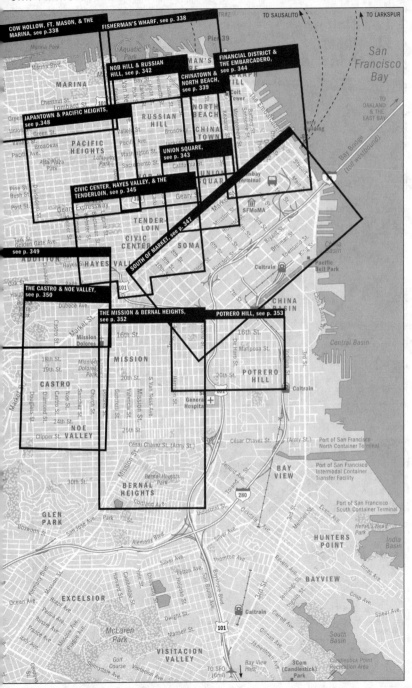

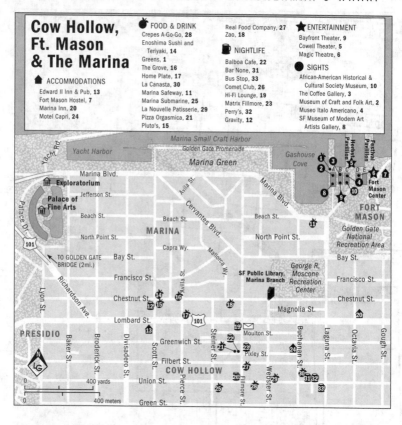

Cow Hollow, Ft. Mason & The Marina

🏠 **ACCOMMODATIONS**

Edward II Inn & Pub, 13
Fort Mason Hostel, 7
Marina Inn, 20
Motel Capri, 24

🍎 **FOOD & DRINK**

Crepes A-Go-Go, 28
Enoshima Sushi and
    Teriyaki, 14
Greens, 1
The Grove, 16
Home Plate, 17
La Canasta, 30
Marina Safeway, 11
Marina Submarine, 25
La Nouvelle Patisserie, 29
Pizza Orgasmica, 21
Pluto's, 15

Real Food Company, 27
Zao, 18

🍺 **NIGHTLIFE**

Balboa Cafe, 22
Bar None, 31
Bus Stop, 33
Comet Club, 26
Hi-Fi Lounge, 19
Matrix Fillmore, 23
Perry's, 32
Gravity, 12

⭐ **ENTERTAINMENT**

Bayfront Theater, 9
Cowell Theater, 5
Magic Theatre, 6

● **SIGHTS**

African-American Historical &
    Cultural Society Museum, 10
The Coffee Gallery, 3
Museum of Craft and Folk Art, 2
Museo Italo Americano, 4
SF Museum of Modern Art
    Artists Gallery, 8

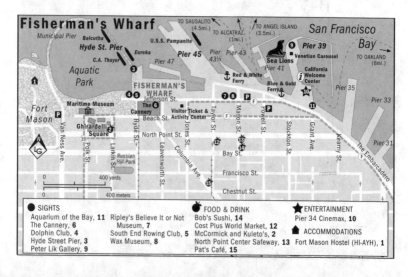

Fisherman's Wharf

● **SIGHTS**

Aquarium of the Bay, 11
The Cannery, 6
Dolphin Club, 4
Hyde Street Pier, 3
Peter Lik Gallery, 9

Ripley's Believe It or Not
    Museum, 7
South End Rowing Club, 5
Wax Museum, 8

🍎 **FOOD & DRINK**

Bob's Sushi, 14
Cost Plus World Market, 12
McCormick and Kuleto's, 2
North Point Center Safeway, 13
Pat's Café, 15

⭐ **ENTERTAINMENT**

Pier 34 Cinemax, 10

🏠 **ACCOMMODATIONS**

Fort Mason Hostel (HI-AYH), 1

Chinatown & North Beach

see key p. 340

NORTH BEACH

CHINATOWN

Coit Tower

Sts. Peter & Paul

Filbert St.

WASHINGTON SQUARE

Union St.

Green St.

Vallejo St.

Broadway

Broadway Tunnel

Pacific Ave.

Jackson St.

Cable Car Powerhouse & Museum

Chinese Hospital

Washington St.

Portsmouth Square

Clay St.

Commercial St.

Huntington Park

Sacramento St.

California St.

CALIFORNIA STREET CABLE CAR LINE

St. Mary's Square

Pine St.

Bush St.

Gateway to Chinatown

MASON STREET CABLE CAR LINE

POWELL-HYDE STREET CABLE CAR LINE

Mason St.

Powell St.

Stockton St.

Grant Ave.

Kearny St.

Columbus Ave.

Telegraph Hill Blvd.

Bonham Pl.

Romolo Pl.

Beckett St.

Wentworth Pl.

Ross Alley

Waverly Pl.

Spofford St.

Joice St.

Stone St.

Stockton Tunnel

TO ① (125yd.) & PUBLIC LIBRARY (50yd.)

TO ㉚ & ㉛ (75yd.) →

Ped Crossing

0 100 yards

0 100 meters

N

Chinatown & North Beach see map p. 339

● SIGHTS

Buddha's Universal Church, **50**	D5
Chinese Cultural Center, **51**	D5
Chinese Historical Society of America, **48**	B5
City Lights Bookstore, **26**	C3
Golden Gate Cookie Co., **45**	C4
Lyle Tuttle's Tattoo Art Museum, **1**	A1
North Beach Museum, **15**	C2
Old St. Mary's, **54**	C6
Sts. Peter and Paul Catholic Church, **3**	B1
Tien Hou Temple, **49**	C5
Volunteer Firemen Memorial, **5**	B1

🍴 FOOD & DRINK

Brandy Ho's Hunan Food, **37**	D4
Chef Jia, **41**	D4
City View Restaurant, **52**	D5
Gelato Classico, **6**	C1
Golden Gate Bakery, **38**	C4
Hing Lung, **20**	C3
House of Nanking, **42**	D4
Italian French Baking Co., **7**	C1
Kay Cheung's Restaurant, **44**	D4
L'Osteria del Forno, **12**	B2
Mama's, **4**	C1
Mario's Bohemian Cigar Store Cafe, **8**	B1
Napoli Market, **2**	C1
Nature Stop, **17**	C2
North Beach Pizza, **9**	C1
Rossi Supermarket, **19**	C3
Sodini's Trattoria, **14**	C2
Stella Pasticceria e Caffè, **16**	C2
Steps of Rome, **23**	C3

The Stinking Rose, **24**	C3
Tandoori Mahal, **40**	D4
Yong Kee, **39**	C4

🍷 NIGHTLIFE

15 Romolo, **27**	D3
Blind Tiger, **25**	B3
Broadway Studios, **30**	D3
Buddha Lounge, **47**	C5
Caffè Trieste, **21**	C3
Hungry i, **28**	D3
Li Po Cocktail Lounge, **46**	C5
Royale, **18**	C2
San Francisco Brewing Company, **43**	D4
Savoy Tivoli, **10**	C2
Spec's Adler Museum, **36**	D3
Tosca Cafe, **35**	D3
Velvet Lounge, **31**	D3
Vesuvio Café, **34**	D3

⭐ ENTERTAINMENT

Bannam Place Theater, **13**	C2
Club Fugazi, **11**	B2
Jazz at Pearl's, **32**	D3
Saloon, **22**	C3

🏠 ACCOMMODATIONS

Grant Plaza Hotel, **56**	C7
Green Tortoise Hostel, **29**	D3
Hotel Astoria, **57**	C7
Pacific Tradewinds Hostel, **55**	D6
YMCA Chinatown, **53**	C6

Lincoln Park, Richmond & Sunset see map p. 341

🍴 FOOD & DRINK

22nd & Irving Market, **16**	E4
Arizmendi Bakery, **24**	F4
Canvas Cafe/Gallery, **20**	F4
Crepevine, **23**	F4
Gastronom Russian Deli and Bakery, **3**	D2
Genki Crepes & Mini Mart, **9**	G2
Hotei, **25**	F4
Kaleo Café, **18**	E4
Kitaro, **4**	E2
Le Soleil, **13**	G1
Lee Hou Restaurant, **8**	G1
Q, **11**	G2
New May Wah Supermarket, **5**	F2
Schubert's Bakery, **6**	F2
Sheng Kee Bakery & Cafe, **17**	E4
Taiwan Restaurant, **7**	F2

Yumma's Mediterranean Grill, **22**	F4
Yum Yum Fish, **15**	D4

🍷 NIGHTLIFE

The Last Day Saloon, **10**	G1
The Little Shamrock, **19**	F4
Pat O'Shea's Mad Hatter, **14**	G2
The Plough and the Stars, **12**	G1
Trad'r Sam, **2**	D2
Yancy's Saloon, **21**	F4

⭐ ENTERTAINMENT

California Contemporary Dancers, **26**	F4

🏠 ACCOMMODATIONS

The Seal Rock Inn, **1**	A2

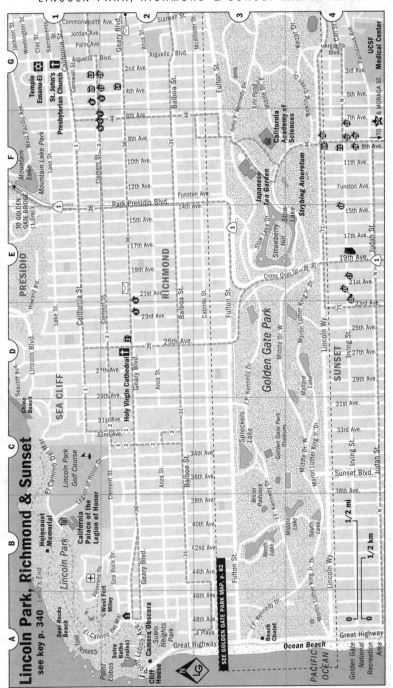

Lincoln Park, Richmond & Sunset

see key p. 340

PRESIDIO

Jackson St.
Washington St.
Clay St.
Sacramento St.
California St.
Commonwealth Ave.
Jordan Ave.
Palm Ave.
Arguello Blvd.
Cornwall St.
2nd Ave.
4th Ave.
6th Ave.
8th Ave.
10th Ave.
12th Ave.
15th Ave.
17th Ave.
19th Ave.
21st Ave.
23rd Ave.
25th Ave.
27th Ave.
29th Ave.
31st Ave.
32nd Ave.
34th Ave.
36th Ave.
38th Ave.
40th Ave.
42nd Ave.
44th Ave.
46th Ave.
48th Ave.

Temple Emanu-El
St. John's Presbyterian Church

Stanyan St.
McAllister St.
Anza St.
Geary Blvd.
Arguello Blvd.
Balboa St.
Clement St.
Fulton St.
Cabrillo St.

Kezar Dr.
Arguello Blvd.
John F. Kennedy Dr.
Lily Pond
Middle Dr. E.
Bowling Green Dr.

Parnassus Ave.
Carl St.
UCSF Medical Center
3rd Ave.
5th Ave.
7th Ave.
9th Ave.
11th Ave.
Funston Ave.
15th Ave.
17th Ave.
19th Ave.
21st Ave.
23rd Ave.
25th Ave.
27th Ave.
29th Ave.
31st Ave.
33rd Ave.
Judah St.
Irving St.

TO 9 & MORAGA ST.

California Academy of Sciences

Japanese Tea Garden
Stow Lake Dr.
Stow Lake
Strawberry Hill

Strybing Arboretum

Cross Over Dr.
Lincoln Wy.
Martin Luther King Jr. Dr.

RICHMOND

Funston Ave.
Park Presidio Blvd.
14th Ave.

TO GOLDEN GATE BRIDGE (1.5mi)

Mountain Lake Park
Mountain Lake
West Pacific Ave.
Lake St.
Howard Rd.
Lake St.
California St.
Clement St.

SEA CLIFF

Seacliff Ave.
Lincoln Blvd.
China Beach

Holy Virgin Cathedral

Geary Blvd.
Anza St.
Clement St.

Golden Gate Park

J.F. Kennedy Dr.
Middle Dr. W.
Mallard Lake

SUNSET

Irving St.
Sunset Blvd.
Judah St.
38th Ave.

Lincoln Park

Lincoln Park Golf Course
El Camino Del Mar
Legion of Honor Dr.
Clement St.
Anza St.
Balboa St.

Spreckels Lake
Golden Gate Park Stadium
Middle Dr. W.
Martin Luther King Jr. Dr.

Holocaust Memorial
California Palace of the Legion of Honor

Veterans Dr.
Sea Rock Dr.
West Fort Miley

Bison Paddock
J.F. Kennedy Dr.

Seal Rocks Beach
Lands End
Sutro Baths (ruins)

Camera Obscura
Sutro Heights Park

Coastal Trail
Point Lobos
Point Lobos Ave.
El Camino del Mar

Cliff House

North Lake
Middle Lake
South Lake

J.F. Kennedy Dr.
Lincoln Wy.
Martin Luther King Jr. Dr.

La Playa
Great Highway

Beach Chalet

Ocean Beach

PACIFIC OCEAN

Great Highway

Golden Gate National Recreation Area

SEE GOLDEN GATE PARK MAP, p. 82

1/2 mi
1/2 km
0   0

RUSSIAN HILL

NOB HILL

Grace Cathedral

Huntington Park

Nob Hill & Russian Hill

● SIGHTS

Bars with a View:
Tonga Room, **28**
Top of the Mark, **29**
Cable Car Powerhouse
& Museum, **20**
Crooked Lombard Street, **1**
The *Real World* House, **3**
San Francisco Art Institute, **2**

🍴 FOOD & DRINK

Bell Tower, **16**
Bob's Broiler Restaurant, **22**
Cala Foods, **27**
The Crêpe House, **17**
The Golden Turtle, **13**
Lemongrass, **7**
Polker's American Cafe, **12**

Real Food Company, **15**
Rico's, **5**
Search Light Market, **10**
Sushigroove, **11**
Swensen's, **9**
Zarzuela, **8**

🍺 NIGHTLIFE &
ENTERTAINMENT

The Bigfoot Lodge, **19**
Bimbo's 365 Club, **4**
Bohemia Bar, **24**

Café Royale, **32**
The Cinch, **18**
Hyde Out, **26**
The Lumière, **25**
Lush Lounge, **30**
N Touch SF, **23**
Red Devil Lounge, **21**
Royal Oak, **14**

♠ ACCOMMODATIONS

The Harcourt, **31**
The San Remo Hotel, **6**

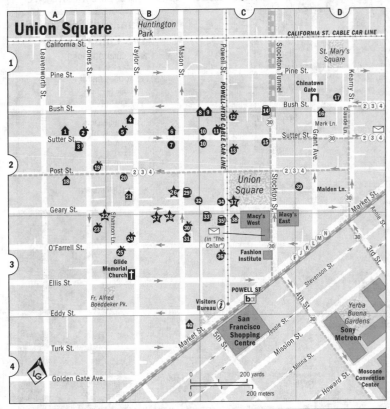

Union Square

● SIGHTS

🏠 ACCOMMODATIONS

🍺 NIGHTLIFE

★ ENTERTAINMENT

🍴 FOOD & DRINK

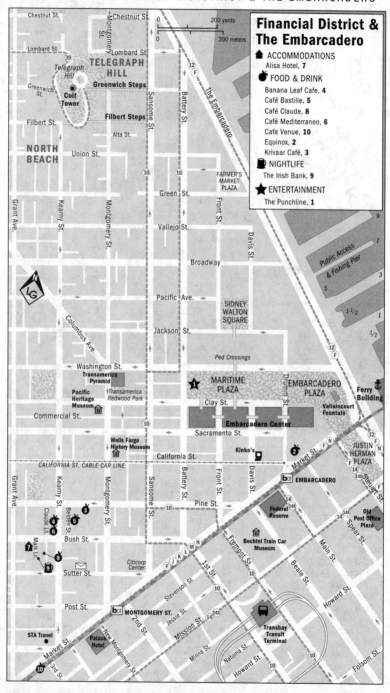

Financial District & The Embarcadero

ACCOMMODATIONS
Alisa Hotel, **7**

FOOD & DRINK
Banana Leaf Cafe, **4**
Café Bastille, **5**
Café Claude, **8**
Café Mediterraneo, **6**
Cafe Venue, **10**
Equinox, **2**
Krivaar Café, **3**

NIGHTLIFE
The Irish Bank, **9**

ENTERTAINMENT
The Punchline, **1**

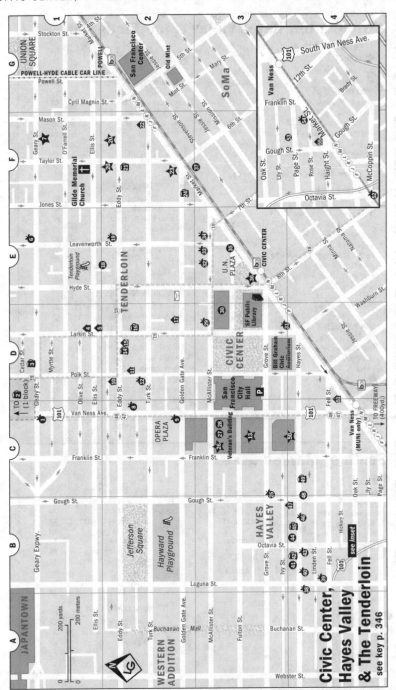

Civic Center, Hayes Valley & The Tenderloin

see key p. 346

JAPANTOWN

WESTERN ADDITION

UNION SQUARE

POWELL-HYDE CABLE CAR LINE

San Francisco Center

Old Mint

SoMa

Glide Memorial Church

TENDERLOIN

Tenderloin Playground

U.N. PLAZA

CIVIC CENTER

SF Public Library

Bill Graham Civic Auditorium

CIVIC CENTER

San Francisco City Hall

OPERA PLAZA

Veteran's Building

HAYES VALLEY

Jefferson Square

Hayward Playground

see Inset

South Van Ness Ave.

Van Ness

Franklin St.

Gough St.

Oak St.

Lily St.

Page St.

Rose St.

Haight St.

Octavia St.

McCoppin St.

Stockton St.

Market St.

4th St.

Jessie St.

5th St.

Mary St.

Mint St.

Powell St.

Cyril Magnin St.

Mason St.

Geary St.

O'Farrell St.

Ellis St.

Taylor St.

Jones St.

Eddy St.

Stevenson St.

Mission St.

Jessie St.

6th St.

7th St.

Leavenworth St.

Hyde St.

Larkin St.

Cedar St.

Myrtle St.

Polk St.

Olive St.

Ellis St.

Eddy St.

Turk St.

Golden Gate Ave.

McAllister St.

Geary St.

Van Ness Ave.

Franklin St.

Gough St.

Laguna St.

Turk St.

Golden Gate Ave.

McAllister St.

Fulton St.

Buchanan St.

Ellis St.

Buchanan Mall

Grove St.

Hayes St.

Fell St.

Oak St.

Lily St.

Page St.

Octavia St.

Ivy St.

Linden St.

Hickory St.

Fell St.

Geary Expwy.

Gough St.

Webster St.

Minna St.

Natoma St.

Washburn St.

Jessie St.

8th St.

9th St.

Van Ness (MUNI only)

TO FREEWAY (400yd)

TO ① ② (1 block)

Grove St.

TO ② (1 block)

200 yards
200 meters

WESTERN ADDITION

Civic Center, Hayes Valley & the Tenderloin
see map p. 345

● SIGHTS

509 Cultural Center, 18	E2
Art Institute of California: San Francisco, 35	E3
Asian Art Museum, 30	D3
Bucheon Gallery, 41	B4
Dudley Perkins Company, 53	inset
Luggage Store Gallery, 37	F3
Octavia's Haze Gallery, 44	B4
Performance Art Library Museum, 27	C3
Polanco, 48	C4
SF Art Commission Gallery, 28	C3

🍴 FOOD & DRINK

Ananda Fuara, 31	D3
The California Culinary Academy, 12	D2
Citizen Cake, 25	C3
Frjtz, 40	B4
It's Tops, 52	inset
Lalita Thai Restaurant and Bar, 33	E3
Max's Opera Café, 9	C2
McAllister's Market and Deli, 32	E3
Millennium, 29	D3
Moishe's Pippic, 46	B4
Momi Toby's Revolution Café and Art Bar, 39	B4
Osha Thai Noodle Café, 6	E1
Powell's Place, 43	B4
Suppenkuche, 38	B4
Taqueria Castillo, 34	E3
Taj Mahal, 19	E2
Thai Bar-B-Q, 8	C2
Tommy's Joynt, 1	C1
Zuni, 54	inset

🍺 NIGHTLIFE

Bambuddha Lounge, 14	D2
Diva's, 2	D1
Edinburgh Castle, 3	D1
Hayes and Vine, 49	C4
Hollywood Billiards, 24	F2
Jezebel's Joint, 16	D2
Marlena's, 45	B4
Place Pigalle, 42	B4
Polly Esther's, 21	F2

★ ENTERTAINMENT

Curran Theater, 7	F1
Exit Theater, 20	F2
Golden Gate Theater, 23	F2
Herbst Theatre, 26	C3
Louise M. Davies Symphony Hall, 50	C4
The Orpheum, 36	E3
War Memorial Opera House, 13	C3

🏠 ACCOMMODATIONS

Central YMCA of San Francisco, 17	D2
Edwardian San Francisco Hotel, 55	inset
The Embassy Hotel, 11	D2
Hayes Valley Inn, 47	B4
HI-AYH San Francisco - City Center, 5	D1
Hotel Essex, 4	D1
Hotel Metropolis, 22	F2
New Central Hotel & Hostel, 51	C4
Phoenix Hotel, 15	D2
Red Coach Motor Lodge, 10	D2

South of Market see map p. 347

● SIGHTS

Academy of Art College Gallery, 3	E1
Pacific Bell Park, 38	E4
Public Art Space, 10	F1
San Francisco Museum of Modern Art, 8	E1
Yerba Buena Center for the Arts, 7	E2
Yerba Buena Rooftop Gardens, 6	E1
Zeum, 30	D2

🍴 FOOD & DRINK

Basil, 21	B2
The Butler & The Chef Café, 36	E3
Cafe Bosse, 11	A2
Caffè Centro, 35	E3
Extreme Pizza, 27	C2
Patisserie Café, 20	B2
Rainbow Grocery, 14	A2
Trader Joe's, 31	B3
Vino e Cucina Trattoria, 34	E3

🍺 NIGHTLIFE

111 Minna, 9	E1
Asia SF, 17	B2
Butter, 16	A2
Buzz9, 4	B1
Cassidy's Irish Pub, 22	B2
The EndUp, 29	C3
12th@Folsom, 12	A2
Hole in the Wall Saloon, 19	B2
Hotel Utah Saloon, 33	D3
Infusion Bar & Restaurant, 37	F3
Julie's Supper Club & Lounge, 25	B2
Liquid, 32	A4
Up and Down Club, 23	B2
Club Six, 1	C1
The Stud, 18	B2
Ten 15 Folsom, 28	C2
Wish Lounge, 13	A2

★ ENTERTAINMENT

Slim's, 15	A2

🏠 ACCOMMODATIONS

Flamingo Inn, 5	B2
Interclub Globe Hostel, 24	B2
The Mosser Hotel, 2	D1
SoMa Inn, 26	C2

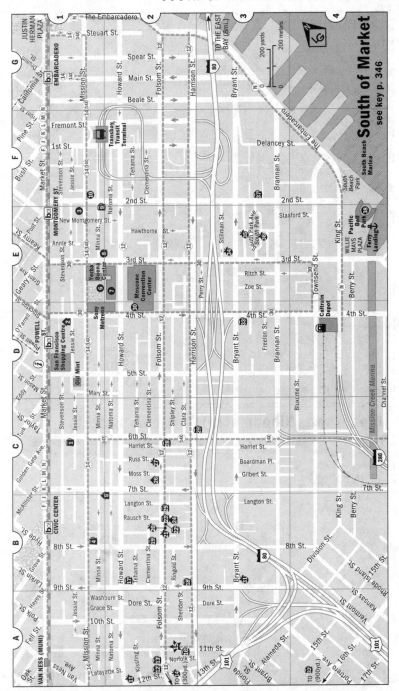

South of Market

see key p. 346

Japantown (Nihonmachi) & Pacific Heights

● **SIGHTS**

Fuji Shiatsu, **13**
Japanese Cultural &
  Community Center, **10**
Kabuki Springs & Spa, **16**
Peace Pagoda, **22**
St. Dominic's Roman
  Catholic Church, **6**
Soto Zen Mission Sokoji
  Buddhist Temple, **12**

🍴 **FOOD & DRINK**

2001 Thai Stick, **5**
Isobune, **21**
Juban, **17**
La Méditerranée, **2**
Mayflower Market, **1**
Mifune, **20**
Mollie Stone's Market, **3**
On The Bridge, **19**
Pizza Inferno, **9**
Sophie's Crepes, **18**

Super Mira
  Japanese Foods, **11**
Tango Gelato, **4**
Trio Cafe, **8**
Umeko, **23**

★ **ENTERTAINMENT**

Boom Boom Room, **14**
The Fillmore, **15**

▲ **ACCOMMODATIONS**

The Queen Anne
  Hotel, **7**

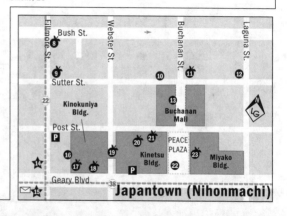

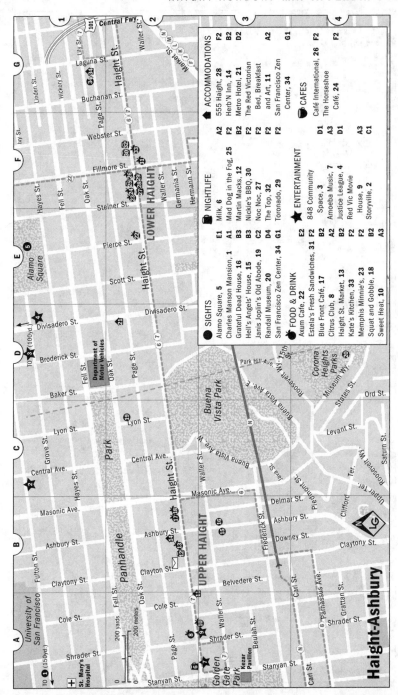

Haight-Ashbury

● SIGHTS

Alamo Square, **5**	E1
Charles Manson Mansion, **1**	A1
Grateful Dead House, **16**	B3
Hell's Angels' House, **15**	B3
Janis Joplin's Old Abode, **19**	C2
Randall Museum, **20**	D4
San Francisco Zen Center, **34**	G1

◆ FOOD & DRINK

Axum Cafe, **22**	E2
Estela's Fresh Sandwiches, **31**	F2
Blue Front Café, **17**	B2
Citrus Club, **8**	A2
Haight St. Market, **13**	B2
Kate's Kitchen, **33**	F2
Memphis Minnie's, **23**	F2
Squat and Gobble, **18**	B2
Sweet Heat, **10**	A3

▲ ACCOMMODATIONS

555 Haight, **28**	F2
Herb'N Inn, **14**	B2
Metro Hotel, **21**	D2
The Red Victorian Bed, Breakfast and Art, **11**	A2
San Francisco Zen Center, **34**	G1

☕ CAFES

Café International, **26**	F2
The Horseshoe Café, **24**	F2

🛏 NIGHTLIFE

Milk, **6**	E1
Mad Dog in the Fog, **25**	A1
Martin Macks, **12**	B3
Nickie's BBQ, **30**	B3
Noc Noc, **27**	C2
The Top, **32**	D4
Toronado, **29**	G1

★ ENTERTAINMENT

848 Community Space, **3**	E2
Amoeba Music, **7**	B2
Justice League, **4**	A2
Red Vic Movie House, **9**	B2
Storyville, **2**	F2
	B2
	A3

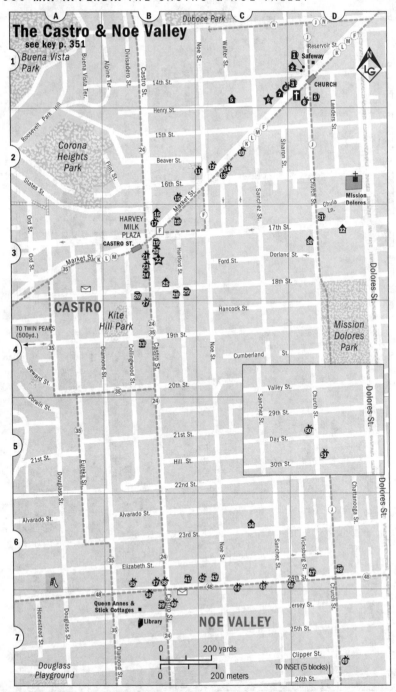

The Castro & Noe Valley
see key p. 351

The Castro & Noe Valley   see map p. 350

The Mission & Bernal Heights   see map p. 352

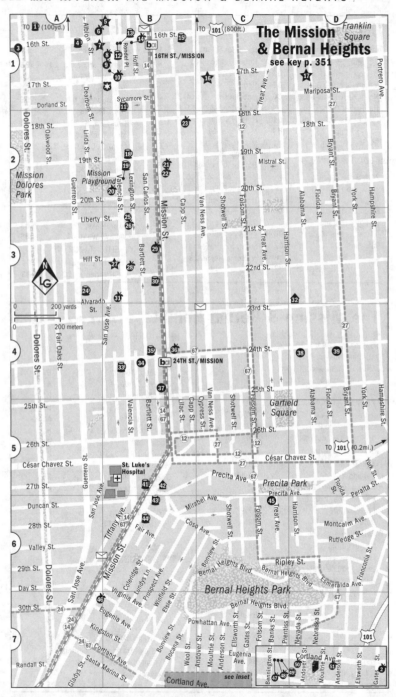

The Mission & Bernal Heights

see key p. 351

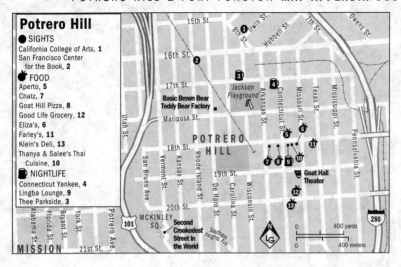

Potrero Hill

● **SIGHTS**
California College of Arts, **1**
San Francisco Center
  for the Book, **2**

🍖 **FOOD**
Aperto, **5**
Chatz, **7**
Goat Hill Pizza, **8**
Good Life Grocery, **12**
Eliza's, **6**
Farley's, **11**
Klein's Deli, **13**
Thanya & Salee's Thai
  Cuisine, **10**

■ **NIGHTLIFE**
Connecticut Yankee, **4**
Lingba Lounge, **9**
Thee Parkside, **3**

**Fort Funston,
Lake Merced
& Stern Grove**

🍖 **FOOD & DRINK**
Ambrosia Bakery, **2**
Jitra, **3**
Taipei Restaurant, **1**

○ Transit Station

the ultimate
road trip

don't trip out planning your big road trip.
put contiki in the driver's seat with a hassle-free vacations designed for 18 to 35 year olds. make new friends, enjoy your free time and explore the sights in a convenient vacation that gives you more bang for your buck... **from only $70/day** including accommodations, sightseeing, many meals and transportation. with contiki leading the way, you can leave the road map at home!

> 7 days **eastern discovery**
new york, washington d.c., us naval academy, kennedy space center

> 10 days **canada & the rockies**
vancouver, calgary, banff national park

> 13 days **wild western**
san francisco, grand canyon, las vegas, yosemite national park

*prices subject to change, land only.

for more info on our trips...
see your travel agent
call 1-888-CONTIKI
visit www.contiki.com

contiki VACATIONS for 18-35 year olds

CST# 1001728-20

> europe > australia > new zealand > america > canada